I0866303

Wings of Argentina

Wings of Argentina

Argentina's Aircraft Industry since 1927

Santiago Rivas

First published 2025 by Crécy Publishing Ltd

© Santiago Rivas 2025

ISBN: 978 190210 9671

All rights reserved. No part of this book may be reproduced or transmitted in any form or by any means, electronic or mechanical, including photocopying, recording, scanning or by any information storage without permission from the Publisher in writing. All enquiries should be directed to the Publisher.

A CIP record for this book is available from the British Library

Publisher's Note: Every effort has been made to identify and correctly attribute photographic credits. Any error that may have occurred is entirely unintentional.

Printed in Lithuania by BALTO Print

Crécy Publishing Limited
1a Ringway Trading Estate
Shadowmoss Road
Manchester M22 5LH
www.crecy.co.uk

FRONT COVER TOP One of the Uruguayan Pucarás, seen on their last days of service in 2016. *Santiago Rivas*

FRONT COVER BOTTOM The new cabin of the I.Ae.37 as installed was different from the blueprints and like the nose of the French Mystére Delta.

BACK COVER TOP The three Pampa prototypes flying together close to the FMA.

BACK COVER LEFT The Pampa III Block 2 serialled A-708, the former EX-04, flying over the glaciers of the southern Andes in July 2023. The plane is now part of the Grupo 10 de Caza of the X Brigada Aérea. *Santiago Rivas*

BACK COVER MIDDLE Plane 59 is one of the last built of the type and had many improvements. While the type could have evolved, the criticism of the locally designed types led to the decision to buy new planes abroad and return to licence production.

BACK COVER RIGHT A-568 and A-585 in flight near Reconquista in September 2018. *Santiago Rivas*

BACK COVER BOTTOM One of the Grob G-120TPs assembled by FAdeA, seen in 2021 flying alongside a T-6C+ Texan II, both being operated by the Military Aviation School of the Argentine Air Force. *Santiago Rivas*

FRONT FLAP TOP The first CBA-123 in flight over São Paulo. *Embraer*

FRONT FLAP BOTTOM The second Guaraní II at Le Bourget.

HALF TITLE PAGE The I.Ae.24 Calquin was one of the types built in large quantities, with 1 prototype and 100 series examples, but its wooden airframe meant their service life was short.

TITLE PAGE TOP The plane c/n 1027 after being upgraded to Pampa III Block 2 and serialled EX-04, seen in 2021. It was later delivered to the Argentine Air Force as A-708. *Santiago Rivas*

TITLE PAGE BOTTOM The second Huanquero prototype and the three pre-series aircraft flying together.

Contents

Introduction

Attempting to write a book about the whole story of the Argentine FAdeA or, as it was originally known, Fábrica Militar de Aviones (FMA, but over the years it has also carried the names IAME, DINFIA, Área de Material Córdoba and Lockheed Martin Aircraft Argentina S.A.), was a huge task and was an ambition I had since I first wanted to be an aviation historian and journalist, more than thirty years ago. The first ideas for this book were drafted in the late 1990s and over the years I collected information, visiting archives, interviewing people and getting all I could to build the puzzle of this story, which now forms this book. While I have attempted to give a complete the history of the FMA, a definitive book is probably impossible as much information was lost over the years and a huge part of the archives were destroyed when the company was privatised in the 1990s. Fortunately, some employees saved some of the archive and another part was preserved in the factory, but in very poor conditions in a room with plans on the floor, some affected by humidity or destroyed over the years. Also, some information was disseminated in different offices of the Argentine Air Force, including its archives, library and technical areas, and a lot of it is in the hands of researchers.

While for some projects a lot of material was preserved, making it possible to reconstruct the whole story, there are some of which nothing was found besides a line in a file or a drawing, or we only know of its existence because the designations were correlative. Theis includes many projects from the 1980s, which include the IA-64, 65, 69, 71 and 72, of which absolutely nothing was found, and it is believed that documentation was destroyed when the company was privatised or sent to an archive of the Air Force without proper identification as there is no trace of it.

The history of the FMA is as complicated as Argentine history itself in the twentieth century, being a story of ups and downs, with times in which the government and the Army (and later the Air Force) was betting on the company's development, and times when there were voices wanting its closure, privatisation or its conversion into a simple workshop. FMA's designs were also sometimes celebrated and other times condemned; sometimes being used for political propaganda, as they were during the rule of General Juan D. Perón, and sometimes being used by those who claimed the country must not produce industrial products and should focus on just farming and mining.

The management of the company, for most of its history, composed of Army and, later, Air Force officers, who often insisted that the factory had to be dedicated to produce aircraft only for the force, thus leading to projects of which very small series were built and were never intended to be sold to other countries. In other times, the management attempted to sell its products on the civil market or, in later years, abroad, with little success. The reasons for commercial failure were various, but the main one was that the managers, until June 1995, were military officers with no experience of sales or post-sale support.

The 1940s and 1950s, when engineers, technicians and pilots from Germany, Italy, France and other countries came to work in the factory, is considered by many as the golden age of the factory, due to the projects developed, including the first Latin American jets. However, was a very poor time in terms of production and delivery of aircraft, as none of the planes developed during the rule of Perón, between 1946 and 1955, were put into production before he was overthrown from power and most of these projects were cancelled. From the 1960s to the 1980s the factory aimed to have a more rational policy on development and production, and three of the most iconic designs were developed – the IA-50 Guaraní II, IA-58 Pucará and IA-63 Pampa – and these were times in which some limited commercial success was obtained.

Now, the factory, under the name Fábrica Argentina de Aviones Brigadier San Martín (FAdeA), is struggling to survive after many years of mismanagement, being used by politicians corruptly or for propaganda and being unable to sell its products, make money or innovate, with the threat of closure on the horizon as it approaches its centenary in 2027.

1 The Factory

1 The origins of the Fábrica Militar de Aviones

The beginning at El Palomar

The origins of the Fábrica Militar de Aviones can be traced back to the beginnings of aviation in Argentina. In 1910, the Compañía Aérea Argentina Sociedad Anónima was created to organise a flying school, obtaining the loan of land belonging to the Argentine Army next to the Colegio Militar de la Nación (Nation's Military School) in the town of El Palomar, close to the city of Buenos Aires. The school was inaugurated on 28 July that year and had an Antoinette and a Henri Farman plane, but also organised a workshop in which the designer Enrique Artigalá developed the first aeroplane built in Argentina, the Argentino I, which never flew despite several attempts. At the same workshop, in early 1911 mechanic Ambrosio Garagiola and workers Pablo Parasovchka and Pedro Rielo started to build a Henri Farman when the Antoinette was lost on an accident. However, the loss of the original Farman on 30 April led to the closure of the school on 5 May and all activities ceased. The Aero Club Argentino, created in 1908, took charge of the airfield and the workshops, while all the facilities were donated by the Compañía Aérea Argentina to the Argentine Army to initiate military aviation in the country. The construction of the Farman continued and in order to finish it, in May they were joined by a new mechanic named Ambrosio Taravella, with the plane being ready by July, powered by a Gnome 50hp engine.

It was decided that the plane would be donated to the Army to become part of its initial fleet, as the Escuela de Aviación Militar (Military Aviation School)

The Farman serialled V, built at the workshops of El Palomar in 1916. The construction of aircraft at that airfield, which included Blériots, Farmans, Caudrons and a Morane-Saulnier, was the first step towards the creation of the FMA.

One of the Caudron G-3s built at the Escuela Militar de Aviación between 1919 and 1920, carrying the initials 'EMA' on the cowling, which was carried by those planes built at El Palomar. Edmundo Lucius is at the middle of the picture, below the initials.

was finally created on 10 August 1912, using the facilities at El Palomar. The plane received the serial I and was the first military aircraft of Argentina.

The four mechanics of the workshop continued working for the school and started a new Farman, which was also serialled I and was delivered in December. As Garagiola kept working as head of the workshop on behalf of the Aero Club Argentino, Taravella was made its manager on behalf of the Escuela de Aviación Militar (which between 1914 and 1919 was named Escuela Militar de Aviación). This meant that the workshop had a civil boss and a military one.

When the First World War erupted in Europe, it became impossible to buy new planes there, so the commander of the school, Lt Colonel Arenales Antonio Uriburu, requested funds to build more planes locally. After his request was approved, the workshops started to build aeroplanes, as well as repairing those in use by the school. The 50hp Gnome engines were also built in Argentina, but by the private workshops of Miguel Mariscal., The Argentine Army also managed to buy three 80hp Gnome engines new in France, despite the war.

The first Farman used the remains of a civil-owned Farman Military type of 1913 that had crashed at El Palomar (that plane had already been rebuilt between April and June 1915 at the request of its owner, Nicolás Valente, who was killed in the second crash on 22 June). Now it was modified by Taravella and became what was called the Farman Tipo El Palomar, with a single tail, a new fuselage and modifications to the wings. It was finished in August and serialled III. In 1916, another three Farmans were built, as well as three Blériot XIs with 80hp engines, serialled 2, 3 and 4, and another three with 50hp engines, also serialled 2, 3 and 4. As the Uruguayan government requested a Farman for their Military Aviation School, the plane that was to be serialled VI was delivered to it in July 1917, together with the Farman serialled V.

In 1915 the Aero Club Argentino ended its involvement in the technical direction of the workshops and, in December, the school contracted engineer Edmundo Lucius as workshop technical director.

By 1916, plans were made to build four 'Blériot Taxis' without wings for ground training, with 25/30hp engines, two Farmans with 100hp engines, three Voisins of 150hp and four Spads of 150hp, but the idea was abandoned due to a lack of materials and because the designs were becoming old.

In 1917 a commission was sent to France, headed by Captain Aníbal Brihuega and including Taravella, to try to get new aircraft for the school and replace the old Farmans and Blériots. They managed to buy two Caudron G-IIIs, one with 80hp engine and one with 100hp, as the war in Europe was finishing, thanks to the help of the Argentine ambassador in Paris, Marcelo Torcuato de Alvear.

The first buildings of the FMA, the first stage to be built, before the inauguration of the factory. The one on the lower left is the administrative building, where the management of the factory still is today. The road below is the route between Córdoba and Villa Carlos Paz, now Route 20/ Fuerza Aérea Argentina Avenue.

They were pressed into service with the Army from August 1919 and materials to build four of 80hp and six of 100hp locally were purchased. These were finished in 1920, while in 1919 a Morane-Saulnier Parasol with 80hp engine was also built.

In 21 March 1919, the Servicio Aeronáutico del Ejército (Army Aeronautical Service) was created, on which depended, among other organisations, the Escuela de Aviación Militar and the Talleres de Aeronáutica (Aeronautic Workshops), meaning that the workshops were no longer part of the school.

In 1921, Edmundo Lucius was sent to Europe and bought thirty-seven Caudron G-IIIs with 110hp Anzani engines, and this was followed by another purchase of five with 110hp engines and five with Gnomes of 80hp. All were assembled at the Talleres de Aeronáutica, and with spare parts that came with them, another four were built, serialled 48 to 51 (the ones purchased in France were serialled 1 to 47), but most of them were delivered to air clubs and civil flying schools to help develop civil aviation in the country and only the planes serialled 5, 16, 36, 38 and 42 served with the Army briefly. The Caudrons received between 1919 and 1920 were all retired by the end of 1921, delivered to civil organisations, and by the end of 1923 the last Caudrons in the Army were also released to civilians.

With the construction of the last Caudron G-IIIs, aircraft production at El Palomar ceased, after building a total of six Henri Farmans, six Blériot XIs, one Morane-Saulnier and fourteen Caudron G-IIIs.

An aircraft factory

In the meantime, Ambrosio Taravella asked to remain in Paris to study aircraft construction and in 1922 he graduated as an aviation engineer, visiting aircraft factories in France, Germany, Italy and the United Kingdom before returning to Argentina, where he was appointed chief of the Talleres de Aeronáutica. He expanded and reorganised it, with the intention of restarting aircraft production, now in series. In Paris he had met retired Major Francisco de Arteaga, who had graduated as an aviation engineer before Taravella, and both concluded that Argentina needed an aircraft factory to be independent from construction abroad. While originally the idea was to expand the workshops at El Palomar, soon it was evident that they needed to build a new factory in a different place, as the air units at the base were also growing fast.

In 1922, Marcelo Torcuato de Alvear, who had met both men in Paris when he was ambassador and was an aviation enthusiast, was elected president of Argentina and appointed Colonel Agustín Pedro Justo as his War Minister, another supporter of the development of aviation. Both agreed to support the idea of creating an aviation industry.

On 30 October 1923 the secret law 11.266 was issued, assigning 15 million pesos for the purchase of aircraft, the development of the aeronautic industry and the construction of workshops. In 1924, Francisco de Arteaga presented a project for the construction of a new aircraft factory, which was approved by minister Justo, and he was ordered to find a place for its construction. He initially analysed the surroundings of the cities of Buenos Aires and the nearby La Plata, but then moved to Rosario, in Santa Fe province, where the local government made a good offer to build the factory there. However, he then visited Córdoba and found the full support of the local government, while the location, in the middle of the country, was strategically better suited.At the beginning of 1925 the location to build the factory was selected on the south-west end of the city, at a place called Las Playas, 5.5km from the downtown, on the road to the town of Villa Carlos Paz. The War Ministry managed the expropriation of the field. In April 1926, de Arteaga finalised the design and on 8 June the Argentine government organised a commission under the head of engineer Domingo Selva of the Army Engineer General Direction to make a plan of

The FMA after the first three stages of construction were finished. The construction more to the left was the hangar for the planes that were being tested before delivery. Now it is used by the Centro de Ensayos en Vuelo of the Argentine Air Force. The big construction to the right of it was the final assembly building, while most of the others were the different workshops.

The third Caudron G-3 with Anzani engine of 100hp, serialled III.

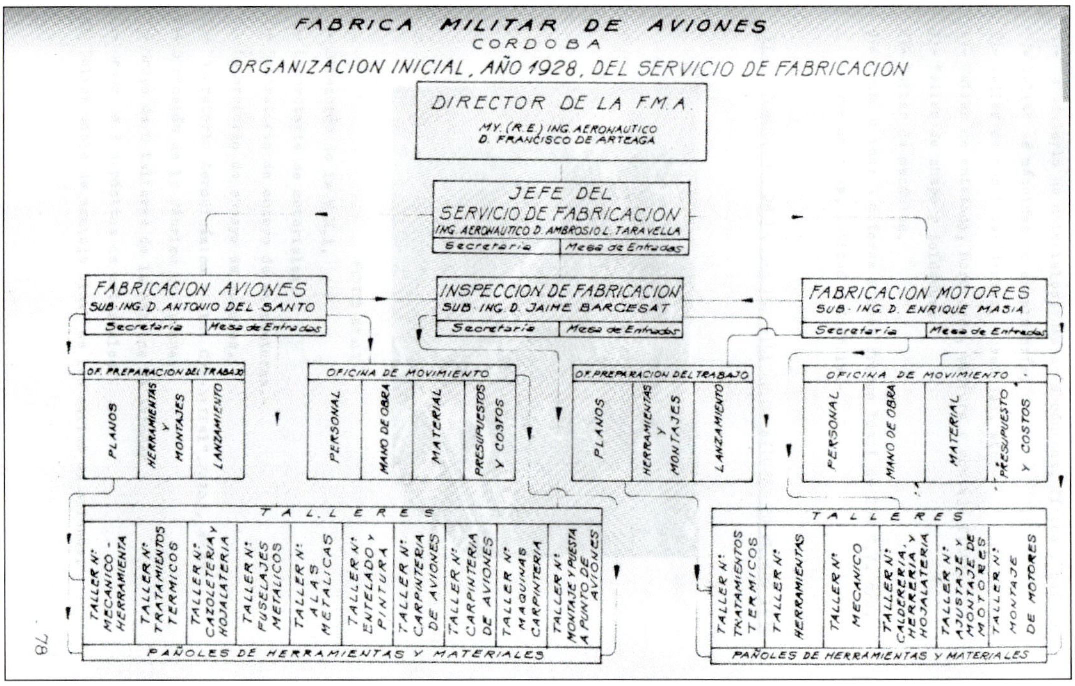

First organisation of the FMA, as it was in 1928.

the works and take charge of the construction of the buildings. In September the work was organised into three stages, with the intention that, after the first was ready, the factory would be ready to start the construction of aeroplanes.

The first stage included an office building to manage the factory, five workshops, a warehouse and an electrical plant. The construction was contracted to DYC-Kerhoff &Widman S.A. and José Luis Pellegrini and on 6 October the first contract for the works was approved, to put in a water supply.

On 10 November, in the presence of war minister General Justo, a ceremony to officially start construction began, while work actually began on 2 January 1927. An unpaved runway 1,000m long and 200m wide was also prepared by levelling the terrain. The runway was inaugurated on 29 June 1928 by Lt Colonel Pedro Zanni in a Breguet XIX. Meanwhile, on 10 January, a commission was organised under Ambrosio Taravella to travel to France and be trained on aircraft construction at the Bréguet factory, while twelve workers, headed by Pablo Parasovchka, went to learn about aircraft engines at Lorraine-Dietrich. Taravella had already been in France since 1925, studying the construction of metal aircraft.On 18 July, a decree by the government authorised the proposal of Francisco de Arteaga to name the factory Fábrica Militar de Aviones (FMA, Military Aircraft Factory), a name by which it was known over the years, despite the designation being officially changed several times.

While originally the factory was run directly by the Servicio Aeronáutico del Ejército (Army Aeronautical Service), on 4 May 1927 military aviation was reorganised as the Dirección General de Aeronáutica, with the Dirección de Aerotécnica as part of it, which was in charge of everything related to aircraft construction and maintenance, so the FMA became dependent on it. Francisco de Arteaga was appointed Director de Aerotécnica.

Meanwhile, on 11 August all the personnel of the workshops of El Palomar were transferred to the new factory, to install equipment and prepare it to open, while on 31 August the commission sent to France was designated as part of the factory, to form the core group that would start production. All personnel were officially designated and on 1 September the first internal organisation of the site was made, with five workshops.

On 26 October, Francisco de Arteaga was also designated as the first director of the FMA. Taravella was designated as head of the Servicio de Fabricación (Construction Service), mechanic Antonio del Santo became head of the Talleres de Aeroplanos (Aeroplanes Workshops), mechanic Enrique Masiá as head of the Talleres de Motores (Engines Workshops), Antonio Muszzopappa as head of the Oficina de Estudios y Proyectos (Projects and Studies Office) and Gustavo Gerock as head of Documentación Técnica (Technical Documentation). The aeroplane workshop was divided into two sections, one for metal planes and one for wooden ones, and the area Montaje de Aviones (Aircraft Assembly) was run by Pablo Parasochka.

Finally, on 10 October 1927, the Fábrica Militar de Aviones was officially inaugurated, with a ceremony in which Francisco de Arteaga acted as host.

The first months were mostly dedicated to organise the workshops, install the equipment and train the personnel, who numbered 193 people by then. Now, the factory was ready to start to build planes, but the first work order, issued on 25 November, was for the construction of three blades for wooden propellers.

2 **Evolution of the FMA, from 1927 to 2023**

The first years

As well as designing the factory, de Arteaga started to plan the aircraft construction. Wisely, as the new operation did not have experience in designing aircraft, he decided to first look for licences outside the country and obtained those to produce the Avro 504R, Breguet XIX, Dewoitine D.21C-1 and D.27, but the Breguet XIX and D.27 were never produced. Also, negotiations took place with the Argentine designer and builder Virgilio Mira, who had developed the Golondrina, a small sport plane, with the intention of producing a series of them at the factory. However, in the end Mira decided to build these in his own workshops.

By January 1928, thirty-eight apprentices were also assigned to the factory to start their training, initiating the growth of personnel numbers.

Meanwhile, on 23 February, the construction of the second stage began, including laboratories to test engines and aerodynamics, and to perform static tests, the aircraft construction office, four new workshops, two warehouses, an engine workshop, a dining room, an infirmary, an entrance guard house, the control tower and a water tower. Shortly after, the third stage was also started and, when completed by the end of 1930, the factory had 27,549m2 of covered surface.

Meanwhile, production began quickly and on 18 July the first plane built by the FMA was presented; an Avro 504N, which flew on 20 August. However, as the factory would experience many times over the years, economic problems arose shortly after as no budget was allocated to it in the Budget Law for 1929 and on 5 January of that year it had to close. It restarted activity on 1 July, while on 4 October a loan was given to the factory to keep it operating until the end of the year.

Exhibition of planes built at the FMA in the early 1930s, with an Avro 504, a Dewoitine D-21, an Ae.C.2 and the Ae.C.1, plus a Lorraine-Dietrich engine.

Despite there being no budget, some tools and equipment were bought, including the first wind tunnel of the Eiffel type, the first in Latin America, with space for models of up to 1.2m wingspan. However, this lacked an engine until 20 August 1936. The Servicio de Estudios y Ensayos (Tests and Studies Service) was established to manage this under the direction of Captain Bartolomé de la Colina.

The production of engines began immediately, with the first Lorraine-Dietrich Type 146 of 450hp, to equip the Dewoitine D.21s, which was unveiled on 15 February 1930, while the first locally built D.21 flew for the first time on 21 October.

In 13 May 1930 Major Bartolomé de la Colina became interim director (confirmed on 16 March 1931) and proposed to change from licence production to the development of local designs, which led to the design and production of the first series of aircraft designed by the factory. This started with the Ae.C.1 (Ae. for Dirección de Aerotécnica, C. for Civil and 1 being the first design) and was followed by the Ae.C.2,

Final assembly line of the Avro 504s at the FMA in 1928.

RIGHT Engine factory around 1940.

BELOW Eiffel wind tunnel today. Now it is not in use but kept preserved.

A factory mechanic works on the construction of a Focke-Wulf Fw 44J. *Life magazine*

Ae.C.3, Ae.C.4, Ae.M.E.1, Ae.M.O.1, Ae.M.Oe.1, Ae.M.Oe.2, Ae.T.1, Ae.M.S.1, Ae.M.B.1 and Ae.M.B.2. This series, which totalled more than 100 aircraft, was criticised by many politicians and in the press because of its quality, without considering that most were experimental aircraft, and some claimed that the factory should return to building under licence, or be privatised or even closed.

The first plane designed by the factory, the Ae.C.1, made its first flight on 28 October 1931, when production of the Avro 504 had ended and that of the D.21 was also nearing the end.

In 1930 the FMA grew until it had 800 employees and at the end of 1931, for the first time, the factory was included in the budget of the War Ministry. However, it did not receive sufficient funding and was forced to operate part-time.

On 6 October 1932, Sergeant José H. Rodríguez, who was testing the FMA aircraft, was officially designated Probador de Aviones en Vuelo (Tester of Aircraft in Flight), being the first with that designation. Later, with the sale of an Ae.C.2 to the government of San Juan province on 26 November 1932, the FMA made its first sale, as all previous aircraft were delivered to the Argentine Army, of which the factory was a part.

With the production of the local types, expanding the type of designs to cover most of the needs of Army Aviation was considered. After the design of the Ae.T.1 light transport, which was planned to be modified into light bomber, and the Ae.M.B.1 light bomber, studies were made for a fighter aircraft. However, the FMA concluded it did not have the capacity for this yet and that it was better to look abroad, something that led to a licence to build the Curtiss Hawk 75-O.FMA also look at building a heavy bomber, considering an aircraft with three engines, a maximum speed of 300km/h and a maximum take-off weight of 15 tons. It is not known if any layout was ever made as any plans to build it were dropped shortly after.

The production of engines was expanded when on 5 October 1934 the first Wright Cyclone of 690hp was finished, to be used on some of the types being produced by the factory.A series of accidents occurred with Army and Navy aircraft, especially with the Ae.M.O. and Ae.M.B. of the Army, which were considered fragile. This led to a meeting of the War and Navy Ministries between 4 and 19 July 1935 in which they explained the problems caused by a low defence budget that impeded the purchase of new aircraft for the forces. While this had a positive result with the issue of law 12,254 that reorganised military aviation and included the expansion of the defence budget from 189 million Argentine pesos to 315 million, it was also concluded that the FMA should return to producing aircraft under licence and stop designing its own aircraft. At the same time it received a bigger budget, making it possible to return to full-time operation.

Licence production for a while

The reorganisation of military aviation also affected the FMA, as on 14 July 1936 the Dirección de Aerotécnica ceased to exist and instead the FMA became the 2° División – FMA, while there was a 1° División containing all the operational units of the Army Aviation. Both were under the Dirección General de Material Aeronáutico del Ejército.

The supersonic wind tunnel, designed by Reimar Horten for the tests of the IA-37 and IA-48 projects.

Now, the factory was reorganised and consisted of the Departamento I Estudios y Experiencias, Departamento II Construcciones Aeronáuticas, Departamento III Inspección, Departamento IV Administración and Departamento V Servicios Especiales.

The Departamento I was divided into the laboratories; library; rules; aircraft projects; and engine projects, while the Departamento II had five areas: aeroplane construction, engine construction, work preparation, sandblasting and galvanising; and casting and forging.

Meanwhile, in 1936 the Argentine aviator Juan Regés Aymá purchased an Avro Cierva C.30 autogiro and, after exhibiting it to the Army, he convinced it to buy two and proposed the construction of them under licence by the FMA. As he received interest from Bartolomé de la Colina and his successor, Major

Production line at the Pabellón 90 around 1946, with I.Ae. DL-22 and I.Ae.24 Calquin.

The tarmac of the factory in the early 1950s with two Bristol 170 Freighters, two Calquins, a Douglas C-47 and a I.Ae.33 Pulqui II, seen from a Focke-Wulf Fw 44J.

Alfredo Paladino, Regés Aymá travelled to London on December to meet Juan de la Cierva and discuss the creation of a company between them to negotiate the licence for the FMA. After reaching an agreement, they met on 8 December and agreed to keep working on the idea, but on the following day de la Cierva was killed in an air accident while flying to Amsterdam, ending this project.In 1937, another licence was obtained to build the Focke-Wulf Fw 44J Stieglitz, followed in 1939 by ones to build the Curtiss Hawk 75-O and the Rhönbussard glider, while five Junkers Ju 52/3ms were also assembled. However, the eruption of the war in Europe, in which Argentina decided to remain neutral, complicated production as it was impossible to get new materials.

That led to the return of local aircraft design, and first the FMA 20 El Boyero light aircraft was developed to promote sport aviation and flew for the first time in 1940, but the plan was that the plane would be produced by private industry. Then, a single North American NA-16-1P was modified with a new wooden wing and became the FMA 21. The names FMA 20 and 21 were given because they were the twentieth and twenty-first types to be built by the factory, including those built under licence. However, from then on those types built under licence were not given such numbers.

On 1 September 1941, the FMA ceased to be under the administration of the Dirección General de Material Aeronáutico del Ejército and instead came under the Dirección General de Fabricaciones Militares, which had under its control all the other factories of the Army. Also, the Departamento II was divided into the Departamento Fabricación de Aviones and the Departamento Fabricación de Motores, which on 1 November 1942 became part of the newly created Servicio de Fabricación, while the Departamento Estudios y Ensayos became Servicio Técnico.

Interestingly, on 5 December that year first engine designed by the FMA was completed, however, it was not an aviation one, but an outboard engine for motor boats. However only one 35hp Surubí experimental unit was built and the project was abandoned.

Instituto Aerotécnico

On 1 September 1943 the FMA returned to the Dirección General de Material Aeronáutico del Ejército and on 20 October the factory name was changed to Instituto Aerotécnico, while it was reorganised into the Servicio Administrativo, Servicio Inspección, Servicios Generales and the Ingeniero Jefe (Chief Engineer) to whom depended the aerodrome, the Servicio Fabricación and the Servicio Técnico. Of the last two, the first was in charge of the construction of aeroplanes, engines and tools, and the second dedicated to experiments, laboratories and design.During that time, the construction of local designs restarted and, under the Instituto Aerotécnico, these began to be designated with the initials I.Ae., the first being the I.Ae. DL-22 trainer. At the same time, the first aviation engine was developed, copying the Wright Whirlwind R975E-3, called I.Ae.R.16 'El Gaucho', to equip the DL-22.

On 6 March 1944 Major Juan Ignacio San Martín was appointed director of the Instituto Aerotécnico, who promoted the growth of the factory and the development of new local designs, starting with the I.Ae.24 Calquin attack aircraft.

Another major step was the construction of the Pabellón 90, a huge building of 12,150m2 to be used for the final assembly of aircraft. The first types

The entrance of the factory by the mid-1950s, with some Rastrojero pick-up and sedan Justicialista cars stored after being built. The big hangars were built in the early 1950s for maintenance work.

to be built there were the DL-22 and the Calquin, followed by the I.Ae.23 (a wooden version of the Fw 44J) and the I.Ae.25 Mañque assault glider.

Another big change occurred on 4 January 1945 when the Secretaría de Aeronáutica was created, making the Argentine Air Force an independent organisation. The force was organised with the Comando en Jefe de Aeronáutica and the Instituto Aerotécnico under its administration.

Now, the Instituto Aerotécnico was divided into eleven Departments, being I Servicio Técnico, with four areas (wings and landing gear, weapons, fuselages and tails), II Servicio Fabricación, also with four areas (aircraft, engines, tools and thermal treatment and foundry), III Gabinete de Estudios e Investigaciones Aerodinámicas, IV Laboratorio de Materiales, V Laboratorio de Motores, VI Laboratorio de Instrumentos, VII Servicio de Inspección, VIII Servicios Administrativos, IX Adquisiciones, X Contabilidad and XI Servicios Generales. The factory had also grown considerably and now had more than 3,700 employees.

Beyond the limits

The end of the Second World War coincided with a big political change in Argentina when on 4 June 1946 general Juan D. Perón became president, after increasing his power during the de facto government established after the coup d'état of 4 June 1943.

Perón wanted to develop industry and address the country's technological lag, so he supported a plan already started in 1945 to attract engineers and designers from the countries that had lost the Second World War to come to work to Argentina.

The country was neutral during most of the war and only declared war on the Axis nations on 27 March 1945. Among the de facto government of General Edelmiro Farrell there were many supporters of Germany and Italy and their fascist ideas, including Perón, who was an admirer of Benito Mussolini. The benign attitude of Argentina to the Axis countries made it attractive to them and some Germans escaped to the country, including some war criminals. Two German submarines surrendered at Mar del Plata submarine base, while still today there are claims that several others were run aground near the coast and its occupants were helped to land by members of the German community in Argentina.

French engineer Emile Dewoitine started to look for a place to work as he had been threatened with prosecution in France for his work with the Germans and had escaped to Spain. However, he was not having any success with developing a new factory, so, in late 1945 he contacted Ambrosio Taravella, with whom he had contact during the negotiations over the licence to build the D.21. Taravella invited him to come to Argentina to work. This idea evolved as the Argentines found there was an opportunity to hire engineers and other experts in Europe.

Between 1946 and 1948 several Germans, Italians and even Polish engineers, technicians, pilots and other specialists travelled to Argentina and most were contracted by the Instituto Aerotécnico, initiating the most interesting era of the factory regarding designs. Among them where the German engineers Reimar Horten and Kurt Tank, with their teams, including pilots, engineers and technicians, while ace Luftwaffe pilot Adolf Galland was contracted by the Argentine Air Force to develop the fighter aviation, which was entering the jet age after the purchase of 100 Gloster Meteor F.Mk.4s that arrived from 1947.

The first design was the I.Ae.27 Pulqui, developed by Emile Dewoitine, which was the first jet aircraft in Latin America, but it was followed by many other designs, like the I.Ae.30 Ñancú of Italian engineer Cesare Pallaviccino, plus the I.Ae.33 Pulqui II jet fighter of 1950 and many others.On 25 November 1947 a new reorganisation took place within the factory, with the creation of the Dirección General de Fábricas, the Dirección General Técnica and the Dirección Administrativa. The first oversaw aeroplanes, jet engines, engines, tools and machinery, propellers and accessories, instruments and equipment factories and the metallurgy department. Interestingly, this new organisation created the Fábrica de Motores a Reacción to build jet engines as Argentina acquired a licence from Rolls-Royce to build the Derwent V engine, although none were built in the end.The Dirección General de Fábricas also created the Private Industry Department, as it was planned that the factory would interact with outside companies, something that had been established with the production of the FMA 20 El Boyero and the failed I.Ae.31 Chingolo and Colibrí projects.

In 1947 the government had developed the Plan Quinquenal (Five-Year Plan) aimed at developing industry and this had a dedicated part for aviation, including the private aviation industry with their own designs or those from the Instituto Aerotécnico, but also with private companies providing parts and components for the aircraft produced by the latter.

The growth of the factory and the design works led to a new organisation on 23 March 1949, with the Dirección General de Fábricas becoming independent of the Instituto Aerotécnico and now being directly under the Cuartel Maestre General de Aeronáutica, to which the Instituto Aerotécnico also reported. Shortly after, on 8 April, the first woman was contracted to work in the factory. Three days later the Laboratorio Experimental de Paracaídas (Parachute Experimental Laboratory) was created, from which on 31 October was created the Fábrica de Paracaídas. By 1950 the factory had 107.695m2 of covered buildings.

Also, work on rockets was taking place and on March 1950 an I.Ae.24 Calquin launched the AM-1 Tábano flying bomb, which was designed as an air-to-air missile but could be also used for air-to-surface missions. While the rocket proved very hard to aim and the project was abandoned, this was the beginning of the development of rockets at the factory, which was continued for more than thirty years.

Aeroplanes but also cars, motorbikes and more: IAME

During those years, the factory grew exponentially and the government wanted to use its experience and capacity to develop other industries, especially cars and agricultural machinery, but also to develop other products. The directors of the factory had told president Perón that they had the capacity to design and build cars, so on 30 November 1951 the Fábrica de Motores y Automotores (Cars and Engines Factory) was created and on 2 December the construction of its facilities began. Shortly after, on 1 February 1952, the production of the first prototype of the Sedan Institec, later called the Justicialista, was started, followed on the 23rd of that month by the first car engine and on 10 March by the Rastrojero pick-up and the Gauchita closed version. After these construction of Puma motorbikes also began.

This expansion led to a big change in the factory, with the creation on 28 March 1952 of the Industrias Aeronáuticas y Mecánicas del Estado (IAME, State Mechanic and Aeronautic Industries), with the Instituto Aerotécnico being part of it, while the aircraft construction area reverted to the name Fábrica Militar de Aviones. The company remained under the administration of the Ministerio de Aeronáutica.

The expansion continued with the construction of the Fábrica de Tractores, which, unlike the others, was outside the facilities and located in the town of Ferreyra, on the south-east of the city of Córdoba. There they built the Pampa tractor.

The Fábrica de Motores a Reacción started to develop its own designs and in 1952 studied the I.A. T-2 jet engine (there are no records of an I.A. T-1 but, as all designations were correlative, this should have existed), but this project was transferred to the Dirección General de Fabricaciones Militares, under the Argentine Army, and was later cancelled.

The focus put on the construction of cars, tractors, pick-ups and motorbikes consumed most of the resources of the factory, which diverted some of the budget originally destined for aircraft construction. Hence, in 1952 aeroplane production was stopped. The end of I.Ae.24 production in 1950 meant series production ceased for some time, while new projects were not ready yet for production.This remained the situation for the next few years, during which the factory became mostly an automotive producer that tested some advanced aircraft but only as prototypes. For those tests, on 29 May 1953 the supersonic wind tunnel was inaugurated, the first of its kind in the southern hemisphere and developed with the support of Reimar Horten.

On 27 May 1953 the Fábrica de Motocicletas (Motorbike Factory) was established at the facilities of the Escuela de Especialidades of the Argentine Air Force, where the Fábrica de Máquinas y Herramientas was also organised to produce tools and machinery. Also, the Taller de Motonáutica (Motor Boats Workshop) was created for the production of small motorboats and sailing boats, beginning in November of that year. IAME also started to produce weapons, starting with napalm bombs, but also rifles and guns.

Between 1952 and 1953 a change in the designation of aeroplanes took place, from I.Ae. plus a number to I.A. (or IA- as was sometimes written) plus a number. However, this was not carried out in an organised way, so some types produced in 1952, like the I.A.34M glider, received the new designation, while there are plans from 1953, including some for the I.Ae.35, with the old designation.

By the end of 1953 IAME was organised into ten factories (aircraft, piston engines, jet engines, instruments and equipment, parachutes, propellers and accessories, machinery and tools, cars, tractors and motorbikes), plus the Instituto Aerotécnico for design and development, with eight departments (aircraft, aerodynamics, flight tests, material tests, weapons, electronics, instruments and equipment, and engines), having almost 10,000 employees. There were almost 250,000m2 of buildings, making it the biggest industrial complex in Latin America.

The growth of the company and the increasing economic difficulties of the country, resulting in reduced budgets, started to have an impact on the factory and on 13 October 1954 part of the Fábrica de Tractores facilities were sold to Fiat, where the Italian company started to produce cars, tractors and other equipment, and this continues today.

Also, to reduce the number of buildings in use, on 4 March 1955 the piston and jet engine factories were merged as the Fábrica de Motores and shortly after the Taller de Motonáutica was closed.

Advertisement of the Plan Quinquenal (Five-year Plan) with the I.Ae.27 Pulqui.

Fewer tests, more aircraft production

On 16 September 1955 a revolution began against Perón and the rebels took control of the Escuela de Aviación Militar (Military Aviation School) that lies next to IAME. Shortly after they gained control of Córdoba city, including the factory. As troops loyal to the government started to converge on the city, revolutionaries used aeroplanes from the school but also some Gloster Meteors that were receiving maintenance at the IAME workshops to attack them. Although there are no records, some pictures and testimonies suggest that the prototype of the Pulqui II was also used against the loyal forces, and the plane received rebel markings. Finally, on 21 September Perón resigned and escaped to Paraguay, meaning the triumph of the revolution and a big change for IAME.

A provisional directorship was established and the factory returned to its name FMA on 30 September, but aeroplane production was still stalled. Between 1951 and 1955 it had only produced three prototypes of the I.Ae.33 Pulqui II, and two of the I.Ae.35 Justicialista del Aire (renamed Huanquero after the revolution), plus two I.Ae.41 Urubú gliders.

Although many aircraft were designed between 1950 and 1955 and a lot of tests were made, the results were extremely poor, as none had entered into production. The new government found that a lot of money and resources had been used on tests, but most projects had been abandoned or had progressed so slowly that they had become obsolete.

Most of the Germans left the factory, some unhappy with their salaries, as the country was experiencing growing inflation, some because they saw their projects were progressing too slowly because the factory was more focused on car and motorbike production. Others were dismissed because of their support of Perón. Only Reimar Horten and his team kept working for the factory and he would do so for many years, contributing even after he retired until his death in Córdoba in 1993.

DINFIA

The new government maintained the production of cars, motorbikes and tractors, but wanted to make the factory more efficient, especially focusing on aircraft production. On 23 January 1957 a new organisation was announced; the state-owned company Dirección Nacional de Fabricaciones e Investigaciones Aeronáuticas (DINFIA, Aeronautics Research and Production National Direction), which was now in charge of the factory.

DINFIA kept the Instituto Aerotécnico and its organisation, but the factories were now under the Dirección de Producción and had a military area with the aircraft, engines and parachute factories, a civil one with the car, tractor and motorbikes factories and a complementary area with the factories of machinery and tools, instruments and equipment and the metallurgy department. The Fábrica de Hélices y Accesorios became part of the Fábrica de Motores. All the aerospace-related activities of DINFIA were organised under the name Fábrica Militar de Aviones, which had its own administration.

The delays in the development of new products led to the decision to obtain licences abroad, and one was bought for the Beechcraft B45 Mentor to replace the cancelled I.A.44 piston engine trainer project, and another for the Morane-Saulnier MS.760 Paris to replace the I.A.45 jet trainer project.

Series production returned to the factory in 1957, with eight I.A.35 Huanqueros and the first six Mentors being built. Also, the focus was put on the civil market, with the development of the I.A.45 Querandí twin-engined light aircraft and the I.A.46 Ranquel light two-seater for crop spraying and tourism.

In 1958 deliveries of the Paris began, the first jet aircraft produced in numbers in Latin America, while, as it was considered that the Pulqui II project was obsolete by then, Reimar Horten was progressing with the development of the I.A.48 jet fighter, with a revolutionary design, but this was abandoned in the early 1960s.

Conservative times but looking to space

On 23 March 1960 the Jefatura de Vuelo (Flight Command) was created out of the Ensayos de Aviones en Vuelo (Aircraft Test Flight) office, but on 9 November 1961 this became the Centro de Ensayos en Vuelo (CEV, Flight Test Centre).

Also, on 3 November that year, the Instituto Aerotécnico was renamed the Instituto de Investigación Aeronáutica y Espacial (IIAE, Space and Aeronautic Research Institute). This was because the focus began to be put on space exploration, which had started on 2 February of that year with the launch of the first space research rocket built by the factory, the Alfa Centauro. That initiated more than twenty years of space exploration with rockets built at the FMA.

Both the CEV and the IIAE reported directly to the FMA, but on 1 January 1963 were transferred to DINFIA and the FMA retained only aeronautics-related production.

Meanwhile, the Fábrica de Tractores was closed on 18 January 1961, when the Pampa tractor production was closed, and the remaining facilities at Ferreyra were sold to Perkins S.A., which started to build engines there. On 27 June 1962, the Fábrica de Paracaídas was transformed into the Fábrica de Armamentos y Equipos.

With the first flight of the IA-50 Guaraní, an evolution of the Huanquero, on 6 February 1962 the factory entered into the production of turboprop aeroplanes, with the Guaraní evolving into the Guaraní II and replaced the Huanquero on the production line. Curiously, in that year, to mark the fiftieth anniversary of the Escuela de Aviación Militar and the first production of the Farman, the factory built a new Farman, using the original plans and engine. The plane flew on 8 September that year.

The 1960s started with the series production of the last Mentors and Parises, the production of the Ranquel and the beginning of the Guaraní II (later G-II). Some other projects started to take shape, now mostly focused on civil aircraft, like the IA-52 light transport, the IA-53 Mamboretá and the IA-54 Carancho glider. A licence to build the Cessna 182-A was also acquired, and production began in June 1966. In 1971 this was expanded to the models 188 and 150. The increase in the number of communist guerrillas in Latin America, as well as in Asia and Africa, led to the interest in developing a counter-insurgency aircraft, with the IA-55 project starting by 1962. This was cancelled in favour of a more powerful design the IA-58 Pucará.

On 6 October 1966 DINFIA started to report directly to the Commander-in-Chief of the Argentine Air Force.

Only aerospace production

After sixteen years in which the company was dedicated to all kind of production, on 31 December 1967 DINFIA ceased to exist. By then the company included the Dirección de Producción, the IIAE and the CEV, plus the FMA as an auxiliary organisation that managed aviation-related production, with the National Direction at Buenos Aires. Now, all the aerospace activities under the Fábrica Militar de Aviones started to come under the direction of the Commander-in-Chief of the Argentine Air Force, including the IIAE and the CEV, while all activities not related to aerospace became part of a new organisation called Industrias Mecánicas del Estado (IME), independent of the Defence Ministry. From then on, although IME production was carried out inside the facilities of the FMA, they were separate companies, until in 1979 all car production ended and IME ceased to exist in 1982.

The FMA now had the Agrupación Aviones from the basis of the Fábrica de Aviones, the Agrupación Motores from the Fábrica de Motores and the Agrupación Servicios from the Dirección de Servicios Generales. The Fábrica de Armamentos y Equipos became Escuadrón Armamentos of the Agrupación Aviones and the metallurgy department became Escuadrón Metalurgia of the Agrupación Motores. The IIAE and the CEV were also part of the FMA and the factory now came under the Dirección de Material of the Argentine Air Force. However, on 27 December 1968 a new name change took place, when the FMA became the Área de Material Córdoba (AMC), with the same status as the two other main workshops of the force, which became Área de Material Río Cuarto in the south of Córdoba province, and Área de Material Quilmes, in the suburbs of Buenos Aires.

Despite this last change of name, which officially lasted until 1995, the company used FMA as its commercial name on its advertising, the designation of its planes as well as in many documents.With the first flight of the IA-58 Pucará on August 1969, a new era began for the factory, which lasted for the whole 1970s, in which Pucará production was the

Aerial view of the factory in 2010. On the left and behind the factory is the Escuela de Aviación Militar. *Santiago Rivas*

most important aspect, while the production of the IA-50 G-II was winding down, finishing in 1975. The other main production during the 1970s were Cessnas built under licence, while the factory was also working on rockets for the experiments of the IIAE and the Comisión Nacional de Investigaciones Espaciales (CNIE).

After the experience with Cessna, in 1972 Argentina tried to expand licence production and negotiations took place with Bell, Hughes, Fairchild Hiller, MBB and Aerospatiale for the construction of helicopters. However, in 1973 the idea was abandoned and, instead helicopter production was undertaken by the private company RACA S.A. with a licence for Hughes 500.

With the Pucará production starting by 1974, the Pabellón 90 was extended to 21,000m2, as the production of other types under study was also planned. The Argentine Air Force was looking for a new trainer to replace its Mentors, a jet trainer to replace the Paris and a transport aircraft, but, after analysing different proposals, only the jet trainer project progressed. This resulted in a deal with Dornier in 1979, which provided a basic design agreed between both companies called the IA-63 Pampa. Dornier also offered to develop a light fighter and to participate in another project of the 1980s, the Avión de Transporte Liviano (ATL). The work with Dornier also meant a complete modernisation of the factory, adding new tools and machinery and working with computers for the first time. The Pampa was the first plane produced to modern quality standards and meant a big step for the factory.Meanwhile, on 8 March 1976 the Fábrica de Armamento was organised again, building different types of bombs, rockets and rocket launchers, and it had new facilities 3km to the west of the FMA.

Also, from 1980 the FMA was working on different ideas with the Brazilian company Embraer, including a possible participation on what later became the AMX programme, but the new government that took over on 10 December 1983 considerably reduced the budget of the FMA. Also, in 1985 the government announced the creation of FAMA S.A. (Fábrica Argentina de Materiales Aeroespaciales) as a private company to develop projects that were to be built by the FMA and that FAMA would sell. Its owners were the Argentine Air Force with 46 per cent, Alenia/Aeritalia & Selenia SpA with 44 per cent and the Argentine company Techint with 10 per cent. The process to create the company was long and it was officially finished on 30 July 1987, with its creation made official on 22 April 1988 by decree No. 492/88.

The Italians were interested on building locally a transport version of the new A129 Mangusta helicopter, called A129 Utility, to sell it to the Argentine Armed Forces to replace the Bell UH-1H and 212, and parts of the ATR 42 transport aeroplane, but in the end the poor Argentine economic situation ended those plans.

Meanwhile, in 1986 Embraer proposed the joint development of their EMB-123 design, which was a

A Pampa during construction, seen around 2006, when production was restarted.

smaller version of their new EMB-120 Brasilia but with its two engines on the sides of the rear fuselage. In 1987 a contract was signed by the two companies and the CBA-123 project was born, which was also called IA-70 by the FMA. While the programme advanced and the first prototype flew in 1990, the Argentine economic problems and the intention of the new government that started in 1989 to reduce spending and also to privatise most state companies slowed progress. By then, Embraer was also in a very difficult situation and by the end of 1991 the CBA-123 programme had almost ground to a halt and it was finally cancelled in 1994.

By that time, the Argentine government had already decided to privatise the company, which had almost ceased all production by 1990, with some Pucarás and Pampas still on the production line, after 103 Pucarás and seventeen Pampas (three of them prototypes) had been delivered.

Meanwhile, on 5 March 1993, the private shareholders of FAMA returned their shares to the Argentine state as the company was inactive and its capital had been consumed. Finally, FAMA was liquidated on 21 October 1998.

Lockheed Aircraft Argentina

The first proposal to take charge of the factory came by the end of 1993 from Pilatus Flugzeugwerke AG, in which the Swiss company offered to buy between 55 to 60 per cent of the shares of the company, with the rest remaining with the Argentine state. However, this was not accepted. In 1994, negotiations with Lockheed began and in June 1995 the company was given to the US concern under a concession contract for twenty-five years, while a five-year maintenance contract for some aeroplanes of the Argentine Air Force was also signed. Now, the factory became Lockheed Aircraft Argentina S.A. (LAASA).

The Fábrica de Armamento was acquired by CITEA in 1994, although this failed in 1996 and the company TALA S.A. took control. In 2019, as the factory was not operating it was returned to the Argentine Air Force but was abandoned and was not put used for production again.

With the purchase of McDonnell Douglas A-4M Skyhawks for the Argentine Air Force, in 1995 another contract was signed with Lockheed for their modernisation planes, with twenty-eight of them upgraded in Córdoba. In 1996, the modernisation of thirty B45 Mentors was also contracted and in 1997, with the merger of Lockheed Corporation and Martin Marietta, the Argentine factory became Lockheed Martin Aircraft Argentina S.A. (LMAASA).

Meanwhile, aircraft production was completely stopped, although there were some unfinished planes on the line and discussions to restart this took place with the Argentine Air Force. It delivered one Pucará in 1996 and another two were sold to the Uruguayan Air Force in 1998 (one of them for use as spares), leaving two unfinished. However, shortly after the production line was removed and the tooling was sold for scrap.The Pampa production line was not disassembled and in 1999 one aircraft, which was almost ready when production stopped in 1990, was delivered and LMAASA announced in 2000 plans to restart production, including new variants. A new five-year maintenance contract was signed, but the economic crisis of 2001 in Argentina stopped those plans. They were restarted with two new contracts signed in 2003, one for maintenance and another for the construction of the Pampas, starting with six new planes of a new variant. This was called AT-63 and later IA-63 Pampa II, and the first of these was delivered in 2007. Some of the original planes were modernised to Pampa II and the factory built another ten airframes with the intention of offering them for export, but no contract was signed.

In 2007, Lockheed Martin informed the Argentine Defence Ministry that it wanted to terminate its contract and return the factory to the Argentine state, as it was not making a profit. The Defence Ministry started to work with Lockheed on the termination of the contract, while trying to encourage interest from Boeing, Airbus and Embraer in a contract to build aerostructures. Finally, on 15 December 2009 the Argentine state took control of the factory again but with no contracts signed.

FAdeA

When the relationship with Lockheed Martin was terminated, the factory was renamed again, now as Fábrica Argentina de Aviones Brigadier San Martín (FAdeA), and continued with the production of the new Pampa, but at a very low pace. A second contract for eight planes was announced in early 2010, and parts for those started to be built in early 2014. The intention, announced in 2012, was to build a total of forty Pampas (including the ten already started by LMAASA), but none was delivered until on 10 October 2013 the first of the ten airframes built by LMAASA was presented as a demonstrator for the Pampa III.

The company developed a plan with different stages, with a short-term intention of producing a two-seat basic trainer, a two-to-four-seat helicopter, UAVs and an aeroplane for crop dusting and firefighting. In the longer term, it intended to develop a four-seat basic trainer and liaison plane, a four-to-six-seat turboprop, a thirty-seat turboprop and bigger aeroplanes under licence.

For the crop duster, the factory made an agreement with the LAVIASA company of Mendoza, which had bought the type certificate of the Piper PA-25 Pawnee and developed the PA-25 Puelche, to assemble the plane from kits provided by LAVIASA, as there was a growing demand for crop dusters.

As there was interest in developing new projects, in 2010 the restart of the IA-73 project, which was under development when the privatisation of the company was decided, was announced. This project, for a basic trainer, evolved when some other Latin American countries became interested and it was named Unasur I in 2012.

Meanwhile, an approach was to China, with the intention of developing some of its projects locally. First, on 10 October 2011, on the eighty-fourth anniversary of the factory, an agreement was announced to assemble the Changhe Z-11 helicopter, while, a year later, during a ceremony to mark the eighty-fifth anniversary of the factory, an agreement was announced to assemble the CATIC JF-17 Thunder Block II multi-role combat aircraft, which was announced as the Pulqui III. The intention was to assemble at least forty, but this did not progress.

At the same time, on that same day, a Z-11 assembled at FAdeA from Chinese components was presented, with the name Pampero. It was tested by the Argentine Armed Forces during 2013, but these demonstrated its performance was poor and the project was abandoned.

Meanwhile, a contract was signed with Embraer in 2011 for the construction of components for the KC-390, namely the spoilers, nose landing gear doors, cargo door, tail cone, flap fairing and electronics rack, and this was ongoing in 2023.

The management of FAdeA between 2011 and 2015 was extremely problematic and the company accumulated a lot of debts, which in 2016 resulted in the directors during those years being prosecuted, accused of corruption, especially its president, Raúl Argañaraz. The company did not deliver any Pampas and the Puelche project progressed very slowly, despite there being a big demand for that kind of plane in Argentina. The IA-73 Unasur I showed no signs of progress by 2014 and was cancelled in 2015.

Meanwhile, in 2015, the experience gained in composite materials thanks to the work on the Embraer KC-390 led to a decision to develop a demonstrator of a light plane with two seats, the IA-100, which flew in 2016. However, tests showed the design needed too many changes.

The main wind tunnel of the factory, built in the late 1940s and beside the building where the Eiffel tunnel is located. This tunnel is still operational, but now belongs to the Centro de Investiación Aplicada (CIA, Applied Research Centre) of the Argentinian Air Force. *Santiago Rivas*

New management arrived when the government changed in December 2015 and Pampa production was restarted, with six Pampa IIIs delivered by 2019. In that year the IA-58 Pucará Fénix programme was launched, to develop an ISR modification for some Pucarás. Also, a programme to modernise the C-130H Hercules of the Argentine Air Force progressed, while one started for fifteen Agusta Bell AB-206s of the Argentine Army. Another modernisation programme, for the Argentine Navy T-34C-1 Turbo Mentors, was developed but did not progress due to a lack of budget. As the factory had a lot of facilities not in use, in 2018 was signed a contract with the German company Nordex to assemble forty-eight wind turbines for energy production and a deal with Etihad Engineering was agreed for the maintenance of Airbus A320s and Boeing 737s at the FAdeA facilities.

Production of Pampas continued slowly between 2020 and 2023, while the IA-100 evolved into the IA-100B Malvina, a basic trainer aimed at the Argentine Air Force. However, the financial returns from of the factory were bad.

Now, FAdeA is on the road to its centenary in times where the company has to define what to do with its future, having lost its reputation after several years of very low-rate production, very few sales and having the Argentine state as its main (and almost only) customer, while governments since 2009 have used it mostly as political tool rather than as an aircraft factory.

2 Local designs before 1940

3 Ae.C.1

The first plane designed by the FMA

RIGHT Construction of the first Ae.C.1, with the fittings for the wing at the place of the spars, and the location of the fuel tanks on the central part of the wing.

When Captain Bartolomé de la Colina was appointed temporarily as director of the FMA on 13 May 1930 (he was confirmed in this position on 16 March 1931), he considered that the organisation's experience with the construction of the Avro 504 and Dewoitine D.21C-1, plus the assembly of some Bristol F.2B Fighters, was enough for it to start the design of its own planes. For that, he contracted several engineers, Desiderio Biró, Juan Peretti, Natalio Trebino, Lorenzo Fontana, Alberto Vanni, Julio Alderete, Mario Rumbo, Pablo Guillot, and Dr Alberto Broglia, and technicians Andrés Levaggi, Juan Córsico, Antonio del Santo and Jaime Barcesat.

With the aim of promoting civil aviation, the first design was attempted as a tourism plane, with three seats, and was designed by a team headed by engineers Fontana and Trebino, supervised by Ambrosio Taravella. The project began in March 1931 and the first part of the design was finished on 24 August of that year; the resultant plane being called Ae.C.1 (Ae. for Dirección de Aerotécnica, C. for Civil and 1 for the first design). While the design was being finished, some parts were built and tested, so by the end of October 1931 the prototype was finished.The Ae.C.1was a light plane with a fuselage of rectangular section made with welded chrome-molybdenum tubes, with low cantilever wooden wings with a Göttingen profile and two main spars. All was covered with fabric and the plane had a closed cockpit with three seats, one in the front and two at the back, with a canopy that slid open to the rear. It was powered by a five-cylinder Armstrong Siddeley Mongoose of 150hp with a wooden two-blade propeller and a Townend ring.

BELOW Tests on the structure of the Ae.C.1 before the construction of the first prototype.

There were many in the Argentine Army who were against the production of indigenous designs and supported the idea of only building under licence, Captain de la Colina decided to make the first flight in private, something made at midday on 28 October 1931, when the Ae.C.1 took to the air piloted by Sargento 1° José Honorio Rodríguez. After the plane landed safely, de la Colina informed the press that the plane was going to be presented the following day in the presence of the War Minister, General Francisco Medina.

During November, the plane was tested extensively and showed good performance, although the instrument panel positioning was changed, so on 15 December Sergeant Honorio Rodríguez and a

ABOVE LEFT Instrument panel of the first Ae.C.1. The closed cockpit offered little visibility outside.

ABOVE RIGHT The first Ae.C.1, called Tenga Paciencia, in front of the FMA hangar.

mechanic named Bussill, flew to Buenos Aires to display it, making the 700km trip in three hours twelve minutes and landing at El Palomar. Six days later the plane was presented to the public and authorities, including the War Minister, the Navy Minister Rear Admiral Carlos Daireaux and the Director General de Aeronáutica, Lt Col Ángel María Zuloaga. During that presentation, the plane was exhibited in flight and also took officials up on flights.

After that, the plane was disassembled and taken to downtown Buenos Aires to be exhibited in an Automobile Salon organised by the Automóvil Club Argentino, which opened on 23 December.

Meanwhile, the Army Aviation took a lot of interest in the plane, not as a light transport but as a trainer to replace the Avro 504, and for that mission they wanted a new design of the cockpit. So, according to the annual memoir of the Dirección de Aerotécnica, another example was built, with two seats in tandem in an open cockpit, with two separated positions, and an Armstrong Siddeley Genet Major with a NACA cowling instead of the Townend ring. It was called the Ae.C.1 Prototipo and was pressed into service with the Army in early 1932, while the other was named *Tenga Paciencia* (Have patience) and was tested with a Gnome Rhône Monosoupape of 100hp that was removed from an Avro 504 when those planes received the Genet Major.

From 5 July 1932 and during the rest of the month, the first Ae.C.1 was exhibited in the Primer Salón de Aeronáutica at the Sociedad Wagneriana de Buenos Aires, together with the prototype of the Ae.C.2, an Avro 504 and a Dewoitine D.21C-1.

To Brazil and back

In 1933 the second plane was chosen to take part with six Ae.M.E.1s, one Ae.C.2 and one Ae.T.1, accompanied by a Junkers F13ge, on a trip to Rio de Janeiro, Brazil, to promote the Argentine Aviation industry, taking advantage of a visit to the country by Argentine president General Agustín P. Justo.

The Ae.C.1 received an extra fuel tank on the rear seat, but, as the fuel was being consumed, the centre of gravity changed considerably and the plane became very hard to control, so the tank was changed to the front seat. The endurance was augmented from four to eight hours.

The Ae.C.1 being readied for a flight. The plane lacks the Townend ring around the engine.

Sargento 1º José Honorio Rodríguez in front of the first Ae.C.1 at El Palomar around 1932. Note the instrument panel is different from the original layout. The plane lacks the cockpit canopy and the Townend ring on the engine. Also, the plane does not have the Argentine roundel on the sides.

Colonel Zuloaga commanded the flight and travelled as passenger of the Ae.T.1, named *General San Martín*. The flight was organised into three escadrilles, one with the Ae.T.1 commanded by 1st Lt Martín Cairó with Sergeant Honorio Rodríguez, technician Octavio Scoppa and 1st Sgt León Castillo as radio operator, the Ae.C.1 with 1st Lt Luis Garramendy, the Ae.C.2 with Lt Carlos Mauriño and the Junkers F13ge with L Nicolás Ferro Sessarego and Sgt José Bauman as radio operator.

Another flight was organised with three Ae.M.E.1s, with the plane serialled 2 with Captain Edmundo Sustaita and Lt Medardo Gallardo Valdez, No. 5 with Lt Pablo Passio and 1st Sgt Luis Ortúzar, and No. 4 with 1st Lt Raúl Pizales and Lt César Lavalle.

The last flight, also with three Ae.M.E.1s, comprised plane No. 3 with 1st Lt Miguel Cardalda and 1st Corporal Nicasio Herrasti, No. 6 with 1st Sgt Miguel Balado and 1st Sgt Ángel Tula and No. 1 with 1st Lt Justo Ossorio Arana and Lt Augusto Bolognini.

On 3 October 1933 at 0745 the flight, called Escuadrilla Sol de Mayo, departed from El Palomar and was escorted for half an hour by three Dewoitine D.25s, three Breguet XIXs and three Junkers K43s. At 1320 they landed at Pelotas, Brazil, having flown the first 690km. At 1500 they took off for Florianópolis, but they had to return because of bad weather and then had to stay in Pelotas until the next day, departing at 0650. However, at 0900 they had to land at Porto Alegre due to more bad weather, taking off again at 1045 and arriving at their next stop at 1405. On the 5th they took off early in the morning and touched down at Santos at 1145, where the Ae.M.E.1 broke one leg of the landing gear while landing. The plane was repaired fast and at 0815 the next day they took off and

ABOVE Officers of the Argentine Army and Navy inspecting the Ae.C.1 at the presentation in El Palomar.

RIGHT The first Ae.C.1 at the FMA. The canopy of the cockpit was made of welded tubes covered with fabric.

The second Ae.C.1, called Prototipo and built in late 1931 for the Argentine Army with the intention of developing a new trainer. The plane had two seats, an Armstrong Siddeley Genet Major engine with a NACA cowling, modifications to the stabilisers and other changes.

landed at 1115 at Campo dos Afonsos airfield in Rio de Janeiro, escorted by a flight of Vought Corsairs of the Brazilian Army.

Zuloaga recalled that:

> My only moment of anxiety during the flight was shortly before arriving at Campo dos Afonsos. Each section had been ordered to transmit anything of importance to the command aircraft. In turn, I called the section commanders every ten minutes. We flew inside a bank of clouds, flew several kilometres over the ocean and at a convenient height, and then, passing over Rio de Janeiro, entered the aforementioned air base in a pre-established order. All sections responded to the command's calls, except the second, despite my insistent calls. Alarmed by this, I resolved to order the successive landing of the first and third sections, and then to devote myself to ascertaining the position of the other. I explored above the clouds, then flew 50km back flying 200m above the water and without losing sight of the coast, which, as we know, is all steep, with very few and small beaches.
>
> I became supremely anxious to know as soon as possible where the second section was. Knowing the expertise of the crews, I was reluctant to think there had been a catastrophe, and consequently I sent a message to the destination base requesting reports. Minutes later I received the good news that the section had just landed, with their only issue being that their radio station was broken.[1]

[1] Ángel M. Zuloaga, *La Victoria de las Alas,* Colección Aeronáutica Argentina, Buenos Aires, 1957

ABOVE The second Ae.C.1 modified as single seater, with an extra tank in place of the front seat.

LEFT The second Ae.C.1 in its final configuration. The plane was retired around 1934, but it is possible some components were used for the very similar Ae.M.E.1.

Some of the planes of the Escuadrilla Sol de Mayo, with the Ae.T.1, three of the Ae.M.E.1s, the Ae.C.2 Tenga Confianza and the Ae.C.1 Tenga Paciencia.

On 15 October they started to return, departing at 0920, carrying Lt Col Ángel Mendes de Moraes of the Brazilian Army and Frigate Captain Ismael Brazil as passengers on the Ae.T.1. At 1223 they landed at Santos and at 1330 they continued to Florianópolis, arriving at 1640, but Ae.M.E.1 No. 1 had to return to Santos because of a fuel leak and Ae.M.E.1 No. 3 had to land at Paranaguá, accompanied by No. 6 and the Junkers F13. However, the latter crash-landed and had to be disassembled to be taken back to Buenos Aires by land. The two Ae.M.E.1s were joined by plane No. 1 and the three had flown to Florianópolis by the end of the day. On 16 October they travelled to Pando airfield in Montevideo, Uruguay, arriving at 1430, after a short stop in Pelotas. A Junkers K43 travelled to support the last leg and at 1550 they took off, arriving at El Palomar at 1744 and thus ending the first flight outside Argentina of aeroplanes built at the FMA.

The fate of the two Ae.C.1s is unknown, but in 1934 they disappeared from all records. As none was lost on accidents, most probably their components were used in the Ae.C.2/Ae.M.E.1, which were similar.

4 Ae.C.2, Ae.M.E.1, Ae.C.3, Ae.C.3G and Ae.C.4

After the experience gained with the Ae.C.1, in early 1932 the FMA decided to develop an improved version to be used as a trainer, with twin controls, both for the civil market and the Army, but also for air mail, observation, police duties and transport. This was powered by a Wright R-540E Whirlwind of 165hp and five cylinders, and a horizontal stabiliser that could be regulated in flight. While the plane was built in the same way, the sides of the fuselage consisted of two panels on each side covered with fabric that were attached to the structure so it could be easily removed for maintenance. Behind the cockpit was a luggage compartment.

Although initially also being called the Ae.C.1, by March 1932 the name was changed to Ae.C.2. A prototype was built and flown on 19 April, flown by Sargento Ayudante Honorio Rodríguez. The plane received a Townend ring shortly after and the construction of another ten airframes began, half of which had been built by the end of the year.

The prototype was sold to the government of San Juan province, the first sale by the FMA, and a big ceremony was organised by the end of December of 1932 for the delivery and the official presentation of the Ae.C.2, in the presence of Argentine president General Agustín P. Justo. At the ceremony, the pilot contracted by San Juan province to operate the plane, Renato Balleri, gave an aerobatics demonstration in it. The Ae.C.2 received the civil serial R226 on 9 January 1933.On 28 March 1933 Balleri started a flight called 'Raid de las 25 horas por la Argentina y el Paraguay' in which he travelled over most of northern Argentina and reached Asunción in Paraguay, in what was the first flight abroad of a plane built by the FMA. Unfortunately, on 28 March 1934, Balleri had an accident at La Paz, Mendoza province, on a flight from San Juan that was expected to stop at Mendoza and then fly to San Luis and back to San Juan. The plane was seriously damaged and not repaired, being officially written off on 18 December 1946 after the Instituto Aerotécnico issued resolution 2527/46 stating that repair was not worth it.

A second plane was delivered by April 1932, but had some differences, as it had a fairing over the fuselage from the tail to the engine, which limited the visibility forward, a pitot tube on the leading edge of the left wing, fairings on the landing gear with bigger wheels for unprepared runways and it lacked the Townend ring. The second pilot position could be covered when not in use.It was given the name *Tenga Confianza* (Have Confidence) and was intended to do a tour of the fourteen provinces of Argentina at that time (the rest of the country, as it was almost unpopulated, was organised into territories governed directly from Buenos Aires and over the years they became another nine provinces).

The tour began at Córdoba at 2230 on 16 June 1932 with the plane flown by Lts Justo Osorio Arana and Martín R. Cairó, who attempted to link all the provinces in less than one day. They headed to the city of San Luis, but they did not land and continued to Mendoza, where they refuelled. A second stage was started and, after flying over the cities of San Juan, La Rioja and Catamarca, they landed at San Miguel de Tucumán, now with Cairó at the controls. From there, after refuelling again and with Osorio Arana flying, they flew over Salta and Jujuy and landed at Santiago del Estero. The next stage was with Cairó flying the plane and they reached the city of Resistencia, from where Osorio Arana took over to fly over Corrientes, Santa Fe and Paraná. They landed at El Palomar in the early hours of 18 June, twenty-eight hours after their departure, having flown about 3,500km with no problems.

The success of the flight was promoted by de Arteaga to show the quality of the planes built by the FMA and the plane, together with the first Ae.C.1, were shown at the Primer Salón de Aeronáutica at the Sociedad Wagneriana de Buenos Aires during July. On 30 July the Ae.C.2was taken back to Córdoba by Lt. Ángel María Zuloaga and Martín R. Cairó.

Shortly after, this Ae.C.2 was painted in a white and red paint scheme and on 18 April 1933 Suboficial

TOP The first Ae.C.2 at the factory when it was delivered to the San Juan government in December 1932.

ABOVE The second Ae.C.2, named 'Tenga Confianza', had a fairing over the upper part of the fuselage and a different cockpit.

LEFT By late 1932 the 'Tenga Confianza' had received a special paint scheme to perform some raids over Argentina. Note the fairings on the wheels and the lack of the NACA ring that the first plane had.

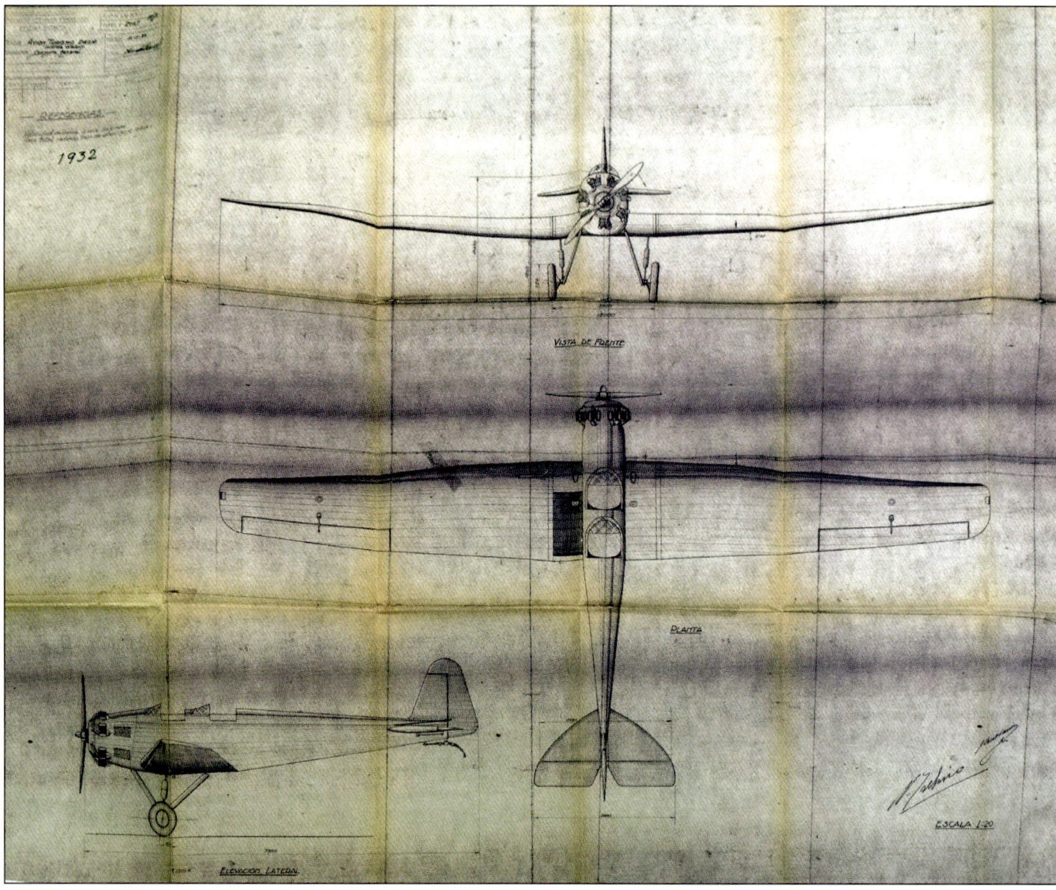

Plan of the Ae.C.2 with 240hp Wright Whirlwind R-760 seven-cylinder engine. The date of the plan is 4 November 1932.

José Honorio Rodríguez, carrying Major Bartolomé de la Colina, made another long flight, going to the east to the town of Rufino, Santa Fe, then to Villa Mercedes, San Luis, and then to Mendoza.

After this flight, the plane was taken from El Palomar to Córdoba on 5 May 1933 by Suboficial Rodríguez and 1st Lt Juan Luis Garramendy. There it was modified with a 240hp Whirlwind R-760 seven-cylinder engine, while the fairings of the wheels were removed and the rear seat was removed to install a 250-litre tank fuel to extend the range to eight hours. After some tests, it was decided to modify the windscreen, also installing a new cowling without the upper fairing to improve visibility.

The 'Tenga Confianza' with the rear seat removed, as well as the fairings for the wheels, and with the new R-760 engine installed.

With this configuration, on 19 June Garramendy started a flight from Buenos Aires to Rio de Janeiro, making stops in Montevideo, Porto Alegre and Santos and returning in the first days of July.

More planes and the Ae.M.E.1

After the *Tenga Confianza*, another plane was finished and flew on 9 October 1932. It had a similar configuration to the first Ae.C.2 but without the Townend ring, some differences on the pilot's cabin and small fairings on the wheels. As it was intended to be used for training, it was called Ae.M.E.1 (Aerotécnica Militar Entrenamiento) and delivered to the Army.

Another five Ae.C.2s were also finished during 1933 and delivered to the Army. They were similar to the Ae.M.E.1 but without the fairings on the wheels. While the Ae.M.E.1 received the serial 1, the other five were-serialled 2 to 6. Although initially being designated as Ae.C.2 as they were to be used at the Escuela de Aviación Militar, they were renamed Ae.M.E.1 shortly after.

The *Tenga Confianza*, together with the six Ae.M.E.1s, took part in the flight of the Sol de Mayo escadrille to Brazil, as described in Chapter 3.

In 1934 another two Ae.M.E.1s were delivered, serialled 7 and 8 and all the Ae.M.E.1s, except the one serialled 2 whose fate is unknown, were sent to

As the visibility to the front of the 'Tenga Confianza' was poor, the fairing between the cockpit and the engine was removed and a new windscreen installed, as seen here. The windscreen was later changed for a bigger one, with the pilot seat higher.

The Ae.M.E.1 had a cabin with improved visibility, a metal propeller and some other small improvements. The plane later received the serial 1.

the Grupo 1 de Observación y Bombardeo at Base Aérea Militar (BAM) General Urquiza, in the city of Paraná, capital of the province of Entre Ríos.

On 6 June 1934 the Ae.M.E.1 serialled 5 had an accident and was written off, while the same happened with No. 6 on 10 September.

During the year, the aircraft were sent to Las Lomitas in the Formosa territory to patrol the border with Bolivia and Paraguay, which were involved in a war over the Chaco area and the Argentine government feared that the area could be used by troops of the belligerent countries or to smuggle weapons. On 9 September 1932 the Argentine Army had created the Destacamento Mixto de Formosa with ground troops and a flight of Dewoitine D.21s and Avro 626 Trainers, based at the new Base Aérea Frontera Norte, and while no activity was recorded at the airfield during 1933, the Ae.M.E.1s were sent in 1934.There is no information about their performance during their deployment, and there is also no record of their activity, as well as of that of the *Tenga Confianza*, after 1935, when one Ae.M.E.1 was tested briefly by the Argentine Navy. The Ae.M.E.1s were officially retired in 1945.

The Ae.C.2 with constructor number 002 (the 'Tenga Confianza' had no constructor number), which was built similar to the Ae.M.E.1 but without the fairings on the wheels and with a wooden propeller. It was later delivered to the Army and renamed Ae.M.E.1, with serial 2.

Ae.C.2 serialled 5 in use by the Military Aviation School of the Argentine Army.

Ae.C.3

Following the development of the previous types, the Ae.C.3 was designed, also being a tandem two-seater with a vertical fin similar to the Ae.M.O.1, a 145hp Armstrong Siddeley Genet Major engine with a Townend ring on a nose longer than the Ae.C.2. It made its first flight on 27 March 1934 with Sargento Ayudante José Honorio Rodríguez at the controls.

The type was planned to be delivered to the air clubs that were being organised all over Argentina, and the Dirección General de Aeronáutica Civil, which was run by the Ministry of Interior, purchased ten to deliver them for free to selected clubs.

A second plane was built and delivered on 12 August of the same year and was delivered shortly

The first Ae.C.3 after leaving the factory.

The sixth Ae.C.3 with the closed cockpit.

after to the Aero Club Posadas, in Misiones territory (now a province).

On 12 November 1934, civil pilot Miguel Vera flew the prototype from the FMA to Seis de Septiembre aerodrome in Morón, in the suburbs of Buenos Aires, to present the plane, while two days later the second Ae.C.3 and the Ae.C.2 *Tenga Confianza* were used by Sergeants José Honorio Rodríguez and Santiago Germanó to fly between Córdoba to the city of Paraná, Entre Ríos province, and Posadas, delivering the plane.

Production of the Ae.C.3 continued during the year, in which sales were made to the Aero Club Argentino for two planes, the both the Centro Universitario de Aviación and the Aero Club Pigüé for one example.Ae.C.3 No. 005 was the third to be delivered, to the Aero Club Pigüé on 9 December 1934, and it received the civil serial R270. It was followed by No. 003 for the Centro Universitario de Aviación on 22 April 1935 and the first for the Aero Club Argentino on 28 August 1935.

The aircraft demonstrated problems with lateral control, had a high landing speed and were considered fragile, suffering some minor accidents that made them unpopular. To promote them, the sixth plane was used by the FMA for demonstrations, starting on 4 March 1935 with a return flight between Buenos Aires and Río Gallegos. Civil pilot Pedro V. Mórtola flew the 5,200km in thirty-seven hours twenty minutes. Later, on 31 March, pilot Carola Lorenzini broke the South American female height record with this plane, reaching 5,380m. For this attempt the aeroplane received a canopy over

BELOW Although the Ae.C.3G was presented as just an Ae.C.3 with a Gipsy engine, in fact it was a totally different aeroplane, with a new wing with flaps, new tail, new windscreens, new landing gear and a different fuselage.

the cabin to reduce the cold. This example was among those sold to the Dirección General de Aeronáutica Civil and on 12 February 1936 it was delivered to Aero Club Coronel Suárez.

The eighth plane was finished with a 145hp Warner Super Scarab engine, which was adopted from then on, and was the second purchased by the Centro Universitario de Aviación. The seventh plane, which was started in 1935, was the last finished with the Genet Major engine and it was delivered in 1936 and used by the FMA for promotion.

Ae.C.3G and Ae.C.4

To improve the performance at low speeds and reduce the landing speed, in 1935 the FMA studied the addition of flaps on the type, with a redesigned wing, as well as a new rudder and stabiliser, a new cabin with a different windscreen, new landing gear and powered by a 130hp de Havilland Gipsy Major engine. Although these developments made the aircraft very different from the Ae.C.3, it was named Ae.C.3G, with the G meaning Gipsy.

The prototype flew for the first time on 21 January 1936 piloted by Lt Pablo Celestino Passio and it was found to be far better than the original Ae.C.3, so production was announced shortly after and construction of another nine was started.

At the same time, during 1935 the development of a new aeroplane began, with the same wing, landing gear and engine but with a slightly different fuselage with different cabin and a new tail, aimed at improving performance. The model, called Ae.C.4, was flown for the first time on 17 October 1936 by Lt Pablo Passio.

The end

Meanwhile, the ninth Ae.C.3 was displayed during the Reunión de Aeronáutica held at Resistencia (Chaco territory) on 12 April 1936. It was piloted by Sgt Santiago Germanó, who won the aerobatics competition. The FMA continued production of the Ae.C.3 during the year and delivered eight with

The second Ae.C.3G seen with an Ae.M.Oe.2. This example and the third had a larger tail and some differences in the cockpit. The flaps adopted by the Ae.C.3G are also visible.

The third and last Ae.C.3G. Note the wheels do not have the fairing that the first Ae.C.3G used.

The Ae.C.4 was the last product of this series, having a different cockpit and tail. Only one was built and it was used briefly before it was scrapped.

Wind tunnel model preserved at the Centro de Investigación Aplicada of the Argentine Air Force of a version of the Ae.C.3G with closed cockpit, which was never built. *Santiago Rivas*

Warner Super Scarabs, while another one was almost ready by the end of the year.

However, the Ae.C.3 proved difficult to fly, especially by new pilots at the air clubs where it was intended to be used for training. This and the several minor accidents suffered and the loss of R284 of the Aero Club Argentino on 13 July 1937 (it was the fourth built), meant that by the end of 1936 the Dirección General de Aeronáutica Civil limited the manoeuvres that could be made in the type. Then, on 15 March 1937, an order was made to ground them, and by the beginning of 1938 the eight planes that the Dirección General de Aeronáutica Civil had delivered to air clubs (a ninth was in use by the directorship) were returned to them and scrapped. The sixteenth Ae.C.3, which was under construction by the end of 1936 and was going to be the last of the ten contracted, was never finished.

The poor reputation of the Ae.C.3 and the military types being built by the factory also affected the much better Ae.C.3G. Only two were finished after the prototype, one in 1936 and the other in 1937, because the Dirección General de Aeronáutica Civil cancelled the negotiations to buy the ten under construction. The three Ae.C.3Gs and the Ae.C.4 remained at the FMA and were used occasionally. The fate of the Ae.C.4 is unknown, while the others were finally retired in 1942.

A wind tunnel model of an Ae.C.3G with a closed cabin is preserved at the Centro de Investigación Aplicada, the site of the factory wind tunnels, but no extra information about that version was found.

5 Ae.M.O.1, Ae.M.Oe.1, Ae.M.Oe.2 and Ae.M.S.1

With the experience gained during the development of the Ae.M.E.1, it was planned to develop a plane to replace the Avro 626 Trainer for advanced training, flown by a pilot and a cadet or an observer. In addition, it was to serve as an observation and light bombing aircraft, carrying the same armament as the Trainer, with the same fuel consumption but with superior performance. During 1933 the Dirección de Aerotécnica (Directorate of Aerotechnics) of the FMA worked on plans to build fifteen observation examples and as many bombing examples in the following year, equipped with the 240hp Wright Whirlwind R-760ET radial engine of seven cylinders with a Hamilton Standard fixed-pitch propeller. They also tested the wing, which was designed in 1932, on 22 August 1933. Meanwhile, the first prototype was ready in December and FMA began manufacturing a series of eleven. The type was a monoplane, tandem two-seater, with an open cockpit, and with a configuration based on that of the Ae.M.E.1, although it was larger and more powerful. The second seat was for an observer or operator, but dual commands could be installed for training.

The first prototype of the Ae.M.O.1 with the machine gun firing forward and the one for the observer installed, as well as the bomb support in the belly.

The Ae.M.O.1 flies

On 24 January 1934 the first Ae.M.O.1 (Aerotécnica, Militar, Observación 1) flew successfully for the first time in the hands of FMA test pilot Sergeant Rodríguez. The tests continued without problems and by July the prototype and the other eleven examples, serialled 1 to 12, were delivered to the Argentine military aviation. The first four were sent to Grupo 1 de Observación y Bombardeo of the BAM General Urquiza, in the city of Paraná, where they served together with the Ae.M.E.1 and Dewoitine D.21. Four (serialled 5 to 8) went to

| Delivery of the second series of aircraft at the facilities of the FMA.

BAM Los Tamarindos in the city of Mendoza and four to the Military School of Aviation, located until 1937 in the BAM El Palomar, on the outskirts of Buenos Aires. According to the records of the units from that year, all the planes met expectations.

These aeroplanes could be equipped with a 7.5mm Vickers machine gun with 500 rounds in the observer's station for defensive air combat. It was planned to equip them with another, with 200 rounds, on the cowling for offensive air combat training, firing synchronised with the propeller, but this was only installed in the first prototype. They could also carry four training bombs of 10kg each, with a Busch sight for bombing training, a Gauman camera behind the observer's post for photo survey training, operated by the observer, or communication equipment in the same place, with an in-flight, unrollable antenna. Also, they could carry special navigation equipment, like a sextant and a small table for charts, for navigation training flights and Holt and navigation lights and batteries for night flights.The fuselage was made of metal tubes covered with fabric, with wooden wings also covered with fabric. There were four fuel tanks on the wings and a gravity tank in the centre, with a total capacity of 300 litres, giving a total endurance of five hours nine minutes and a range of 1,000km.

The plane had a cruise speed of 190km/h at sea level, a maximum of 209km/h at 500m, a maximum speed of 250km/h in a dive and a stall speed of 90km/h. The time taken to climb to 5,000m was forty minutes and the service ceiling was 6,200m. The take off distance was 100m and for landing was 200m without using brakes. The empty weight was 965kg and the maximum 1,434kg.

The first series production planes had a modified machine gun mount for the observer, with better ability to fire in all directions.

The plane serialled 14 with the radio installed. Those planes received a generator with a small propeller to give power to the equipment.

The second Ae.M.O.1, as well as the first prototype, had a back seat without the ring for the machine gun.

Meanwhile, at the FMA construction progressed of a second series of fifteen (serials 13 to 27) and the construction of a similar-sized batch began (28 to 42), all with some changes, especially a redesign of the tail, a larger vertical and horizontal stabiliser with straight edges and the last series incorporating a NACA speed ring to improve performance, plus wheels with hydraulic brakes tested on plane No. 28. In addition, to improve performance, they began the design of a new version, working on the first aircraft of this new series, with a cowling for the engine, a larger join of the wing with the fuselage and a windscreen in three flat pieces, instead of a single one. This version was named Ae.M.Oe.1 to differentiate it from the others and it flew for the first time on 5 July 1934.

In 1935 the twenty-nine Ae.M.O.1s of the second and third series were delivered, reaching the 41st example. The first Ae.M.Oe.1 received the serial 42, while a series of another five was under construction.

The Ae.M.O.1 enters service

During that year the BAM Urquiza received more aircraft and integrated the Grupo 3 and 4 de Observación, in which they replaced the Breguet XIX and some Dewoitine D.21s in this task. At the Military Aviation School they joined the Avro Gosport and Avro Trainer but although they took over many of their functions, they never came to replace the British types and the two eventually retired together.

The BAM Los Tamarindos also actively employed its Ae.M.Oe.1s for observation, training, light bombardment and liaison tasks.

From 25 September 1935, by Order of the Day 2090 and by Resolution of the Minister of War S-9075-Cde. 13.380 (MG) R-888 (D.G.Ae.), all Ae.M.O.1s were redesignated Ae.M.Oe.1s, to homogenise the designation, although they maintained their differences with the newer model.

In 1936 the number of aircraft built reached forty-seven with the delivery of five Ae.M.Oe.1s. Construction began of the last series of fourteen examples and these, designated Ae.M.Oe.2, incorporated more innovations, with a larger tail and a horizontal stabiliser with straight edges. The first of them, serial 48, entered service at the beginning of 1937, but would be lost in an accident on 18 November in Campo de Mayo. This cost the life of the mechanic of the plane, while the pilot managed to escape by parachute.

Accidents and modifications

Other fatal accidents led to the loss eleven aircraft between 1934 and 1937 and led to a harsh questioning of the activity of the FMA and its products. This culminated in 1938 in the ending of home-developed projects and the return of licensed manufacturing, in addition to the purchase of numerous models abroad. Because of its slow speed and difficult handling, the type was called 'Tronco' (Trunk) by its pilots.

On 17 November 1936 a batch of 7.65mm and 11.25mm Madsen machine guns was purchased to equip the Ae.M.O. and the Ae.M.B.1 bombers, replacing the 7.5mm Vickers with the 7.65mm Madsen in the Ae.M.O.s. However, only the Ae.M.O.1 used the machine guns and no data is known regarding their use in the Ae.M.Oe.1 and Ae.M.Oe.2. One example was tested at that time with a rear machine gun in a simpler mount than the mounting of the Vickers and another in the cowling.

As many design deficiencies were found that led to many of the accidents, during 1937 all Ae.M.O.1s of the first series were decommissioned, leaving only four in service for the parade over Buenos Aires on 9 July, Argentine Independence Day, when the Ae.M.O. flew in greater quantity, reaching forty-eight aircraft of

The planes modified with the new tail were also designated Ae.M.Oe.2, although they were originally built as Ae.M.O.1s or Ae.M.Oe.1s.

The plane serialled 41 received a NACA ring, which was the basis of the development of a cowling installed in the Ae.M.Oe.2.

The plane 42 was the first Ae.M.Oe.1 but received all the modifications of the Ae.M.Oe.2, including the new tail and new engine installation with a modified nose and a cowling. After 1944 all planes received a modification of the serials, adding letters. 'Ea' meant Escuela Avanzada (Advanced School) and was added to the Ae.M.Oe. serials.

LEFT One of the Ae.M.Oe.1s with an engine cowling but still with the small tail.

BELOW LEFT Plane 59 is one of the last built of the type and had many improvements. While the type could have evolved, the criticism of the locally designed types led to the decision to buy new planes abroad and return to licence production.

BELOW Side and upper view of the Ae.M.Oe.2.

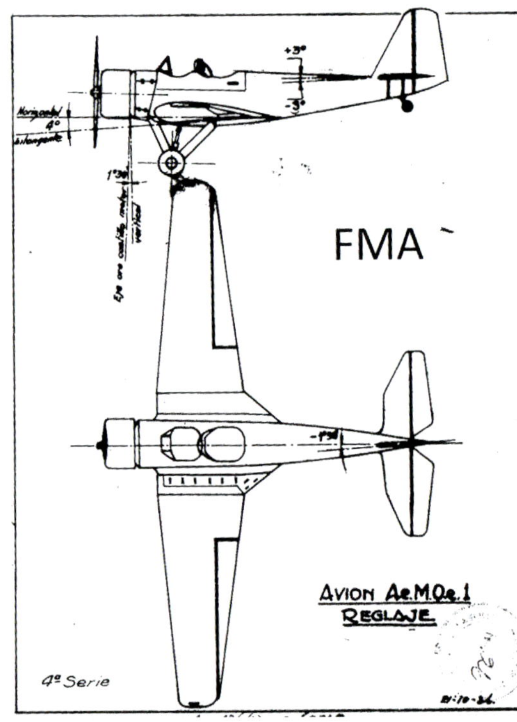

A big formation for an air parade, with nine Ae.M.Oe.1s, all wearing a NACA ring, two Junkers K43s and the Ae.M.S.1, the only known picture in which this latter type is seen flying. The Ae.M.Oe.1s serialled 31, 32, 33, 35, 36, 37, 38, 39 and 40 are seen. The picture looks as if it was taken from another Ae.M.Oe.1.

The Ae.M.T.1 was initially called Ae.M.O. con cabina and later Ae.T.3.

the fifty that were in service at that time. Also, after the parade, No. 16 crashed on the waterfront of Buenos Aires, causing the death of the pilot.

In order to improve the performance of the Ae.M.Oe.1s, during 1938 the FMA modified eighteen Ae.M.Oe.1s into Ae.M.Oe.2s (only the tail was changed), work that was continued in the following years and reached almost the entire fleet. In addition, most examples were transferred to the Escuela de Aviación Militar (thirty in 1939), leaving only a few in the BAM Urquiza and the BAM El Plumerillo (ex Los Tamarindos) for liaison and observation.

Into the 1940s

Due to the problems of fragility that the type demonstrated, the Reserved Order 2 of 18 March 1941 was issued, by which the Ae.M.Oe.2 would be used exclusively for local training flights with strict prohibition of aerobatics.

At that time, the effects of the Second World War were felt in Argentina in the impossibility of importing strategic materials, and the operational status of the weapons systems of the Army Aviation Command (Army Air Forces Command until 1943) had become reduced, especially in terms of the main combat aircraft. For this reason, which led again to the construction of local designs such as the I.Ae. DL-22 and the I.Ae.24 Calquin, in 1943 it was decided to group the workshops by type of aircraft. Work on all the Ae.M.Oe.1s and 2s were now carried out at BAM Urquiza, where most of the fleet now served, next to the Ae.M.B.2, and they received new radio equipment at the end of the year.

When 1947 began, the Argentine Air Force only counted in its fleet twenty-one Ae.M.Oe.1s and 2s, although many of them did not fly. The annual report of Grupo 1 de Observación specified that 'the main material is the DL. The Ae.M.B.2 and Ae.M.Oe.2 no longer have a reason for their existence because they do not adapt to the specialty of the Group. The Taylorcraft and Boyero are very useful for liaison.' Thus, in 1947 thirteen of the twenty-one aircraft were decommissioned and in 1948 at the General Urquiza Military Air Base the Ae.M.Oe.1 and 2 gave their last year of service. Between the beginning of the year and 31 May, aircraft 31, 36, 38, 39, 47, 51, 54 and 55 were decommissioned.

The remains of some aircraft were used in the technical schools of the FAA but little by little they disappeared and now only a fuselage of an Ae.M.Oe. is preserved at the Museo de la Industria in the city of Córdoba.

The Ae.M.O. marked the end of an era of experimentation in the factory, whose objective was to open the way to the construction of high-performance aircraft and had to suffer the harsh criticism of those who did not see that, although it was a more difficult path, national industrial development was the only way to have autonomous air power.

The Ae.M.T.1/Ae.M.S.1

In 1934, after a proposal by engineer Alberto Roque Macías, who was a forerunner of Argentine aviation but also a member of the Argentine Red Cross, the FMA designed and built a modified Ae.M.Oe.1 for medical evacuation, with the intention of building a series of planes to deliver them to the aeroclubs. It incorporated a 30hp Wright Whirlwind R-975 engine, and although it maintained the configuration of the wings, the tail and the landing gear of the Ae.M.Oe.1, the cabin was completely closed and could carry a doctor and four stretchers. This aircraft was originally called the Ae.M.Oe. con cabina (with cabin), later the Ae.T.3, but it finally flew on 21 November 1935 as the Ae.M.T.1 (Aerotécnica Militar Transporte 1). Shortly after it was renamed the Ae.M.S.1 (Aerotécnica Militar Sanitario 1), it flew for the first time and five days later was delivered to the Military Aviation School for evaluation with serial 01. It later went to the Grupo 1 de Observación.

The sole Ae.M.S.1 ended its days used to drop paratroopers, with all the interior of the rear cabin removed to carry up to five troops. Its small door and the need to walk over the wing to jump made the operation very complicated and by 1946 it was grounded and retired in 1947.

On 19 December 1935 it was officially unveiled at El Palomar and captain Pedro Castex Lainfor flew Argentine president General Agustín Pedro Justo.

In 1936, ten wings were built for more Ae.M.T.1s, but no more of the type were built and most probably those wings were used on the Ae.M.Oe.

In 1944, as the plane was no longer used for medical evacuation, it was sent to the newly created Escuela de Tropas Aerotransportadas (Airborne Troops School) at Córdoba, which was inaugurated on 11 October 1943. The Ae.M.T.1 performed the first paratrooper dropping in Argentina on 30 November 1944. Major Ibarra; Captain Valarche; 1st Lieutenants Lima and Bonafina; Lieutenants Riportella, Binotti, Mendizábal, Roca and Balmaceda Moreno; 1st Sergeant Mario Galasso and Sergeant Roberto Camossa jumped from the plane, which was flown by pilot auxiliary NCO Jorge Gallo. The paratroopers, who used a single modified back parachute (from those used on the seat of aeroplanes), crouched through the reduced door of the plane and, after leaning on the wing, jumped in a difficult and risky manoeuvre.

The plane was criticised because of its small size, small door and the difficulties of jumping. By 1946 the Ae.M.T.1 had been grounded and on 8 August 1947 it was officially retired and scrapped shortly after.

6 Ae.T.1 and Ae.T.2

After its experience with the Ae.C.1 and Ae.C.2, the FMA decided to develop a larger type for transport, with the intention of offering it to the Aeroposta Argentina S.A. airline, which was flying from Buenos Aires to Río Gallegos, on the southern end of the Patagonia, with old Latécoère Laté XXV aircraft. Also, the Argentine Army was developing its own transport aviation with the Junkers F13, K43 and W34 and needed more aeroplanes.

The new project was initiated in May 1932 and named Ae.C.X, to powered by a 300hp Hispano Suiza engine. It carried two pilots and four passengers with up to 15kg of luggage each, having a luggage compartment besides the passenger cabin, with an opening to the left. The passenger cabin had access doors on both sides, in the middle of the cabin.

The plane was expected to have a wingspan of 17.3m, a height of 3.9m, a length of 9.64m, a wheelbase of 2.7m, a wing area of 35m2, with a horizontal empennage area of 5.2m2 with the fin area 2.1m2. The empty weight was expected to be around 1,200kg with the ability to carry a payload of around 800kg. The approximate maximum speed would be around 210km/h with a cruise speed of 175km/h and a stall speed of 70km/h. It was planned with a service ceiling of 6,500m, an endurance of five hours and a range of 1,000km.

Construction would be of wooden wings, with pine structure and stringer souls and ribs of plywood birch, covered with fabric, with the leading edge in birch plywood. The fuselage was made with steel tubes covered with metal on the sides of the cabin and fabric on the tail and on the top of the cabin. The construction was analogous to that of the Ae.C.1 and Ae.C.2, with a fuselage structure of welded chrome molybdenum steel tubes, the engine mount entirely of pylons and Duralumin sheeting analogous to that of the Dewoitine D.21 and attached to the fuselage with four pins.

The landing gear was equipped with Dunlop low-pressure wheels and Sandow shock absorbers with brakes.

Structure of the Ae.C.X built to test the systems and accommodation, equipped with the Hispano Suiza engine.

Construction of the first Ae.T.1, where the passenger cabin could be seen, as well as the luggage compartment that was behind on the right side.

The first Ae.T.1. The plane copied the cabin layout of the Junkers F13, of which the Argentine Army operated three.

The first Ae.T.1 at El Palomar together with four Junkers K43s.

ABOVE Cockpit of the second or third Ae.T.1, which had different windshields, similar to the one on the Junkers W34.

Entrance to the passenger cabin, where the wooden seats in the front part could be seen.

Luggage compartment on the right side of the plane. The passenger cabin had doors on both sides.

The design work took 6,838 hours and static tests were carried out on a front wing spar and a No. 1 master rib, as well as some other minor elements, all with satisfactory results.

Also, a structure of the fuselage, with the Hispano Suiza engine installed, was built for ground tests.

The construction of the aircraft developed slowly due to the lack of wood for the wings, which was only obtained in mid-December. The lack of plans for the undercarriage or wheels much delayed its study and construction.

The construction of the rest was done without major setbacks and the aircraft was built on a 45 per cent by the end of 1932.

In 1933 the design was renamed the Ae.T.1 (the T was for Transporte) and it was also planned to be eventually converted into a light bomber, copying the idea from the Junkers W34 and K43. Also, because the FMA was building the 450hp Lorraine-Dietrich 12 Eb engine of under licence, it was decided to install this instead of the less-powerful Hispano Suiza. It would drive a Reed two-blade, fixed-pitch metal propeller. It was equipped with radio, the first plane built by the FMA with this equipment, although the Ae.C.1, Ae.C.2 and Ae.M.E.1 also received it shortly after for the flight of the Escuadrilla Sol de Mayo.

The new design had a wingspan of 17.30m; length of 9.70m; height of 4.36m; wing area of 37m2; tail area of 2.20m2; stabiliser surface area of 5.20m2; and wheelbase of 3m. It had an empty weight of 1,750kg with a total weight of 2,810kg and wing load of 76kg/m2 and a load per horsepower of 6.25kg/hp. The maximum speed was 225km/h, the cruise speed 195km/h and the landing speed 90km/h. The service ceiling was 6,000m with six hours of endurance and 1,170km range.

Finally, on May 1933 the plane was ready and on the 18th of that month it was flown for the first time by Sargento Ayudante José Honorio Rodríguez.

As the tests passed without incident, it was decided to use the plane as part of the flight of the Escuadrilla Sol de Mayo, and see how it performed on a long endurance flight. On 25 August the Ae.T.1 took off from Córdoba piloted by Major Aníbal Barros and Suboficial José Fernández, and it headed to El Palomar on a non-stop flight of 650km. From there they continued to the city of Paraná, in Entre Ríos province, and back to Córdoba, covering almost 1,400km.

For the flight of the Escuadrilla Sol de Mayo, described in Chapter 3, the plane was named *General San Martín* and acted as command plane for the flight.

At the same time, another two Ae.T.1s were started and received some minor modifications. The second, named *Dean Funes*, had a slightly larger passenger cabin, with the rear bulkhead installed more to the tail, with the third window to the aft of larger size. Also, the fin was larger, to improve lateral control, and the windscreen for the pilots was improved. The third plane was named *Jorge*

Newbery and had an extra round window on the left for the radio operator. Later on, *Dean Funes* also received this extra window. These two aircraft were finished in 1934.

Experimental airline

After the success of the tour of the Escuadrilla Sol de Mayo, the head of the factory, engineer Bartolomé de la Colina, asked the War Ministry for permission to organise an experimental airline between Córdoba and Buenos Aires using the Ae.T.1s. The request was approved in decree 34,776 on 18 January 1934 and the Dirección General de Aeronáutica of the Army created the Sección Experimental de Transporte Aéreo (SETA) to control what was named Líneas Aéreas Experimentales de Transporte, commercially known as Aero Argentina. The idea was that, if successful, the airline would be converted into a state-operated airline independent of the Army. Civil pilot Pedro Mórtola was appointed as its head, and he was also its pilot, together with civil pilots Carlos D'Alkaine, Miguel Vera, Dante Corucci and Isaac Díaz Villafañe. Army pilots Francisco José Vélez, Oscar Cairo and José Honorio Rodríguez were also part of the airline. Radio operators Manuel Otero, León Castillo and Ernesto Algaba also joined.

An agency called Eves was in charge of selling the tickets, at 55 pesos for a single fare or 400 pesos for chartering the entire flight, while they also were authorised to sell individual flights on the Ae.C.2 between Córdoba (operating from the FMA) and Buenos Aires (El Palomar) for 200 pesos. The government of Córdoba also agreed to pay a monthly subsidy of 10,000 pesos during the first three months.

Three regular flights per week were organised, departing Córdoba on Mondays, Wednesdays and Fridays and returning on Tuesdays, Thursdays and Saturdays, and the first flight was on 8 February of that year with *Jorge Newbery*, piloted by José Honorio Rodríguez and Miguel Vera.

On 27 June, the *General San Martín* broke the speed record between the FMA and El Palomar, José Honorio Rodríguez piloting the trip in two and a half hours.In May, the subsidy ended, but the FMA continued operating the airline until July, when it stopped the service. However, on 1 September the flights were restarted after receiving an extra subsidy but now flying only twice per week. As no more subsidies were received, the services were stopped on 1 October, ending the experiment after flying 282 hours over 46,720km, carrying 197 passengers and 2,151kg of cargo.

During the operation of the airline, the towns of Villa Dolores, Mina Clavero and Cruz del Eje, which were on the western side of the hills of Córdoba province and had poor connections to the provincial capital, asked that services were opened to link those cities with Cordoba, but there was no support from the provincial or national government to make this possible.

The first Ae.T.1 with the designation 'Prototipo' added on the tail.

The second Ae.T.1, named 'Dean Funes', with the logo of the Aero Argentina airline. Note the third window is larger than in the first plane and the tail is different. Also, the windscreen was based on the one of the Junkers K43.

A passenger climbs into the cabin of the third Ae.T.1, named 'Jorge Newbery'. Note the logo of Aero Argentina on the fuselage.

On December 1934 the name Aero Argentina was made official and the airline was authorised to open the route between the cities of Córdoba and Salta.

Meanwhile, in May 1934, contact was made with Aeroposta Argentina to sell the Ae.T.1 as a replacement for the Laté XXV and on 9 June a flight tested the route to Patagonia that Aeroposta was flying. Piloted by Rufino Luro Cambaceres, the *Dean Funes* took off from the FMA, making a first stop at Aeroposta airfield in General Pacheco, near Buenos Aires, to pick up the president of Aeroposta and a local director of Air France, Colin Jeannel, the son of the Argentine president, Eduardo Justo and Lago Fontán. They reached Ushuaia, the first commercial aeroplane to reach the southernmost city in the world, and on 15 June they started the return flight, travelling the 1,620km between the cities of Río Gallegos and Bahía Blanca non-stop in five hours forty-nine minutes at an average speed of 264km/h. In total, they flew more than 7,600km. Cambaceres considered the plane to be suited for Patagonia, but requested that the wing area was increased and the landing speed reduced.

In September 1935 the Ae.T.1s were transferred to the Grupo 1 de Observación at El Palomar, flying together with the Junkers F13 and Junkers K.43 at the Escuadrilla de Exploración, but they were grounded on 25 July 1936 by Decree 86,976. At least the *Dean Funes* was used for ground training and they were officially retired in 1945.

Ae.T.2

After the flight to Ushuaia, an agreement between Aeroposta Argentina and the FMA was signed in October 1934 in which the factory would build a bigger aeroplane, named Ae.T.2, with a greater wingspan, a Wright Cyclone R-1820E1 600hp engine and a bigger cabin. The structure was built in 1935, but the project was abandoned shortly after. Although no plans of the Ae.T.2 survive, nor pictures of the structure built, it is very probable the design was the same as the Ae.M.B.1, which had been under development since 1932 and flew for the first time in 1935.

7 Ae.M.B.1 Bombi and Ae.M.B.2

A bomber

The limited attack capacity of the Ae.T.1 was never used because of the development of a bigger plane, the last of this series. The Ae.M.B.1 light bomber was designed to replace the old Breguet XIX biplanes, in service since the end of the 1920s. Although the idea was to build a fighter too, this development was cancelled because, due to the limited experience of the company, it was impossible to build a fighter with the same characteristics of those in service around the world. The design works began in 1932 and in the following year construction of the first prototype began, however its completion was delayed in 1934 because of the lack of some materials, like aluminium tubes. Also, the Messier landing gear and the Hamilton Standard propellers did not arrive in the country on time. During this period, two scale models of the Ae.M.B.1 were made and modified, adaptable wings were built and the blueprints of the experimental union of the wing and fuselage. Also, it was projected to install a Townsend speed ring.

At the beginning of 1935, after 38,000 hours of work, the first prototype of the Ae.M.B.1 was rolled out. It was cantilever monoplane with a low, wooden wing and conventional fixed landing gear, a Wright Cyclone 6R-1820F3 715hp nine-cylinder radial engine with compressor and reduction box, moving a three-blade Hamilton Standard 3.8m-diameter propeller. The pilot's cabin was open, but the plan was to close it with a movable canopy, so it was equipped with the necessary rails. The windscreen was of a single piece. It also had dual control and the fuselage was made with chrome-molybdenum tubes covered by Duralumin on the

The first prototype in its initial configuration.

cabin and with fabric on the tail. The other crew members were a bomber, a gunner, a wireless operator and, in some cases, a mechanic. Also, on observation flights it could carry two observers. For this mission, in the ventral opening for the gunner a vertical camera could be installed. Fabric covered the wings, tail and all movable surfaces.

On 9 June 1935 the prototype flew for the first time, beginning a series of flight tests that led to some modifications, like first the adoption of a NACA ring and later a change of landing gear. Because the gear legs gave big wind resistance, it was studied to cover them, doing some plaster covers to test the different configurations before installing a definitive one. Other changes were the addition of flaps to the wings and Flettner servo tabs to the tail.

Then the armament was installed, comprising a dorsal open position, using two Lewis .303 British machine guns in a turret from a Breguet XIX. Between the tail and the wingtips were the radio antenna cables.

Tests were satisfactory but the modifications continued. The tail was changed for a bigger one to improve lateral control and the union of the wing and fuselage was modified to improve access to the cabin, made through a small door on the left side. The NACA ring was changed for a big cowling and a window below the cockpit, close to the pedals, was removed. After that, the landing gear cover was changed for a larger one and the dorsal machine guns were removed.

By the end of 1935 the Ae.M.B.1 was exhibited during the finalisation of the Military Aviation School courses, at BAM El Palomar, in Buenos Aires.

After the last modifications, the type reached the definitive configuration, with which the first series production planes left the FMA. The cockpit was enclosed with the installation of a new windscreen and upper windows, the window between the cockpit and the door was reduced to the same size as the one on the door. New armament was installed, comprising a closed dorsal turret armed with two 7.65mm Madsen machine guns and another two on the cowling and in the ventral position. The maximum bomb load was 450kg. The fuselage covering was changed from aluminium to fabric to reduce weight.

The prototype with a Breguet XIX machine gun mounting, with two Lewis guns.

Accident of the prototype, with serial 201, note the turret installed, the upward-opening door and new canopy.

While tests were being carried out, during 1935 the series production of fourteen planes began, the first three 60 per cent finished by the end of the year and the others at 25 per cent.

The prototype with the new and definitive tail.

Structure of the series production Bombis.

A series production Ae.M.B.1.

Starting the engine of a Bombi.

The Bombi in service

Deliveries of the Ae.M.B.1 to the Argentine Army Aviation began, including the prototype serialled 201, at the beginning of 1936. Aircraft 202 to 209 were delivered to the 2° División de Material Aeronáutico del Ejército (Army Aeronautical Material 2nd Division) on 6 March 1936, followed by 210 and 211 on 10 April. The type was exhibited officially to the authorities and the press on the 12th of that month, creating a good impression. On 20 May the last aircraft were delivered, serialled 212 to 215. Initially six went to the Grupo de Bombardeo of the Regimiento Aéreo 3 at BAM Los Tamarindos, in Mendoza city, which was officially created on 14 July 1936, and the others joined the Regimiento Aéreo 1 at BAM El Palomar.

During the acceptance flights, on 20 May the aircraft serialled 203, flown by Sergeant Julio Arrieta, had an accident at the runway of Fábrica Militar de Aviones after the landing gear collapsed.

The first operational accident was on 2 May at 1145. After a normal landing at BAM Los Tamarindos, while taxiing in a left turn, 207 lost the left wheel because the undercarriage was not strong enough. The landing gear, the pitot tube (installed below the left wing) and one propeller blade were broken. The aircraft was being flown by Major Alfredo Pérez Aquino, and also on board were Captain Enrique Guntsche and two passengers. The plane had only flown for twenty-one hours and thirty-five minutes and the repair cost was 2,600 pesos.

One month later, on 17 June at 0835, 214 had an accident at Los Tamarindos. In this case, after landing, the right landing gear leg broke on the unprepared surface. It was crewed by the two pilots and one passenger and the repair cost was 2,700 pesos.

The life of the bomber, named Bombi by the crews, was complicated, mainly due to lateral instability problems caused by the dorsal turret, which generated turbulence over the rudder and made turns difficult, mainly at low speed. Also, the landing gear had problems because the legs were weak, and the crews protested because of the low speed of the type.

On 9 July 1936, while taking off from El Palomar, the aircraft serialled 210 was lost, although the crew escaped. It was the first plane officially written off, on 29 April 1937 by Boletín Militar Reservado (Reserved Military Bulletin, BMR) 1087. On 21 September, 207 lost the left wheel while landing, and a similar accident occurred on 26 September to 203, the same day that 209 has an accident while landing. All were repaired.

Two days later, 214 lost the right wheel on landing and on 19 October 212, which was assigned to the Escuela de Aplicación de Aviación where pilots and mechanics were trained on the type, had an accident while landing, without injury to the crew.

This series of accidents became more serious when on 21 December 207 crashed near Despeñaderos, in Córdoba province. The pilot, co-pilot, two observers and the wireless operator jumped using parachutes but the mechanic died in the plane, the only fatal victim in all the service life of the Bombi.

Shortly before that, on the 17th, the Madsen 11.25mm and 7.65mm machine guns were purchased for the Ae.M.O.1s and Ae.M.B.1s. The 11.25mm guns replaced the ventral and front machine guns to give more defensive capacity. The others equipped the dorsal turret, unarmed until then.

In the following year, the continuous failures to the landing gear led the FMA to test a new type for the Bombi, fleet of which was now part of the Grupo de Observación y Bombardeo of the Regimiento 1. Other work undertaken by the FMA were tests of a 12.7mm Colt machine gun in the cowling (although this position was later eliminated), a study of the Bofors bomb launcher for bombs of 20lb to 200lb under the fuselage, the adaptation of the Calderoni 'wasps' nest' for forty-eight 4lb incendiary bombs and studies of a ventral door with curtain seal to use the bomb sight, the telescope and the ventral machine gun in normal conditions. Also, the manifold and the oil radiator were changed and a new longer cowling was tested, although sometimes the Bombi flew without it.

The accidents continued when on 12 January 1937 the landing gear of 206 broke. Because of this situation, on 1 March Orden Reservada 3 (Reserved Order) was issued and the Ae.M.B.1s were grounded until the problems with the landing gear, which showed little elasticity and was impractical for unprepared runways, was corrected. This grounding was temporary and the planes flew again sometime later.

On 5 June 1937, according to Boletín Militar Reservado 1293, aircraft 201 took off from El Palomar heading to Paraná, on Entre Ríos province, with a stop at Tortugas. Arriving at the intermediate stop the aircraft had some technical issues, so the crew landed in the town of Galvez, where they

The turret is clearly visible in this view.

A Bombi with the Madsen machine guns installed in the turret.

The Bombi 205 with the two Madsens in the retractable turret tested on the aircraft.

The 204 after modification with the removal of the turret. The ram generator of the Telefunken radio is clearly visible over the wing.

O-212 after the final modifications, with a lower fuselage top and a new undercarriage, in a lower and advanced position. The plane also has a different engine cowling and radiator.

refuelled and took off at 1710. The plane was crewed by Sargento 1° Pelliza, and Sergeants Algarate and Abrallay and Cabo 1° Maciel. They arrived at Regimiento 2 at BAM General Urquiza, in Paraná, at 1830 during darkness and after attempting to land without visibility, they crashed 500m before the runway because of a poor appreciation of their altitude. The engines became detached and ended up some metres from the plane, and the crew was injured. *La Razón* newspaper reported the following day that the plane had to fly from El Palomar to Paganini to stay for the night, but landed at Saenz and at 1730 departed to Paraná. The Bombi, which was the prototype, was destroyed and written off, reducing the fleet to twelve examples.

Despite of this, on 9 July, during the Independence Day celebrations, there was a big flypast involving 112 Army aircraft and all the Bombis took part, the only formation they made with twelve planes.

From Ae.M.B.1 to Ae.M.B.2

Because of the problems caused by the accidents, on 5 February 1938, under BMR 1235 modification of the type was authorised, with a resulting change of name from Ae.M.B.1 to Ae.M.B.2. To fix the problem of the landing gear, a change was ordered, including the fairings. The fuel tanks and the tailskid were modified, while an emergency door was installed. The turret was eliminated to fix the problem of the poor lateral control, after an unsuccessful test of a retractable turret installed in aircraft 205. Also, the recoil of the machine guns had been found to constantly damaged the mountings on the turret, leaving the ventral 11.25mm machine gun as the only defensive weapon. The top was also modified after the elimination of the turret, but not all the planes kept the same kind of top as some received modifications

An Ae.M.B.1 in its early days

ABOVE Bombis flying during a flypast in 1938. The second plane has its turret retracted.

LEFT Two Bombis during a deployment, note the turret of O-205 is retracted.

The first prototype in its initial configuration.

Workshop at the FMA with two Bombis (202 and 206) sharing the hangar with a Martin 139, Northrop 8A, Fw-58 Weihe, Junkers F.13, Curtiss Hawk III and 75-O, Fw 44J and an Ae.M.Oe.2

later. The main door was enlarged and became rectangular, when initially it was almost triangular. This made it possible to abandon the aircraft more quickly during an emergency. The modification work took five hours per plane and this was undertaken at the FMA, as were the test flights. Later, at an unknown date, the landing gear and its fairing was again changed for a lower one, which was moved forward.

Bombi being repaired, with the engine clearly visible. *Time-Life*

During this year nine aircraft of Regimiento 1 de Observación y Bombardeo of El Palomar were modified, but only 208, 209, 211, 212 and 213 were in service. On 8 October 1938 BAM Villa Mercedes was created in the city of the same name in San Luis province and Bombis 208, 209, 211, 212 and 213 were taken there one year later to be part of the Grupo de Observación. No. 212 was transferred directly from the FMA, where its modifications had been completed. Nos 204 and 214 were still in the workshop. During trials prior to their delivery, 203 suffered a rupture of the landing gear on 16 February 1939.

The Bombi is not a bomber any more

During 1940, Bombi 212, which was still commissioned at Fábrica Militar de Aviones, made 122 parachutist droppings, inaugurating a new use for these planes. They began to be relegated from bombing tasks to observation, mainly because of the purchase of thirty Northrop 8A attack planes and twenty-two Martin 139WAA (B-10) bombers. These types were far more modern, with better performance for attack and bombing missions than the Ae.M.B.2, which had a maximum speed of 285km/h and a cruise of 240km/h at 2,100m with a range of only

600km. The Northrop 8 reached 355km/h at 2,651m, with a cruise speed of 321km/h and a 1,900km range, while it had a bomb load of almost double that of the Bombi, better defensive armament and agility. The B-10 could carry 2,000lb of bombs at a cruise speed of 313km/h at sea level and a maximum of 370km/h at 3,500m, with a 2,240km range. Also, the bigger fuselage of the Argentine plane made it good for other jobs, including observation, parachutist launch, liaison and transport, keeping a secondary attack capacity. The purchase of those imported planes together with the Curtiss Hawk was because of the continuous failures of the locally developed types, caused by limited experience in construction and in many cases due to the operational use of prototypes and experimental planes. Also, these home-grown types had modest performance compared with the new aircraft constructed in Europe and the United States.

In 1942, some Bombis were sent to the Grupo 1 de Observación for photo survey duties and received a curtain system for blind flight and K3B photographic cameras.

In 1944 the type was used for navigation, observation, radio communications instruction and photography, and received an equipment to extend the telephones from the wireless operator position to the pilot and co-pilot.

That year, by Reserved Order 58, the serials of all the Army Aviation planes were changed, receiving a letter before the number to indicating their mission. B was for bomber, C for Caza (Fighters), a system still used today by the Argentine Air Force. By this order, the Ae.M.B.2s received O for Observation, and the survivors became O-202, O-203, O-205, O-206, O-208, O-209, O-211, O-212 and O-214.

During 1944, 211 was sent to the Escuela de Tropas Aerotransportadas (Airborne Troops School) at Córdoba, with the Ae.M.S.1, with the Bombi carrying five paratroopers seated on the floor.

During 1945, year of the creation of the Fuerza Aérea Argentina, along with all the Army units, the Bombis began to be transferred to new units for a big variety of tasks, while they began to be relegated from the observation task after the arrival of the first I.Ae. DL-22 trainers, which were also used for this mission. O-211 continued at the Escuela de Tropas Aerotransportadas together with the Ae.M.S.1 and although both types were criticised by paratroopers because of their cramped space, low interior height, and low door and lintel over the floor, O-205 and 208 were sent to the Instituto Aerotécnico for modification to be used by this school.

O-202 of the Grupo 1 de Observación was sent to BAM Coronel Pringles, where it received Telefunken Stat 274AF short- and long-wave radio equipment, as used in the Northrop 8s, and these started to be used on towing target missions. Later in the year, three aircraft were sent to Agrupación Entrenamiento at El Palomar, where they were modified to act as crop dusters and participate in the fight against the locust with equipment installed

The fuselage of one of the planes used by the Escuela de Paracaidistas was used until the 1970s for ground training. It was later replaced by a structure, still called Bombi, but the remains of the plane were scrapped. *Archive Walter Bentancor*

on the ventral opening and a 400kg tank for insecticide inside the fuselage. The aircraft served in this new role for a while, returning to Grupo 1 de Observación on 21 February 1946, when the equipment was installed in the Avro Trainers.The type was retired in 1948, when the last two were decommissioned, but the fuselage of one aircraft at the Escuela de Paracaidistas of Córdoba was mounted on a structure and from there the pupils practised the jumps. After some years it was planned to be replaced by a Vickers Viking fuselage, which was taken to the training ground but never used. By 1970, this Bombi fuselage was still in use by the Regimiento de Infantería 2 Paracaidista of the Army. It was replaced by an aluminium structure that still keeps the Bombi name, and is still used today, although those who use it usually don't know the origin of the name.

The Bombi was a noble plane that symbolised the maximum design ability of the FMA in the 1930s, although it arrived a little late and with the common problems of an industry with little experience, soon being overtaken by more modern types. When it left service in 1948 (although there are references of a Bombi flying sporadically until 1950), the Instituto Aerotécnico had been testing one of its masterpieces, the jet fighter I.Ae.27 Pulqui, first Latin American jet, for more than a year. Thirty Avro Lincolns and fifteen Lancasters, the biggest strategic bombing force in Latin America, then formed the bomber force of which the Bombis had once been a part.

3 The wooden years

8 FMA 20 El Boyero

After the failure of the design of the Ae.C.3 and Ae.C.4 in the 1930s, civil aviation in Argentina was still lacking basic trainers to train new pilots. The Focke-Wulf Fw 44J Stieglitz built under licence by the factory was considered too advanced for basic training, as was stated on the VII Conferencia Nacional de Aeronáutica, when the Aero Club Argentino, headed by engineer Julio Argentino Noble, led a request to the Fábrica Militar de Aviones to develop and build a new aircraft for elementary training that could be also used as a private tourer.

The factory accepted the request and by the end of 1939 engineer Juan A. Peretti and professor Clodoveo Pascualini started the development of the new plane, which was called FMA 20 as it was the twentieth type constructed by the factory including those built and assembled under licence, and was named El Boyero.

ABOVE The first prototype of the FMA 20 El Boyero just after leaving the workshops of the FMA.

LEFT The first prototype of the El Boyero after being fully painted. The plane changed hands many times and still flies in private hands.

The FMA 20 serialled LV-YSJ is one of the planes of the first batch of eight units delivered by Petrolini Hermanos in 1949, originally with the serial t-20. The plane was painted in yellow, with the Argentine flag stripes on the wingtips. In 1956 it was delivered to the Aero Club Curuzú Cuatiá in Corrientes province as LV-ZLI.

Two prototypes were built, both equipped with a 50hp Continental A50 engine with a two-blade wooden propeller, and the first of them flew for the first time on 2 November 1940, followed by the other in early 1941 As the factory was dedicated to the production of the Curtiss Hawk 75-O and the Focke-Wulf Fw 44J, and because it was intended to develop private industry, by the end of 1940 the War Ministry began to tender for the award of the production of the plane. This was won by the company Sfreddo y Paolini Sociedad Anónima, which had its workshops at Morón Aerodrome, near Buenos Aires.The second prototype, now serialled LV-YGA, was delivered to Morón and an order was placed for 160 aeroplanes. However, the lack of materials because of the Second World War ended the project and the prototype was sold to Juan Barcia on 11 January 1944.

The FMA continued using the first prototype, which was later serialled T-01, and by 1945 became t-01, when the lower-case 't' was applied for a short period for liaison aircraft (instead of Tango-01 it was Tanguito-01), but in 1945 it was stored.

With the war over, in 1946 the government decided to revive the project and a contract was now signed with the company Petrolini Hermanos, which received the first prototype after it was re-engined with a 65hp Continental A65, and it was used as a basis for the series production, until it was returned to the factory in 1947 and assigned to the Grupo 1 de Observación of the Argentine Air Force on 7 October. In 1955 the plane was delivered to the Ministerio de Aeronáutica and became LV-ZLF on 8 March 1956, being delivered to a flying club. It still survives with a private owner.

By then, the plane was designated I.Ae.20 El Boyero, according to the new designation in use by the Instituto Aerotécnico.

Petrolini signed contract 706 with the Secretaría de Aeronáutica for a first series of one prototype, 120 planes of series production for the Dirección General de Aeronáutica Civil for distribution to flying clubs, thirty unassembled planes for use as spares and twenty-five for the Argentine Air Force.

The prototype was readied at the workshops of the company in Paso del Rey, near Buenos Aires, on 3 October 1947 and flew shortly after as LV-NZP at the nearby Merlo aerodrome. Production began immediately, with a second plane delivered on December 1947. However, output continued at a slow pace because of problems importing the requested materials, which were to be paid for by the Secretaría de Aeronáutica but it lacked sufficient funds.

Finally, on 14 January 1949 the first eight series production planes with military serials t-18 to 23 were presented at Aeroparque domestic airport in Buenos Aires, in the presence of General Perón and his wife Eva Duarte. Production during 1949 was also slow, but accelerated in 1950 and on 29 September 1952 aircraft c/n 129, the 127th built by Petrolini, was delivered. Another fifteen planes, with c/n 066 to 080, also received military serials, from t-26 to t-40.

One of the FMA 20 El Boyeros, formerly t-26, transferred to the Argentine Army in 1956, with serial AE-4 Ob. The plane was retired in 1965.

The aircraft t-18, t-21, t-25, t-26, t-39 and t-40 were delivered to the Argentine Air Force and others also went to air clubs. On 19 January 1956 t-18, 21, 26, 39 and 40 were transferred to the Army and received the serials ME-2 Ob to ME-6 Ob. These were the first aircraft with the recreated Army Aviation, which had ceased to exist when the Air Force was created in 1945. Shortly after they were re-serialed AE-2 Ob to AE-6 Ob and on 17 September 1959 AE-2 Ob, AE-3 Ob and AE-6 Ob were transferred to the Gendarmería Nacional as GN-1P to GN-3P respectively. The three planes with the Army were retired by 1965 and those of the Gendarmería were also retired around this time.

A few El Boyeros are still flying in private hands.

ABOVE One of the three El Boyeros transferred from the Army to the Gendarmería Nacional in 1959, which were the first planes of the force. They served until the late 1960s.

RIGHT The FMA 20 serialled t-20 had the constructor number 008 and after brief service with the Grupo 1 de Observación of the Argentine Air Force it was handed over to the Dirección Nacional de Aeronáutica Civil as LV-YSJ.

The first FMA 20 El Boyero seen in 2011, now with serial LV-ZLF. The plane is still being flown from General Rodríguez Aerodrome, in Buenos Aires province. *Santiago Rivas*

9 FMA 21 and I.Ae. DL-22

Improvements to the NA-16

As the Second World War progressed it become more difficult to get spares for the thirty North American NA-16-1Ps and one NA-18 that the Argentine Army had purchased in 1936, especially when it came to major parts for planes that had accidents. As part of the US intention of getting Argentina on the side of the Allies, Major John Cannon suggested the delivery of fifty North American BT-9s to add them to the fleet of NA-16s, together with twenty-three Douglas A-23s, eight Lockheed A-29s and twenty P-36 Hawks, as well as delivering to the Navy thirteen Vought OS2U-3 Kingfishers and eight Consolidated PBY-5 Catalinas or Naval Aircraft Factory PBN Nomads. However, the Argentine decision to remain neutral led to the US government not approving this idea, as well as the Argentine request to buy spares.

This situation led to the idea of making parts locally, but it was very hard to get the necessary metals, so it was decided to study the use of local wood. In the meantime, in 1941 the FMA began to work on a project called FMA 21, which was the attachment of a wing based on that of the Curtiss Hawk 75, but built in wood, to the fuselage of an NA-16. The wing included a retractable landing gear, the first designed and built in Argentina, and was built in early 1942, with tests performed during the second half of the year and in early 1943.

Meanwhile, the NA-16 serialled 323, which had suffered an accident by the beginning of 1943 at the Escuela de Pilotos Militares, was sent to the Instituto Aerotécnico to be repaired and, according to Chapter 5 of the Memoir of the Escuela de Pilotos Militares of 1943, was converted into the prototype FMA 21.

This plane made its first flight at the Córdoba factory on 14 May 1943, with Lt Osvaldo Mauro Rovere at the controls, and was then flight tested during the rest of the year. By that times, a plane was needed not only with better performance, but also in bigger numbers because of the growth planned for the Comando de Aviación de Ejército.

Wind tunnel model of the FMA 21. Note the detachable fin, which has a rudder completely different from that of the NA-16 and more similar to the one adopted on the DL 22.

The FMA-21 during trials at the FMA. *Santiago Rivas*

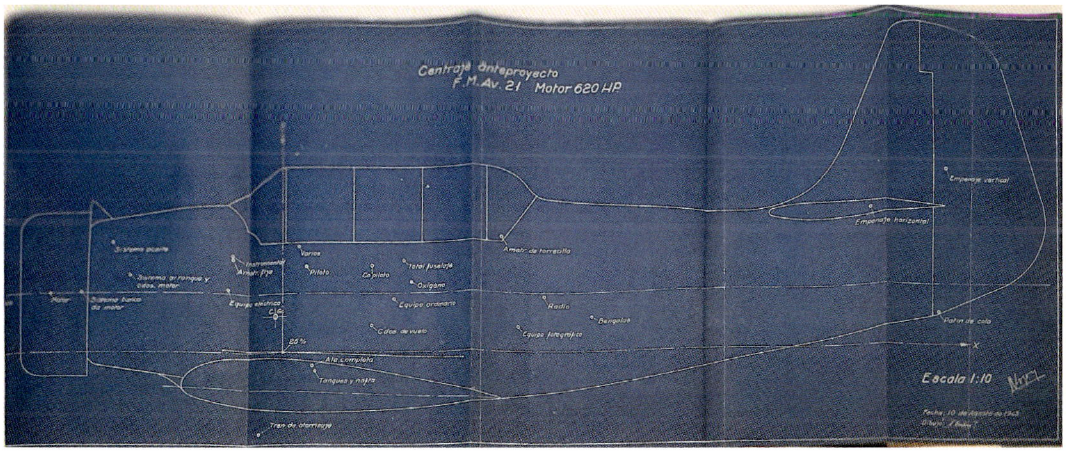

Balance plan of the FMA 21 from 10 August 1943. Interestingly, the plan shows the plane with a modified rudder and describes it as 'Anteproyecto F.M.Av. 21'. Thirteen days later, the project IDD 22 was revealed, with a new wooden fuselage, but as an evolution of this idea.

The FMA-21 painted in white on the fuselage and light blue on the wings, a scheme also used by the DL-22s. *Santiago Rivas*

The DL-22 is born

Owing to the problems of buying planes similar to the NA-16 in other countries because of the Second World War, it was decided to develop a new aircraft from the FMA 21. Initially, it was planned to modify the other NA-16s and add some improvements, for which the design was improved during 1943 and, most significantly, a new rudder and stabiliser was designed and tested in the wind tunnel.

Structure of the FMA I.Ae.DL-22. *Santiago Rivas*

Construction of the DL-22 prototype with Whirlwind engine. *Santiago Rivas*

Plans for the improved FMA 21 evolved until August 1943, but as the force needed a larger quantity of planes, it was decided to leave the idea behind and start with the development of a new plane, based on the NA-16. The project was first called IDD 22 and later I.Ae. DL-22, the study of which entered the Projects Cabinet of the Instituto Aerotécnico on 23 August 1943.

As it was not possible to get additional Whirlwind engines nor a similar one and the FMA had the capability of building them, it was decided to work on a local version of the engine used by the NA-16, which was called the I.Ae.R.16 El Gaucho and was the first aeronautical engine designed and built in Latin America. The nine-cylinder engine reached 450hp at 2,250rpm and was basically a copy of the Whirlwind. As it was not possible to get light metals like Duralumin, the decision was taken to build the plane with local wood, as previously a study was made to use it in aeronautical construction and it was tested on the wing of the FMA 21.

In March 1944 static tests of the new plane began and these ended in July. At the same time, construction started of the first prototype, which was to be equipped with a Whirlwind engine as the El Gaucho was not ready yet. After only twenty-five days of work, the first I.Ae. DL-22 was finished, while construction of the first four series production examples was started.

On 17 May, 1st Lt Rovere carried out the first flight and twelve days later the official presentation of the type was made in Buenos Aires, in the presence of War Minister Colonel Juan D. Perón. On its return, on 1 June, the plane made a direct flight between Buenos Aires and Córdoba (700km) at an average speed of 300km/h.

Immediately after an order was given to produce 100 examples, which were to be used at the Escuela Militar de Aviación (EMAv) to complement the NA-16 and at the Grupo 1 de Observación, where they would replace the Ae.M.Oe.2, Ae.M.B.2, Fw 44J and Avro Trainer. Work on the new planes began two months later, when the production line at Hangar 90 of the FMA was prepared. Many private companies were also contracted to provide parts to augment the production rate.

Some days later, on 27 June, the first El Gaucho was started up for the first time and after ground running it replaced the Whirlwind in the prototype, being tested successfully in the plane.

The prototype was officially taken on charge at the Comando de las Fuerzas Aéreas Militares (the new name for Army Aviation) on 3 August 1944, together with the first four series production planes, those receiving the serials 701 to 704. Initially the prototype did not carry a serial, but it was later serialled as 0 and finally as 700. By the end of the year the FMA reported that the series of 100 planes was at a 30 per cent completion overall.

The evaluation of the model indicated that the DL-22 was completely aerobatic, without limitations, with a maximum dive speed of 450km/h and a level speed of 400km/h at high altitude and 290km/h at 450m. The stall speed without flaps and with maximum weight was of 120km/h, the cruise speed was of 240km/h, the endurance was four hours fifty minutes including twenty-five minutes of reserve, as fuel consumption was 75 litres per hour, and the range was of 1,100km. The empty weight was of 1,800kg, with a payload of 600kg, reaching a MTOW of 2,460kg.

Construction was made of wood with the wings using a sandwich covering. The fuselage was semi-monocoque with a chipboard cover. The landing gear was retractable, and either electrically or manually operated.

It was armed with a Lewis 7.65mm machine gun in the observer's position and two under the wing, each with 450 rounds, while it could carry three 50lb bombs or nine of 15kg.

Meanwhile, on 26 August 1944 the Reserved Order 15 was issued to solve the problem of identifying aircraft caused by the use of different models with the same numbers, with the solution the use of letters before the number, specifying the type of plane. The Comandante en Jefe de Aeronáutica (Aeronautics Commander in Chief) ordered that 'to the planes currently in service with the Comando de las Fuerzas Aéreas Militares and the Dirección de Institutos Aeronáuticos, a characteristic will be added, consisting of one or more letters, according to their speciality'. Among the letters for the planes were the following: E.e.- Escuela Elemental, E.a.- Escuela Avanzada, O- Observación.

As a result, the NA-16s were serialled E.a.-301 to 331 and the DL-22s became E.a.-700 onwards. Although the DL-22s used by the Grupo 1 de Observación should in theory have used the letter O-, they kept the serials as if they were trainers.

The first prototype showing the Pratt & Whitney engine taken from the NA-18 serialled 301. *Santiago Rivas*

Presentation of the DL-22 first prototype. *Santiago Rivas*

DL-22 production line at the Hangar 09 of the FMA. Behind them is the I.Ae.24 Calquin production line. *Santiago Rivas*

At the Fuerza Aérea Argentina

On 6 January 1945 the Comando de las Fuerzas Aéreas Militares finally became an independent force, when the Secretaría de Aeronáutica was created as an independent office of the War Ministry and, subordinate to it, the Fuerza Aérea Argentina (FAA).

During the year, the first series of DL-22s started to be delivered, reaching the serial E.a.-750. Aircraft E.a.-706, 707, 709, 712, 718, 720, 721, 722, 723, 724 and 724 were delivered to the Grupo 1 de Observación, at Paraná, and E.a.-715, 716, 717, 725, 727, 729 and 730 to the newly created Grupo 2 de Observación, at BAM Reconquista, to the north of Santa Fe province. Also, the Agrupación Entrenamiento (at Paraná) received E.a.-708, 713, 714, 719 and 726 and the Escuela de Aviación Militar all of the others, totalling twenty-three planes, except the prototype, E.a.-705, which was retained by the FMA for tests, and those examples donated to foreign countries, described below.

Foreign deliveries

From the planes of the first series, it was decided to donate one each to the Peruvian, Chilean and Brazilian Air Forces with the intention of getting their interest on future purchases. Unfortunately, this decision had no effect, as the United States started to deliver huge quantities of trainers of the Texan family to all the Latin American countries, leaving no possibility of the Argentinian product

The first prototype with the Alvis Leonides 503 engine tested. *Santiago Rivas*

FAR LEFT Delivery of the Peruvian DL-22 at El Palomar Air Base in Buenos Aires. *Santiago Rivas*

obtaining orders. The plane with the constructor number (c/no) 002 was donated to the Chilean Air Force and was received at El Bosque Air Base, in Santiago, on 20 August 1945, where it started to operate with the NA-74s and AT-6s of the aviation school. However, due to its difference from the other models and a lack of spares, the plane only flew briefly and was then retired.

At the same time, aircraft c/no 010 was donated to the Peruvian Air Force and 011 to the Força Aérea Brasileira. The last was delivered by an FAA pilot on 16 July 1945, received the serial FAB 1436 and was used, also for a short time, at the Academia da Força Aérea at Campo dos Afonsos, Rio de Janeiro. It was retired on 7 July 1947. The plane for Peru was

ABOVE The plane delivered to Brazil as a gift during the delivery ceremony at El Palomar Air Base. *Santiago Rivas*

accepted on 13 April 1946, and collected by Captain Roberto Borton and NCO Oscar Almirall of the Peruvian Air Force, departing BAM El Palomar on 27 May. The plane was kept operational at the Escuela de Aviación Militar at Las Palmas, but mainly used for liaison, and was retired by the end of 1952 having accumulated few flying hours.

At the same time, the Argentine Navy became interested in the type and in 1945 signed a letter of intention for ten examples, asking for one to be delivered so it could be evaluated. E.a.-705 was delivered with a Cheetah engine and was tested at Base Aeronaval Punta Indio until November 1945, when it was returned. No orders followed because the wooden construction was not considered suitable for use in a maritime environment.

Other engines

Operation of the DL-22 during the first months determined some troubles with the El Gaucho engines and led to the decision to test other ones, as now the war was over they were available on the international market.Also, in August 1946 the plane

The Chilean DL-22 shortly after its arrival at El Bosque Air Base in Santiago. *Patrick Laureau*

E.a.703 shortly after being built. The plane later received a Cheetah engine and after that a Whirlwind from a retired NA-16. *Santiago Rivas*

was tested with a 2M-D-30 variable-pitch propeller built of wood and metal made by the Instituto Aerotécnico, which provided better performance than the original wooden one.

Initially, it was decided to test the Pratt & Whitney R-1340-41 Wasp used by the NA-18 serialled E.a.-301, which had stopped flying recently, and this was the same engine used by some versions of the North American SNJ. The DL-22 prototype received this engine, which was tested for a while at the beginning of 1946 but the idea was not pursued. Meanwhile, the FMA built forty-one El Gaucho engines in 1945, out of a series of 100 that was completed in 1946, while a second series of 180 was started.

Among the agreements made with the British government for the provision of aircraft and equipment was included a project to build the seven-cylinder Armstrong Siddeley Cheetah Mk.XXV engine in Argentina. It was decided to test it on the DL-22, installing them in the prototype and the aircraft serialled E.a.-703 and 705. The engine bedplate and cowlings were redesigned and a Rotol two-blade wooden propeller installed. According to the factory, the performance reached was superior than with the El Gaucho, because the engine reached 475hp at 2,700rpm.

After some initial tests, an engine with serial 90048 was installed in DL-22 E.a.-802 and used on 26 February 1947 to determine the performance, with pilots Comandante Osvaldo Rovere, 1st Lt Edmundo Weiss and Suboficial Mayor Fermín Gentile in charge of the test flights.

The maximum speed at 1,220m was 301km/h and the cruising speed at 1,500m was 280km/h. The aircraft had a range of 1,228km and a maximum endurance of four and a half hours.

Shortly after, in 1948, a nine-cylinder 540hp Alvis Leonides 503 engine was also tested, the same used on the Percival Provost, with a Rotol three-blade propeller built by the FMA. With this engine a maximum speed of 375km/h at 450m was reached, with a cruising speed of 305km/h and a ceiling of 6,000m, but the plan to use this engine was not pursued and the prototype received the Cheetah again. On 24 April 1946, the aircraft was sent to Chile to take part in a sports competition. It was flown by Captain Osvaldo Rovere, with Suboficial Principal Alfredo Dalton as mechanic, and it returned home on 9 May. The Alvis Leonides engine is currently at the Museum of the Centro de Investigación Aplicada in Cordoba.

Finally, it was decided that the second series of 100 planes would be delivered with Cheetah engines, but they were all purchased in the UK. Also, because of the availability of Whirlwind engines from the NA-16 and other types, some DL-22s in the first series received this engine between 1946 and 1948. It is possible to identify these as E.a.-704, 709, 716, 717, 723, 724, 725, 747, 752, 753, 754, 787, 793 and 796 in the FAA registers.

E.a.-746 also without the E.a.- letters, in front of Hangar 90 of the FMA. The plane is equipped with the machine guns in the wings and in the observer position, and also has the rails to fire three rockets under each wing. Note the tube-type sight in front of the windscreen as originally used. The pilot had to align the two ends of the tube, which had the sights, with the target when the weapons were aimed. *Santiago Rivas*

Operational service

Meanwhile, during 1946 the remaining fifty planes of the first series were delivered, and a new series of 130 aeroplanes (later reduced to 100) was started, which was at a 25 per cent by the end of the year. By that time, the planes had no weapons, but those with the observation groups received a photo machine gun and plans started to be developed to install machine guns, bombs and rockets, while they were painted with the dark green and light blue paint used by the other combat planes in the air force. Also, E.a.-760 received a radio. According to Grupo 1 de Observación memoir for 1946, the performance of the DL-22s was good.

In the meantime, the fleet of NA-16s was kept at the EAM, including the FMA 21 serialled E.a.-00, although this was never painted on the plane. All the DL-22s of the unit were painted in white on the fuselage with the wings and stabilisers in light blue, with the sun on the tail, forming the Argentine flag.

According to the annual memoir, the DL-22s did not have all their instruments fitted, especially in the second position, and they did not carry equipment for instrumental flight training, although the hoods were being made at the EAM. The intercoms were old and not electric, making it very difficult to hear the other pilot. Crews also complained that there was no fuel indicator, making navigation flights difficult.

The Grupo 2 de Observación was the sole unit equipped entirely with DL-22 and during 1946 they tested a Lear Matic navigation equipment with a fixed wave transmitter in E.a.-756, but the results were poor as the equipment had an error factor of 10°.

The Agrupación Entrenamiento had some trouble with a lack of spares. It became clear that parts of the planes were not all of equal size, making it difficult to interchange them between examples, and also making repairs difficult as many items had to be made at the factory to fit the particular aircraft.

Twenty of the second series were delivered between 3 January and 14 March 1947, all for the EAM, which, by the end of the year had seventeen NA-16s, thirty-five DL-22s and the FMA 21.

With the intention of improving the performance of the remaining NA-16s and thanks to the good results of the FMA 21, the FMA planned to modify another plane to this standard in the following year and to modify all the remaining NA-16s, but this plan was cancelled in the end because the priority was given to DL-22 production. Besides that, the FMA produced twenty El Gaucho engines, which were only used as spares as the DL-22s delivered from that year used Cheetah engines.

By that time advanced training was made carried out first with an instructor in the NA-16 and DL-22, and after flying the Fw 44J the pilots then flew alone in the NA-16 or the DL-22. This was followed by instrument flights in the NA-16, formation flying in the DL-22, aerobatics in the Fw 44J, night flying in the NA-16 and finally navigation in the DL-22.

The first planes delivered to the observation units received the serials without the letters E.a.- painted on them, although they had them in the official records. They were applied during 1945 and 1946. Note the different sight installed in front of the cockpit, in which the pilot had to have the target inside the smaller circle when the weapons were aimed. *Santiago Rivas*

At the same time, it was decided to deliver two planes to the Dirección General de Aeronáutica Civil, to provide advanced training for civil pilots, so the aircraft with c/nos 080 and 081 were-serialled LV-XZL and XZI respectively and delivered on 2 September 1947. The first of them was destroyed on 19 March 1948 when a storm threw it against Airspeed Consul LV-XYN. On 7 June the same year the other DL-22 had an accident at San Fernando aerodrome, in Buenos Aires, and was written off.

E.a.-747 was modified in 1947 with a fixed landing gear with the intention of producing a

One of the very few colour pictures of a DL-22 in service, this time E.a.-870. *Santiago Rivas*

DL-22 LV-XZL after being destroyed by a storm which made the plane lay over the Airspeed Consul LV-XYN at Morón Air Base in 1948. *Santiago Rivas*

The only photo known of the sole example equipped with fixed landing gear. The wing was modified and did not have the space to house the wheels when retracted. It is supposed that the model was intended to be offered for export as a low-cost version. *Santiago Rivas*

cheap version for export. It received a new wing without the space for wheels, but after being tested it was returned to its original configuration.

By that time, the end of the war had brought the possibility of importing Duralumin again, so the FMA began to study the production of a metal-built version of the plane and a wing was built in metal to test the structure. The aim was to build a third series of 100 examples completely in metal, but at the same time an offer was received for the purchase 100 Percival Prentice T.Mk.1s at a very low cost, as part of the payment for the debt the United Kingdom had with Argentina for supplies sent during the Second World War. The offer was accepted and the planes started to arrive in 1948 to be assembled at the FMA and finishing. The deliveries ended any plans to build a metal version of the DL-22.

By 1948, because the DL-22s were being produced together with the I.Ae.24 Calquins, there were problems on the production line due to a lack of space in Hangar 90 at the FMA, where they were assembled, and this causing some delays in deliveries. Meanwhile, the second series of 180 El Gaucho engines was completed on a 50 per cent.

With the aim of increasing the combat capacity of the DL-22, in 1949 rocket launchers for 11kg A3F rockets, built locally, were developed and tested, with three carried under each wing.

Meanwhile, on 15 March 1949 a reorganisation of the force took place with the creation of the Brigades, which grouped all the air units on each base. The Agrupación Entrenamiento became part of the I Brigada, at BAM El Palomar; the Grupo 1 de Observación was now part of the II Brigada; and the Grupo 2 de Observación became part of the III Brigada. The EAM kept the same organisation.

During 1950 there were no changes in the organisation, but the force was organised into Commands, so the II and III Brigades came under the

E.a.-841 armed with machine guns in the wings and equipped with the rails to fire rockets. The type was used extensively in combat at Córdoba during the revolution of September 1955. *Santiago Rivas*

A group of DL-22s preparing for take-off from the Escuela de Aviación Militar. *Santiago Rivas*

Comando de Exploración y Enlace, while the EAM and the Agrupación Entrenamiento were subordinate to the Comando de Institutos Aeronáuticos Militares.

During that year, the factory delivered the DL-22 E.a.-841 to the FAM and from E.a.-861 to 900 to the Agrupación Entrenamiento, but for a brief period the E.a.-873, 876, 882, 883, 884, 887 and from 889 to 894 served at the Regimiento 1 de Bombardeo to help train crews. Those were the last DL-22s delivered and the production line was then closed. Meanwhile, for unknown reasons, the FMA 21 was retired together with the DL-22 prototype, but the latter was put back into service sometime later.

At the Agrupación Entrenamiento, DL-22s started to share the training duties with seventy Fiat G-46s that started to arrive from Italy, which had better performance, besides being all metal. Of the DL-22s in the unit, eighteen were equipped with 7.65mm machine guns in the wings.

During 1955, there were 141 DL-22s on Air Force strength, but by the end of the year four had been retired and many sent to storage. The wooden construction of the planes and their age started to cause trouble, especially with those based at Reconquista and El Palomar where the wet weather

Two planes of the Grupo 1 de Observación in flight. Note that E.a.-759 has the letters painted and E.a.-776 does not. *Santiago Rivas*

A DL-22 of Grupo 1 de Observación, catching a towed target at Paraná Air Base.

The last surviving DL-22, E.a.-701 at the National Aeronautics Museum. *Santiago Rivas*

caused deterioration of their structures. Because of that, the Air Force began to seek a replacement. As the DL-22s had a short life ahead and a solution was needed fast, it was decided to look for a foreign type that could be produced under licence. The Beechcraft B45 Mentor was chosen and seventy-five examples were built by the FMA, as well as another fifteen built in the USA (of which six were assembled by the FMA).

In 1957 the new Mentors entered service and the DL-22s started to be replaced. They flew until October 1958 and were officially retired on 31 December that year.

Unfortunately, only one example of the DL-22 was preserved, E.a.-701, which is currently at the National Aeronautics Museum at Morón Buenos Aires, after being completely restored by the beginning of the new millennium.

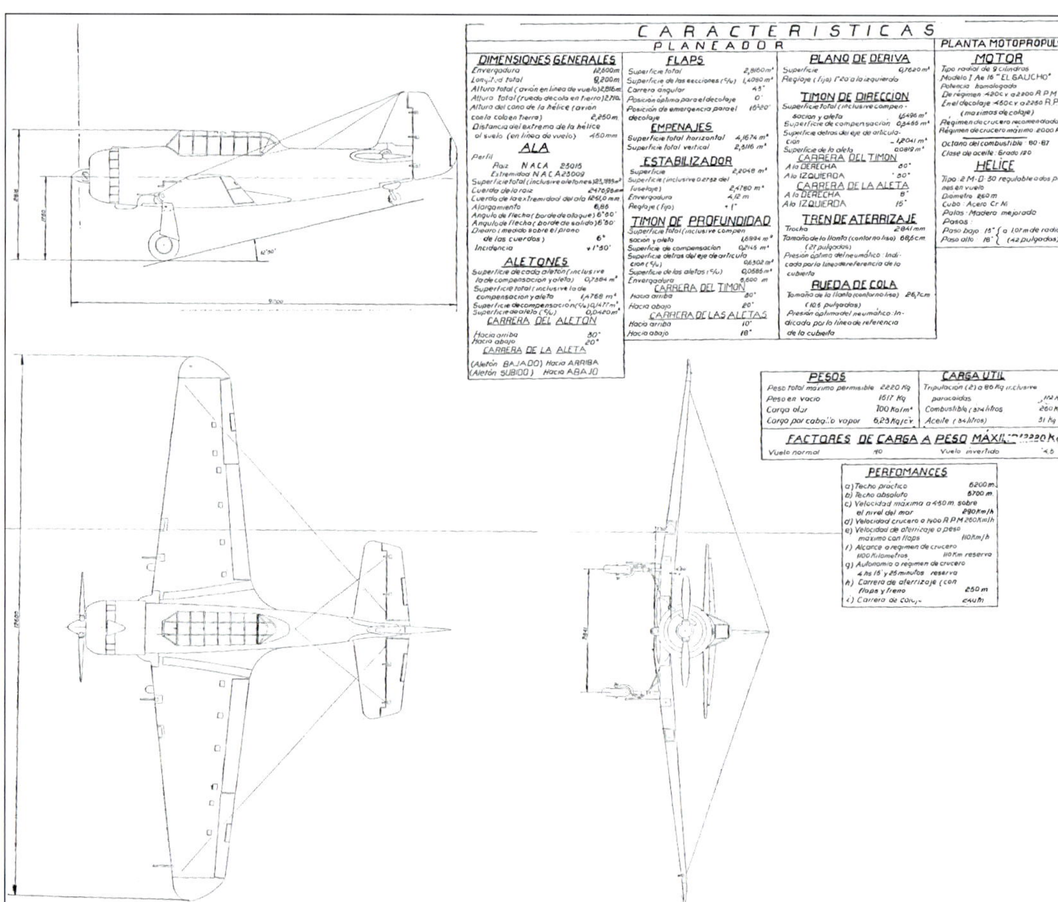

Three views of the FMA I.Ae. DL-22 made by the factory.

10 I.Ae.23

Argentina encountered problems getting parts from Germany to build the Fw 44J under licence after the outbreak of the Second World War, and as it intended to continue the series beyond the initial 190 to be delivered, during 1942 the Instituto Aerotécnico started the development of a local version, the I.Ae.23. This would use local resources to build the wooden parts and a monocoque fuselage completely made of wood, instead of tubes and fabric. It also featured a licence-built Sh-14 engine and locally built metal pieces. The prototype was finished by mid-1945, sporting a blue livery and carrying no serial, although Ee-0 was allocated. On 7 July it made its first flight in the hands of Santiago Germanó.

The FMA I.Ae.23 was a locally built Fw 44 in which the fuselage was completely built of wood and the wooden parts were built using local wood instead of European. The plane received the serial 0 and was tested from 1944 to 1947, when it was used for ground training until 1948. *Fábrica Militar de Aviones*

Testing was successful, but by the time the I. Ae.23 was ready for production the Instituto Aerotécnico was no longer interested on continuing production of the model, as the Argentine Air Force was now looking for a new basic trainer and there were too many Fw 44Js stored. The sole example was transferred to the Comando de Institutos Aeronáuticos Militares on 16 April 1947 for ground training after flying only seventy-four hours fifty minutes. It was officially retired on 27 January 1948.

11 I.Ae.24 Calquin and I.Ae.28

A replacement in difficult times

In 1944 the Commander in Chief of Aeronautics, still under the administration of the Argentine Army, studied the possibility of replacing the service's Northrop 8A attack bombers. Thirty of the type had been incorporated in 1938 and although they were fully operational, they had already become outdated with respect to the attack aircraft that were used in the Second World War and that later would be received by the Latin American countries that had supported the Allies, including A-20 Havocs and B-25 Mitchells. Argentina's neutrality during the conflict meant they could not obtain these types and strategic materials such as Duralumin could not be obtained to manufacture them locally. Faced with this situation, and thanks to the experience acquired in the construction of the I.Ae. DL-22, which was based on the North American N.A.16 although made of wood and incorporating the first engine designed and built by the FMA, it was decided to develop an attack and bomber type on a similar basis.

On 25 August 1944, the División Planes y Ensayos (Plans and Tests Division), under the Departamento de Servicios Técnicos (Department of Technical Services) of the Instituto Aerotécnico

Assembly of the wing and fuselage of the first prototype of the Calquin.

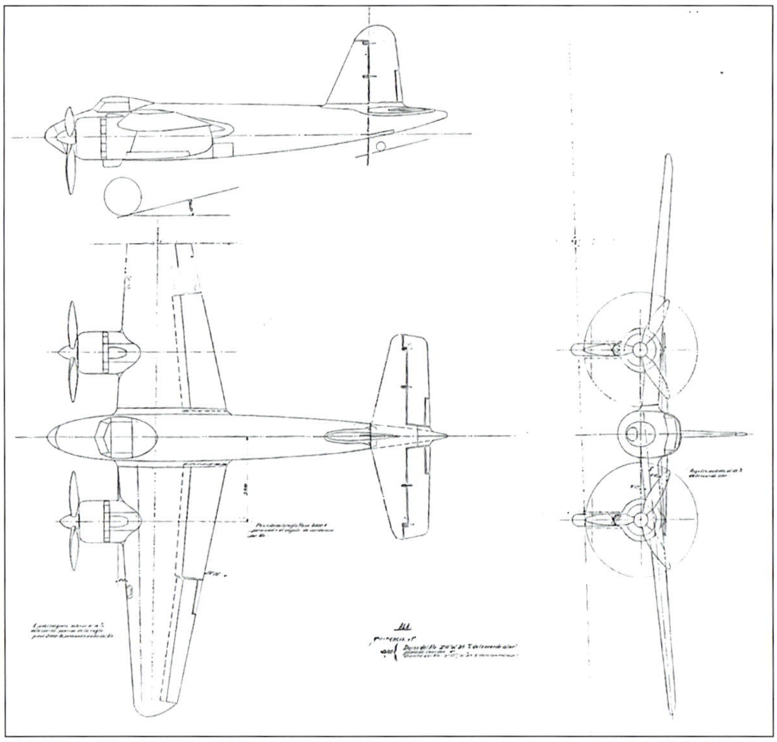

Three views of the Calquin.

(Aerotechnical Institute), began work on the new model, called DL 24 but later IAe-24 and named Calquin (Golden Eagle in the language of the Araucanian Indians), which had some similarity to the de Havilland D.H.98 Mosquito. Thanks to the studies carried out by the director of the Instituto Aerotécnico, Major Engineer Juan Ignacio San Martín, on the wood suitable for aeronautical use that was available in the country, it was not difficult to determine which would be used for the different parts. The goal was to achieve a simple, lightweight structure that met the necessary conditions of strength and rigidity.

The aircraft

The result was a twin-engine, two-seat attack and bomber aircraft. It was powered by two Pratt & Whitney R-1830-65A Twin Wasp model S1C3-G radial engines of 1,200hp at 2,700rpm at take-off, 13,000cc and fourteen cylinders in double star that drove three-bladed metallic Hamilton Standard Hydromatic 23-E-50 (later model 33-D-50) propellers with variable pitch and constant speed. With these engines it was only possible to reach a maximum speed of 440km/h, which greatly limited the type's capability. The cruise speed was 380km/h and endurance with full bomb load was two hours twenty minutes, but for long-range flights it was planned to install an extra tank in the bomb bay

Diagram of the structure and components of the Calquin.

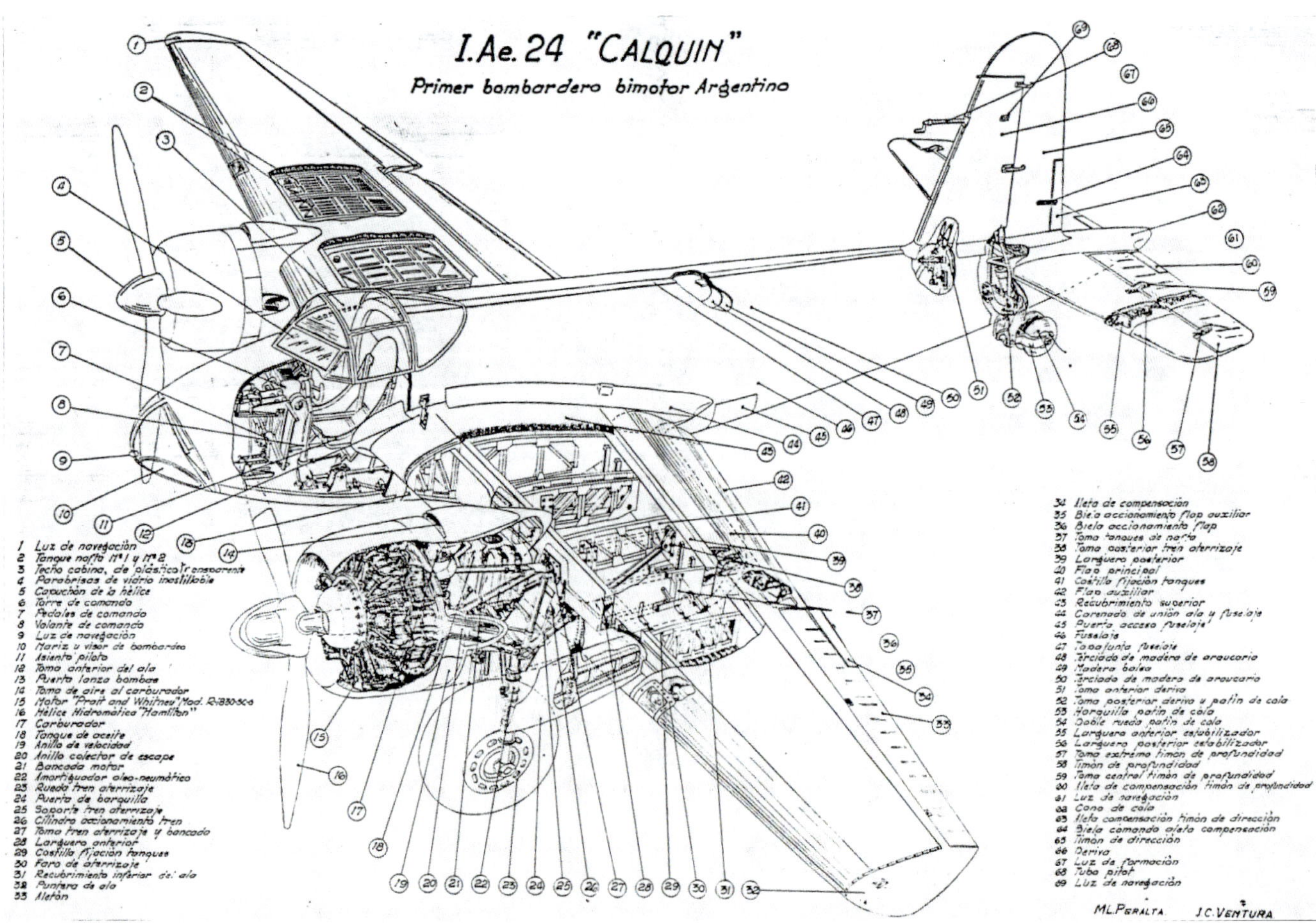

with 600 litres of fuel, making for an endurance of four and a half hours.

Another problem that arose was the aerodynamic resistance generated by the radial engines, when the Calquin had been designed similar lines to the Mosquito, which had Merlins with inline cylinders that produced less resistance. If a Calquin's engine stopped at low speed, an asymmetrical thrust was produced that caused the plane to 'screw up', inexorably causing a crash.

The Calquin had a fuselage built with two symmetrical halves, of oval section formed by seven cedar frames with plywood coating and four cedar and mañio stringers. The coating was on birch plywood plates filled with balsa wood. Between the first frame and the nose were the positions for the pilot and co-pilot/observer/bomber, who were seated side by side. Below them were communications equipment, oxygen and internal weapons. Behind the cockpit, below the wing spars and up to the second frame was the bomb bay, with a fuel tank on top. Behind it was a small luggage hold.The nose and cockpit were plexiglass, except for the windscreen and side panels, which were bulletproof. Access to the cockpit was through the roof, which opened in three pieces and could be ejected in flight by the crew. It was reached by two retractable ladders, housed in the fuselage, at the height of the wing. The entrance to the bomber's position in the nose was via the co-pilot's seat.

The cantilever wing had two one-piece stringers built in mañio. It had a strong coating similar to the fuselage except for the rectangular centre area, which was open at the bottom. The wing housed

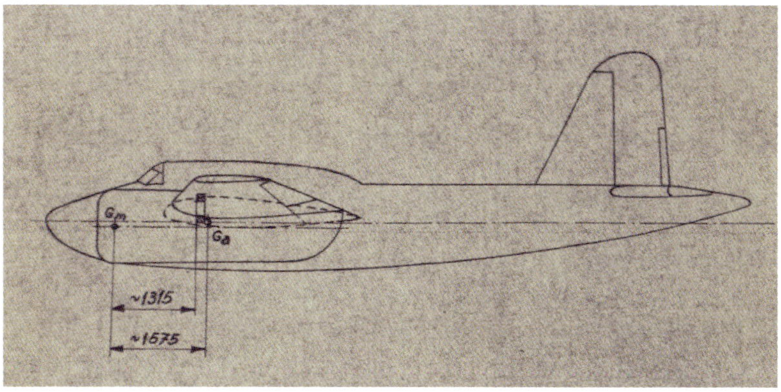

Side view from a plan of the FMA, with the original layout for the area of the cabin.

the fuel tanks, which were not self-sealing and their lids closed the central area. The leading edge was made of plywood, as were the tips, which were not structural. Both the wing and fuselage had fabric as a coating, to provide greater strength.

The ailerons, equipped with tabs, occupied approximately half the trailing edge of the wing, while the rest was occupied by a slotted wooden Lagman flap that had a smaller auxiliary flap attached. The flaps could be used as aerodynamic brakes under 240km/h. The stabiliser and tail were also cantilever structured, while the rudders were made of wood covered in fabric with tabs. The retractable landing gear was conventional, with a tailwheel, and the main units were housed in the engine nacelles. Both main wheels had two oleo-pneumatic shock absorbers and air brakes.

The control surfaces were moved by cables, while the flaps, like the doors of the bomb bay, the landing gear and the brakes, were powered by a

Calquin assembly line in Hangar 90 of the FMA. This hangar was inaugurated in the mid-1940s for the production of the DL-22 and the Calquin.

The first prototype during the first test flights. The plane has a camouflaged paint scheme, which was not used in the series models except for A-49, which used it experimentally.

high-pressure hydraulic circuit, with an accumulator and manual emergency circuit for landing gear and brakes operation. The Calquin was the first Argentine aeroplane to have such a system, designed locally.

The engines were mounted in nacelles made of Duralumin, this being the only major metal part of the aircraft apart from a cover under the nose where the machine guns and bomb bay were positioned.

The Calquin was equipped with a camera, radio equipment, direction finder and survival material.

In flight, the type was difficult to control, although there were those who acquired great expertise in it. It was unstable on all three axes and, although some authors specify that the landing gear was lowered only at the end of the approach due to the high risk of stalling, the flight manual states that the landing gear could be lowered to a maximum of 240km/h, while the landing speed without flaps was 100km/h less and does not indicate any special procedure for landing. The manual also prohibited all types of aerobatic manoeuvre and advised not exceeding 450km/h in a dive.

The Calquin is built

In April 1945, only three months after the creation of the Argentine Air Force on which the factory now depended, the manufacture of the first prototype began, and according to the annual report of the Instituto Aerotécnico by 31 December it was 80 per cent finished.

On 25 February 1946 ground tests began with a set of wings, empennage, fuselage, flaps, engine bed, landing gear and other parts, all separately, culminating successfully on 8 June, while the prototype received the finishing touches before its first flight.

In the following days the I.Ae.24 Calquin prototype (without a serial, according to the General Directorate of Aeronautical Material of 1947) began ground tests prior to the first flight, which took place on 4 July in the hands of Captain Edmundo Osvaldo Weiss, chief test pilot of the Instituto Aerotécnico. Then, at 1017 on 8 July, the prototype was flown by Commodore Juan I. San Martín and Captain Osvaldo Mauro Rovere, chief test pilot of the Instituto Aerotécnico, to the El Palomar Air Garrison, near the city of Buenos Aires. It arrived at 1215 in the middle of torrential rain to be presented to Air Force authorities. This trip also aimed to show the Calquin in flight in the parade for Independence Day, which was due to be held the next day but for weather reasons finally took place on 11 July. On that occasion the inhabitants of Buenos Aires were able to see the prototype for the first time, only seven days after its first flight.Given the success achieved so far, flight tests continued and when these had reached 100 hours without problems, the construction of a pre-series of ten aeroplanes began. These would serve to adapt the pilots to the new type, in addition to evaluating the response of the materials and construction techniques during operational service. The designers also took

Construction of the last Calquin, serialled A-100.

A-49 experimented with camouflage in two shades of green at the top and light blue at the bottom.

advantage of the visit of a de Havilland Mosquito, which arrived in Buenos Aires on 3 October 1946 to participate in the Aeronautics Week and then visited the FMA. There engineers studied it and as a result they adopted some improvements in the Argentine type. The pre-series aircraft incorporated some improvements over the prototype, including new propellers, different tyres on the main landing gear, a redesigned tailwheel, new oil radiator and shorter engine exhausts.

I.Ae.28

Given the possibility that existed at that time after the end of the war to acquire Rolls-Royce Merlin 604 engines and metal for the construction of aircraft, at the beginning of 1946 the Instituto Aerotécnico began the development of the I.Ae.28, which would be a Calquin with the British engine. The Secretaría de Aeronáutica 1946 Memoir describes the project:

Schemes of the I. Ae.28, which added Merlin engines and other improvements. *Archive César Arregues*

Study, project and construction of a fighter and light bomber, using native woods, this study carries the number I.Ae.28 It was started during 1946 and consisted mainly in designing and building an aircraft based on the I.Ae.24 modifying its structure in such a way as to allow the adaptation of the Rolls-Royce Merlin 604 liquid-cooled engines, and therefore of performances and characteristics superior to those of the I.Ae.24 Calquin with the Pratt & Whitney R-1830-65 A. The type of construction is similar to that of the Calquin with the difference being the modifications that were essential to adapt the new engines; fully metallic control surfaces to prevent deformation; adaptation of the radiators on the leading edge of the wing; a change of the landing gear; an increase in fuel capacity and a total change of the fuel and oil circuits. At the same time, modifications have been introduced aimed at facilitating the maintenance that experience has advised during the use of the Calquin aeroplane.

The Merlins were dispatched between 21 and 29 June 1946. In total, 960 plans were made, which made up 60 per cent of the necessary documentation (plans and project descriptions), and a 1:1 scale wooden model. According to calculations, this version would reach 650km/h. One hundred aircraft were planned to be manufactured, after the first series of the I.Ae.24, also of 100 examples, with Pratt & Whitney engines. By November 1946, tests began of some parts of the plane, including parts of the wing made of wood of mañio and lenga beech.

The possibility of equipping the type with the Bristol Hercules then used by the Vickers Viking and Bristol 170 Freighter that had just been received by the Air Force was evaluated. However, the advanced state of development of the I.Ae.30 Ñancú led to the

TOP Part of the mock-up of the I. Ae.28 project. *Archive César Arregues*

ABOVE View from top of a Calquin.

One of the very few colour pictures of a Calquin.

Installation of spraying systems on a Calquin, using two of the underwing pylons for rockets, used for unknown duties, most probably to fight locusts. This was a huge problem in Argentina in the late 1940s and different solutions for air spraying were tested.

Instituto Aerotécnico to announce the cancellation of the I.Ae.28 shortly after due to the better performance of the new design. Similarly, the I.Ae.30 would not be mass produced, mainly due to the large number of fighter and attack aircraft available, which far exceeded the number of pilots and ground personnel available to the force. This meant that a large number of almost all the types newly acquired post-war would remain in storage. As an example, the 100 Calquins replaced the survivors of thirty Northrop 8As. This happened in all units as not only did the most advanced aircraft such as the Gloster Meteor arrive, but the quantities multiplied compared with previous types.

This also meant, both in the case of the Calquin and other types, that many machines that suffered minor accidents were never repaired and ended up being decommissioned.

Tests

Meanwhile, on 10 July 1946 the first pre-series Calquin, serialled Ex.-06, was delivered. However, after flying for just five hours and ten minutes it suffered a minor accident due to material failure and although it could be repaired it never was. On 8 September, all other aircraft of the first series (Ex.-01 to 10), except Ex.-08 and 09, were delivered. On 7 November, by Reserved Order (OR) 454, they were assigned to the Grupo Experimental (Experimental Group) that had been formed at the Regimiento 1 de Bombardeo at BAM Coronel Pringles, in Villa Mercedes, in San Luis province. The unit would aim to test the Calquin to determine the best modes of operation and maintenance, analyse the possibility of manufacturing errors and, above all, evaluate the

A-72, equipped with four 12.7mm machine guns.

A-58 with the rockets installed and the engines running, before taking off in one of the tests at the factory.

impact of weather on the plane, given its wooden construction.

From these tests it was determined that when aircraft remained parked outdoors all inspection covers had to be sealed with gummed paper. However, the weather in the area and that where they were destined to be based, the Regimiento 3 de Ataque, part of Air Bombing Command, in the city of Mendoza, was quite benevolent to wood due to the low percentage humidity.

The evaluation aircraft were at Coronel Pringles from February 1948, when they were transferred to Mendoza to begin replacing the Northrop 8A in attack missions. Their serials were changed from Ex.- for Experimental to A- for Attack. The Northrops were then assigned to Grupo 1 de Observación 1 at BAM General Urquiza in Paraná. Alongside the Calquins the last remaining Martin 139WAA (B-10) bombers that the force possessed operated for a time.

After the Grupo Experimental finished its tests, on 4 March 1948 the factory released a document governing its use of weapons, signed by engineer Antonio Sablich, Chief of the Projects Division, 1st Lt Alberto Chavez, Chief of Testing of the I.Ae.24 Calquin, and engineer Natalio Trebino.

For bombing missions, the armament consisted of four Browning M-2 or Argentine built DL 12.7mm machine guns with a total of 1,680 rounds and 350kg of bombs in five options: the first was with one 250kg and two 50kg bombs, the second was with three of 100kg, the third was one of 100kg and four of 50kg, the fourth was with six 50kg bombs and the fifth was with seven groups of small bombs totalling 350kg.

For attack, the plane could carry the four machine guns plus two Hispano 804 20mm guns in the nose, the latter with 200 rounds. With this load, the endurance was two hours forty minutes.

For assault missions (interdiction) it was planned to arm the Calquin with the machine guns plus ten 80mm and two 210mm rockets under the wing, but those rockets were never mounted and instead they used up to ten 105mm A3F rockets.

The machine guns could be also replaced with a total of four Hispano 804 20mm guns in the nose. It could carry two different types of shooting sights, both removable, one for dive bombing and strafing and one for horizontal bombing.

Meanwhile, at the beginning of September 1947, the first prototype was sent to Buenos Aires to participate in an aeronautical exhibition that would take place from the 29th on 9 de Julio Avenue, where the new types that the Air Force had acquired would be exhibited. These included the modern Gloster Meteor IV fighter, Avro Lincoln bomber, the I.Ae.27 Pulqui jet fighter and many other aircraft. On the

Front of A-58 with one of the two types of sights used by the type. Both were removable. This sight was for horizontal bombing.

A-72 flying over the hills of Córdoba province.

Crews standing with a Calquin with the markings used by the revolutionaries in the revolution against Perón in September 1955. The letters MR meant 'Movimiento Revolucionario'.

Bomb bay of the Calquin.

afternoon of 8 October, the Calquin's return to the Instituto Aerotécnico was organised, for which it was to take off from an improvised runway on Edison Avenue, in the port of Buenos Aires. As it was rolling, a railway line that crossed the street diverted the aircraft's wheels and the right wing hit a train loaded with alcohol. An engine broke off and hit one of the wagons, which caught fire immediately. Both the pilot, Captain Roberto Borton, and the co-pilot, Chief Petty Officer Antonio Mina, were unharmed, although the plane was lost.

For this reason, Ex.-08, whose delivery had been on 21 September 1946, stayed at the Instituto Aerotécnico for evaluation, while Ex.-09 was modified to dual control for training flights, a change that would later be made to all the aircraft of the Experimental Group.On 17 January 1948 the German engineer Kurt Tank, who was contracted by the Argentine government to work at the FMA, made the first of a series of thirteen flights in Ex.-09, with the last on 13 March.

Tank specified in his report that:

> Take-off is simple, with or without flaps, as it hasn't tendency to deviate, even with moderate lateral wind. After the take-off strong vibrations on the plane are perceived, from the disequilibrium of the wheels. Stopping them, those vibrations disappear. The raise of the wheels is extraordinarily fast without a big displacement of the centre of gravity to the tail. The same to put the flaps in flight position. Because of this, a night or bad weather take-off can be made without trouble.

Referring to the stall tests, he said that 'with a weight of seven tons and the centre of gravity displaced to the back due to the lack of military equipment (guns) that displaces it to the front, the plane has no tendency to fall laterally, even when a yaw to the right or left is made at stall with the engines in slow motion'. He remarked that the plane responded to commands during the stall. The descent speed in these conditions was of 10 to 15m/s at a horizontal speed of 160 or 155km/h. He added: 'With full power there is always, when stalling, a fall to the right, without flaps at 140km/h and with flaps at 125km/h. Nevertheless, there is no risk of entering a spin. Moving the ailerons slightly to the front is enough to regain full control of the plane.'

He highlighted that this good performance in the stall meant that the engines considerably affected the air flow on the central part of the wing, and that could be the reason for the low climb rate.'Landing is very easy. Crossing the limits of the field with the engines at reduced power are enough for 190/200km/h to touch down at 160km/h with flaps fully down. At landing there is also no tendency to deviate and, because of the good effect of the brakes, it can stop fast,' explained Tank in his report and he added that, while the forces needed on the controls were not high on speeds up to 450km/h, the force to be applied to the rudder was high, as well as on the brakes. Also, he explained that the aircraft was not flown over that speed because above 350km/h vibration of the stabilisers and ailerons began and increased with speed, causing resonance problems. He recommended not starting series production of the stabiliser until it could be modified to eliminate this problem, which he suggested was caused by lack of resistance of the ailerons and stabilisers and of equilibrium of their weights. On his sixth flight, on 16 February, this problem was solved by improving the weight distribution on the ailerons, noting a minimum vibration at 360km/h that was solved by accelerating the plane.

On his last flight, he checked the climb rate, which was 2.6 minutes to reach 1,000m, 8.2 to reach 3,000m, 16.5 to 5,000m and 31.5 to climb to 7,000m. The operational ceiling was calculated at 8,400m and the maximum at 9,000m, but Tank added that 'speeds at higher altitudes couldn't be measured because the oxygen provision was not enough'.

Regarding the flight, Tank stated:

> The flight performance is bad, considering the power available from the engines, both while climbing and in fast flight. The engines can't be considered as high-performance engines ... the pass of the air through the engines is too big, especially on fast flights. The engine flaps can be installed for a narrower opening and be stiffer so as to not be opened by the air on fast flights. The passage of the air through the oil radiator is made in a very unfavourable way. Over the wing, big apertures are formed between the sheeting of the engine cowling and the wing covering, which could have an effect on the climb performance. The performance could be improved in many other areas (fittings, screw fixing, apertures, etc.).

In the reports of his flight tests he detailed other aspects of the evaluation, starting by saying that the aeroplane did not have its own ladder to climb or descend from the cabin and suggested that one be installed, something that was adopted. He considered the seat as comfortable and that most of the instruments and commands were well placed, except for the one for the landing gear and fuel controls, while the fuel indicator was not in a good position. Visibility was considered good but he asked for special windows on the sides that could be opened when the windows were dirty. He concluded that the plane 'fundamentally has good flight conditions and the deficiencies that still existed could be easily be corrected'.

Tank also suggested an extensive programme of tests with weapons before starting series production, but this did not take place and construction began while those tests were undertaken with the one of the series production aircraft, serialled A-33. It was the first equipped with the 12.7mm machine guns and the Hispano 804 20mm guns. Later, in early 1949, pylons were also tested to launch up to ten locally built A3F rockets under the wings, in addition to the respective firing tests with bombs.

From 30 June 1948 to 31 August Tank made four test flights in A-14, followed by one in A-31 on 9 September, six in A-35 between 5 and 21 October and two in A-34 on 13 and 22 October.

Meanwhile, Ex.08 and 09 were delivered to the Air Force on 5 April 1948 with the serials A-08 and 09, followed during the year by the first series production aircraft. Regimiento 3 de Ataque received A-08, 09, 12, 15, 16, 18, 19, 20, 21, 22, 24, 25, 26, 27, 28, 29 and 32 on 2 October.

Sometime before, on 20 April 1948, the first fatal accident occurred in the I.Ae.24 when Ex-07 was lost in El Algarrobal, Mendoza, causing the death of Lieutenant Sebastián Cupani and Ensign Aldo Berterreix. The accident occurred during a training flight when, shortly after taking off and when about 100m high, the plane lost stability and crashed. This episode would be the first of a long series of accidents that would cost the lives of forty-one crew members and led to the Calquin being unloved by the Air Force. It was for that reason that some called it 'Nardo' (cemetery flower).

The Calquin began to participate in the most important exercises of the Air Force as the new pilots were trained, demonstrating that it was a good platform for close air support and attack, and very robust and simple to repair thanks to the type of construction.

During 1948, aircraft up to A-47 were delivered and five entered service with Grupo 2 de Observación at BAM Reconquista.

Meanwhile, the aircraft serialled A-10 remained at the Instituto Aerotécnico and between October 1948 and the beginning of 1949 it was used alternately with a Northrop 8A and a Martín 139WAA to tow the glider test aircraft for the I. Ae.33 Pulqui II jet fighter. It was then transferred to Mendoza and replaced at the Instituto Aerotécnico by another Calquin, A-35.

During the first half of 1949 more machines were delivered to the Regimiento 3 de Ataque until they reached the serial A-60. According to the annual report of the Instituto Aerotécnico, at the end of the year there were twenty I.Ae.24s on the assembly line that were 80 per cent complete, the fuselages for the entire series were at 95 per cent and the wings at 75 per cent. Modifications were made to the flight controls, carburettor air intake and the movable fins of the engine cowlings. Dual control was installed in two aircraft and in others machine gun controls were added. Two received Collins 185 radio transmitters and sixteen received Bendix MN 31 radio compasses. The annual report concluded that given the production cadence, despite the large size of the factory's Hangar 90, where the machines were produced, there was little room to produce the DL-22 and Calquin together. In any case, during 1949, twenty-six aircraft were delivered and another fourteen were pending delivery.

The next delivery, from A-61 to 84, would be made to the Grupo 2 de Observación during 1950. The rest of the I.Ae.24s, up to a total of 100 aircraft, were delivered in the course of 1950 to the Regimiento 3 de Ataque, except for A-77, 88, 95, 97 and 100 that, although they were completed that year, would only be delivered on 30 April 1951.

During 1950 the Instituto Aerotécnico also worked on a bomb carrier for two bombs of 100kg, four of 50kg or eighteen of 13 to 15kg, while transforming five machines into dual control for training.

Air-to-Air missile

The most interesting project in which the Calquin participated was the launch test of the AM-1 Tábano (Gadfly) air-to-air missile, developed at the Instituto Aerotécnico by the División Proyectos Especiales (Special Projects Division) No. III. This project began with the constitution of this division by Order of the Day 1115 of 12 August 1947 and was run by the Polish engineer E.N. Kulcycki. The liquid-fuelled rocket engine with 335kg of thrust was developed by engineer Ricardo Dyrgalla, with which the Tábano

The Tábano air-to-air experimental missile in the belly of a Calquin. One launch was made before the programme was abandoned.

Wind tunnel model of an early design of the I.Ae.24, with a different tail and with the longer fairing on the upper part of the fuselage that appears in the earlier plans.

A proposed transport version of the Calquin found in the archives of former FMA technician César Arreguez. *Archive Arreguez family*

reached a speed of up to 900km/h for thirty-five seconds. Later it was planned to use a mixed propulsion system featuring the rocket and a pulse jet. It was guided by radio and the shape of the missile, called at that time an airmobile bomb, was that of a small aircraft, with wings, tail and stabilisers. The first ground tests were carried out on 20 October 1949 and then Captain Edmundo O. Weiss, chief test pilot of the Instituto Aerotécnico, made some launches from the Calquin serialled A-72, with the first on 18 March 1950 using a Tábano without the engine, followed later by a launch of one with the engine, in which the rocket climbed in a chandelle and then almost hit the Calquin. Other flights of the Tábano with the explosive warhead were made by Captain Villegas of the Air Force, but the result obtained was not as expected as the rocket was very hard to guide to the target. The project was cancelled shortly after. The launches were photographed from a Spitfire PR. Mk.XI, the former LV-NMZ, used by the factory, and another Calquin, while a Morane-Saulnier Criquet was used to search for the remains of the missile once it fell to the ground.

The Calquin needed modifications to its bomb bay to take the missile, since it was too long at 2.45m. It was necessary to install a pylon through the doors of the hold and the missile was carried in the belly. A-72 remained at the FMA for use in tests until shortly after it was sent to the School of Non-commissioned Officers of the Air Force to be used in ground training.

More tests

In June 1954 A-58 began to be used in the evaluation of the A3F rockets developed by IAME (Industrias Aeronáuticas y Mecánicas del Estado, the former Instituto Aerotécnico) and the Dirección General de Fabricaciones Militares (General Directorate of Military Fabrications) in Córdoba. After ground testing, the first launches were carried out by Captain Jorge Conan Doyle and 1st Lieutenant Ruberto Pío Uriz. These were made with live ammunition, firing them one by one, in pairs and in salvos. The rocket was equipped with a 105mm field artillery grenade, with a salvo from an aeroplane being equivalent to the fire by a ground battery with ten guns of the same calibre. According to the project notes, they would be used to attack concentrated targets in horizontal and low flight, or in steep dives, being more accurate than bombs against moving targets. The rocket launcher was built by IAME and could carry up to five rockets under each wing.

During 1956 the Ministry of Aeronautics acquired 200 A3F rockets to use in the Calquin, continuing with the normal use of these weapons. By this time the fleet was down to sixty, although by 21 March 1957 it had decreased to forty-nine, four of them in storage, demonstrating that the decrease of the fleet was constant and that the end was near.Thus, on 30 December 1957, by Secret Day Order OS57-9J, rectified by OS 58-1J, it was specified that the amount of Calquins on strength was twenty-nine and that 'they will remain in activity until they have to receive a Major Inspection or Major Repair, at which time they must be discharged and dismantled'.

In 1958 only twenty-five aircraft started the year, but in April almost all the examples were decommissioned and in May the last two were retired, ending the operation of this twin-engine attack aircraft.

The surviving aircraft had their engines, instruments and everything that could be used removed, after which most were destroyed, many of them in firefighting drills at different air units. A-72 survived as a ground training aircraft at the School of Non-commissioned Officers of the Air Force (ESFA) and when the National Museum of Aeronautics was established in 1963 it began to manage its transfer. The aircraft was prepared by the ESFA for transfer by land, but was then abandoned and in April 1967 during a fire practice at the I° Air Brigade of El Palomar, in front of the entrance to the Military School, the last of the 101 machines built was burned.

12 I.Ae.25 Mañque

While the Second World War was unfolding, the Argentine military followed closely all its developments and started to think how its own industry could produce some of the weapons being used and to develop different capabilities for its forces. As an example, based on information on the Sherman tank, the Argentine Army developed the DL 43 Nahuel tank, which was similar and used a Lorraine-Dietrich engine of the type built by the FMA. Also, the experiences of paratroopers and air assault led to the creation of the Military Paratroopers School (in which the Ae.M.B.2 Bombi and Ae.M.S.1 were used for the first jumps) and interest in assault gliders was developed, based on the German, British and US experiences.

On 14 January 1945, while the war was still raging, work began to develop a transport glider based on the North American Waco CG-4A, which received the name I.Ae.25 Mañque (Vulture). The result was a very similar product, with a smaller glazed area in the front cabin.

The construction was carried out with Argentine woods of mañio, guatambú, and araucaria fibres mixed with glue, which possibly did not give it an appropriate weight for its intended purpose. Inside the nose was a turret of steel tubes, at the top of which was the tow cable hook. It had dual steering, detachable seats and spoilers that increased the glide ratio from 1/15 to 1/8.

The cabin could carry two pilots and thirteen fully equipped soldiers, one jeep type vehicle, or one 75mm Krupp gun with its crew and ammunition.

Between June and August 1945 some structural tests were undertaken on two wings, the first of 480kg and the second of 358kg with an improved structure but keeping the same aerodynamic design.A prototype was built, with the fuselage being completed in early August 1945 and tested on the 6th and the 7th, specifically to prove the resistance to torsion and the strength of the structure while being towed, with a roll out, once completed, on the 11th.

The glider made a series of short test flights towed by a Martin 139WAA, taking off in less than

Fuselage of the Mañque used for structural tests. Note the badge with a vulture painted on the side.

Another view of the fuselage of the I.Ae.25 Mañque used for ground tests before being assembled for the test flights

The only Mañque built, seen at the FMA. The glider performed just a few tests and later it was used for ground training until it was scrapped.

100m. While there are no reports on the result of the project, very few test flights were made between 1945 and 31 November 1949, when the project was officially cancelled. The glider was then transferred to the 13th Infantry Regiment of the Argentine Army, located at Córdoba, which was the first unit dedicated to airborne operations, for experimentation. Experience in the Second World War had shown that, while the glider was a good tool for air assault, it was very dangerous and vulnerable to anti-aircraft artillery.

In 1946, plans were developed to transform the Mañque into a powered aeroplane with Gipsy engines, for use as a transport. A tunnel wind model of the glider with engines was built and wooden nacelles were also built to be tested on the prototype, but they were never installed and the project was cancelled.

It was painted olive green and carried under the cockpit on the port side the drawing of a black vulture on a white circle. In an interview, Brigadier Ojeda recalled that engineer San Martín was unable to get the indispensable nylon rope for towing the glider, and for this reason a flexible steel cable and Sandows cushioning was used.

There are no reports that the Mañque ever flew after its delivery to the Army and it was scrapped shortly after.

Wind tunnel model of the proposal with Gipsy engines to convert the Mañque into an aeroplane, an idea that was abandoned shortly after.

4 Beyond the limits

13 **Dewoitine's projects: I.Ae.26, I.Ae.27, I.Ae.28 and I.Ae.29**

At the end of the Second World War, the world was astonished by the performance of jet aircraft and all the aviation powers wanted to develop and build them. Argentina had become a powerful country, which was neutral during most of the conflict but supplied food and other goods to the United Kingdom. The military shortages that came as a result of the war, when no equipment could be bought in Europe and the United States, had convinced the government that had ruled the country since a coup d'etat in 1943 that local industry must be developed and that the new technologies that emerged in the war must be adopted. The best way to do so was to contract some of the engineers, pilots and other experts from the defeated countries, which were being hunted by the winning powers to take them home to work with them, but many wanted to look for other horizons, to countries where they could develop their research but where there was no anger against them.

When the Third Reich's defeat became evident, some Germans started to see Argentina as an option, as the country had a community of German immigrants, was rich, had some industrial development and did not take part in the war. However, together with the Germans were engineers and technicians from other countries who had worked for the Axis powers during the war and feared being prosecuted.

After working in France for the Spanish company Hispano Suiza, which in 1943 was absorbed by Hispano Aviación, in 1944 French national Emile Dewoitine travelled to Seville in Spain to develop several aircraft there, as he was being accused of collaboration with the Nazis. However, by the end of 1945 he decided to talk with his Argentine friend, engineer Ambrosio Taravella of the FMA, with whom he had worked on the deal for the licence production of the D.21, to negotiate with the

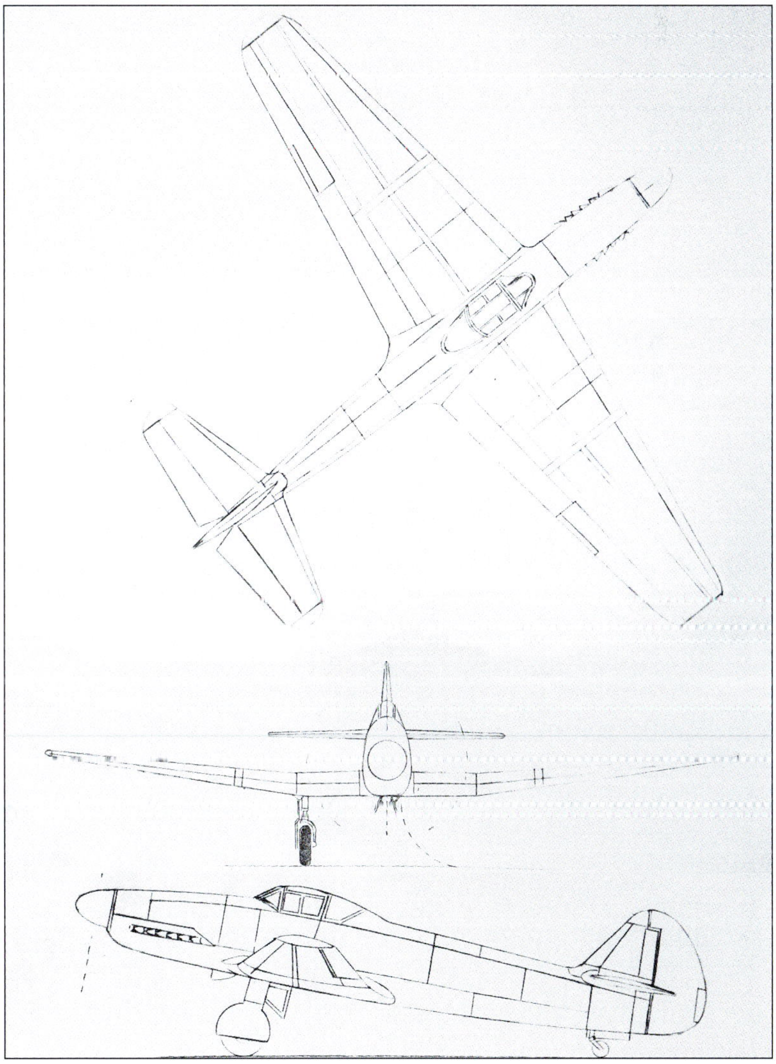

Three views of the Dewoitine D-600, which received the designation I. Ae.26 at the Instituto Aerotécnico.

I.Ae.27 mock-up, where can be seen the smaller air intake and the shape of the canopy, with little view to the rear.

Argentine government for a contract to work at the FMA and develop a series of aircraft.

Dewoitine at the FMA and the I.Ae.26

From 1942 Dewoitine had been working on the project D-600 for a fighter jet to be built by Hispano Suiza under the designation HS-50, which was based on the D-551 that was suspended when France surrendered in 1940, and equipped with the Hispano Suiza 12Z engine that developed 1,300hp at 18,000ft. When by 1944 Hispano Aviación started to produce the Messerschmitt Bf 109 under licence, interest in the HS-50 by the Spanish Ejército del Aire disappeared. However, the company decided to continue with the development to offer the model to Latin American air forces, which could not buy new aeroplanes from the major powers because of the war.

Construction of the fuselage of the first prototype. Some parts had to be modified to use the remains of the construction of the Curtiss Hawk 75-O due to the lack of materials.

The aircraft was redesigned, with a longer nose to increase the internal fuel, with a fourth tank of 305 litres under the cockpit. As a result the aircraft went from a length of 8.769m to 9.60m. The weapons were also modified, with one central 20mm Hispano 804 gun with 80 rounds, plus two on the wings also with 80 rounds each and two 12.7mm machine guns with 875 rounds each. The resultant plane had a weight, with equipment, of 3,238kg, 435kg more than the original project.

On 26 September of 1944, Emile Dewoitine gave information to the Argentine aeronautic attaché in Madrid, Captain Ismael Núñez, to enable it to build the type under licence in Argentina, and also suggested installing a Rolls-Royce Merlin engine.

The project was analysed during 1945 and the D-600 received the local designation I.Ae.26, but in late 1945 Dewoitine was told that Argentina was no longer interested in a propeller fighter as it was negotiating the purchase of Gloster Meteors (and the possible licence production of 200 of them). However, but because of the possibility of acquiring Rolls-Royce Derwent V jet engines of 1,585kg thrust, the FMA asked Dewoitine to design an interceptor with the aim of building 100 planes, equipped with that engine, with a planned armament of two 20mm guns and two 12.7mm machine guns, a speed of 800km/h and an endurance of one hour.

The I.Ae.27 Pulqui

Dewoitine started the development of the model D-700 immediately, working from the basis of the D-600. On 28 May 1946 he arrived in Buenos Aires and on 26 June signed a fourteen-month contract with the I.Ae. to start the detail work on the D-700, which was going to be called I.Ae.27 Pulqui (Arrow in the language of local aborigines). He was going to receive a monthly fee plus a percentage of the value of each of the 100 planes to be produced if the prototype was successful. Later on, the contract was extended to 30 September 1947. He considered that he was going to need sixteen months to develop the aircraft before starting series production.

In addition to Dewoitine, the design group included Argentine engineers Enrique Cardeillac, Norberto Morchio, Humberto Ricciardi and another forty-seven from the best of the I.Ae.

Cockpit of the I.Ae.27 Pulqui.

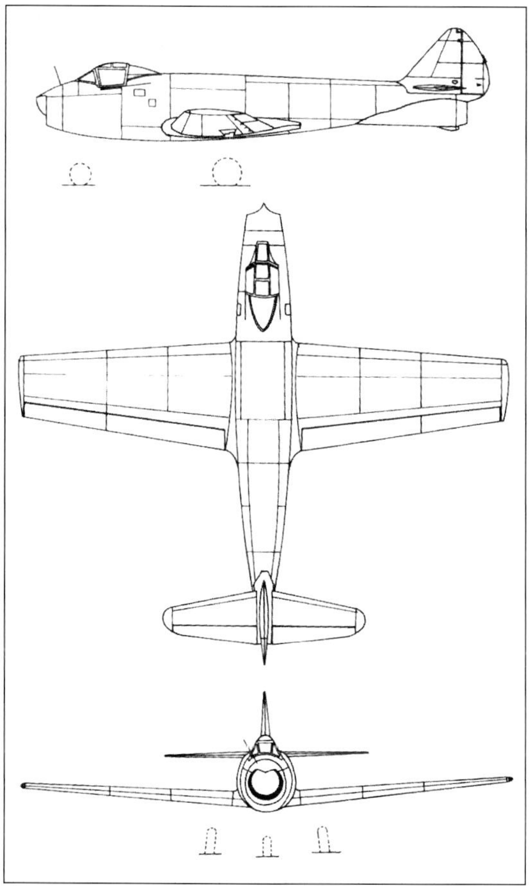

Work commenced by late 1946 using a 1:10 scale drawing that Dewoitine made with a pencil and that was placed in the middle of the design room. Morchio and Ricciardi made all the calculations, supported by Dewoitine, and in September that year began the construction of the first parts. As there were only a few materials, some parts left over from the construction of the Curtiss Hawk 75-O were used and the design had to be adapted to the equipment and material available. A wooden mock-up was built to test the placing of the engine, the cockpit design and the interpretation of the blueprints. This had almost the same cockpit as on the D-600 but with less visibility to the rear.

In spite of the problems of working on a jet for the first time, one year after the beginning of the project the prototype was finished, with a new canopy for better visibility, a new and bigger air intake and other modifications.

By the end of July 1947, the aircraft was rolled out from the South Hangar of the factory for tests before the first flight. However, when an attempt was made to start the engine, the Rolls-Royce technicians who travelled Argentina to verify the installation of the Derwent V discovered that because of the long exhaust, it was impossible to do it because of the counter-pressure it produced. To find a solution, a circular exhaust was cut below the fuselage, which was opened by a man before the engine start and closed shortly after.

First Flight

After these problems, all was ready for the first flight. Initially it was planned to carry this out on 9 July, Argentine Independence Day, but tests were delayed and 18 July was chosen, although bad weather then prevented the flight. Because of the short length of the runway at the FMA, the take-off would take place on the runway of the Escuela de Paracaidistas (Paratroopers School, near the FMA), which was longer but of grass. Vicecomodoro Paradelo Malcolm was the chief of the operation to carry the Pulqui by truck from the FMA to this school.

Finally, more than a thousand people were awaiting the first flight of a Latin American jet on 9 August 1947, including Brigadier General Bartolomé de la Colina, commander of the Argentine Air Force, and Comodoro Juan Ignacio San Martín, director of the FMA. A few minutes before the flight the technicians discovered that the front landing gear shock strut had lost pressure, so the flight was delayed for a short time until they fixed the problem in front of the public.

The instructions for the first flight were to climb to 4,500ft at less than 350km/h and at a rate of less than 30ft per second, with the landing gear down. After that the pilot had to follow level flight at less than 350km/h, turning with no more than 30° of bank and watching the indicators and the response

FAR LEFT Three views of the I. Ae.27 Pulqui.

ABOVE From left to right, Norberto Morchio, Eduardo Fernández, Humberto Ricciardi, Luis Michell and Enrique Cardeillac, all participants on the Pulqui project. Note the plane lacks the doors for the nosewheel which were installed later, nor the roundel and flag which weren't yet painted on the tail.

BELOW First take-off of the first jet aircraft built in the Southern Hemisphere on 9 August 1947.

RIGHT The Pulqui after receiving the definitive doors for the nosewheel.

BELOW The Pulqui with the initial doors for the nosewheel, of smaller size and only covering a part of the hole.

of the aircraft. If everything was going right the flaps had to be tested at less than 220km/h, and also the response of the aircraft at low speed (190km/h). After twenty minutes the Pulqui was scheduled to land at about 220km/h. The pilot was to be 1st Lt Edmundo Osvaldo Weiss.

Despite these restrictions, immediately after the take-off and because of the excellent response of the controls, Weiss made a chandelle climb, turning with more than 30°, reaching 45° of bank, but the aircraft suffered no problems and the flight was a success. After this flight there was some others before more static tests took place. After the fifth flight, the plane was shown to the press for the first time.

In the meantime, it was decided to show the Pulqui in an exhibition at the 9 de Julio Avenue in Buenos Aires, between 7 and 30 September 1947, where the Air Force would exhibit all its new aircraft. This included the Avro Lincoln, Gloster Meteor, DC-3, Fiat G-46, Bristol 170 and many others.

The Pulqui over the Pampas. It was the only jet aircraft designed by Emile Dewoitine to be built

The Pulqui after a belly landing on 15 July 1955.

To get the plane to Buenos Aires the Pulqui had to land at Marcos Juárez city aerodrome to refuel and then at President Rivadavia airport at Morón, in the suburbs of Buenos Aires. There the jet gave some flying displays and it was then taken by land 20km to the 9 de Julio Avenue, in downtown Buenos Aires. In the exhibition, the Pulqui was shown mounted on a stand with the gear up.

To return the plane to Morón, the transfer started at sunrise to avoid the traffic of Buenos Aires. The convoy was preceded by a car, a truck towing the Pulqui and another Jeep containing engineer Ricciardi, chief of the operation. While going along Libertador Avenue, at an intersection, a taxi passed between the first car and the truck, making the latter brake. The mechanic driving the Pulqui could not stop and the aircraft hit the back of the truck, smashing the front landing gear, its doors and part of the structure. The journey continued with the nose of the plane lying on the back of the truck, and it arrived in Morón many hours later.

Ricciardi estimated that it would take a month to repair the aircraft, because in Morón there were only a few tools to work with, but thanks to the dedication of the technicians, the work was finished in only one week. After some test flights by Weiss, the Pulqui returned to Córdoba.

Some modifications were made, like the shape of the wingtips and new front landing gear covers. After that, on December the plane resumed flying, while a second airframe was being finished for static tests.

Meanwhile, by the end of September the contract with Dewoitine ended and he decided not to renew it, with the aim of developing his own company to produce the plane. Shortly after, the Spanish Air Ministry became interested in the Pulqui and requested asked it was possible to buy acquire aircraft by the end of 1948, or to get the licence to build the type.

In October 1947, Dewoitine proposed to the government the construction of a factory near Buenos Aires, called Dewoitine Argentina SRL, to build the Pulqui, together with the twin-engined transport D-710 and the D-720 jet fighter (described below).

Dewoitine asked for a contract for 200 aircraft and financing to build the factory, but after negotiations, Brigadier de la Colina, as Secretary of Aeronautics, and Emile Dewoitine, signed an agreement in which land was to be granted to Dewoitine for twenty years to build the factory and runways on a field of 200 hectares near the city of Bahía Blanca. There he would build thirty Pulqui Is for a total cost of 7,350,000 Argentine pesos, plus 300,000 for the development of the D-710. He was also authorised to work on the development and construction of cars, buses, trailers, trains, steam and hydraulic turbines, engines, machinery, bombs, ammunition and other products. Delivery of the first Pulqui would be in fourteen months, followed by two in the fifteenth month and three each month after the sixteenth month, but Dewoitine considered that it was impossible to meet those dates and that the number of aircraft contracted for was for too few.

Nevertheless, Dewoitine organised the company, with Brigadier General Ángel Zuloaga, Vicente Curto, Luis Felipe Ferrari, Jorge de Atucha and Bartolomé Luis Ginocchio as partners, and the trading name was Aviones Dewoitine.

The Plan Quinquenal (Five-Year Plan) developed by the Argentine government for 1947 to 1951 included the production of sixty aircraft at the factory in 1949, forty in 1950 and eighty in 1951.

Tests by Kurt Tank and cancellation

As German engineer Kurt Tank had arrived in Argentina in early 1948, he was asked to help on the project and test fly the Pulqui. He made his first flight on 19 July 1948 and after it he suggested some modifications, including the elimination of the mechanism that connected the flaps to the ailerons

After 1955 the plane received the designation painted on the sides, now as I.A.27, as by then the designation was changed from I.Ae. to I.A. Also, copying the British use of the 'P' on the sides of the prototypes, the plane received it inside a yellow roundel. The picture shows a minor accident in which the nosewheel retracted, on a date and location unknown.

The I.Ae.27 prototype today at the Museo Nacional de Aeronáutica, after being completely restored.

during landing. Another problem he found was that the undercarriage shock strut movement was made using tubes linked by a system of stretching with connected slots, instead of a torque scissors link. This system suffered problems during the landing tests because they were carried out on a grass runway and dust got into the slots, mixed with the oil, and formed a paste that impeded the shock strut movement. The solution was a leather-made coverage.

A new flight was made by Tank on 3 August in which he reached 700km/h in level flight and this was followed by a third and last on the following day.

On 8 August 1948 the official presentation of the aircraft took place and the twin-engined I.Ae.30 Ñancú fighter at the Aeroparque (the domestic airport) of Buenos Aires, in the presence of president Perón. The Pulqui flew together with the Ñancú with lieutenant Luis Valoni at the controls.Shortly after, on the 21st of the month, the aircraft made its only exhibition outside the country, when it was taken to Montevideo, Uruguay, together with Bristol 170 Freighter serial T-39.

On 4 September, tests on aerobatic flight took place and while recovering from a manoeuvre at high speed, one of the big inspection covers on the side of the fuselage broke and was lost, forcing an emergency landing but without more major damage. A structural inspection was made and after some successful test flights after that, Tank suggested the type be adopted as an operational trainer for jet pilots, before they went on to more capable aircraft. The Pulqui had shown itself to have a performance below expectations, not reaching the expected 800km/h (Tank's flight at 700km/h was the fastest made). Moreover, at high speeds, the plane was unstable and sometimes vibrated a lot, on one occasion landing without paint on the wing. Also, the design made it impossible to install internal guns for lack of space, and it was not possible to convert it into a two-seater. Hence, on 27 October 1948 it was decided to abandon further development and use the I.Ae.27 as a research aeroplane.

The Pulqui continued test flying and to support the I.Ae.33 Pulqui II project, as was the case during a flight on 24 July 1952, when it acted as the chase plane. In 1953 it was exhibited again in Buenos Aires for the Semana Aeronáutica (Aeronautic Week). On 15 July 1955, while being flown by Captain Carlos Alesina, the landing gear retracted when the aircraft touched the runway while landing. Although this resulted in a belly landing, the damage was not heavy and it was repaired shortly after. The Pulqui was flown sporadically until late 1960, when it was retired and was put into storage. In March 1962 it was transferred to the recently created National Aeronautics Museum in Buenos Aires, where it was taken in 1963. After thirty-six years being exhibited in the open, in 1996 the aircraft was restored and today it is exhibited in perfect condition indoors at the new location of the Museum at Morón Air Base. The Pulqui's engine, Rolls-Royce Derwent c/n 10,004, which is exhibited together with the plane, flew for the last time in Meteor C-051 on the last flight of the Meteors on 29 December 1970.

Other projects by Dewoitine – I.Ae.28 and 29

On 18 March 1947, Brigadier Bartolomé de la Colina asked Dewoitine to develop a light twin-engine aircraft, with a preliminary study to be presented on 31 December 1947. The specifications according to the letter Sae 13151/25 included full metal construction, excluding the control surfaces, of monoplane configuration, with retractable landing gear, Armstrong-Siddeley Cheetah 25 engines of 385hp at 2,300rpm (the ones already in use by the DL-22) with Rotol propellers, two pilots and capacity for eight passengers with 20kg of luggage in a cabin at least 1.70m high. The plane should be also able to carry a radio with at least 600km range. The performance should be at least a cruising speed of 260km/h at an altitude of 2,100m with engines running at 2,100rpm, a practical ceiling with cargo of 5,000m (2,500m on a single engine), a take-off run of 500m with an obstacle of 15m (1,200m with an engine failure at the beginning of the climb) with the same conditions for landing. The rate of climb was to be 260m/min at ground level (40m/min with one engine) and the range 1,000km with cargo.

Dewoitine named the design D-710 but received the designation I.Ae.28 from the factory, the same used on the cancelled improved version of the Calquin of 1946, and on 19 August he signed a contract to develop the model in six months.

He aimed to build it on the factory he wanted to set up in Buenos Aires but progress was slow and he presented the project in 1948, based on the D.700-T2 he had originally developed in Spain but was never built.The D-710 differed essentially by having a trapezoidal flat wing with a constant dihedral of 4 per cent, as well as an ovoid-section fuselage 2.1m high and 1.7m wide. The wingspan was 20.41m and the wing area was 36.65m2.

Together with the required Cheetah XXV engines, he also studied a way to install the 426hp Alvis Leonides LE 1M, which was also tested in the DL-22, and the more powerful 440hp I.Ae.R.19 El Indio developed by the Instituto Aerotécnico.

With the Cheetah the type was expected to carry 580kg of fuel, reach a speed of 310km/h and cruise at 260km/h; with the Alvis Leonides it was 755kg of fuel, 337km/h maximum speed and 283km/h cruise speed; and with the El Indio the figures were 800kg, 347km/h and 291km/h respectively.

Shortly after, he redesigned the project, to be equipped with Cheetah XXV engines, with a different wing with 37.4m2 area, a fuselage 1.65m wide instead of 1.7m. Its performance, with a total weight of 4,500kg, would be 302km/h maximum speed at sea level with maximum power and 2,500rpm and 284km/h at 2,300rpm; 295km/h maximum speed at 2,000m of altitude with 2,300rpm, 289km/h at 3,000m and 282km/h at 4,000m; cruise speed at 2,100rpm of 246km/h at ground level, 268km/h at 2,000m, 265km/h at 3,000 m, 256km/h at 4,000 m; rate of climb at 2,300rpm with two engines: 4,500m/min at ground level, 326m/min at 2,000m, 200m/min at 4,000m; with a single engine: 125m/min at ground level and 65m/min at 2,000m; practical ceiling: 7,100m (3,950m with one engine).

The work to finish the project was calculated by Dewoitine as likely to take 85,000 hours for the detailed design, 100,000 hours to build the prototype and 25,000 hours per aircraft for a series production of 100 examples.

While there are no details, a wind tunnel version of what looks as an improved design, with a more aerodynamic windscreen, is preserved at the Centro de Investigación Aplicada of the Argentine Air Force, which now occupies the wind tunnels of the factory.

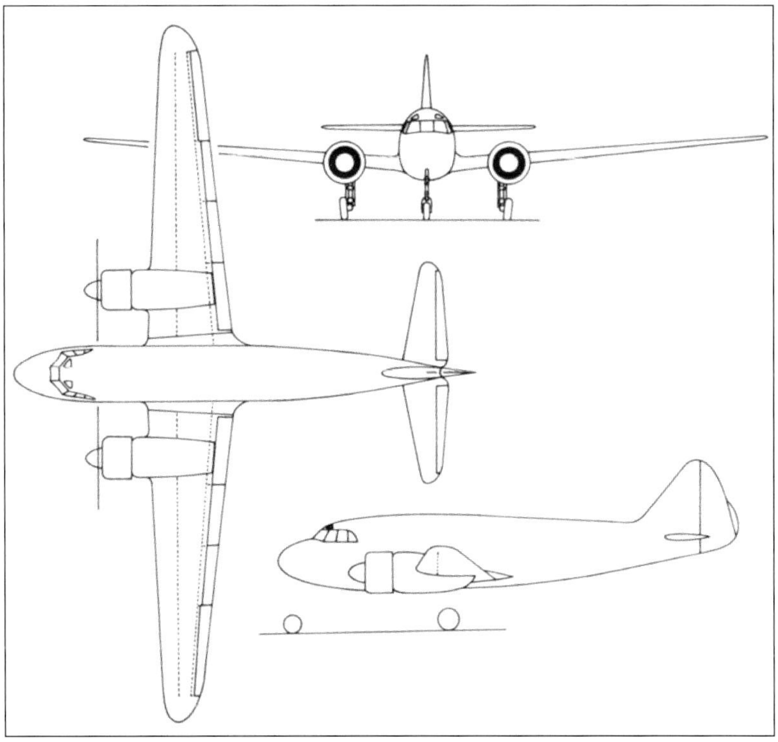

Three views of the Dewoitine D-710, which received the designation I. Ae.28.

Wind tunnel of one of another version proposed of the D-710, called locally I.Ae.28, missing the engine nacelles. Note the windscreen is completely different from the other layouts of the project. The model is currently at the Centro de Investigación Aplicada of the Argentine Air Force.

As the I.Ae.27 Pulqui project was not reaching the desired performance, Dewoitine started to work on an improved design, which he called the D-720. He expected to have this ready in eight months, after 20,000 hours of work, with another engineer and nine draughtsmen, plus 24,000 hours to build a prototype and then 6,000 hours per aircraft for during series production. He proposed the type to

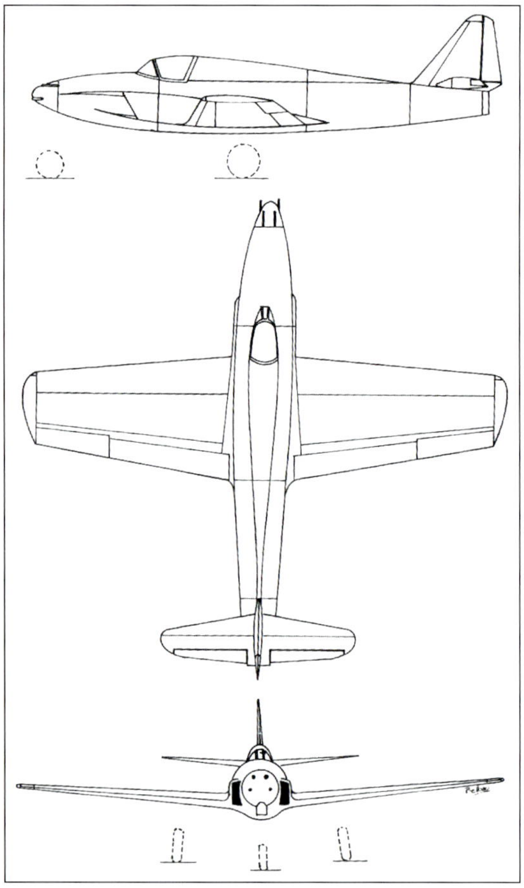

Three views of the Dewoitine D-720, named I.Ae.29 by the FMA. *Drawing by Sergio Bellomo*

the Argentine government, and it received the designation I.Ae.29.

The design was very different, with the air intakes on the side of the fuselage and four 20mm guns on the front. It had a new tail and two internal fuel tanks, one behind the cockpit and one under it, with a capacity of 135 and 270 litres respectively, with two additional tanks in both wings, one of 130 litres and one of 100 litres.

The trapezoidal wing was originally the same as the I.Ae.27, with a wingspan of 11.25m, but it was later reduced to 9.50m, with a wing area of 17.60m2. The fuselage length was of 9.78m, with a conical body of a diameter not exceeding 1.22m. The cockpit had a canopy that ended on the rear part on a fairing with the shape of a water drop that ended at the base of the tail.

Model of the Dewoitine D-720 or I.Ae.29.

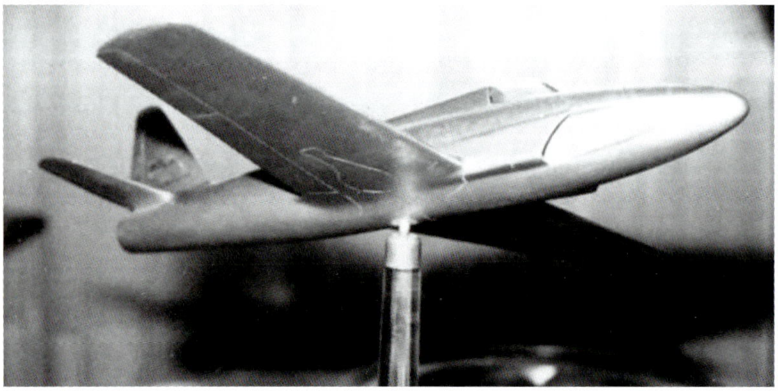

Take-off weight would be 3,346kg, broken down as follows: wing 550kg, fuselage 250kg, empennages 84kg, landing gear 225kg, armour 60kg, for a total of 1,169kg in the airframe. Engine 600kg, accessories 26kg and nozzle 60kg for a total of 686kg in the engine installation. Plus, 900kg of fuel, 120kg of equipment, 370kg of guns and ammunition and 100kg for the pilot with his equipment.

Dewoitine delivered a preliminary proposal by the first half of 1948 and the type was considered in the Five-Year Plan, but when on 7 October 1948 the government decided to cancel the contract with Dewoitine, the I.Ae.28 and I.Ae.29 projects were also cancelled. By that time, Kurt Tank was already working at the FMA with a more technically advanced proposal, the IA-33 Pulqui II.

Just a proposal

After the end of his contract with Argentina, Emile Dewoitine stayed in Argentina until 1952, looking for new opportunities and trying to get interest from the Argentine government to develop his factory. Also, on 20 February 1948 he was sentenced in France to twenty years in prison and forced labour for his collaboration with the Vichy government, so he was reluctant to return to Europe.

During this time, he started the development of two new projects, the D-730 and D-740 interceptors, using the Rolls-Royce Nene engine. They were similar, but the first had a straight wing, while the D-740 had a swept one, but both had the same fuselage 9.6m long, 1.2m diameter, air intakes on the sides and part of the belly and an exhaust under the tail. The glazed cockpit had a fairing on the back that ended on a beam supporting the empennage and placing it out of the exhaust cone of the jet nozzle. The vertical tail had an angle of attack of 40°. The wing of the D-730 was of trapezoidal shape and had a wingspan of 10m and area of 16m2, while the D-740 had the same area, but with an angle of attack of 36° 30' and only 9.25m wingspan. In both cases, they carried all the internal fuel. The stabiliser of the D-730 was trapezoidal, and that of the D-740 was swept. The height was only 3m.The weapons were planned to be four 20mm guns or two of 30mm.

The D-730 was expected to have a weight in flying order of around at 4,024kgm, being 1,970kg empty (1,270kg for the equipped airframe and 700kg for the engine installation) and 2,054kg of payload. Maximum planned speeds were 910km/h at ground level, 900km/h at 4,500m and 860km/h at 9,000m, while the climb rate was expected to be three minutes eight seconds to reach 4,500m and eight minutes to 9,000m. The practical ceiling was 14,000m with a range of 800km at a cruising altitude of 4,500m, and 1,058km at 9,000m. With additional jettisonable underwing tanks the range could be extended to 1,550km at 4,500m and 2,100km at 9,000m.

While Dewoitine received no interest from Argentina, which was working on the Pulqui II and other jet projects, in 1951 he restarted work with Iberavia in Spain, after they had collaborated on a design in 1946 that was never built.

Iberavia was interested in developing a new plane, which Dewoitine called the D-750, to participate in a tender launched by the Spanish Air Force to replace its Fieseler Storch. The intention was to develop an aircraft of two or three seats, with a maximum speed of at least 175km/h, a stall speed of less than or equal to 60km/h; an initial rate of climb of at least 200m/min; a practical ceiling not less than 4,500m, a take-off in less than 190m with an obstacle of 15m, landing at less than 160m after crossing an obstacle of 15m, and an endurance of at least two and a hours.

The type was named the I-18 by Iberavia and in 1952 Dewoitine decided to abandon his plans to try to establish his company in Argentina and emigrated to Spain. By then, Iberavia had been purchased by AISA (Aeronáutica Industrial Sociedad Anónima), who called this project the AVD-12. Meanwhile, he offered the D-730 and D-740 to the Spanish Air Force, but the projects did not generate interest and he abandoned them shortly after.

The AVD-12 was named XL-10 by the Spanish Air Force and competed with the Dornier Do 25, called the XL-9. Initially, both were to be powered by the 150hp ENMASA Elizalde Tigre G. IV. The first prototype AVD-12 (D.750-1 for Dewoitine) revealed that the engine power was not enough and it was replaced by the 225hp Continental O-470J on the second prototype, designated AVD-12C, which first flew in 1956. The AVD-12C was designated D.750-2 by Dewoitine.

A fatal accident in the second prototype and some shortcomings of the design led to the decision to choose the Do 25, which in the end evolved into the Do 27. This led Dewoitine to offer the type to

Drawing of the Dewoitine D-740, which he projected while he was still living in Argentina but did not generate interest in the Argentine authorities. He also tried to get interest from the Spanish Air Force, without success.

Mitsubishi, to be built under licence in Japan, but in July 1956 he again contacted the Argentine Ministerio de Aeronáutica, through his company Aviones Dewoitine, which still had an office in Buenos Aires. He offered the production under licence at IAME of 200 AVD-12Cs with Gipsy engines, as his company had been appointed by AISA as the exclusive representative for South America. On 27 February 1957 he received a final reply from Brigadier General Pedro Domínguez, president of IAME, stating that under the current political and economic situation in Argentina it could not take on such 'a complex operation'. Dewoitine then tried to interest Chile in the type, but this also failed. The failure of all his projects after the Second World War led Dewoitine to decide to end his career as aeronautical engineer shortly after.

Dewoitine's last proposal to the FMA was the licence production of the Dewoitine D-750, called AVD-12C by AISA in Spain. He made it by July 1956, but in February 1957 he received a negative reply. Shortly after he retired from aircraft engineering.

14 Pallavecino's projects: I.Ae.30 Ñancú and jet derivatives

With Ricardo Lezón

The growth of the FMA factory, its reorganisation and the increase in the quantity and quality of facilities, could not have been achieved without improving the technical level of its engineering staff. This goal was reached and overcome thanks to the incorporation of a group of professionals who were hired in the countries that lost the war. This was thanks to the remarkable work of the Delegación Argentina de Inmigración Europea, which, since 1946, made successful contacts with professionals who offered their services to work outside France, Germany or Italy, convincing them of the benefits of living in a distant country, neutral, and as prosperous and promising as Argentina. The delegation worked closely with Argentine embassies in Europe (mainly in Rome and Madrid). In the spring of 1946, Brigadiers Bartolomé de la Colina and Juan Ignacio San Martín arrived in Europe to oversee the programme, which achieved success hiring German engineers Reimar Horten, Kurt Tank, the French Emile Dewoitine and Italian Cesare Pallavicino, among many others. All these professionals went to Argentina and took their own team of technicians.

Construction of the first prototype of the Ñancú.

Towards the end of 1946 Italian engineer Cesare Pallavicino, who had been in Argentina since the previous summer together with a large group of Italian technicians and craftsmen largely from the Caproni Cantieri workshops, assumed the technical direction of the Instituto Aérotecnico, while at the same time Brigadier Juan I. San Martín was in charge of national aeronautical production. He was preparing to initiate a vast production programme, and it was expected that the aforementioned group of Italian technicians and workers would cooperate.

Ing. Pallaviccino was assigned to Grupo División de Tareas Especiales No. 2. Formed on 5 June within the Instituto Aerotécnico, the unit was composed of four engineers and a dozen designers, the latter unsuited for the task. Ing. Pallaviccino solved the problem by bringing in four members of his group

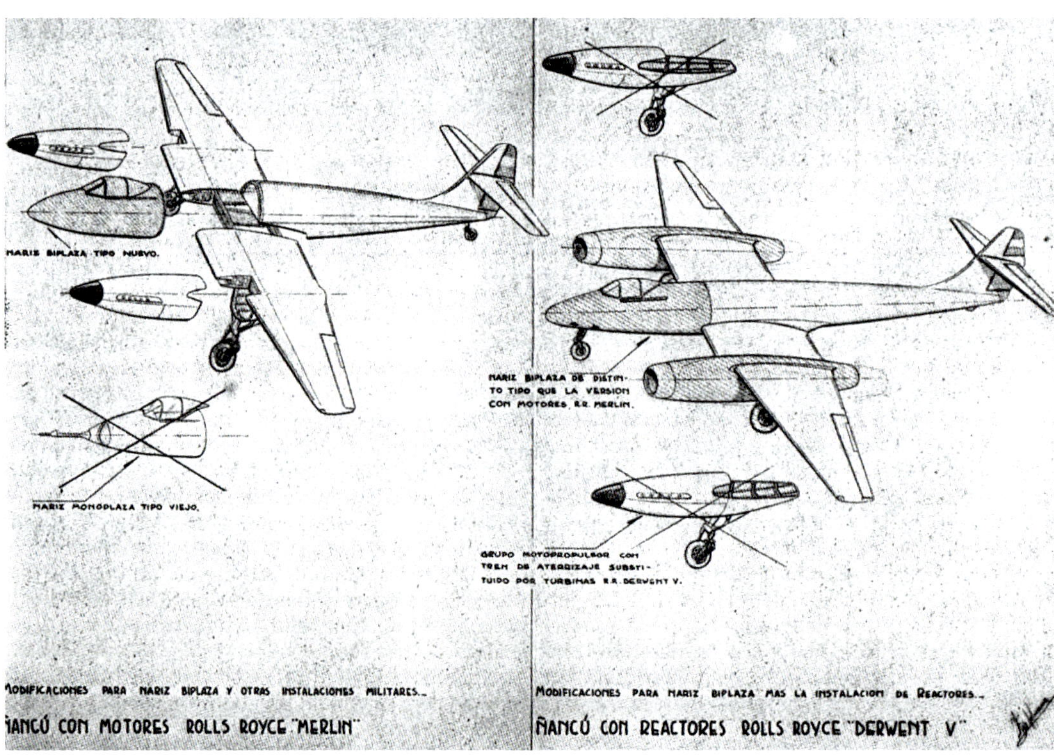

Cesare Pallavicino's proposals to convert the Ñancú into a jet fighter, on which he worked at the same time as he was developing the plane.

who were used to his working methods. He also invited students from a technical school. During his stay in Argentina, Ing. Pallaviccino also taught aeronautical radio engineering and aeronautical engineering at the Universidad de Córdoba.

Early in 1947, the Fuerza Aérea Argentina headquarters issued a requirement for a heavily armed, single-seat day and night fighter. Ing. Pallaviccino submitted preliminary drawings for a twin-engined fighter with the most heavily concentrated mounting possible for four 20mm guns, a good all-around view for the pilot and a clean minimum-drag airframe. The new aircraft received the official designation IAe.30 Ñancú (Hawk in Araucarian).

The Ñancú was a good example of the excellence that can be obtained when close collaboration exists between the aircraft designer and the engine manufacturer. Related to this, when the design of the IAe.30 was laid down in February 1947, the decision was taken to use Merlin 130 series engines. The Merlin 134/135s were specially developed variants of the Series 100 engines and were specially prepared for installation in the de Havilland Hornet, the first twin-engine British aircraft to have handed airscrews.

By June 1947, progress on the IAe.28 was quite well advanced, but there was little enthusiasm for it. At the same time, the Instituto Aeronáutico started to work on the IAe.30 and the IAe.28 project was cancelled.

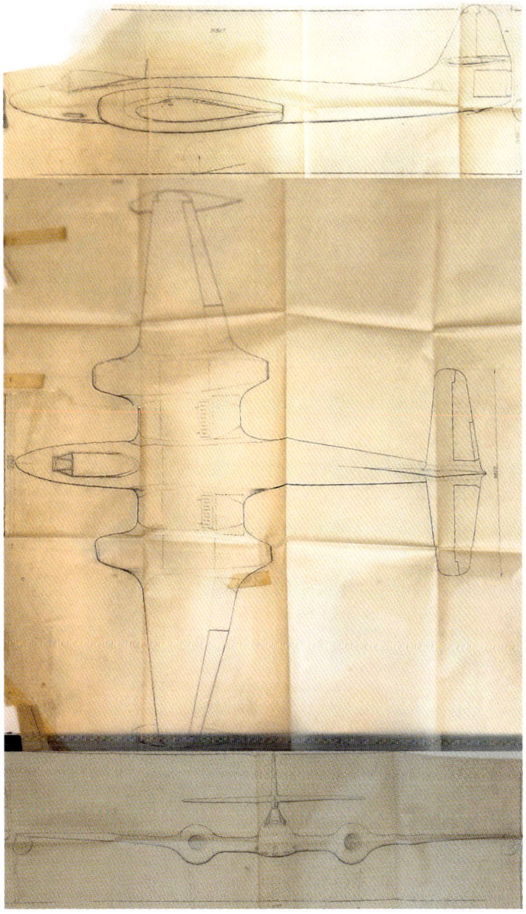

One of the layouts of the proposed jet version of the Ñancú, dated 24 November 1947.

The aircraft

The streamlined semi-monocoque fuselage was designed in two primary sections, the front and rear fuselage with integral fin. Ing. Pallaviccino adopted the pear-shaped cross section used in the Caproni Ca.331.

The IAe.30 wing was a one-piece cantilever structure comprising two spars. The wing's taper was kept as sharp as possible to conserve the aircraft's roll performance and the tip was squared to permit the aileron to extend outboard as far as possible, again to enhance roll quality. The control surfaces were metal covered and Alclad ailerons and hydraulically operated split tabs, divided by the engine nacelles, were fitted.

The tailplane and fin were cantilever all-metal structures consisting of two spars. The fin was built integrally with the fuselage. The rudder and elevators had controllable and automatic trim tabs.

The landing gear consisted of two retractable single-wheel units one under each engine nacelle, and a retractable tailwheel. Wheel forks had oleo pneumatic shock absorbers. The main wheels turned 90 degrees when raised to lie flat in the engine nacelles. Dunlop brakes and AH8208 wheels were fitted. The retractable tailwheel had a Dunlop wheel and also used a rubber compression shock absorber.

The IAe.30 was powered by two Rolls-Royce Merlin 134-5/135-5 twelve-cylinder, vee-type, liquid-cooled engines, which were fitted with Corliss throttles to give less throttle torque and a clean intake at full throttle conditions.

Four engines were purchased for the Ñancú and two starters were sent with them. They were de Havilland Hornet power plants built and converted at Derby. The suffix -5 denoted the customer, Instituto Aerotécnico. These were two-stage, two-speed units with supercharger and intercooler, using a downdraught air intake and reverse coolant flow, and both were mounted in 'power plant' nacelles.

Originally manufactured by Rolls-Royce at the Derby works as Merlin 130s (c/n 234729 and 234799) and 13s (c/n 236702 and 236026), the engines were converted to 134/135s under Contract No. 479 dated 25 March 1947. On the completion

Design of the installation of the six Hispano Suiza 20mm cannon in the belly of the Ñancú, as was originally planned. The jet version of November 1947 had the same layout.

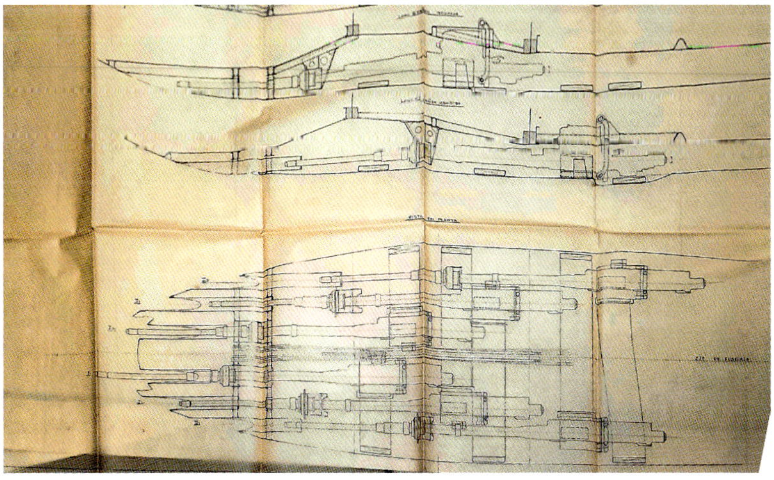

The first prototype just after being rolled out from the factory. It still lacks any paint and the undercarriage doors.

of tests, the engines were renumbered, packed in crates and readied for shipment. Merlin 134-5s Nos 309001 and 309003 were dispatched on 23 May 1947, while Merlin 135-5s Nos 309002 and 309004 were dispatched on 30 May 1947.

The Merlin 134-5 had a reverse-rotating propeller shaft, and both engines drove four-bladed de Havilland Hydromatic 4/4000/5 constant-speed, narrow-cord, full-feathering propellers 12ft 0in in diameter.

The controls for the engines and propellers, as well as the hydraulic system, were the same as for the de Havilland Hornet.

The engines were mounted low to obtain a smooth airflow over the wing, with their exhaust being ejected below; the positioning of the nacelles allowed for a relatively short landing gear leg for easy stowage when retracted, and gave the pilot a completely unrestricted view over the top surface of the wing.

The engines were mounted on steel tube frames attached to the front spar and to the undercarriage fixed structure. The coolant radiators and oil coolers were housed within the forward section of the wing profile between the fuselage and each engine nacelle. The temperature was thermostatically controlled and the carburetor air intake was ducted from an opening in the leading edge of each wing outboard of the engine.

The fuel load was contained in four pairs of wing tanks and two fuselage tanks. All these tanks were self-sealing and were vented to atmosphere. Each pair of wing tanks were interconnected, there was one pair of tanks outboard and one inboard of each engine.

Communications and navigation equipment included an AN/ART 13 Collins radio transmitter and a Bendix MN 31 radio compass.

Alternative guns arrangement were examined. The original proposal had six 20mm Oerlikon guns,

The I.Ae.30 Ñancú at the factory during the first trials.

but the Argentine Air Force requested a change to Hispano HS 804 guns with 600 rounds for each gun mounted under the nose. Due to the bigger size of these guns, the number was later reduced to four. In addition, a 250kg (550lb) bomb could be carried under the fuselage or five 83mm rockets could be fitted under the outer wings. Also, extra drop tanks were planned to be carried under the wings and a proposal was made for a version armed with a torpedo carried under the belly, where a maximum of 1,000kg could be loaded. However, the prototype was never armed.

The Instituto Aerotécnico assigned its own construction number, IA 30/MD/01, and the Fuerza Aérea Argentina assigned the military serial I-101, but it was not used.

Test pilot Edmundo Weiss and Cesare Pallaviccino in front of the Ñancú on 16 July 1948, two days before the first flight.

First flight

On 10 July 1948, the prototype was rolled out for systems and fuel flow checks, engine runs and taxiing. The sixty-minute taxi run included undercarriage adjustments and enabled take-off run estimates. Following preliminary ground handling and taxying trials, the I.Ae. technicians examined the aircraft. The only snag they found was a failure in the undercarriage retraction system. Following adjustments, the aircraft was declared fit to fly.

The next day the local press announced the roll out of the new fighter. Three photographs and a short description were published in *Democracia* newspaper. The paper described the Ñancú as one of Argentina's fastest machines and also informed the readers that its latest Rolls-Royce Merlins produced 1,800hp and would achieve 700km/h at 27,500ft. 'This technical and industrial effort will place the local aeronautical industry at the front line by matching the performance to the de Havilland Hornet, rightly identified as the fastest ever piston-engined fighter, with a maximum speed of 700km/h.'

Early in the morning of 18 July, the aircraft in bare metal finish sat outside the Instituto Aeronáutico hangar undergoing final preparations for its maiden flight. The pilot detailed to test the Ñancú was I.Ae. Chief Test Pilot 1st Lieutenant Edmundo O. Weiss. The previous year, he was sent to the UK to evaluate aircraft and was assigned to de Havilland's facilities at Hatfield, where he tested various types, among them Hornet F.3 FX386.

The I.Ae. technicians began their external checks, starting with the cockpit and working around the Ñancú in a clockwise direction. Meanwhile, another group checked the Merlins' fuel, oil and glycol coolant levels, the exhaust manifolds and intercoolers.

With the external airframe, undercarriage, radiators and cockpit inspected, and flying controls tested by the I.Ae. technicians, they started and warmed up the engines, checking the magnetos, engine temperatures and various power settings.

After brief preliminaries, 1° Tte Weiss climbed into the cockpit of the Ñancú, strapped in and started the engines. When he was satisfied that all was as it should be, he indicated he was ready to taxi and waved 'chocks away'. The ground crew pulled the chocks away from the wheels, freeing the

The Ñancú taxies for its first flight on 18 July 1948.

After some flights, the plane received a slightly improved streamlined canopy and the front doors for the undercarriage.

throaty Merlins driving their massive 12ft de Havilland propellers. He gave a burst of power to break the inertia and get the prototype taxying quickly to the end of the airfield (the 'ready to boil' Merlins warmed up quickly on the ground and it was recommended that the aircraft be faced into wind during all ground running).

On the far side of the airfield, the Ñancú was moving forward. Faster and faster, it sped across the grass, slap into the wind and tail up. But it did not leave the ground and 1° Tte Weiss brought it back to the take-off position. There was nothing amiss. The test pilot had raced across the airfield with both Merlins at full power to sample his fore and aft control. He was satisfied. Again, the Ñancú began to move forward. At 1100 Weiss took off after a 300m ground run. During the twenty-minute flight a speed of 370km/h was attained. A failure in the retraction system persisted and the pilot had to land at the Escuela Militar de Paracaidistas airfield.

The I.Ae.30 had gone from the drawing board to first flight in just eleven months thanks to the greatest foresight, skill and initiative of the Italian team led by Pallaviccino validly assisted by engineers Gaviraghi and Ferretti, technicians Pietro Montano, Quarti (formerly Caproni's designer), Targhi, Bardi, Trabalza, Fossatti, Cerrutti, Pastorino, Saldin and Moldano, and around sixty specialised Italian workers. The debut of the Ñancú was covered by the main local papers.

Five further flights were conducted between 18 and 30 July and it was reported that it was impossible to retract the undercarriage. In addition, the ailerons were reported as being heavy. Following adjustments, the undercarriage problem was solved and the aircraft was ready to be sent to Buenos Aires.

Debutant

In August 1948, the Argentinian government announced that a display of new aircraft was to be held at Aeroparque domestic airport in Buenos Aires. It included the I.Ae.27 Pulqui I, I.Ae.30 Ñancú and Vickers Viking T.1 serialled T-64, recently ordered for President General Juan Domingo Perón.

On the morning of 8 August, the gleaming prototype sat on the ramp at the I.Ae. waiting for its pilot. At 1200 after charts and log sheets had been prepared and the preliminary checks completed, he climbed into the cockpit. Completing final checks, 1° Tte Weiss ordered chocks away and taxied to the end of the airfield. At 1320 he took off and set off for Buenos Aires. Flying at 18,700ft and using 60 per cent of the maximum power available, he covered 650km in fifty-five minutes at an average speed of 650km/h, with peaks of 780km/h due to a strong tailwind.

At 1415, fifteen minutes before the ETA, a silver shape approached the Aeroparque from the north-west, breaking the speed record between those two cities, which the Ñancú still has for piston-engine aircraft. After his appearance over the airport, Weiss flew over at about 5,000ft at a speed of some 480km/h, then approached the control tower at a height of 2,000–3,000ft before turning the Ñancú so tightly at such speed that vapour trails streamed from the wingtips. That was followed by a normal circuit and landing.

1° Tte Weiss emerged from the tiny cockpit and climbed down the ladder to be received like a hero by Secretario de Aeronáutica Brigadier César R. Ojeda and Brigadier Juan Ignacio San Martín.

The next day, the Ñancú and Pulqui I were displayed for President General Juan D. Perón, his wife Eva Duarte de Perón, Secretario de Aeronáutica César R. Ojeda and his staff, Instituto Aerotécnico chief, Brigadier Juan Ignacio San Martin, engineer Césare Pallavicino, Argentine Army officers, the British Air Attaché Air Commodore Henry Edward Walker and Civil Assistant Air Attaché R.H. Van Dyke and Argentine's government representatives. After the display, 1° Tte Weiss and engineers Pallaviccino and Ferretti were met by President General Perón, who congratulated them for the success of the flight and decorated Pallaviccino for his contribution to the local aviation industry. The Ñancú must have made a good impression, as the next day the government ordered 210 of the type. It was obvious that the I.A.e 30 was an extremely 'hot' aeroplane. The I.Ae. began negotiations with Rolls-Royce Ltd for 430 engines and spares.

Farnborough?

Due to the outstanding performance, the government, always alert to the value of propaganda, asked Pallaviccino to display the aircraft in Europe. The trip coincided with the first SBAC air show to be held at Farnborough between 7 and 12 September 1948.

The Society of British Aircraft Constructors (SBAC) had staged six exhibitions and flying displays between the wars, and its first two post-war events were held at Handley Page's Radlett airfield near St Albans. These were the days of early post-war prototypes, a number of which progressed no further for various reasons. Some were built for specific research purposes, while others, it was hoped, would receive production contracts. At that time all the aircraft displayed had to be British

The plane taxiing at Aeroparque Jorge Newbery after its flight from the factory, in which it broke the speed record between the cities of Córdoba and Buenos Aires.

manufactured and powered by British engines. The I.Ae.30 would have the rare privilege of being one of the first foreign aircraft to be displayed there. The first leg was to be from Buenos Aires to Rio Janeiro, then on to Natal and the Canary Islands, then to Dakar and finally London.

The normal fuel load for the Ñancú consisted of 2,977 litres, giving a range of 2,700km. Since the distance from Natal to Dakar was 3,000km, the I.Ae. fitted a 600-litre tank in the fuselage. This contributed to a total of 3,300 litres and a range of 3,600km.

Two Fuerza Aérea Argentina Avro Lancastrian IVs with serials T-65 and T-66 were assigned to assist the prototype en route. One of the Lancastrians was used to assess fuel consumption ahead of the ferry flight. T-65 was flown from Córdoba to Morón airport on 17 August 1948 and readied for the long flight to Dakar.

Taking off from Morón airport the next day, the Lancastrian, crewed by Capitán L.A. Lafuente (commander), Capitán J.C. Villa (first pilot), Alferez L.A. Castagnino, Suboficial Auxiliar R.A. Bolla (mechanic) and Suboficiales Auxiliares B.A. García and B.A. Iñon (wireless operators), reached Natal (Brazil) after an eleven-hour five-minute flight. Then, on 20 August, it covered the 3,000km between Natal and Dakar in

A colour video still taken at the factory in 1949, with the Ñancú together with a DL-22 and a Calquin.

One of the few colour pictures of the Ñancú, taken in 1949.

The Ñancú had an elegant design and was a very fast and manoeuvrable aircraft, but arrived late for its time, when fighters were starting to use jet engines.

eight hours thirty minutes piloted by 1° Tte S. Posadas. The return flight to Natal on 22 August took seven hours fifty-five minutes, with the last leg completed the next day in thirteen hours.

On their return to Córdoba the crew of T-65 set about preparing operational procedures based on the information they had gathered from the trip. The technical information and fuel consumption of the aircraft was documented.

However, although a presidential government decree dated 6 September 1948 authorised the trip, it was cancelled due to the lack of time available to prepare the aircraft. Pallavicino was also strongly opposed to the plan, as he considered the aircraft was not ready and the pilot needed navigation training.

Unfortunately, for Pallaviccino his disagreement with the management meant he lost his position as a director, although he was then assigned to oversee the development of the prototype and the mass production of the Ñancú.

Testing times

Although the I.Ae. test pilots Teniente Luis Valoni and Sub-Oficial Jorge Villegas carried out test flying, 1° Tte Weiss was the main pilot.

Other snags encountered on the first flight were still to be overcome in September, when the aircraft

Kurt Tank at the controls of the Ñancú. He made an evaluation flight of the plane and made several recommendations.

underwent brief handling trials at Córdoba in the hands of the I.Ae. pilots. They reported favourably on the handling but criticised some features, including the heaviness of the controls in the three axes of flight at high speed and a lack of balance in the ailerons.

By early September 1948, the aircraft had completed thirty-four flights. On 10 September, the aircraft was flown by Kurt Tank. The flight was devoted to check handling characteristics. At 1350 he took off and climbed majestically into the crisp winter air. He checked the aircraft performance during a fifty-minute test over the I.Ae. aerodrome. The resulting report addressed to eng. Pallaviccino agreed with the previous criticisms and began complaining about the layout of the instruments:

> The arrangements of instruments and throttle levers do not correspond to the requirements of a modern fighter. A complete revision is required.
>
> Taxi and take-off is normal and there is no swing. This is an advantage of the counter-rotation of the propellers.
>
> Deficient harmonisation of rudder and elevators was evident once the aircraft gained speed after retracting the undercarriage. Their forces remained normal, while the aileron forces increased excessively, so it was possible to act at 300 m.p.h. An existing turn to the left could not be stabilised at once, as the Flettner tab control was misplaced. Also, the effectiveness of stabilisation is very low. The aircraft was stabilised with the use of the entire deviation margin.
>
> After achieving an equilibrium in the three axes, the stability conditions were provisionally evaluated at 8,200ft.
>
> Vertical axis: The return to the normal position is aperiodic after applying a strong stick force.
>
> Longitudinal axis: The aileron control is heavy at high speed. The aircraft recovered slowly but unequivocally after each turn keeping the stick fixed. This test must be repeated with aileron control forces corrected.
>
> Transverse axis: There is sufficient static and dynamic longitudinal stability at the gravity centre.
>
> After throttling back, the plane maintained the direction through slight movements even with the propeller in low pitch. After trimming the aircraft around the vertical axis applying the Flettner tab, the aircraft flew in a straight line. The engine's performance was increased to reach the primitive speed (370km/h) at 508ft. The single engine performance of the aircraft is very good.
>
> A further test showed height can easily be maintained on either engine at moderate altitudes at power well within the weak mixture range.

Wooden mock-up of the improved Ñancú, with new tail and new nose.

> The deployment of the undercarriage was fast and the reaction of the aircraft was normal in terms of longitudinal inclination when lowering the flaps.
>
> The behaviour during landing is normal and the efficacy of the elevators is sufficient for a three-point landing.

On completion of the test flight, Tank recommended:

> Reduce considerably the force of the ailerons and adapt them to the elevators.
>
> Decrease the sensitivity of compensation.
>
> Increase the sensitivity of the aileron compensation or reverse the direction of command of the servo tab (Flettner). After this modification, the speed must be considerably increased during the test, in order to allow the necessary harmonisation of the control forces.

Showing off the Ñancú

In October 1948, the Bolivian government announced that the Feria Industrial Internacional was to be held at El Alto, near La Paz, to commemorate the 400th anniversary of the country (in fact, since the Spanish occupation of the territories). Several countries were invited, including Argentina, and the Argentine authorities, eager to show their new aircraft, set out a plan: send a delegation that included Instituto Aerotécnico representatives and the Ñancú to be displayed to potential buyers and evaluate the aircraft's suitability to the demanding operational requirements in Bolivia, especially at high altitude, since El Alto airport is at more than 13,500ft.

On completion of an overhaul, engine checks and a test flight, 1° Tte Weiss set off for El Alto, accompanied by the I.Ae. delegation in the Fuerza Aérea Argentina Douglas C-47 serialled T-20. The flight was witnessed by participants and public in the Gran Premio de la América del Sur del Turismo Carretera (Buenos Aires–Caracas 15,000km race). Many years later the locals remembered the shiny aircraft flying under the puna's (arid plateau's) crisp blue sky.

The remains of the Ñancú after its accident, which occurred by the end of 1951. By then, Pallaviccino had already left the factory and the programme was being left behind in favour of jet projects.

It was scheduled to demonstrate the aircraft on 4 November. At 1100 Weiss took off and carried out his performance according to the flight plan. Once he completed it, he added two more pieces to his repertoire. He made a low pass with the landing gear extended and another with a feathered propeller. Later he climbed and disappeared in the clouds, only to reappear in a rather aggressive dive and aimed directly at the grandstand, where the people watched in amazement. During that dive, Weiss again set a new record for a twin-piston engine aircraft, as the Ñancú reached 885km/h. After landing, he was received by the local authorities and a crowd of onlookers. Everybody wanted to meet the brave pilot.

On the Bolivian altiplano, with elevations of 13,500ft and temperatures nearing 20° C, the Ñancú's performance proved to be exceptional.

Upon its return from Bolivia, some modifications were made to the prototype. The original one-piece windscreen was replaced by a flat armoured front windscreen with two curved Perspex side panels and the addition of a modified Mk IV-E sight, as it was planned to equip the plane with weapons to start trials.

The aileron controls were extremely heavy at high speed and therefore spring tabs were fitted in order to provide improved lateral control at speeds up to the maximum permissible. Brief handling trials were made on the Ñancú to investigate the effect of the spring tabs ailerons on its handling characteristics and these showed they gave a considerable improvement in the rate of roll at high speeds. The prototype retained the original Perspex nose cone and the large probe for trials.

By that time, a second prototype was being built, while a third was planned, the last to be of the proposed I.Ae.30B two-seat version that would be a night fighter equipped with radar, two extra 20mm guns in the nose and capacity for up to twenty 75mm rockets under the wing. Also, on the drawing board of Pallaviccino a series production version was taking shape, leading to a wind tunnel model and a full-scale wooden mock-up. This added some design revisions: a solid nose to house the Hispano guns and the 760 rounds of ammunition; a lower tailplane and extended dorsal fin, beneficial at low speed in a single-engine condition; a single-piece rudder; and a reshaped canopy with improved vision, with capacity for a second crew member behind the pilot. A plan for a 1/43 scale model of this version has been found, dated 3 February 1947, which means this modified version was planned around that time.

The end

The aircraft was now deemed satisfactory with good manoeuvrability and overall performance, especially on take-off and landing. Ground handling proved to be easy. The improved Ñancú would meet the FAA's needs.

In early April 1949, Rolls-Royce informed I.Ae that it was not able to meet the request for the Ñancú's engines. However, the company did made a lucrative deal for licence production of the Derwent V turbojet, and the supply of machine tools to manufacture it.

The I.Ae.30 Ñancú in its final configuration, with the belly tank and the new armoured windscreen.

The Ñancú in flight with the new armoured windscreen. Pallaviccino started to develop a new and bigger canopy, while he expected to add a second crew member.

The Ñancú continued flying well into 1951 and on 4 December 1951 it was transferred to the Grupo 3 de Caza to start operational tests in 1952. It was allocated the serial I-101, which was never painted as the prototype suffered an accident in February 1952, when I.Ae. test pilot Capitán Carlos Fermin Bergaglio cleared the aircraft for a flight test. On landing, he realised he was high on the final approach. He misjudged his height over the airfield and did not add power in the flare as the aircraft stalled before then cartwheeling. The pilot suffered minor injuries but the sole Ñancú was destroyed.

By this time, progress on the IAe.33 Pulqui II jet fighter was quite advanced and the authorities decided they no longer wanted the IAe.30, giving instructions to cancel the programme.

Sadly, the Ñancú went from a cutting-edge fighter at its conception to a wrecked carcass on a forgotten part of the I.Ae. airfield. After the removal of salvageable components, the aircraft was towed away and scrapped.

Wind tunnel model of the improved design with the new cockpit and canopy for two crew members.

Other proposals

As well as the built version, the planned two-seater and the improved version for series production, Pallavecino worked on other variants of the I.Ae.30. They include what he called the I.Ae.30 Tipo B, which was more similar to the de Havilland Hornet, also with two Rolls-Royce Merlin 604 engines, of which three different layouts have been preserved. One had with a wingspan of 16m, a length of 11.55m, a height of 4m, a wheel track of 5m, a wing area of 32m2, an empty weight of 5,000kg and a maximum weight of 7,790kg, and it was armed with four Hispano Suiza 20mm guns. The fuselage was of almost round section.

Another layout had a more triangular section, a length of 11.26m with the same wing, a height of 3.3m with a wheel track of 4.6m. While the empty weight was the same, the maximum was 8,340kg. The third layout had a different wing and a tail like the Mosquito but no data is known.

The I.Ae.30 Tipo C was more radical, adding a tricycle landing gear and the addition of a Rolls-Royce Derwent V engine inside the fuselage, plus the two Merlin 604 engines on the wings, which were slightly bigger than the first two layouts of the Tipo B. The fuselage had a round section, with the jet engine intakes on the sides, over the wings,

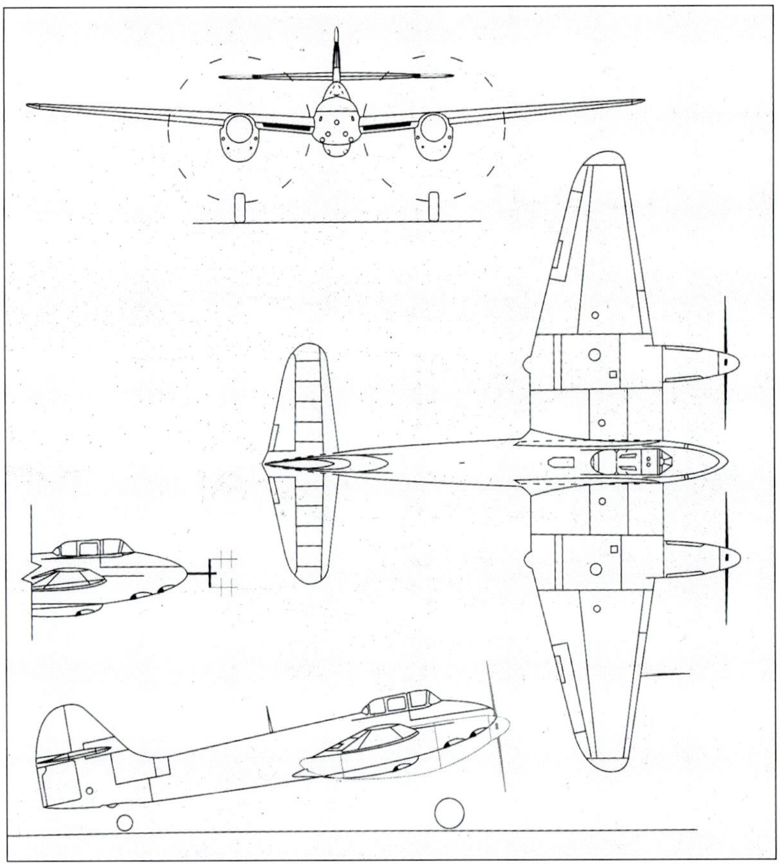

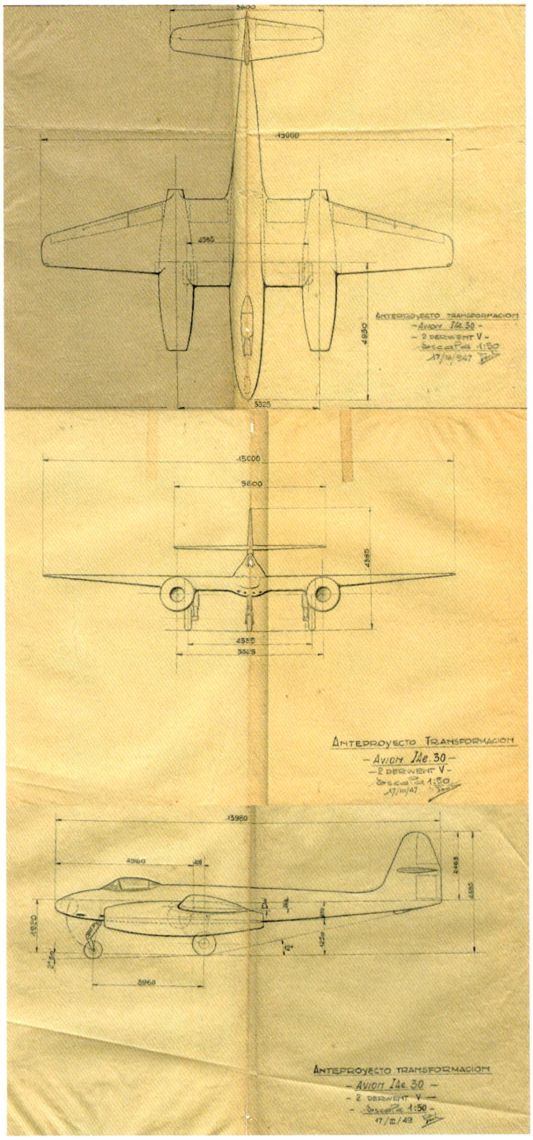

ABOVE Three views of the I.Ae.30B night fighter version.

RIGHT Three views, two dated in 1947 and one in 1949, of the jet version of the Ñancú.

BOTTOM RIGHT Plan from February 1947 of a 1/43 model of the series production Ñancú, where the new design of the tail is seen.

BELOW Projected installation of a torpedo on the I.Ae.30 Ñancú.

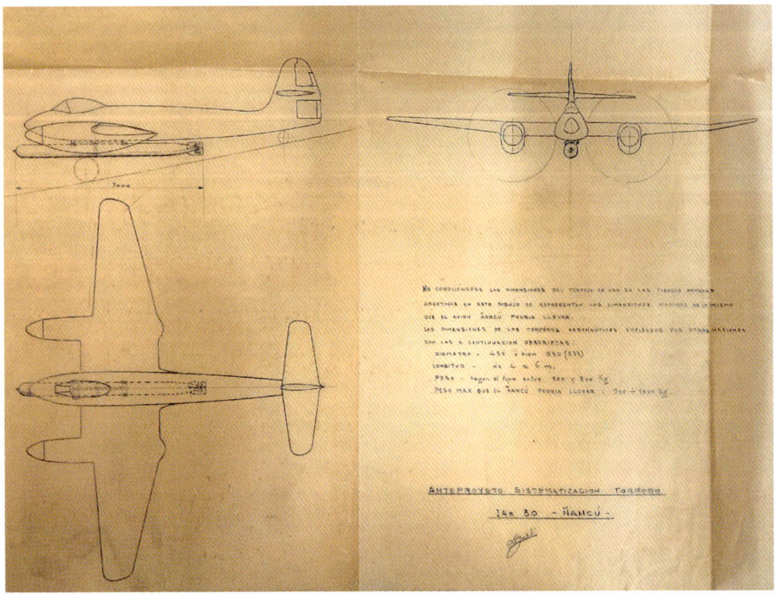

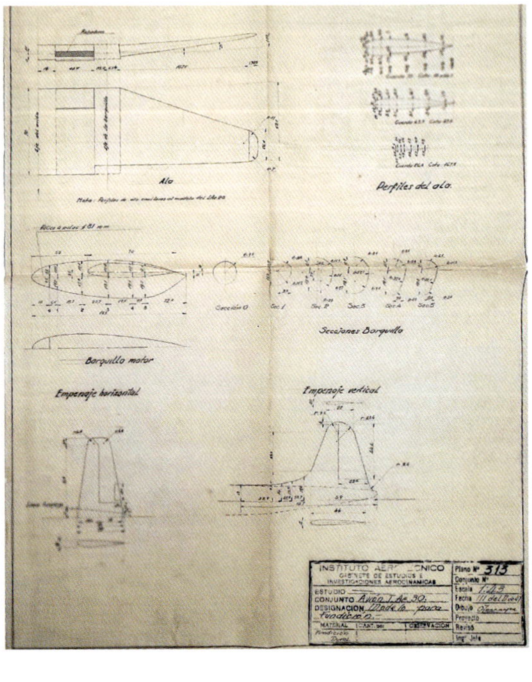

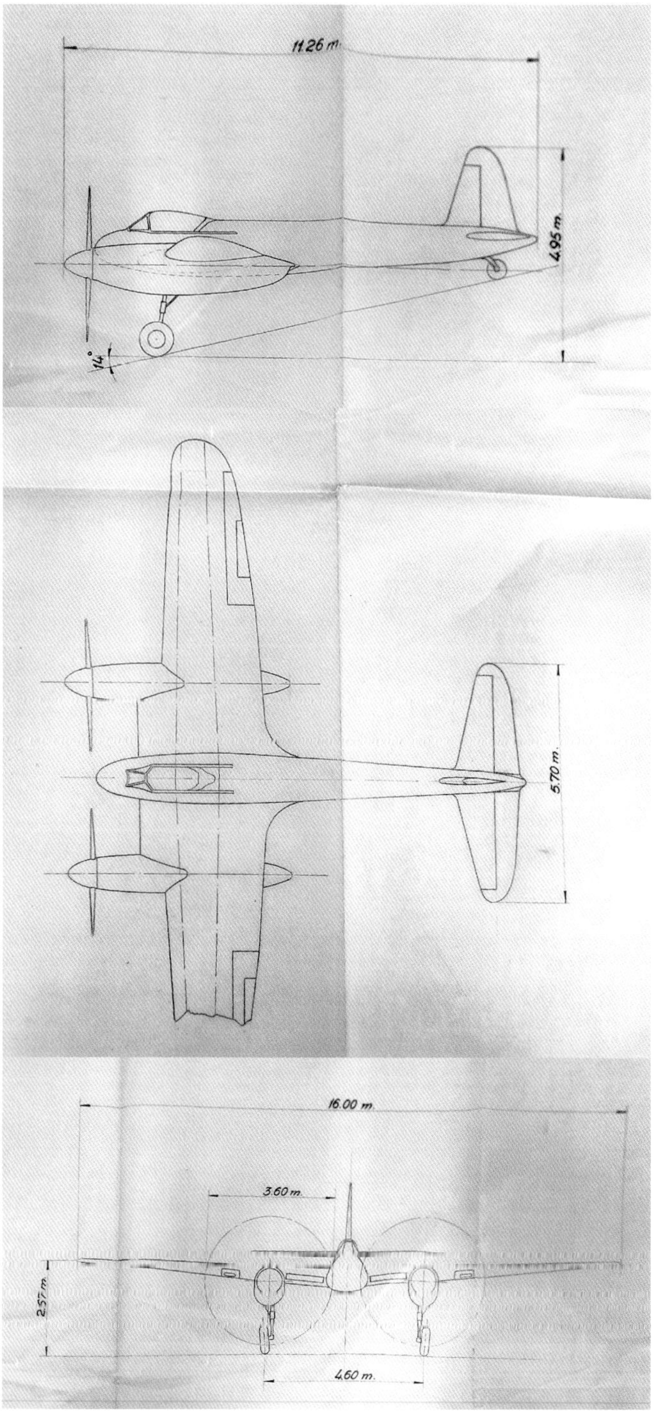

Three views of the third proposal of the I.Ae.30 Tipo B.

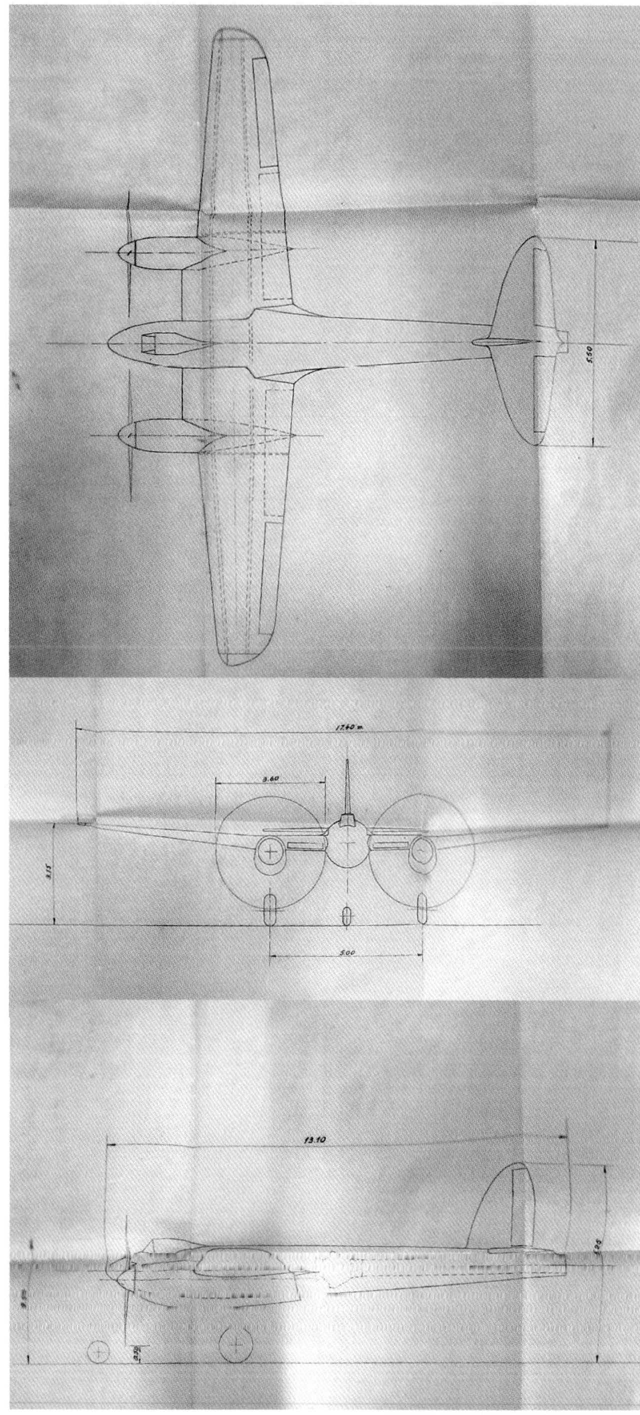

Three views of the I.Ae.30 Tipo C proposal, with the addition of a Derwent V engine.

and the tail was redesigned. It had a wingspan of 17.4m, a length of 13.1m, a height of 3.5m and a wheel track of 5m, a wing area of 38m2, an empty weight of 6,400kg and a maximum one of 19,790kg.

On 17 March 1947, Ing. Pallaviccino submitted the drawings of a jet variant of the Ñancú, to be powered by two Derwent V engines of 3,500lb thrust. Adapting the Ñancú to these engines required a complete alteration to the nose and produced a slim and elegant-looking aircraft. The conventional gear configuration was changed to a tricycle arrangement and the fin and rudder were also modified. The changes reduced the empty weight by 25 per cent, so there was more fuel capacity. The armament was four 20mm cannons and the result was a plane that looked very similar to the Gloster Meteor.

An improved layout is on a plan dated 24 November 1947, in which the aircraft resembled a

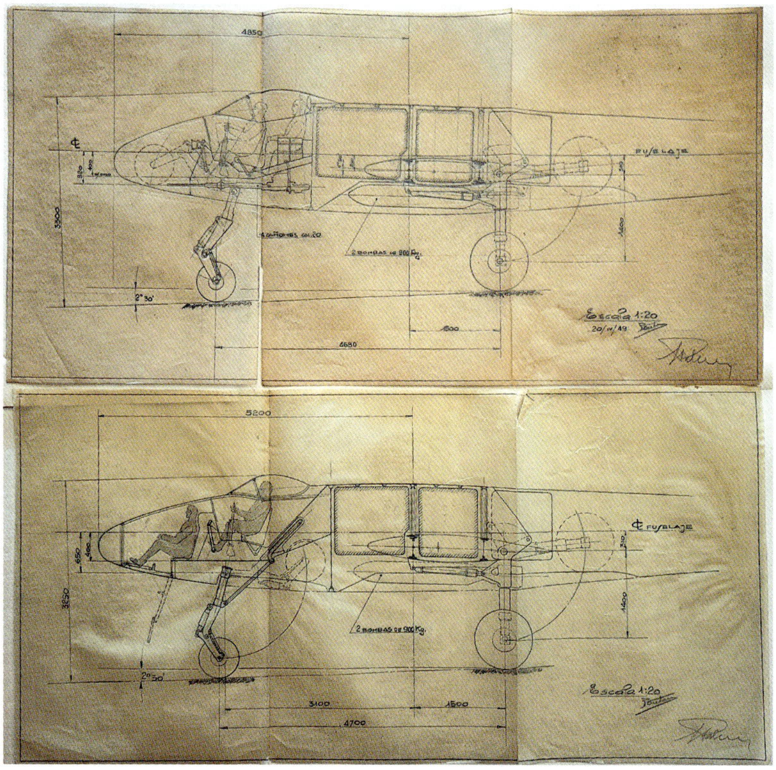

Two possible layouts for the front part of the bomber proposal. One has the observer in the nose and lacks the 20mm cannon, while the other has the cannon and the observer goes behind the pilot.

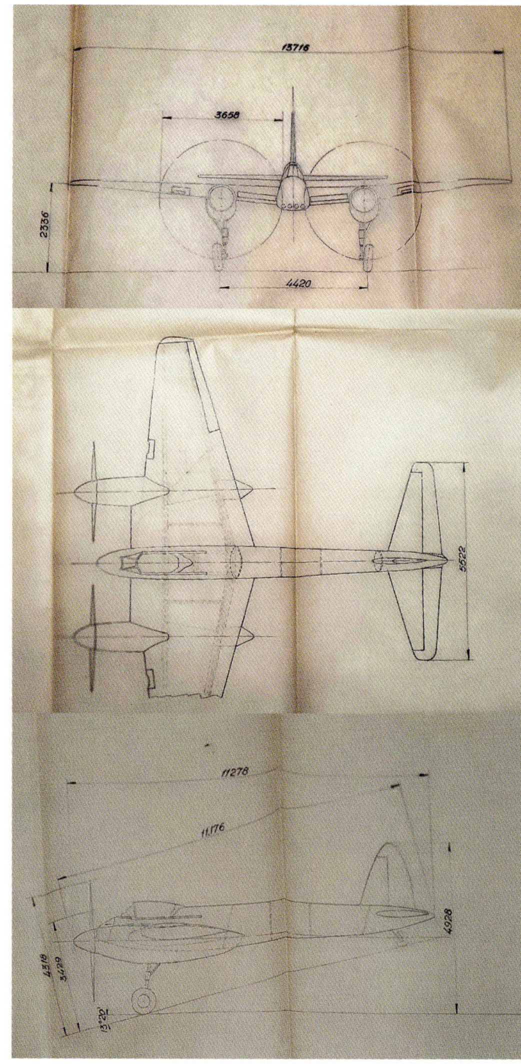

Three views of one of the I.Ae.30 Tipo B proposals, with different wing and a tail like the one of the Mosquito.

Three views of another proposal for the I.Ae.30 Tipo B.

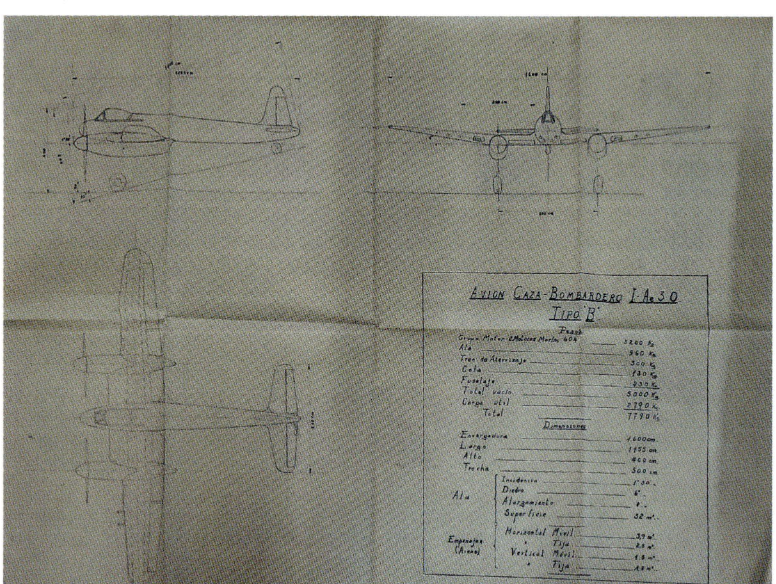

Meteor, but with the Ñancú tail and an improved cockpit canopy. This design had six 20mm guns in the lower part of the front fuselage.

Also, in drawings made in March 1949, a seat for an observer was added behind the pilot and there was a 750-litre fuel tank behind the cockpit.

Together with this proposal, in April of the same year Pallavicino worked on a twin-engine, two-seat bomber based on the other jet project but bigger and heavier. The tail and wing were changed and the landing gear was a bicycle type below the fuselage, with a small wheel below each engine. He proposed two possible cabin layout options, one with the observer behind the pilot and the nosewheel retracting into the nose, and one with the observer in the nose and the nosewheel retracting backwards. A bomb bay was also included under the fuselage fuel tanks for two 900kg bombs (the maximum bomb load was 2,000kg).

The plane had three fuel tanks in the fuselage and eight in the wings like the other proposal. It also had four 20mm internal guns in the nose and could carry up to twenty 75mm rockets. Interestingly, it was planned to equip the plane with a radar. It would have an empty weight of 6,130kg and a MTOW of 13,070kg.

Although these projects were analysed by the FMA management, they were not accepted and did not receive any official designation by the factory. Cesare Pallaviccino left Argentina in the spring of 1950.

15 I.Ae.31 Colibrí, Chingolo and other ideas

By the end of 1946, Emile Dewoitine was asked to prepare a request for proposals for a basic trainer for civil aviation, with the aim of building the prototypes at the Instituto Aerotécnico and then handing over series production to private industry. While the intention was to deliver the new planes to the aero clubs, by the beginning of 1947 the Argentine government had purchased 150 Miles Magisters in the United Kingdom with the same purpose.

The project continued with different proposals, all of which received the designation I.Ae.31.

Only a few plans remain of the first, all dated October 1948 with no extra information. It was a four-seat plane with tailwheel undercarriage, of which it was proposed to build a version with a radial engine and one with an inline power plant.

While the planes were intended to be built by private industry, the personnel of the factory that took part in the projects asked for a licence without salary to win the contracts and build the planes in their workplace.

Thus, the second project and one of the two types to be built was named I.Ae.31 Colibrí and it was designed by engineer Salomón Kogon, who worked at the Instituto Aerotécnico, and used the Ae.C.3G as a basis, which also used some parts that were in the factory. It was a tandem two-seater monoplane for elementary school and acrobatics.

The cantilever wings were constructed with two stringers of cedar wood and covered with araucaria and fabric, with a NACA 23012 profile. The wing was bolted at four points to the fuselage, which was constructed of welded chromium-molybdenum tubes. The covering for this was mixed, with the canopy and the lower part made of Duralumin panels and the rest fabric.

The tail was built of wood, while the rudder was made of welded tubes covered in fabric. The landing gear was fixed and independent, with oleo-pneumatic shock absorbers and mechanical brakes and tailwheel. The cabin had tandem seats and dual control.

The private workshops of Hipólito Goberna, another employee of the factory at Córdoba, built three aircraft under the direction of two brothers named Minoldo, also factory workers.

The first plane flew on 18 September 1947 in the hands of 1st Lt Edmundo Weiss. It was powered by a Blackburn Cirrus Major III air-cooled, inline, four-cylinder engine of 155hp at 2,400rpm, although the design was for an engine of 250hp. This left the aircraft with a big problem with the centre of gravity, as the engine was far lighter than planned. Ballast was added in the nose to fix this, while the other two built had different rear fuselages to reduce weight and improve the visibility to the rear.

Shortly after its first flight, the first prototype was exhibited in Buenos Aires at the Aeronautic

First prototype of the I.Ae.31 Colibrí. The design was based on that of the Ae.C.3G and used some remains of their production.

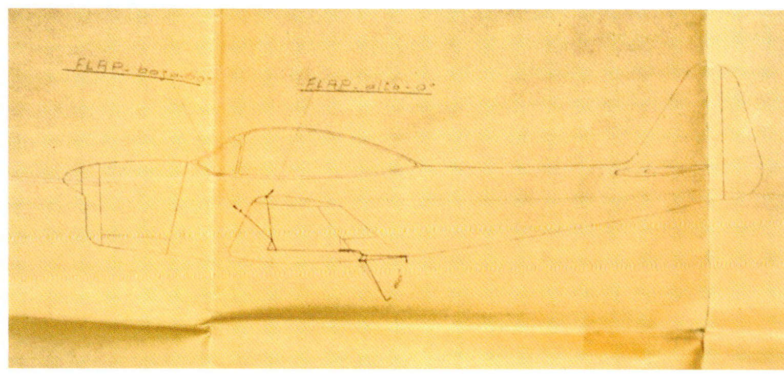

Side view of the inline engine version of the I. Ae.31 proposal. Unfortunately, no more information was found.

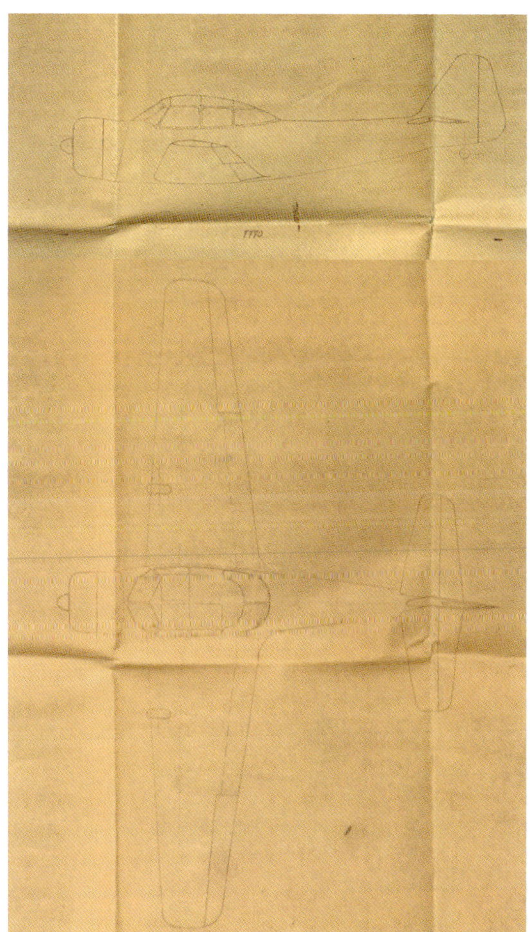

Two views of the I.Ae.31 proposal with radial engine and four seats.

The Colibrí during a test flight.

The third Colibrí, with a different rear part of the fuselage and cabin, seen in front of Hangar 90 at the factory.

Exhibition that took place at 9 de Julio Avenue, where new aircraft that were being imported or built in Argentina were shown.

The aircraft could also be equipped with a de Havilland Gipsy Major X engine of 145hp at 2,550rpm driving a manual, variable-pitch de Havilland twin-blade propeller. Fuel capacity was 135 litres, the maximum speed was 240km/h and the service ceiling was 6,500m.

The third project was named the I.Ae.31 Chingolo and it was similar in concept to the previous one. It was designed by Ernesto Vicente, who worked at the factory and asked for a licence to work privately on the project. Although he was contracted to build three aircraft, only one was finished in the workshop of Mario Vicente Construcciones Aeronáuticas S.A. (Córdoba province) because of the long delays experienced in construction. This was also a basic training, tandem two-seater, with a cantilever low wing and conventional fixed landing gear. The engine was the Blackburn Cirrus Major III and the wing was in one piece, with the central part passing inside the fuselage, with two spars and wooden covering. The wing profiles were 23009 and 3015 without torsion. The fuselage was covered externally by Duralumin sheet around the cabin and fabric at the rear. The Duralumin panels could be removed for maintenance. The first flight was in 1949.

The plane reached a maximum speed at sea level of 230km/h, with a stall speed of 65km/h, a service ceiling of 5,180m, four hours of endurance and a range of 800km.

The lack of interest in the types due to the purchase of the Magisters (which were later followed by 100 Percival Prentices for the Air Force, plus a huge quantity of Piper J-3s and other types) and the poor performance of them led to the abandonment of the project. The Chingolo was delivered in 1950 to the Ministerio de Aeronautica, which had retired it by the end of 1955, but there is no information if it ever flew during that period. All the aircraft were scrapped.

The only I.Ae.31 Chingolo was similar to the Colibrí and had the same engine.

16 I.Ae. 32, I.A.44 and I.A.45 trainers

During the late 1940s and early 1950s there were three designs for trainers for which there is very little information. The first was the I.Ae 32, which included some different proposals and was started by 1948, being an advanced training aircraft that complemented the I.Ae. DL-22. It would have been powered by a 620hp I.Ae.R.19 El Indio engine with a Rotol wooden propeller.

One of the proposals for the I.Ae 32 was submitted by Kurt Tank and the other by Italian engineers Angelo Miele and Massimo Arbitrio. Miele, who had born in Italy in 1922 and arrived in Argentina in 1947, worked briefly in the I.Ae. until moving to the United States in 1952, where he had an outstanding career as an engineer and teacher. His proposal for the I.Ae.32 is his only known design in Argentina.

The proposal by Tank was a three-seater, with two side-by-side seats in front and a third in the back, so that it could also be used for liaison. The fuselage length, according to one plan, was 5.167m, and the wingspan 8.366m. Tests were carried out in the wind tunnel, and this model, with a longer fuselage, is preserved in Córdoba. A modified version was proposed, named Modelo III, with only two seats side by side, by February 1949.

Wind tunnel model of Tank's I.Ae.32 project proposal. *Santiago Rivas*

The proposal by Miele and Arbitrio was like a bigger DL-22, with two seats in tandem. According to one of the plans, the dimensions were 8.8m length, 12.6m wingspan, 4.095m height and 1.225m wheel track. In a document about the initial studies it is 9.18m long and 3.91m high, with an 11.75m wingspan and a wing area of 21m2.

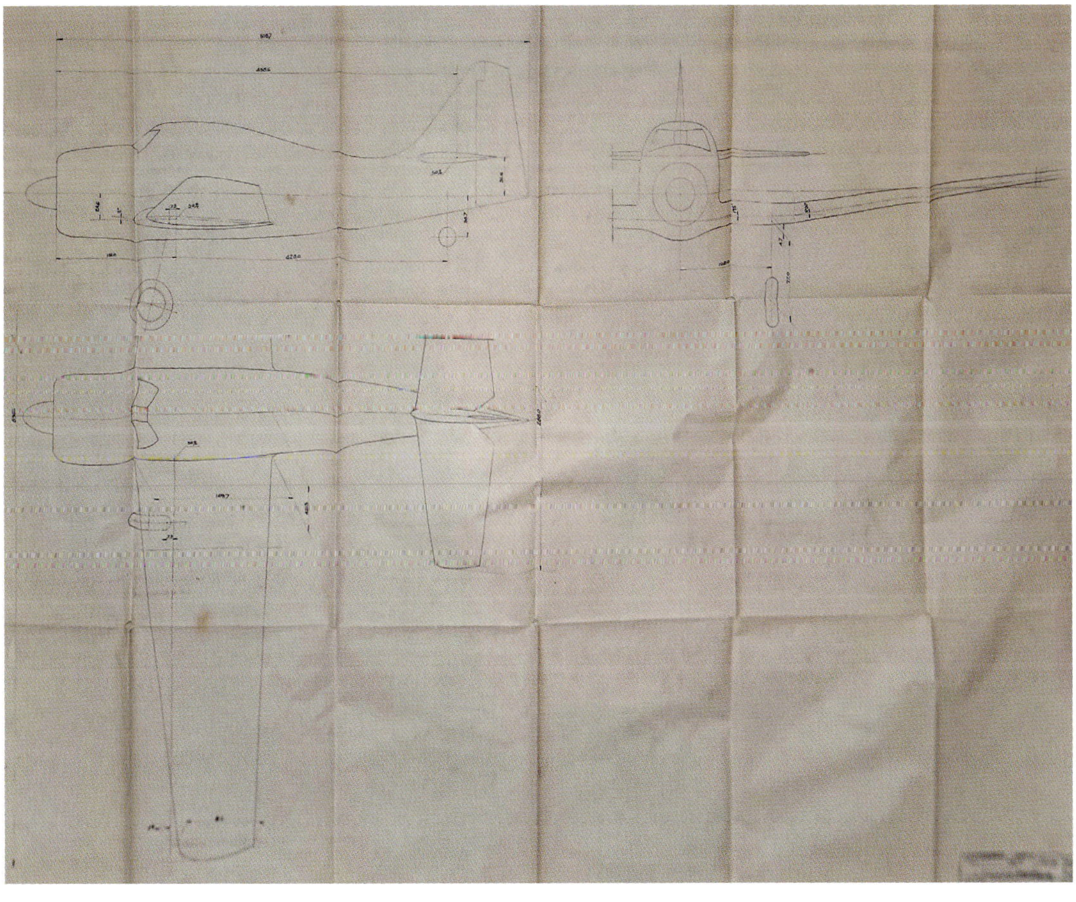

Three views of Tank's first proposal for the I.Ae.32.

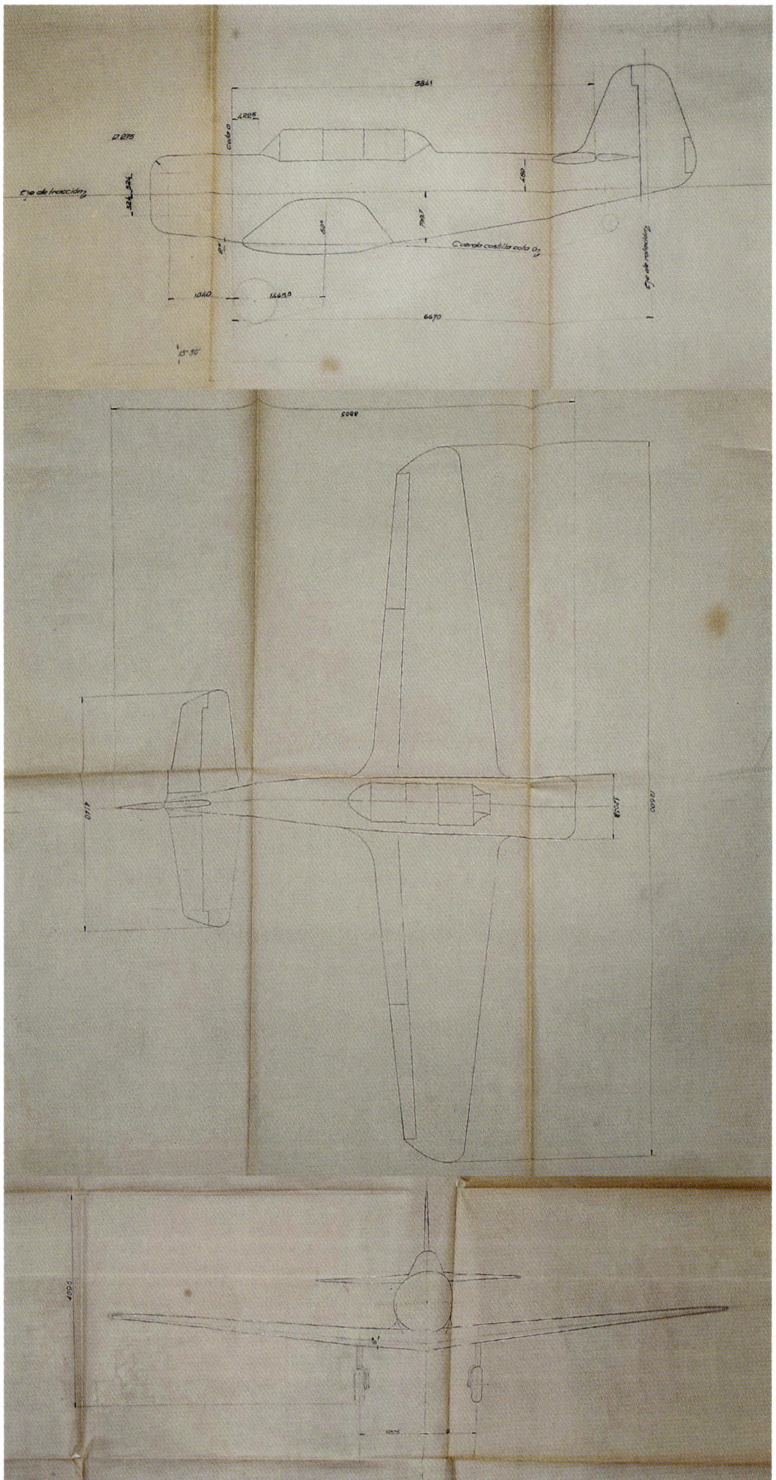

Three views of the I.Ae.32 proposal by engineers Angelo Miele and Massimo Arbitrio.

It was expected to have a maximum speed of 357km/h and cruise at 337km/h, a stall speed with flaps at 50° of 116km/h and 135km/h without flaps, a range of 1,280km with fifteen minutes reserve, four hours of endurance at economic cruise speed, a maximum ceiling of 7,050m, a climb rate of three minutes twenty seconds minutes to reach 1,500m and thirty-six minutes two seconds to reach the operational ceiling of 6,675m.

The project was compared with the Avro Athena, Boulton Paul Balliol, Hawker Hurricane Trainer, Percival Prentice, de Havilland Chipmunk, Morane-Saulnier MS.474, SIPA S.10, Fiat G-46, Fiat G-55AM, Fokker S.11, Pilatus P.2, FMA I.Ae. DL-22, Fairchild XNQ-1, North American T-6 Texan and North American NA-142 (T-28 Trojan).

Despite some progress, interestingly, Argentina had already accepted in 1946 an Italian proposal to supply seventy Fiat G-46s at a very attractive price, although the type had yet to fly but did so on 25 June 1947. The Fiats started to arrive in early 1949, when the I.Ae.32 project was cancelled.

Continuation with the I.A.44 and a jet trainer

Tank continued to work and in 1953 proposed the I.A.44 to replace the I.Ae. DL-22, which due to its wooden construction showed signs of wear. Building on the experience gained in the DL and I.Ae.32 project, the designer would apply the construction methods to a much more modern aerodynamic design that revealed its origins in the studies of the Focke-Wulf Fw 190. The project, proposed and conducted by Tank, was publicly announced by President Juan Perón in September 1953 and its entry into service was expected in 1958.

The aircraft would be a tandem two-seater with a semi-monocoque fuselage built using wood of national origin. It would have retractable tricycle landing gear and be powered by a national engine, the 650hp I.A.R.19CR El Indio or the 840hp I.A.R.19C, with a metal three-blade propeller.

The detailed design progressed rapidly and, after 60,000 man hours, all the plans had been completed, while another 200,000 man hours were budgeted to build two prototypes. However, various factors would have conspired from December 1953 to reduce the momentum and support for development work. One of them was that the Tank team was dedicated to the Pulqui II project, and another was that with the arrivals of the Percival Prentice T.Mk.1, the DLs were being replaced. Finally, the departure of Tank to India in early 1955 ended the project. Its place was taken by the American metal Beech B45 Mentor trainer, which was built under licence from 1957.

The last trainer project of those years was named I.A.45, a designation that was also used for another project later on. Only a drawing of the I.A. 45 trainer survives today in the files of the factory, where it can be seen that it was a jet trainer with some resemblance to the Aermacchi MB-326. The two pilots were seated in tandem, the air intakes were next to the wing roots and the engine was in the rear fuselage, with extra fuel tanks on the wingtips. The drawing is dated 18 November 1953 and no further information was preserved.

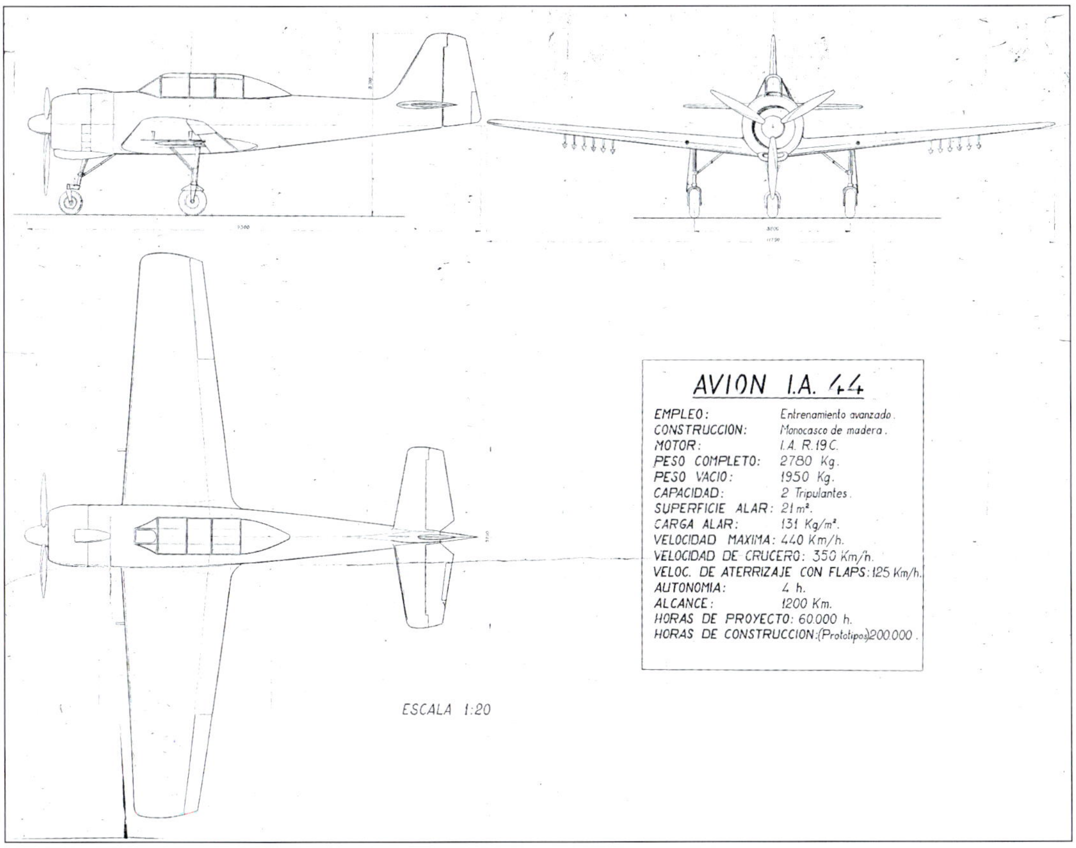

Three views and specifications of the I.A.44 project.

A drawing of the I.A.45 proposal that is in the files of the factory.

17 I.Ae.33 Pulqui II and I.A.40

In 1947, after Emile Dewoitine left the I.Ae.27 Pulqui project, engineer Norberto Morchio became the head of the Departamento de Proyectos Especiales (Special Projects Department), with the collaboration of the engineer Ricciardi. Before the year's end, the director of the factory, Juan I. San Martín, gave the order to construct a new aeroplane to reach the world speed record.

Morchio and Ricciardi started with the Pulqui, trying to improve the existing aircraft, but the limitations showed that it was better to start with a new project with swept wings, laminar outlines and a 2,070kg thrust Rolls-Royce RN.2.41 (Nene 2) engine.

At the beginning of 1948, they built a scale model that was designated IAe-27a Pulqui II (very similar to the later Mystere II of Dassault) with swept wings of 33 degrees and trapezoidal surface, tailplanes in the middle of the vertical fin and wings of NACA 16009 laminar outline.

First glider of the Pulqui II, with the initial tail design. Note the skid on the belly, as the glider had no landing gear.

Second glider of the Pulqui II, with modified tail, similar to the one used on the prototypes.

The Germans

The experience with Emile Dewoitine and Cesare Pallaviccino showed the Instituto Aerotécnico that there was a big opportunity to employ some of the main advances made in the Second World War and boost considerably the capacities of the factory, quickly moving up from slow, piston-engined aircraft to new advanced designs. The Argentine government learned that, although the United States had contracted many German engineers, Russia had captured many others and a few were collaborating with British industry (which was only contracting a few as advisors), there were many others who were looking for a job in the aviation industry.

The problem was that the Allies did not allow the Germans to leave their country if they did not have a contract with one of the Allied nations, so there was no possibility of contracting them and taking them to Argentina legally.

By 1947, Reimar Horten and Kurt Tank, including most of the team that worked with the latter at Focke-Wulf, were preparing to travel to China to develop the local aviation industry for the nationalist government. However, the Chinese civil war, which ended in 1949 with the defeat of the nationalists, ended their plans, so Tank started to look for other alternatives.

As Argentina had been neutral during almost the entire Second World War (the country declared war on the Axis countries only on 27 March 1945), had a small German community and the government of General Edelmiro Farrell was close to the fascist ideas, some government officials and military officers escaped to Argentina in 1945 by submarine. Two of them, U-530 and U-977, surrendered at the Mar del Plata Naval Base, but others were beached on the coast and their occupants then settled in Argentina with the support of the government.

This, and the acceptance of Germans in other Latin American countries such as Brazil and Chile, led Tank and other engineers and pilots to look for opportunities on the continent, at the same time that Argentina was looking to learn as much as possible from the experience of those who had been involved in the war and was willing to contract as many engineers and pilots as possible. So, after learning about the interest of Tank's team in Latin America, they offered them a contract and started to make a plan to transport them from Europe to Argentina.

Tank was contracted in mid-1947, together with another sixty engineers from Focke-Wulf, who included Paul Klages, Karl Thalau, Wilhelm Bansemir, Ludwig Mittelhauber, theoreticians Gotthold Mathias and Herbert Wolff and gas dynamics specialists Otto Pabst, plus pilots Otto Behrens and Hans Ulrich Rudel.

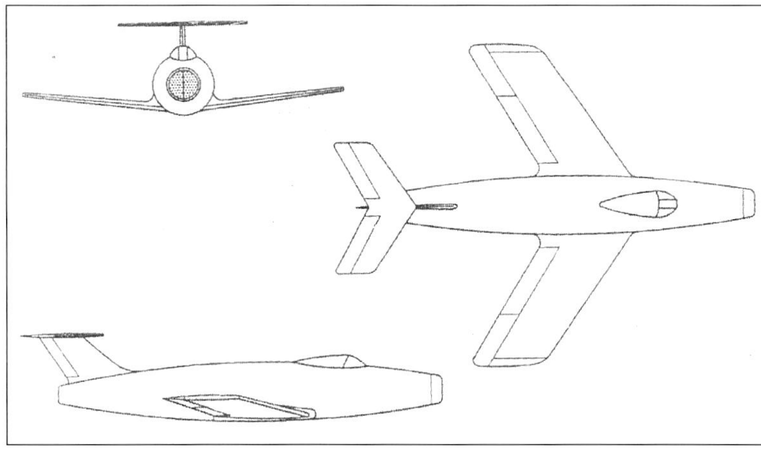

ABOVE LEFT Model of the first I.Ae.27a Pulqui II design made by engineers Morchio and Ricciardi.

ABOVE RIGHT Three views of the second I.Ae.27a Pulqui II design by Morchio and Ricciardi, with T tail.

They travelled to Denmark, where they received Argentine passports with new names and birthplaces in Argentina. From there they travelled to Rome, where they flew to Argentina in aircraft of the Flota Aérea Mercante Argentina (FAMA) airline, which had just started flights to Europe with Avro Lancastrians and Avro Yorks.

Once in Argentina, Tank was invited to meet General Juan D. Perón, who had become president on 4 June 1946 and immediately after had presented a Five-Year Plan to develop the country, in which he included a special chapter for the development of aviation, including the industry. He told Tank about his interests and the German replied that he could help to develop a jet fighter, a basic trainer, a reconnaissance aircraft, a bomber and a jet passenger aircraft. Perón gave his support, but said that he must develop the aircraft progressively, as the factory, which was already working on the projects of Dewoitine and Pallavecino, as well as building the Calquin, did not have the capacity to develop all of them at the same time.

When Tank was leaving for Argentina, he tried to convince Reimar Horten and his brother Walter to come with him, but they were not convinced. However, Horten kept the idea in his mind and after trying unsuccessfully to get a job in the British aviation industry, in October 1947 he decided to go to Argentina. However, he had to find a way to contact Tank or the Argentine government.

After the Allies found out about the escape of Tank and his team to Argentina, they tightened the controls to stop other Germans travelling to the South American country, so it was not going to be easy for Horton migrate. However, in early 1948 Horten managed to travel to Austria and from there he crossed the border with Italy and went to the Argentine embassy. After informing the staff he wanted to join Kurt Tank, he was invited to travel to Argentina and offered a contract at the Instituto Aerotécnico and a flight to the country in a FAMA aeroplane. Horten arrived in Argentina in May 1948 and went to Córdoba to meet the other Germans there.

By that time, other teams were joining them, including those from Henschel, which included Ernst Henrici and his brother, Dieter and Goets Mandel, Polish rocket specialist Ryszard Dyrgalla and other engineers with experience on rockets.

Three views of the tail-less fighter design proposed by Reimar Horten.

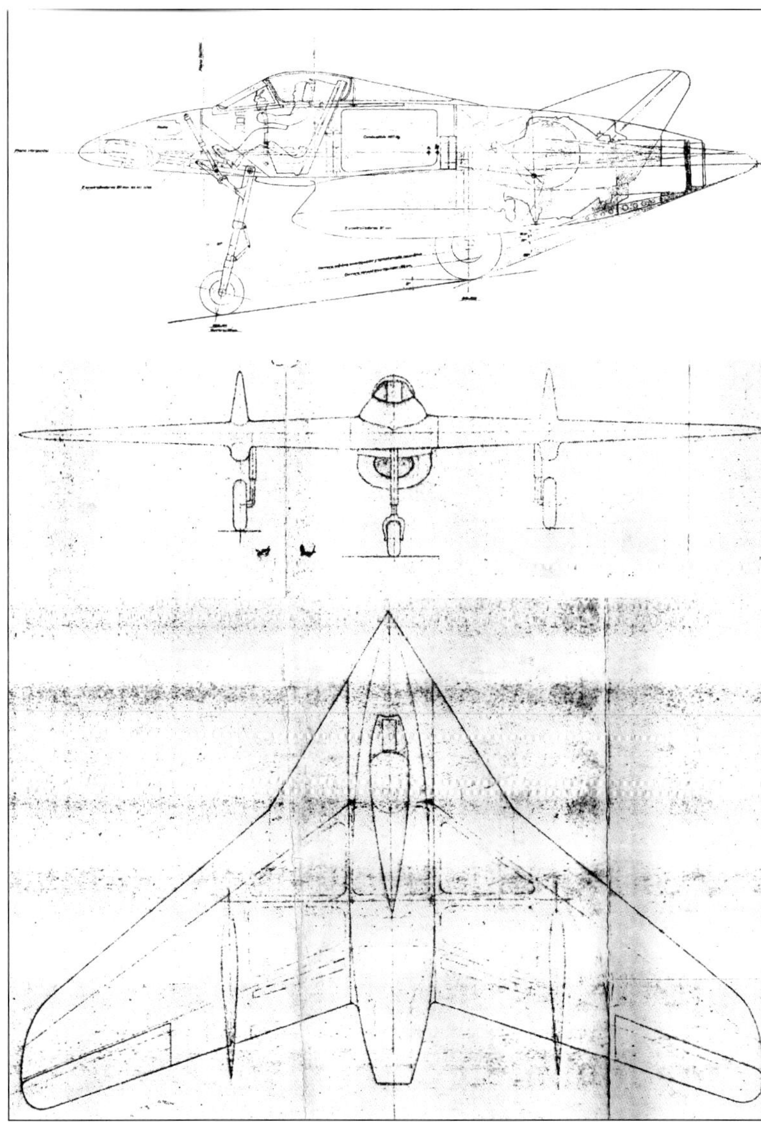

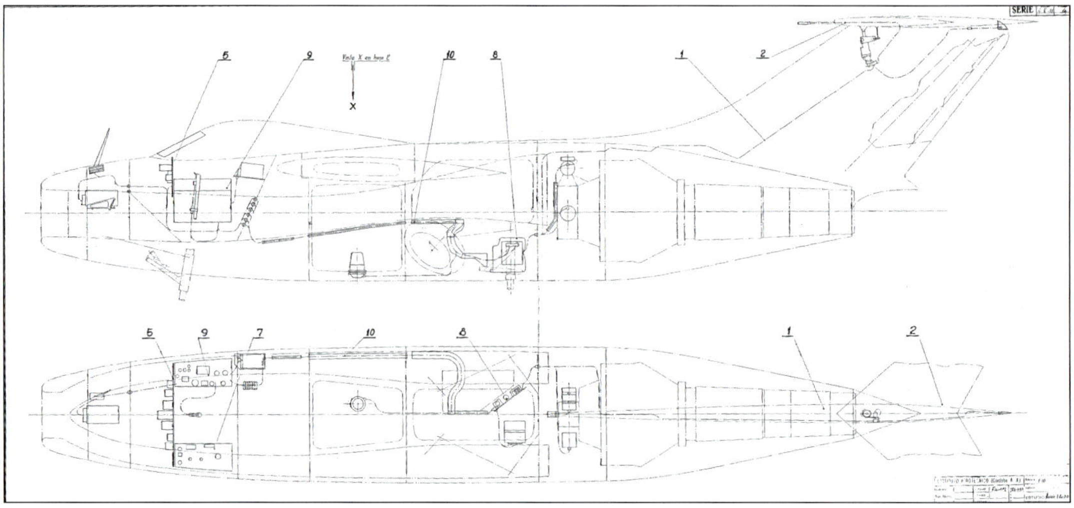

Equipment installation of the plane E-2 in its final configuration, as it was in March 1955.

Also, former pilots including Werner Von Baumbach and Adolf Galland joined them by 1948 to advise the Argentine Air Force on new bomber and fighter tactics developed during the war.

The new jet fighter and Kurt Tank

Tank travelled to Argentina with a bag carrying the microfilms of the design of the Focke-Wulf Ta 183 jet fighter that was designed by Hans Multhopp, as he personally had never designed a jet aircraft before.

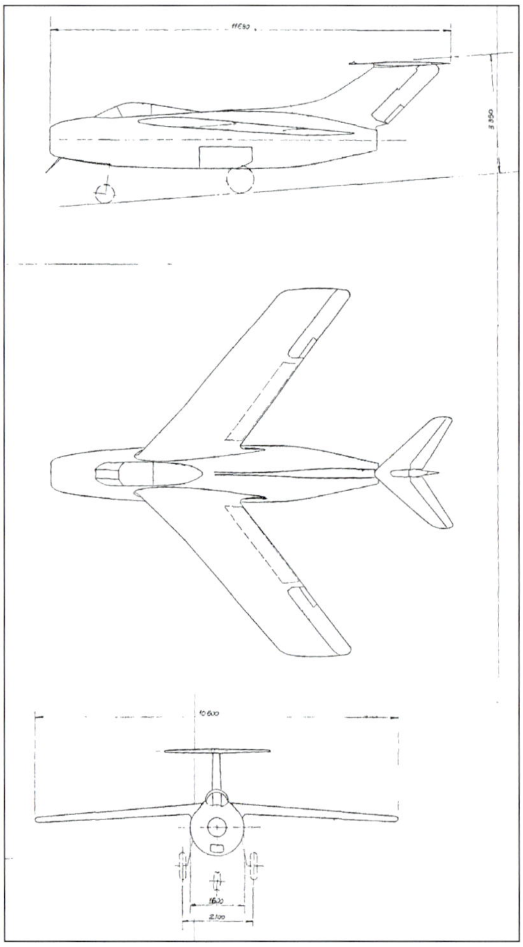

Three views of the Pulqui II as per the first prototype's initial configuration.

The Ta 183 was born by the end of 1944 when the Luftwaffe awarded contracts to Focke-Wulf Flugzeugwerke, Junkers, Blohm & Voss, Messerschmitt and Heinkel to develop a new light fighter. Focke-Wulf had the advantage of the experience of Otto Pabst's experiments on the dynamics of air at transonic and supersonic speeds during 1942 and 1943. The engineers developed eight designs, named P I to P VIII, some to use a Heinkel He S 011 engine and some with a Jumo 004, but only the P V, designed by Multhopp, was advanced enough to fulfil the Luftwaffe's needs. Multhopp considered that the fighter should be capable of operating at transonic speeds and developed a 40° swept and thin wing to be installed on the upper part of a short fuselage with an air intake in the nose and a swept tail with the elevators on top, making a V.

Early in its design engineers were worried about the possible problems of flutter and Dutch roll that the high wing could cause. Also, engineer Dietrich Fiecke, who analysed the design, considered that 'the poor ratio of slenderness of the fuselage and the bulbous nose could lead to compression shocks at even relatively low speeds, resulting in a large increase in drag'. He also considered that the large surface area of the swept and upward-protruding tailfin caused a high amount of drag[2], and drag could be also induced by compression shocks at the elevator roots, even at relatively low speeds.

Those problems were to be faced by Tank when developing the Ta 183 into the Pulqui II.

Defining the Pulqui II

By the end of 1947, Morchio and Ricciardi had finished their proposal and a meeting was organised at the I. Ae., at which Tank and some of the other German engineers were present. After the proposal was examined, Tank showed the Ta 183 project and the

[2] Article 'Stand der deutschen Jagdflugzeug – Entwicklung zu Kriegsende' by Dietrick Fiecke – June 1953.

possibilities of both ideas were discussed. Engineer Juan Ignacio San Martín proposed the formation of two groups to develop both projects, one to work under Morchio and the other headed by Tank.

Morchio and Ricciardi's project continued but with some changes, including a T-tail, and another scale model was built and tested in the wind tunnel. Because of the proximity of the wings to the ground, they changed to a high wing. Meanwhile, Kurt Tank was working on his project based on the Ta 183, but he completely redesigned the fuselage, making it far longer to reduce the drag problems expected, and adapted for a Derwent V or a Nene II centrifugal jet engine. The elevators lost their dihedral and the tail now had T shape.

The cooperation between both groups was important and by mid-1948 they met and San Martín ordered them to now work together on one project because the differences between the designs were so small.

The main differences were in the landing gear and the fuselage, so they adopted Tank's fuselage and the IAe 27a undercarriage, while the wings were designed by Horten, who had just arrived in Argentina. From this moment on, the project was designated IAe-33 Pulqui II and Tank remained as the project director. Morchio and Ricciardi left the project shortly after.

In October 1948, with the help of Horten, a glider made of wood and fabric was built to complete the aerodynamic tests carried out in the wind tunnel. On the 30th of the month German test pilot Otto Behrens (Tank's test pilot) made the first flight, towed by the FMA 21 prototype. Three more flights were made on 9 November by Behrens and after that it was decided to make some modifications to take account of the lessons learned. These included the rudder and improvement to the union of the wing and the fuselage. A new flat windscreen was installed to avoid reflection, and to aid this the upper part of the nose was painted black.

The first prototype being finished.

On 19 November flights were resumed in which the glider climbed to 4,000m, followed by two other flights on 25 and 26 of that month. On some occasions the glider was towed by a Northrop 8A-2 or by a Martin 139WAA bomber.

It was determined that the design needed some changes and a new glider with more modifications was built. The changes were especially to the tail and the wing, which received a negative dihedral. The tail changed from a parallelogram to a trapezoidal one, with 35° of sweep instead of 55°, a total surface of 3.95m2 instead of 3m2 and with a rudder with a surface of 1.38m2 instead of 1.02m2.

On 21 January 1949 the second glider flew for the first time, again with Behrens at the controls, followed by other flights on 4 and 11 February, 4 and 5 March and 8, 13 and 20 April, when it was

Ground tests of the engine of the first prototype.

Comparison of the four proposals discussed in March 1949 for the new jet fighter.

	Pulqui II	Mittelhuber	Horten	Klages
Wing area	25.1m2	20m2	32.4m2	45m2
Wingspan	10.6m	9.5m	12.6m	13.5m
Wing sweep	40°	35°	32/35°	51/35°
Elevator surface	3.2m2	2.95m2	3.2m2	-
Elevator sweep	45°	40°	45°	-
Tail surface	3.75m2	2.15m2	3.75m2	1.98m2
Tail sweep	55°	45°	55°	53°
Weight, equipped	4,600kg	4,100kg	5,000kg	4,600kg
Crew	1	2	2	2
Armament	2 20-mm Hispano Suiza			
Fuel	1,200kg			
Maximum speed	880km/h	1,003km/h	952km/h	915km/h
Climb rate	20m/s	26.5m/s	19m/s	22.5m/s
Time to reach 12,000m	21.5 min	13.4 min	22 min	16.6 min
Service ceiling	13,200m	14,700m	13,900m	15,000m
Range	1,180km	1,560km	1,230km	1,490km
Endurance	1.76 h	1.96 h	1.88 h	2.06 h
Landing speed, full weight	189km/h	195km/h	173km/h	144km/h
Landing speed, empty	166km/h	171km/h	155km/h	127km/h

concluded that no more flights were needed and that flight tests should continue with the prototype. The glider flew well and showed no major problems.

After the tests, by the beginning of 1949 construction started of one airframe for static tests and a prototype for flight trials. The static frame was destroyed after passing the limits of resistance.

Alternatives

Although Tank was progressing with his project, three of the other German engineers – Ludwig Mittelhuber, Paul Klages and Reimar Horten – presented alternative proposals, which were compared in a memo on 11 March 1949. Unfortunately, no plans of these projects survived, except for some data that is described in the file where the four projects were compared. What can be deducted is that Klages' design had no elevators and could have been a delta or a flying wing, while Horten's shared the tail with the Pulqui II. All models were to be powered by a Rolls-Royce Derwent V.

Meanwhile, Horten started to criticise the design made by Tank, as he considered it had some aerodynamic shortcomings. This led to discussions between both designers and ended in the rupture of their relationship and the relegation of Horten by Tank within his team. Horten then decided to produce his own fighter jet proposal and he presented what he called the Caza sin cola (tail-less fighter) to Brigadier Juan I. San Martín and Aeronautics Minister Brigadier César Ojeda in Secret File N° 339 of 19 October 1949. The file also included the design of a twin-engined flying wing for advanced training and surveillance, a small transport flying wing, both described in Chapter 21, and an observation and training flying wing with two El Gaucho engines, described in Chapter 43.

The Caza sin cola was an evolution of his idea of the H X proposal made to compete with the Volksjäger project in Germany during the Second World War, but now with the engine intake in the belly instead of the sides of the rear part of the cockpit, a new canopy design, two vertical fins and the use of a Nene 2 engine instead of the planned BMW 002, Jumo 004 or Heinkel-Hirth 011 turbojets.

The fighter project used a double delta wing with 58° of sweep on the central part and 40° on the outer wings, with two spars, while the trailing edge had ailerons and flaps, which also acted as elevators. It also had two vertical fins, one on each wing, below each was the main landing gear. It used the cockpit and landing gear of the Pulqui II and a Derwent V engine. The thick wing allowed it to carry four fuel tanks between the fuselage and the tails, while there was another tank between the cockpit and the engine.

Armament consisted on four Hispano Suiza 20-mm guns, two in the wings and two below the air intake.

Horten estimated 20,000 hours of work would be required to build a test glider and another 100,000 hours for a wooden mock-up. According to the designer's calculations, based on the use of

The Pulqui II being readied for its first flight at the Escuela de Paracaidistas.

the Derwent V, the fighter he proposed would have a higher ceiling, lower landing speed and higher maximum and ascensional speed than the I.Ae.33 Pulqui II.

The aircraft would have a wingspan of 12m, a fuselage length of 7.50m and a total length of 8m, with a wing area of 39m2 and an elongation of 3.7, with a wheelbase of 5.32m. The empty weight was of 3,300kg, with 2,000kg of fuel capacity and a total weight of 5,700kg. Maximum speed would be 970km/h at 5,500m, with a landing speed of 140km/h, a range of 3,400km and a service ceiling of 14,200m.

As the Pulqui II had advanced much further, the project was not approved. Despite this, Horten kept working on it for some time, until on 4 April 1951 it was finally abandoned.

The Pulqui II flies

With the availability of the more powerful Rolls-Royce Nene 2 engine of 2,070kg of thrust instead of the 1,587kg of the Derwent V, it was decided to use that engine in the new fighter, while production of the prototypes was being prepared. After new calculations for the new engine were made, construction started.

The Pulqui II was equipped with a new Martin-Baker Mk.1 ejection seat, being one of the first aircraft in the world to use such a device. This was the first type produced in series by Martin-Baker and was not fully automatic, having an explosive charge that ejected the seat and the pilot from the aeroplane. Two drogue chutes then stabilised the seat and the pilot then had to release the seat and open the parachute manually. While this seat was a great advance, it had many limitations, especially at lower altitude as the pilot would need some time to release the seat and open the parachute.

By the beginning of 1950, the first prototype (designated E-1) was finished and it started ground tests prior to the first flight. Although Tank wanted either himself or Otto Behrens to carry out the first flight, the Instituto Aerotécnico determined that Edmundo Weiss would be the pilot.

On 16 June the Pulqui II was taken to the Escuela de Paracaidistas for its first flight. Weiss flew for twenty-eight minutes and found no major problems, but he stated that the rudder started to vibrate when the aircraft was travelling at over 350km/h and was extremely sensitive over 500km/h. He also reported that the plane was very stable, but some

Edmundo Weiss is already in the ejection seat prior to the first flight, with the safety pin of the seat being removed by German engineer Werner Ruth.

Kurt Tank at the cockpit of the first prototype Pulqui II after receiving the reinforcements to the canopy. He was the first to use a plastic helmet to fly in Argentina.

instruments failed and others were uncomfortable to watch or use due to their position.

On 19 June a second flight was made, now with Otto Behrens at the controls, taking off at 1705 from the Escuela de Paracaidistas with 4,950kg of weight and using only 650m of runway. At 350km/h, Behrens raised the landing gear, finding the control was too far from the pilot and was difficult to reach. Also, the left wheel did not lock so he kept the hydraulics working to keep the wheel up. He then reached over 710km/h and found there were some oscillations due to the over-compensation of the rudder. At that speed, Behrens heard a bang and decided to reduce speed and pass over the runway, believing the left wheel door was partially open. Observers on the ground told him that was the case, so he manoeuvred to land. At 400km/h he lowered the gear and at 350km/h he put down 25° of flaps. He reached the runway threshold at 200km/h and 5m high and touched the ground at around 180/190km/h about 200m after the beginning of the runway, however the plane bounced lightly up to 30cm of height and for a length of 100m. After touching the runway again with the main landing gear it jumped again, this time for a shorter time but higher. On the third and fourth jumps, the plane hit the ground on three wheels, with the pilot feeling a hard impact of the nosewheel. The fourth jump was higher and steep and the Pulqui II started to turn to the left. Although the pilot again tried to land, it fell hard, breaking the left shock absorber and hitting the ground with the wingtip. The plane made a turn of 150° and the front wheel collapsed rearwards, making a hole in the fuselage and into the cockpit, but not hitting the pilot, who immediately shut down the engine and the electric systems and abandoned the plane.

Despite his landing accident, which Behrens considered was because the shock absorbers were not working well, he found the plane easy to fly, with good visibility, low noise in the cabin, with a temperature of about 25°C while flying at 4,500ft. However, he reported that the system to open and close the canopy was poor and must be changed.

The aircraft was repaired during the next four months and after that Tank resumed testing with the third flight on 23 October at 0815. Tank also found a tendency to oscillate and roll to the right as he increased speed, but this almost disappeared once he had compensated, although he had to keep pressure on the ailerons for the whole flight. The Pulqui II again bounced on landing, but only once, with Tank noting an asymmetric behaviour of the wheels until speed was reduced.

The Pulqui II during its presentation at Aeroparque Jorge Newbery in Buenos Aires on 8 February 1951.

The first Pulqui II seen at Aeroparque Jorge Newbery on 8 February 1951.

On 11 November at 1011 Tank performed the fourth flight, after making some adjustments to the ailerons to correct the tendency to roll and to the landing gear. Now, there was no tendency to roll to the right, but a small one to roll to the left.

Tank then carried out low-speed tests, taking the plane down to 240km/h at 6,000ft, then pulling the stick back to reduce more, until the controls were soft at 210km/h and the plane tended to raise the nose and roll to the right or left. Then, he made another test with the landing gear and flaps down and the controls went soft between 175 to 180km/h, finding it was very easy to leave this situation by simply moving the stick forward. This time, there was no bouncing during the landing.

As the plane tended to flare on landing, it was decided to move the centre of gravity forward, so two of the four Mauser MG-151/20 20mm guns were installed in the nose. A thinner leading edge on the wing close to the root was also adopted, because the wingtip had previously stalled at the root. This permitted the airflow to separate sooner at low speeds.

The rudder also was changed to solve lateral instability problems. The undercarriage shock absorber was changed and the height of the front landing gear was reduced. By this time a fairing had been installed above the engine exhaust and the cockpit canopy was modified with the addition of two structural reinforcements to avoid deformation of the Plexiglas when the cabin was pressurised.

The guns were installed only as ballast, as they lacked the electrical system and the sight was not installed, as weapon tests were not planned at this stage. The Instituto Aerotécnico started to work on the construction, under licence, of a local version of the Mauser gun, designated the I.Ae. Mk.151.

On 16 November, Tank made the fifth flight of the plane, with a new improved rudder, and again he found some oscillations. These could not be solved before the next flight, which took place on 21 November. On 23 November, the seventh flight took place, during which tank found that the oscillations were reduced, and on 4 December, on the eighth flight, he reached 800km/h. Two days later Tank took the prototype to 920km/h, or Mach 0.77, without problems, landing for the first time on the runway at the factory after thirty minutes. Tank found that now the tests were progressing, he could make future flights from that runway.

On 13 December, Tank made the tenth flight was made and the Pulqui II was shown to the Aeronautics Minister, Brigadier César Ojeda. The hydraulic system again failed and the landing gear retracted partially, but as the aircraft flew normally, Tank made the demonstration at slow speed and also performed some tests. Ojeda asked if the plane

The first prototype in flight after being modified in November 1950.

Engine tests on the second prototype being made by Behrens at the factory.

was ready to be exhibited in Buenos Aires and he was told that it was possible in one month.

On 20 December Tank reached Mach 0.89 or 1,020km/h at 7,200m, the highest altitude at which the plane had been tested until then, and he found the controls were soft at that altitude. After that, he landed at Pajas Blancas, the civil airport of Córdoba city. After two and a half hours he took off again with the intention of making more tests between 6,000m and 8,000m, but a lack of oxygen prevented that and he returned to the factory. On his report of the flight, Tank said the Pulqui II could be considered as tested sufficiently for a demonstration in Buenos Aires.

The next flight was on 24 January 1951, when Tank made low passes over the factory at speeds of up to 830km/h at 220m before landing in Pajas Blancas. Then, he made a flight of one hour eight minutes to test the fuel system, to check its readiness before the flight to Buenos Aires. This began at 0912 the following day, when Tank left Pajas Blancas heading to Morón airport, but as the orders from the control tower were not clear, he decided to land at Ezeiza international airport, arriving after seventy-eight minutes, of which thirty-two were tests over Córdoba. Later that day, he flew to Morón and on 30 January he went to the Aeroparque Jorge Newbery, Buenos Aires' domestic airport, where the Pulqui II was going to be exhibited. During that flight, Tank tested the rolling ability performing four of them.

Because of bad weather, the exhibition was delayed and on 2 February Tank flew back to Morón, returning on the 7th to have the aircraft ready.

On 8 February 1951 the Pulqui II was shown to president Perón and more than 20,000 people who went to Aeroparque. This time, Tank flew from Aeroparque, starting with a flypast at almost 1,000km/h, followed by one at 210km/h with the landing gear down and a third, also at 1,000km/h, which ended with a steep climb performing two rolls and then landing. When Tank descended from the plane, he was congratulated by Perón.

After taking the plane back to Morón on 9 February, Tank returned to Córdoba on 17 February and on 30 March the tests continued, with another flight on 3 April. On the 5th another two test flights were made before going again to Buenos Aires, landing at Aeroparque.

On 6 April, the Pulqui II was exhibited to Prince Bernhard von Lippe-Biesterfeld of Holland, who was visiting Argentina, and he showed interest in the type because his country needed modern fighters. Finally, the Netherlands bought the Gloster Meteor F.Mk.8.

After going to Morón on 7 April, on the 9th Tank returned to Córdoba flying at 6,300m. However, as he as landed, he touched the runway with the front wheel at 200km/h, bounced and landed hard with the three wheels, bounced again

Behrens climbing into the third prototype at the factory shortly before his death. The Porsche 356 in the picture belonged to engineer Jürgen Naumann, of Tank's team.

The second prototype at the factory in its final layout.

and fell, breaking the main landing gear. Again, a failure of the struts was discovered.

The plane was repaired and flew again on 29 and 31 May with Tank at the controls. By then the Argentine Air Force had designated Commander Carlos A. Soto (commander of the Regimiento 6 de Caza Interceptora, equipped with Gloster Meteors) and Captain Vedania Mannuwal to fly the Pulqui II as they were experienced fighter pilots. It was considered that, at that stage of the tests, they should check the plane and make their own suggestions for any improvements needed. So, after Tank's flight on the 31st, Soto made a flight in the morning and he noticed some hard vibrations close to the speed of 1,000km/h, caused by the Flettner positioning, while on one turn at low height, the plane turned on its longitudinal axis when the pilot moved the rudder, caused by rolling movement due to slide slip.

Soto landed and then Captain Mannuwal was told not to use the rudder to turn, while the Flettners were regulated again. He was also told not to fly over 600km/h and 1,500m. He took off on the thirty-fourth flight of the Pulqui II and, without taking care of the advice, Mannuwal, one of the most experienced Meteor pilots of the FAA, began aerobatic manoeuvres. During one of them the wing separated from the fuselage. The pilot ejected inverted but, as he was not trained in the use of the Martin-Baker Mk.I ejection seat, he did not separate from it and was killed when he hit the ground without opening his parachute. The cause of the accident was that the welding of the joint pin that held the wing was defective. Mannuwal's ejection was the first in the southern hemisphere, and one of the first uses of the Mk.I seat.

New prototypes

The construction of the second prototype (E-2) had already started at the time of the loss of the first aircraft and on 25 September 1951 Tank flew it for the first time. This aircraft had a modified and bigger rudder to improve lateral stability, as well as new design of the nose landing gear strut. The exhaust fairing was also bigger and there were three structural reinforcements for the canopy. After that first flight, the aircraft was used for ground tests and then loaded on a truck and to Buenos Aires to be exhibited as part of the government display at the intersection of Florida and Charcas streets, in downtown Buenos Aires. In January 1952 it was shown at the Alas Argentinas exhibition at Mar del Plata city, where it was also taken by truck. After that, it returned to the workshops for the rudder to be changed and other adjustments to be made.

A third prototype was also started, with more improvements, including more fuel in a new wing with eight tanks, to augment the range from 2,030km to 3,090km.

In the meantime, an LGW-Siemens K-23/1 autopilot, used in the Focke-Wulf Ta 152, was tested in the

The fourth prototype (E-5) shortly after leaving the workshops, without paint.

FMA I.Ae. DL-22 serialled Ea-886, with the intention of using it in the third Pulqui II. The second and third prototypes were also equipped with spoilers, as the type proved difficult to slow down when descending.

When the second prototype returned from Mar del Plata, it was decided to change the tail, the spoilers, the position of the Flettners and the electrical system for the guns, and add a second pitot tube on the left wing. So it was sent to the workshops and later used on the ground to test the spoilers, not flying again until 18 May 1953.

The third prototype (serialled E-3) was ready by mid-year and was equipped with a new wing with eight rubber fuel tanks, while the canopy lacked the reinforcements that were installed in the first two examples. This aircraft flew for the first time on 18 July 1952, on what was the first flight test of the spoilers. Tank was at the controls and he saw that these behaved well and reduced the jumps on the runway during landings, although they were not properly adjusted. He made a second flight on 21 July and another on 22, while on the 23rd Tank flew the third prototype together with the I.Ae.27 (now called Pulqui I), with Captain Carlos Bergaglio at the controls. The Pulqui I was used as a chase plane to observe the Pulqui II extending and retracting the landing gear, flaps and spoilers. The flight lasted twenty-five minutes.

On 24 and 25 July, Tank made two other test flights in the third aircraft and after that Behrens resumed flying. He found this aircraft much better than the first prototype and it was flown again by both pilots on the 31st of that month, then by Tank on 6 August and by both on the 18th. Behrens performed the thirteenth flight of the third prototype on 20 August, when the elevator locked in the descent position and there was no way to unlock it. He reduced power and managed to make a hard landing, but without causing heavy damage to the plane.

Both Tank and Behrens resumed flying on the 26th to test the K-23 autopilot, which worked properly. The same test was repeated by them on the following day and on 10 and 12 September Tank made two extra test flights.

A visit of president Perón was planned for 11 October and it was decided to give display with Behrens at the controls. On the 9th, he took off on a test flight as some repairs had been made. After the take-off, Behrens reported that the plane was making a strange noise and was very difficult to control. He dived over the runway and after that he ascended to 2,400ft, the plane stalled and started a lateral spin that he could recover only when he was very close to the ground. However, the Pulqui II then hit the ground, killing the pilot instantly.

The fourth prototype during engine tests at the factory.

Tests resume with the second prototype

The accident was a big blow to the programme, which was progressing slower than expected, but the second prototype was returned to service after its modifications. In the meantime, parts were also started for another three planes. When the Instituto Aerotécnico enquired about ordering more Nene II or Nene IV engines, Rolls-Royce stated that the more powerful Nene VII was now available, but it would need some modifications to install it into the Pulqui II. The Instituto also asked for the cartridge starting system to be changed for an electric one.

In May 1953 the plane was readied and flew again for the first time on the 18th with Tank at the controls, with a Gloster Meteor flown by 1st Lt Luis González as chase plane, followed by another flight the following day. They performed three more test flights with the Meteor as chase plane between 18 and 19 August and some more modifications were included, including an electrical engine to help move the rudder, improving the control. González, together with 1st Lt Jorge Conan Doyle, were trained

to fly the aircraft from 20 August until, on 18 September, it was taken to Buenos Aires for the Aeronautic Week and then returned to Córdoba. On 14 December it was sent to Mendoza to participate in the Feria de las Americas.

In an interview with Tank by author Wolfgang Wagner in 1979,[3] he said that on his first flight in the plane:

> I climbed to about 8,000 metres' altitude in barely six minutes and was a bit proud to have launched what was probably the fastest fighter in the world at that time together with my colleagues so far away from home. We were able to realise what we'd only been able to dream of long before with our Ta 183 model experiments at Focke-Wulf. I trimmed the aeroplane for level flight and pulled the throttle back to idle, checked my bearings and found that I was near the airfield at an altitude of 9,000 metres. Another tug on the safety harness and a glance at the canopy eject lever. It took a while for the speed to bleed off. Slowly I approached stall speed. However, with the Pulqui II a stall didn't announce itself by a shudder or sudden drop off onto one wing or any type of unusual behaviour at all. I held the stick, but the machine never nosed over to pick up speed. Suddenly, I had no control effect whatsoever. The stick could be moved around freely as though the plane were on the ground. An eery silence pervaded the cockpit. Only two of the gauges were behaving crazily: the climb rate indicator and the altimeter. The climb rate needle twitched at 'falling', while the altimeter unwound rapidly – 8,000 metres, 7,000 metres … It became clear to me that I was falling almost straight down like a rock with the plane in a perfect normal flight attitude – nowadays we can this a superstall – and the aircraft failed to react to any inputs … 6,000 metres. I moved the stick around, nothing … 5,000 metres. 'Bail out' went through my mind. But before that another try at the engine; the turbine was still running – they could easily have gone out during the rapid descent. I slowly pushed the throttle forward, then pulled it back – then the machine began pumping. I noticed a bit of pressure on the ailerons, but the aeroplane still didn't respond to controls. Once again, I pushed the throttle forward and pulled it back, forcibly pulled the stick to one side, the wing lifted and the machine dropped over onto its side, nosed over, picked up speed and I was able to pull out as though nothing had happened. I climbed out to 500 metres in order to reflect on the cause of this unusual behaviour. I would have to repeat the whole spectacle, for only in this way would I be able to get to the root of the matter. Was it chance,

Although there are no records of the plane being used in the revolution, there are statements indicating its guns were used during those days and the plane received the marking used by the rebels, a cross over a V. All aircraft available at the factory and the military aviation school were used, so most probably the Pulqui II saw action during those days.

[3] Published in *Kurt Tank: Focke-Wulf's designer and test pilot*, by Wolfgang Wagner, Schiffer Books, Atglen, 1998.

The fourth prototype taking off from the runway of the Escuela Militar de Paracaidistas on its first flight on 18 September 1959 piloted by Lt Roberto Starc.

Starc being prepared for his first flight in the Pulqui II.

or did this fall happen as a result of a particular flight attitude? I pushed the throttle lever forward and climbed to an altitude of 9,000 metres. Again, I put it into a stall and I was at once whistling straight down like a rock with the plane still maintaining a level attitude. But this time I immediately began pumping the throttle and quickly regained control of the machine. One thing was obvious to me: the tail must have fallen in the airflow's dead zone and downdraft, for the aeroplane refused to react to anything. As I landed, I became aware of the fact that for the first time I'd built an aeroplane which could be deadly.

This is not logged in the reports of Tank's flights in the first prototype, in which he never tried stalls nor reached that height, so it must have occurred during the flights with E-2 or E-3 between 1952 and 1955. This occurred because of the T-tail design, which with angles of attack between 15 to 20° and slow speeds the airflow separated completely and could even flow forward, losing all effectiveness of the rudder and elevators.

By the end of 1953 the aircraft returned to the workshop to receive the new wing with the internal fuel tanks as the E-3 had, one wing fence on each wing and four fences on the rear fuselage. Works to pressurise the cockpit was also carried out, including

The last prototype of the Pulqui II during one of its few flights.

a new canopy without reinforcement. Four Hispano Suiza HS404-TI80 guns of 20mm were installed, the same used on the Meteors, which replaced the Mauser guns and included a GGS-Mk.IVE sight and Omera T20 camera.

In 1954, 1st Lt Jorge Conan Doyle became the FMA test pilot's chief, with Lieutenants Luis Gonzalez and Rogelio Balado, although Kurt Tank continued making test flights. After the modifications, flight tests were resumed and firing carried out with the internal 20mm guns. For this, two holes were made to expel the cases. Pressurisation tests also began, with Doyle reaching 45,000ft. On 2 October, Tank reached a top speed of 1,080km/h in level flight, but he had to reduce power when one of the landing gear covers opened. That was the fastest speed reached with the Pulqui II.

As the project was going well, production of 100 examples was planned, including a version with a radar in the nose and an IFF in the tail for night operations, which would also be equipped with air-to-air missiles. Moreover, there was interest in buying the type from many countries.

Tank leaves the project

Meanwhile, in January 1955 Kurt Tank's contract ended, although he kept working at the factory. He asked the government for a much higher salary that what he was being paid under the former contract. The factory management rejected his request and discussions continued, while Tank made his last two flights in the Pulqui II on 10 and 24 March 1955 to test the autopilot and the pressurisation system of the cockpit. Then, he travelled to Germany and then on 19 June to the United Kingdom to visit Rolls-Royce and negotiate for new engines, including the Avon, to equip the I.Ae.36 passenger aircraft project. While he was in Bonn, he met the Indian Minister of War Mahavir Tiagy, who offered him the opportunity to go to India to develop the local aviation industry. His contract had not yet been renewed in Argentina, where there was also growing political instability in the country (on 16 June there was a failed coup against Perón). Also, an economic crisis had slowed the programmes at the factory, which also diversified its production to cars, motorbikes and other products, leading to the delays in the test programme of the Pulqui II and the initiation of series production.

Tank decided to travel to Bangalore, India, to visit the factory of Hindustan Aeronautics, and he was impressed with what he saw. He also received an offer to work in Germany in a factory to be built in Kaltenkirchen, but then he was told that this would be delayed until at least the following year, so Tank decided to accept the Indian offer and did not return to Argentina.

Meanwhile, between 16 and 21 September 1955 a violent revolution overthrew president Perón. The

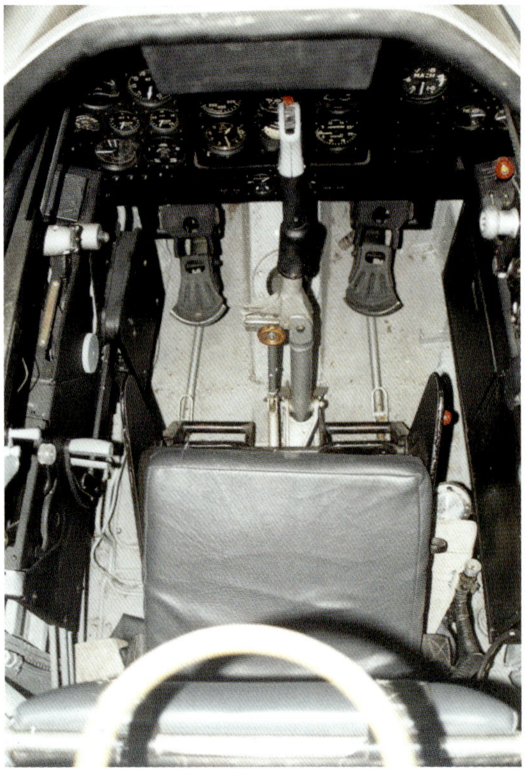

Cabin of the Pulqui II, with the Martin-Baker Mk.I seat visible.

Military Aviation School, next to the FMA, was taken by the rebels and aircraft from the school and the FMA were used in combat. Although little is known about the activity of the Pulqui II, the second prototype received the markings of the rebels, a Catholic cross over a V painted on the fuselage, and it and 20mm guns were used against the government forces, together with four Meteors that were being overhauled when the revolution started. On the parade to celebrate the victory of the revolution in Córdoba city, the Pulqui II participated with Captain Jorge L. Suárez at the controls. Its guns had been used recently, as they had scorch marks around the ports.

The revolution against Perón meant trouble for the programme and the pilots González and Conan Doyle had left to join the Air Force, leaving Balado as the only test pilot.

Some engineers on Tank's team left the country, while the government preferred to focus on the series production of other projects, including the IA-35 Huanquero.

The Pulqui II project continues

The factory management decided to keep working on the Pulqui II, as the development was well advanced, but support from the new government was diminishing as they saw that more than five years had passed since the first flight and the aeroplane still was not ready for series production.

In 1956 a flight was planned to show the capabilities of the Pulqui II and encourage the government to continue with the project. The flight would be from Córdoba to Buenos Aires with a full load of ammunition, making three shooting passes over the VII Brigada Aérea at Morón Air Base and returning to Córdoba. The idea was to show the ability of the Pulqui II to escort the Air Force's Avro Lincoln and Lancaster bombers, something unique for a fighter in the world at that time, because it would only use internal fuel to fly 1,600km.

To reach the target, the oxygen system was changed for one from a Gloster Meteor that was being checked at the FMA. As this would be the first time the aircraft would take off with a maximum load, the flight would start at the Pajas Blancas international airport in Córdoba. The pilot was Rogelio Balado.

On 9 November 1956 Balado took off and flew to Buenos Aires at 33,000ft. Thirty-five minutes later it attacked targets installed on the side of the runway with its guns and started to return home. The pressurisation system began to fail close to its destination and the pilot started to receive less oxygen, but he managed to return to Córdoba. Instead of landing at the FMA, he made for the runway at the Military Aviation School, which is besides the factory, touching at more than 200km/h and bouncing two times, breaking the landing gear. The Pulqui II ran off the runway and was 60 per cent destroyed. Balado was glad that he had changed his soft helmet for a plastic one just before the flight as this saved his life, although he was severely injured.

The commander of the Argentine Air Force, Brigadier Ahrens, asked the FMA management about the possibility of building 100 Pulqui IIs. FMA replied that there were wings and fuselages to build ten aeroplanes in a short time. As the FMA had the licence to build the Nene II engine, the factory could make the aircraft in five years, but an offer from the United States for 100 F-86 Sabres with Orenda engines began to compete with the Pulqui.

In spite of this, it was decided to finish one of the three prototypes that were under construction, using the fifth airframe (E-5), with parts of E-4 and E-6 and some parts recovered from the wreck of E-2. E-6 was originally intended to be the first of a pre-series production batch. E-5 and E-6 were also modified to use the Nene VII engine with more power, but had no other differences from E-2. However, the work to finish the new aircraft took two years. Although the aircraft had the installation for the guns, it was never fitted with them nor their operating systems.

Finally, on 18 September 1959 the new aircraft flew for the first time with 1° Lt Roberto Starc at the controls and a Meteor as chase plane. It was tested by Starc and Lt Sergio García during the year, being exhibited in Buenos Aires on 24 May 1960. However, by that times the design was not as modern as it was in 1950.

A new government came to power in 1958 with a leaning to the USA and it received an offer for twenty-eight F-86F-40 Sabres at very low price, which was accepted. The aircraft were received in

1960 and this killed the Pulqui II project. Starc and García made twelve flights (ten Starc and two García) during which they never exceeded 700km/h and never forced the plane above 70 per cent of its capacities. In late 1960 they made the last flight. The aircraft was stored and in 1964 it was transferred to the National Aeronautics Museum. After the restoration of the IAe-27, the Pulqui II also received attention and is now on display in the new facilities of the museum at Morón in excellent condition.

The I.A.40 Pulqui III

In 1954, Kurt Tank, seeing the advances in fighter aircraft after the Korean War, started to work on the I.A.40 Pulqui III, a supersonic two-seat interceptor with two Bristol Siddeley Orpheus 703 for the prototype and two Rolls-Royce Avons or Armstrong Siddeley Sapphires with afterburner on the sides of the fuselage, with swept wings and tail, and armed with four Hispano Suiza 20 or 30mm cannon. Wind tunnel tests were made and the scale model is preserved today at the Área de Material Río Cuarto of the Argentine Air Force. Tank was progressing with this project when in 1955 he left Argentina and went to India, where he proposed it to the management of the new Hindustan Aeronautics. They approved the proposal and the plane evolved to become the HF-24 Marut, but equipped with Bristol Orpheus engines.

Meanwhile, in Argentina, during 1956 and 1957 wind tunnel tests of the I.A.40 continued without Tank and the project evolved to become a night fighter. Nine flights with launched scale models were made, but work had ended by the end of 1957 because it was decided to focus on Horten's projects.

The fourth prototype is currently on exhibition at the National Aeronautics Museum of Argentina at Morón Air Base, together with other types built by the FMA over the years. *Santiago Rivas*

Wind tunnel model of the I.A.40 Pulqui III, which later evolved to become the Hindustan Aeronautics HF-24 Marut in India. It is preserved at the Centro de Ensayos de Armamentos y Sistemas Operativos (CEASO) of the Argentine Air Force at Área de Material Río Cuarto. *Santiago Rivas*

18 **Glider flying wings: I.Ae.34 Clen Antú and I.Ae.41 Urubú**

While working with Tank on the Pulqui II design, Reimar Horten was authorised by Juan Ignacio San Martín to continue the work he had started when he was very young on the development of flying wing gliders, as long as this work did not affect the Pulqui II programme. Also, shortly after his arrival, he had joined the Club de Planeadores Cóndor in the town of Zárate, in Buenos Aires province, restarting flying and also interesting club members in his flying wing designs.

Based on the experience of the H IV glider that he built in 1941, with a high aspect ratio and 20m wingspan, which was followed by the H VI that flew briefly in 1945, he designed what he called the H XVa. It received the designation I.Ae.34 Clen Antú (Sun Ray in Araucanian) from the Instituto Aerotécnico during the second half of 1948. The aim was to provide the glider clubs of Argentina with a two-seat tandem glider trainer, able to fly for long periods, with good visibility. It should be suitable to be used by students for solo flights, capable of aerobatic manoeuvres and with a structure that could be easily modified into a motor glider.

The I.Ae.34 was a flying wing with a single spar, and consisted of three parts; a small fuselage in the middle, 60cm wide, with a cabin, and two wings, each covered with plywood, with elevons and flaps on the training edge. The elevons were balanced with lead weights. Ball bearings supported all the pushrods. Drag rudders retracted flush into the wingtips and terminal speed airbrakes were installed near the wing roots. The wing could be removed by four people in a few minutes. The all-wood central section had two tandem wheels near the centre of gravity, with a skid in front, to enable it to make off-field landings without danger off flipping over. The rear seat was located 30cm above the front one, giving both pilots an identical view. A single instrument panel was visible from both cockpits. Provisions for oxygen and seat parachutes were included and the rear control stick could be removed for passenger flying.

The construction of the prototype was problematic, as the wood available was not of the same quality that Horten was accustomed to use in Germany and the glue that was prepared at the Instituto Aerotécnico also was of poor quality and had usually already started to harden when it was delivered.

Horten started to build three prototypes, with the first being ready by January 1949, but the first flight was delayed when the factory management

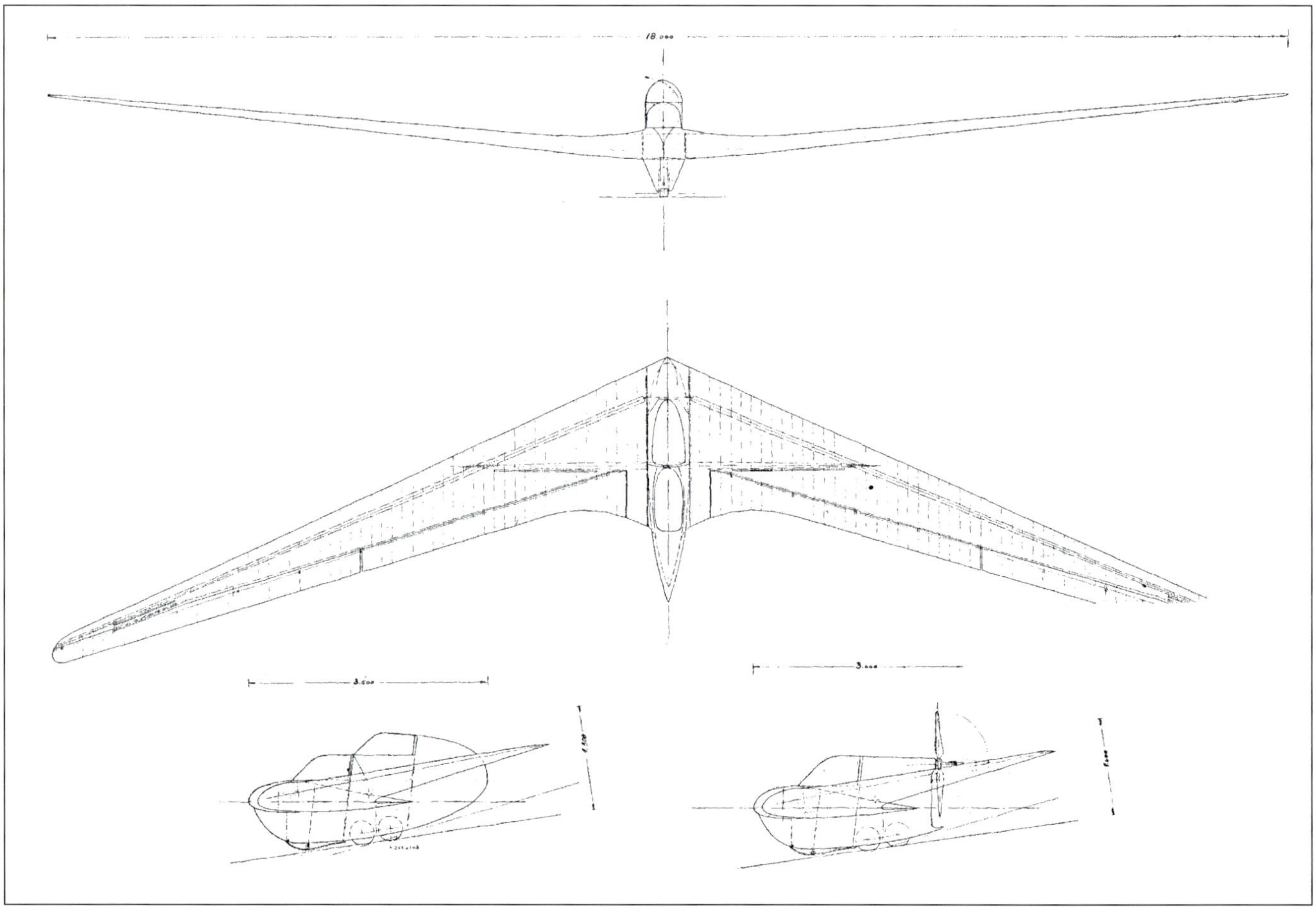

Plan of the I.Ae.34 Clen Antú, with a side view of the idea to convert it into a motor glider.

decided to send it to an exhibition in Córdoba city with the Pulqui II glider. The I.Ae.34 returned in March in very poor condition after a month being exhibited outside and had to be completely restored.

Finally, on 20 June 1949 the first flight was made by test pilot Edmundo Osvaldo Weiss, being towed by a Morane-Saulnier MS.502 Criquet that had been delivered to the factory for this purpose and which then served there for several years. Weiss considered that the glider flew very well, so between 11 and 14 October Aeronautics Ministry Brigadier Mayor César Ojeda invited a group of glider pilots from the Club Argentino de Planeadores Albatros to test the Clen Antú. However, after making some flights from the runway at the factory, always towed by the Criquet, it was evident that they needed special training to fly the flying wing. Interestingly, although the glider was a two-seater, the invited pilots flew alone. One of the invited pilots, Manuel Fentanes, remembered: 'The task of flying this glider was not easy, since adaptation training was needed. The position of the pilot was sitting very straight on a seat parachute. The rudder pedal was operated by pressing down, they were independent but they could operate simultaneously. These did not move a conventional rudder, but they operated air brakes located close to the wingtips, making it difficult to maintain level flight. Downward visibility was almost nil. Another problem was following the towing plane.'

In 1951 Horten was authorised to organise his own team, so shortly after he was joined by two of his collaborators, engineer Karl Nickel and pilot Hans Scheidhauer, while he tried to convince his brother Walter to come but he refused. They were called the 'Grupo Horten'. However, despite all the work to improve the Clen Antú, the glider was still difficult to control, especially at low speed, making landings very complicated, so the factory decided to not build more examples.

On 25 November 1951, the second example, now serialled LV-X-12, had an accident at Merlo aerodrome while being flown by Enrique Hörhammer and Manuel Fentanes. Fentanes remembers that they 'flew for over an hour. Upon returning to the airfield, we were short on approach due to a strong headwind, we could barely skip telephone wires, but immediately stalled and hit the ground. The Clen Antú was totally destroyed, but we escaped unharmed.' He also recalled that 'on another flight I had difficulty in lowering the nose to "see" the towing plane … While trying to track the tug plane, pressing either foot at altitude I was careless and I almost made the tug plane stall. The Clen Antú was unstable, it required between 50 and 100 hours of training to be able to say the pilot really controlled it.'

Later, on 11 November 1953, Hans Scheidhauer and Héctor Bravo performed a long-distance flight, flying 320km in the third Clen Antú.

In order to address the criticism of the glider's handling characteristics, in 1955 Horten started to work to improve it, testing different modifications. This included the addition of a small lifting surface below

Construction of the first two Clen Antús at the Instituto Aerotécnico. The glider had a metal tube structure for the fuselage, but all the rest was made of wood.

The first prototype of the Clen Antú being readied for a flight.

Glider pilot Gisela Hilger preparing for a flight in the Clen Antú. She was the daughter of Germans and was a renowned glider pilot in Argentina in the 1940s. When Reimar Horten arrived in the country, she was appointed as his translator. This evolved into a love story, as they got married and had two sons together, living in Córdoba until Reimar's death on 14 August 1993.

A Clen Antú flying over the suburbs of Córdoba. The glider had poor characteristics at low speeds, which were criticised by the pilots who flew it.

The second I.Ae.34 Clen Antú seen with the first single-seater, called I.A.34M, still with serial number 4. Interestingly, the single-seater was among the first types of the factory with the new designation without the 'e'. The canopy of the cockpit of the single-seater had a large windscreen, which was later changed for a smaller one. The undercarriage is totally different from the two-seater.

the wing, near the trailing edge, on the first prototype, which was then named I.A.34B, already without the 'e' under the new designation system of the factory. According to the Ministerio de Aeronáutica's annual review, twenty-three flights were made in the I.A.34B, and plans were made to modify one of the two examples as a single-seat motor glider, with a 20 to 30hp engine, but this was abandoned.

The third Clen Antú was delivered to the Club de Planeadores Córdoba, based at Marcos Juárez, and serialled LV-X-13, until 1953, when it was returned to the factory. The second aircraft was lost in an accident and the remaining gliders stopped flying in the early 1950s and their final fate is unknown.

I.A.34M

Between 21 and 25 March 1951 the Primer Congreso Argentino de Vuelo sin Motor (Engine-less Flight First Argentine Congress) was organised at Villa Rumipal, near the city of Córdoba, in which Horten explained the attributes of the Clen Antú. The Aeronautics Minister, César Ojeda, asked him to develop a single-seater version to participate in the World Soaring Championship that would take place in Spain in 1952. Horten accepted and started the design of what he called H XVb, which was known by the factory as the I.A.34M.

The first glider, built using the unfinished airframe of the fourth I.Ae.34 (which initially had the c/n 4, later changed to 1 once the designation was changed to I.A.34M, and was serialled LV-X-14), flew for the first time on 19 October 1951 and the second (serialled LV-X-25 and later LV-XXB) on 9 February 1952, having the same wings as the two-seaters, but with a different cabin and landing gear, which had a main fixed gear and a small retractable nosewheel. The first glider initially had a bigger canopy with a better view, but it was changed for a smaller one that had better aerodynamic performance and this was also installed in the second one.

To test their performance before going to Spain, in March 1952 they both took part in the IV Concurso Nacional de Vuelo a Vela at Trenque Lauquen.

Pilots Eduardo Bazet and José Ortner were selected to fly the gliders in Spain, and the tournament started on 3 July 1952 at Cuatro Vientos airfield near Madrid. However, the Clen Antús performed poorly as they were still difficult to control and the pilots did not have much experience in them. On the first day, while on a training flight, Ortner had an accident and damaged the second glider beyond repair, while Bazet had an accident while landing during the fourth official test and could not continue.

The second glider was repaired and had resumed flying by late 1953. It was later exchanged with the Club de Planeadores Córdoba for the third Clen Antú, which returned to the factory. This single-seater Clen Antú took part in the XII Concurso Nacional de Vuelo a Vela of 1962 at the Aero Club Junín, flying in the hands of Guillermo Horrocks, who finished twenty-second.

This glider flew on for a time until it was stored. In 2000 it was re-covered and donated to the Museo de la Industria of Córdoba, who restored it completely and it was handed over to be exhibited on 19 December 2006.

Just an idea

In 1953 Reimar Horten proposed another version of the Clen Antú equipped with an engine, but this time with a small Turbomeca jet. This was not approved by the factory, but Horten started to work on the idea of designing a small jet engine based on the supercharger turbine of a radial piston engine. However, work on this idea was also stopped in 1954.

The I.A.41 Urubú

When Horten designed the Clen Antú, he also worked on an idea of a version with side-by-side seats, called the H XVc, which was based on his X XII motor glider trainer project flown in 1944. Horten had sent some incomplete plans to Germany, where four were built from 1951 and the first was flown on 20 May 1952 at Tübingen. However, as the unrefined plans were completed by the constructors, their performance was not good. At the same time, those who flew the two-seat Clen Antú complained that when flown by a single pilot the centre of gravity moved forward too far, making it harder to fly, so they requested a side-by-side solution. The Instituto Aerotécnico asked Horten to develop a glider to fulfil what the glider pilots were requesting, so he presented the H HXc, which was named I.A.41 Urubú (Vulture in Araucanian).

The first flight of the first prototype was made by Hans Scheidhauer on 29 September 1953, but it was only a short one to test the controls, so the first official flight was on 4 December of that same year, also by Scheidhauer.

A second example, designated I.A.41B, was finished and flown on 7 March 1955, while construction of another two was started. This second example was delivered to the Instituto Argentino de Vuelo a Vela (INAV), which had its aerodrome at La Cruz, Córdoba province. With this plane, on 20 August 1955 Scheidhauer reached an altitude of 6,200m and after that he developed the idea of crossing the Andes with the glider, something never done before.

To attempt this, in September 1956 Scheidhauer made a 1,000km flight from Córdoba to the city of San Carlos de Bariloche on the Urubú, towed the whole time by the Morane-Saulnier Criquet used by the Instituto Aerotécnico. He flew with a Slingsby Sky 34 glider, serialled LV-EEN, which was flown by

ABOVE First prototype of the Urubú, with the fairing that covered the main landing gear, which was not used on the other examples. Also, the canopy opened upwards and backwards, but this was changed on the second example because of the risk of losing it if it opened in flight.

LEFT The sole-surviving Clen Antú, preserved at the Museo de la Industria in Córdoba after being fully restored.

The two I.A.34M Clen Antú in Spain, with the first seen at the forefront.

The Urubú being towed by the Criquet over the Andes returning from Chile after the first crossing of the mountains by a glider made in October 1956 by Hans Scheidhauer.

The first Urubú prepared for stall tests. The glider was tested exhaustively to check it did not have the same problems as the Clen Antú at slow speeds.

Claudio Dori and towed by a Boeing Stearman 75. Due to bad weather, they had to wait until 30 October to attempt the crossing. They then made a three-hour flight from Bariloche to land at the town of Ensenada in Chile, making the first crossing of the Andes by glider. They were followed twenty minutes later by the Sky.

Fifteen days later the gliders returned towed by the Cricket and the Stearman.

By then, the construction of the third and fourth Urubús was 90 per cent complete and they were tested during 1957. However, only the third example was flown, on 17 December 1958, and the other was never finished.

Although the glider had far better performance than the Clen Antú and was very easy to fly, the lack of trust in the flying wing layout caused by the former led to gliding schools taking no interest on the Urubú, so no orders were placed.

The Urubú was used to make tests of the limits of the displacement of the centre of gravity of the glider, with a 50kg ballast on the right seat to replace the second pilot. It was also used to test two small fins installed next to the wingtips, which were part of the tests for the I.Ae.38 programme.

Horten also proposed a motor glider version of the I.A.41 Urubú, with a pusher propeller, like the H XII, but the idea was never approved even though the structure of the Urubú was originally planned to receive an engine behind the seats.

The gliders were flown for some time but the fate of the first and the third is unknown. The second was transferred in 1965 to the Museo Nacional de Aeronáutica, but it was stored at the Club de Planeadores Los Caranchos in Córdoba for many years and deteriorated. In 1996 it was finally taken to the museum in Buenos Aires and a complete restoration process began, being finished in 2001. Since then the glider has been exhibited at the museum.

The second Urubú at the Museo Nacional de Aeronáutica, with one of the vertical fins close to the wingtip used to test their performance as part of the I.A.38 project.

19 I.Ae.35 Justicialista del Aire, Huanquero, Pandora, Constancia and I.Ae.39

Among the engineers that were contracted with Kurt Tank in 1947 was Paul Klages, who was responsible of many of the designs of Focke-Wulf-Flugzeugbau AG under the direction of Tank, including the Fw 44 Stieglitz and Fw 58 Weihe. He had left Focke-Wulf in 1935 to go to AGO Flugzeugwerke and then in 1939 to Focke, Achgelis & Co. GmbH, where he worked on VTOL aircraft concepts. However, in 1944 he returned to Focke-Wulf. Klages attempted to escape to Argentina via Denmark, as did the others of Tank's team, but he was captured by the British and sent to prison in Neuengamme. He was released after a few months and on 17 May 1948 he arrived in Buenos Aires, going to Córdoba to work at the Instituto Aerotécnico with Tank.

Besides collaborating with Tank, Klages proposed some projects, including some VTOL ideas, which were not accepted, except one for a light transport equipped with two I.Ae.R.16 El Gaucho engines, of which only two plans exists today, but which indicates one is the third and the other the ninth layout. The design had a low wing, a T-tail, and was 13.93m long, of 4.75m high and with a wingspan of 19m. It had a glass nose common on some Second World War German types, the third having three windows on the sides of the passenger cabin and the ninth having a bubble window on top for astro navigation and four windows on the sides, while the entrance was in the belly at the back of the cabin.

This idea evolved in 1950 into a much-improved design, thanks to the availability of the more powerful I.Ae.19 El Indio engines (later I.Ae. R-19 SD/1 and I.Ae. R-19A) developed by the company from the basis of the Wright Cyclone engine, which was already built under licence by the factory.

The El Indio was developed in 1946 by engineer Raúl A. Magallanes and the first was started for the first time on 12 June 1947, reaching 620hp. The tests continued with three more engines built in 1948. The radial engine of nine cylinders and 19.4 litres was soon improved to reach 680hp and later the I.Ae. R-19 SR/1 version (later I.Ae. R-19C) was developed with a planetary system reductor that made 750hp possible at 2,350rpm. The first version was equipped with a Rotol RA.25635-1 propeller and the second with a RA.25826.

By 1950 the engine was ready for use and Klages redesigned his proposal into a slightly bigger plane, with a new, bigger wing, a new windscreen but keeping the all-glass idea, two tails at the ends of the horizontal stabiliser and some other differences. The plane was planned to be a multipurpose one, used for passenger transport, attack, medical evacuation, aerial photography and training, and once its proposal was approved by the I.Ae., it was designated

The first prototype of the I.A.35 flying over Córdoba close to IAME. Around 1955 and 1956 the prototypes received a P painted next to the type, like the British used on their prototypes.

I.Ae.35 (around 1953 this changed to I.A.35). An executive and commercial transport version was also designed for the growing national and foreign airline market. During this year the first wind tunnel tests were made and a wooden mock-up was built with two 20mm guns and a dorsal turret.

The idea was accepted by the government that although the Argentine Air Force was receiving large quantities of de Havilland Doves, Beech AT-11s and Airspeed Consuls for training, light transport, medical evacuation and photography, the new type presented

Layout 9 of the first proposal made by Paul Klages for a twin-engined, multi-purpose aircraft equipped with El Gaucho engines.

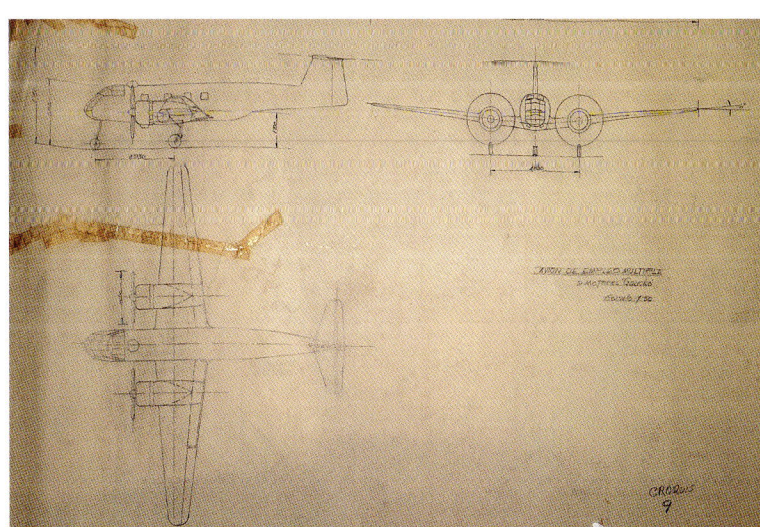

RIGHT Plan from 22 July 1953 with the different versions initially proposed for the I.Ae.35.

BELOW Plan of the I.A.35-D1 proposal, dated 19 February 1954, which kept the wings of the I.A.35 but with a new fuselage and tail.

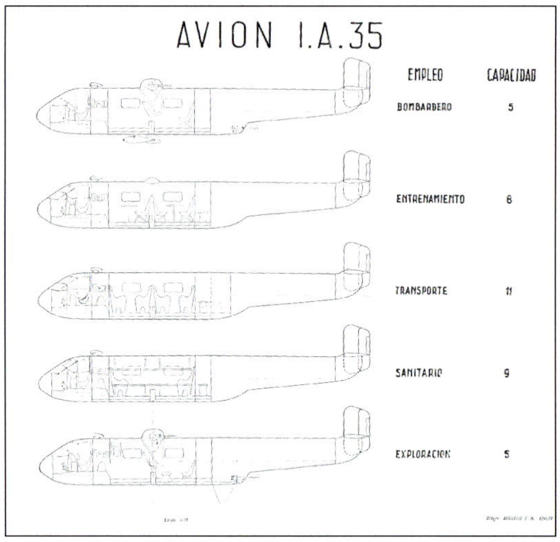

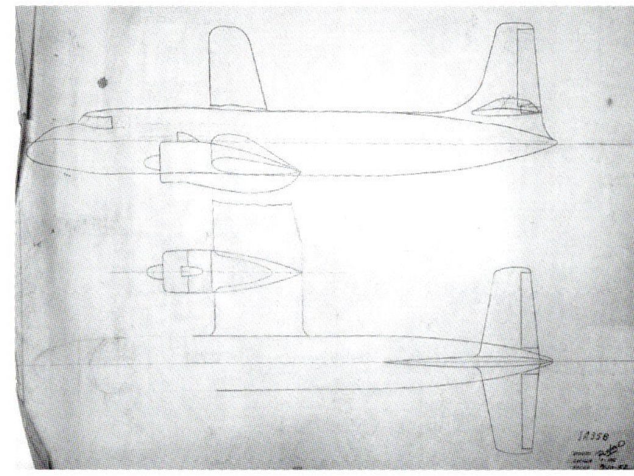

Three views of the proposed I.A.35B version dated 9 October 1957, slightly similar to the proposed I.A.35-D1. This version evolved later into one of the proposals for the I.A.47.

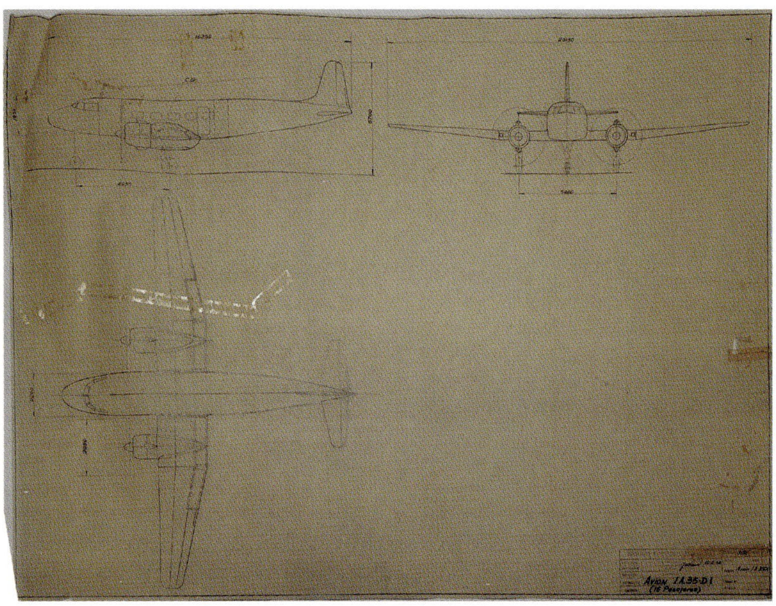

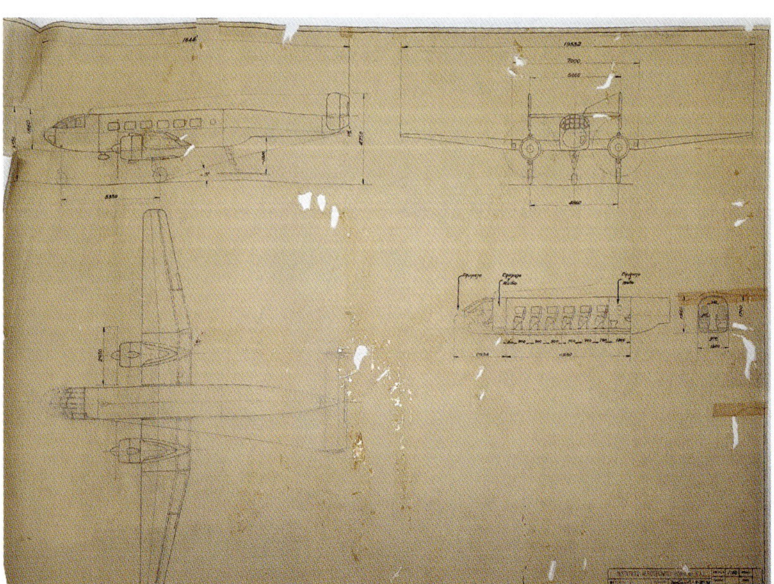

Plan of the I.A.35-E proposal with a longer fuselage with twelve passenger seats and a bigger toilet.

the possibility of having a modern plane completely built in the country as was the case with the DL-22. The I.Ae.35 would use locally built engines, too.

The aircraft had a semi-monocoque fuselage, with the wings and tail and built of Duralumin. It had cantilever wings with a 7° dihedral, and a NACA 633-218 profile section at the join with the fuselage and 631-212 at the wingtip.

There was a crew of three including a mechanic/radio operator. In the original design the plan was to install two 20mm guns in the nose in the attack version, later replaced by two 12.7mm machine guns. The fuselage was of four parts: the cockpit, centre section, tail boom and extreme tail. The wing had a central section including the engine nacelles and two outer sections.

Different versions were planned, which were:

- Tipo I with basic equipment and empty cargo cabin.
- Tipo Ia for bomber training, equipped with a dorsal turret and capacity to carry bombs under the belly and the wings, two 12.7mm machine guns on the sides of the fuselage plus a rear-facing machine gun in the opening of the access door, for which the door and its ladder were removed. It also had four seats in the main cabin.
- Tipo Ib for advanced training, with a bubble window on top for navigation and eight seats with working tables in the cabin.
- Tipo II for exploration and reconnaissance, with the dorsal turret and the rear gun position but without the front-facing machine guns nor the capacity to carry bombs.
- Tipo III for light transport, with eight seats in the cabin.
- Tipo IV for medical evacuation, with four stretchers and two seats.

Structural tests airframe at the factory.

The first prototype of the I.A.35 at Aeroparque Jorge Newbery airport in Buenos Aires.

The first prototype after receiving the new nose, with the name 'Pandora' slightly visible on the side of the cockpit.

Side view of the first prototype of the I.A.35. The windscreen was completely redesigned for the series production planes.

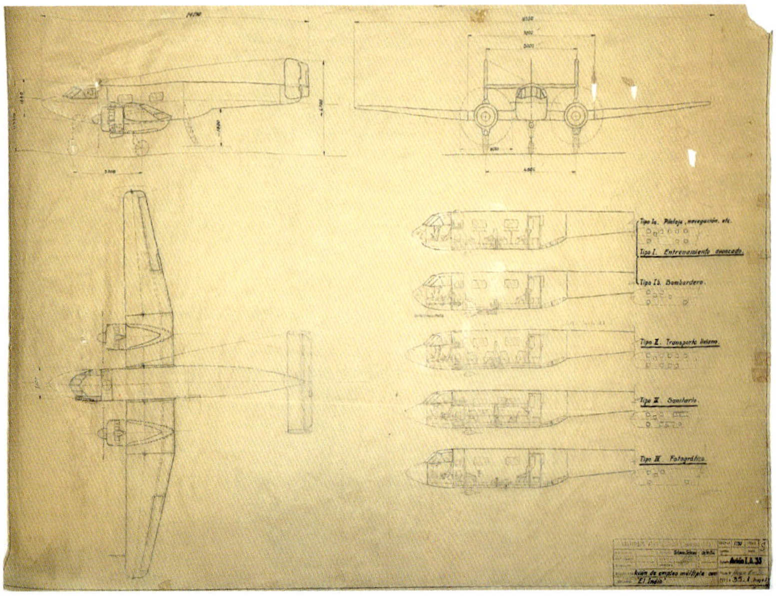

Plan from 18 June 1954 with the different versions proposed, now with the new design of the nose, both with metal or glass.

In 1952 the construction of three airframes started, one of which was used for static trials until it was destroyed during torsion tests, while in September of the following year the first prototype was finished, equipped with I.Ae. R-19A engines. On the 7th of that month it made the first flight with test pilot 1st Lt Jorge Conan Doyle at the controls. Some days later, on 21 September 1953, during the Aeronautic Week, the I.Ae.35, the type now named Justicialista del Aire to honour the Justicialista party created by Perón, was presented to the president and the aeronautical authorities and causing a great impression due to its performance and construction.

More ideas

A plan dated 19 February 1954 shows what is called an I.A.35D-1 design to carry fifteen passengers, which kept the wings and engines of the I.A.35 but had a new fuselage, a new metallic nose and a smaller windscreen. It would have had a wider fuselage of 2.2m, with four windows and a door to the left and five windows to the right, and a new single tail, with lower stabilisers. The I.A.35D-1 was to be 16.25m long, 5.7m high and with wingspan of 20.13m. Unfortunately, no more information is available on this proposal.

The first prototype, now as Pandora, with a new paint.

There is also a plan dated 9 March 1954 for a version called I.A.35E, which followed the same design as the I.A.35 prototype but with a longer fuselage with twelve seats and a toilet.

The existence of these proposals designated I.A.35D and E suggests that there were proposals called I.A.35B and C, but nothing has been found about them, except for a layout of an I.A.35B dated 1957. This was a slightly bigger plane, similar to the I.A.35D-1 in conception, and keeping the wing of the I.A.35, with a new tail and new engine nacelles.

At the same time, the second prototype was being built, but with a different windscreen than the first, with fewer pieces, and the versions were renamed as follows:

- Tipo Ia for pilot and navigator training, with bubble window on top of the cabin behind the cockpit, eight seats in the rear cabin, with tables.
- Tipo Ib for bomber training, with front-facing 12.7mm machine guns with 250 rounds that could be reloaded in flight, two pylons for bombs under the fuselage and one under each wing.
- Tipo II for light transport, with eight seats.
- Tipo III for medical evacuation, with four stretchers and two seats.
- Tipo IV for photo survey, with an opening for a Fairchild 225 camera in the belly and two seats for the operators.

While tests of the first prototype and construction of the second were progressing during 1954, in early 1955 a pre-series of three aircraft was started and they were expected to be delivered to the Argentine Air Force to start the training of new crews. Series production of 100 aircraft was also ordered.

The fall of Peron's regime after the Revolución Libertadora of September 1955 paralysed the programme and in early 1956 Paul Klages left Argentina for Spain, to work with Willy Messerschmitt at Hispano Aviación.

In 1956 the new management of the factory decided to keep working on the I.A.35 and changed the name of the military version from Justicialista del Aire to Huanquero. At the same time, the first prototype was modified with the same windscreen as the second one, but with a closed nose, being named Pandora, with the intention of offering it as a civil transport.

The second prototype was finished in the Tipo I configuration, but the bubble window was relocated backwards to the place originally intended to accommodate a dorsal turret, while the original place for that window was used for an emergency

ABOVE TS-12, originally serialled S-12, received a metal nose in the late 1960s. Here it is taxiing at Buenos Aires in 1968. *Alberto Martín*

LEFT The second pre-series aircraft, serialled E.a.-003, seen in the town of Dolores, Buenos Aires, in its initial configuration in 1957, before it was modified with the metal nose. Note the lower bubble window on the top of the fuselage.

The third pre-series aircraft, serialled E.a.-004, in flight. This plane was later re-serialled E-504 and later was modified for photo survey as F-23, operating until 1971.

E-532 was the last Huanquero produced, delivered in 1962. It is seen at the IV Brigada Aérea of Mendoza, but it was serving at the II Brigada Aérea. The plane has two SCAR rockets on the wing pylon and remains of smoke on the guns, showing they had been used shortly before.

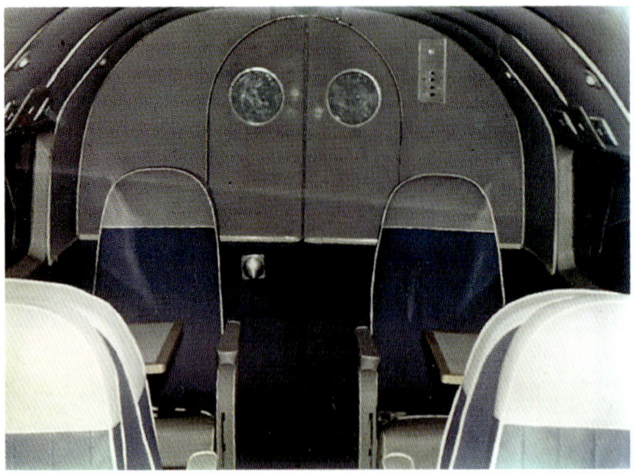

Interior of the Constancia. *Photo archive Eduardo Ruiz*

exit. By the end of 1956, the three pre-series production aircraft were 92 per cent finished and the first series of ten were 59.2 per cent complete.

Also, the designations of the types were modified, the Tipo Ia becoming Tipo I, the Ib becoming Tipo II, the III and IV keeping their designations and the original Tipo II becoming Tipo V. This latter version was modified with a more aerodynamic metal nose instead of the glass one.

The second prototype received the serial E.a.-001 (E.a. meaning Entrenamiento avanzado, advanced training) and the three others were E.a.-002 to 004, with E.a.-002 flying for the first time on 29 March 1957, followed shortly after by the other two, all built in the Tipo I configuration. By 1958 E.a.-003 had been modified to the Tipo V version, with the metal nose and the removal of the bubble window, which was later also removed on the other three planes. All were equipped with dual control so they could be used for training.

In August 1957, E.a.-001 visited Montevideo, Uruguay, to take part in the II Exposición Aeronáutica, organised in front of the Municipal Palace of the city, together with aircraft of the Uruguayan Air Force and Naval Aviation.

By the end of 1957 the aircraft of the first series (construction numbers 4 to 13) were 90 per cent finished and the seven of the second series (14 to 20), initiated that year, were at 70 per cent.

Transport versions

The transport prototype, Pandora, received a special paint scheme with the upper part and the nose in white and a white line from the cockpit to the wing on a curve. It also had anti-glare paint in front of the

The Pandora in its final configuration, with the colours of the II Brigada Aérea of the Argentine Air Force, having received the engine mounts and nacelles of the rest of the I.A.35. Here it is seen after its accident on 12 August 1968 at Aeroparque Jorge Newbery. Despite the plane suffering only 5 per cent damage, it was not repaired.

The I.A.35-X-III Pandora after being completely modified, with new nose landing gear, an extra window in the passenger cabin, new engine nacelles and other changes.

Roll out of the I.A.35 Constancia at DINFIA. The plane received the serial LQ-FMA. Although this and the Pandora were intended to be sold on the civil market, they were not successful. *Photo archive Eduardo Ruiz*

The first plane delivered with the Tipo II configuration was E.a.-005, used by DINFIA for promotion with this paint scheme and designated I.A.35-II. The plane was the first to use the weapon pylons and received for some time extra fuel tanks on the wingtips, which were not adopted by other planes.

View of the I.A.35-II in which the underwing pylons can be seen with SCAR rockets, and four 50-kilo bombs under the fuselage. The plane has the opening for a camera on the belly, behind the bomb pylons, to be used for photo survey missions.

Installation diagram for the two Browning 12.7mm machine guns. The ammunition boxes could be changed in flight once they were emptied.

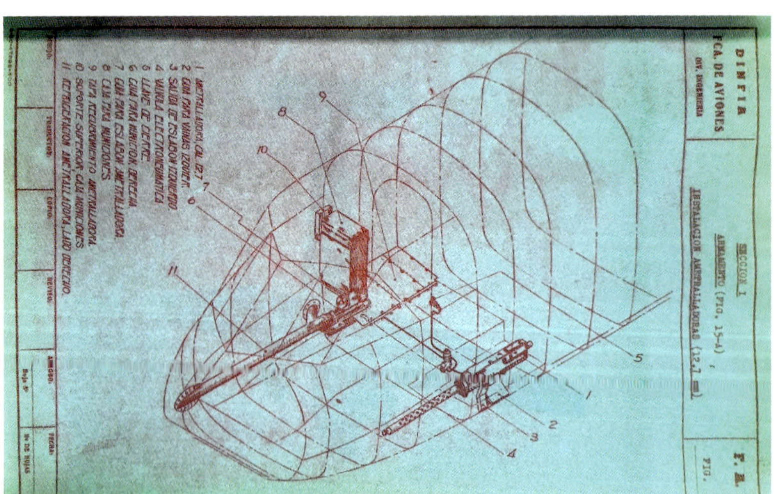

Sight on the I.A.35-II for rockets and machine guns, with the weapons panel on top.

Bomb sight, installed in a window in the nose of the plane.

windscreen. However, the design was not considered suitable for the commercial market because of its austere military origin, so in 1959 it was decided to develop an improved version. The engineers of the Instituto Aerotécnico organised two teams, one led by German engineers (no names appear on the documentation) and one by Argentine engineers.

The first worked using the first prototype, which received a nose like E.a.-003 (re-serialled E.a.-043 in 1958), I.Ae. R-19C engines of 720hp, a new nose landing gear with two smaller wheels, new redesigned engine nacelles, a third smaller window on the sides of the cabin and a small round one on the left side next to the toilet. In the cabin, a total of ten seats were installed with a small bar. The aircraft was rolled out in early 1960 and made its first flight on 28 May of that year, named I.A.35-X-III Pandora and with the serial T-550. Sometime later, the nose landing gear was changed again, returning to the original one of the Huanquero. After being evaluated by DINFIA, it was delivered to the Argentine Air Force in 1962, but the engine nacelles were also changed for those of the Huanquero. It was finally retired in 1968 after a minor accident.

The second group developed a different version, which was named Constancia, with a different metal nose and a new windscreen with two windows on the sides and two on the front. It also had a VIP interior. This aircraft made its first flight on 10 October 1959 with the serial LQ-FMA and remained in use by DINFIA until it crashed on 21 July 1963 near the city of El Dorado, Misiones, with eight occupants killed and one survivor. This was the only fatal accident in the history of the I.A.35. Meanwhile, a version with a longer fuselage, for fourteen passengers, was proposed, but never went beyond an idea.

Series production

Meanwhile, at the beginning of 1958 the first series production plane was finished, which was the first delivered of the Tipo II variant, now called I.Ae.35-II, for attack and bombing training. Besides the weapons of this version, two extra fuel tanks were added on the wingtips, while underwing pylons were installed that could fire one 5in rocket or four of 2.25in (a baggage container was planned to be carried there too, but it was never made) and four under-fuselage pylons for two 100kg bombs or four of 50kg. This plane was later serialled E.a.-005 and after tests it never used the extra tanks again. By mid-1958, together with Ea-001 to 004 and Ea-006 to 010 (of version II), it was delivered to the IV Brigada

E-503, formerly E.a.-003, seen at Aeroparque Jorge Newbery in Buenos Aires, with its development, the I.A.50 G-II behind, seen in 1968. Note the side window with a bubble and the two radiogoniometers for improved navigation, suggesting the plane was modified for photo survey. *Alberto Martín*

F-26 was one of the planes converted for photo survey in 1962. *Alberto Martín*

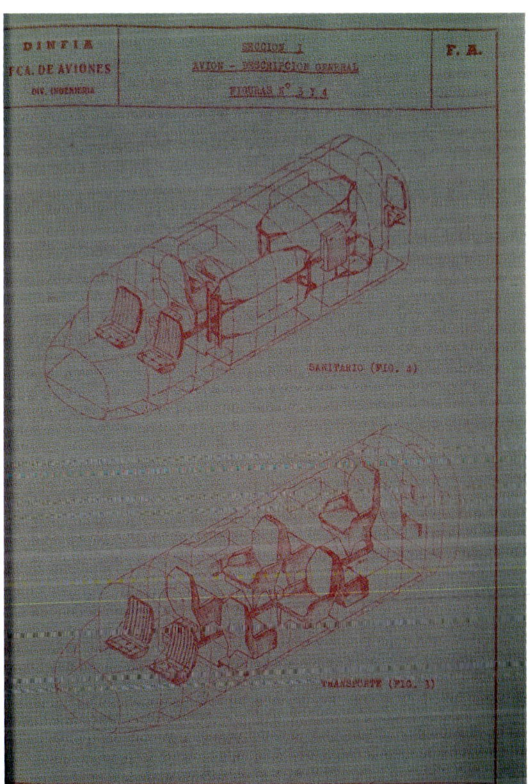

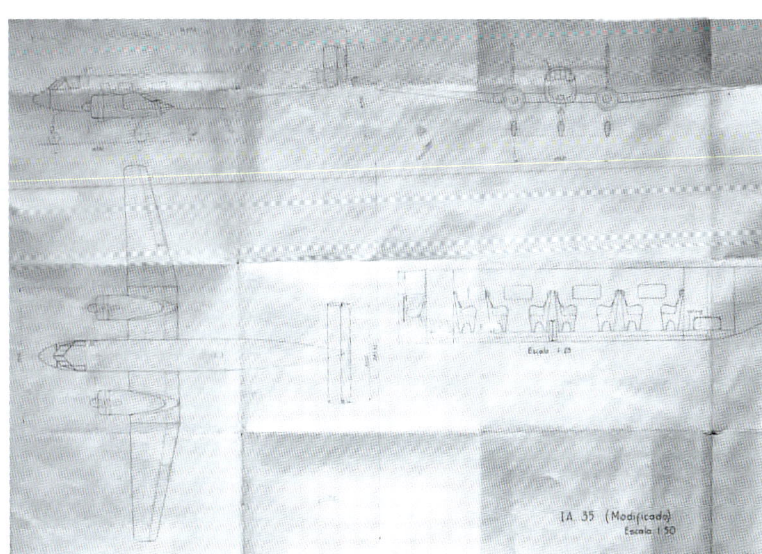

ABOVE Internal layout of the medical evacuation and transport versions.

RIGHT Plan of the proposed longer version for fourteen passengers. *Archive Ricardo Burzaco*

S-14 used for medical evacuation, seen at Aeroparque Jorge Newbery of Buenos Aires in 1968. *Alberto Martín*

ABOVE LQ-GMF with the badge of the Centro de Ensayos en Vuelo (Flight Test Centre) and the metal nose that the plane received in the 1960s.

Aérea of the Argentine Air Force at Mendoza city. This unit was retiring its last I.Ae.24 Calquins and were also receiving the first Morane-Saulnier MS.760 Parises built under licence by the FMA.

The next examples to leave the factory were five of version III (ambulance) in September, serialled S-11 to 15. During 1959, the IV Brigada Aérea continued receiving aircraft, up to E.a.-019, and on 17 June 1959 E.a.-001 to 019 were re-serialled E-501 to 519 (Ea-003 had the serial Ea-043 by then but became E-503). Deliveries continued and E-520 to 522 had been accepted before the end of the year.

Shortly before the end of the year, E-501, 502, 504, 506 and 513 were transferred to the II Brigada Aérea, of Paraná, Entre Ríos, where they were modified for photographic survey, becoming F-501, 502, 504, 506 and 513.

To demonstrate the capabilities of the Huanquero, on 11 July 1959 DINFIA held a firing demonstration with Huanqueros and Parises at the Escuela de Aviación Militar. The Huanqueros used were Ea-016, 017 and 018. On the first pass an I.Ae.35 dropped four 50kg bombs from 400m and at 265km/h, on the second Ea-016 and 017 fired their machine guns and Ea-018 launched eight 2.25in SCAR rockets in pairs, and on the last pass 017 launched rockets in pairs, 018 fired its machine guns and 016 launched all its rockets at the same time. SCAR training rockets were modified by Departamento Armamento of Instituto Aerotécnico of DINFIA with TNT warheads.

End of production

In 1960 only one plane was delivered, serialled E-523, and it was followed in 1961 by production up to E-529, with those from E-526 being equipped with R-19C engines, which were later installed in all the other planes.

In the late 1960s and early 1970s there was a lot of smuggling activity in northern Argentina, with planes flying from Bolivia and Paraguay with illegal cargo. To fight them, the Huanqueros of BAM Reconquista were used, as the case of A-317, carrying the inscription 'Represión del contrabando, cumpla las indicaciones' (Repression of smuggling, follow the instructions), intended to be read by the pilots of intercepted aircraft. *Photo archive Daniel Gómez*

ABOVE An I.A.35 Huanquero taxiing in at Buenos Aires in around 1972. An I.A.50 G-II is visible in the background. *Alberto Martín*

LEFT Huanqueros flying over the southern part of Tierra del Fuego, close to the city of Ushuaia, in the early 1970s, near the end of their career.

TS-12 received a new nose and windscreen in its later years, as seen here in 1972 during an aircraft exhibition at the Sociedad Rural campus in Buenos Aires. *Alberto Martín*

A Huanquero flying over the Pampas in the late 1960s or early 1970s.

In 1960 the national director of DINFIA, Brigadier Mayor Pereira, asked captain engineer Héctor Eduardo Ruiz, chief of Agrupación Reparación de Aviones, to study changing the engine of the Huanquero to the 870hp Turbomeca Bastan III turboprop. Ruiz worked on the aircraft with construction number 39 that was being finished at DINFIA, and as a result it was decided to suspend construction of the Huanquero, with production now planned to reach just forty-three aircraft instead of 100. It was decided that the last Huanquero would be E-532 (c/n 38),[4] with E-530 to 532 being delivered in 1962. The last of them left the factory on 16 July 1962. The following aircraft, of which four were already under construction, would be of the new Guaraní version (described in Chapter 28).

Based on this work, in June 1961 Reimar Horten worked on a proposal to change the engines of the existing I.Ae.35s to the Bastan and made a plan dated 28 June, keeping the rest of the plane unmodified, but this was not approved and the idea was abandoned.

Meanwhile, at the operational units all continued normally, with the Huanqueros serving mainly at the II Brigada Aérea for photo surveillance, the V Brigada Aérea of Villa Reynolds, San Luis province, for attack and light transport, the Destacamento Aeronáutico Militar (DAM) Reconquista, Santa Fe province, for the same mission and the DAM Mar del Plata, for liaison and light transport. Also, the I Brigada Aérea, the Taller Regional Río IV and the Comando General de Defensa Antiaérea had one aircraft. The ambulance versions were in service at the II Brigada, the V Brigada and DAM Reconquista.

By the end of 1961 another serial change took place when E-505 and 511 received the serials T-551 and 552 respectively, flying in the I Brigada Aérea together with T-550. Also, E-530 was delivered to DINFIA in February 1962, receiving the serial LQ-GMF and receiving sometime later a metallic nose. E-521 and E-526 to 529 were modified for photo survey and re-serialled F-20 and F-26 to 29 respectively. Also, F-501, 502, 504, 506 and 513 received the serials F-21 to 25 respectively.

Interior of a I. Ae.35 Huanquero for medical evacuation. *Archive Eduardo Ruiz*

[4] The quantity of aircraft built is a matter of discussion. In the archives of the FMA the quantities are two prototypes, one airframe for static tests, without a construction number, three pre-series planes with construction numbers 1, 2 and 3, and thirty-five series production aircraft, ending with the construction number 38, giving a total of forty planes that flew. However, in the units' annual reports only thirty-nine flying Huanqueros can be found (E-501 to 532, S-11 to 15, LQ-FMA and the first prototype, later T-550).

With the increased activities of guerrillas in Argentina, in the late 1960s the planes were all sent to the II Brigada Aérea and Base Aérea Militar (BAM) Reconquista and the serials of those, being in the E-5XX or T-5XX range, were changed to A-3XX, alluding to the attack mission.

The last modification of a Huanquero also took place in the late 1960s, when the example serialled TS-14 and used medical evacuation received a new nose, similar to the Constancia LQ-FMA.

Finally, the retirement of the type was scheduled for 31 December 1973 and the last flight of the type occurred when in March 1974 A-316 flew to the Museo Nacional de Aeronáutica.

I.Ae.39 project

At the same time of the development of the I.Ae.35, two other projects were proposed by Paul Klages, the first of which received the designation I.Ae.39 around 1951, but detailed design began in 1953. This was a derivative of the I.Ae.35 for eighteen passengers, with I.Ae. R-19C El Indio engines, of which only one drawing is known. This shows an aircraft with the same configuration as the I.Ae.35 but with a wider and longer fuselage, with six windows on each side. In the records of the factory for 1954 it is stated that a wooden model for wind tunnel tests was going to be built and in the one for 1955 it is reported plans were made and tests carried out on a model of the I.Ae.39. The project was abandoned shortly after when Klages left Argentina.

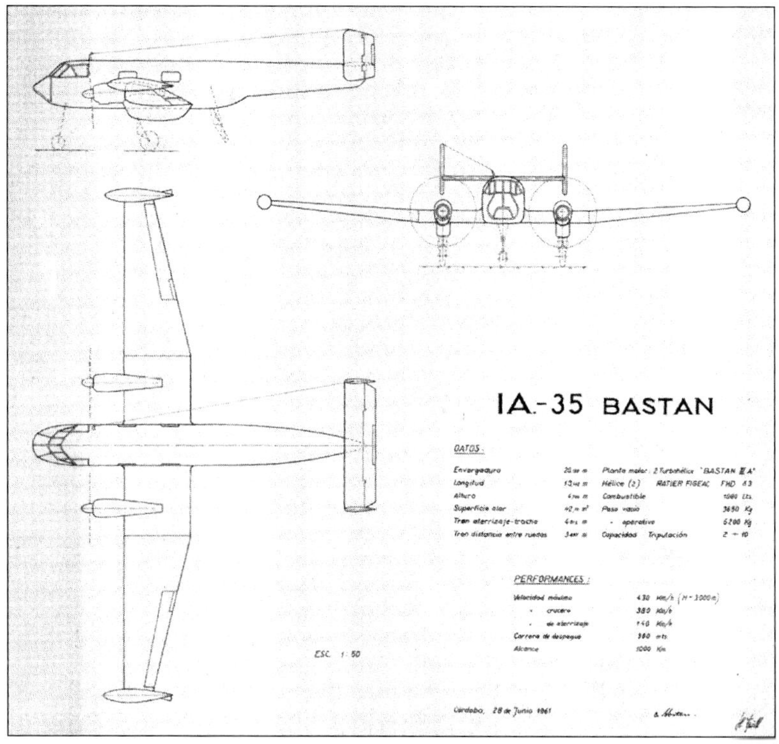

TOP RIGHT Three views of the proposal by Reimar Horten to modify the Huanqueros with Bastan engines, dated 28 June 1961. *Archive Diego Horten*

RIGHT Scheme of the proposed I.Ae.39 based on the I.Ae.35 but with a bigger fuselage for eighteen passengers.

BELOW Interior layout of the I.Ae.39 proposal.

20 I.Ae.36 Cóndor II

In 1948, among the projects that the Instituto Aerotécnico wanted to develop, the idea of a jet passenger aircraft started to evolve, with the intention of using it on transatlantic flights from Argentina to Europe, which were starting to be made by the local airline FAMA (Flota Aérea Mercante Argentina) with Avro Yorks and Lancastrians. Both Reimar Horten and Kurt Tank made their proposals, both having the same position of the engines, which were expected to be five Rolls-Royce Nene IIa of 2,267kg of thrust each or seven Derwent Vs of 1,590kg of thrust, all inside the rear part of the fuselage, with the air intakes in a ring around the fuselage.

Horten proposed a flying wing idea, with the wing on top of the fuselage and a small vertical fin on the tail. The fuselage was thin at the front, where the cockpit was located, and then became much wider in the area for the passenger cabin, which was lower than the cockpit and under the wing, and had thirty seats and a toilet. The crew was projected as five.

The wing area was 212m2, wingspan 32m and the height 5.9m. It had a payload capacity of 25 tons, plus up to 21 tons of fuel, and a maximum take-off weight of 57 tons. The cruise speed was expected to be 900km/h and a normal range was 5,900km, with a maximum of 7,750km.

Kurt Tank presented a more conventional design, with a low swept wing of 35° and a tail like the one of the Pulqui II. It had thirty seats for passengers, two fuel tanks and a space for the main landing gear separating the cabin from the engines, which were about 12m behind the end of the cabin, thus reducing the noise level for the passengers.

Its construction was to be all metal, and the fuselage was composed of eight compartments. The last of them was the tail segment, which was attached to the main fuselage, housing the engines with a common exhaust nozzle and the possibility of being easily removed to leave the engines exposed for maintenance. The front wheel had to rotate 90° when retracted.

The plane was 33.3m long, with a wingspan of 31m, a height of 7.65m, a wheelbase of 7.26m, and a fuselage diameter of 3.3m.

Both were designed with strong landing gear and big wheels with low-pressure tyres, be able to operate from unprepared runways, as there were not too many paved runways in Argentina by then. They also had pressurised cabins to operate at high altitude.

After studying both proposals, Tank's was chosen, but work progressed very slowly, despite wind tunnel models being made and tested, because he and his team were focused on the Pulqui II programme.

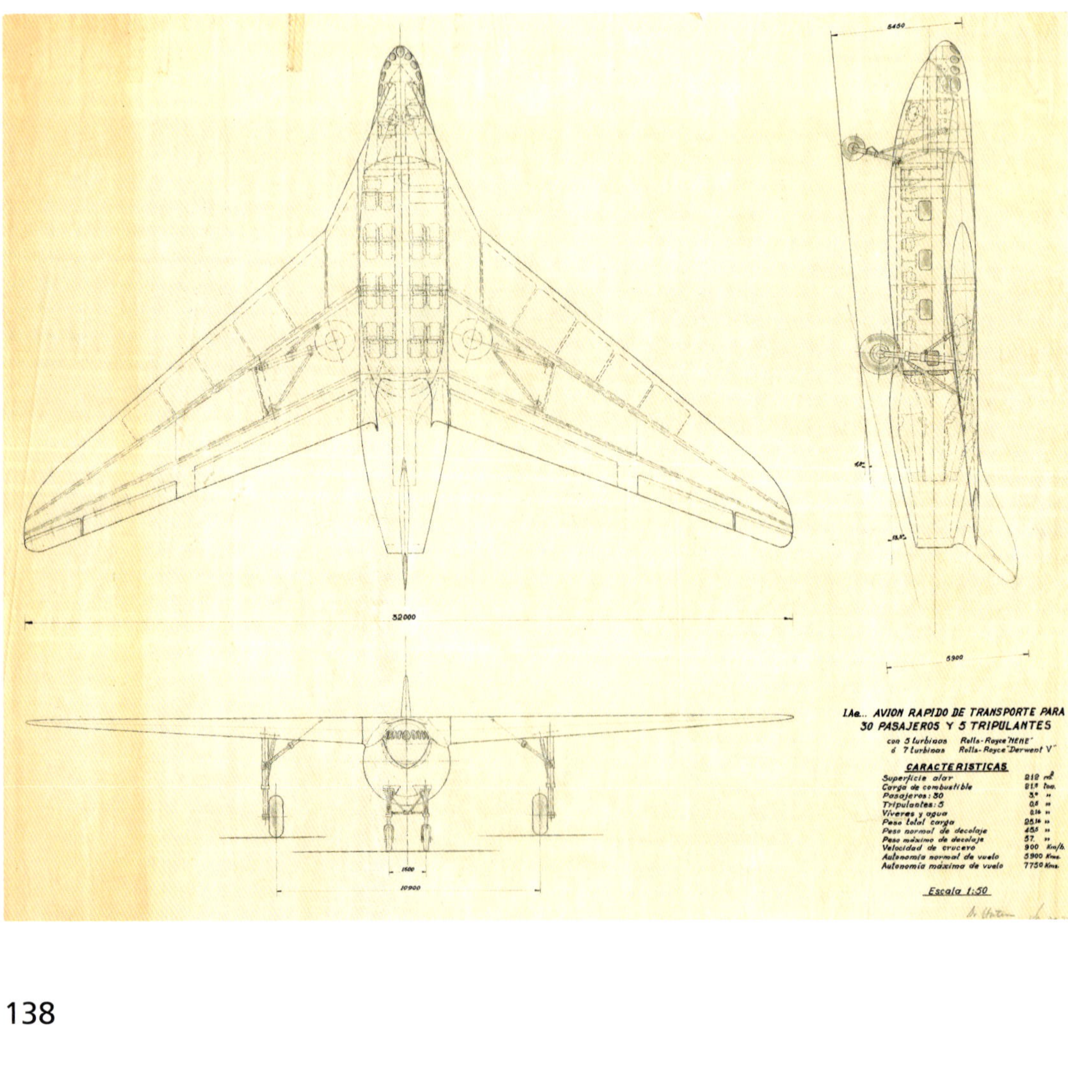

Reimar Horten's proposal for the passenger jet idea of 1948, with the type of flying wing he also used for the 'Caza sin cola' project. *Archive Diego Horten*

Modifications

By 1952 the project had received the designation I.Ae.36 and Tank unofficially called it Cóndor II as he considered it the successor to his Fw 200 Condor project from the 1930s. It was completely modified, with a longer fuselage of 29.66m instead of 27.05m, to carry up to forty passengers in a 10m-long cabin, instead of the 8m of the original version, as it was considered that, on transatlantic flights between Argentina and Europe in 1950, there was a need to carry twenty-nine passengers. However, by 1952 this was between thirty-two and thirty-five and this was expected to reach forty in the near term. The total length of the plane was now 34.80m.

The wingspan was increased to 34m with the possibility of adding extra fuel tanks on the wingtips, reaching an area of 120m2, and the sweep was increased, the height was now 9.5m and the wheelbase was reduced to 6m. The wing consisted of a central part, built also as a fuel tank with a 9,600-litres capacity, and two outer parts, also with the space to carry fuel, with another 5,900 litres each, totalling 21,400 litres, plus 3,800 in the fuselage.

Also, using results from the development of the Pulqui II, the tail was modified, with a lower stabiliser, just above the engine exhaust.

One of the main changes was made to the engines, as now it was planned to install the new SNECMA ATAR 101C turbojet of 2,800kg of thrust, reaching a total of 14,000kg instead of 11,300kg. The smaller diameter of the engines made also made it possible to reduce the diameter of the fuselage in this area, reducing air resistance.

The engines were arranged like a five-pointed star, with one on top, and with an inclination of 10° from the longitudinal axis of the plane. To prevent the loss of thrust from the engines and take advantage of the dynamic flight pressure, it was necessary to remove the boundary layer in front of the air intake. In front of each inlet a channel was provided for the suction of the boundary layer and these five channels flowed into a common channel, which was simultaneously a tube that supported the weight of the engines and reached the exit of the turbine nozzles. The jet of the turbines would produce a strong suction of the boundary layer, which would be mixed with the exhaust gases. This reduced the air resistance of the fuselage by the aspiration of the boundary layer, and reduced the resistance of the engines by them not having nacelles. Increasing the air flow and the resulting performance of the jet would reduce fuel consumption, and if an engine failed there would be no alterations to the flight axis. If an engine failed or needed to be stopped, its air intake could be closed. The covering of the fuselage around the engines had inspection hatches for maintenance.

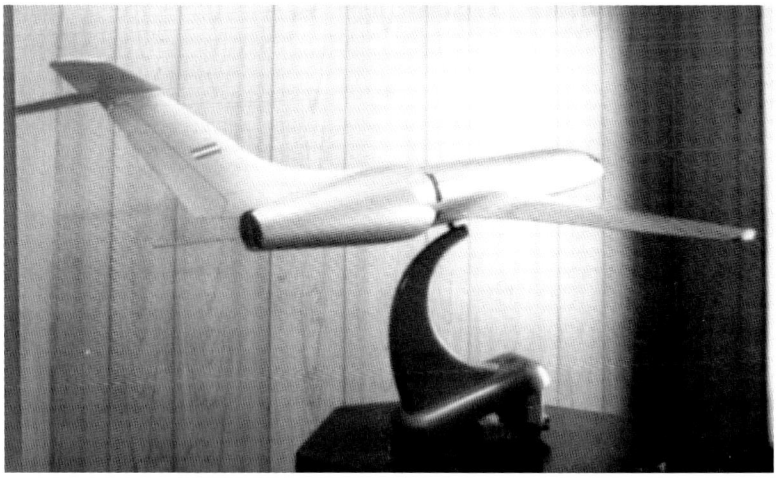

Model of the I. Ae.36 in its first configuration with a T tail. *Archive Ricardo Burzaco*

The project also considered the possibility of using other engines of more power, including three Bristol Olympus of 4,800kg of thrust each, which could reduce the fuel consumption by 25 per cent, increasing the range by 30 per cent.

The landing gear was also changed from single big wheels to two smaller ones in both the nose and main gears.

The nose would have a radar and a landing light, while an autopilot was planned. The crew comprised a pilot, co-pilot, mechanic, and radio operator. The cabin was pressurised, and expected for an overpressure of 0.65 atmospheres to have at 16,000m the conditions found at 2,500m.

The front part of the passenger cabin had a wardrobe for the crew and one for the passengers, plus a small bar with a refrigerator, a toilet, and a seat for a stewardess. The area for the passengers was divided into five small cabins, each with two rows of four facing seats with a folding table between them. It was expected there would be the possibility to configure the cabin with seats that could be converted into beds, for a total of thirty passengers, or it could be configured with all the seats looking forward or rearward. The possibility of showing movies during the flight was also considered. In the rear of the cabin was a second toilet. The luggage was carried in a compartment below the passenger cabin, which was also

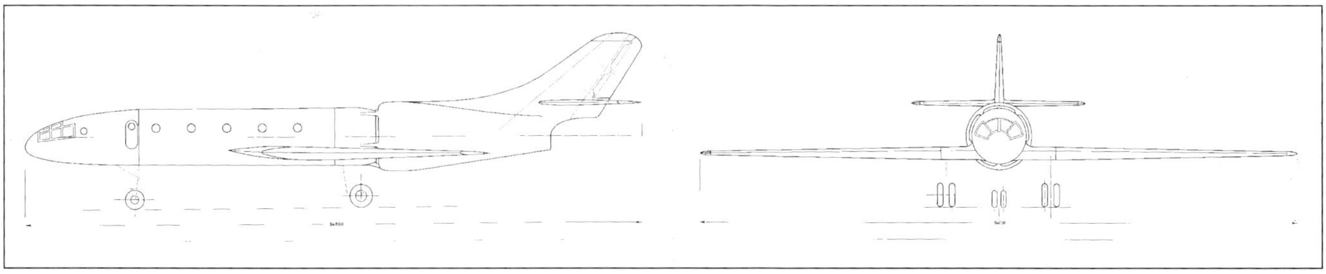

Views of the improved design of 1952 for Atar 101C engines or Bristol Olympus, with new tail and landing gear design.

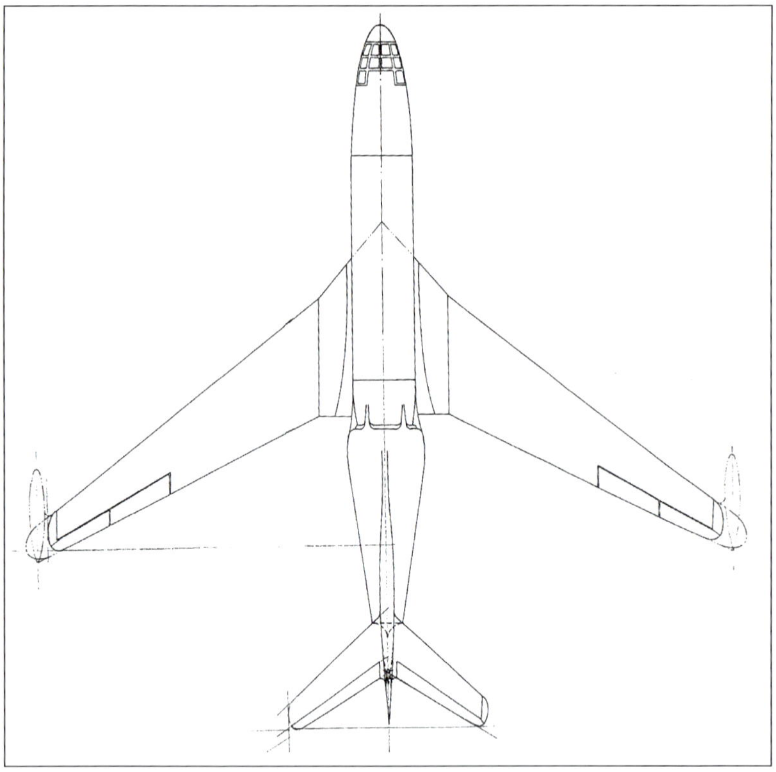

ABOVE LEFT View from above of the design of 1952, with the wing modified at its root and including the extra tanks on the wingtips.

ABOVE RIGHT Model of the later version, but with the horizontal stabiliser in the middle of the vertical fin.

pressurised, had a volume of 17.3m3 and a capacity of 2,700kg.

Behind the cabin was a fuel tank with 3,800 litres of capacity, some of the aircraft's systems and the space for the main landing gear.

Calculations were made that the plane could fly a leg between Natal and Dakar of 3,100km carrying a payload of 4,500kg, this being equivalent to forty passengers and 1,200kg of luggage. If Bristol Olympus engines were installed, the range would be 4,430km.

The empty weight, equipped, was 28,000kg, while the maximum take-off weight was 48,400kg, with a typical payload of 4,000kg plus 16,000kg of fuel (20,000 litres). Extra fuel tanks with another 5,000 litres could be installed in the central part of the wing, increasing the maximum take-off weight to 52,500kg and increasing the range to 4,350km. With Olympus engines this figure was of 5,655km.

The plane was expected to have a cruise speed of 900km/h and a maximum speed of over 1,000km/h, with a service ceiling of about 46,500ft. In case of engine failure, the airliner would fly with only two of them, keeping a speed of 550km/h and a height of 18,000ft, and it being possible to fly up to 1,600km before landing.

Construction of the first prototype began in 1953, but progress was slow and work stopped when Kurt Tank left the country in 1955. The project was cancelled, with the built parts, which were mostly of the rear fuselage, scrapped.

21 **I.A.37, I.A.48 and other Horten jet flying wings**

Researching fast flying wings

Reimar Horten, along with his brother Walther, had been working since the 1930s on the development of flying wings to reach high speeds, advancing in the study of large sweep angles up to the H XIII model, a glider with a wing with 60° of sweep that flew satisfactorily about twenty times. From this derived the H XIIIb fighter project proposed together with the H X for the Volksjäger programme of the Luftwaffe, which was never built.

Parallel to these investigations with high-angle swept wings, other investigations were made into high-speed flight.

As a delta wing approached the speed of sound, the wing root experienced an increase in aerodynamic drag, before the wing itself and. On the other hand, with the increase of the sweep angle there was a drop in the maximum lift, so it was logical to think that the solution to the problem was to increase the sweep angle at the root of the wing. Thus, for example, with a swept wing with an angle of 35° combined with a root of more than 60°, there was an increase in aerodynamic drag, initially at the root, when approaching the speed of sound. To investigate the flight qualities of aircraft of this type, they modified an HO-II glider, in which the swept angle of the root was combined, also mounting on it the air intakes for turbines. The results of these tests served as the basis for the H X project.

Meanwhile, the Hortens began to design a glider to evaluate a wing with 70° of sweep, but the end of the war stopped the work, which Reimar Horten resumed as soon as he arrived in Argentina. There, together with the engineer José Krasinski and mathematician Karl Nickel, he began to study different wing configurations in the wind tunnels of the Instituto

LEFT AND FAR LEFT
Different shapes of wings tested by Reimar Horten on the wind tunnels of the Instituto Aerotécnico. At least eighteen of them still exist. *Santiago Rivas*

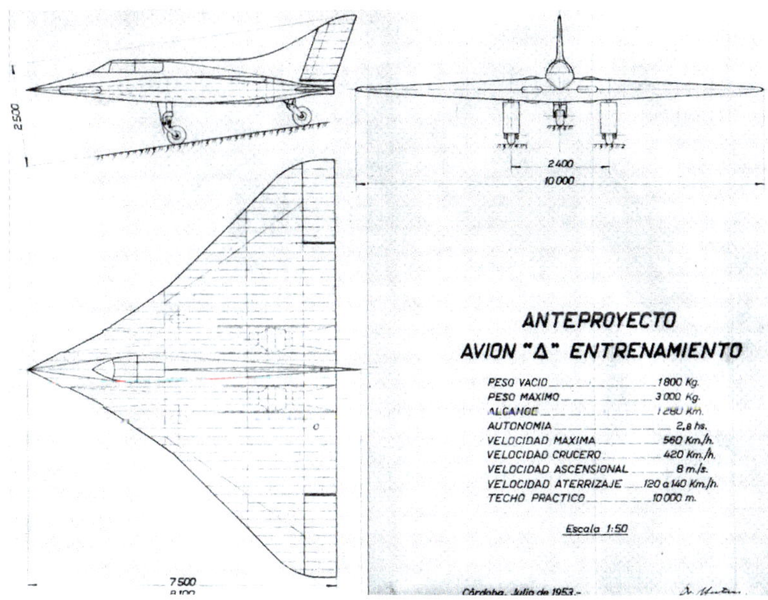

Aerotécnico, also working actively on the design and construction of the supersonic tunnel. Currently, in the facilities of the Centro de Investigación Aplicada of the Argentine Air Force, which occupies the factory's wind tunnel buildings, at least eighteen models of different wing configurations that Horten evaluated in the wind tunnel are preserved.

Aeroplane proposals

Meanwhile, as stated in Chapter 17, Horten had submitted in 1949 a proposal for an advanced training and reconnaissance aircraft powered by a Derwent V engine and two seats in tandem. Although the project was abandoned in 1951, in 1953 Horten returned to the idea of a delta-wing training jet, with two air intakes in the wing root, as proposed in the HO-II project, with a tandem two-seater cabin built in wood and metal, powered by two Turbomeca Marboré II turbines or with pulse jets that were being developed at the Fábrica de Motores a Reacción of IAME. The aircraft would have an empty weight of 1,800kg and a maximum of 3,000kg, a range of 1,280km, a maximum speed of 560km/h, a cruise of 420km/h, a landing speed of between 120 and 140km/h and a climb rate of 8m/s, with a service ceiling of 10,000m.

At the same time, in 1949 Horten had also presented a project for an advanced transport and training aircraft for two pilots and up to eight passengers, with the same wing configuration and vertical planes as the Caza sin cola, also powered by a Derwent V engine, where only the cockpit changed. This project was not approved.

Using as his H X project for the Volksjäger programme as a basis, Horten presented on 11 August 1952 another proposal, this time for a single-seat

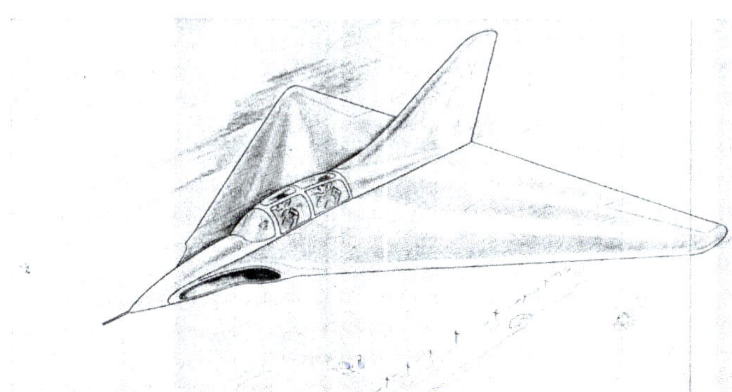

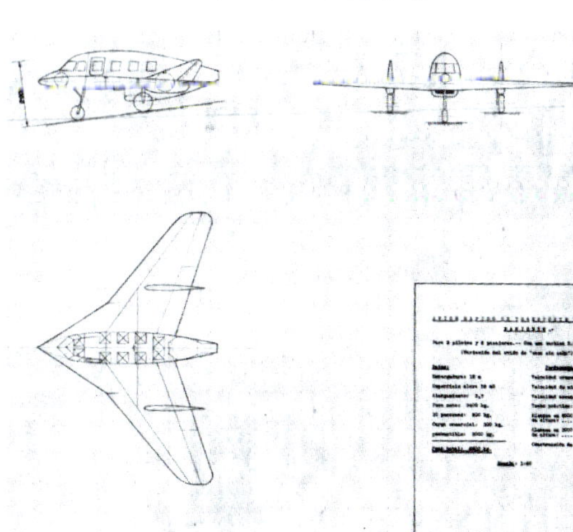

ABOVE AND LEFT
Three views and a diagram of the proposed training jet with delta wing of 1949 and again in 1951. *Archive Diego Horten*

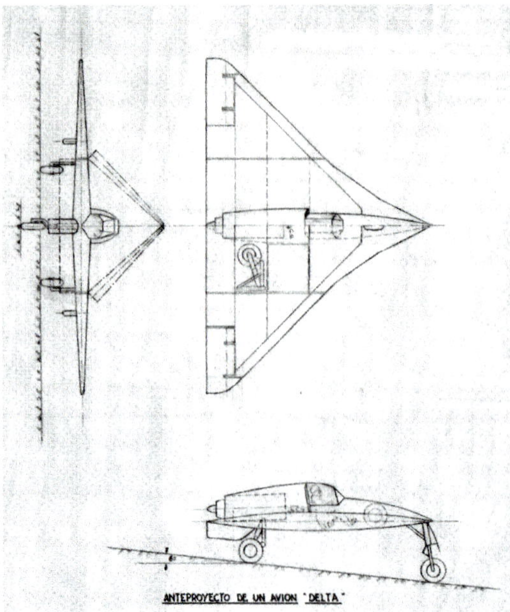

Based on the H X proposal for the Volksjäger programme in Germany, in 1952 he proposed this flying wing trainer made in wood. *Archive Diego Horten.*

training flying wing made of a metal structure covered with wood, with folding wings, and that could be equipped with a Turbomeca Marboré II turbojet or an Aspin II turbofan, both of 350kg of thrust. The plane was 5.5m long and 2.1m high. It had a wingspan of 8m, a wing area of 21m2 and an empty weight of 700kg. With Aspin II engines the performance expected was a service ceiling of 10,000m, a range of 1,760km, a maximum speed of 435km/h, a take-off distance of 430m, a landing speed of 93km/h and an endurance of four and a half hours. With the Marboré II engine, the plane was expected to reach 14,000m, have a range of 1,260km, a maximum speed of 565km/h, a take-off distance of 350m, the same landing speed and an endurance of two and a half hours. This project was not approved either, even though the Argentine Air Force was showing interest in a jet trainer for the pilots that went on to fly the Meteor and it was expecting to receive the Pulqui II soon.

Launching a delta-wing model at San Roque Lake around 1953.

Supersonic interceptor

While his proposals for jet flying wings were not approved due to the focus on the Pulqui II and the car and motorbike production at IAME, Horten continued his research on high-speed flying wings to reach supersonic speeds. In 1953 he started to work with 5 to 20kg models, which were launched on the shore of San Roque lake, near the city of Villa Carlos Paz, where Horten went to live, which was very close to the east of the factory. With them he estimated stability data and compared it with what he found in the wind tunnel, making more than 200 flights in which the models were launched at more than 200km/h. Some of the models were full delta wings and some had air intakes for jet engines, as well as two exhausts. He also tested the use of leading edge flaps (slats) on some of them.

Horten also studied the different possible engines that such an aircraft would need to reach supersonic speeds, considering ramjets, but he considered these had not been studied sufficiently and should be combined with a jet. He considered that the pulse jet, as used in the V1 flying bombs, produced enough power and could be used together with a ramjet, but they consumed too much fuel. He concluded that only a turbojet could produce enough power and have low enough fuel consumption to fly for an hour at very high speeds in the stratosphere.

In 1953, together with Karl Nickel, Horten made the first layouts of what he projected as a supersonic interceptor, to be equipped with two I.A.T. 22 turbojet engines that were being proposed by the Fábrica de Motores a Reacción (which were never built in the end) and to reach supersonic speed would also have a liquid fuel rocket with 1,000kg of thrust. The aircraft was expected to have a maximum speed of around 1,300km/h, with a cruise of 1,100km/h, a maximum range of 2,000km and two hours' endurance, a landing speed of 150km/h and a service ceiling of 15,000m.

Interestingly, during those years, Horten exchanged a lot of mail with Willy Messerschmitt and Marcel Dassault, the first of whom had been working since 1952 on the Hispano Aviación HA-300 supersonic jet project, and the second was working on the MD.550 Mystére Delta, both making use of delta wings on designs that were similar to what Horten was developing.

In 1954 a wooden glider was built with a metallic airframe covered with wood, to test the results obtained with the launched models and in the wind tunnel. It was designated I.A.37 and it was basically a delta wing, with symmetric profile (the upper and lower sides were identical) with the pilot in prone position because the intention was to test the wing without the alterations that a cockpit could make to the air flow. This position was also chosen because, for take-off and landing, due to the design of the wing, the plane must fly at very high angles of attack, so a pilot in normal position would have very reduced visibility. For a powered prototype, Horten considered that, because it was not possible to use an ejection seat, the whole cabin must be used as an escape system at high altitudes, with a parachute used to land.

The wing was 10m long with a span of 11m. It had a sweep angle of 63.5°, with an area of 48m2.

In May 1954 the glider was exhibited for the first time and on 1 October it made its first flight, towed by a Junkers Ju 52/3m serialled T-153. The pilot was Captain Conan Doyle, but on the following flights 1st Lts Balado, Rossell and González and German pilot Hans Scheidhauer of Horten's team all piloted the aircraft. Flight performance was excellent, especially during take-off and landing, which were very smooth with a short run with the nose up, so a longer nose landing gear was adopted.

After some tests, it was decided to build a powered prototype, but the problem was that the I.A.T. 22 turbine project was progressing too slowly and there were no other engines powerful enough and with the reduced size planned to fit in the spaces reserved for the two engines on the prototype.

Flying testbed

This meant that in 1955 the project was reformulated, with the decision to keep the I.A.37 for experimentation equipped with a single Rolls-Royce Derwent V engine in a modified fuselage. As it was not possible to reach supersonic speeds with this engine, the aim of the test version would be to study the characteristics of flight at subsonic speeds with delta wings and research the necessary specifications to develop a supersonic aeroplane. With the Derwent V it was expected to reach a speed of 800km/h and have a service ceiling of 11,600m, with a landing speed of 110km/h.

The change of engine meant a modification was made in early 1955 to the belly of the glider with a fairing for the space of the Derwent V, but when in July a storm damaged the tail of the Ju 52/3m used to tow it, the flights were stopped. Also, the revolution of September and the change of government meant that work was suspended as occurred with all the other projects while the factory was restructured and all the work carried out between 1946 and 1955 was analysed.

During that time, Horten decided to make two big changes. One was to alter the position of the pilot from prone to seated on an ejection seat in a pressurised cockpit. The other change was to modify the landing gear with a big nosewheel located almost in the centre of the plane, and two smaller wheels under the wings.

To reduce the take-off and landing speeds, it was considered that the plane must have a high angle of attack, to take advantage of the lift of the wing and the power from the engines. For that, the rear landing gear was located closer to the trailing edge

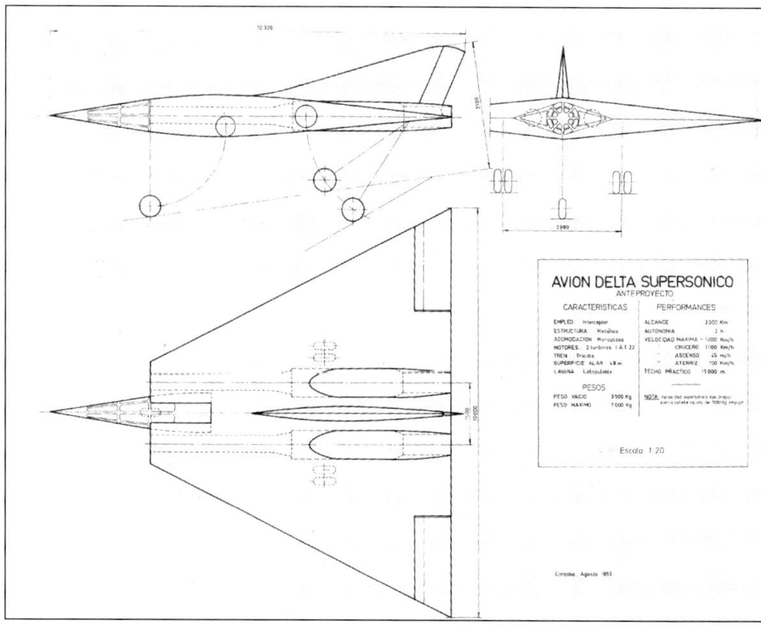

Initial design of August 1953 for a supersonic jet fighter that evolved to become the I.A.37.

and only supported 40 per cent of the weight of the plane, while the nose landing gear was close to the centre of gravity and supported 60 per cent. Also, there was a system to extend the nose undercarriage leg, so the plane on the ground had an angle of attack of 4°, but for take-off and landing this could be extended to 23°. The calculations made stated that, with no angle of attack, the plane must have a landing speed of 250km/h, but with 23° it could make a three-point landing at 129km/h or, with a maximum angle of attack of 32°, touching first with the rear wheels, it could approach at 117km/h.

To improve the visibility of the pilot in flight and while taxiing with high angles of attack, windows were planned to be installed on the sides of the cabin, and another window was planned for the floor of the cabin with the installation of a vertical photo camera in place of the guns.

Work on defining the characteristics of the first prototype with all these changes began in April 1956, while it was decided that, besides the use of the I.A.37 as a test bed, the type could be also used for training, for which six different versions were planned:

The first to train experimental pilots to fly delta-winged aeroplanes, with a single seat and the ability to perform aerobatics.

Construction of the I.A.37 glider. The structure was of metal, covered by wood. *Archive Diego Horten*

The I.A.37 glider was built with the same shape of the original project for an interceptor, with the jet exhaust for two turbojet engines. As was adopted by IAME in those times, the prototypes received the letter P behind their designation.

The second would be a two-seater for basic training on jet aircraft, without ejection seats.

The third would be single-seater with a Martin-Baker ejection seat described in 1957 as a model 'D/Sk/2511' but it must have been a type between the Mark 2 to 5, which were the ones available between 1953 and 1957.

The I.A.37 glider with the air brakes deployed. Behind is the Avro Lincoln serialled LV-ZEI, which was modified as a transport.

When it was decided to equip the I.A.37 with a Derwent V engine and use it only as a subsonic testbed, the glider received a fairing on the belly to simulate the installation of the engine.

This version was planned for training in fighter and attack manoeuvres and would be able to reach up to 1,100km/h or Mach 0.93 in a dive.

The fourth would be for gunnery training, both for air to air and air to ground, armed with two Hispano Suiza 804 20mm guns.

The fifth would be to train the firing of rockets of different calibres, with a maximum speed of 800km/h.

The sixth and last would be for reconnaissance, with the installation of a photo camera instead of weapons.

In July 1956 the glider, which had been grounded for a year by then, was sent to the workshops to receive the new cockpit with the pilot seated, with the work being finished in November.

However, no flights were made until at least March 1957, leading to a complaint by the head of the factory, and testing was resumed during the year. Horten worked from February with ten draftsmen to decide the final design of the prototype, estimating that he would finish the blueprints by May 1958. He suggested that, if by February 1958 there could be 150 workers available to start the construction of the prototype and an airframe for static tests, they could both be ready for December of that year, making the first flight before the year end.

In 1956 Horten had started to work on a more advanced design, with which to attain supersonic speeds using more powerful engines, in which he expected to use a Rolls-Royce Avon with afterburner or something similar. Wind tunnel tests were made for this model, but no further work was carried out, and Horten decided to move on with a completely different design.

The I.A.37 glider flew for about fifty hours between 1957 and 1959, but Horten could not get the support he requested to produce his final design in 1958, although he continued with wind tunnel tests in 1959, planning the construction of the prototype in 1960. In the end the project was cancelled in that year. The glider was scrapped after 1962.

Personnel of IAME posing with the glider after the new nose was installed.

Four-seat versions

Based on his studies with the I.A.37 project for training, in early 1957 Horten developed a proposal for a four-seat plane for training and liaison, changing the forward fuselage for a bigger one, with a pressurised cabin. It had the singularity that, to improve visibility on during take-off and landing, which was poor due to the high angle of attack, the whole cabin could be inclined nose down, using a hydraulic piston to move it. The engines would be two small turbojets like the Turbomeca Marboré II that he already considered for his flying wing trainers. The landing gear was similar to the final proposal for the I.A.37, to be extended during take-off and landing. However, there were some modifications, as the extensible main wheel under the belly was not stored in the fuselage and remained retracted under the belly. Also, the rear undercarriage was much smaller, with its function mainly being to keep the plane stable on the ground.

This proposal evolved into a different one in October of that same year, in which the engine was again a Derwent V, so the rear fuselage was enlarged, and the landing gear was more like that on the I.A.37. Also, the cabin was redesigned, with a new nose, windscreen, and side windows. The length was 8.165m and the height 3.31m with the nosewheel in the horizontal position.

Although this aircraft was not intended for supersonic flight but had a delta wing that had limitations at low speeds, as well as the described high angle of attack needed for take-offs and landings, Horten started to work on a more conventional solution, with a normal swept wing instead of a delta one. This plane had an annular air intake for the engine, behind the cabin and all around the fuselage, a T-tail, and a fuselage 8.4m long, a total length of 9.75m and a height of 3.5m.

On 20 December 1957 Horten presented a study comparing the delta solution and the conventional one for his four-seat jet. In his comparison, he stated that the plane was intended to carry four people up to 3,000km. Now, both planes had the same cabin design and engine intake, which was the same as the conventional wing proposal, with the delta version being much shorter than the previous design.

The type with a conventional wing had 2,400kg of empty weight, a wingspan of 9.4m, a wing area of 18m2, a fuel capacity of 1,650kg and a take-off weight of 4,450kg. The glide distance to height loss ratio was expected to be 13.6, the take-off distance of 880m without wind, needing a speed of 226km/h. It would be able to reach a speed of Mach 0.9, have a maximum ceiling of 13,000m, a landing speed of 171km/h and a fuel consumption for a flight of 1,500km of 0.64kg/km.

The delta version had an empty weight of 2,050kg, 8m wingspan, a wing area of 21m2, 1,150kg of fuel capacity and a take-off weight of 3,600kg. The glide relation was expected to be 13.06, the take-off distance of 640m with no wind, with a speed of 213km/h. It would be able to reach a speed of Mach 0.92 with a 15,000m maximum ceiling, a landing speed of 147km/h and fuel consumption for a flight of 1,500km of 0.43kg/km.

Horten's conclusions were that, while the construction of both planes was equally complex, the delta design was 110 to 130km/h faster at

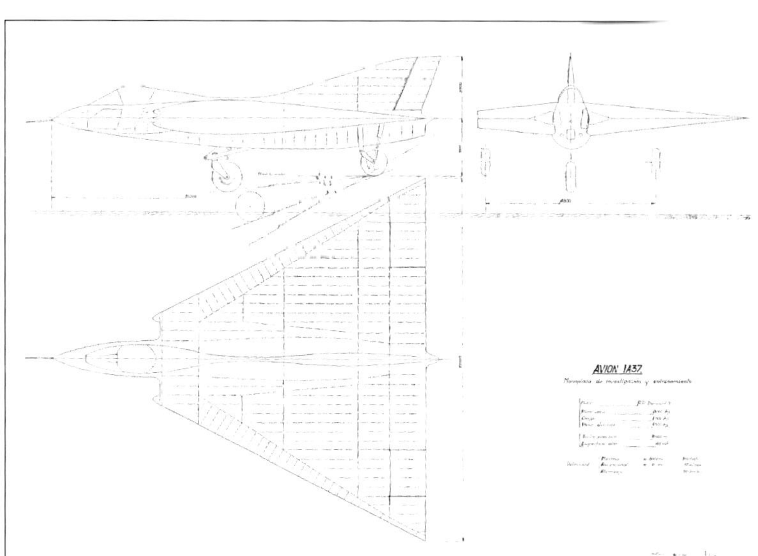

Three views of the I.A.37 made on 18 January 1958, with the new nose and new landing gear in retracted and extended positions. Note the side windows drawn on the sides of the cabin and the opening below the cabin, seen in the front view, for the camera for photo reconnaissance versions.

The I.A.37 with its new nose looked completely different to the original glider. Despite progress on the design, budget cuts from 1958 onwards led to the cancellation of the project in 1960.

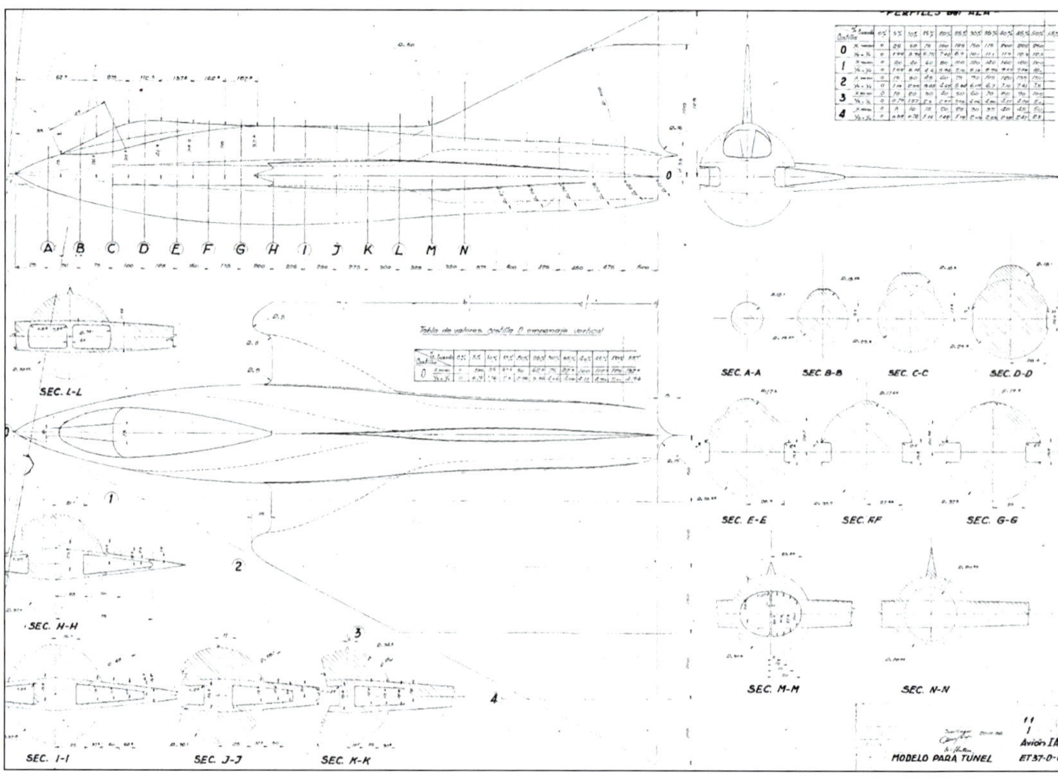

LEFT Three views for a wind tunnel model of an idea by Horten to make a bigger I.A.37 to equip it with more a powerful engine for supersonic flights.

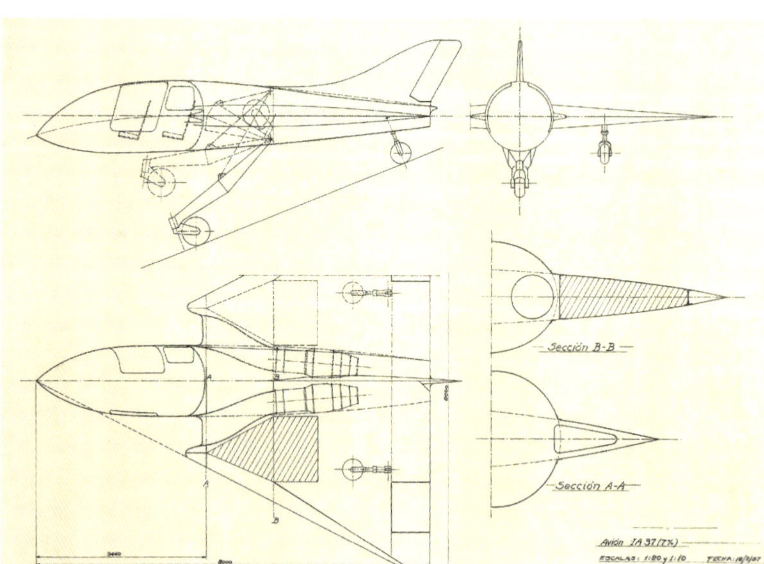

BELOW The first idea for a four-seat training and liaison version of the I.A.37, dated 12 February 1957. *Archive Diego Horten*

cruise speed, with lower fuel consumption and a slower landing speed.

In the end, none of the proposals received the approval of the factory and they were abandoned.

I.A.48

After progressing in his studies of supersonic flight and seeing the limitations of the I.A.37 project, in 1958 Horten started to work on a much more advanced two-seater design for multiple purposes, with an ogival delta wing with a sweep of 66° 15' at the root, a surface area of 43.08m2 and a wingspan of 7m. It would have been powered by two Rolls-Royce Avon RA.16 engines each of 4,082kg of thrust (a version of the Avon intended for the Comet and later cancelled) in nacelles mounted under the wing, like the engines of the B-58 Hustler. The fuselage of 14m of length would accommodate two pilots with ejection seats, with a fuel tank behind

In October 1963 Werner von Braun visited Argentina and DINFIA. In the picture, he is being shown a model of the I.Ae.37.

Comparison of the delta-wing and conventional-wing proposals for the four-seat plane.

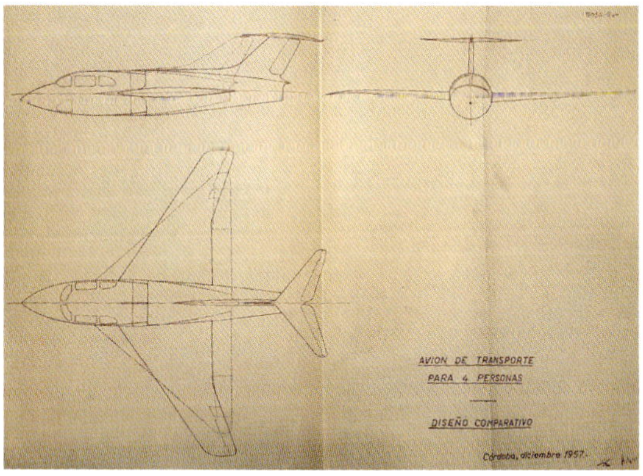

the cockpit for 5,000 litres. The total height of the plane was 4.19m.

The empty weight given in one of his reports was 7,000kg, with 800kg of weapons, 200kg for the crew and 4,000kg for the fuel, making a total of 12,000kg.

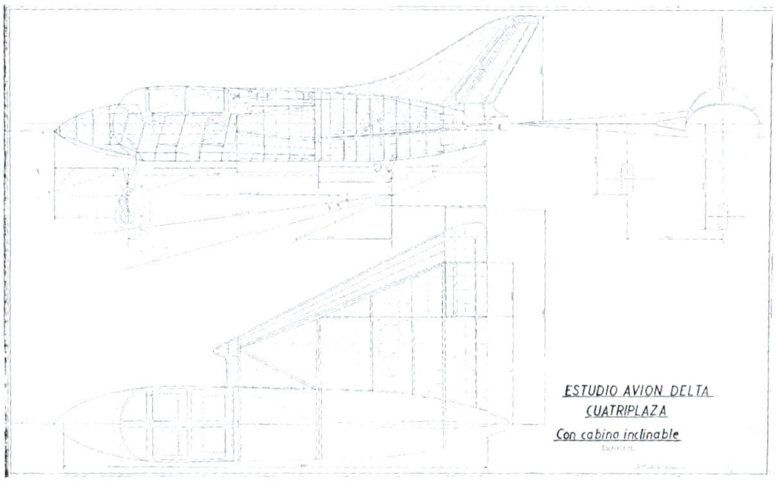

Second layout for a four-seat version of the I.A.37, where the inclinable cabin is shown.

In another report he stated an empty weight of 6,000kg, 10,000kg of fuel, 600kg of weapons, 200kg for a single pilot and a total weight of 16,800kg.

The aircraft was expected to reach 2,000km/h at 11,000m, a cruise speed of 1,700km/h and a dive speed of 2,500km/h, with a climb rate of 70m/s, a service ceiling of 20,000m, an endurance of two hours and a range of 3,200km. The take-off speed was 220km/h and the landing one 150km/h.

The weapons planned were four 30mm cannon or two cannon and two 400kg bombs.

Work progressed on the design during 1959, including wind tunnel tests, and the Argentine Navy showed some interest in operating the type off its recently purchased ARA *Independencia* aircraft carrier. However, the carrier was too small and the catapult not powerful enough for this design, so Horten proposed a system to tilt the exhaust of the engines up to 45° to the ground to increase the lift at slow speed. The project was too ambitious at a time when budget cuts were made in defence after Arturo Frondizi became president of Argentina in May 1958, and the I.A.48 project was cancelled in 1960 together with work on the I.A.37.

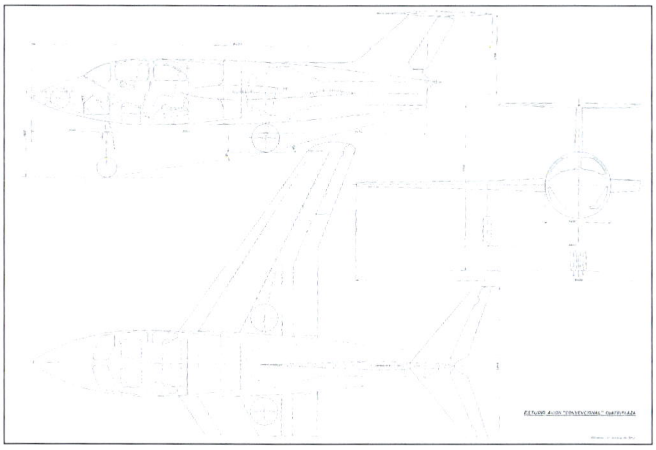

Conventional version of the four-seat jet plane, with a different wing, a T-tail and annular air intake for the engine.

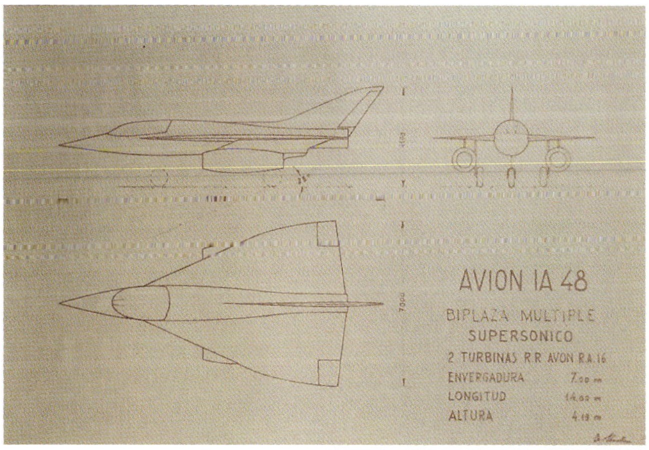

Three views of the I.A.48 project.

22 I.Ae.38

Reimar and Walther Horten started working on big flying wings when in 1939 their brother Wolfram, who was carrying out maritime reconnaissance patrols over the sea before the Second World War started, asked them to develop a new type with better performance for that mission, as if war broke out they would be much needed. Reimar then developed the H VIII, which was a flying wing with a 40m wingspan, powered by six Junkers Jumo 210s of 650hp, and with the capacity to fly for up to twenty-four hours with three crew members, but the project was never built.

Between 1943 and 1945 they returned to this project, but now for transport missions, adding a fuselage with a cargo hold in the centre of the wing and using six Argus S-10 engines.

Later on, in late 1944, they were asked to design a long-distance bomber capable of carrying up to 4,000kg of bombs to a distance of 11,000km, to reach New York from Germany. Unbeknown to them, the payload was expected to be an atomic bomb. They designed the H 18 as a flying wing powered by six Junkers Jumo engines, but after the Luftwaffe included Junkers engineers plus some from Messerschmitt on the project, they decided to locate the engines under the fuselage instead of putting them inside, and added a vertical fin. The Hortens called this new design the H 18-B, which had a 40m wingspan, with four Heinkel-Hirth HeS 011 turbojets placed under the fuselage in nacelles that also contained the fixed landing gear. Although their design was finally chosen and Herman Göering approved further works in March 1945, asking for a prototype to be ready before the year end, all work ceased when the war ended in May.

After they were captured, they were taken to London in April and, with the British interested in developing a transatlantic passenger aircraft, on 27 August the Royal Aircraft Establishment (RAE) asked them if they could use the basis of their H VIII to design such aircraft. After they accepted, in September they were contracted to develop the plane at the AVA facilities they had in Göttingen, Germany. By December they presented a proposal

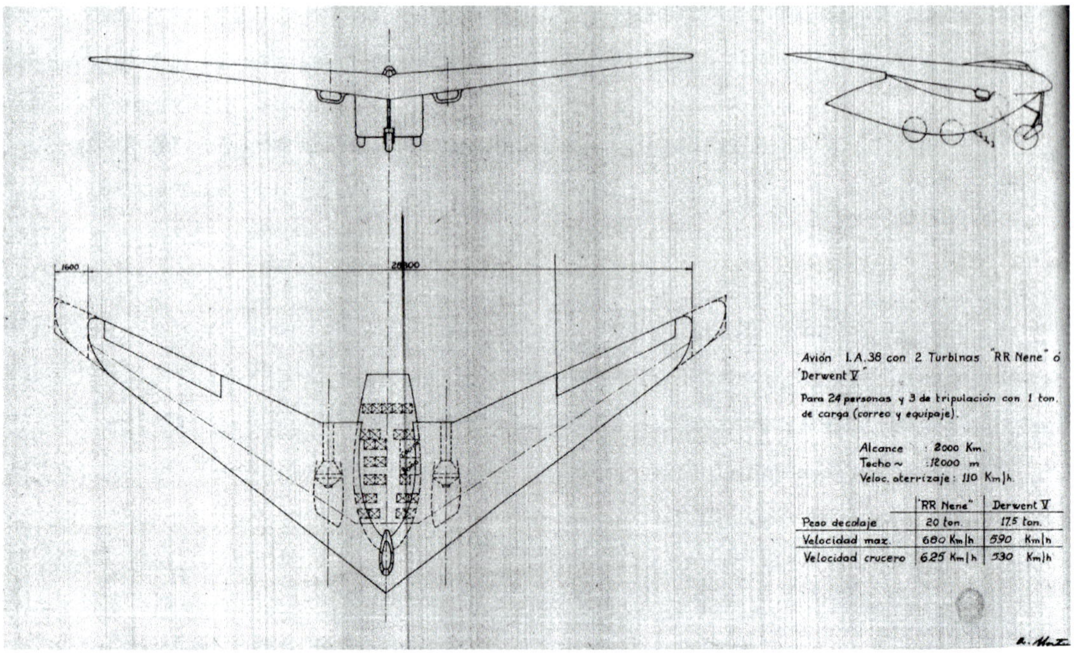

Plan of the proposed jet version of the I.Ae.38, with Derwent V or Nene II engines, for twenty-four passengers. *Archive Diego Horten*

Side view of the fuselage of the I. Ae.38, with the details of the cockpit and the cargo hold.

for a flying wing based on the original H VIII design but with an 80m wingspan, with a capacity of 102 passengers carried within the wing, with windows only on top of the fuselage and in the leading edge. The crew would be in a small cabin above the wing.

The layout did not convince the British, who asked that all the passengers have windows, so they returned to the layout of the cargo H VIII developed between 1943 and 1945, but changed the engines for four Rolls-Royce Merlins driving contra-rotating propellers, and increased the size of the cabin, which was capable of carrying up to forty-eight passengers seated in day flight configuration or twenty-four when arranged for overnight travel, all in private booths with sliding doors on the lower level. The upper level had a lavatory, lounge area with tables and chairs and a kitchen area. Passengers would climb aboard via a stair that unfolded from a hatch beneath the nose. The aircraft had a wingspan of 48m and a wing area of 363m2. Horten also planned to develop a version that could be used as a flying wind tunnel, with a fuselage open at the front and back for the wind to pass through it, and models placed in the middle of it for testing.

Although the landing gear and parts of the wings had already been built, in December 1946 the British cancelled the project, as well as all other work with the Horten brothers.

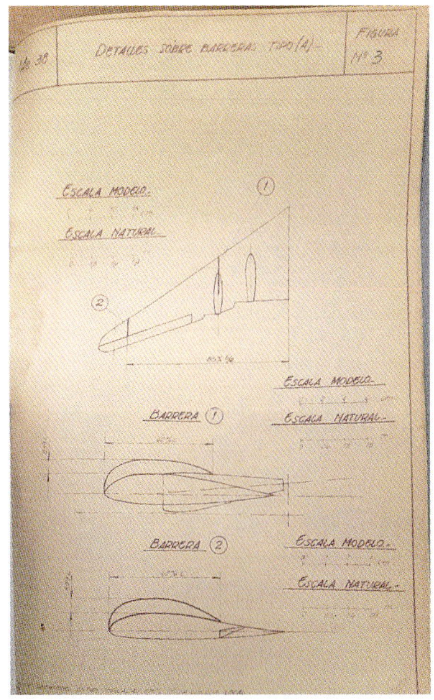

First configuration of the barriers, with two over the wing.

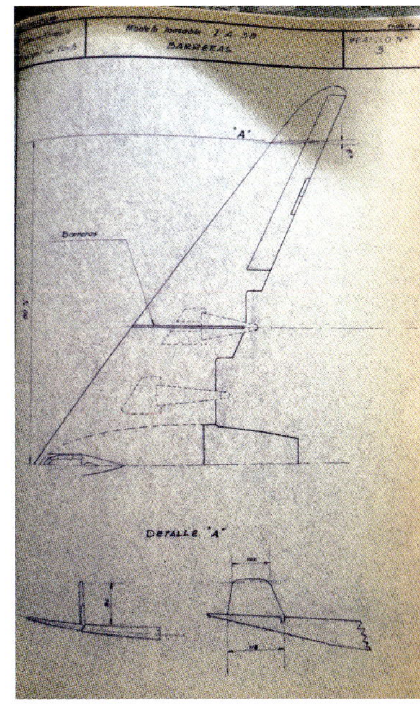

Third configuration with the four barriers all over the wing.

Follow-up in Argentina

In 1950, when Reimar was already in Argentina, he was asked to meet Air Ministry César Ojeda at his summer house in Santa Rosa de Calamuchita, 120km from Córdoba. In his book *Nürflugel,* Horten recalled:

> With my current and new employees, I was supposed to live and work here. I should visit Córdoba only once a week and La Cruz is only 30km south of here. An institute for gliding was to be established in La Cruz, of which I was appointed technical director and board member. His [Ojeda's] plane would be at my disposal for the flights to Córdoba or La Cruz.
>
> He complained that in the province of Misiones the orange harvest was rotting, while for the capital Buenos Aires, oranges had to be imported. Truck transport was not possible in the long term due to the lack of asphalt roads. He could also not use his bomber fleet for transport. There were hardly any airfields and the few there were soft at that time of year, at least unsuitable for the four-engine Lancasters and too far away from the plantations.

Wooden mock-up of the I.Ae.38.

Test of the installation of the El Gaucho engines on the I.Ae.38. Each engine was equipped with a fan on the axis that went to the propeller, to create an air flux to cool the engine. The fan consumed about 100hp and failed regularly, so they were removed for the third and fourth flights.

Ojeda told him that there was the same transport problem in the south, from Mar del Plata to Bahía Blanca, with the fish that were landed in those harbours.

Couldn't the 1,000km distance be bridged quickly and cheaply with a 10-ton glider in tow behind the four-engine bombers? The Me 321 carried 20 tons, he was satisfied with 10 tons. In order for the cargo to be retracted into the hull from behind, the minister suggested the tail-less design. In my reply, I expressed concerns about the great effort involved in towing and instead recommended that the aircraft be equipped with engines for take-off, even from dirt roads (Me 321 – Me 323 Gigant). Because of the hot and humid climate, the aircraft would have to be made of metal.

Installation of the main landing gear, with its strut system with five struts. The wheels were those used on the I.Ae.24 Calquin.

Reimar idea's was approved, and he started to work on what became the I.Ae.38. While Ojeda was replaced in his post on 2 October 1951, the work continued, but with less support, so progress was very slow.

In addition to the official task of fruit and fish transport, with the I.Ae. 38 the reserve pilots can also use it to practice and a car can also be carried for government visits within the country.

For the metal construction, we first had to train the people. The production of steel parts, fittings, etc. was only possible to a limited extent due to the lack of machines. For example, we dispensed with easy dismantling and only provided for separation points for the main parts of the airframe. This also ensured that the aircraft could not be taken to exhibitions in towns and villages [referring to when the I. Ae.34 was damaged when exhibited in 1949].

While the H VIII was basically a double-size H III from the shape of its wings, the I.Ae.38 was a double-size H II, with a swept angle of 36.5°, but the root profile had been reduced to 18 per cent thickness and the trailing edge of the wings had been extended. The wingspan was 32m, and the wing area was 132m2. The gondola-shaped fuselage (as on the H VIII) was accessed through a double tail door, which could also be opened halfway during flight to drop parachutists and parachute loads. Horten also considered the plane could be used to supply Antarctic bases and meteorological stations in the Andes, as the plane could be equipped with skis.

He also planned in 1951 to build a second I.Ae.38 for use as a flying wind tunnel, as he had originally planned on the H VIII, but this idea did not progress because in 1953 the big wind tunnel of the factory was made available for them. Also, a plan from 12 July 1951 shows a proposal for a passenger version with two Rolls-Royce Derwent V or Nene II jet engines, 28.8m of wingspan, with capacity for twenty-four passengers and three crew members, plus 1,000kg of cargo, with 2,000km of range, 12,000m of service ceiling and a landing speed of 110km/h. With Derwent V engines it would have a take-off weight of 20 tons, a maximum speed of 680km/h and a cruise one of 625km/h, while with Derwent V those values were 17.5 tons, 590km/h and 530km/h respectively. This idea did not progress as IAME was focused on the I.Ae.36 proposal of Kurt Tank.

Landing flaps were attached to the side of the fuselage, which extended automatically at 145km/h. For landing, additional spreader flaps were used and they increased the maximum lift coefficient to 1.65. The cargo hold had a floor area of 15m2 with a volume of 30m3. The pilots' cabin was on top of the fuselage, with two seats in tandem, an opening canopy and a door on the floor under the co-pilot seat to allow access to the cargo hold.

By 1952 the initial layout was finished, with a wooden mock-up being built while construction of the first prototype began, with the wings and the rear part of the fuselage, including the cargo door, being finished by September 1952. The project was announced in 1953, but continued at a very slow pace, as was happening with most other projects. The prototype was almost ready in 1955, when all work was stopped during the revolution of September. When all projects were analysed during 1956, the directors of DINFIA started to give strong support to Horten to continue with the I.Ae.38 and works were restarted, but again, very slowly.

Due to lateral oscillations found in the wind tunnel tests due to an excess of stability, different configurations of barriers over the wing were tested on launched models in 1956. First, a vertical barrier was installed over the external engines and two similar ones at 80 per cent of the wingspan, followed by the installation of four smaller ones that ran from about a third of the chord to the trailing edge, two in the same position of the former and two between them. Another test was made with the four barriers but running all over the upper part of the wing, from the leading to the trailing edge. In the end, a barrier was adopted over the external engines and two bigger vertical fins at an 80 per cent of the wingspan.

These modifications were added to the prototype during the year, but it still was not finished and readied for the first flight.

The landing gear consisted of five identical wheels, those used on the I.Ae.24 Calquin, a steerable and retractable nose wheel and four non-retractable main wheels. Each of the two tandem main landing gears was cushioned with five identical shock absorbers, while the nose wheel received two. On the main landing gear on each side, two wheels sprung against each other at the rear via a swivel bulkhead with four shock absorbers. The fifth shock absorber determined the position of the pair of wheels to the aircraft. It was connected in such a way that it had the greatest initial

The I.Ae.38 being built, seen around 1955 at one of the hangars of the factory. Due to its size, the assembly was not carried out in Hangar 90 like all other planes built since the 1940s. A lot of Puma motorbikes, built at the factory and widely used by the employees, can be seen at a side of the hangar.

The I.Ae.38 at the factory runway, most probably during taxi tests.

View of the front part of the I.Ae.38. The fuselage had a big window on each side. The access to the cockpit was through the hole of the nosewheel and the cockpit was not accessible from the cargo cabin.

spring travel when touching down for landing and then, as a result of the angular shift, only experienced small working distances. This avoided jumping of the aircraft during landing.

In addition, the fifth shock absorber was connected to a compressed air system that allowed the pilot to change the pressure before take-off (after loading the machine) until the nose wheel lifted off while standing and then put the line back under a defined pressure for take-off. In this way, he determined the exact centre of gravity.

Horten calculated that they needed an engine power of 3,000hp in order to be able to meet the required performance and four I.Ae.R19C El Indio engines of 750hp were selected, but these were not available for the prototype as all production of the El Indio was directed to the use on the I.Ae.35 Huanquero. Hence, the I.Ae.38 had to be equipped with the less powerful I.Ae.R16 El Gaucho with a maximum power of 450hp, but with only 320 available because the system to cool the engines consumed part of the power. Horten explained:

> A fan mounted on the engine shaft coupling (as on the H VII) cooled the engine during stationary operation and start-up. The pressure screw was driven by shafts. We were not allowed to import a foreign aircraft engine of the 750hp class, as the prestige of our own engine production would have suffered. This enabled us to improve the performance of our I.Ae.38.

Side view of the I.Ae.38. The plane had huge spoilers on the sides of the fuselage to land at very slow speeds. The air intakes to cool the engines are visible, as well as the ladder for the crew in the nosewheel well.

With El Gaucho engines, the plane would have an empty weight of 7,500kg, so to carry 10,000kg of cargo plus the two crew members, only 800kg of fuel could be carried, for a maximum take-off weight of 18,500kg. However, with El Indio engines, the empty weight would be 8,500kg but 2,000kg of fuel could be carried, giving an endurance of up to ten hours, for a maximum take-off weight of 20,700kg. The wing load with the El Gaucho was of 65kg/m2 and a power load of 9.0kg/kW, while with the El Indio it was of 172kg/m2 and 9.1kg/kW respectively. The take-off distance with both was the same, 470m, but the maximum and cruise speeds were 250km/h and 220km/h respectively with El Gaucho and 320km/h and 280km/h with El Indio.

The four engines were equipped with two-blade, fixed-pitch Rotol engines with some modifications.

In 1958 Horten proposed installing turboprops, but this was not approved.

Between 1957 and early 1960 works were stopped and only on 8 February 1960 were the four engines installed, with El Gaucho serials 127 and 137 on the left wing and 131 and 124 on the right one, with engine tests started shortly after. Engine 137 showed vibration problems and was removed on 21 September, with engine 136 being installed on 23 November.

On 30 November 1960 the first high-speed taxi runs were performed by pilot Rogelio Balado, with the plane having a weight of 9,800kg in total and making some small jumps. It was noted that the nosewheel left the ground at 120km/h and the main gear at 150km/h. Balado stated that the plane was extremely stable in direction while taxiing and that visibility was very good from the cabin. The exhaust of the four engines were melted during the tests due to poor design and materials, so they were rebuilt with stainless steel to an improved design.

A few days later, another similar test was made, making jumps after a run of 600 to 700m, but the propeller of engine 1 broke, because they were units with many years of use. On 8 December the prototype was taken by land to the runway at the Escuela de Paracaidistas in preparation for the first flight.

On the following day, Balado performed the first flight, but due to the pitch angle of the propellers at 13°, which were positioned before take-off and could not be changed in flight, the plane stop climbing after reaching 30m as it could not gain more speed, flying at that altitude as if it was its maximum ceiling. That caused the pilot to fly with the engines at the maximum 2,300rpm, despite only reaching 50 per cent of the maximum power. Besides that, the plane performed well, with no tendency to stall. The weight of the plane was 9,200kg. After the flight, the pitch angle was changed to 14°.

One day after, they made the second flight, with a weight of 8,800kg, lifting off after 450m and climbing at 1.5m/seg, reaching a height of 300m and reducing the engines to cruise power.

After the flight, Flettner servo tabs were added to the vertical fins, together with some minor repairs.

The fans to cool the engines suffered problems with the blades and these had to be changed.

After those two flights, tests continued on the ground, with the engines reaching 1,800rpm, and the propeller pitch angles, with Horten finally considering 16° the best. During engine runs in January 1961, engine No. 2 suffered vibration and variations in the rpm, but despite the work to repair it, the problems continued until on 7 April the engine did not start, so it was decided to replace it. The engine serialled 123 was sent as replacement, but it was in poor condition and needed repairs, so it was finally installed on 20 May, being tested, without the cooling fan, on 26 and 27 May.

The plane was then considered ready to resume flights, but on 5 June another test with the four engines was made and all had some minor problems. Horten decided to remove the remaining cooling fans while the engines were repaired. On 3 July the engines were run again, but No. 4 failed. After repairs, on 4 and 5 July tests were made with the engines and none failed, but on the 6th engine No. 4 stopped abruptly when one of the gears broke. On the following day, the director of DINFIA ordered the ending of all work on the I.Ae.38, but after that the prototype performed two other flights before the end of the year, on unknown dates, and on the last one of the engines exploded due to structural failures and the plane had to make an emergency landing.

Although it was obvious that the problem was the engines and that the plane would have far better performance if the more powerful engines were installed, by the end of 1961 it was decided to cancel the programme and the I.Ae.38 prototype was donated to the National Aeronautics Museum at Buenos Aires in 1962. It was never taken there and was sent to the Escuela de Suboficiales for storage, but remained in the open and deteriorated, being scrapped two years later.

After the cancellation of the I.Ae.38, Reimar Horten returned to Germany, but in 1964 he went back to Argentina to keep working for DINFIA as a consultant and helped develop many other projects. In the 1970s he returned to work on his own project for the factory, the IA-59.

Landing from its first flight, during which it was unable to fly above 30m due to the angle of pitch of the propellers.

The I.Ae.38 had a rear ramp that could be used to drop paratroopers or cargo. The nacelles of the engines are clearly visible here, too.

The I.Ae.38 abandoned at the Escuela de Suboficiales between 1962 and 1964.

23 I.Ae.42 and I.A.43

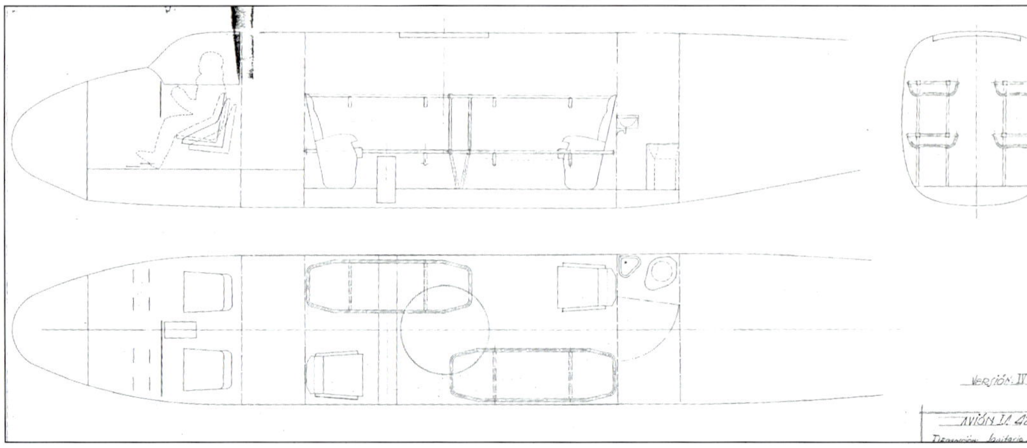

Layout of the fuselage of the medical evacuation version of the I. Ae.42

These two projects were developed in the early 1950s and not much information was found on them, especially regarding the I.Ae.42. Interestingly, while the first still used the designation I.Ae. on the documents, the second is the first to be found with the new designation of I.A.

I.Ae.42

This was a multipurpose plane project of which only a few plans were found, all dated between February and March 1952, and could have been a competitor against the I.Ae.35 as it was also planned with versions for gunnery, bombing and navigation training, medical evacuation, photo survey and transport, with a cabin of almost the same size. Although no plans include the design of the wing nor the tail, very probably it was a twin-engine plane using I.Ae.R19 El Indio engines and probably had two tails. The shape of the fuselage resembled that of the B-25, but with a low wing.

The pilots sat side by side and had a glass nose to carry a navigator or a bomber with the aiming equipment. For medical evacuation, it was able to carry four stretchers and two assistants, while for photo survey and navigation training a version was planned with the navigator in the nose, capacity to carry two or four bombs on pylons under the fuselage, six seats and a vertical camera in the rear cabin.

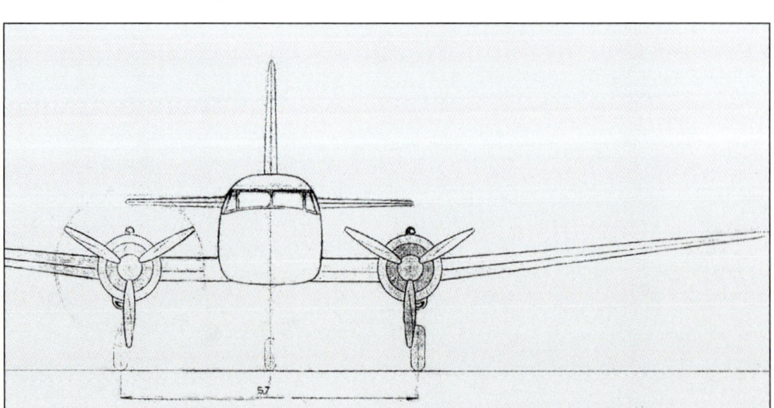

A view of the I.A.43.

The bomber and attack training version carried the bomber in the nose, a turret on top of the fuselage with a machine gun, a ventral position with another machine gun in the rear part of the fuselage, aiming backwards, capacity to carry two or four bombs and two machine guns in the fuselage aiming to the front, for strafing.

I.A.43

In 1952 the Instituto Aerotécnico began studies of a twin-engine passenger aircraft for short distances, of all-wood construction, equipped with I.Ae.R.19C El Indio engines. Work continued throughout 1953 and a mock-up was built to evaluate the layout of the cabin, although in 1954 it was cancelled.

During the initial work to define the type of aircraft, designers studied the passenger aircraft for existing subsidiary lines in Europe and the United States, especially the de Havilland Heron and the Handley Page Marathon I. They also analysed the basic requirements for this type of route, conducting a study of the conditions of the commercial air market to help develop a suitable passenger aircraft.

To the reality of the North American and European market, they added the requirements in Argentina, since although an export model was intended, the main market was expected to be at home. In the United States, in 1951 certain parameters had been established for aircraft of subsidiary lines, which were a range of at least 560km, a take-off run of less than 1,000m at sea level, no fewer than twenty-four passengers and 320km/h cruising speed. As for the range, if the action of headwind and the fuel reserve to reach an alternative at 200 or 300km were considered, the average range was 350km. In Argentina, this made it possible to cover routes such as Córdoba–Rosario, Buenos Aires–Rosario, Rosario–Santa Fe or Córdoba–Río Cuarto. However, after considering the possibility that the model could replace the DC-3 on some routes and the greater distances between many cities, it was thought that the I.A.43

Plan of the bomber training version of the I. Ae.42.

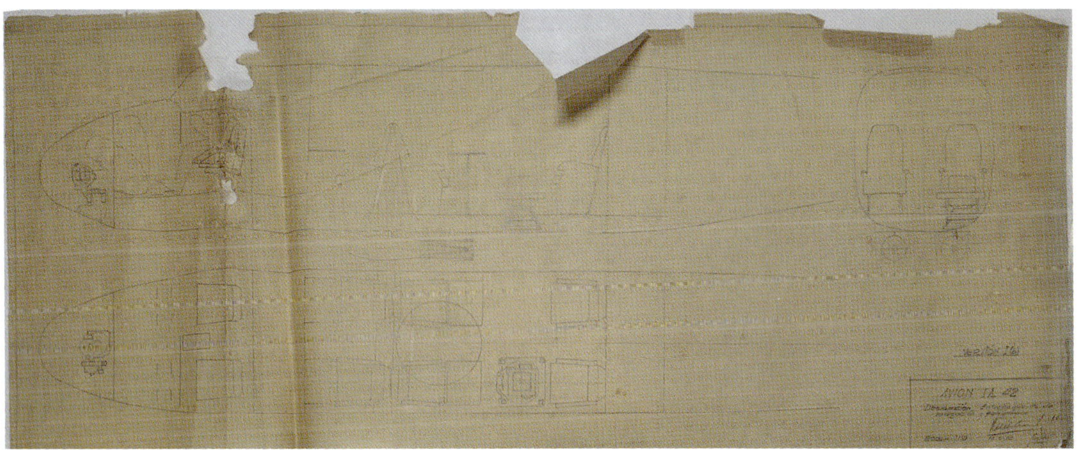

Plan of the navigator training and photo survey version of the I. Ae.42.

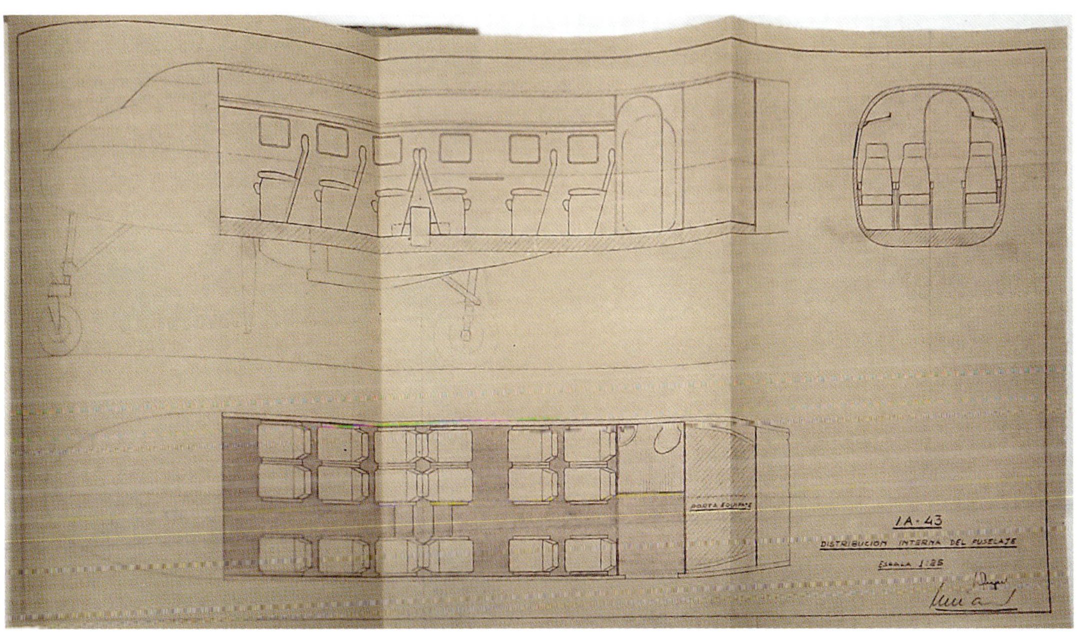

Cabin layout of the I.A.43.

would have a range of 650km, so that considering the reserves and headwinds, the maximum range should be 1,000km.

The take-off distance was calculated to be 800m, while the type was designed to carry eighteen passengers in rows of three, in order to minimise variations in the centre of gravity when a passenger moved in flight. For greater economic efficiency, the crew was reduced to two, eliminating the radiotelegrapher and without space for a stewardess, who had to sit in one of the passenger seats.

To reduce the complexity of the aircraft, it was decided to use materials from other types, such as the wheels of the Gloster Meteor. The aircraft was a low-wing cantilever monoplane with a single spar, with a wing of rectangular central part and trapezoidal outer parts. It was planned to build the prototypes with a wing in one piece, while if the need to transport a wing demanded it, its division into parts was to be studied.

The fuselage was formed by a single set of cylindrical section of semi-monocoque wooden structure, with reinforced floor for the possibility of using it for cargo transport, with a door at the rear of the cabin, where the luggage hold and the bathroom were also housed. The engines were attached to the wing by a bank of welded steel tubes, attached with four pins to the wing structure, where the flame protection was also located. The nacelles were made of aluminium alloy. On the leading edge of the wing and empennages, de-icing systems were to be installed.

To facilitate maintenance and repairs, the construction of the central plane was dihedral free, to easily allow the changing of the different parts of the landing gear, the fuel tanks and the engine mounts.

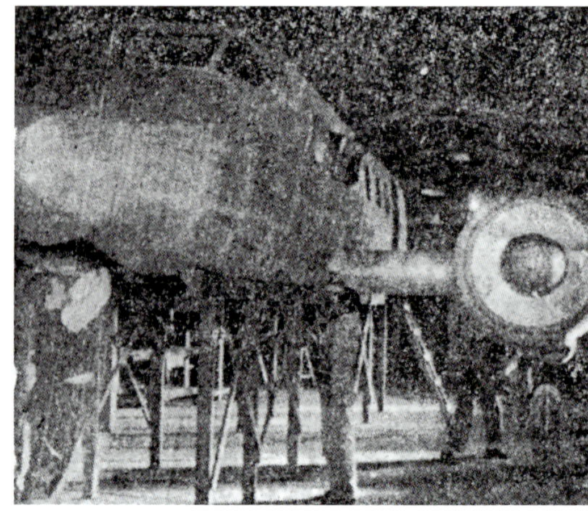

The only known picture of the mock-up of the I.A.43.

24 I.A.45 Querandí

On 20 November 1953, during the Civil Aviator Day, General Perón announced the development of two new civil aviation projects, the first being an aircraft for air taxi companies and the second a light two-seater for flying schools, tourism and crop dusting. For the first of them, different options were analysed, including a single engine of 130hp or two of 90hp, and it received the designation I.A.45, with budget for its development being allocated for the period 1953–57 of the second quinquennial plan. The second project was named I.A.46, described in Chapter 25.

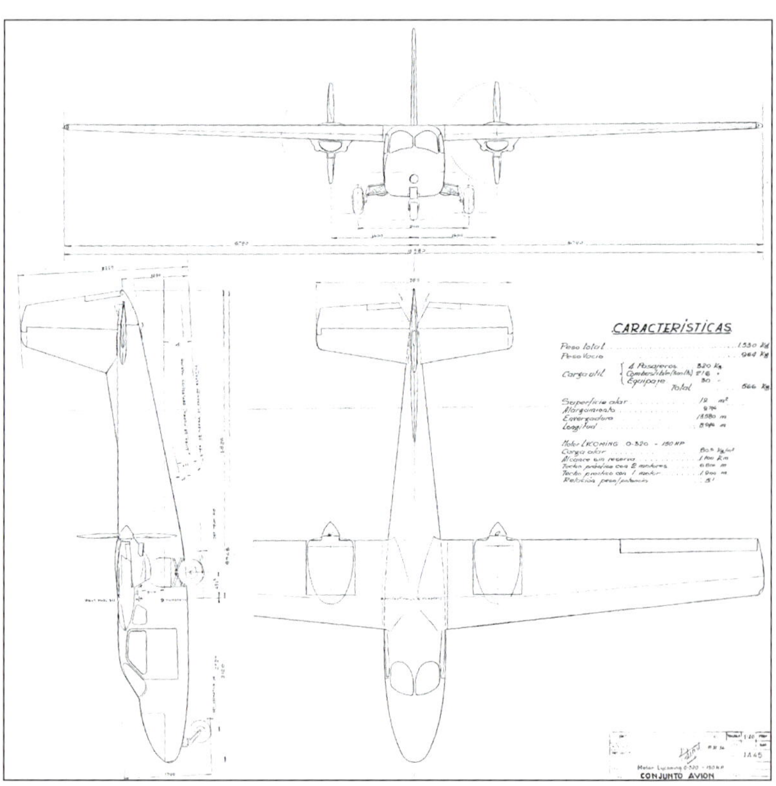

Plan dated 11 November 1956 of the proposed variant of the I.A.45 with a single vertical fin.

In 1954, the Dirección General de Aeronáutica Civil made a survey among air taxi companies and other operators of light aircraft, with the consensus being that they wanted an aircraft with six seats and two engines. IAME then asked engineer José Elaskar, who had been working in the factory since the 1940s, to be in charge of the project, starting with the evaluation of different alternatives and then with the basic design of the plane, but work progressed slowly and stopped after the revolution of September 1955. However, in 1956 the continuation of the project was approved, with the construction of some wind tunnel models and other models that were launched at Lago San Roque with the same catapult that Karl Nickel built for the tests of the I.Ae.37 models.

Elaskar made an elegant design with the capacity for five people. It had a high wing and two Lycoming O-320 engines of 150hp each, which drove Hartzell metal two-bladed propellers of variable pitch and constant speed in pusher position. The I.A.45 had two vertical fins, although Elaskar also analysed a version with a single one. The retractable landing gear had articulated quadrilateral suspension.

In addition, the location of the engines allowed a quieter cabin, and its large wingspan was studied to allow flight with a single engine at 2,000m high.

A first prototype was built and flown for the first time on 23 September 1957 by Captain Pedro Luis Rosell, who explained how his flight was:

> That day we planned to overcome all the minor difficulties and we would taxi, as long as the weather conditions allowed it, because at mid-morning a strong south wind began to blow that worsened at noon.
>
> Hours slowly passed until we were able to help push the plane on to the test pad. I settled into the cockpit and, next to me,

The first I.A.45 prototype just after the roll out, without any markings.

was the engineer Elaskar, designer of the prototype.

I started both engines and waited the necessary time for their warm-up, after which it was necessary to check the correct operation. The pressures, temperatures and revolutions indicated by the instruments coincided with the limits given by the engine operating manual. This showed that it worked properly and would allow us to continue with the programme. I had the wheel chocks removed, starting the roll towards the runway.

Only now could I see that the brakes on the aircraft were not working properly and that it would be necessary to take account of these details for successive taxies; and

ABOVE The first prototype on its first trials. The markings with the X between the letters and numbers were used on some prototypes in the late 1950s, being seen also on the last Pulqui II and on the I.A.46 Ranquel prototype.

Rear view of the first prototype of the Querandí.

Detail of the main landing gear of the Querandí.

The access door of the I.A.45 was big enough to enter both the front and rear rows of seats and also made it easy to place a stretcher inside.

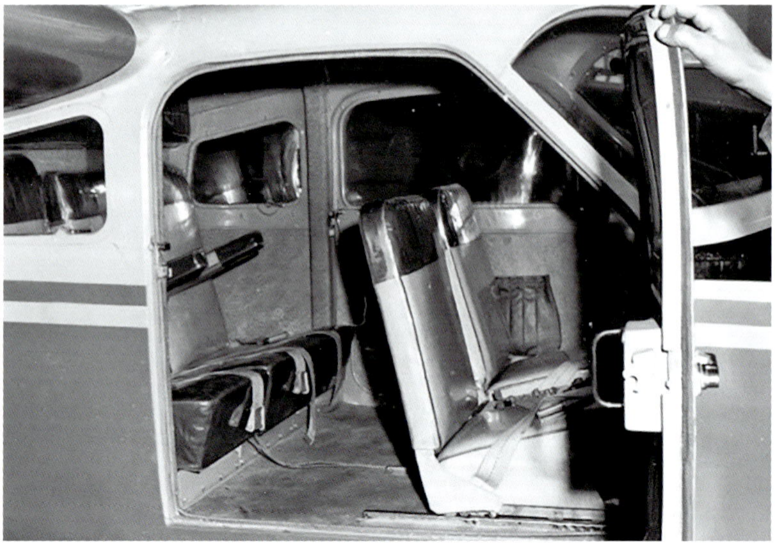

also, in the take-off attempts I planned to practice. Although I did not plan to use more than half the length of the runway in these attempts, it should be noted that with full load the plane takes off in 270m, so I could travel in the air about 500 to 600m, without having to land again. At the end of the runway, increase the power of the engines to 50 per cent. The speed of the plane grew rapidly; A few rudder strokes kept it in a straight line and at 60km per hour I began to slowly lift the nose wheel, running a distance over the main landing gear until I reached 100km per hour.

For the first time I judged that it was enough, I reduced both engines and drove the flaps to create more drag. A few metres after the middle of the runway, the plane was almost stopped in its run. The wind, which made us think about stopping the rehearsals, had calmed down completely, so I went to the opposite end of the runway of the first attempt to repeat the experience. Only then did I remember that engineer Elaskar was next to me and waiting for my news of what I had perceived on the first run. Although I drew few conclusions from such brief experience, I communicated them, receiving in response a real bombardment of questions impossible to specify because it was not yet within my reach to answer them.

We were back at the end of the runway, ready for a new run. The grass began to slide under the wheels and the speedometer exceeded the previous mark, now reaching 120km/h. At that moment the plane left the ground under its own power, rising rapidly to about five metres, where I restored the flight line, continuing with a prolonged glide until it touched the ground again. Practically, we had flown for the first time, even though this flight was only a small jump of little importance.

I was now in a better position to form a more complete concept of the sensations obtained, which I communicated to my companion. The rudder reacted in a very sensitive way, which is why, and without my intention, the plane had taken off from the ground in this second run. As it was necessary to gain a better knowledge of the plane, we completed four more 'jumps', all commanded at will, arriving by such empirical means to determine the take-off speed of 110km/h as the most appropriate, data that was quite close to that established with greater accuracy in subsequent tests.

With the enthusiasm that is evident when a task of our liking is carried out without abnormalities, we had forgotten that the time would not allow us, with safety, to continue with the trials, so we returned to the test line. When the engines were stopped, we were soon surrounded by engineers and operators; All expressed their joy at the good behaviour of the plane they had built and, in addition, each one asked about their specialty to clarify doubts and corroborate the operation of the systems designed, built, or armed by them. As always, when a nucleus of spectators sees things from afar, we hear comments of all kinds; Some wanted us to believe that we had reached more than 20m in height; others said that the machine had been 'crushed' in one of the jumps, with the possibility that the landing gear had some failure. But no one was to blame for this. The group of observers was more than 600m away, so the valuation of measures was very uncertain. For my part, I was very satisfied with the plane in general and happy to have passed another stage to be able to make the first flight in private. We had solved this by virtue of the good performances obtained in the runs. It only remained to get more braking power from the plane, and specialised personnel immediately focused on the task. It was also necessary to specify the flight with the authorities of the Fábrica Militar de Aviones, and we presented ourselves determining that the flight would take place, if the weather conditions were propitious, the next day at 7.30.

A cool, calm and sunny morning fulfilled our hopes for Monday. However, when I arrived at the hangar my illusions seemed to be frustrated. The plane was on jacks and a swarm of workers was spinning busily on a lathe. In search of data, I verified that the brakes were the cause of such a situation. It was useless to ask the commander of the hydraulic circuit area how long the task would take, because I got the usual answer: 'Ten more minutes and it will be ready.' This, in exact and aeronautical language, is equivalent to not knowing at what time something can be solved. Thus, in steps of ten minutes we arrived at 9 in the morning, the time when they began to lower the plane from the jacks and move it to the runway.

On this first flight I was also accompanied by the engineer Elaskar. We boarded the plane, fastened our parachutes, and set off. The running of engines, checking, a check of the flaps and moving surfaces indicated that everything was OK. We closed the doors; signalled for the chocks to be removed, and we were linked by the radio with the control tower that authorised the taxi. The operation of the brakes had improved a little, but not as convenient as expected. In the runway end, I tested the engines again without finding problems.

I applied full power, the plane picked up speed, and before running 300m we were in the air. Past the limit of the field, we continued to climb to 200m. A gentle turn to the left, maintaining the flight line, placed me in a safety sector, which, in case of failures, would allow me to return to the runway without setbacks. The plane was flying well, its centred commands and the beauty of the morning allowed me to enjoy this first flight. Flying over the runway, we passed in front of the hangar where the prototype had been built. The workers, at the door of it and with their arms raised greeting us, was another demonstration of the pleasant moment we lived. Engineer Elaskar didn't speak, he just watched. He is also a pilot and understood that no communication was needed at that time. After a few manoeuvres we performed the pre-landing. Landing gear down, flaps,

The first prototype of the I.A.45 after being painted. The mainwheels had no cover when retracted.

The first prototype in the early 1960s, with a new paint scheme, including a big Argentine flag on the rudder and nose art. It also has the designation I.A.45 X-I, as the second prototype was designated I.A.45 X-II.

> propeller pitch and with 140km/h we crossed the edge of the field. The runway was approaching gently until landing. Once the plane was stopped, we drove to the test line where the authorities of the Fábrica Militar de Aviones were, receiving their congratulations. In this way the IAe-45 fulfilled its first flight and with it the factory had put one more plane in the sky.

The plane was officially presented on the thirtieth anniversary of the factory on 10 October 1957, receiving the name Querandí (the name of the aborigines that lived in the Pampas) but flight tests progressed slowly due to the budget cuts that the factory had suffered since 1958. The type proved very stable, especially at slow speeds, and was very easy to fly.

Three pre-series planes were started during 1957 and by the end of the year they were 87 per cent completed, incorporating some improvements, but work was stopped in 1958.

The first of them was finished and designated I.A.45 X-II and later I.A.45B (with the first prototype being named I.A.45A), featuring changes especially to the windscreen and the windows on the sides, which were bigger and could not be open. Also, the engines were changed for the more powerful Lycoming O-360 of 180hp of four opposed horizontal cylinders and cooled by air, driving the same type of propellers, and circular doors were added to the main landing gear to cover the wheels entirely, which were exposed on the first prototype. Fuel consumption was of 39.7 litres per hour per engine

This prototype flew for the first time on 15 November 1960 with captain Roberto Starc at the controls.

In February 1962, the flight tests were completed and it was recommended that the model receive its certification so series production and sales could be started. As the factory was run by military personnel who did not know how to sell aeroplanes in the civil market, DINFIA had no success with the sale of the Querandí, despite series production being planned. By then, the factory had to compete with the import of US-built types, from Piper, Cessna, Beechcraft and other factories, that offered proven designs and, in some cases with good financing, while the factory never made agreements with banks to offer financing.

In 1965, as a law to protect the local industry was issued, offering subventions and financing, an attempt was made to revive the project, with the I.A.45B receiving extra fuel tanks on the wingtips and the experimental registration LV-X-29, but, again, the factory was not successful in selling the plane and the Querandí project was finally cancelled shortly after, with the two prototypes being scrapped. The two other pre-series production examples started in 1957 were never finished.

The plane

The fuselage was metallic, semi-monocoque in structure. All the movable parts of the tail were covered in fabric.

Elaskar explained in an article he wrote[5] that:

> when initially establishing the requirements of the I.Ae.45 aircraft project, the propeller was not thought of being behind the wing, but that solution was born from the need to

[5] El porqué del I.Ae.45 by engineer José Elaskar at Revista Nacional de Aeronáutica, November 1958.

The first prototype of the Querandí in front of the control tower of the factory, which is still in use today.

The second prototype of the I.A.45 had larger windscreen and side windows, as well as more powerful engines. The main wheels had doors that covered them when in flight.

satisfy other more important conditions for an aircraft of this type, such as accessibility to the interior for a patient on his stretcher. Carrying a patient on a stretcher aboard a small plane requires juggling and four or five people to do it safely and without excessive inclinations that are harmful to the patient. Sometimes it is impossible to do it with some seriously ill people. In the I.Ae.45 this can be executed with only two people and the stretcher perfectly level.

In a twin-engine with tractor propellers and high wing, the door must be under the wing, the only possible place, and it would have been excessively small unless the fuselage was designed enormously large for an aircraft of that size, to the detriment of weight and performance. With the low wing the accessibility problem is even greater because you must walk over the wing. In addition to this accessibility advantage, the rear propeller allows the noise source to be moved away from the cabin, not to mention that the position of the engines to the rear increases visibility in all flight conditions. On the other hand, it prevents the propeller disc from sweeping the immediate area to the passenger cabin, which would be inevitable with front propellers and even dangerous in certain conditions.

The high wing adopted – almost two metres above the ground – prevents tall grass from affecting take-off conditions with the strong resistance they would produce; on the other hand, the height protects it from dents or breaks caused by logs, bushes, etc.; All this, without considering the already known advantage of greater longitudinal stability at large angles, and greater visibility in flight than the low wing.

'The wing … it looks like that of a glider, why?' is a common question from someone who critically walks his eyes along the large wingspan of 13.50m of the IAe-45. The wing has an elongation – ratio of span to the medium chord – somewhat greater than the generality of aircraft of that size, and this is due to the favourable influence that elongation has on the service ceiling of the aircraft, in particular with a stopped engine, and that according to the initial requirements established should not be less than 2,000m; the elongation of 9 that the IAe-45 has is precisely the one that satisfies these conditions, as has been proven in flight tests. The profile of the wing belongs to NACA 2300, and of very good behaviour in lift and resistance. We were also trying to use laminar profiles – of low aerodynamic resistance – but they were discarded from the beginning because in certain conditions of the wing surface – dirt, mud, crushed insects – they have as much or greater resistance than the common profiles, also affecting the lift.

The wing structure is monospar with a resistant and hermetic leading edge so that inside it contains the fuel – 150 litres in each wing, which can be increased to 200 – representing a solution widely used in modern aircraft.

The breakage of the landing gear means serious damage to the aircraft, propeller and sometimes damage to the occupants. To gain experience in the behaviour of the landing gear, and gain time at the same time, even before the first flight, the construction of a test vehicle was advanced, equipped with the IAe-45 gear, which was subjected to intense tests of 'torture' in

In 1965 the second prototype of the Querandí received the experimental serial LV-X-29 and extra fuel tanks on the wingtips. The lack of sale success meant that the programme was cancelled shortly after and the two prototypes scrapped.

terrain especially worsened for this purpose, thus fulfilling hundreds of hours of violent reeling, equivalent to thousands of landings.

The nose wheel is also articulated according to the same criteria. Both the main and nose axes have classic pneumatic oil damping, with the advantage that the shock absorbers only work axially and are not subject to any bending force. The retraction and extension of the landing gear is ensured by three almost independent systems: hydraulic pressure from an engine-driven pump, hydraulic pressure from a pressure accumulator, and emergency pneumatic pressure, provided by the pressurised air reservoir.

But even in this condition it is comforting to know that the I.Ae.45 has the belly planned and calculated to land with the gear undeployed, with almost no deterioration, without the propellers touching the ground – they are at more than 15cm when the plane is resting on the ground, with the front landing gear inside – as it could be verified the day that a curious person activated the gear with the plane stopped on the ground and the engines worked. Ten minutes later the plane was flying.

Special consideration has been given to the overload imposed by turbulent gusts, of the type to be found in the south of the country, and it being able to support the structure, with all certainty, with vertical gusts of up to 20m/sec, which are the most severe. The load factor of the aircraft is 6, that is, it is calculated to support six times its weight in any of the flight conditions it may encounter.

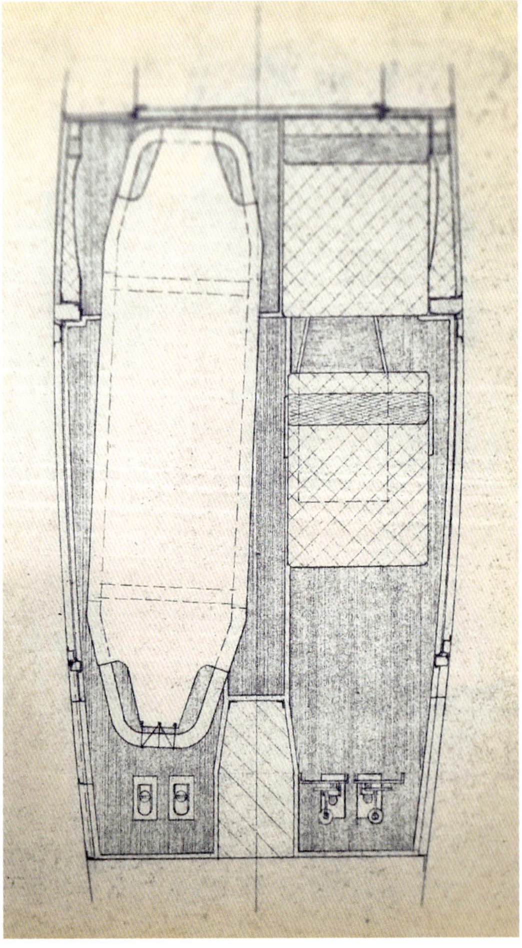

Internal layout of the medical evacuation version, with capacity of up to two stretchers, a pilot and a doctor.

The cabin, with a volume of 4m3, has dual controls and accommodates the pilot, co-pilot and three passengers or pilot and four passengers or pilot, two stretchers and a doctor. The possibility was also considered of carrying up to six people, but this cabin layout was never installed. The big access doors and low height of the cabin floor in respect to the ground made access very easy. The cockpit was equipped for IFR flight.

25 **I.A.46 Ranquel, Super Ranquel and I.A.51 Tehuelche**

Together with the announcement of what became the I.A.45 Querandí, on 20 November 1953, during the Civil Aviator Day, General Perón also announced the development of a light two-seater aeroplane for flying schools, tourism, and crop dusting. The first layouts were made by engineer in 1954, but the project was stopped in 1955 and resumed in 1956 after the factory was reorganised. José F. Elaskar, head of the Departamento Aviones, was in charge of the project, but he appointed engineer Oscar Horacio Elorza to head the design team. The plane, designated I.A.46, evolved from a two-seater to a bigger plane with three seats, one in front for the pilot and two in the back, passing from an initial engine of 90hp to a Lycoming O-320 of 150hp and a Sensenich two-blade, fixed-pitch metal propeller.

The type had a high wing with two spars, with a structure made of aluminium alloy tubes covered in fabric, with a NACA 23012 profile. It has Frise ailerons and internal flaps, the fuel tanks were housed inside the wing and had a total capacity of 140 litres. The fuselage was built of welded steel tubes and covered in fabric, as was the tail. The landing gear was conventional and fixed, with hydraulic disc brakes.

For training, the plane could be equipped with dual commands in tandem, while for crop dusting the plane received a 380-litre tank for liquid or solid products to be sprayed, as well as the spraying system, with a bar under the wings for liquids with a small propeller to move the pump, or a dusting system with an opening in the belly for solids.

The first prototype shortly after its first flight, equipped with the crop-spraying system. The Ranquel was widely used on this task, as well as glider towing. The prototype wears its first paint scheme and the markings I.A. X 46 on the fuselage.

By mid-1957, construction of the prototype began and was finished by early December. Serial P01 made its first flight at the factory on 23 December 1957, with Pedro Luis Rossell at the controls. After that, it was named Ranquel, the name of the original people of south-central Argentina.

The flight tests evolved without trouble with the first prototype and a second that was finished during the year, which received the serial 001, and the type was certified in 1958 At the same time, production of

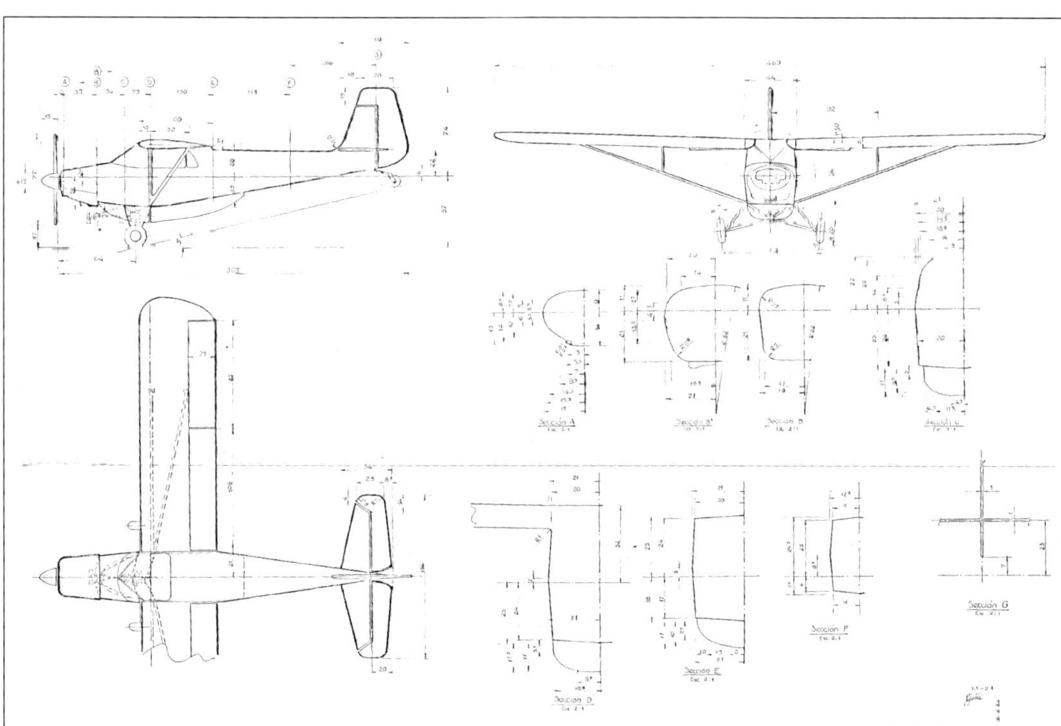

A plan for a wind tunnel model of the Ranquel, with the three views of the plane.

The Ranquel could be equipped with a crop-spraying tank in the belly with a capacity for 420 litres, which could be released in flight in case of emergency. The development of this tank, replacing the one installed behind the pilot's seat, made it possible to retain the rear seats for passengers when not spraying.

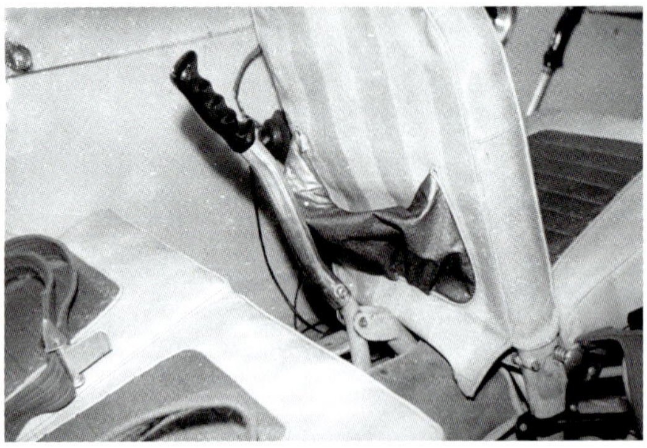

Ranquel cabin with dual controls. The rear seat had the capacity for two passengers.

a pre-series of ten aircraft began, later expanded to eleven. The price calculated by DINFIA for the basic aircraft was of $10,000, plus about $650 for the liquid spraying system for agriculture.

In 1959 plans were developed for another series of ninety aeroplanes and a follow-on one of 300, while on 31 October 1959 the pre-series aeroplanes were delivered to de Secretaría de Aeronáutica, who sold them to private owners with financing.

Despite this good start, the production of the first series was delayed until 1961, when parts for forty-five planes were built, but none were finished, despite a plan to deliver all of them that year.

Also, in 1961 two new versions were planned, one with four seats, which was cancelled the same year, and one with an engine of 180hp for glider towing. This was at the request of the Federación Argentina de Vuelo a Vela (FAVAV, Argentine Soaring Federation), which wanted an aeroplane to tow the gliders that would take part in the Gliding World Championship in 1963 in Argentina. One of the prototypes was equipped with a 180hp Lycoming O-360 and tested by the FAVAV, who, at Merlo aerodrome, near Buenos Aires, also evaluated other aeroplanes built locally that could be used in this task, these being the Macchi MB-308G, Aero Boero 95, Lockheed Kaiser 60 and the Avi-205. The 180hp Ranquel proved to be the most efficient for glider towing.

In 1958, when a second prototype was built, the first one received the markings I.A.46 X-I, while the other was X-II. The plane is equipped with the spraying bomb and propeller, but without the bar for spraying.

I.A.51 Super Ranquel and Tehuelche

After the tests of the I.A.46 with the 180hp engine, DINFIA developed an improved version with that engine, with an all-metal wing structure, a different fuselage structure, new cowling, fairings covering the main wheels (later removed), a new bubble windscreen, some differences to the tail and other minor changes. This version was initially called I.A.51 Super Ranquel, but when the plane was presented it was named I.A.51 Tehuelche. The prototype was started in May 1962, being finished in early 1963 and flying for the first time on 16 March 1963 with experimental serial LV-X-26. But the plane came too late for the world championship, which took place on February of that year. While the plane was certified, in the end it was never built in series. The prototype continued flying at the CEV until in 1981 it was given to the Club de Planeadores Tucumán, where it crashed on 20 October 1988 and was not repaired.

I.A.46 Ranquel Modelo 66 or Super Ranquel

In 1962 the first nineteen series production I.A.46s were finished and sixteen of them were delivered to civil operators, mainly glider clubs, and some of them were used with success during the world championship that took place in Laguna de Gómez, close to the town of Junín, Buenos Aires province.

Curiously, until then, the first prototype flew without any serial, until the civil authorities requested it to be officially registered and on 3 October 1962 it became LV-HOG.

To promote the Ranquel, on 4 May 1963 German pilot Hans Scheidhauer repeated the flight that in 1932 the Ae.C.2 Tenga Confianza made over the (by then) fourteen provinces of Argentina, making the same stops on a single day. Scheidhauer used aircraft serial 033, which was registered LV-IAE for the Instituto Aerotécnico.

Due to the limitations of the plane with a 150hp engine and after the successful tests with the 180hp engine and variable-pitch propeller, in 1965 DINFIA decided to offer a version with that engine, which flew for the first time on December 1965. It was named I.A.46 Modelo 66, but it was known also as Super Ranquel. The plane reached a maximum take-off weight in the passenger version of 1,050kg and of 1,100kg for crop spraying. For glider towing it reached a climb rate of 4m/s at sea level and 2.35 between 600 to 1,000m towing gliders of 360kg of weight, while the maximum towing capacity was of 504kg. While it was never used for medical evacuation, the plane could carry a stretcher, while it was also designed to receive a vertical camera for photo survey operations at up to 5,000m.

The planes that were still being built with the 150hp engine were now called Ranquel 150.

Deliveries of the I.A.46 Ranquel 150 continued at a good rate until 1968, when they started to slow down, mainly because the factory obtained the licence to produce the Cessna 150 and 182, and only four planes were delivered in 1969, two in 1970 and the last two in 1972, after 116 were built. Also, a total of sixteen Super Ranquels were delivered between 1965 and 1967, the last of them to the Argentine Air Force for glider towing. Only twenty-nine Ranquel 150s and one Super Ranquel were delivered with crop dusting equipment, but over the years another sixty-two were converted for that mission, most of them receiving the 180hp engine.

The plane proved very robust, easy and cheap to maintain, and over the years many received modifications, including engines of 210 and 235hp, and at least one was equipped with a different landing gear, while many received the bubble windscreen like that of the Tehuelche, which improved the pilot's view and reduced the noise of the wind. Only one was exported, second hand, to an owner from Paraguay, equipped with a 210hp engine.

Currently, a few are still flying, while the remains of the first prototype are abandoned at Mar del Plata Air Club.

Second prototype of the Ranquel, which received the constructor number 001, meaning that it was built as a pre-series plane.

The sole prototype of the I.A.51 Tehuelche, with 180hp engine, new bubble windscreen (later adopted by most of the Ranquels), fairings for the wheels and a tail with a small fin at the beginning. While no more Tehuelches were built, the engine and windscreen were later used by the Super Ranquel and retrofitted to most of the Ranquels.

The last production Super Ranquel seen in 2010. The plane originally received the serial LV-JFG and later became PG-423 with the Argentine Air Force. The plane was used for glider towing at the IV Brigada Aérea at Mendoza and later at the Military Aviation School next to the factory. It is currently at the National Aeronautics Museum. *Santiago Rivas*

26 I.A.47

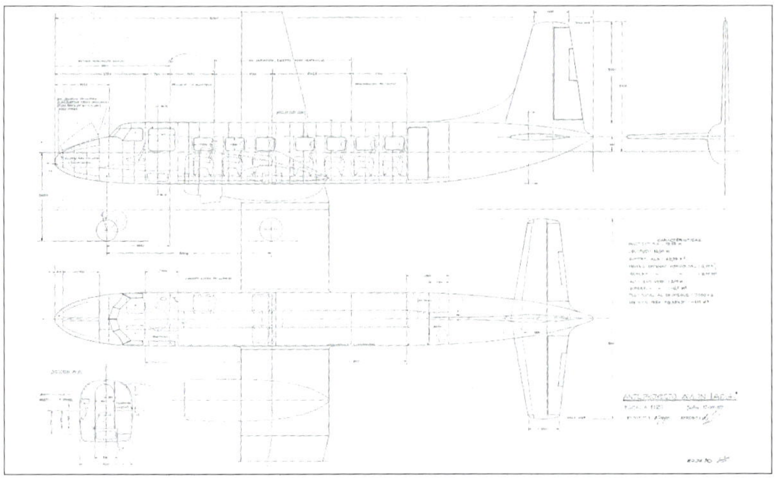

Plan of the first design with the I.A.47 designation, very similar to the I. Ae.35B proposal.

Curiously, there are three projects of aeroplanes with this designation, all very different and of which very little information is available. The first of them was an aircraft derived from the I. Ae.35B proposal of October 1957 and the only plan available is from 17 November 1957, so most probably, as the plane was very different from the I.Ae.35, it was decided to give it a new designation. The wing was the same as of the I.Ae.35, with El Indio engines but with slightly different nacelles. The fuselage had the same section, but with an entirely new nose and rear area, while it was longer. The nose housed the communications and navigation equipment, while the cockpit was for two pilots, behind whom was a luggage compartment and a small foldable seat. The cabin had space for fourteen seats, with another luggage compartment and a toilet at the rear end. A single door was installed to the right in the rear. The tail had a single fin, with a low stabiliser.

The design had a wingspan of 19.53m, a length of 16.5m, a wing area of 42.3m2, with a maximum take-off weight of 7,000kg.

This project was cancelled shortly after, most probably since the decision to develop a turboprop version of the I.Ae.35 was taken.

The next design with the I.A.47 designation was a family of jet transports proposed by Reimar Horten in August 1960. They included five possible versions, the smaller being one for twenty seats with two Rolls-Royce Derwent engines. Another version was for forty-four passengers with a swept wing and one for forty-six passengers with straight wing, both with two Bristol Orpheus. The biggest was one for fifty passengers with two Rolls-Royce RB163 Spey of 5700kg of thrust each. The fifth was the more radical one with a delta wing and two Pratt & Whitney JTF-10A-1 of 3,742kg of thrust each, with capacity for forty passengers and four crew members. Of this version, a three-view plan still exists, with some technical data, including the length of 21.6m, a wingspan of 15m, a height of 6m and a wing area of 107m2. The empty weight was 10 tons, with capacity for 4,000kg of fuel and 4,700kg of payload, with a maximum take-off weight of 19.46 tons. It was expected to have a service ceiling of 12,000m, or 6,000m with one engine, a take-off run of 1,532m with a 15m obstacle, and a landing run of 1,594m. The climb rate was of 19m/s and the landing speed was 233km/h with 30 per cent of fuel. At 7,600m height, the cruise speed was of 890km/h with 80 per cent of thrust, with an economic cruise of 745km/h. The range with 80 per cent of thrust was of 1,956km and the maximum was of 2,310km.

The five proposals of Reimar Horten that received the designation I.A.47, from August 1960. *Archive Diego Horten*

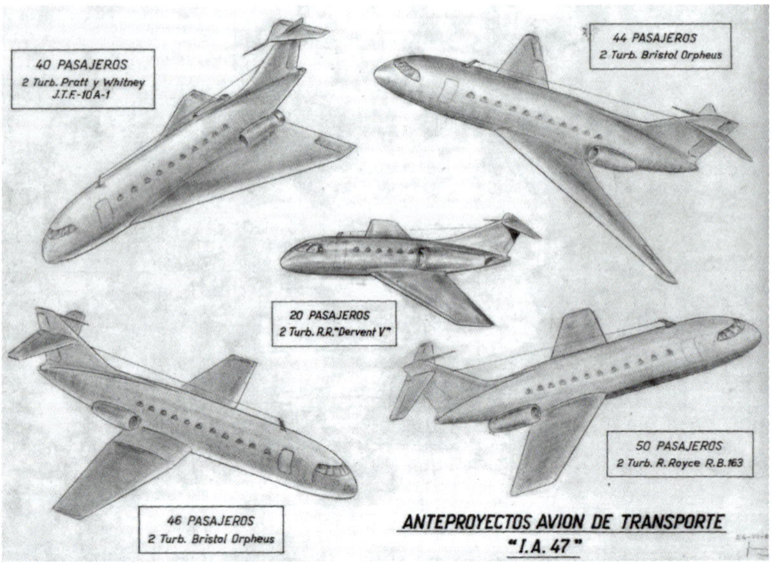

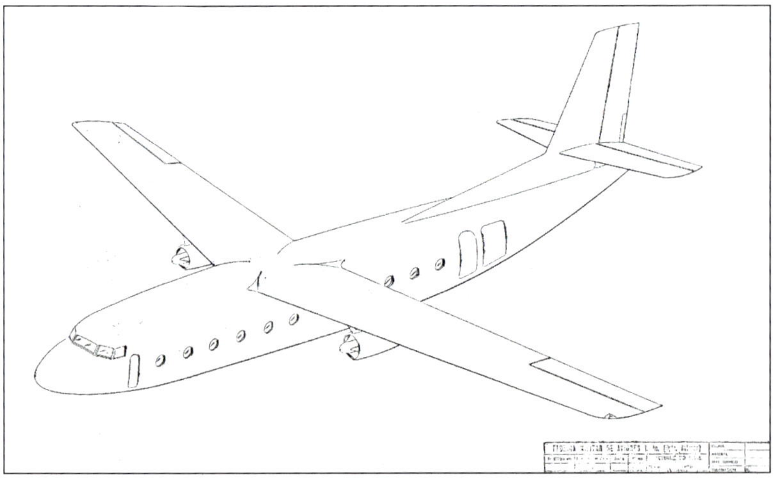

Jet version of the 1961 proposal with the I.A.47 designation.

The five proposals had the same fuselage, only varying in its length, as well as the wings and tail, with the engines on nacelles on the sides. The internal layout considered rows of four seats, with a toilet and bar on the rear, inside a pressurised cabin. It also had a cargo hold in the belly for the luggage, with an entrance from the nose landing gear bay, and another in the back for mail, with a door on the belly.

Horten's proposals were not approved and another project was developed with the I.A.47 designation, with plans dated from 24 March to 7 April of 1961. This design resembled in some ways the Fokker F27, with a high wing and two engines, with a turboprop version with two Rolls-Royce Dart RDa.7/1 of 1990shp on take-off and 1,325shp for continuous operation, and a jet one with Bristol Orpheus BOr.12 of 3,088kg of thrust.

The plane had a length of 23.5m, a wingspan of 26.8m, a height of 7.7m and a wing area of 74m2. While both had capacity for forty passengers and three crew members, the turboprop version had an empty weight of 9,900kg, a capacity of 3,000kg of fuel, a payload of 3,800kg, for a maximum take-off weight of 17,000kg.

At 6,000m of height the cruise speed was of 460km/h, with a range of 1,500km. The take-off run was of 760m, and of 950 with a 15m-high obstacle. With one engine stopped, it was of 1,300m and 1,600 with a 15m-high obstacle.

As the main wheels retracted into the fuselage, this meant that the cabin was divided into two, with the rear part being a little bit higher. For cargo, the plane had a door on the left side of the front fuselage, but only the front part of the cabin could be used for cargo because of the division, with capacity for 3,000kg and 31m3, with the rear part used to carry sixteen passengers. At the rear of the cabin, there was a toilet to the right and a passenger door to the left, and a luggage compartment at the back with 9.5m3 of volume, with its own door.

This project was also cancelled shortly after, when budget cuts forced the factory to reduce considerably the number of projects.

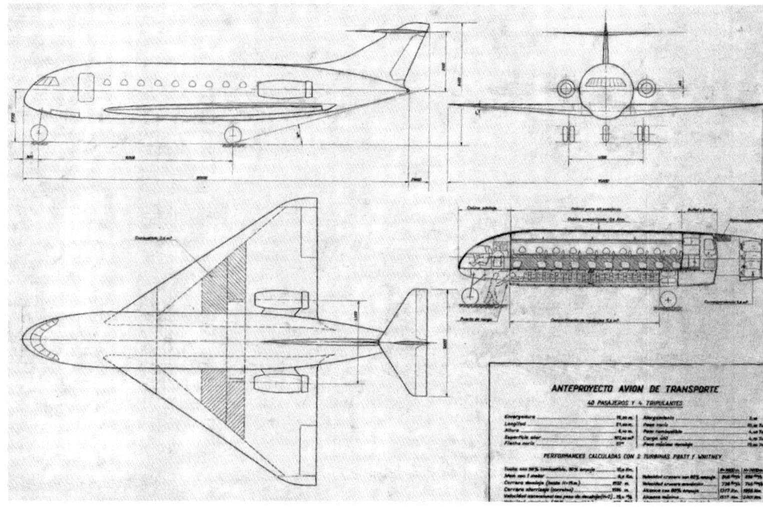

Jet version of the 1961 proposal with the I.A.47 designation.

Plan with the three views of the proposal for the I.A.47 of 1961 in its turboprop version.

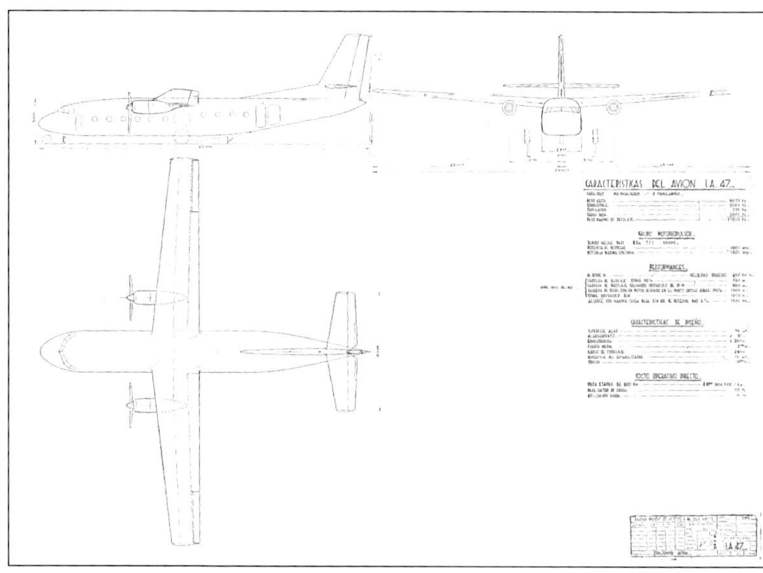

Cargo and passenger layout of the I.A.47 of 1961. Due to the space needed for the main wheels, cargo could only be carried in the front part of the cabin.

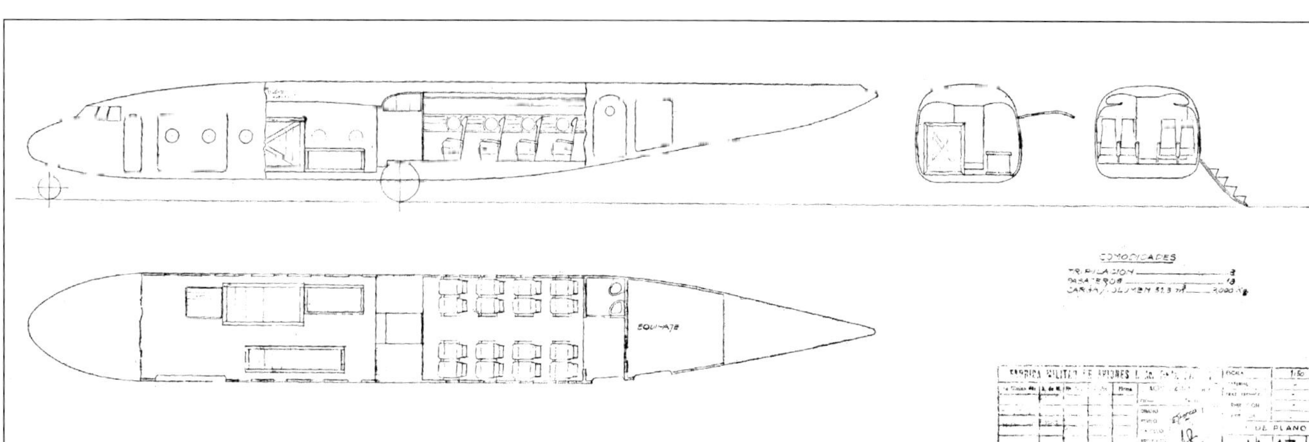

5 Conservative times

27 I.A.49, I.A.54 Carancho and I.A.56 gliders

I.A.49

With the huge development of soaring in Argentina and in response to the requests of glider pilots, in early 1959 Reimar Horten proposed a high-performance glider more conventional than its flying wings, having a wing with laminar profile with a wingspan of 20.7m, a wing area of 10.66m2 with an elongation of 40, a load factor of 9 and using a NACA 65618 profile. The empty weight was of 250kg, with a maximum of 350kg. The gliding relation was of 46 with a minimum descend rate of 0.45m/s.

Work on development was approved and the type received the designation I.A.49, with wind tunnel tests being made, but in 1961 the project was cancelled.

Another glider design, designed by the Dirección de Investigaciones, received the same designation, being more conventional, with a wingspan of 19.12m, a wing area of 21.12m2 and a dihedral of 7°. The fuselage was a metallic monohull. It was expected to have a maximum speed of 230km/h, a cruise one of 130km/h and a landing speed of 90km/h. This proposal was cancelled before a prototype was built, too.

RIGHT Cockpit of the I.A.54 Carancho.

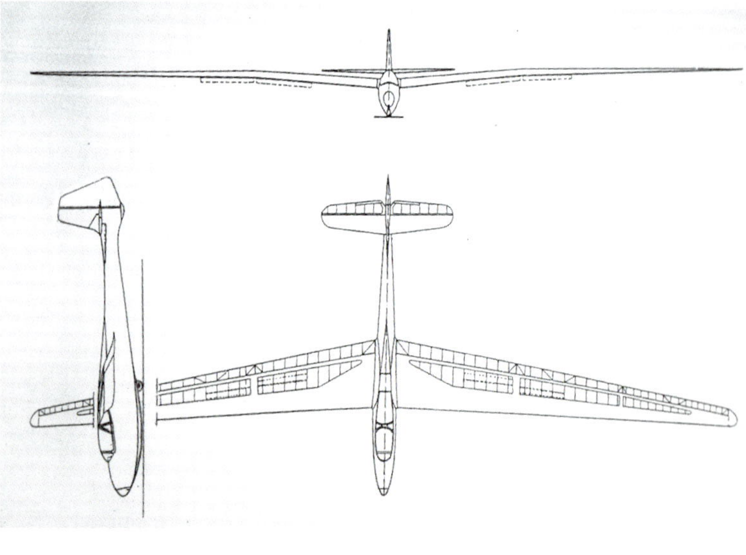

A design made by the Dirección de Investigaciones for a more conventional glider with the designation I.Ae.49.

I.A.54 Carancho

In 1963 engineer Ricardo Emilio Olmedo proposed the development of a new glider with laminar profile created by Horten (designated IIAE 45-789-5418), more conventional than Horten's design, with two seats, and this proposal was approved and received the designation I.A.54.

A prototype was built in 1954 using the fuselage of the Dittmar Condor IV serialled LV-EHI that was the property of Club de Planeadores Los Caranchos, based at the Military Aviation School, by whom the glider was named Carancho, but it was also known as Condor V. The original glider had had an accident and its wings were damaged, so it received the new wings with a laminar design designed by Horten and they were made of wood. The prototype was flown for the first time in late 1964 by NCO Alfredo Figueroa and was later tested by civil glider pilot Reinaldo Picchio, being registered as LV-X31 on 5

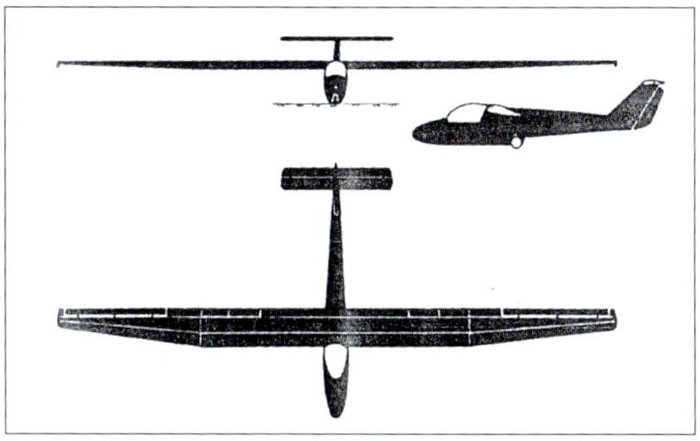

March 1965. The new wings improved the gliding ratio by a 15 per cent compared with the Condor IV. The glider had a maximum speed of 240km/h, a gliding ratio of 34, an empty weight of 340kg with a maximum of 548kg, a length of 8.4m, a wingspan of 19m, and a wing area of 20.6m.

After the tests, it was delivered to the Club de Planeadores Los Caranchos to be tested by them and participated on the National Gliding Championship of 1966 at Rafaela, Santa Fe. During the tournament, on 11 February, Reinaldo Picchio had to make a landing on a crop field and the glider suffered extensive damage to the wings, being sent to the factory and stored. After a few years later it was decided to repair it and send it to the National Aeronautics Museum, but this did not take place and the glider was scrapped in the early 1970s.

I.A.56

In August 1965 engineer Olmedo agreed with the president of the Federación Argentina de Vuelo a Vela (FAVAV), engineer Tulio Calderón, that they should send a survey to all the gliding clubs of Argentina about what they wanted from a standard-class glider. With the results, Olmedo came up with the design of a single-seat glider with wooden wings with 15m of wingspan, IIAE 45-789-5418 laminar profile, a fuselage made of steel tubes covered with fibre on the cabin and fabric on the rear part.

After the basic design was settled, Olmedo met with some of the most important glider pilots of Argentina and discussed the possibility of the Argentine state paying half towards the purchase price. However, the pilots were not very enthusiastic and preferred to import gliders from Europe, so the project was abandoned shortly after.

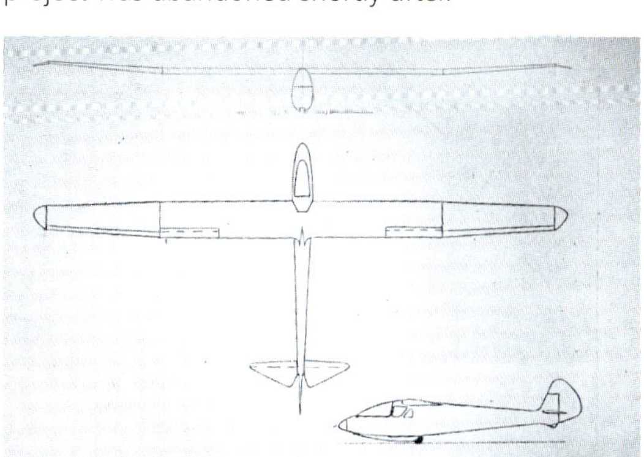

ABOVE RIGHT The only I.A.54 Carancho glider, which used the fuselage of a Dittmar Condor IV glider with a new wing.

ABOVE LEFT Three views of the I.A.56 proposal.

BELOW Three views of Horten's proposal for the I.Ae.49 glider. *Archive Diego Horten*

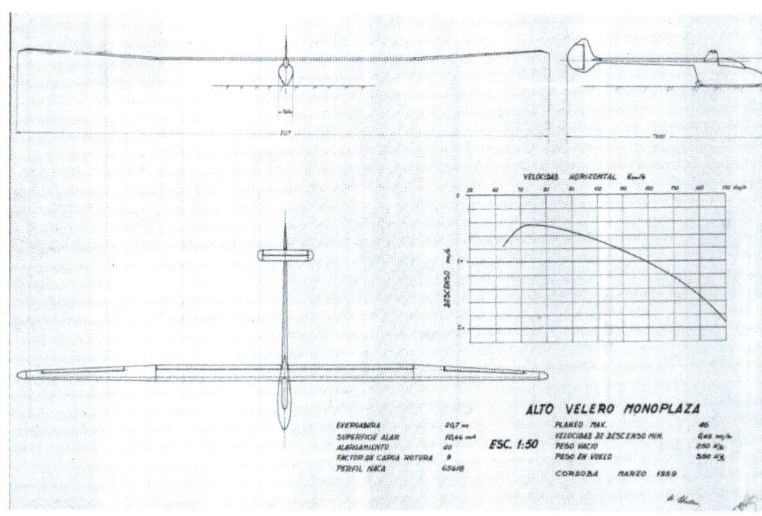

Wind tunnel model of Horten's I.Ae.49, preserved at the Centro de Investigación Aplicada of the Argentine Air Force. *Santiago Rivas*

Three views of the I.A.54 Carancho.

28 I.A.50 Guaraní I, Guaraní II/G II, Guaraní III, Guaraní IV

As was described in Chapter 19, the development of turboprop engines at the end of the 1950s led the request to be made at the beginning of 1960 by DINFIA's national director, Brigadier Mayor Juan Carlos Pereira, to the chief of Agrupación Reparación de Aviones, captain engineer Héctor Eduardo Ruiz, to change the El Indio engines of the I.Ae.35 for the Turbomeca Bastan III turboprop of 870shp. Pereira gave Ruiz the installation manuals provided by Turbomeca and the engineer organised a team with Rudolf Freyer to make the aerodynamic calculations, plus Reimar Horten with a team of six other engineers and three assistants were added by Day Order 798 of 29 December 1960. Ruiz, Horten and Freyer made an extensive analysis of the performance with both engines and test pilot Rogelio Balado, who was director of the Centro de Ensayos en Vuelo, was asked to make a report on the flight performances of the I.Ae.35 with El Indio engines and the possible improvements of using a turboprop engine.

The analysis considered that the modifications were feasible and it only needed 4,500 work hours to modify the tooling, which was finished in forty-eight days, followed by thirty-two days to build parts, forty-three to assemble the sets and fifty-two for the final assembly, meaning 8,700 working hours to finish the first plane. They would need just 6,500 for the second, 5,800 for the third, 5,300 for the fourth and 5,000 for the fifth.

Ruiz worked from the basis of the I.Ae.35 Tipo V transport, not only adding the turboprops, but also adding a third window on each side of the passenger cabin and lengthening them all and adding round ends. He modified shape the of the windscreen and made a more radical change to the rear part of the fuselage, to allow for a door on the left side instead of one in the belly. The first drawings of the new version, which Ruiz named I.Ae.35 Constancia II, were made in April 1960, with the Bastan engines in nacelles under the wing and the escape to the outer sides, maintaining the wings, tail and central fuselage of the I.Ae.35 with a new nose and rear fuselage, new landing gear and many internal improvements. Later on, the engines nacelles were installed over the wings, with the exhaust to the rear, increasing the clearance of the propeller to the ground.

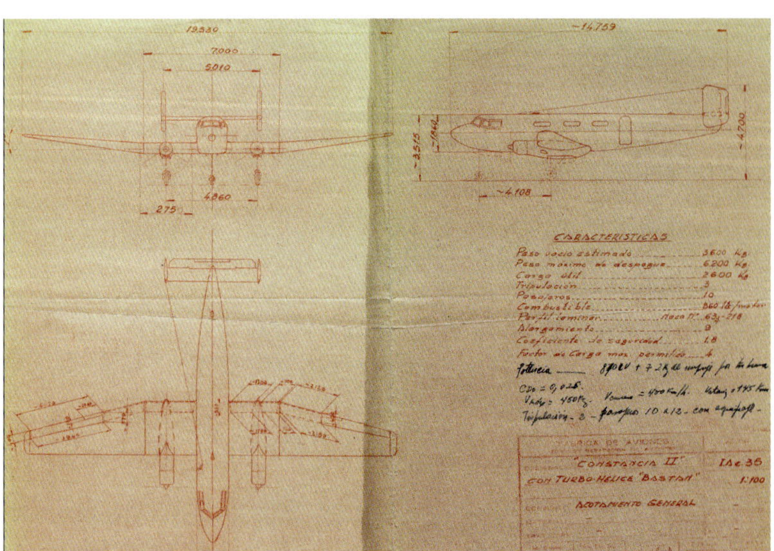

Three views of the Constancia II design, with the original position for the engines, with hand annotations made by Héctor Ruiz. *Archive Eduardo Ruiz*

In August 1961 it was decided that the I.Ae.35 production would end at airframe construction number 38 and the five airframes still in construction were going to be finished with as the new version. One of them, with serial 39, would be the prototype and the others would serve as a pre-series aircraft.

At the same time, the team also started to work on a different version, with a single tail, which was named Constancia III and models of both the Constancia II and III were built, but shortly after the names were changed to I.A.35T Guaraní I and II respectively.

In a memo on 18 September 1961, the plans for the works to be done were presented, describing that they included the 'verification and documentation of the prototypes of the aeroplane Guaraní with a tail of two vertical fins and a tail with one vertical fin (central)'.

The unfinished airframe of the I.Ae.35 serialled 39 was used first to make a mock-up of the new nose and cabin and the rear part frames were modified to have the shape of the new tail and the side door. Also, the engine installation was tested with the new space for the landing gear. After that, the modification of the plane began, to become the first prototype of the I.A.35 Guaraní I, receiving a new nose, completely different from that of the former I.Ae.35, and the new tail. The central fuselage was extensively modified and was slightly longer, while the wing kept 84 per cent of the original one, only changing in the area of the engines. In total, it was considered the new plane retained 32.35 per cent of the original I.Ae.35.

Finally, by the end of 1961 the prototype started ground tests and it was planned to make the first flight in the first half of January 1962. This was delayed until 6 February, when flew for the first time with serial LQ-HER (for Héctor Eduardo Ruiz), commanded by Rogelio Balado, and became the first turboprop aeroplane made in Latin America.

As the serial LV-HER was in use by a civil Macchi MB-308, DINFIA was informed by the Registro Nacional de Aeronaves that they could not use LQ-HER and the plane was assigned the experimental serial LV-X23. However, this was never painted on the prototype and was cancelled on August 1964.

A second flight was made on 7 February, followed by another on the 12th and then two

5 CONSERVATIVE TIMES

FAR LEFT Factory model of the Constancia II in its initial configuration. *Archive Eduardo Ruiz*

LEFT Factory model of the Constancia III, which was redesignated Guaraní II. *Archive Eduardo Ruiz*

more on 10 March, followed by two on 17 and 18 April respectively. On May, test flights were made on the 5th, 15th and 16th. To present the plane, on 23 May the prototype was taken to the VII Brigada Aérea at Morón, near Buenos Aires, where it was shown to the commander-in-chief of the Argentine Air Force, Brigadier Mayor Cayo Alsina, the Naval Aviation Commander, Capitán de Navío Jorge Bassi, and other authorities.

Meanwhile, on March 1962 the order was given to start work on the first two pre-series planes, to avoid stopping work at the factory between the end of the Huanquero production and the start of the Guaraní line. The first of them, sometimes described by the Centro de Ensayos en Vuelo and DINFIA as the second prototype, was originally designed to be the first with a single vertical fin.

By then it was also decided to change the engines for the more powerful Bastan IV, but shortly after it was decided that the engine to be used on the series production aeroplanes would be the Bastan VI, which had 930shp of power, plus 75kg of thrust, with Ratier Figeac FH86 three-blade propellers with variable pitch. So, on 4 August 1962 the purchase of four Bastan IVs and thirty-six Bastan VIs was approved.

The test flight programme continued with two more flights on 7 and 12 June and then the plane was grounded until 17 September, flying again the next day and finishing the first stage of tests with a flight on 18 October. Those tests were aimed at verifying the basic performance of the plane, the flight conditions with a single engine and the maximum take-off weights in different conditions. A report was delivered in December 1962 by Rogelio Balado and engineer Miquel De Virgilio, sub-director of the Centro de Ensayos en Vuelo.

During the tests, the empty weight of the plane (with 44 litres of oil, 20 of hydraulic fluid and 20 of non-drainable fuel) was of 4,230kg, while the internal fuel was of 1,800 litres, for a total weight of 5,656kg. That left a payload capacity of 844kg for a maximum take-off weight of 6,500kg.

The minimum control speed with one engine was established as 169km/h, the stall speed with 45° of flaps and landing gear down was of 137km/h, and the type reached a maximum cruise speed of 447km/h with 6,000kg of weight between 3,000 and 4,000m of height, with an economic cruise of 300km/h, with which the plane had a range, at 5,000m height, of 2,297km. At maximum cruise speed the range was 2,194km.

While it was considered that the plane had better flight characteristics than the I.Ae.35

Before the first prototype of the Guaraní was built, a mock-up of the cabin was made using the unfinished fuselage of the I.Ae.35 that was going to be used in the prototype. *Archive Eduardo Ruiz*

Mock-up of the Guaraní cabin covered with fabric. The design was slightly different from what was built in the end. *Archive Eduardo Ruiz*

Construction of the tail of the first prototype of the Guaraní, with the lower structure modified from the original one of the I.Ae.35. *Archive Eduardo Ruiz*

Modification of the Guaraní I prototype into the Guaraní II, with the new tail.

Huanquero and fully fulfilled what was expected, with level speeds higher than what was calculated, the tests determined that the minimum control speed could be reduced on the version with one vertical fin, thus reducing the take-off speed and distance. That version was also expected to have better stability and control, so it was decided to cancel the version with two vertical fins and develop only the Guaraní II.

This led to the decision to modify the Guaraní I into the first Guaraní I, and it received a new tail with 52° of swept and a far bigger size than the original two, new brakes and other improvements, including the modification of the emergency exits on the central windows of the passenger cabin, which were made larger. Also, the weight was reduced by changing the materials of several parts and a de-icing system was added provided by the French company Kleber-Colombres.

The prototype was modified between January and March 1963 and, as now it was considered a different plane because it only maintained 20 per cent of the original I.Ae.35, on 27 March the administration of the factory requested the Instituto de Investigaciones IIAE assign a new model number to the type, to avoid confusion on the plans and part numbers. Thus, on 1 April the reply came with the new designation I.A.50 Guaraní II, and the prototype then received the new constructor number 00, received the serial LV-X27 on 4 April and two days later made its first flight with now Vicecomodoro Balado at the controls.

In the meantime, on 4 January of that year, the Dirección de Producción of DINFIA received the order to produce a first series of twenty Guaraní IIs, but the contract for the planes, which in the end included the prototype and another nineteen, was not signed until 6 September 1965. Meanwhile, since the design was almost ready, in March 1963, Horten, Freyer and part of the team stopped working on the project, with just a small team headed by Ruiz remaining.

Prototype of the I.A.50 Guaraní I at the runway of the Military Aviation School. *Archive Eduardo Ruiz*

The Guaraní I flying over the San Roque dam lake during its flight tests. *Archive Eduardo Ruiz*

While the flight tests evolved during the year, on 11 December the Guaraní II was presented to the Argentine president Arturo U. Illia, with the plane flown by Captain Juan Carlos Moroni. Also, around that date, the prototype received the Bastan IV engines.

Also, during that month the Guaraní II made its first flight outside Argentina, when it visited Asunción in Paraguay for the Aeronautical Week at the international airport of the city, performing a flying display.

Versions

Like the I.Ae.35, the I.A.50 Guaraní II was also planned in different versions, although they did not have an official designation. All had a toilet in the back, in front of the door, and a luggage compartment, in the left area between the cockpit and the passenger cabin, with the radio equipment to the right.

The passenger variant could carry ten people in individual seats but there was also an economic transport with six individual seats plus two rows of three seats, each one in front of the other in the front part of the cabin.

There was a VIP variant with four seats in the rear part of the cabin, with folding tables between them, plus two rows of three seats in the front part, a configuration already used in the Guaraní I prototype.

For medical evacuation it was planned to carry six stretchers plus two doctors, which was never used operationally.

There was a photo survey version, with an opening in the belly for the camera, which could be a Wild RC-8 or RC-9, and another for a periscope for navigation during the photo shoot. The camera operator was in a seat over the main wing spar, which as in the I.Ae.35, crossed the cabin through the middle. Also, this version carried three oxygen tanks for operations at high altitude.

A troop transport version was planned, with two rows of seats, one of eight seats and the other of seven, but this configuration was never used.

Also, in February 1963, following the idea of the I.Ae.35 as a multipurpose plane, Ruiz made various proposals, including one for attack and counter-insurgency, called Guaraní III Versión Armamento. It was basically a light bomber, in which the passenger cabin space was dedicated to the bomb bay,

The first prototype, already as a Guaraní II, at the factory, with a Huanquero seen inside the hangar. Both types co-existed for ten years in service. *Archive Eduardo Ruiz*

The first prototype of the Guaraní II on the apron at DINFIA, wearing the original serial LV-X27. *Archive Eduardo Ruiz*

without the traditional windows and with two bomb bay doors per side, which could carry twenty 50kg bombs. In addition, it carried two Hispano Suiza DCA-804 20mm guns in fairings on both sides of the fuselage and four underwing rocket mounts, with a capacity for eighteen SCARs or twelve T-10s. The upward view of the cabin was also improved, with a larger Plexiglas surface. The bombing sight was at the rear of the plane, where the 'bomber' station was also located with two round windows on the sides of the fuselage. This idea was shelved, since the original design of the plane did not make it very suitable for the type of war that was already looming in the 1960s and the FAA preferred to aim for a design born for the attack mission.

Another proposed version, called I.A.50-A, was for anti-submarine warfare, maritime patrol and attack, with a MAD on the rear end of the fuselage, search radar and ECM systems on the belly. It would have had two positions for the operators, one for the radar, ECM and MAD and the other for the active sonobuoys, eight sonobuoy dispensers with a rack to carry more, plus 5kg bombs, oxygen system, life raft and life jackets, APU and heating system. In addition, four 12.7mm machine guns on the sides of the nose, two bomb bays on the sides of the front cabin, each for two 200kg bombs, a searchlight on the right wing, extra fuel tanks in the wings and four underwing pylons, each for up to 200kg. Despite the type looked interesting, the Argentine Navy had just received its first Grumman S-2A Trackers, capable of operating from the ARA *Independencia* aircraft carrier, so they did not show much interest on the proposal.

Three views of the maritime surveillance and ASW variant proposed.

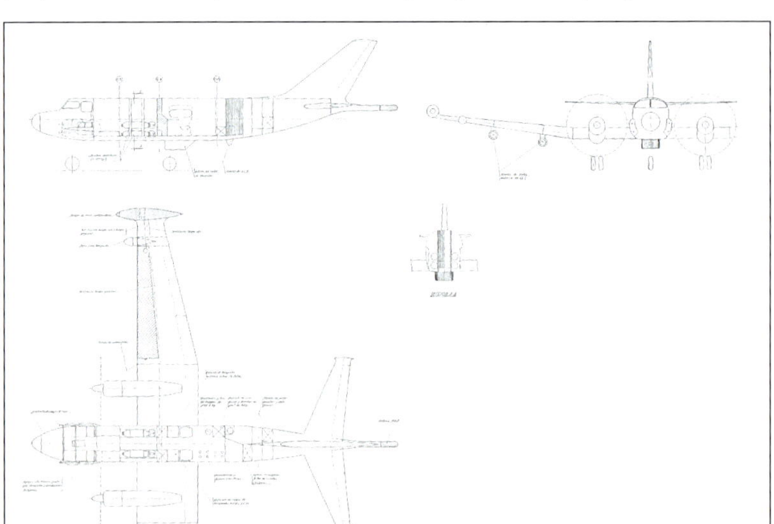

Shortly before those two armed versions were proposed, Ruiz started to work on a passenger variant, initially called Guaraní III, as is written on a model that was built by then, with a much longer fuselage, with 17,166m of length, keeping the same wing and tail, and having a semi-pressurised cabin. The plane had an extra door behind the cockpit, on the left side, and nine windows of almost triangular shape on each side, one for each of the eighteen passengers. When the armed version was called Guaraní III, this one became Guaraní IV, as appears on a plan dated 18 October 1963, but this idea was left behind shortly after.

Second plane

Production of the other planes progressed slowly, and Ruiz decided to modify the windscreen to increase visibility and because the one used on the prototype was not strong enough. Although the second and third planes were initially built with the structure around the windscreen to receive the original one, they were modified before being finished.

Thus, the second Guaraní II, which was considered the second prototype or the first of the pre-series, was finished on October 1964 and received the serial LV-X30 on 4 November. It received a special paint scheme with the words 'Guaraní II' big on the sides of the fuselage. Flew for the first time on March 1965.

This plane was used for the second stage of the flight tests because it had some improvements to the trim, but LV-X27 was also used in some of the tests, too. The plane demonstrated vibration problems in the tail, so from 1963 DINFIA started to study the possibility of performing such tests abroad.

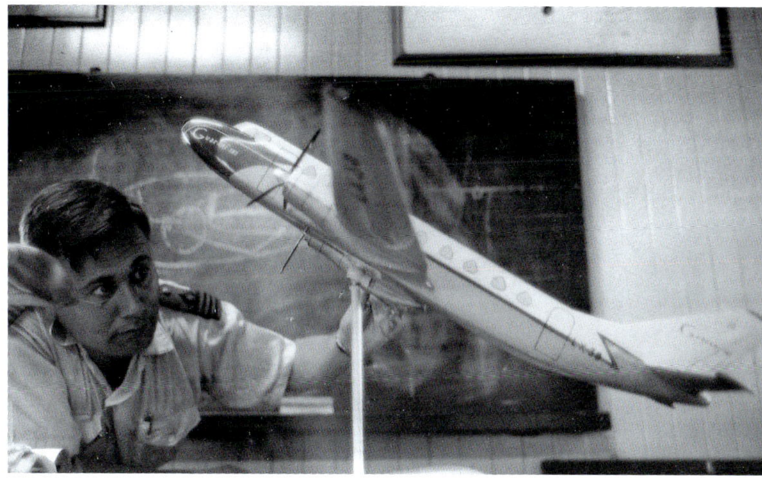

Héctor Ruiz looking at a model of the proposed Guaraní III with a longer fuselage. *Archive Eduardo Ruiz*

Plan of the Guaraní IV, which was the new designation of the longer I.A.50. This idea was abandoned shortly after. *Archive Eduardo Ruiz*

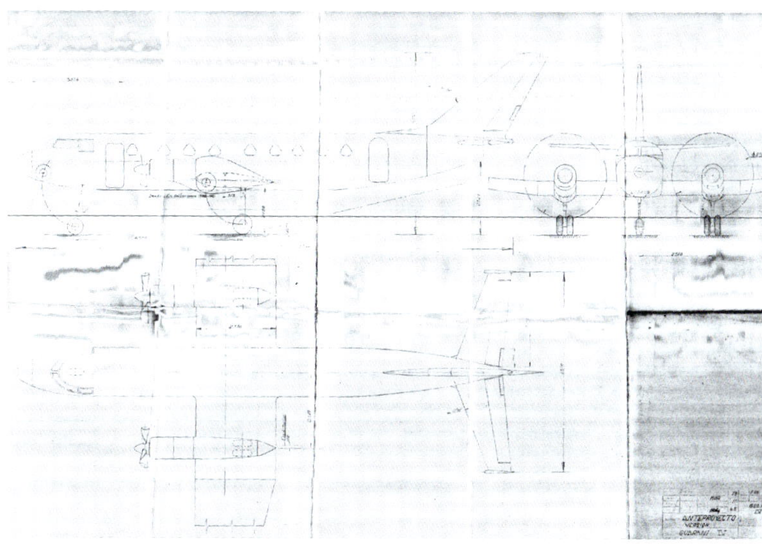

To France – Operación Ensayo

In September 1964, the founder, president and general director of Turbomeca, Joseph Szydlowsky, visited the factory and, due to the need to resolve the vibration problems, he suggested the aircraft be flown to the Centre d'Essais en Vol (CEV) in France for flutter and vibrations tests and also to achieve the international certification of the plane with the aim of exporting it. Also, he suggested sending a French test pilot to make a preliminary evaluation of the plane. DINFIA approved the idea and plans were made to send the plane to France, called Operación Ensayo, to perform the flight tests at Bretigny-sur-Orge and the static tests at Istres-Le Tubé.

In January 1965 French engineer and SNCASE chief pilot Jacques Lecarme arrived at the Argentinian CEV to evaluate the Guaraní II, and he recommended that to augment the stability in a spin and reduce the oscillations at low speeds, a ventral fin could be added to the rear, like the one used on the Beechcraft King Air. This fin was tested during the first months of 1965 on LV-X27, but not only did it not improve the flight quality, it worsened it, so it was removed.

The ferry flight to France was a challenge, not only because no aeroplane built in Latin America had done it before, but also because for the crossing of the Atlantic extra fuel tanks had to be installed. LV-X30 was chosen for the mission, for which the plane received a modification to the paint scheme on the nose and the new serial TX-01, while it also received

The second Guaraní II at Le Bourget.

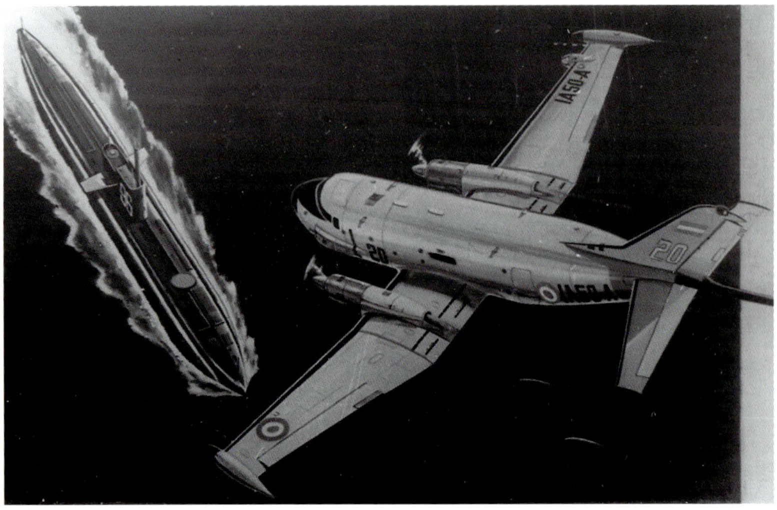

Drawing of the I.A.50-A version proposed for maritime surveillance and ASW. *Archive Eduardo Ruiz*

Three views of the attack proposal of the I.A.50, called Guaraní III Versión Armamento.

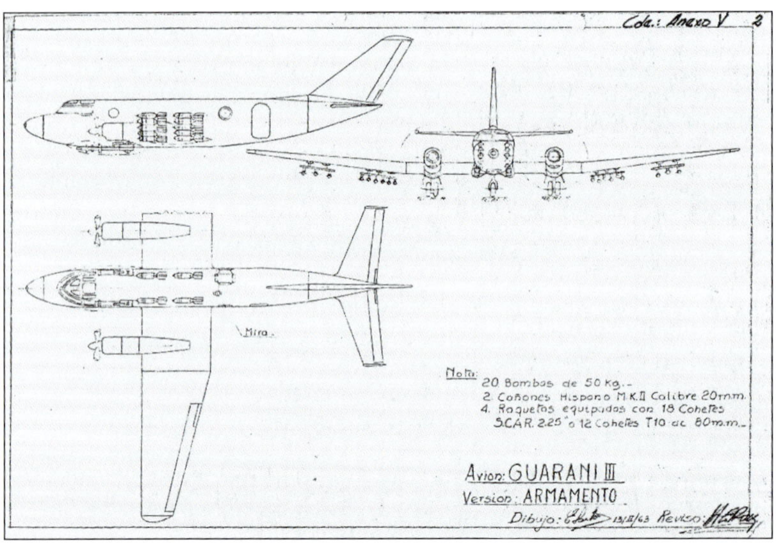

some modifications to its equipment. For the crossing of the Atlantic, three tanks of 500 litres each were designed and built to be installed on the floor and sides of the cabin, plus another, with rectangular shape, of 276.3 litres of capacity, to be installed below the extra tank installed in the front part of the cabin.

Also, it was decided to add a Kolsman sextant and a Bendix RDR-1E navigation and meteorological radar in the plane, which was installed in the nose, moving some of the instruments originally located there to the racks behind the cockpit. Also, the landing light was installed on the nose landing gear instead of the nose of the plane. This was later adopted by all the other planes and retrofitted to the first prototype, too. The plane was also as equipped with a life raft, six life vests and survival equipment in case it had to ditch in the Atlantic.

A crew for the trip to France was organised, headed by Rogelio Balado with Captain Ramón Ameodo as co-pilot, 1st Lt Roberto Mela as navigator and Captain Héctor Ruiz as flight engineer. Vicecomodoro Luis Rossell, Captain Carlos Alberto Maiztegui and civil employees Blas Ambrogio, Roberto Bengolea and Orlando Petrey also were part of the commission to France but did not fly in the Guaraní II.

The crew analysed four alternatives for the Atlantic crossing, all departing from Recife in north-eastern Brazil; one being Ascension Island–Conakry, another with stops at Ascension and Dakar, the third with stops at Ilha de Sal and Dakar and the last trying a direct flight to Dakar. In the end, they chose to land at Dakar, with an alternative at Ilha de Sal, due to the airport infrastructure, despite that route demanding more time flying over the sea, as it was 3,160km from Recife to Ilha de Sal.

Between 13 and 19 May 1965 the plane was tested with the new equipment and also to test the endurance with the extra tanks, which occupied most of the rear cabin, and it reached up to ten hours of flight.

On 21 May 1965 the team left DINFIA towards the Aeroparque of Buenos Aires, from which they flew on the next day to Rio de Janeiro and then to Recife. They had analysed if it was better to cross the Atlantic during the day or during the night, with Mela suggesting that it was better at night as they could use the stars for a better navigation, but Balado preferred to do it in daylight to have better visibility if they had to ditch. The crossing of the Atlantic started before dawn, to avoid the high temperatures of the day due to their heavy take-off weight. The crossing was with good weather, with only a few clouds while crossing the Equator. They landed at Dakar after nine hours fifteen minutes, with forty-five minutes of fuel remaining, making the first Atlantic crossing of a Latin American-built aeroplane.

On 24 May they took off from Dakar to Las Palmas in the Canary Islands, and then to Madrid, following on the next day to Paris Le Bourget.

It was decided to take advantage of the trip and also show the plane at the XXVI Salon International de l'Aeronautique et l'Espace at Le Bourget between 11 and 21 June, being the first Latin American plane to be shown at the exhibition on the ground and in the air. The extra tanks were removed and twelve seats were installed in the cabin. After that, the plane went to Istres for airframe vibration tests performed by the ONERA (Office Nationale d'Etudes et Recherches Aéronautiques) between 7 August and 15 September and engine tests by the Centre d'Essais de Propulseurs (CEP) between 10 October and 9 December. Then, it went to the CEV in Bretigny-sur-Orge, where it was flown for more than 200 hours, obtaining in the end the French AIR-2051 certification (similar to the CAR-4b1 of the FAA). In France the plane received a liquid oxygen system, to replace the gaseous oxygen tanks, making it possible to fly higher on the return flight and consume less fuel, reaching an endurance of almost up to twelve hours.

Finally, after almost nine months in France, on 13 February 1966 the TX-01 and its crew started the return to Argentina, with a first stop at Madrid and

Construction of the second prototype or first pre-series plane. The mid fuselage and the wing were originally made to be an I.Ae.35 and were modified. The cockpit still has the original shape of the windscreen, which was modified before the plane was finished.

then at Las Palmas, following on the next day to Dakar. On 15 February they made the flight to Recife and continued to Rio de Janeiro, while on the next day they went to Montevideo, despite it not being originally planned, because they had to wait until making the final leg to Aeroparque for the official reception. On the 18th they flew back to DINFIA, finishing the Operación Ensayo.

TX-01 continued being used for tests, which were finished by mid-1966, and on 5 August 1966 a commission was created to analyse all the technical reports produced during the tests. On 29 August they made their final report, suggesting some changes, including the change of the engines for the Bastan VI, as was already planned. Then, on 17 October 1966, TX-01 was delivered to the Argentine Air Force, with serial T-124, to serve at the Escuadrón III of the I Brigada Aérea at El Palomar, wearing a new paint scheme, although the official transference was only made on 30 December. By then it was decided that the Guaranís would have serials running from T-111 onwards.

Installation of the Bastan engines on one of the first Guaranís. Originally the prototype used the Bastan III, later changed for Bastan IV, but in the end the type used the more powerful Bastan VI. Archive *Fernando Benedetto*

Production

The second pre-series plane (c/n 02), which was assigned the serial LV-X32 for the tests, was presented on 27 October 1965, during the thirty-eighth anniversary of the FMA, with a special colour scheme and named *Patria* (Homeland). It was intended to operate it as presidential plane, but in the end it was never used for that mission. The plane flew on July 1966 and kept flying with the factory until 13 December of that year, when it was transferred to the Argentine Air Force with serial T-112 to serve with the I Brigada Aérea. It was the fourth I.A.50 Guaraní II in operational service, as the first series production machine (c/n 03) was finished on June 1966 and delivered to the Air Force on the 28th of that month, with serial T-111. On 25 October, T-113 was delivered, followed by T-114 on 1 December.

Although the plan was to deliver the first twenty (including the prototypes) to the Argentine Air Force in 1967, production progressed slowly due to delays by the providers of some equipment that came from abroad, so in 1967 only five Guaranís were delivered, with the first being the T-115 (c/n 07) on 23 March. This was followed on 22 August by the first for photo

Cockpit of one of the first Guaraní IIs. The controls were changed over the years. *Archive CEV*

Installation of the extra fuel tanks in the cabin of TX-01 for the flight to France. *Archive Eduardo Ruiz*

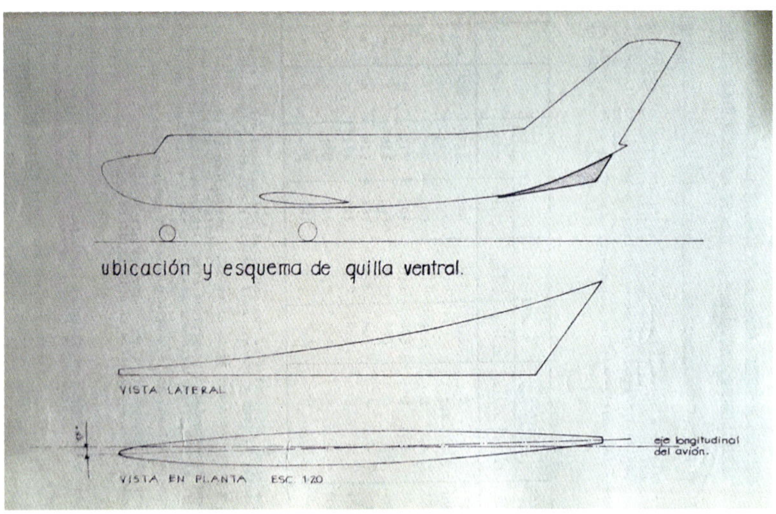

Disposition of the ventral fin that was tested in early 1965 on LV-X27. No picture of its installation is known. *Archive CEV*

Diagram of the installation of the four extra fuel tanks for the Atlantic crossing, with two ahead of the main spar (one on top of the other) and two behind. *Archive Eduardo Ruiz*

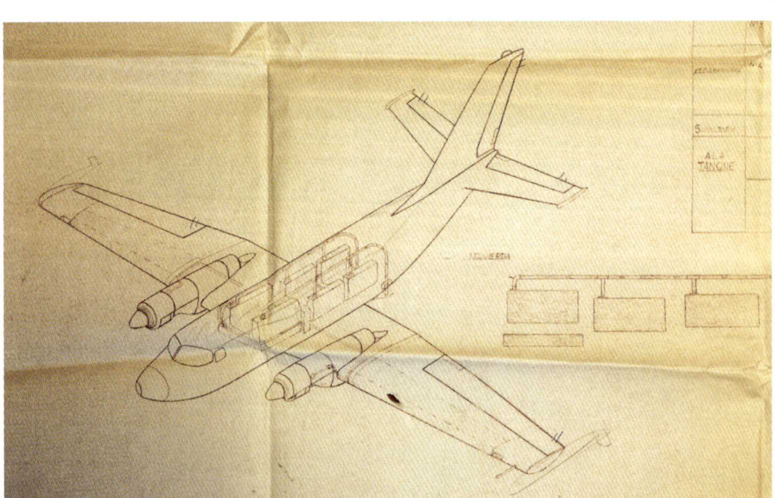

survey (c/n 06), serialled F-31, and ending with T-118 (c/n 10) delivered on 19 December. All were sent to the I Brigada Aérea, except F-31, which was sent to the II Brigada Aérea, the unit of the Argentine Air Force dedicated for photo survey and reconnaissance.

The other ten were almost finished, all between 84 to 99 per cent of construction, but waiting for some parts.

T-115, before delivery, was used on February 1967 for tests of the air flux around the nose of the plane in different configurations.

On 28 March 1967, T-112 suffered a minor accident when, due to hard vibrations, the stabilisers were extensively damaged, although it could land without major problems. This also stopped production until it was determined that, being a pre-series plane, some structural parts were different from the series production, so the line restarted work. Because of this, it was decided to assign the airframe with constructor number 18 for use on static tests. Although some improvements were made during the tests, the type still suffered from some vibration problems in the tail.

On July 1967 the first prototype, which received a new paint scheme, was used for vibration tests, evaluating the air flux on the rear part of the fuselage. At the beginning of 1968, it was re-serialled TX-110.

Deliveries continued in 1968 with aircraft T-119 to T-123, with T-122 being configured for VIP flights for the Commander in Chief of the Air Force. It was equipped with four seats in the rear part, with folding tables in the middle, a radio syntonizer and a telephone, plus two extra passenger seats in the front, with another one for the waitress and a small bar. This plane was also the first to be equipped with the 300-litre extra fuel tanks on the wingtips.

Meanwhile, on 11 May 1967 the Brazilian Aeronautic Direction requested a quote for fifteen aircraft with basic configuration with ten seats. The company informed Brazil that the first two could be delivered in the second half of 1968, taking them from the series being built to the Argentine Air Force, with all deliveries lasting between twenty-four and thirty months. However, in the end the Brazilians decided to cancel the purchase as the country was developing its own light transport, which became the Embraer EMB-110 Bandeirante, which flew in October 1968.

Finally, the first series was concluded in 1969 with the deliveries of T-125 (c/n 16), F-32 (c/n 17) and F-33 (c/n 19).

To Antarctica

After the successful flight over the Atlantic Ocean, another long-distance flight was planned, this time to fly over Antarctica, for which the first prototype was equipped with radar and extra fuel tanks in the cabin plus the two wingtip tanks, to have a range of 4,000km. The plane also received red stripes to make it more visible in case of an accident over the ice.

The T-111 was the first Guaraní II destined for operational service with the Argentine Air Force, delivered in 1966. In 1970 it went to the Federal Police until 1981, when it returned to the Air Force as T-123. It was scrapped before 2005.

With Commander Roberto Starc as pilot, Captain José Videla as co-pilot, Commander Héctor Ruiz as engineer and Captain Ramón Campos, they took off from Río Gallegos, Santa Cruz province, at 9.53 on 15 November 1968, heading south to fly over Tierra del Fuego and then over the Drake Passage. They flew over Deception Island and then reached the Argentine Teniente Benjamín Matienzo Base on the Antarctic Peninsula, flying over it and then heading back, arriving to Río Gallegos at 15.40, after five hours fifty minutes hours of flight. The operation was supported by the Douglas DC-6 serialled TC-55 and with its success they became the first aeroplane built in Latin America to fly over Antarctica.

This experience led to the interest of the possible use of the Guaraní II on Antarctic operations, so Héctor Ruiz started to work on the design of skis and a modification of the landing gear to operate them. The plane serialled T-125, which was being finished by the factory, was chosen to be modified and by early 1969 it was ready for the tests. Several flights were made to test the performance of the plane with the skis, but they never received the Teflon material needed to prevent the skids freezing to the ice and the programme was cancelled shortly after, as the Argentine Air Force was receiving de Havilland Canada DHC 6 200 Twin Otters prepared for Antarctic operations, with more cargo capacity than the Guaraní II.

Damage caused to T-112 due to heavy vibrations on 28 March 1967. This accident led to the decision to stop the production line briefly and to dedicate the airframe with c/n 18 for structural tests. This aircraft was later lost on in accident with 35 per cent damage at Paraje Bahía Solano, near the city of Comodoro Rivadavia in Chubut province. *Archive Eduardo Ruiz*

Tests performed on 24 February 1967 with T-115 before delivery, to evaluate the air flux around the nose of the plane. *Archive Eduardo Ruiz*

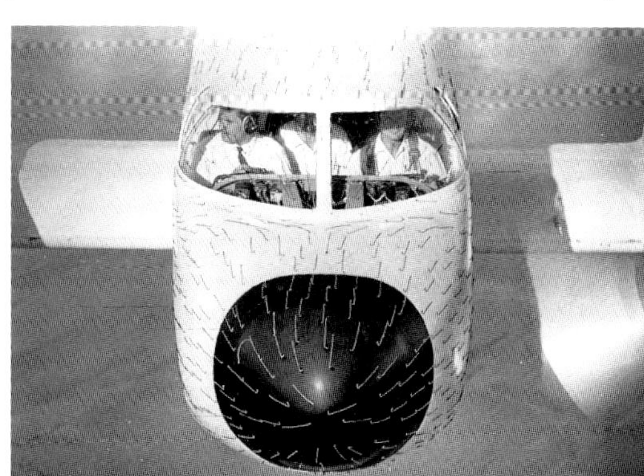

From Guaraní II to G.II and second series

By the end of the 1960s, a company that had registered the name Guaraní sued the now FMA (DINFIA had ceased to exist on 1 January 1968 when the car production was separated from the aircraft one) for the use of the name, so on 22 June 1970 the

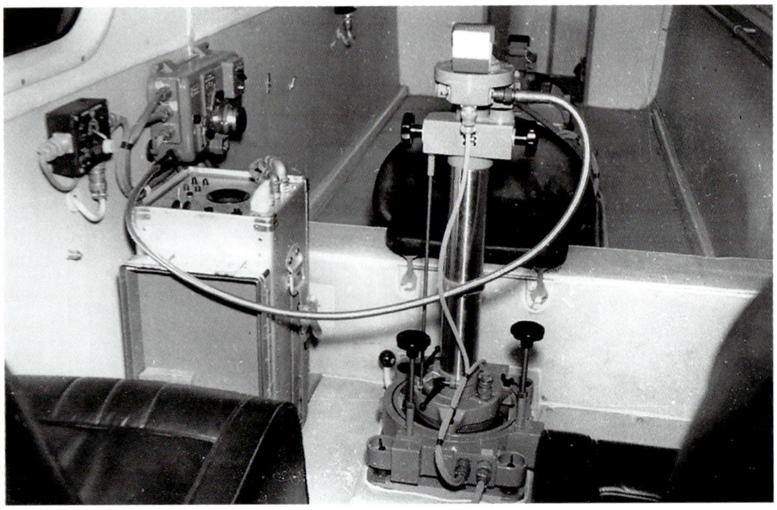

Navigation periscope for the photographer in the extended position and with the cover slid, used in the photo survey versions. *Archive Eduardo Ruiz*

Navigation periscope for the operator of the cameras in the photo survey aircraft. The plane still does not have the liquid oxygen tanks that were installed for high-altitude photography. *Archive Eduardo Ruiz*

factory had to change the name to I.A.50 G-II, which was communicated by Resolution No. 210, but it was known unofficially as Guaraní until its retirement.

Meanwhile, by August 1968 Héctor Ruiz was ordered to prepare a second series of the I.A.50 and he made a plan, which was finished on 6 September, in which he specified the first plane could be delivered in one year, with deliveries of one plane every thirty-five days and with construction demanding 77,000 men hours.

This second series, interestingly, was not aimed only to the Air Force, but also for other customers. The Argentine Air Force was wanting six, two of them for the Comando de Regiones Aéreas and to be for the verification of radio aids at civil aerodromes. The Argentine Navy also showed interest in five aeroplanes in 1968, reduced in 1969 to two, but with modification for operations over the sea and specific equipment. The Dirección de Aviación Civil was interested in two, while the provinces of Buenos Aires, Córdoba and Corrientes also requested offers to equip their Aviation Directions. The same happened with Obras Sanitarias de la Nación, the company in charge of the water distribution, Fiat Concord, the company Fairey Survey SA, IKA Renault and the Instituto Nacional de Vitivinicultura (dedicated to wine production research).

Twenty Bastan VI engines were ordered in 1969 and it was considered equipping the planes with Ratier Figeac FH 206.2 propellers of four blades of 2.55m of diameter, but this was left behind as they could provide only a limited increase in performance but would generate logistic problems by having aircraft with different propellers.

In the early 1970 a contract was signed for the production of the second series of ten planes, which was later extended to fifteen, of which at least eight

5-T-30, only Guaraní II operated briefly by the Argentine Navy. The force showed interest in the type at the beginning, but in the end they bought the Beechcraft Queen Air.

The first prototype was re-serialled TX-01 when the second prototype was delivered to the Argentine Air Force as T-124. It was also modified with the new windscreen around 1970 and was the first one to receive the new stabilisers with 14° of positive dihedral. Here it is flying with one of the planes dedicated for radio aids verification and is equipped with an air data probe. *Archive Eduardo Ruiz*

were expected to be sold to other customers.

The first of the new series (with constructor number 20) was a new special version for radio navigation aids verification, especially the new ILS systems installed since 1969 in different airports of the country, but also VOR, DME and VASI systems. The aircraft was delivered on 22 December 1971 to the VII Brigada Aérea of the Argentine Air Force at Morón, near Buenos Aires, for use by the Comando de Regiones Aéreas, which was the organisation within the Air Force in charge of civil aviation. The aircraft, with serial VR-15, received two antennas on the sides of the nose, plus another on top of the cabin and the consoles to register what the antennas detected. The system was provided by the French company Sofreavia. The aircraft c/n 22 was also delivered in this configuration, with serial VR-16. They performed this mission until December 1986, when it was planned to modernise their systems, but this did not take place and, instead, on 15 March 1990 they were transferred to the II Brigada Aérea with serials T-110 and T-129 respectively, configured as transports.

On 22 August 1983, with the intention of adding a new mission to the G-II, although it was originally in the plans when the type was designed, parachutist jumps were made from T-114, by removing the door, but the risk of hitting the stabiliser was high, so this

T-122, which was built with VIP interiors, seen in August 1996. This was the first Guaraní II to be delivered with the extra wingtip tanks. After its retirement it was donated to the Aeroclub Argentino but when the club closed the plane remained abandoned and currently is in very poor conditions. *Santiago Rivas*

T-125 flying with the skis and the gear down during tests. Due to the incorporation of the Twin Otters by the Argentine Air Force, prepared for Antarctic operations, and the limited cargo capacity of the Guaraní II, the idea was dropped. The skis are currently stored at the Centro de Investigación Aplicada of the Argentine Air Force, next to the factory. *Archive Eduardo Ruiz*

was never repeated.

As the problems with vibrations were still not solved, in the early 1970s the prototype received modified stabilisers with 14° of positive dihedral, but this was not adopted on other examples until in 1987 the Argentine Air Force started to modify their planes at a slow rate, finishing in 1999 with T-110. Finally, on 7 January 2007, the I.A.50 G-II was retired from service by the Argentine Air Force, with F-31 being the last of the type in service. Currently, seventeen still survive, but some are in very poor condition or abandoned.

To other operators

The first operator of the I.A.50 G-II outside the Argentine Air Force was the Policía Federal Argentina, who on 31 December 1970 purchased T-111, which was delivered to the Escuadrón Aéreo of the force on 31 August 1971 with serial LQ-JXN. The plane was used until on 18 June 1981 was sold back to the Argentine Air Force, which serialled it T-123.

The next to be delivered to another operator was also one from the first series. Due to the interest of the Argentine Navy, the plane serialled T-113 was loaned in 1971 to that force, to be used by the Segunda Escuadrilla Aeronaval de Sostén Logístico Móvil of the Comando de Aviación Naval, receiving the serial 5-T-30 and being used until 5 June 1972, when it was returned to the Air Force as T-113. In the end, the Navy did not buy the I.A.50 and went for the Beechcraft B50 Queen Air instead.

Meanwhile, as was planned, most of the planes of the second series were delivered to other customers as, besides VR-15 and 16, the only others from the fifteen of the series that originally went to the Argentine Air Force were c/n 26, which became T-126 and since its delivery on 22 December 1972 was used to carry the commander in chief of the force; c/n 33, which was going to be delivered to another customer as LV-LAN but in the end went to the force in 1974 as T-128, and the last G-II built (c/n 34), which was delivered on 20 January 1975 for photo survey as F-35. (T-114 was modified for photo survey in 1971 and re-serialled F-34).

The first aircraft of the second series to be sold was c/n 21, which was negotiated with the Argentine Army in 1971 and even received the serial AE-1001, but in the end the contract was cancelled and the plane was again offered for sale. It was bought by the Servicio Penitenciario Federal, in charge of federal prisons, which received it on 13 January 1972 with serial LQ-JXY, using the plane until its retirement on 18 June 1993.

The next operator was the government of Córdoba province, which purchased three to be flown by the Dirección General de Aeronáutica. They were c/ns 23, 28 and 31, which received the serials LQ-JZS (shortly changed to LV-JZS on 14 April 1973), LQ-LAF (changed to LV-LAF shortly before delivery) and LV-LAL. The purchase of the latter was cancelled and it then went to the Argentine Air Force as T-127 in 1974. The other two planes were used to provide air services between the cities of Córdoba and Villa Dolores, but also in brief operations to other cities of the province. In 1979 the government decided to cease their operation and in 1980 both were resold to the Argentine Air Force, which serialled them T-112 and T-114 respectively.

The Ministerio de Bienestar Social (Social Welfare Ministry), which was creating an air branch of the new Dirección Nacional de Emergencias Sociales (Social Emergencies National Direction) in the early 1970s to provide medical evacuation and social assistance throughout the country, purchased c/n

VR-15 seen around 1988 with the last paint scheme used with that serial, copied from the one used by the two Learjet 35As that performed the same mission. When it was transferred to the II Brigada Aérea as a transport, it kept this scheme for a while. *Alberto Martín*

LQ-JXY, originally destined for the Argentine Army, was purchased by the Federal Penitentiary Service for the transport of prisoners. The plane served with this organisation until its retirement in 1993, when it was donated to the National Aeronautics Museum. *Alberto Martín*

The first Guaraní II for the government of Córdoba province was LV-JZS, named Inti Huasi. In 1980 it became T-112 with the Argentine Air Force.

24. It was delivered on 4 August 1972 with serial LQ-MBS, re-serialled LV-MBS on 7 February 1973 and went back to LQ-MBS in the early 1980s. It was retired in 1995 after a minor accident at San Fernando International Airport in Buenos Aires.

The government of Salta province purchased another example (c/n 25) for the Dirección Provincial de Aviación Civil, it receiving the serial LQ-LAD on 6 December 1972 and later LV-LAD in 1973. It was used extensively for air services over the province and to carry officials, having duplicated avionics and a system to start the engines at high altitudes, as it was used regularly at airfields around 4,000m of height. It was used until September 1983, when it had an accident and was written off.

While the province of Mendoza negotiated two planes and one was delivered to be tested in 1973, the deal was cancelled and the plane (c/n 30), with serial LV-LAJ, was delivered on 26 December 1973 to the Dirección Provincial de Aeronáutica of Catamarca province, together with c/n 32, which was serialled LV-LAM and delivered on 28 June 1974. They performed regular flights between the capital of the province, San Fernando del Valle de Catamarca, to small towns on the Andes mountains. On 17 June 1980 they were sold back to the Argentine Air Force with serials T-113 and T-111 respectively.

The other province to buy the I.A.50 G-II was Entre Ríos, which purchased two in 1972. It received c/n 27 on 15 February 1973 as LQ-LAE (becoming LV-LAE shortly after) and c/n 29 on 10 October of that year as LV-LAI, but while waiting to receive those planes, in 1972 the Argentine Air Force loaned T-119, which received the serial LQ-JZO (changed to LV-JZO) and was used until late 1973, before returning to the air force. They served at the Dirección de Aeronáutica Provincial, which in 1967 had created the Línea Aérea Provincial de Entre Ríos, LAPER, to fly from Paraná city to other cities in the country and also within the province. In 1977 LAPER shut down but the planes continued making official flights for the provincial government until in 1983 it created Servicios Aéreos Provinciales de Entre Ríos, SAPER. It only operated briefly during the year but was then restarted in 1986 on a non-regular basis. Finally, in 1988 Líneas Aéreas Entre Ríos was set up, which operated the G-IIs until LV-LAI was retired in 1992 and LV-LAE was written off after an accident on 23 January 1994.

The main problem for customers outside the Argentine Air Force was poor customer support by the factory and lack of spares, which were more evident by the late 1970s and led to the decision of the Federal Police and the governments of Córdoba and Catamarca to sell their planes to the Air Force. Also, as was usual at the factory, a poor sales team and financing were crucial in the failure to sell the G-II to private customers or to export the type.

The G-III

In 1964, Héctor Ruiz started a draft of an aeroplane much bigger than the Guaraní II and with pressurised cabin. It was 22m long, 7.95m high, had a wingspan of 27.5m and a fuselage 2.3m wide. The wing area

LQ-MBS was delivered to the Ministerio de Bienestar Social and served in medical evacuation and social assistance until it had an accident in 1995 and was written off. Currently it is being used for ground training at the Escuela de Suboficiales of the Argentine Air Force in Córdoba. *Alberto Martín*

Before being converted for photo survey, T-114 briefly wore this paint scheme, which was originally adopted by the Fokker F27 and DHC-6 Twin Otters and was later also used by the Fokker F28.

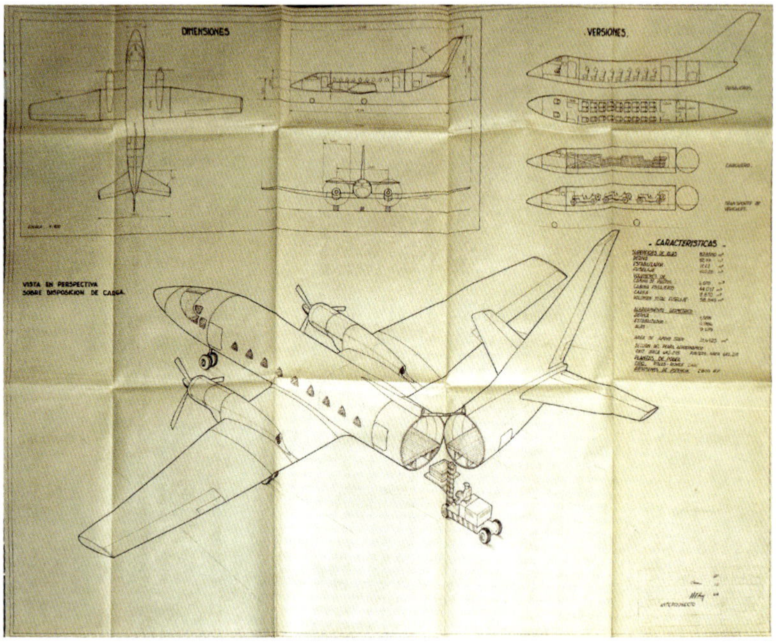

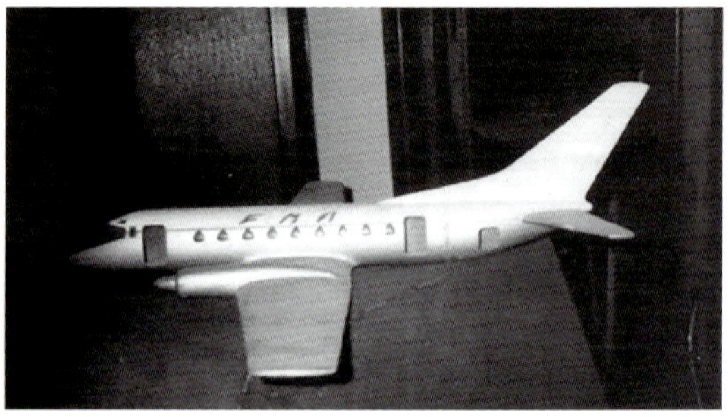

ABOVE Factory model of the proposed G-III shown in 1972.

LEFT Scheme of the draft made by Héctor Ruiz, dated 20 October 1964 for its pressurised turboprop, which in the 1970s he intended to develop as the G-III. *Archive Eduardo Ruiz*

was 82.83m2 . While the tail had a similar design to the Guaraní II, the rest was totally different. Like the original Guaraní III, the windows would have an almost triangular shape.

The passenger cabin had a volume of 44.017 cubic metres and the rear part of the fuselage could be opened to one side to permit the loading of large cargo or vehicles, with space for up to three jeeps, for example. For passenger cargo it would have capacity for twenty-seven passengers with a toilet and a cargo hold of 8.87 cubic metres. It was going to be powered by two Rolls-Royce RB.53 Dart turboprops of an unspecified type, but Ruiz stated they would have a total of 2,800hp of power, so most probably he was thinking of the RDa.3 of 1,480hp and 1,345shp.

This idea did not progress, and Ruiz shelved it for some time, but he saw that the market needed a small turboprop with pressurised cabin, something that was not possible with the fuselage section of the Guaraní II, despite his attempts with the original Guaraní III (later called Guaraní IV) proposal. So, in 1970 he presented a plan for a family of aircraft to be developed in which he included what he called

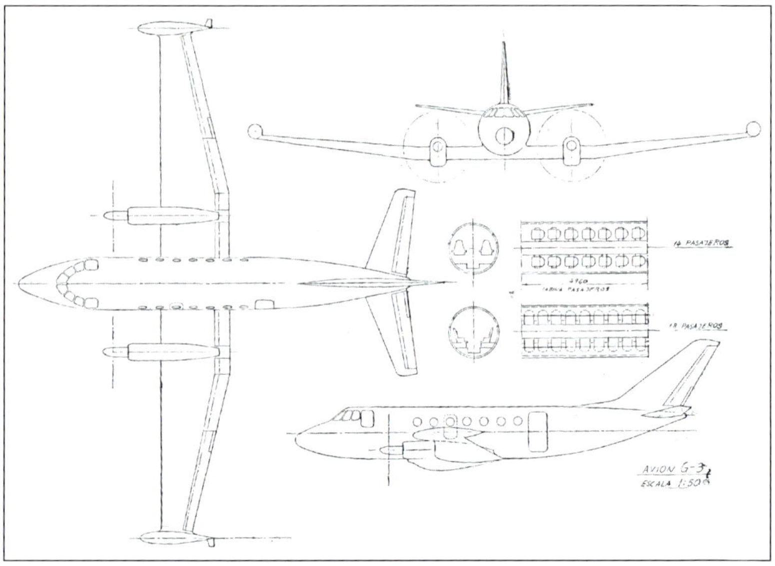

First layout of the pressurised G-II from 1970, called G-III or G-3.

The first prototype, as TX-01, seen in Buenos Aires in the 1970s. It is now a monument at the town of Tancacha, Córdoba, with fake serial T-121. *Alberto Martín*

One of the two Guaraní IIs that belonged to Entre Ríos government, already with the colours of Líneas Aéreas Entre Ríos, LAER, after 1988. *Alberto Martín*

as 'pressurised version of the G-II', stating it was a plane to carry twenty-five passengers at around 580km/h. That plan also included the development of an improved version of the I.A.53 Mamboretá, the I.A.60 attack plane and different versions of the I.A.58 Pucará, plus an idea for a transonic bomber.

Interestingly, for this plan, he included a picture of the scale model of his proposal from 1964, but three-views of a much smaller design, which used the wings and tail surfaces of the G-II, Turbomeca Astazou engines, and a new fuselage with round shape and capacity for fourteen passengers. Another plan was made, probably before this one, in which the fuselage more resembled the G-II and shows also a high-density cabin layout with eighteen seats on two rows on the sides of the cabin. A plan dated 2 November 1970 shows a more aerodynamic fuselage design. At the III Aerospace Technology Symposium, which took place in April 1972, the model of the 1964 project was shown with the designation G-III, indicating that Ruiz had returned to this idea instead of just a pressurised version of the G-II.

In a plan he presented in November 1973 for the development of the FMA for the next fifteen years, he proposed to start the design in that year, while he revealed that preliminary calculations had already been made in 1973. In that report he included also the development of a jet light liaison plane based on the Pucará, a subsonic bomber (the I.A.60 project) and a supersonic fighter, whose first pre-series example was expected to be ready by 1989. He also included the improved I.A.53 Mamboretá, the I.A.58 Pucará and the jet version of the Pucará. For the G-III he stated that it would need 420,000 direct man hours between 1974 and 1976 to develop the plane, plus 850,000 indirect ones. He expected to have the prototype ready to fly in 1975.

The second Guaraní built was delivered to the Argentine Air Force as T-124, with a white nose despite the rest of the paint scheme being the regular one used by most of the force's Guaraní IIs. *Alberto Martín*

In 1983, tests were made to drop paratroopers from the I.A.50, but the danger posed by the low stabiliser and the small size of the cabin, plus the need to remove the door before the flight, ended the idea.

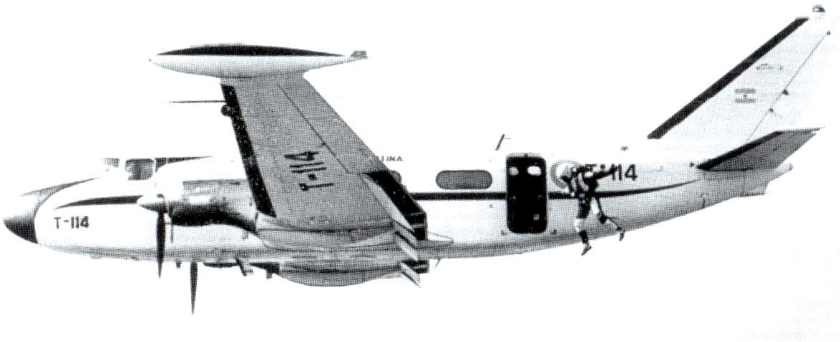

29 I.A.52

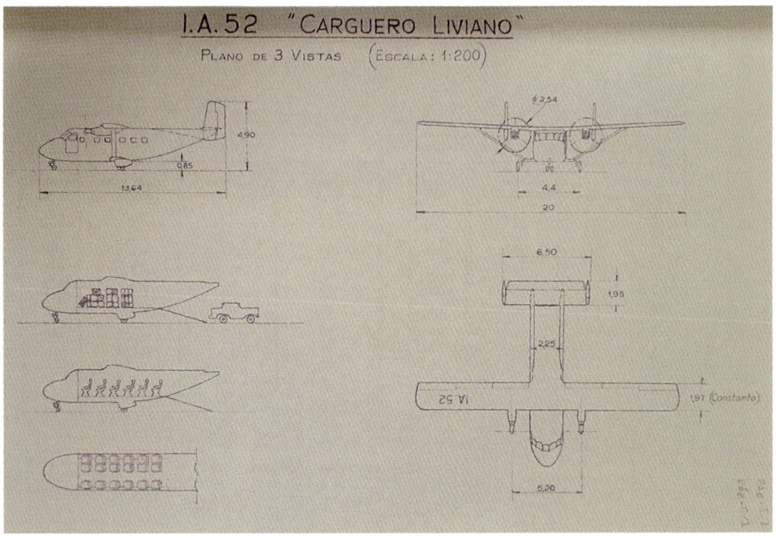

Three views and cabin configurations of the I.A.52.

In 1962, the Grupo de Desarrollos Aeronáuticos of the IIAE saw the need for a light transport aircraft to operate in regions with poor airport infrastructure but also a lack of proper roads or railways, for which they started to work on a proposal to fulfil that need. The project, designated I.A.52, was started with engineer Ricardo Olmedo heading it. The design was based on the Shorts SC.7 Skyvan, whose prototype was being built by then, and the plane was expected to carry 1,330 kilos or twelve passengers up to 1,160km, or a maximum load of 2,040 kilos or eighteen passengers only 111km, at a height of 3,000m and a cruise speed of 282km/h with a reserve for forty-five minutes of flight. It was to be powered by two Turbomeca Astazou II turboprops of 640shp at 43,000rpm, with Ratier Figeac three-blade propellers of 2.5m of diameter. It would have two fuel tanks on the wings, for 215 litres each, plus one in the central part of the fuselage for 770 litres, for a total of 1,200 litres (935kg).

It was planned in passenger, cargo, ambulance and military versions and, for cargo, the floor was prepared to resist a load of 1,000kg/m2, especially in the case of vehicles, having a rear ramp for the loading of cargo, which was planned to be opened in flight to drop parachutists or cargo, and as an option a hoist to move the cargo inside the cabin could be installed. Also, it would have a door on the left side of the cockpit for pilot access. In the case of passengers, it would have six rows of three seats, with a toilet in the back. For medical evacuation it was planned to carry twelve stretchers and an assistant, and as military transport it was expected to carry up to sixteen paratroopers and their equipment. It was also planned to divide the cabin by an attachable wall to carry passengers in the front part and cargo in the rear.

The cost of the plane was calculated on being 205,600 USD, of which 30,700 was calculated for the engines, 6,500 for the propellers and 25,000 for the communications equipment.

The type was a monoplane with high cantilever wing, made of aluminium alloy, with a mount on each side, having a main spar and a secondary one. All moving surfaces were to be built and covered with metal.

The fuselage was also completely made of metal, with cantilever construction in the cabin and nose and semi-monocoque construction in the cargo area. The tail had a horizontal stabiliser linked to the fuselage by two short booms and had two vertical fins, of cantilever construction.

The landing gear was fixed but the nose one, with two wheels, could be optionally retracted forward.

The avionics would include a Bendix radar and autopilot as options, while it would have two VHF and one HF radios, two ADF, one VOR/ILS and one DM.

The wing would have 20m of span and 39m2 of area, while the design would be 13.64m long and 4.90m high. The wheelbase was 4.4m, with a distance of 4.8m between the nosewheel and the main wheels.

The passenger cabin would be 6m long, with a maximum width of 1.92m and a height of 1.8m, with an area of 11.5m2 and a volume of 21m3, while for cargo, using part of the ramp, the volume was 26m3. The cargo door would be 3.25m long, 1.86m width and the height of the threshold 0.86m high.

The empty weight of the cargo version was to be 3,000kg and the passenger one was 3,250kg, while the payload, including fuel, was 2,015kg for the passenger version and 2,065kg for the cargo one.

The maximum speed was expected to be 347km/h at 2,000m, with a never-exceeded speed of 438km/h. The economic cruise speed was to be 282km/h and the stall speed of 110km/h with 60° of flaps, with a climb rate of 8m/s. The take-off distance, with an obstacle of 15m, was 470m, and it needed 445m to land in the same conditions. For ferry flights at 7,000m, using oxygen for the crew, the range could be up to 1,700km with reserves or 2,000 without them.

In 1963 wind tunnel tests were conducted with models, one of which still survives at the Centro de

Scale model of the I.A.52 showing the possible cargo that could be carried on the plane, which included long loads thanks to its rear ramp. *Archive FAdeA*

Investigación Aplicada of the Argentine Air Force, and a wooden mock-up of the fuselage was built. Also, construction of the prototype parts began to be built in 1964, as it was planned to make the first flight by 1965.

Finally, because an analysis of costs and possibilities of selling the type showed that there was a small margin, and due to the economic situation of the country, by the end of 1964 the project was cancelled and the mock-up was scrapped, although there was a demand for such a type of aircraft.

ABOVE LEFT Wind tunnel model of the I.A.52 preserved at the Centro de Investigación Aplicada of the Argentine Air Force. *Santiago Rivas*

ABOVE RIGHT Construction of the mock-up of the I.A.52.

30 I.A.53 Mamboretá

After the use of aeroplanes in crop dusting to control locusts in Argentina in the 1940s and 1950s, the country also started to incorporate aircraft for crop spraying to protect the huge agriculture production of Argentina. As was happening around the world, but especially in the United States, the use of aircraft to protect crops was growing fast and development of new dedicated aeroplanes began in the 1950s. By the early 1960s, a lot of Piper PA-25 Pawnees began to be imported to Argentina, as well as some other types, and DINFIA saw that there was a big demand for crop-spraying aircraft. While since 1962 the I.A.46 Ranquel was being sold for this duty, it was in fact an aeroplane designed for light transport that had a version dedicated to crop spraying. It was evident that a specialised type was more efficient.

In 1963, engineer Captain Ricardo Olmedo, whose team at the Grupo de Desarrollos Aeronáuticos had nothing to work with after the cancellation of the I.A.52, proposed to develop a crop-spraying aircraft and, after insisting on it to the head of DINFIA, the idea was approved. On 1 October 1964, Olmedo and engineer Justo Demetrio Díaz started to work on the project, who had no official designation yet, and carried out a poll of the crop-spraying companies all over Argentina to see what their needs were and what they expected from a plane developed for them.

The project was designated I.A.53 Mamboretá (the name of the praying mantis insect given by the Guaraní aborigines) and by the end of 1965 three airframes were started, one of them for static tests and the other two to serve as prototypes, with constructor numbers 1 and 2. The second prototype was the first to fly, on 10 November 1966, with Commander Pedro Luis Rosell at the controls, followed by the other, which received the experimental serial LV-X33, on 17 November. The second prototype received the serial LV-X35 on 20 October 1967, although by then it had been flown for almost a year.

The Mamboretá was different from most crop sprayers by having the tank for agrochemicals in the belly, under the cabin, which was planned to carry two seats, for a pilot and a passenger, as in many cases, especially in the north of Argentina, the planes operated on runways or even roads far from their bases and they needed to carry someone to assist with the operation on the ground, who

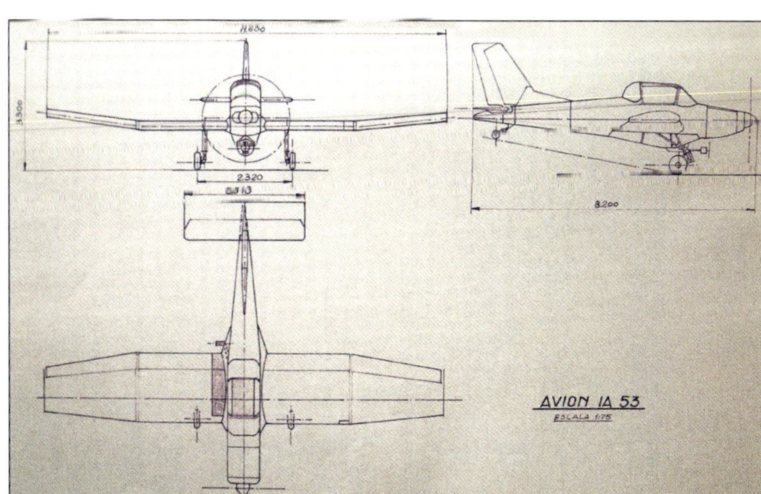

Three views of the initial design of the Mamboretá.

ABOVE LEFT The first prototype with the first canopy used on the cabin, with the rear part as it was in the three views. Although the rear view was better, the turbulence created behind the canopy affected the efficiency of the rudder. It also has the original large tank on the belly.

ABOVE RIGHT The first instrument panel installed in the prototypes, which was very simple and had few instruments.

marked with flags the places on the field to be sprayed. The tank was for 650 litres, and the spraying system, which could be Britten-Norman, Sorensen or Trans-Land, was on the trailing edge of the wing. The engines to be installed could be a Continental O-470-E of 200hp, an O-470-M of 240 or a IA-470-D of 260hp, but the prototypes were equipped with the Lycoming O-540-B2B5 of 235hp, driving a McCauley A200 FM-9047 two-blade metal propeller of fixed pitch.

Initially, the type had a cabin that ended in curved Plexiglas on the back, but after some test flights this revealed turbulence issues, which affected the rudder, so it was replaced by a fairing that extended almost to the tail. Also, the instrument panel was replaced by a larger one with more instruments and an improved disposition.

The plane was all metal, with a structure of steel alloy tubes covered with aluminium panels. The tail had big inspection accesses on both sides to improve maintenance. The cantilever wing was made of aluminium alloy, as well as the stabiliser and tail. The wingtips were designed to be conventional or receive vertical plaques.

Maximum speed was 200km/h and cruise speed was 178km/h, while stall speed at maximum weight was 84km/h. Service ceiling was 4,300m, with a climb rate of 230m/min, a take-off distance with an obstacle of 15m was 350m and the range with 75 per cent of power was of 600km. The empty weight was of 804kg and the maximum take-off weight was of 1,520kg, with capacity of 560kg of chemicals to be carried in the tank, but the maximum load allowed to carry only 41kg of fuel.

The I.A.53 was 8.20m long, with a height of 3.3m, a wingspan of 11.6m and a wing area of 21.52m2.

After evaluation by the test pilots of the CEV and also civil pilots dedicated to crop spraying, it was considered that the plane had some deficiencies in flight performance and also limitations to the maximum weight.

The factory expected to get the certification of the type in 1967 and DINFIA expected to sell at least 300 of the type, but this did not progress due to the deficiencies found in the design.

In 1968 LV-X33 was modified, with the reduction of the size of the tank for chemicals, changes to the tabs and the flaps and a modification of the spraying bar, which was located higher and just behind the trailing edge. Also, the landing gear received a fairing to increase the speed of the plane while reducing the resistance, a step and a handle were added on one side

The Mamboretá had big inspection covers on the sides of the tail to facilitate maintenance.

LEFT The first prototype of the Mamboretá, already with the serial PGX-01, landing at the FMA in the mid-1970s.

BELOW One of the two Mamboretá prototypes, after the serial was changed to PGX.

to facilitate the access to the cabin, a hook for glider towing was added, and an indicator of the quantity of liquid on the tank of chemicals was also added.

By 1970, engineer Héctor Ruiz proposed an extensive modification of the design, with an lengthened fuselage to carry the tank for chemicals between the engine and the cabin, as was the use on most agricultural aircraft, with a cabin for a single seat and a modified tail and stabiliser.

This design was modified again in 1973 with a fuselage shape resembling a Piper Brave and the horizontal stabilisers were more similar to the ones of the original Mamboretá. The engine was changed for a Continental Teledyne Tiara of 285hp. It had two fuel tanks, one on each wing, with 75 litres of capacity each. The plane would have an empty weight of 1,000kg and a MTOW of 1,800kg, with a fuel tank of 160 litres and a tank for chemicals of 650 litres. The wingspan was 11.83m and the length 8.42m. With full load, the maximum speed was expected to be 220km/h, the cruise speed with 75 per cent of power was 210km/h, the stall speed was 110km/h and the climb rate of 4m/s, while at minimum weight those values were 240km/h, 230km/h, 85km/h and 7m/s respectively. The service ceiling was of 4,500m and the type needed 530m to take off with a 15m obstacle and 250m to land.

The plan was to deliver the two prototypes to a private company that would build the new fuselage and tail and it would then get the rights to produce the type. However, at the same time, DINFIA had decided that it was a better solution to get the licence

The cabin of one of the Mamboretá prototypes after it was modified with a bigger instrument panel for more instruments. Note the plane has a gunsight installed.

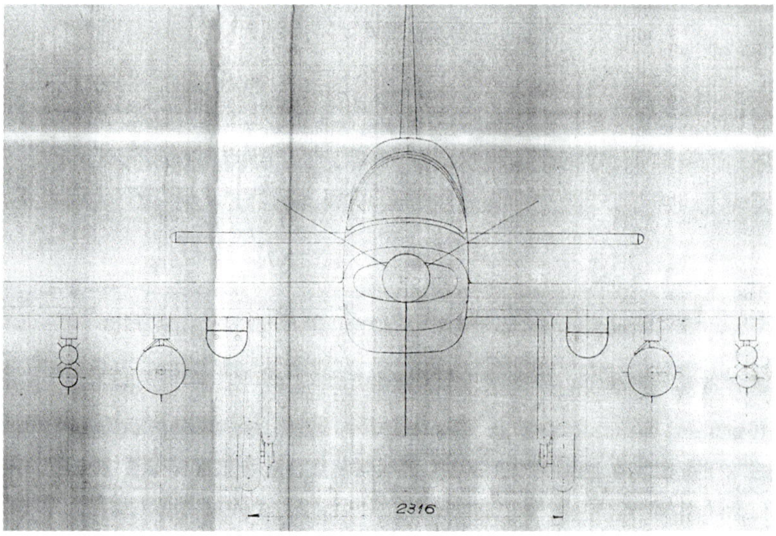

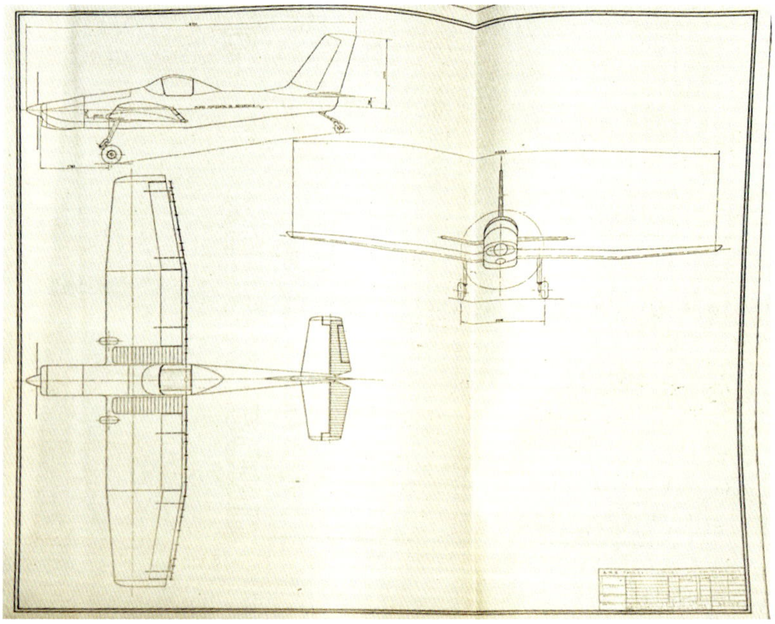

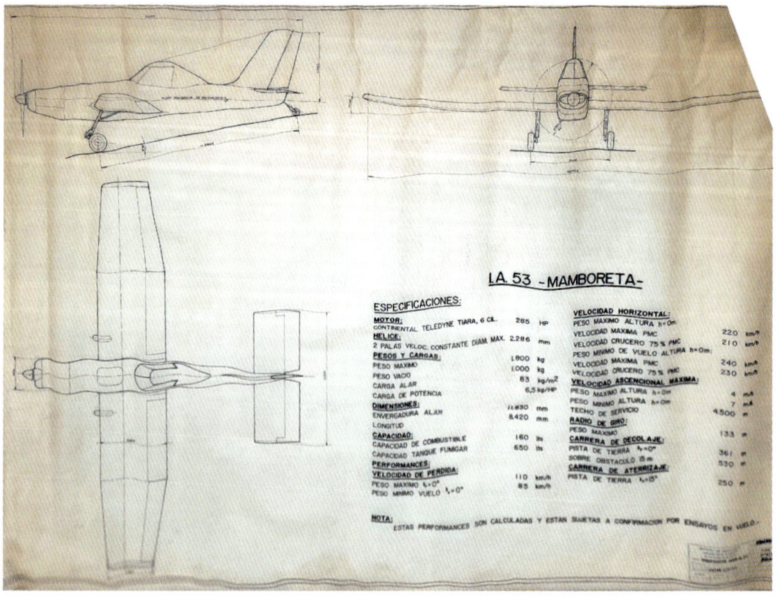

to produce a proven design and in 1972 the company had already purchased the rights to produce the Cessna A188B Skytruck. Also, the only other company in the country producing agriculture aircraft by then, Aero Boero, had flown in 1972 the AB-206AG, which was similar to the new proposed I.A.53, and it intended to build in series, so it was not interested in the Mamboretá (in the end the AB-206AG was cancelled, too), so the I.A.53 was finally cancelled.

Interestingly, when the first agreement with Cessna was made for licence production of the Cessna A182, in 1965, it was going to receive the designation I.A.53, before the Mamboretá project began, but the factory decided to keep the original designation.

The two prototypes were delivered to the Argentine Air Force in 1970 with serials PGX-01 and 02 and used for training at the CEV and glider towing, with at least one of them receiving a shooting sight. Finally, in 1976 they were retired and PGX-02 was scrapped, while PGX-01 was delivered in 1980 to the National Aeronautics Museum, where it is preserved today.

Armed Mamboretá

In December 1966, engineer Captain Justo Demetrio Díaz and engineer Billy Juan Mauricio Montico prepared the development of a COIN version of the Mamboretá, using the weight that the crop duster had available to carry the chemicals and the extra passenger to carry weapons, although they kept the back seat for shuttle flights or for an observer.

The study considered that the plane with a Continental IO-520-A or a Lycoming IO-540-B1A5 engine could be equipped with a fixed armament capacity of 96kg consisting of four 7.62mm machine guns in pods under the wings and 208kg of launchable weapons such as T-10 rockets and 50 or 100kg bombs on four underwing pylons. The idea was for it to be used for armed reconnaissance and target marking, as well as light attack. In addition, 60kg of armour would be added to the crop duster. This version was expected to have a maximum speed of 285km/h, a cruise of 250km/h, a climb rate of 240m/min, a stall speed without flaps of 100km/h, a service ceiling of 5,600m with maximum weight, a take-off run with a 15m obstacle of 330m and a landing one, with the same obstacle, of 340m. While the empty weight was also of 1,000kg, the maximum was of 1,500kg.

While the project was viable, the cancellation of the Mamboretá also meant the end of this idea.

TOP LEFT Front view of the armed Mamboretá proposal, with four underwing pylons for rockets or bombs and the pods for machine guns.

CENTRE LEFT Proposal of 1970 for a much-improved I.A.53.

LEFT New proposal of a modified I.A.53 dated 1973.

31 I.A.55 COIN projects

With the emergence of rural guerrillas after the Second World War, especially in Latin America, the Argentine government began, like the rest of the region, to develop strategies to face this type of unconventional and certainly complicated war.

Anticipating a growth in guerrilla activity, and also with the objective of equipping the other Latin American nations with an aircraft dedicated exclusively to the anti-subversive fight, the Argentine Air Force (FAA), through DINFIA, at the beginning of 1963 faced the development of a counter-insurgency aircraft, holding a contest between the Grupo de Desarrollos Aeronáuticos and the Dirección de Fabricación. The decision as to the winner was made by the German engineer Reimar Horten together with Estanislao Krazinski. Two proposals were presented; the one by the Grupo de Desarrollos Aeronáuticos of the engineers Commander Ricardo E. Olmedo (head of the department), Commodore Antonio R. Mantel, Federico Seufert and Justo Demetrio Díaz; and the other, from the Dirección de Fabricación, led by Commander Héctor Eduardo Ruíz, administrator of the factory. Both were a tandem, low-wing, conventional two-seater. The first would be equipped with a 675hp Turbomeca Astazou X engine and the second with a 660hp Astazou XI.

In addition to the version for the Air Force, an embarked one was also foreseen, to operate from the aircraft carrier ARA *Independencia* of the Argentine Navy, in the style of the US Skyraider, replacing the North American T-28P Fennec as a training and light attack aircraft. The aircraft could also be used for advanced training in the Air Force, complementing the Mentors and replacing the T-28A. However, the design of both proposals differed greatly, the former being a W-wing design, while the latter was highlighted by a very small section fuselage and an unusually large cockpit dome, which would give great visibility to the pilots, although it reduced their protection.

Both, conceptually, were very similar to the Morane-Saulnier MS.1500 Epervier, which had first flown in 1958 and of which only two prototypes were produced before it was abandoned. The French type flew with a 370hp Turbomeca Marcadou, changed for a 650hp Bastan I, then a 700hp Bastan II, a 750hp IIB, an 800hp III, a 986hp Bastan IV, a 1,080hp Bastan VI, a

Plan of the I.A.55 proposal by the Grupo de Desarrollos Aeronáuticos, dated 26 June 1963.

Drawing of the proposal made by the Dirección de Fabricación for the I.A.55, but curiously showing the designation I.A.47, never used for this project. This is the proposed naval version, seen with only one seat and six machine guns in the wings *Archive Eduardo Ruiz*

Drawing of an anti-tank version of the I.A.55 of the Dirección de Fabricación, showing the designation I.A.57, which in the end was used for another project. The plane is armed with two miniguns in underwing pylons and has a single seat and retractable landing gear, not planned in the original idea. *Archive Eduardo Ruiz*

Commander Héctor Eduardo Ruíz with a model of his proposal for the I.A.55 project. *Archive Eduardo Ruiz*

600hp Astazou XIV, a 800hp XVI and finally a 980hp Astazou XVI G.

The FMA's close relationship with Turbomeca and the French industry, due in large part to the work with the IA-50 G II, led to the French options being analysed in the development of a local COIN aircraft, especially with regard to the power plant.

Regarding the work at DINFIA, the team that evaluated both projects declared the winner the project led by Ricardo Olmedo, which was named I.A.55, and in July 1963 development work began. Although the manufacture of a prototype was announced, the design was not enough to satisfy the needs of this type of war, since the armament and armour capacity was very limited due to the low power of the engine, something that had been evidenced in the French competition. For this reason, the I.A.55 project was abandoned by the end of 1964.

32 I.A.57

In 1963, the director of the air transport company CATA, Roque Pugliese, asked engineer Ricardo Olmedo, in charge of the Grupo de Desarrollos Aeronáuticos, to develop a two-seater light aircraft for the civil market, that would be built by the private industry. Olmedo drew a design with a low wing, two seats side by side, with a monocoque structure and all-metal construction, with an empty weight of 390kg and a MTOW of 650kg, having a wingspan of 8.3m, a wing area of 10.79m2 and a length of 6.08m. The engine would be a Continental O-200 of 100hp or a Lycoming O-235-C1B of 108hp with four cylinders horizontally opposed and air cooled, driving a McCauley fixed-pitch propeller of 1.85m of diameter. The landing gear was tricycle, and the plane was expected to be fully aerobatic.

Work progressed slowly and by early 1966 the basic design was ready, but it was cancelled shortly after, when the factory decided to prioritise the licence agreement with Cessna to produce the Cessna 182, 150 and 188.

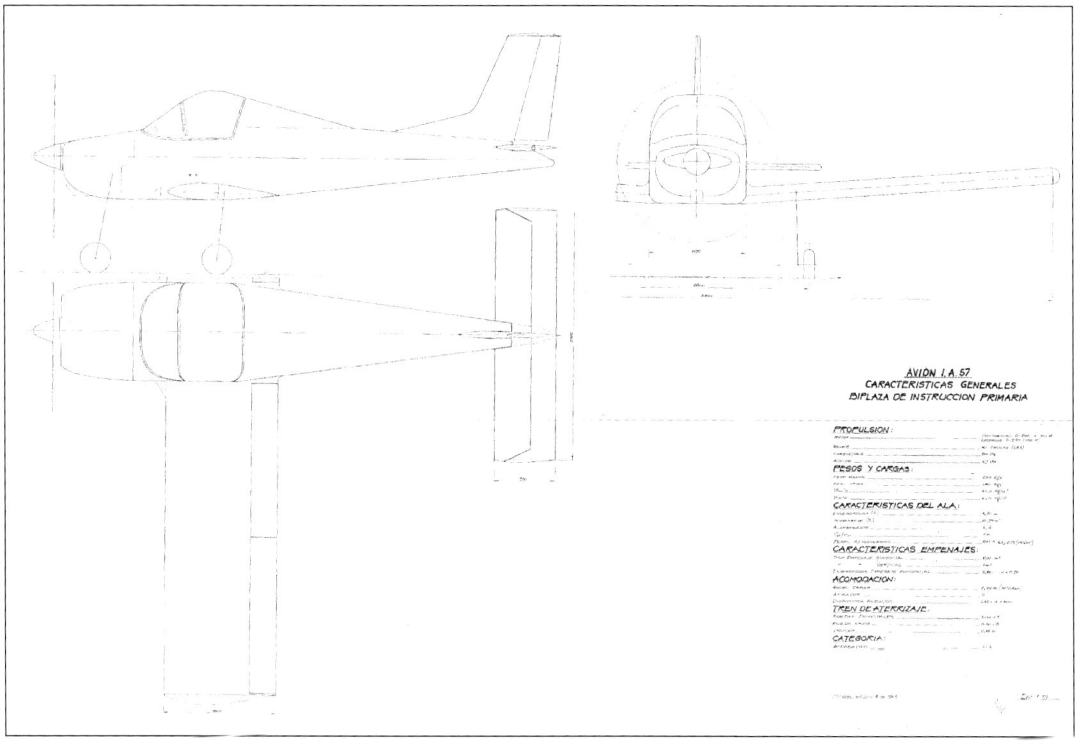

Plan of the I.A.57 proposal dated 8 October 1965 that never went beyond a draft.

33 **IA-58 Pucará and derivatives**

The A. X2

After the I.A.55 project was cancelled and due to the need for an aircraft for COIN missions with better performance, in 1965 Commodores Carlos Washington Pastor and Antonio R. Mantel prepared a requirement for an aircraft that also had to carry out offensive reconnaissance missions and tactical fire support both on land and at sea, with secondary missions of photographic reconnaissance and training. The project was named A. X2 and shortly thereafter received the designation I.A.58.

In August 1966 the work team of the Grupo de Desarrollos Aeronáuticos of the IIAE was organised, led by Commander Ricardo E. Olmedo, together with Captain Justo Demetrio Díaz and the Commander Juan M. Beverina, who directed the Aerodynamics Department of the IIAE.

On 11 August that same year, Captain Díaz presented his preliminary proposal, classifying the A. X2 as an offensive reconnaissance and fire support aircraft on land and sea, counter-insurgency (COIN), although he also highlighted that it could perform light transport missions, training, and photographic reconnaissance. Among the participants in the proposal was Dr Reimar Horten, who provided advice on aerodynamic issues.

The proposal was based on the OV-10 Bronco, which was entering service in the United States at the time. The project was practically the same, although equipped with two Turbomeca Bastan VI-C of 1,000 shp and Ratier Figeac FH 146 propellers of 3.2m in diameter and reversible pitch, only it did not have the same visibility of the North American model. The wing would have four sections of 'double-slotted' flaps to improve the STOL characteristics, in addition to the deflection of the propeller flux.

Some deficiencies of the OV-10 were taken into account, where the arrangement with blown flaps made it possible for the plane to roll over the axis in case an engine stopped when operating at maximum power with flaps down, such as take-offs. For this reason, the engines had to be interconnected so that, in case one stopped working, the other turned that propeller. The Bastan engines did not convince,

Second design of the A. X2 with the extra weapon sponsons. *Archive Santiago Rivas*

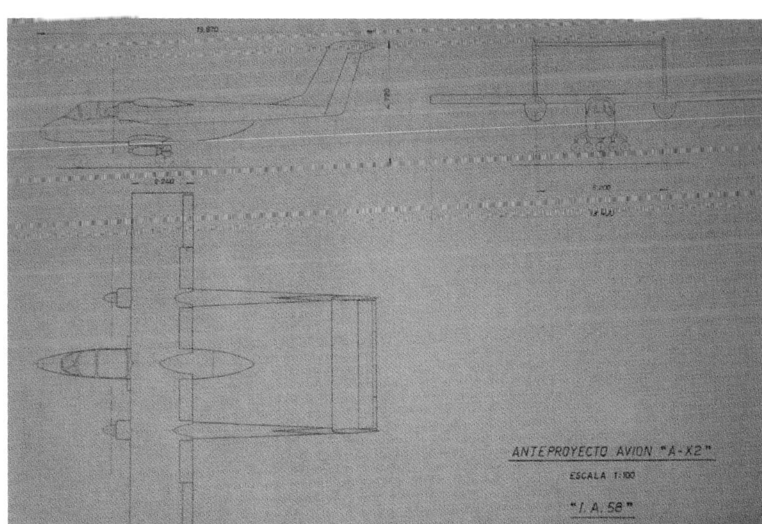

Once the design based on the Bronco was abandoned, engineer Olmedo used the front part of the fuselage with a new wing and tail, as can be seen in this artist's impression. *Archive Eduardo Ruiz*

Three view of the A. X2 design by engineer Olmedo. *Archive Eduardo Ruiz*

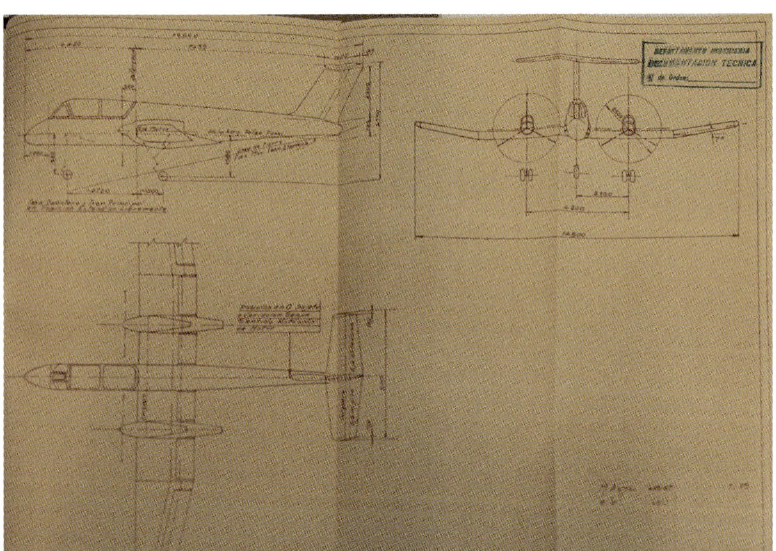

although they were known by the force, because they did not allow inverted flight as they were designed for civil use.

Like the US-built aircraft, the A. X2 also had a rear hold with a resistant floor, although larger, in this case being 3.55m long by 1m wide (with a maximum width of 1.1m) and a minimum height of 1.26m, which could carry up to seven soldiers or three crew members and six paratroopers (the third crew member as jumpmaster). The cargo cabin floor would be 1.10m high with the plane on the ground, facilitating loading and unloading, counting on the tail cone as a cargo door, opening to one side, but, unlike the Bronco, it would also have a side door on the left side, 0.6m wide, for passenger access or paratrooper launching.

For passenger transport, a configuration with a double seat in the front, four individual seats and an optional basic one was envisaged. For paratrooper transport a longitudinal seat for six troops was foreseen. For cargo, it would have fixed tie-down supports, which would also be used to attach the seats. It could carry packages up to 3.5m long, 1.2m high and 1 wide.

It was planned to have a non-pressurised cabin, air conditioning, two VHF sets, an intercom, and a weather radar. The two pilots would have Martin-Baker ejection seats, although the model was not determined. Behind the second seat would go the electronic equipment, accessible from the cargo hold. The air conditioning, electrical and hydraulic systems would go in the tail booms.

A cruising speed at maximum continuous power of 460km/h with external loads and 498km/h without loads was expected, although it was estimated that, if a better aerodynamic coefficient was achieved, it could reach 540km/h with external loads. The stall speed was 91km/h. The take-off run on unpaved runways, with maximum weight and flaps at 30°, was expected to be 150m and the service ceiling would be 9,400m. The maximum weapons load was estimated at 1,764kg and the maximum range in ferry flight, at 680hp of power in each engine and 6,000m above sea level, would be 3,303km. The empty weight was estimated at 2,770kg, with a payload of 2,230kg and a gross weight of 5,000kg.

The aircraft would have a length of 13.87m, a height of 4.72m, a wingspan of 13.4m, a wheel track of 5.12m and a horizontal tail wingspan of 4.92m.

The armament would go on five pylons, one under the centre of the fuselage with 1,000kg capacity, two on the sides and another two in stub wings (similar to those of the Bronco, which could be removed if necessary, all for 450kg of weapons).

Four 12.7mm Browning AN-M3 machine guns with 360 rounds each were planned to be installed. Up to six 7.62mm Minigun SUU-12/As were envisaged, five on the weapons pylons and one on an XM-5 mount for shooting from the rear side door. It could also carry up to five AN-M3s in SUU-12/A pods, with 750 cartridges each, one in each pylon. The use of up to two M51 Vulcan 20mm guns, with three or six tubes, was envisaged on the internal side pylons. Those pylons could also carry 20mm single-tube guns. It could also carry a 40mm XM-75 grenade launcher on the central pylon and another on the rear side door.

The possibility of equipping it with air-to-air and air-to-surface missiles was foreseen, which should be defined with the Argentine Air Force. It was also planned to install armour to withstand shots of up to 7.62mm from 100m away.

It was also planned to be able to install three floats, one central and two on the sides, instead of the wheeled landing gear, for operations in the water, as well as the possibility of installing skis to operate in snow. The installation of JATO units was also envisaged to shorten the take-off distance.

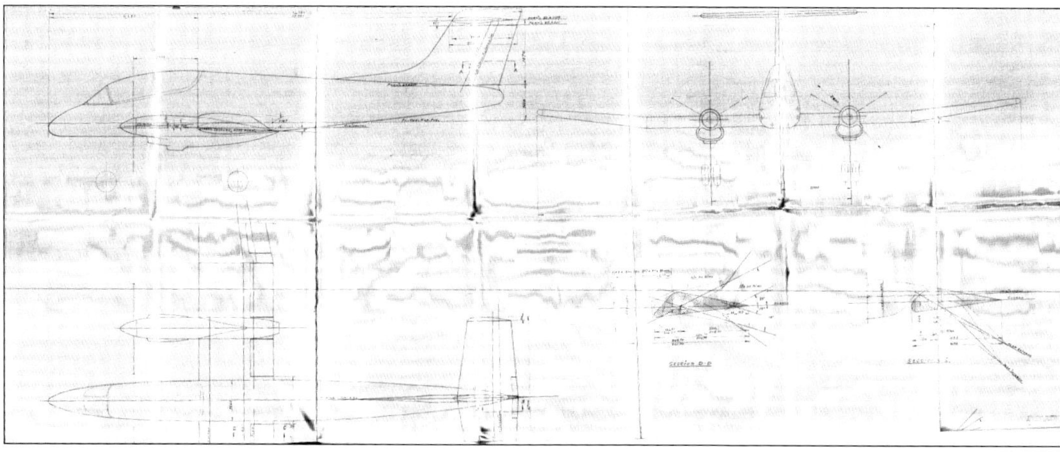

Design of the Pucará with Pratt & Whitney PT6A-32 engines. *Archive Eduardo Ruiz*

Redesign

Meanwhile, on 11 July 1967 there was a restructuring in the factory, which ceased to be called DINFIA when it was separated from the automobile manufacturing concern and became the Area de Material Córdoba (AMC), although it was commonly still called the FMA, dependent on the Air Force Material Command.

At that time, both the Grupo de Desarrollos Aeronáuticos and the Grupo Fabricación became part of the Departamento Ingeniería de Desarrollos (Development Engineering Department), leaving the IIAE only for missile and space studies. Engineer Commander Ruíz was appointed as head of this department.

The results of the first studies of Captain Díaz's project showed several deficiencies that led to a complete redesign, which Olmedo presented to Héctor Ruíz in that same month of 1967. This was approved by Ruíz as administrator of the factory and consisted of a more conventional design, low-wing cantilever, maintaining the design of the front part of the fuselage but with a new rear part and with a single T-tail. It would be powered by two Garrett TPE-331-303s of 845shp (although the possibility of using 1,000shp engines was considered), with a maximum fuel capacity of 2,245 litres in a fuselage tank and three in each wing, with the aim of reaching a maximum ceiling of 9,500m, with a ferry range of 3,500km. It would have a take off distance of 250m and a landing distance of 510m, with a minimum turning radius of 150m, a minimum control speed of 146km/h and a maximum of about 477km/h. The empty weight was 3,070kg and the payload, including fuel and pilots, was 2,130kg or 2,430kg with overload, reaching a maximum take-off weight of 5,500kg on prepared runways or 5,200kg on unprepared ones.

A maximum capacity of 1,500kg of armament was calculated, including 137kg of internal weapons. The latter would include four 7.62mm Browning machine guns, two on each side, in a fairing on each side of the fuselage with a total of 2,000 rounds, plus two 20mm guns in removable under-belly fairings with 600 rounds in total. In this way a narrower fuselage was obtained. In addition, it would carry two Aero 7-A1 underwing pylons for 500kg each and one Aero 20-A1 ventral for 1,000kg of weapons, which was expected to include TERs (Triple Ejector Racks) and MERs (Multiple Ejector Racks) and could include 25, 500 and 1,000lb bombs, T-10, 2.75in or 5in rockets, napalm bombs, torpedoes and training bombs.

A weather radar could be installed on the nose and a Librascope-type sight was envisaged. The design also included a 1m3 compartment with a reinforced floor, above the wing structure, in the central fuselage, for the transport of equipment, tools, engines, fuel and lubricants, or even for the evacuation of personnel. The dimensions were a length of 13.54m, wingspan of 14.5m and a height of 4.71m.

Olmedo's project also contemplated three versions. The I was an attack aircraft with naval capacity, with two Martin-Baker 0/100 ejection seats, complete de-icing systems on wings, empennage and engines, oxygen equipment, HF equipment and provision for IFF system and weather radar. Version II was an air-to-ground attack single-seater with an ejection seat, with the possibility of adding a second crew member in a fixed seat,

Engine nacelle design for the Pucará with Bastan VI engines. *Archive Eduardo Ruiz*

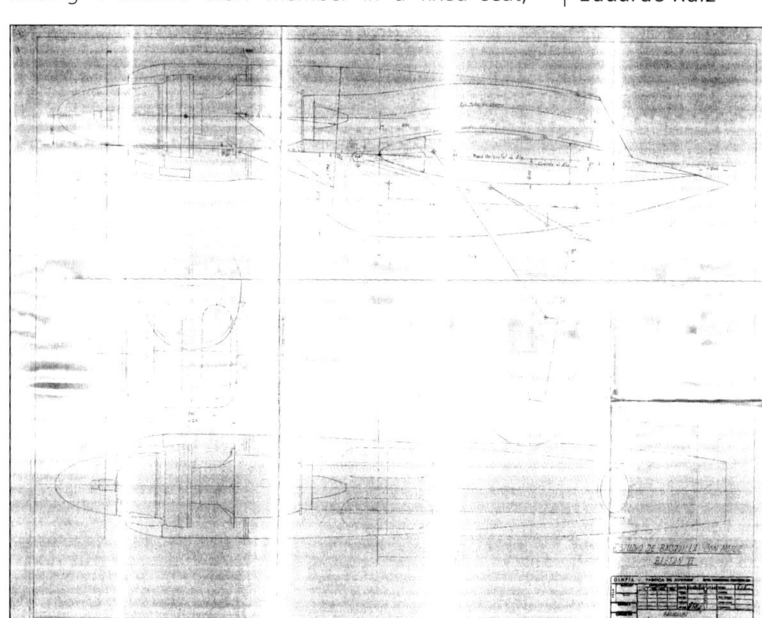

The glider flying close to the FMA. The cables installed to keep the strength of the structure of the tail are visible, as are the brakes on the rear part of the fuselage. *Archive Santiago Rivas*

without de-icing system, oxygen for one crew member and also provision to install IFF and radar. Version III was for training, with fixed seats, without de-icing equipment, oxygen, HF radio, nor provision for IFF or radar.

During that year the project was presented to the Commander in Chief of the Force, Brigadier General Teodoro Álvarez, who authorised the construction of the prototypes and a glider, despite the opinion of some officers to put it aside and buy the Bronco.

Gliders

As soon as the new design of the A. X-2 was defined, a mock-up of the fuselage was built, to evaluate the cabin design. Reimar Horten was in charge of building, with staff from the School of Apprentices of the AMC, a wooden glider of the single-seater variant, with a fixed landing gear. In November 1967 the glider, serialled A-X2, was completed and tests began on taxiing towed by a Kaiser Manhattan automobile loaned by IIAE engineer Apóstoli. After these tests were completed, on 27 December it took flight for the first time under the command of Commander Roberto Starc, towed by a C-47 serialled TC-27 of the CEV, flying for forty minutes after releasing the tow and then reaching 3,500m above sea level. First, evaluations of the general flight conditions were carried out, followed by tests at low speed, flaps, centring, aerodynamic flow tests and flutter. By then, the plane had been internally christened I.A.58 'Delfín' and during the evaluations, Captain José B. Videla joined Starc.

The second glider flying after the modifications of the main landing gear and fake propellers. *Archive Carlos Ay*

The first prototype, now with the serial AX-01, flying over the plains of eastern Córdoba province. *Archive Eduardo Ruiz*

The results of the tests highlighted that in the glider construction stage, the low structural rigidity of the fuselage had become evident, which made it necessary to brace the empennage by means of six tensioners and made evident the need to modify the final configuration of the fuselage. Despite this, it was decided to carry out the first flights with the glider to determine the corrections to apply. In the first two flights a strong tendency to the right, inefficiency of the aerodynamic brakes and a heavy nose was found. On the third flight, longitudinal instability was found when flying at low speed, it was considered that the control lever was very high and the visibility to the sides was not good due to the width of the cabin. After that flight, the rudder was changed to one with a greater chord, although in the next two flights it was found that the improvement was not sufficient. In addition, stalls began to be evaluated without flaps, with 15° flaps and with flaps all down. On flights 10 and 11, the aerodynamic flow around the engine nacelles and the wing-fuselage junction were analysed, finding strong turbulence at the rear of the nacelles. Then, only one additional test flight was made on 12 March and, in total, eighteen hours fifteen minutes were reached.

Meanwhile, on 29 January 1968, the general details were presented to the FAA Command according to the requirements and it was decided to rebuild the glider with what was learned, opting for a complete redesign of the fuselage, tail and engine nacelles.

However, on 15 March of that year, Olmedo left the project after several discussions with engineer Héctor Ruíz about the configuration of the plane, who remained in charge of it until its completion.

Now under the direction of Ruíz, the glider was redesigned and became a two-seater with a totally new fuselage and tail, with the stabiliser in fixed position, and enlarged engine nacelles, so that they were ahead of the leading edge of the wing. The speed brakes on the tail cone were modified and the position of the second pilot was slightly elevated, to improve his forward visibility. Only the overall wing design remained unchanged. In February, in addition, the design of the powered prototype began, which would not have too many significant changes with respect to the last version of the glider. For this, different engine manufacturers were asked to propose their alternatives to propel the aircraft.

Selection of engines

As part of that process, on 29 February 1968, United Aircraft Corporation responded to Commodore Horacio Guerra of the FMA by offering two 750shp Pratt & Whitney PT6A-29 engines on loan, one to be delivered in May and the other in November of that year, with repayment (or loan extension) in June 1969. United Aircraft's proposal stated that, if the tests were successful, the company would bring both engines to the PT6A-32 standard (specific for

AX-03 seen around early 1977, wearing the serial in smaller size and the name Pucará on the upper part of the fin. In the rear cockpit, an unknown instrument, most probably for tests, is installed. The size of the serials was changed by 1975. *Archive Eduardo Ruiz*

One of the very few pictures of the first three prototypes together at the FMA. *Archive Santiago Rivas*

the I.A.58, which was never produced in the end) and sell them to the FMA. If not chosen, the agreement stipulated that the engines would be brought up to the PT6A-27 standard and sold to the FAA for use in Twin Otters. The FMA stated that to accept the proposal United Aircraft had to guarantee the delivery of engines with more than 1,000shp, dimensions equal to the -29 and a weight no more than 20 per cent higher, before May 1970.

At the same time, the provision of 1,000shp Bastan VID engines such as those used in the IA-50 Guaraní II as standard was being negotiated with Turbomeca, although, given the aforementioned engine limitations, Turbomeca offered to develop an improved version of the Astazou XVI model, which had better features than the XIV initially offered. In this case, the manufacturer covered development costs, the engine was named Astazou XVIG-01, offering 1,021shp of power, and five engines were provided free of charge for testing.

The first prototype, with the air data probe. *Archive Santiago Rivas*

As part of this process, Ruíz worked on the design of the nacelles for the four engines that could propel the plane, since the PT6A, the Bastan and the Astazou were joined by the Garrett AiResearch TPE331-O3H-U303, of which the manufacturer delivered the first three engines produced (serial numbers P-04001 to 3). The nacelles for all were designed, but the Bastan option was scrapped for the reasons stated and the PT6 because United Technologies did not yet have ready the proposed version, even though it planned to have the prototypes by December 1968, certification in June or July 1969 and deliver them in August 1969. The company promised to be able to modify the -29 engines so that they reached 1,010shp by increasing the temperature of the compressor, which would be modified. In addition, the option of adding two additional stages to the turbine was proposed, lengthening the engine by 3.5in, to reach 1,100shp.

Thus, it was decided to advance only with the Garrett and Turbomeca options, for which the wind tunnel trials of different bench alternatives began.

At the same time, Ruíz had abandoned Olmedo's ideas of a single-seater version, a turboprop trainer and the naval version, despite from the beginning of the design, the possibility of equipping it with two 600lb torpedoes on the underwing pylons or one of 1,200lb on the ventral pylon was envisaged.

The glider flies again

After the modification of the glider, on 25 July 1968 it flew for the first time under the command of Commander Starc, towed by Douglas C-47 TC-27, freeing itself from the tug aircraft at 3,500m above sea level. The tests carried out were like the previous ones, reaching 104 flights with a total of sixty-one hours ten minutes. On the seventh flight, on 5 August, ten pressure taps were added to the fuselage, connected to alcohol tubes located in the rear cabin, with which the pressures reached were measured. On the tenth flight, a camera was added to take images of these tubes during the flight. The last flight was on 8 May 1969, piloted by Starc. During the tests, segments of the propeller blades were added in the feather position and the main landing gear was modified with dual wheels, for better performance on unprepared runways.

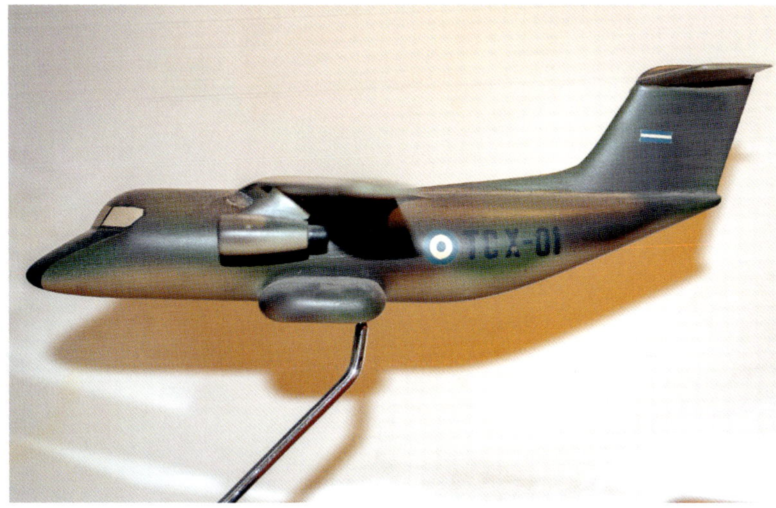

Light jet transport proposal made by engineer Héctor Eduardo Ruiz as part of the family of planes based on the Pucará. This proposal only kept the tail of the original design. *Santiago Rivas*

Plans of the first ideas for a light transport and observation aeroplane based on the Pucará. *Archive Eduardo Ruiz*

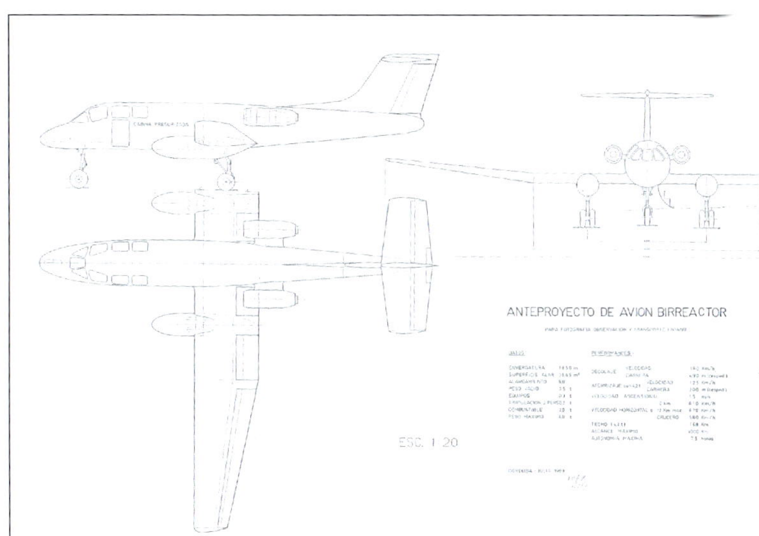

Prototypes

To evaluate the performance of the two chosen engines, it was decided to equip the first prototype with two Garrett TPE331-O3H-U303 840shp engines and Hamilton Standard 33LF-337 variable-pitch three-bladed propellers and the second with the Astazou XVIG-01 and three-bladed Ratier Figeac propellers with reversible pitch, which allowed the elimination of spoilers.

In September 1968 the first prototype began to be manufactured, serialled A-X2, like the glider. The structure was designed by German engineer Rudolf Freyer, one of the few remaining in the FMA from Kurt Tank's design team. It was also equipped with HSA (Folland) 4GT/1 Type 40 ejection seats.

Although the first flight was planned to be made on 10 August 1969, the Air Force Day, the prototype was completed and taken to the FMA runway only on the 16th, and three days later the engine and taxi tests began, carrying out the first private flight on the 20th, under the command of Major (a rank that replaced Commander) Starc, taking off from the factory runway. For this the prototype did not have the internal weapons or the external pylons, the landing gear covers, the rear ejection seat and some other elements. The two Hispano Suiza 20mm cannon in the lower part of the fuselage and the four Browning Model 1919 7.62 × 51mm machine guns on the sides of the fuselage were never installed in this prototype, although they were already defined as the internal armament of the Pucará (the guns that would be used were the remnants of those that had been purchased for the Gloster Meteors, the IAe-33 Pulqui II and the dorsal turret of the Avro Lincolns, as there were more than 400 unused ones in storage). There would be three weapon pylons; one under the fuselage and two under the wings, at the junction of the central plane with the external sections of each wing, with a total capacity for a maximum of 1,500kg. Unlike Olmedo's initial project, the cannon would not go in removable ventral fairings, but rather inside the fuselage and would be fixed. In the same way, the machine guns would not be in fairings that would protrude from the sides of the fuselage, but the fuselage was wider, and the guns were inside. The opening to be able to place an engine in the fuselage and transport it was eliminated, although a cover was placed in the belly to access the fuselage and thus be able to access the equipment.

On 21 August 1969, the second flight was made in private with the presence of the Commander-in-Chief of the FAA, Brigadier General Jorge Miguel Martínez Zuviría. Then the prototype went into the workshop to undergo some adjustments based on what was found on the first two flights. In addition, doors were added to the landing gear, the second seat was installed, and weapon pylons, although the underwing ones did not have the attachments to carry loads or landing lights in the front.

On 6 October the plane flew again, returning with some minor faults, which were corrected and the next day it made its fourth flight without incident. On 8 October it flew twice, signalling some faults on the main gear doors and the engine fuel system. The next day it made two more flights.

On 10 October 1969, the baptism and official in-flight presentation took place before the defence

A pilot boarding AX-03 on the apron of the Centro de Ensayos en Vuelo (Flight Test Centre) inside the factory. *Archive José Martínez*

minister, Dr José R. Cáceres Monié, on the forty-second anniversary of the FMA. That day the plane changed its name from Delfín to Pucará, which in the Quichua language of the Incas and Aimará is the name of the fortresses that they built in the past, in the north-western area of Argentina.

On 20 October, test flights were resumed, this time in the rain, which made it possible to verify the need for a windscreen wiper, in addition to detecting that the cabin gasket was not totally waterproof and water was entering. Shortly after, Major Sergio García and Captain José B. Videla joined the flights.

On 28 November, the order OPS69-15 was issued for the change of the prototype serial to AX-01 because the AX-2 designation had already been dropped. However, this change became effective on the plane only on 18 May 1970. Meanwhile, on 16 February 1970, the type's first long-duration flight was made, reaching three and a half hours, which was followed by another of four hours forty-eight minutes on the 21st of that month.

On 30 March the prototype reached 100 flight hours, so it went for a check, which lasted until June. On 26 November that year, the first flight was made with new Hartzell HC-B3TN-5C/T10282 HB propellers and the next day the first flight with weapons was made, with two nineteen-tube 70mm rocket launchers, one on each underwing pylon, and six loads pretending to be 115kg bombs in a MER on the ventral pylon.

At that time, the second prototype was started, with Astazou engines and a 20cm longer fuselage, and this made its first taxi on 9 September 1971. It took to the air for the first time on 15 September with the serial AX-02, under the command of Major García, and completed first a fifteen-minute flight, followed that same day by another of half an hour. After all the systems had been fine-tuned, the first test flight (number 17 of the plane) was carried out on 14 October, initiating a preliminary test programme with this aircraft and its engines. In addition, on 23 October, it flew to the VII Air Brigade, in Morón, Buenos Aires, and then to the nearby I Air Brigade in El Palomar, where it was exhibited. The next day it flew to Ezeiza International Airport ,where it was showed to the Argentine President, General Roberto Levingston, later returning to the I Air Brigade. The next day it started the return to the AMC, but due to bad weather had to land at the airport in the city of Villa María, in the province of Córdoba, being able to fly to its destination before the end of the day. On 30 October the test flights were resumed, which ended on 6 November after a total of forty-four flights (sixteen of them for tests) with a total flying time of thirty-four hours five minutes.

Pucará AX-01 taking off using three JATOs. This system was only used for tests and exhibitions, but made it possible to take off in only 50m. *Archive Santiago Rivas*

At that time different versions were proposed. On the one hand, engineer Ruiz suggested that some Pucarás be delivered in a single-seater version, eliminating the second seat, the instruments and controls, but with all the fittings to be able to add them if necessary. In a study from around the end of 1971 the weather radar is referred to as optional equipment of the plane, which was installed twice, as will be seen later. This indicates that said installation was something planned from the

ABOVE A drawing made by Héctor Ruiz of an idea of an executive jet using the wings and tail of the Pucará. Unfortunately, only this drawing was found in his archives. *Archive Eduardo Ruiz*

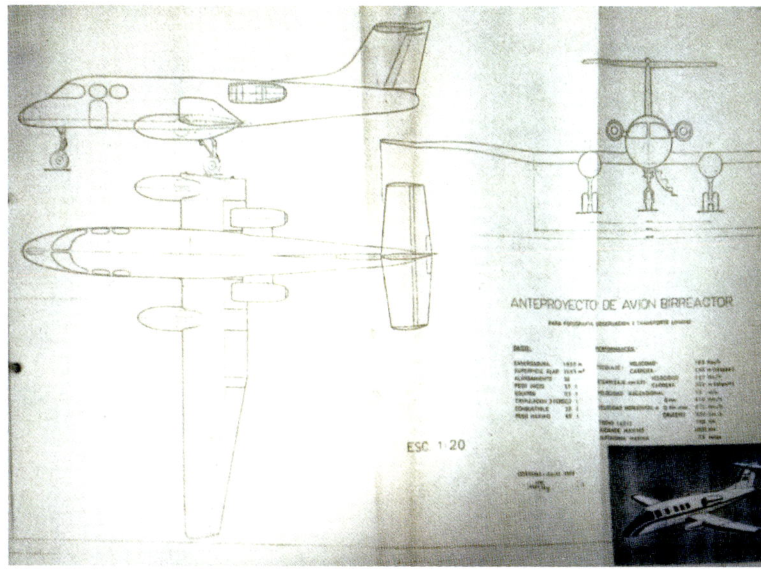

TOP RIGHT Plans of the light transport and observation plane but with a different window design. *Archive Eduardo Ruiz*

RIGHT A model of the first jet version proposed in 1969, with a plane of smaller size. Note the plane is armed with rockets, as was also proposed for light attack. *Archive Eduardo Ruiz*

beginning and not only carried out for those particular cases. It is also interesting, when describing the armament configurations, that a so-called B-2 configuration is included, with the plane carrying a 1,000kg torpedo, as well as rockets and ammunition for the 20mm cannon.

Astazou selection

After the test flights carried out, in May 1971 the report on the evaluation of the Garrett and Astazou engines was submitted to the Material Command of the Argentine Air Force, to determine which of the two should be finally adopted by the aircraft.

According to the report, the Garrett engine could deliver up to 840shp (for up to five minutes) at take-off and 770shp at cruise, with a torque limiting of 2,363in/sq ft, and fuel consumption at take-off of 276 litres/hour and at cruise of 264. The weight of the engine was 156kg and, with its accessories and propellers, it reached 355kg.

In turn, the Astazou delivered up to 965shp in take-off (without limitation in terms of time) and 890 in cruise, with a torque limit of 2,575 lb/sq ft, a consumption in take-off of 294 litres/hour and in cruise of 265. For its part, the engine weighed 143.5kg and, with propellers and accessories, 335kg.

In the Pucará, the Garrett supported up to 7Gs upwards and 1.5 laterals, while in the Astazou the limits were 10 and 5 respectively.

For its part, while the Garrett engine was widely used, the Astazou XVI-G was a new model and there was little history of its long-term performance.

In the flight tests, AX-02 showed a service ceiling in attack configuration, armed with bombs, weight equivalent to the cannon and machine guns

The IA-58B tunnel model with Garrett engines as it is today. *Santiago Rivas*

The IA-58B was an attempt to develop a version of the plane with Defa 552 cannon of 30mm instead of the Hispano Suiza of 20mm.

and their ammunition, with two pilots and full internal fuel, with two engines, of 8,280m, against 6,680 of AX-01, and of 5,340m against 5,000m with one engine, but the tests were done with a bigger fuel load in AX-02, so the difference was estimated to be even greater. AX-02 reached a maximum speed at sea level of 482km/h against 432 of AX-02. The take-off run was 600m on AX-02 and 830m on AX-01, while the landing run was 440m and 523m respectively. In addition, AX-02 could meet the requirement of a turning radius of 150m flying with the internal weapons (they were not installed, but the equivalent in weight), against 190 in AX-01 due to its lower power.

The range of AX-02 with an extra tank, totalling 2,580 litres, flying at an altitude of 5,000m and 402km/h was verified at 3,400km, although in AX-01, with 2,485 litres it was between 2,630 and 3,400km, but it was indicated that the necessary power tests at different heights in said prototype had yet to be completed. The maximum endurance with extra tanks in AX-02, with a consumption of 116 litres/hour per engine, was ten hours ten minutes, while in the AX-01, with a consumption of 128 litres/hour per engine, it was nine hours thirty-seven minutes.

At the same time, it was found that the power delivered by the Astazou was guaranteed by the manufacturer, which was not the case with the Garrett engines, which, moreover, easily exceeded torque and temperature and complicated the operation.

On the other hand, given the small number of flights carried out with AX-02, a margin of error of more or less 10 per cent was estimated and it was suggested at the same time to make a more complete study of both aircraft in all kinds of situations, such as acrobatic flight, inverted, shooting and bombing, training and instruction, to reach between 150 and 200 hours.

On the other hand, the Garrett engines had presented a large number of faults during the tests, delaying them a lot, and these ended on 17 March 1971, after 167 flights and a total of 175 hours, without achieving complete tuning of the engines on the plane. That same day AX-02 reached eighty-seven flights and eighty-five and a half hours, having tuned the Astazous, for which the two planes entered a check.

Another aspect considered was the cost of the engines and their accessories, estimated at $57,305 for the Astazou and $69,187 for the Garrett.

For all this, the selection of the Astazou engine was recommended, as it was considered to be better adapted to the operation of the aircraft, especially in combat missions, where maximum performance was required. Thus, it was decided that AX-01 be modified with the installation of said engines and on 21 June AX-01 made its last flight with Garrett engines, having accumulated 204 and a half hours in 190 flights, removing the Garrett engines on the 25th. As the plane was 20cm shorter, the engine supports had to be installed further back

AX-03 while preparing to depart for Le Bourget in 1977. Note the radar installed in the nose and the plane carrying one 1,135-litre and two 320-litre fuel tanks. *Archive José Martínez*

A-501 at Aeroparque Jorge Newbery of Buenos Aires. *Alberto Martín*

than in AX-02, to keep the centre of gravity in the same location. This aircraft received Hamilton Standard 23LF-3335 propellers, with the installation of the new engines finished on 8 February 1972. AX-01 returned to test flights on 21 April 1972, with its first flight with Astazous piloted by Vice Commodore Roberto Camblor.

In May of that year, the type's first flight outside the country was made, when AX-02 flew to the Asunción del Paraguay International Airport to show the model to the Paraguayan Air Force, something carried out on the 15th.

Meanwhile, on 3 June 1971, C-130E Hercules serial TC-63 took AX-02 to France to carry out, at the Turbomeca facilities, structure vibration tests with the new engines, returning on the 24th aboard the same aircraft.

In addition, that year and after the first evaluations of the CEV, the FAA ordered a series of thirty aircraft that was later raised to 100, starting the assembly line in 1972.

The tests continued with the two prototypes during 1972, at the same time that the third aircraft (AX-03) began to be manufactured, also equipped with the Astazous and with a modified nose, adopting the final shape. In addition, the outer wing tanks were eliminated because they had a bad influence on the roll. This was the first example equipped with full armament from the start, including a Matra SFOM 83A-3 sight and Bendix AWE-1 firing programmer. Due to budget problems, the completion was delayed and AX-03 made its first flight only on 8 December 1973, while serial production was postponed until June 1974. The plan called for the delivery of the first aircraft before the end of 1974, another four in 1975, fourteen in 1976, thirty-six in 1977 and 1978 and nine in 1979, finishing before June of that year.

While this was happening, in 1973 in Hangar 90 of the FMA, the manufacture of the first series aeroplanes was being prepared, and the aerodynamic studies were finished.

On 4 April 1973, AX-02 carried out a JATO take-off and during that year undertook tests with the weapons, including two conventional 115kg bombs, 70mm LAU-60 rockets, T-10 and SCARs rockets and an experimental six-tube rocket launcher for ground tests. It also tested the strength of the self-sealing tanks, internal armour and armoured windscreen against the impact of different-calibre projectiles, demonstrating great resistance to light weapons fire. Given the delay in the completion of AX-03, during that year AX-02 was modified to receive the fixed armament of cannon and machine guns.

On 16 April 1974, AX-01 was presented to President Juan D. Perón at BAM Mariano Moreno, in Buenos Aires, including a take-off using JATOs from the apron itself, in just 55m, which was carried out by Vice Commodore Camblor. In May it was also presented to authorities of the Libyan Air Force, who were interested in the type, and in October to the Bolivian Air Force, one of those forces that showed the greatest interest in the Pucará from the beginning. Shortly thereafter, AX-01 received a large aerial data probe in its nose to continue testing.

For the Argentine Air Force day of that year, on 10 August, the three prototypes deployed to the VII Air Brigade in Morón, Buenos Aires, where they participated in the parade headed by the new president, María Estela Martínez (Perón's widow and vice-president until Peron's death on 1 July 1974), in one of the largest exhibitions of the force in its history.

On 15 September, the BAM Reconquista, which would be the unit that would fly the Pucará, formed the Pucará Task Force under the command of Major

A-539, now as AX-06, with the original Garrett engine nacelles.

José M. Ignes Rosset and on 15 October, with Captain José Ignacio Igarzábal and 1st Lieutenant Hugo Palaver instructing, the first training flights began in Córdoba prior to the reception of the first series aircraft, using the AX-01 and 02 prototypes, with the last pilots finishing their adaptation flights on 13 December.

On 8 November 1974, the first series production aircraft flew for the first time, which initially had been manufactured to be the fourth prototype, serialled A-501, with Vice Commodore Camblor at the controls. Its second flight was carried out on the 13th by Captain Horacio Oréfice and it was presented two days later during the forty-seventh anniversary of the factory. This aircraft, among other differences, had the Martin-Baker APO-6A 0-0 ejection seat. Thus began the evaluation flights by the CEV, which lasted until 31 July 1975.

Due to the interest shown by Bolivia, on 20 March 1975 AX-02 was exhibited there, although the purchase was not made in the end. It was once again officially offered to the Argentine Naval Aviation Command as a light embarked attack aircraft to replace the T-28 Fennec, without arousing much interest.

In 1976, 700 flight hours were allocated for the two prototypes that flew at the factory, since in November 1975 AX-02 had stopped flying and had become a platform for ground structural tests, being subjected to efforts until its destruction, leaving only the forward part of the fuselage preserved for many years in the III Air Brigade. In this regard, it must be borne in mind that its airframe had been subjected to structural stresses during the vibration tests in France, which is why it was grounded.

International exhibitions

As part of the FMA's attempt to sell the aircraft abroad, it was planned to exhibit it at the 32nd Le Bourget Salon in Paris, which would take place between 2 and 12 June 1977. With that goal in mind, from 10 to 28 April, tests were carried out with AX-01 and 03 to evaluate the possibility of flying the Pucará to Europe. With the planes equipped with three additional tanks, they made non-stop flights departing from Córdoba and passing through the cities of Santa Rosa, Neuquén, Bariloche, Bahía Blanca, Ezeiza, Rosario and Paraná to return to Córdoba eight hours later, having travelled 3,200km. With this, the Pucará's ability to cross the Atlantic in flight was proven, a task carried out by AX-03 manned by Vice Commodore García and 1st Lieutenant Germán Spika, accompanied by the C-130H Hercules serialled TC-64, which carried in its hold A-507. They left Córdoba on 14 May at 0830, making the first stopover in Porto Alegre, after flying two and half hours to cover the distance of 1,260km. Then they made the first long-duration part, flying directly to Recife, at 2,970km, which required seven hours forty minutes of flight and where they had to land by instruments. The crossing of the Atlantic was the riskiest stage, although they were able to complete it without setbacks. They arrived at Salt Island by instruments after another seven hours forty minutes of flight that required them to cover 3,070km. The next leg of the flight was also over the sea, although shorter, to Las Palmas (Canary Islands), 1,490km away, arriving after three hours fifty minutes and again landing by instruments. From there they continued to Seville to complete the last stretch over the sea, landing three hours twenty minutes later after flying over 1,335km. The last leg was to fly to Pau-Uzein in France on 19 May, covering 835km in two hours and landing at 0930. To accomplish this flight, the aircraft received a VOR/ILS, two ADFs, two VHF, INS Litton LTL-72, a Bendix RUR-160 weather radar in the nose, and Bendix DPR-600 transponder. At the Turbomeca plant in that town, AX-03 was checked and A-507 was assembled, them both flying to Le Bourget in Paris on 29 May.

After the exhibition, between 15 and 29 June AX-03 went to Cazaux to test the guns and the SC-PT-303 firing programmer from Sistemas y Controles company (which would not be adopted in the other aeroplanes). In reference to the guns, vibration tests were carried out, one for toxicity of gas emissions in the cockpit and one 'explosive'.

The latter, according to the report carried out by the French Center D'Essais en Vol, CEV, aimed to analyse the risk that the gases from the cannon may ignite during firing, both due to heat or a spark from the aircraft electrical equipment. Twelve tests were carried out on the ground, with bursts of up to 2.5 seconds where no risk of gas explosion was detected, both with the barrel ventilation system open and closed. Then two test flights were made, at 1,500m of altitude and at speeds between 150 and 240 knots, making twelve bursts of between 0.7 and 1.9 seconds, in which no risks were detected but the test clarified that it was necessary to take the results cautiously due to the short duration of the bursts. Regarding the cockpit gas tests, high levels of toxic gases were detected when shots were fired over a period of more than twelve seconds. Thus, it was recommended that a pilot keep his oxygen mask on and open the vents to the maximum, with some reforms to the ventilation system of the guns also considered. It was indicated that machine guns possibly generated more vibrations in the instrument panel than cannon, since their muzzles were closer to it. On the other hand, they pointed out that the measurements detected when firing the guns indicated the possibility of untimely disconnection of the connectors of some instruments. It was recommended that tests were carried out on the ground with the firing of all the ammunition and others in flight with shots of long bursts. Two flights were also recommended to detect the possibility of ignition of gases at altitudes of up to 10,000ft and between 130 and 350 knots.

The test report indicates that the aircraft was equipped with two internal cannon and weapon pylons (one Aero 7A-1 ventral and two Aero 20A-1 under the wings), but not the machine guns, which may have been retired before the flight to France.

In addition, the installation of different weapons was tested on the ground, some already approved by the French Service Technique Aeronautique, others in process and others not approved. Among the approved were SAMP BD 10 general-purpose bombs of 125kg for training, the SAMP model 25 of 250kg, Matra LR-F2 rocket launchers (of six tubes of 68mm) and the universal adapters AUF-1 for these arms (an adapter for the electrical connection of the plane was needed to be built, since it had ten connectors against nineteen of the AUF-1 and voltage differences) and the Alkan 65 adapter for Lacroix Bavar practice bombs (it also needed an electrical adaptation). Among those in the approval process were the Alkan Type 530 cartridge launcher for forty cartridges of 74mm, BLG grenade launchers (later named Beluga, with 151 grenades of 1.2kg and 66mm in diameter), Durandal anti-runway bombs of 198kg and Matra LR-F8 rocket launchers, while the unapproved ones were 120kg SAMP and 250kg SAMP EU2 bombs, 125kg super-braked Matra and thirty-six-tube Matra 155 rocket launchers for 68mm SNEB rockets.

The CEV recommended a flight test campaign after the adaptation of the AUF-1 pylon, which was not carried out. Also, the addition of the shot-by-shot option for launching rockets. Only the Alkan 530 was adopted by the FAA (although using MERs and TERs of US origin) and the French CEV report advised its use in six launchers, with Lacroix Type 314 anti-vehicle

The Pucará at Farnborough '78

The IA-66 at the factory.

grenades, using the launch of five grenades per second, two containers at a time, at a speed of 240 knots, a height of 200 to 220ft and a range (if fired sideways on TER or MER racks) of 240 to 250m, with a lateral inclination between 0° and 15° to increase or decrease the range of the cartridges. Thus, a coverage of 2,500 × 60m of surface was achieved.

Although there are no records that indicate that it was carried out, a plan was made at the FMA to translate all the external inscriptions of the plane into French, for the tests to be carried out in France.

AX-03 then flew to the Turbomeca factory in Pau-Uzein to test the engines and their performance on the I.A.58, beginning the return to Argentina on 10 July, to arrive in Buenos Aires on 18 July.

On its return it was planned to transform AX-03 into the IA-58B prototype, although in an accident that occurred on 4 October, the aircraft was completely destroyed, causing the death of Captain Schmidt. Because of this, A-509, re-serialled AX-04, in November 1977 was assigned to the CEV for weapons tests, including a ventral pod with a DEFA 553 30mm cannon and the Alkan 530 containers to launch Lacroix 314 anti-vehicle and F130 smoke cartridges.

Given the success of the demonstration at Le Bourget, in 1978 it was planned to send the Pucará to the Farnborough exhibition in the UK, for which A-519, which was being tested by the CEV before its delivery, was modified as had AX-03 for the previous crossing of the Atlantic. On 18 August A-19 departed flown by Major Carlos Digier and 1st Lieutenant Germán Spika, supported by Hercules TC-61, and after a successful exhibition between 3 and 10 September, it returned on the 20th to Córdoba.

In 1979 AX-01 stopped flying and was used for static displays, being decommissioned in October 1980.

Into service

On 20 August 1975, A-501 and A-502, completed in July, were officially delivered to BAM Reconquista to form Escuadrón I de Ataque. By the end of the year the planes, plus A-503 and AX-03, were used from the Escuela de Aviación Militar (EAM), to perform attack missions against the guerrillas of the Ejército Revolucionario del Pueblo, who were operating on the jungles of Tucumán province, starting their missions on 11 December, until the 17th of that month, when they finished the operations.

Deliveries continued in 1976 with A-504 and 505, but progressed slowly through 1977, with those up to A-524 (A-521 was not used) in 1978. Of these, those with construction numbers 013, 014, 017 and 018 were originally produced for a contract with Mauritania for four aircraft, which were to be the first to be exported. However, this contract was cancelled after the first had already received the African air force's colours and serial 5T-MAB. Thus, 017 and 018 were delivered to the FAA with serial numbers A-514 and 515, and 013 and 014 as A-518 and 517 respectively. This led to a change in the serial numbers of those aircraft originally assigned A-517 to 519 (c/n 021, 022 and 023), which became A-520, A-522 and A-523 respectively. The aircraft with c/n 019 became the new A-519. A-518 entered FAA service in the camouflage originally painted for Mauritania, which it retained for a time and it distinguished it from all other Pucará aircraft.

In March 1980 A-539, which was under evaluation at the CEV, was taken under the command of Captain Carlos Tomba to participate in the FIDA show in Santiago de Chile, flying Chilean

Pucará A-582 seen on 18 May 2021 during one of the test flights of the MET-1 version of the INVAP pod.

A-577 as the first IA-58D Pucará, seen at the ceremony marking thirty years of the type in 2005. *Santiago Rivas*

Air Force personnel during the exhibitions. This aircraft participated during the year in an evaluation in Iraq, for which it was transported aboard C-130 TC-61. There, among other demonstrations, a combat exercise against helicopters was conducted by Major José Ignacio Igarzábal. At the time, the Iraqi government was very interested in the Pucará. This visit took place before the start of the Iraqi invasion of Iran in September of that year. On its return, the aircraft was sent to the factory to be converted into the IA-66.

On 16 March 1980, a flight with the call sign 'Huayra' was flown to Montevideo, Uruguay, to participate in the Uruguayan Air Force Day, the first time the Pucará visited that country.

Shortly afterwards, on 31 May, a tour of South America began using the A-534 and 541 aircraft under evaluation by the CEV, with Captains Carlos Tomba, Jorge Benitez and Fillipi, supported by C 130 TC-67. The first display was carried out at Palanquero base (Bogotá, Colombia), followed by another at El Libertador base (Maracay, Venezuela), Las Palmas (Lima, Peru), Nhu Guazú (Asunción, Paraguay) and São José dos Campos (São Paulo state, Brazil). On 3 July, the aircraft returned having successfully completed the demonstrations, in which they used real weapons equipped with a MER with six 125kg bombs and two TERs with two LAU-61 rocket launchers for nineteen FFAR 70mm (2.75in) rockets.

During that year, the FMA completed twelve of the twenty-one aircraft planned, while throughout 1981 the nineteen aircraft planned were completed, up to A-569, c/n 070, and the final assembly of 072 began. The aircraft originally serialled as A-542 to 544 and 546 to 548 were sold to the Uruguayan Air Force, so those serials were never used by the FAA.

In 1982 the type was used extensively in the Malvinas/Falklands war, operating from BAM Malvinas at Puerto Argentino/Stanley, at BAM Cóndor at Goose Green and at the Estación Aeronaval Calderón at Borbón/Pebble Island.

IA-58B

In 1976, development began of the IA-58B, which was a Pucará fitted with two 30mm DEFA 553 cannon with 280 rounds each, in place of the 20mm Hispano Suiza. It would also have the addition of HF, IFF/SSR, DME, tactical VHF/FM, while the VOR/ILS, DF and VHF equipment were duplicated. Because the cannon and ammunition took up more space, the belly of the fuselage had to be modified and the fuselage became bulkier.

During 1978, the production aircraft 025, originally serialled A-525 and later re-serialled AX-05, was modified as the IA-58B prototype, starting flight tests on 15 March 1979 under the command of Major Carlos Digier.

That same year it was decided to present it at the Le Bourget exhibition, for which it was fitted with Omega navigation equipment, and weather radar was planned to be installed, but on 1 June

The IA-58C with Major Horacio Orefice at the controls during one of the test flights. *Archive Eduardo Ruiz*

1979, A-519, with CEV pilots Major Carlos Digier and Captain Germán Spika at the controls, crashed at Cerro Ancasti in Catamarca during tests of the Omega system, causing the death of both pilots.

AX-05 was finally sent disassembled in a C-130, where it was displayed on the ground between 8 and 17 June. It was then taken to Cazaux for testing of the guns, where the results showed that they generated vibration when fired, although this did not significantly affect the aircraft's controllability, while there were problems with the cabin insulation, into which smoke from the firing of the guns entered. The test schedule would be completed in October 1980, on AX-05's return to Argentina after 150 hours of flight. In addition, the cruise speed was 5.5km/h less and the stall speed 115km/h with gear and flaps down.

During 1981, a study was made to install a Saab RGS-2 air-to-air and air-to-surface gunsight in the IA-58B, which was carried out shortly afterwards, and it was also planned to install Garrett TPE-331-11U engines, for which tests were carried out in the wind tunnel. The idea of the re-engining was to facilitate marketing, since Venezuela, one of the most interested countries, demanded that the engines be replaced as they preferred power plants of US origin.

Initially it was thought that aircraft from c/n 042 would be delivered as IA-58Bs with Garrett engines, but delays in the installation of these power plants led to the decision that only aircraft from 060 would be delivered as such. Finally, in 1981 the programme was abandoned because the problems of vibration and smoke ingress in the cabin could not be solved, so this prototype was retired on 7 November 1982.

IA-58C

On 12 June 1979, engineer Alberto Yeraci, head of the FMA Fuselage Projects Section, presented a proposal for three possible single-seat variants of the Pucará, all designated IA-58C.

The aim was to achieve a more versatile and lighter aircraft, at a lower cost and whose design would also improve on the flight characteristics of the two-seater aircraft. Yeraci proposed two alternatives for the location of the pilot's seat, in the pilot's position in the two-seater or in the co-pilot's position, as it could not be in an intermediate position due to the location of the propellers.

The first alternative, which he called IA-58CI, retained the two-seater configuration and only removed the seat and instruments from the rear seat, but incorporated a new canopy with individual openings for each pilot and a fixed section in the middle. The second, called IA-58CII involved a single canopy for the pilot and a cover on the co-pilot's seat, so that this could be replaced to accommodate a canopy to revert to the two-seat configuration without major structural changes.

The third configuration, called IA-58CIII, envisaged installing the pilot's position in the rear position, with a cover on the original pilot's station, and using the space for avionics or armament.

The first version reduced the weight by 156kg and the cost by $58,500, the second by 171kg and $65,050 and the third by 240kg and $70,000, to which should be added a reduction of about 90kg in the weight of the co-pilot and his equipment.

While the early versions had the advantage that they could be converted back to two-seaters, they did not allow the use of the rear space except for avionics, since the installation of a fuel tank there would lead to variations in the centring of the aircraft as the fuel was consumed. In addition, the elevated location made it difficult to maintain whatever was installed there.

In the IA-58CIII version, however, while it was not possible to convert it back to a two-seater without structural changes, the forward space was considered ideal for installing armament or avionics, due to its easy accessibility. While this version would require some additional tooling, it could be produced along the same lines as the two-seaters. In addition, pressurisation was considered feasible without structural changes, given the small size of the cabin.

Although the downward forward visibility angle was reduced with respect to the two-seater, it was maintained at 15°, which allowed the firing of all the intended weapons. The position of the propellers in front of the cockpit was considered not to significantly affect vision, although it could be a nuisance during night landings due to the reflection of the landing lights on the blades. This could be solved by painting the blades black or changing the position of the lights. For both this version and the IA-58CII, it was considered possible to redesign the fuselage fuel tank to increase its capacity.

An interesting aspect is that they were all planned with similar armament to the IA-58B, with two 30mm cannon instead of the 20mm, although in the diagrams presented, the IA-58CIII is not shown with the machine guns.

Although the idea was not taken forward at that time, the South Atlantic War experience led to it being taken up again in 1983, when the AMC carried out preliminary feasibility studies for three versions of the Pucará, which appear in the factory's memoirs of that year as IA-58B rear single-seater, IA-58C rear single-seat with 30mm cannon (basically the original IA-58CIII) and IA-58 Malvinas, front single-seat with cabin redesign and 30mm cannon (based on the other two ideas from 1979).

From these ideas, the rear single-seat IA-58C was chosen, although it was decided to keep the 20mm cannon, due to the problems encountered on the IA-58B, and add a 30mm DEFA 553 cannon above the nose, the ability to launch Matra Magic air-to-air and Martin Pescador radio-guided air-to-surface missiles. Airframe 043, originally to be built as an IA-58B, was modified and publicly presented on 10 October 1984 as a mock-up of the IA-58C, known as Pucará Charlie.

In 1985 the aircraft was completed as the prototype of that model and re-serialled AX-06. A new

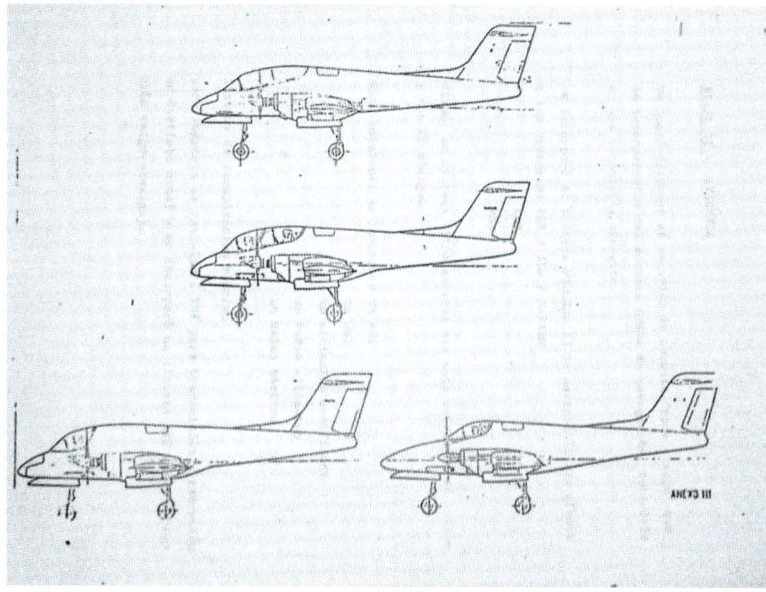

Layout of the IA-58A and the three IA-58C proposals considered in 1979.

Blueprint with the scheme of installation of the Kevlar plates planned as armour for the IA-58E version, to replace the original metal armour. This was not adopted on the modified planes.

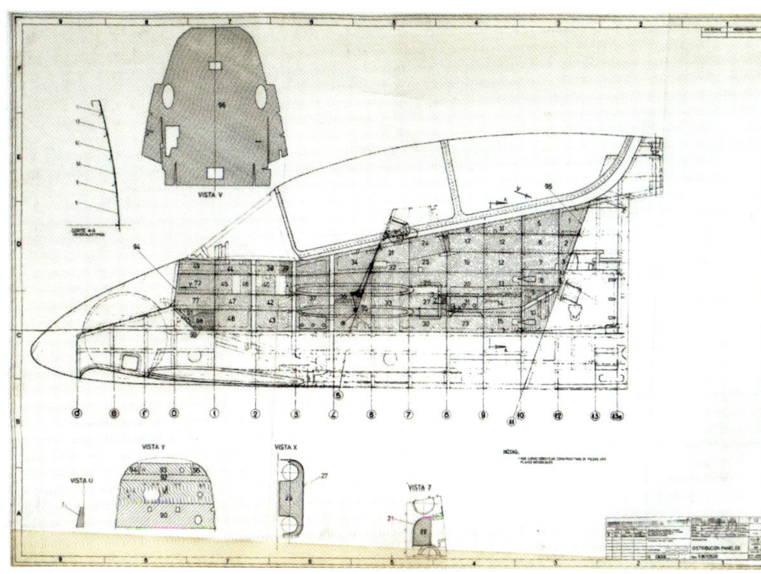

installation was made for the French DEFA 30mm cannon with 270 rounds, the two upper machine guns were removed, although the idea was to keep them, and a Saab RGS2/A sight, coded altimeter, accelerometer and variometer were installed. The first flight was made under the command of Major Horacio Oréfice on 30 December 1985.

During 1986 AX-06 received Collins equipment such as an Electronic Horizontal Situation Indicator (EHSI), VHF (AM/FM) AN/ARC-186(V), VOR/ILS/MK VIR-32, ADF, DME, gyro unit and Photo Sonics camera. In addition, extra Kevlar armour was added to the cockpit sides, Garrett air conditioning, APU and cockpit instruments and commands were redistributed. It was planned to lengthen the exhausts to reduce the

A-545 being used for tests of the Martín Pescador in 1982, with the intention of using the missile against British forces in the Malvinas/Falklands War.

infrared signature and to fit the Pampa's avionics. In addition, it was to receive Omega, HUD, chaff and flare launchers, radar warning receiver (RWR), IFF and radio altimeter, for which the wiring was laid, but never the equipment.

Up to 12 November 1986, sixteen flights were completed, all under the command of Major Oréfice, of which the first five were for qualitative evaluation, from the sixth to the ninth for calibration, and the remaining flights were for air-to-air and air-to-ground firing in Río IV (Córdoba).

However, due to budget cuts, the programme was relegated in the following years and the aircraft flew just a few more times, until in 1995 AX-06 was finally retired, since the IA-58C programme had been cancelled and because it was not compatible with the rest of the aircraft in several aspects. After being completely cannibalised and remaining outdoors in the factory facilities until 2002, it was restored and transferred to the Aerospace Technology Museum of the Area de Material Río IV.

The FixView POA pod developed for observation with a 360° gimball, batteries and wireless connection with the console on the cockpit, to facilitate the installation. *Santiago Rivas*

Other tests

To replace A-519 in tests, A-530 was commissioned to support the ongoing trials with the Pucará and in 1981 received a Garrett cabin heater, with a SEMCA one installed in A-511 and a Hamilton Standard in A-520 to evaluate them and thus improve the comfort of the pilots. This idea was shelved in 1988 and taken up again in 1995 on A-584. A Crossor IFF transponder and later a Siemens SIT-4211 were also evaluated, although neither would be finally adopted due to a lack of budget.

Also, a study to install the 'Martín Pescador' short-range, air-surface, radio-guided missile developed by CITEFA (Centro de Investigaciones Técnicas de la Fuerzas Armadas, Centre for Technical Research of the Armed Forces) took place. This weighed 150kg and had an operating range between 2.2km to 9.2km with a normal range of 6km, whose trajectory was covered in just eleven seconds. It had a 220mm diameter, a length of 3,000mm and a speed of Mach 2.3. The corresponding installation was carried out on the AX-04 and tests achieved successful results.

These tests were also carried out on A-545 during the Malvinas/Falklands War, until it crashed in Flor de Oro, Santa Fe, on 2 July 1982. The missile system was never adopted by the Air Force, despite the fact that Naval Aviation had been using it since 1973.

Torpedoes

During the war, the use of torpedoes was proposed, with the provision of MK-13s by the Argentine Navy, who used them in the ten Higgins-class torpedo boats that had been in service until 1966, and more than forty units were available. They were used to test the launching from the Aero 20A-1 ventral pylon of Pucará AX-04, which had been equipped with a film camera to follow the launching. This work began on 21 May at Comandante Espora

AX-04 at Base Aeronaval Comandante Espora during the first tests of the torpedo on the Pucará.

Naval Air Base, with the first launch the following day, which was unsuccessful, as was the second, carried out on the same day. In both launches, the exercise torpedo was used and in all cases the device was destroyed on impact with the water due to the high launch speed. This was due to the fact that the torpedo model used had been designed to be launched from the four cradles on the deck of the torpedo boats, which had a speed of about 50 knots. In the Navy they had also been used from Martin Mariner seaplanes and Catalina amphibians, in straight and level flight and whose speed for a successful launch was at the time of launching approximately 95 knots and 20m high.

In the case of the Pucará, the launch speed was much higher, and the correct angle of release was not set, which is why the first attempts failed. The aircraft was then transferred to Trelew to continue testing alongside A-566. On 24 May, the first successful launch was made in the San José Gulf, using the flight profile of a PBY-5A Catalina as an example. On 10 June, the first launch was made with a torpedo equipped with a warhead, against a cliff in the Puerto Santa Cruz area at a speed of 120 knots. Although another launch was planned four days later, it was cancelled due to the end of the war. Another idea was to adapt Mk.12 anti-ship mines, but the end of the war also put a stop to the project after the first trials.

IA-58G and IA-66

At the request of Venezuela, which was interested in purchasing twenty-four aircraft, in 1981 the IA-58G project was developed, consisting of a Pucará with 1,000shp Garrett TPE-331-11-601W engines and Dowty Rotol R 316/4-82-F/6 four-blade propellers, on which the FMA, AeroFalcon of Argentina and Volpar Inc. of the United States worked together. Although it was initially planned to install these engines in AX-05, in order not to slow down the trials with the 30mm cannon, it was decided to modify A-539 after its tour of Iraq. The central wing was changed and the engine cowlings were redesigned to install the Garrett engines and the heating of the same brand. This work was carried out by Volpar and the A-539 wing assembly had to be sent to the United States, where engineers Frank A. Nixon and A. Chana worked on its modification. On 20 August 1980, the wing assembly was delivered to the United States and sent back to Córdoba in an FAA Hercules. The installation of the wing with the new spars was carried out between 6 and 9 October and on the 13th the aircraft flew for the first time with Vice Commodore José Videla at the controls. Shortly afterwards, on the 28th of that month, the aircraft was re-serialled AX-06 and received the new designation IA-66. Early trials indicated the need for some major changes to the wing, so the wing assembly of aircraft c/n 042, in the process of manufacture, was sent to Volpar in 1981. There, a

A-561 flying with the MQ-2 Biguá. This example has a different nose with a camera.

new engine mount and cowlings were made, returning to the country on 8 July 1981. At that time, after thirty-seven test flights, the aircraft entered the workshop to receive the new wing, returning to testing on 29 September.

The original plan was to build 200 units in 1982 to be sold abroad as training and attack aircraft. The IA-66 had a minimum take-off run of 240m or 490m with a 15m obstacle, 86m assisted by JATOs and 155m with obstacles. Work on two pre-series aircraft was started and it was envisaged that four could be delivered to the Instituto Nacional de Aviación Civil (INAC, National Institute of Civil Aviation), based in Morón, Buenos Aires province, for advanced training, equipped with full instrumentation in the rear seat. Although the results were satisfactory, as the aircraft vibrated less (in 1981 they had received McCauley propellers), had lower noise levels and had autonomous starting, the performance was inferior in terms of fuel consumption and take-off and landing performance. They also had some vibration problems and no fuel system for inverted flight, as well as the engines being heavier and the nacelles reduced the view to the sides. Added to this, the country's economic situation and the cancellation of the contract with Venezuela led to the project being abandoned and AX-06 was retired in 1984, after flying for the last time in April of that year after 170 hours of testing, while the pre-series aircraft were completed as IA-58As.

The engines were sold to the Lapa airline for use in their Fairchild Metros, while the aircraft went to the FMA to return to its original configuration with a new wing, receiving the serial A-607, although it was never delivered back to the FAA. The engine nacelles remain abandoned at the factory.

Final deliveries

After the war, the factory delivered the aircraft A-563, 572 and 573 on 28 June 1982, followed on 15 July by A-564, 567 and 568 and on 12 August by A-560, 569 and 575. Deliveries continued in December 1982, with the arrival of A-570, 571, 574 and 577 on the 14th and A-578 on the 29th, already covering fifteen of those lost in the war. The FMA finished the fourteen planned aircraft, also registering A-583 from the workshop on 29 October, starting the assembly of the aircraft serial 088 (A-588) and also building an airframe for fatigue tests, with 087 delivered on 16 September.

The fleet continued to increase in 1983 with the delivery of A-579 and 576 on 16 February, A-580 and A-582 on 16 March, and A-583 on 20 April, with the FMA completing nine of the ten planned.

In 1983 studies were carried out to install the GGS Mk.IVE air-to-air sight, night sights and the possibility of equipping the planes of the IX Brigada Aérea with Matra R550 Magic air-to-air missiles.

In 1984, the FMA planned to deliver A-596 to A-608, of which they had already begun to build up to A-601. However, the budget cuts that began with the inauguration of President Raúl Alfonsín on

10 December 1983 overturned these plans and none were delivered. At the end of the year production of the planes with serial numbers 096 to 100 were at 62 per cent and 101 at 5 per cent. Assembly of the others had not been started. The main problem was the lack of engines and propellers, which prevented completion.

That year Pucará A-591, which was delivered to the workshop but had not been delivered to the Air Force, was sent in March to participate in a new edition of the FIDA fair, at the El Bosque Air Base, in Santiago de Chile.

While the FMA plan in 1985 was to finish seven aircraft, up to c/n 108 (A-608), the lack of engines and propellers again paralysed production, leaving c/n 096 to 104 at 62 per cent, 105 at 3 per cent and assembly of the rest unstarted. Additionally, A-595 (c/n 095), which was 90 per cent complete, had its engines removed for use in other aircraft that were in service.

In addition to constant budget cuts, which forced all funds to be diverted to the IA-63 Pampa trainer programme, which was starting flight tests, the Argentine Air Force no longer had the need for an anti-guerrilla plane. Now the Pucará only served as a close air support aircraft, supporting combat rescue missions and patrolling the borders in search of illegal flights. For this reason, the assembly line was suspended and then the FMA, through the recently created Tecnología Aeroespacial (TEA S.A.), a company owned by the factory and destined to sell its products, began to negotiate the sale of the Pucará abroad.

In 1986 the assembly of the aeroplanes progressed a little, but none was finished. Meanwhile, in that year, A-561 was delivered by the FMA and sent to the CEV for weapons tests, because AX-04 used for that purpose had entered a main check that was never finished.

During 1987 the FMA also continued without being able to finish the series, although it made some progress in the assembly of aircraft 106 to 108. On 5 August 1988, A-584 was finished by the FMA, which was delivered to the III Brigade shortly after, while A-585 and A-588 to A-597 remained in the workshop with completion at between 75 and 90 per cent. In May of that year, the missing engines and propellers arrived, and manufacturing continued, albeit slowly. However, A-588 received engines from an aircraft in service to be presented that year at FIDA 88, in Santiago, Chile, then returned to the FMA to be readied.

Thanks to the arrival of the missing material, in 1989 the 108 series production airframes were completed and between June and October the production line was removed, to make way for the Pampa. Similarly, the tail of the 108th aircraft was used to replace that of A-563. At that time a plan was made to deliver four in three months and then one per month, with the assembly line in hangar 36 of the factory. A-585 and 595 were ready, while A-588 was finished and ready for check flights by the Air Force and to be officially received.

In March 1990, the Pucará participated again in what was now called FIDAE in Chile, with A-594 together with the first prototype of the IA-63 Pampa (EX-01).

At that time, President Carlos S. Menem began a much more marked cut of the Armed Forces' budget, affecting the FMA again, while the units practically stopped flying. The manufacture of the Pucará, which had been reactivated, was again suspended, delivering the planes up to A-604 at a very slow pace.

In 1992 A-561 was sent, in March, to participate in the FIDAE 92 fair in Chile, now held at Los Cerrillos Air Base, in a new presentation of the aircraft abroad.

In 1995, the FMA was handed over in concession to Lockheed Aircraft Argentina Sociedad Anónima

A-505 operating on the highway between the cities of Córdoba and Villa Carlos Paz, which was under construction when the tests were made by this plane and AX-03 in 1976. *FMA*

Pucarás CA-604 and 605 flying armed, one with bombs and the other with rocket launchers. *Peter Steinemann via Carlos Ay*

(LAASA, later Lockheed Martin, LMAASA), although the delivery of the pending aircraft remained delayed. In 1996 A-595 and 604 were delivered, and shortly the latter after was re-serialled A-504.

In 1996 a Pucará again participated in the FIDAE fair in Chile, now with A-584. Forest fires in the vicinity of the city of Bariloche in January of that year, which destroyed several houses, led to the evaluation of options for fire-fighting aircraft, and the Argentine Air Force raised an idea for the Pucará Hidrante, using a modified ventral fuel tank to drop water, although the idea was considered unsuitable and none was modified for this.

Project 'Halcón del Sur'

At the beginning of 1985 the FAA signed a contract with the Italian company Meteor SpA, the Argentine Quimar S.A. and Pacific Aerosystems Inc of the United States, which teamed up to develop a new high-performance airborne attack and reconnaissance system called the 'Halcón del Sur'. Said system consisted of the integration of a mother plane (carrier or launcher), which was a Pucará, together with the MQ-2 Biguá multirole system, a RPV (Remoted Piloted Vehicle) based on the Italian Mirach 100, powered by a Meteor TRS-18-076 turbojet, manufactured at the FMA. The Biguá could be launched both from the ground and in flight and could be used as a target for conventional weapons, surface-to-air missiles or air-to-air missiles, while pretending to be an attacking supersonic aircraft. The Biguá measured 4.32m long and had a wingspan of 1.8m. It flew at 900km/h, had an endurance of one hour, an empty weight of 220kg and a maximum weight of 281kg.

In war it could be used for reconnaissance, during which the Pucará would maintain control over the Biguá and could then be relieved by another machine until the RPV was recovered to the landing zone, where it parachuted down. It could also be controlled from the ground by an Alamak mobile station.

Another function was for many of them to saturate enemy defences, pretending to be attacking aircraft during the penetration strike aircraft, while it was possible to modify the Biguá to be used as a cruise missile.

The payload was 35kg and could consist of a vertical camera for reconnaissance at high altitude or a panoramic one for low altitude, as well as infrared sensors, video cameras, electronic intelligence equipment and countermeasures.

The experiments began in Córdoba by the CEV, using A-561, between 23 July and 2 August 1985, with four launches over La Perla Firing Range in Córdoba. These were followed by those carried out on 13 and 28 August when six flights were made with a Biguá to test the qualities of gliding and control, recovering it without problems. In all cases, the Biguá had neither an engine nor a payload and only the aerodynamic behaviour was evaluated.

Subsequently, the propelled prototypes were fine-tuned and on 5 July 1988 the tests were restarted at BAM Chamical (La Rioja province), beginning with ten fine-tuning flights with the Biguá and the ground guidance systems. Then, on 20 July, the first test launch was carried out, but the Biguá was destroyed due to problems with the parachute. On 27 July, the system was publicly presented to the Minister of Defence, Horacio Jaunarena, using the Biguá serial number 00446, at an altitude of 2,000m and 2km from the base. After a first launch where the Biguá had to be recovered due to some problems, another was carried out, where the image transmission systems were successfully tested and then the RPV was recovered at the same base.

Although around 1989 the Biguá was also mounted on A-585, there are no records that it was launched from it. Unfortunately, the budget cuts that followed led to the programme being postponed and finally cancelled in 1990.

As a test airframe used by the CEV, A-561 received a data acquisition system, which years later was replaced by a more modern one, which not only allowed it to record a large amount of information, but also to send it to a ground station. The most modern equipment sends all the information collected in real time, as well as the parameters of the engine and instruments and the position of the aircraft.

Roberto Quiroga, who from 1996 to 2004 and from 2007 to 2012 was assigned to the CEV and flew A-561, explains that the plane 'had many sensors and an electrical system designed to withstand the electrical load of the data recording system. In the lower hatch in the belly, in the standard Pucará there is a box where things are stored when the plane moves. We had a tray there and we put all kinds of sensors. So, if a new brake block had to be evaluated, for example, the undercarriage legs were instrumented with temperature, pressure sensors, etc., and the cables were routed to the recorder.'

In addition to the data acquisition equipment, the aircraft received two VHFs (the Pucará had only one), a VOR, ILS, a transponder and an IFF (which was later removed). Then the other planes received a transponder and the idea of adding GPS was mooted, so A-561 was modified to receive it.

On the left side of the nose, a sensor that measures skidding, whether the plane is flying from side to side or straight, was installed, along with an angle of attack sensor.

At that time, when the CEV was testing a real-time telemetry system in Pampa prototype EX-03, the Air Force asked to make a similar system for all the force's aeroplanes, including the Pucará, so equipment was tested in A-561 that transmitted the aircraft's GPS position in real time. The problem was that the VHF equipment had to transmit all the time, so it overheated and had to be cooled. In addition, because the VHF had visual range, it was not suitable for long flights, so it was finally put aside and only adopted for the planes of the Military Aviation School.

Start-up pod

The Pucará, due to its type of engine, a direct turbine, at the time of start-up has a very high battery consumption, in addition to the fact that they suffer a very large voltage spike, reaching 800 to 900 amperes. For this reason, if the battery is not in good condition, it is not possible to start the aircraft, with the high consumption also causing premature wear of the nickel cadmium unit, which had a high cost. If it was possible to start an engine with a low battery, ground crews had to wait a while to start the second one, since the generator did not directly assist the other engine but charged the battery and only with an acceptable level of charge could the start-up of the other engine be

Pucará A-568 after a night sortie in Reconquista in 2018. *Santiago Rivas*

initiated. This meant that on each deployment ground starter equipment had to be carried.

The V Air Brigade had developed a starter for the A-4 Skyhawk using a supplementary tank, to which wheels were also added and could be mounted on one of the aircraft's pylons, so it could be deployed with the aircraft.

Copying the concept, it was decided to develop an external battery pod, but using gel batteries, which in the late 1990s were a novelty. Regular lead acid batteries could not be used in a plane capable of inverted flight, as the electrolyte leaked, but gel could be used. Roberto Quiroga, who participated in the pod test flights, explained that 'the problem was that these batteries needed a slightly more elaborate charger than what was commercially available. An electrical engineer at the CEV designed that charger. Tests were made, including the destruction of some batteries in the tests. And then we started doing tests in the Pucará. Trials were made to get the pod to start up ten times before needing a recharge. Initially it was thought to put it in a 318-litre tank, but there weren't that many, and we found a napalm bomb in a tank, they put the legs on it, the entire structural part inside to charge the batteries, and we did it.'

After testing, it was shown on the Air Force Day on 10 August 1999 and sent to the III Air Brigade, along with a second pod that was made. 'There were no longer napalm containers of that model to make a third one. The tank had to be remanufactured, that changed the game a bit. Also, the batteries were expensive. And the problem was that when they got to Reconquista, people did more start-ups than they had to, they didn't charge the batteries well and they started having problems. They finally stopped using them. One of the prototypes was returned to us, the other was destroyed, and we continue to use it for maintenance in the hangar. It was good, but the budget to buy more batteries or make the containers was never obtained,' added Quiroga.

Pucará 2000

As part of the extension contract of the concession that the Argentine government granted in 1999 to Lockheed Martin to operate the FMA, the development of the Pucará 2000 was foreseen, which would consist of the modernisation of the aircraft still in service. This plan initially envisaged the replacement of the engines with some variant of the Pratt & Whitney PT6, and changes to the avionics, instruments and weapons systems, for which the addition of new pylons was studied. Budget cuts forced the suspension of the engine replacement, although some variants of the PT6 had already been studied, and the programme was finally cancelled at the end of 2001. This plan included the completion of A-606, 607 and 608 as the first examples. These aircraft would require some minor structural changes that had been incorporated into the operational aircraft over the years.

IA-58D

After the cancellation of the Pucará 2000 project, the Air Force decided in 2002 to move forward with the simpler IA-58D project, called 'Pucará Delta'. This consisted only of changing some cockpit instruments and radio navigation equipment, such as: Collins VHF 22B, Marker CTL 22 and 32, VIR 32, RMI 30, Garmin 150 XL GPS and a Litton HSI. The plan was implemented during 2003, with the first aircraft being officially presented on 27 October 2003. A-590 was used to test the installation of the components, while A-577 was the first of the modernised series, which had some of its components changed at the request of the Air Force and was delivered on 2 June 2005, after a period of testing. The second IA-58D was A-524, followed by A-534, A-504, A-582 and A-580. However, due to the fact that the programme did not fully satisfy the force and budget cuts, only A-577 received the complete instrumentation of the new version and the others received only the GPS and the structure was only prepared to receive the other equipment, which was never installed. In addition, the paint scheme was changed to air superiority grey, with no serials or insignia. Given the criticism of the programme, it was cancelled shortly afterwards.

IA-58E

Since the beginning of the new millennium, when Safran (formerly Turbomeca) stopped producing spare parts for the Astazou engines, various alternatives began to be analysed. Initially, Safran's proposal to sell the rights and tooling to build the engines and their parts in Argentina was analysed, but poor management by the Ministry of Defence led to the decision not to accept the offer.

Later, when in 2009 the factory returned to Argentine state ownership, now under the name Fábrica Argentina de Aviones Brigadier San Martín, FAdeA, a new plan was developed to modernise the aircraft and install new engines, along the lines of the FAS 1160 programme developed since the beginning of the new millennium on the basis of the Pucará 2000 idea. The aim was to modernise a dozen aircraft to serve for up to thirty more years. This was possible because, despite their age, many airframes did not even have 1,000 hours flown and the biggest problem was the need to replace some components that were obsolete.

Thus, the IA-58E version was born, starting with stage 1, which was communications, in which the UHF and HF were changed, two VHFs and a latest-generation IFF were added, and the communications console in the cockpit was changed. The aircraft serialled A-568 was the prototype of this modification and carried out test flights from the end of 2009 and during 2010.

After the certification of this stage, A-568 returned to the factory workshop for the second stage, where the IA-58E project included the

A-568 and A-585 in flight near Reconquista in September 2018. *Santiago Rivas*

replacement of the navigation equipment (ADF, VOR, ILS, DME, etc.) by a Honeywell HG-764 EGIR (Embedded GPS/INS and Radar Altimeter) for both inertial and GPS navigation, plus a radio altimeter (the same used in the Pampa II) was installed in the aircraft, and a Garmin 150 GPS.

To view the information from such equipment, the Centro de Investigación y Desarrollo de Tecnologías Aeronáuticas (CITeA, Centre for Research and Development of Aeronautical Technologies) of the FAA's Dirección General de Investigación y Desarrollo (General Directorate for Research and Development) and the National University of Río Cuarto developed a multifunction panel that allowed the representation of a mission generated in the Ground Mission Planning System, showing the aircraft's position in real time, as well as its altitude, speed and heading.

At that time, Captain Arturo Medici, from the Argentine Navy, had developed mission planning and navigation software called CALNAV and worked with CITeA to solve some of its problems, after which it was adopted by the FAA. Thus, they studied installing the CALNAV software on the Pucará, which ran on Windows and would work with the EGIR information.

The information was displayed superimposed on maps or charts. The system had a data input consisting of a USB port where the mission to be flown could be uploaded, then the crew could manipulate and represent the information coming from the aircraft's inertial control unit in different ways by interacting with the touch screen.

The equipment with the multifunction display was built in the Area de Material Río Cuarto, using aeronautical standards, and had, in addition to the screen, a computer and a Garmin GPS inside, as well as a connector to communicate with the EGIR.

To evaluate the multifunction panel, a prototype was installed in the front seat of A-568, under the sight, for which the instrument panel was modified, with the upper frame raised to allow the display to enter and changes to the faults light panel, which went from being in two parts to one, with all the lights together and in a different place from the other aircraft.

The aircraft also received new camouflage in 2012 in three tones of green, with a grey belly, which set it apart from the rest. A-568 was also fitted with an Electronic Attitude Director Indicator (EADI) and Electronic Horizontal Situation Indicator (EHSI) in the central part of the panel, while the speedometer, altimeter and variometer remained analogue. In addition, the fuel quantity and flow indicators were changed to digital, but were cumbersome to use, and it received a new oxygen system. The aircraft returned to flight in June 2015 after also receiving the new instrument panel with the multifunction display.

A first flight was made in which the equipment performed well, including a climb to 6,000m to see if the capacitors of the multifunction display withstood the low pressure and there were no problems.

Subsequently, in 2016, it was decided to change the LCD screen for an LED one, with lower power consumption, less weight and size and better performance, which allowed a saving in space in the box containing all the equipment.

The results were satisfactory, and it was decided to build a pre-series of eight, but when the system was operationally evaluated by the Argentine Air Force it was discarded after a few flights, as it did not meet the operational requirements, the software had problems and the visual interface was rather primitive. It was considered that it needed to evolve before it could be considered for operational use.

This project also contemplated a third stage, in which it was planned to change the engines and add a HUD with a multifunction display similar to those used in the Pampa II. Although it was not planned to install equipment such as RWR, all-weather capability, chaff and flares, it was planned to add Kevlar and high-impact ceramic armour in the cockpit area, replacing the original aeronautical steel, as well as adding it to the engine nacelles, but this idea was abandoned.

For the engines, the Honeywell TPE-331 and versions of the Pratt & Whitney PT-6 with the same power as the Astazou were evaluated to minimise modification to the aircraft. The plan was for all three stages to be completed in 2012 and to begin re-engining the aircraft in service in 2013.

Thus, although A-524, A-571, A-575, A-580, A-582, A-583, A-585 and A-588 were modified with the new communications equipment of this version, they did not receive the modifications of the second stage, so A-568 remained different from the rest, returning to the III Air Brigade at the end of 2017. A-551, 567, 584, 592 and 595 were to be modified but the work was cancelled.

IA-58F

For the Argentine Air Force's participation in Exercise Salitre 2009 in Chile, the force raised the possibility of deploying Pucarás with some communications equipment upgrades. Given that there was neither time nor funds to quickly upgrade the aircraft with the scheme proposed for the IA-58E version, in 2009, before the factory was returned to the state, a simplified communications modernisation version was proposed, which was called IA-58F. However, since the upgrade could not be carried out in time to have the aircraft ready for the exercise, only A-4AR Fightinghawks were sent. This project was cancelled, and it was decided to go ahead with the IA-58E.

New modernisations planned

At FIDAE 2010, the manager of FAdeA's Pampa line, Gualberto Natali, asked whether the possibility of remanufacturing the Pucará was being considered, replied yes, but only after the modernisation programme was completed, 'because today there is no aircraft of this type and there is a need for it. There is talk of a Super Pucará, which would mean reopening the production of the Pucará, but with techniques that are 40 years more advanced. The Pucará has a lot of welding, both spot and cord welding, all the welded parts would be redesigned, we are already redesigning many parts and making them by numerical control. Some of this is being applied during modernisation.'At the time, the aim with the modernisation was to update thirty aircraft to fly until around 2040, although initially only sixteen were to be re-engined due to the limited budget. In addition, an offer was made to modernise the Uruguayan aircraft, but this was not successful.

With the development of the IA-63 Pampa III, between 2015 and 2016 it was proposed to modernise the Pucará cockpit by installing the systems of that version, provided by Elbit Systems, with a full glass cockpit with three 5in × 7in screens, mission computer, INS, datalink, upfront control panel and HUD, but after some discussions with Elbit this was also discontinued. A mock-up of the HUD and upfront control panel was obtained, but one of the problems was that the instrument panels of the Pucará were too small for the displays and the HUD, which did not allow a comfortable and safe cockpit, so a total redesign of the panels was necessary. Another HUD was considered, but it implied a higher cost and there would not have been compatibility between the Pampa and the Pucará.

IA-58H Pucará Fénix

In 2012, the selection of the new engines that would equip the aircraft was made, first prioritising the Honeywell TPE-331, returning to something similar to the IA-66 project, but the company's management decided to opt for the Pratt & Whitney PT-6A-62, despite the fact that technical experts had recommended going for the Honeywell. The reason given was that the PT-6A was a much more widely used engine in Argentina, which made it easier to obtain spare parts.

A-561, which was still in service with the CEV, was modified to take the new engines. Its wing was sent to Israel in December 2013, where IAI carried out the design and built the new nacelles, and the work was completed in March 2015. Once sent back to Argentina, the wing was installed and on 24 November 2015, the aircraft, now serialled AX-561, made its first flight with the new designation IA-58H Pucará 2. In addition, some obsolete systems were replaced, such as the fuel, hydraulic, oxygen and pneumatic systems, among others.

The installation of these engines entailed some problems, because the aircraft was not built in series and each one had some differences, making the modification very complicated. In addition, the nacelles were larger, reducing the view to the sides, the side exhausts caused problems to the fuselage due to heat and the four-bladed Hartzell propellers had no reversible pitch for braking.

These criticisms and the high cost of the project (some $45 million was spent on the modification) led to the decision in 2016 to halt work, although in June of that year AX-561 received an air data probe in its nose, with which it resumed test flights. After a

The IA-58H Pucará Fénix received camouflage in tones of grey. *Santiago Rivas*

few flights, it took off again in early 2017, but flew for a short time and the programme was cancelled.

In any case, flights with the prototype were resumed in July 2018, with a plan to do some additional testing for thirty-five flight hours but the flights were suspended shortly thereafter without reaching those hours.

Meanwhile, a group of retired Argentine Air Force officers were looking at alternatives to modernise the Pucará, including the possibility of returning to the Honeywell engine installation, but their proposal, submitted in late April 2019, was rejected due to the long time needed to have the new modification certified, while the original aircraft were to be retired in six months thereafter.

At the same time, the force's UAV programme was making slow progress on the development of the MALE Vigía UAV, but one of its payloads, the FixView FV-300 gyro-stabilised multi-sensor turret, was already developed and operational on civil helicopters, and the company had already developed some years ago the idea of installing the turret on a pod to be used by aircraft such as the Pucará. As the force had already contracted FixView for the UAV programme, there was a great need for increased border control and the IA-58H was available, so the idea arose to use the work already done on the pod for the UAV and the FixView idea to modify the aircraft for the surveillance role. The Pucará's endurance of up to eight hours made it a good platform for such a mission.

In June 2019, FixView began work on the production of what they called the Pod de Observación Aérea (POA), which includes an FV-300 turret, its batteries for seven hours of operation and a wireless connection, weighing 50kg. This means that the only modifications to the aircraft are the fittings to attach the display and the joystick to operate the turret from the rear cockpit. The display has a wireless connection to the pod and both the display and joystick can be easily installed, as they only need a 14 volt connection to the aircraft.

After the aircraft was displayed on 8 August 2019 during Air Force anniversary celebrations, with a mock-up of the pod, it was officially unveiled on 4 October with the operational pod, with the new designation IA-58H Pucará Fénix and serial OVX-501 (received in June).

Two new projects to increase the aircraft's capability were announced at the same ceremony in October 2019. One is a new pod developed by local company INVAP, with all the equipment of the POA but adding a synthetic aperture SLAR (Side-Looking Airborne Radar), which was christened POD Inteligencia, Vigilancia y Reconocimiento – Radar Aerotransportado Banda X Argentino (ISR – RAXA, Intelligence, Surveillance and Reconnaissance – Argentine X-Band Airborne Radar). As part of this project, the Pucará Fénix aircraft will receive a data link to send the information to the ground or another aircraft.

Thus, it was decided to integrate the FV-300 turret into the new pod, which would initially use a 318-litre fuel tank, to which the turret, radar antennas and equipment would be fitted. With the FAA's approval of the project, the company produced the MET 1 (Technology Evaluation Model), which only carries the radar antenna on one side. Evaluation flights began on 6 May 2021, using aircraft A-582. The flights continued until the end of that month and then

A-568 after being modified into the prototype of the IA-58H, initially called Pucará II. *Santiago Rivas*

additional ones were carried out at the beginning of July, thus completing the first stage of the project. With these results, INVAP planned to produce the MET-2 which will no longer use a 318-litre tank, since it was found that it was not easy to install the equipment in it, but a specific structure will be designed for the pod. The MET-2 should have the antennas on both sides and the FV-300, which would define the final configuration, to be evaluated in the MET-3, which would be the final product. Currently, the project is progressing slower than expected and the MET-2, planned for 2022, was not finished.

The concept of a communications intelligence pod, using the container of a LAU-60 rocket launcher, was also unveiled in 2019, but is at a very early stage of development by INVAP.

In 2019 the Argentine Air Force requested the development of reversible pitch for the propellers, which became available in early August 2019 and during 2020 certification work began, although it was delayed by the COVID-19 pandemic until mid-2023. Although the engines are less powerful than the Astazou, the four-bladed propellers compensate for this and the aircraft performs very similarly to the originals, although it has certain limitations in high-altitude flight and a slower response, as it is not a direct turbine.

The Argentine Air Force decided to convert three additional aircraft, but maintaining the attack mission and only the prototype will be used with the pod, with the possibility of adding more if the budget allows, trying to reach a total of twelve. In November 2020 the Chief of the General Staff of the FAA, Brigadier Xavier Isaac, announced plans to modify a second series of Pucará Fénix to be based at BAM Mar del Plata and to be used for maritime patrol missions, but this plan was discontinued by 2022.

On the other hand, in order to modernise the cockpit, part of the programmes FAS-1160-1A and part of what was the -1B, which led to the IA-58E but were not installed on that aircraft, were applied but with newer systems. The new instrument panel adds two Electronics International MVP-50T screens with engine indications, a Garmin GPS and EHSI and three Aspen Avionics Evolution navigation displays. The rear cockpit will have the pod screen instead of the instruments and a joystick to control the pod sensors. For now, the aircraft assigned to be converted into the Pucará Fénix, in addition to the prototype, are 571, 582 and 585. A-568 was sent to the factory but as is different from the others, it has not yet been included in the plans.

Failed exports

Poor sales management and a lack of security in the provision of spare parts after sales, added to the lack of credit from state banks, meant that exports were minimal.

As soon as the Pucará was developed, the FAA decided that it was a product that could be successful abroad, given that there was a growing demand for anti-guerrilla aircraft, especially in small air forces in Latin America, Asia and Africa. Thus, a sales campaign began, frustrated in most cases due to lack of experience.

In 1978 the first export contract was signed with the Force Aerienne Islamique de Mauritanie for its Escadrille de Surveillance for $10.8 million for four aircraft, although it was cancelled shortly after due to financing problems. The original plan was to buy

twelve aeroplanes and of the aircraft already built, one was painted in the colours of that country, receiving the serial M1/5T-MAB, the flag and the roundel.

In March 1983 a pre-contract was signed with the Central African Republic for two planes for $9.5 million, with the intention of expanding the order to twelve examples, although the contract was not finally signed.

At that time, the Venezuelan Air Force was interested in the plane, despite the fact that in 1973 they had received a batch of sixteen Rockwell OV-10E Broncos. However, they preferred a power plant other than the Astazou, because the Pucará's version was not used by any other aircraft. Thus, the FMA together with Volpar Inc. proposed the IA-66 to satisfy the Venezuelan demand. In 1982, a group of FAV officers visited Argentina and were able to analyse the Pucará, beginning negotiations for a batch of twenty-four IA 66s worth $110 million. It was intended that they would be assembled in Venezuela, using parts manufactured in Córdoba, although it was not possible to resolve the financing issues and the purchase was cancelled in February 1984.

Venezuela would regain interest in the Pucará when the FAV considered they needed a light attack and counter-insurgency aircraft to combat drug trafficking and illegal mining. Thus, the general commander of the FAV, Division General Luis Monserrat Pérez, reported that they had selected the IA-58A Pucará (with Astazou engines), from which they aimed to buy twenty aircraft for a total of $60 million that included spare parts, engines and training for pilots and mechanics.

At the same time, Rockwell proposed a modernised version of the OV-10D, which they christened the OV-10G, of which they would deliver a batch and also modernise the surviving OV-10Es. Although the FAV preferred the Pucará, the negotiations were halted again due to financing, when Venezuela proposed that the planes be discounted from a loan granted by Venezuela to Argentina, which was not accepted by the FMA. Finally, the FAV ended up buying from the USAF a batch of eighteen OV-10As without modernisation.

Also, around 1983, the Dominican Air Force expressed interest in twenty-four aircraft, although the idea did not prosper either.

The FMA, through the Tecnología Aerospacial (TEA SA) company, began to manage the export of the model, which is why on 29 March 1985 a contract was signed with Iraq for twenty planes with an option for another twenty for $3.8 million each, but the contract was cancelled due to pressure from Iran, which was, in turn, negotiating the purchase of sixty at a cost of $283 million. Although by decree 987/85 a plane was transferred to Iraq, it was never delivered.

In June 1985, TEA made a quote to Bolivia for twenty planes in exchange for natural gas, and in 1986 a pre-contract was signed for twelve machines for $52 million, but this was not signed. In August a new fruitless offer was made, this time to Paraguay for eight Pucará in exchange for electricity from the Yaciretá hydroelectric dam, which this country built in conjunction with Argentina.

Meanwhile, in June 1985, by decree No. 333/85, the export of fifty aircraft, plus fifty fuel tanks and a batch of spare parts and tools to the Syrian Air Force, for a total of $159,730,000, was authorised through the company Crowning International Corporation.

A-518 was originally built for Mauritania and received the colours, serials and markings of its Air Force, but the contract was cancelled and the plane was delivered to the Argentine Air Force, wearing the desert camouflage for some time. It was used for a photo session armed with 125-kilo bombs and INC-220 napalm bombs.

FAU 227 in flight, seen on 28 May 2013, close to its base. *Santiago Rivas*

According to the decree, the contract had already been signed, but it was cancelled shortly thereafter.

The offers continued with another of six aircraft to Zaire in October 1986 with a pre-contract signed for $26 million, cancelled shortly after, the same happening with an offer to Nigeria for twelve Pucará and several Hughes 500D helicopters made in Argentina by RACA, all frustrated. The government also authorised the sale of the plane to Yugoslavia and China.

At the end of April 1987, five officials from the Iranian Air Force visited the FMA and then the III Air Brigade to learn about the use of the plane, since they were now evaluating the purchase of fifty planes, twenty-five of them second hand, for $160 million. This visit was followed on 21 May by three representatives from Mauritania, a country that was once again interested in the plane, although the Argentine government did not authorise the sale.

Throughout the 1980s TEA S.A. made offers to the Ivory Coast, Saudi Arabia, El Salvador, Egypt (for fifty aircraft), the Philippines, Gabon, Honduras, Indonesia, Libya, Morocco, Nicaragua, South Africa, Singapore and Thailand. Finally, in September 1991, a pre-contract was signed with Paraguay for four planes for $11.6 million, although the sale did not progress either.

Many years later an interest in the Pucará arose from an unexpected country. In 2007 the US Navy had launched the Imminent Fury programme, with the objective of providing the forces deployed in Afghanistan with a light attack aircraft with ISR (Intelligence, Surveillance, and Reconnaissance) capability, which was what the special forces most demanded. Thus, in 2008 they bought an Embraer EMB-314 Super Tucano, which they began to evaluate, but found that the Brazilian type had some deficiencies for combat, such as being single engine, with little armour, little endurance and little internal armament. Thus, they began to analyse the options in twin-engined aircraft, which only existed in the OV-10 Bronco and the IA-58 Pucará, so in 2010 contacts were initiated between the US government and FAdeA. In 2011 US personnel visited the factory with the intention of analysing the possibility of obtaining some aircraft and the licence to develop a new platform based on the Pucará.

Unfortunately, there was no interest from FAdeA in advancing with an agreement, considering that the company was not in a position to offer aeroplanes or to give a licence, so there was no progress.

In 2019 there was another visit to FAdeA by interested parties, this time from the United Arab Emirates. Although the company tried to interest them more in the IA-63 Pampa, the visitors focused mainly on finding out if the company could sell them the licence for the Pucará or produce it again, to which they were answered in the negative. Despite this, in 2023 they visited the factory again, interested in the modernised IA-58H Pucará Fénix, but they were not convinced by the modernisation of the cockpit.

Exports

The first export was achieved when six aircraft, with an option for another two, to be delivered by April 1981, were sold to the Uruguayan Air Force for $9,329,443.27. The aeroplanes had originally been manufactured within the batch for the Argentine Air Force and were assigned the Argentine serials A-542, A-543, A-544, A-546, A-547 and A-548; with constructor numbers 042, 044, 045, 047, 048 and 049 respectively. Of these, A-542 was even painted in Argentine colours. The aircraft were re-serialled FAU-220, FAU-222, FAU-223, FAU-221, FAU-224 and FAU-225 respectively and were sent to the facilities of Chincul company, in San Juan, to be painted with a scheme in two shades of green and light brown, with the belly in light grey. In addition, a Litton LTN 211-27 inertial navigator was added to them.

The first two Pucará were delivered to the FAU as FAU-220 and FAU-221 on 12 May 1981. The planes became part of the Grupo de Aviación No. 1 Instrucción y Entrenamiento of Brigada Aérea II based at the military airfield 2nd Lieutenant M.W. Parrallada in Durazno, where they served throughout their career under the local name of A-58.

In addition to the weapons purchased in Argentina, the FAU initially used 250kg AN-M64 bombs left over from the P-51D Mustang and PG-125 general-purpose 125kg bomb produced in Argentina. They were later equipped with 500lb Mk-82 and 250lb Mk-81 bombs with normal tails or Snakeye-type braked tails, INC-220 napalm bombs, LAU-66 rocket launchers with nineteen tubes and LAU-68 with seven, ARM-657 Mamboretá with 57mm Aspid rockets and AF/B-37K launchers for BDU-33/B practice bombs, to which they later adapted 12lb practice bombs produced in Uruguay. Aspid rockets were used for both training and target marking. Meanwhile, in early 1986 they began to evaluate the use of MK-24/SUU-25B lighting flares in four-tube containers, each with two flares, with the first launches on 10 April 1987.

On 11 September 1998, the Argentine Air Force loaned A-574 to the FAU, which received the serial FAU-226. The aircraft operated in Uruguay until it was returned on 27 February 1999. The aircraft returned to Uruguay on 6 July 2000 and again operated as FAU-226 until June 6, 2001.

At the same time, in March 1998, a cooperation and logistical exchange agreement had been signed between the FAA and the FAU, where the former promised to deliver two IA-58 Pucará airframes (A-605 and A-606) that were incomplete and stored, in exchange for spare parts, two incomplete T-34A Mentor airframes that had been Spanish and two fully operational T-34As. In 2001, A-605 was transported in a Uruguayan C-130B Hercules to Durazno in 1998.

There, it was completed with elements of FAU-221, which was decommissioned. Once delivered, it became FAU-221, although shortly afterwards it was re-serialled FAU-227, making the first flight on 14 April 1999 with Major Sergio González and 1st Lieutenant Rodolfo Pereyra. Meanwhile, A-606, after remaining in LMAASA, had all the components that the Uruguayans needed removed and then it was again assigned to the FAA, although it was never completed.

On 11 February 2002, the Argentine Air Force returned to lend a Pucará, this time A-571, which was also serialled FAU-226 and remained in Uruguay until 13 February 2003.

The lack of spare parts, especially for its Astazou XVI-G engines, led to the fleet's operability gradually declining and by 2016 only FAU-227 remained operational. The decision was made to withdraw the type from service definitively on 17 March 2017.

Colombia

At the beginning of 1989 the Argentine government offered the donation of Pucará constructor nos 077, 079 and 080 to the Colombian Air Force (FAC), which had been completed in 1982 but were still in the factory. For unknown reasons, the aircraft 079, 080 and 081 were finally delivered, although the serial numbers were not changed administratively. Thus, 077, which was assigned the serial A 576 for the Argentine Air Force, was re-serialled as A-580, while A-580 (c/n 081), which in 1985 had suffered an accident with 32 per cent damage and was in the FMA after being repaired, was delivered to Colombia. The other two planes had been assigned the serials A-578 and 579, which were ultimately not used.

The aircraft received a complete overhaul and were painted in Colombian colours, receiving the serials FAC 2201, 2202 and 2203 (previously A-580, 578 and 579 respectively).

The Colombian Air Force also began to negotiate the purchase of another nine Pucarás, to complete a squadron of twelve aircraft, but economic and political problems in both Argentina and Colombia delayed the negotiations until in December 1991 the United States delivered twelve Rockwell OV-10 Bronco to the FAC, followed by another three in 1993, ending negotiations for more Pucarás.

FAC2202 at Apiay, with an AC-47 Fantasma gunship at the back. On night operations they used to fly together, with the Fantasma dropping flares for illumination, as well as acting as a command post. *J. Domínguez*

ZD485 at the Air Tattoo in the UK in 1983.

Towards August 1989, Colombian personnel travelled to Argentina to train on the type and in December they ferried the planes to Colombia, where they entered combat against the guerrillas at the Escuadrón de Operaciones Especiales 314 in the Comando Aéreo de Combate 2 (CACOM-2) in Apiay.

The planes went out of service by the end of 1991 due to lack of spares, but in 1995 they were recovered with the help of Uruguayan personnel. However, by 1996 they were grounded again and were retired.

Sri Lanka

In November 1992 an export contract was signed and the aircraft from c/n 100 to 103 were sold to Sri Lanka for $11 million. The Sri Lanka Air Force (SLAF) needed the plane to fight against the guerrillas of the Liberation Tigers of Tamil Eelam (LTTE) group. The four aircraft received a Trimble GPS and communications equipment of a different model than the one used by Argentina, which is why initially the FMA named them IA-58SL, but later only IA-58L.

In Sri Lanka they were assigned to the 1st Flying Training Wing of Anduradhapura together with the Siai-Marchetti SF-260TP and W for training and light attack, with some de Havilland Chipmunks also still operational. The CA-602 was re-serialled shortly after arriving as CA-605. Two planes were shot down by the guerrillas and the other two operated until late 1997, being officially retired in 1999.

United Kingdom

Although it was not a sale, at the end of the Malvinas/Falklands war, the Royal Air Force (RAF) took over several abandoned Pucará aircraft with different degrees of damage and took them for evaluation. Three aeroplanes were selected for tests, with A-515 being chosen to fly, as it was complete, while the aircraft intended for use for spare parts were A-533 and A-549. They were taken on 1 August 1982 to the Aeroplane & Armament Experimental Establishment (A&AEE) at Boscombe Down. The aircraft received the British serial ZD485, while A-533 received ZD486 and A-549 became ZD487, although the latter two were never painted. Tests took place from February to September 1983, including participation in the International Air Tattoo at Greenham Common on 23 and 24 July.

Aircraft family

By 1968, Ruíz began to devise the development of a whole family of aircraft based on the Pucará, but changing the turboprops for two Turbomeca Astafan I or IV jet engines of 1,200kg of thrust each, which shared some components of the combustion chamber with the Astazou turboprop. The idea was to be able to achieve a higher speed, ideal for the missions that it was expected to fulfil.

In June 1968 Ruíz submitted his proposals, working on them throughout 1969. Although he failed to get these projects authorised. In November 1973 he presented the plan again, but he also added the IA-60 project for an advanced training and attack jet and the idea of also developing a transonic attack aircraft. At the same time, he and Reimar Horten worked on the redesign of their training aircraft proposal, now with smaller dimensions.

Observation and light transport twin jet

At that time, Ruiz was working on the study of the pressurised G-III and, based on these studies, he proposed a version of the Pucará jet, but this time with the wing and tail of the IA-58, but with a new, wider fuselage, to carry a pressurised cabin for four seats, with the pilots in tandem and two passengers behind, accessing the cabin through a door and side ladder. In addition, he adopted the landing gear of the IA-50 G-II. In total, it was planned to use 40 per cent of the components of the IA-58.

Of this proposal, as seen in the plans, he proposed two versions, where basically only the arrangement of the windows varied, in one case with a three-piece windscreen and rectangular side windows, and in the other case with a design similar to the Learjet 21, both for the windscreen and the side windows.

These proposals also modified the wing, which went from a wingspan of 14.55m to 18.50, with a wing area of 35.65m2. A maximum speed at sea level of 610km/h and of 670km/h at 12,000m was expected, with a cruising speed of 580km/h, a maximum ceiling of 16,800m, a range of 4,000km and an endurance of seven and a half hours.

Also, as seen in the document in which the engineer Ruiz presents his proposal for a family of aeroplanes, a version with more seats was planned, possibly for four or five passengers. As Ruiz explains in said work, the objective was to achieve an aircraft similar in performance to the Cessna Citation, but with a lower development cost by using components from the Pucará, the G-II and the G-III project.

The plan proposed by Ruiz was to start development during 1976, to have a prototype ready in 1977 and another, in addition to a test cell, in 1978, but the project was not approved.

Assault transport

Under that name, as it appears in Ruiz's proposal for a family of aircraft, or under the name 'Anteproyecto Carguero' as it appears in the plans, the project was developed for a light transport aircraft, which retained only the Pucará's empennage, with a completely new fuselage and high wing, a side-by-side cabin for two pilots and a cargo hold with a rear ramp. Ruiz expected a market of at least seventy-five to eighty aircraft and also planned to develop a passenger version to cover regional routes in the civil market.

The aircraft would have an overall length of 22.43m, a wingspan of 26.7m and a height of 8.12m. The cargo cabin would be 8m long and the fuselage would be 3.3m wide and 2.95m high. For its size, the aircraft was slightly larger than a CASA C-212, but with Astafan turbofans and a pressurised cabin, which would give it considerably better performance in terms of speed and service ceiling.

Jet trainer and tandem observation trainer

Another version was intended as a jet trainer, with Astafan Is, to replace the Morane-Saulnier MS.760 Paris in fighter pilot training. The landing gear was located in wing fairings that replaced the nacelles of the turboprops and the jet engines were located on both sides of the fuselage, slightly behind the wing. Preliminary estimated characteristics were an empty weight of 3,500kg, a maximum take-off weight of

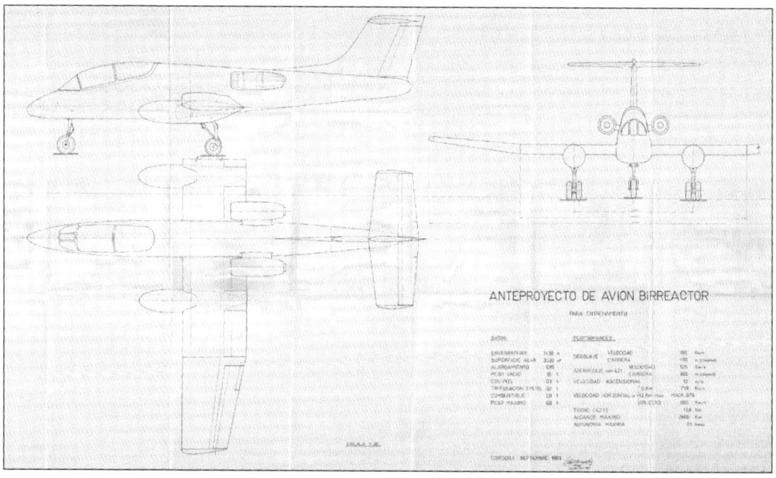

First proposal for a jet engine Pucará for advanced training. *Archive Eduardo Ruiz*

6,000kg, a speed of Mach 0.73 or 750km/h at sea level, a cruise speed of 680km/h, a service ceiling of 13,500m, seven and a half hours' endurance and 3,600km range, thanks to an internal fuel capacity of 2,000 litres. The dimensions were similar to those of the Pucará.

With the same design, he also proposed a version for photography and observation, without too many changes beyond the equipment for camera operation, although the project was abandoned without any studies on the location of the cameras.

Among the existing drawings are some with the engines located further forward, with the air intakes just behind the leading edge of the wing and the exhausts just behind the trailing edge, although these drawings are undated.

In the work plan submitted by Ruiz on 24 September 1969, he envisaged being able to produce a test glider in 1970.

Although the idea did not prosper, in November 1973 it was again put forward by Ruiz in response to an operational request from the Air Force Air Operations Command, which called for the 'preliminary study and preliminary design of an advanced training aircraft suitable for use in aero-tactical procedures'. The objective was for the aircraft to replace the Morane-Saulnier Paris for advanced training at the Military Aviation School and for the Curso de Estandarización de Procedimientos para Aviadores de Combate (CEPAC, Combat Aviator Procedures Standardisation Course), where future fighter pilots complete the last stage of their training before moving on to operational units. In addition, it had to be capable of performing tactical support missions in combat operations in short- and medium-range missions, with the capacity to operate on unprepared runways of up to 1,000m, a maximum operational ceiling of no less than 8,000m with maximum payload, a flight range of 1,600 nautical miles and a radius of action in Hi-Lo-Hi profile of 600 miles, capable of +7 and -3.5Gs. It was also intended to be a twin-engined, two-seater in tandem, capable of being flown by a single pilot, with 0-0 ejector seats, and with an armoured and pressurised cabin. The fixed armament required was to be two 30mm cannon and two 7.62mm machine guns internally or in pods, plus

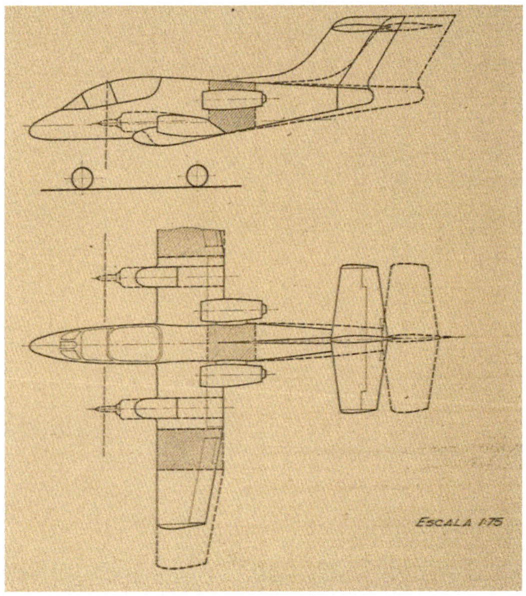

A comparison of the fuselage and wings of the Pucará and the smaller trainer proposed in 1974. *Archive Eduardo Ruiz*

five weapons pylons, with at least three of these capable of carrying supplementary tanks. The gunsight was to be of the predictor type, for air-to-air combat and with a depth deflection system for air-to-ground firing, while it was to have mounts for up to four JATO rockets, without affecting the armament pylons. It had to have a flare launcher and be able to carry an air-to-air gun pod on the ventral pylon, as well as a photographic pod. The requirement was for a total of 100 units, to enter service between 1978 and 1980.

In the work plan proposed by Ruiz, the aim was to carry out the development during 1975 in order to have a prototype in 1976, hoping to be able to start series production in 1977. At the request of the FAA, the work was entrusted to Reimar Horten together with Dr José Pedro Tamagno and engineer Carlos Paoletti, who in March 1974 presented their proposal for a new version of the jet trainer. In addition to the change of engine, now the Astafan IV of 1,200kg of thrust each, with the aim of increasing manoeuvrability, they proposed to reduce the size of the aircraft. Part of the wing between the landing gear nacelle and the outer wing joint would be eliminated, as there was no tapering of the wing. Thus, it would have a wingspan of 11.94 m instead of the original 14.5m, extending the inner wing flap to the outer wing and eliminating the outer flap. The engines were located on the sides of the fuselage as in the 1969 proposal, but the fuselage was shortened by 1.6m to 12.4m. These changes, however, meant only a 25 per cent alteration to the construction of the aircraft, allowing much of the existing tooling to be used.

It was planned to produce two versions: a two-seat training version with less armour and a single-seat attack version with more armour. The first was expected to weigh 584kg less than the Pucará and the other 573kg less than the IA-58A, making 3,287kg and 3,276kg, respectively, compared with 3,820kg for the IA-58A. The armament capacity remained the same as the Pucará, with up to 1,560kg, as did the internal armament.

In order to maintain the critical Mach number of the aerofoil at Mach 0.64, which was set until studies could be carried out to achieve Mach 0.68 (with up to M 0.70 at certain angles of incidence), air brakes were added to the rear fuselage area.

The proposed characteristics did not convince the FAA, which was looking for an aircraft with higher performance. This led engineer Ruiz to work on a new idea, also based on the Pucará, which received the name IA-60.

34 **IA-59 jet aircraft and IA-59 flying target**

There were two projects that received the designation IA-59, one of them being a series of transport aircraft proposals and the other being a drone for use as target for anti-aircraft artillery training.

Tactical transport

In 1971, a team of the factory headed by Reimar Horten started to work on a draft of a multipurpose light transport plane with the aim of having a single platform that could be used for a wide variety of missions, including passenger, executive and troop transport, reconnaissance, bombing and training. The intention was also that the type could be easily adapted from one mission to another. The team explained that, while the design would not an optimum design for each mission, it would be possible to reach the minimum standards for them.

The design had two engines on the sides of the fuselage, with a fuselage 14.9m long, a height of 5.4m and a wingspan of 15m.

The draft aimed for a plane with three possible transport configurations, the first with up to 1,000km range, with capacity for twenty passengers and 500kg of luggage, non-pressurised cabin with an operational ceiling of 9,000ft and cruise speed of 800km/h. The second was to have up to 2,000km range, with a pressurised cabin to fly at 27,000ft at a cruise speed of 800km/h, while the third was a military transport with a range of up to 3,000km, carrying up to thirty people and 500kg of equipment at a height of 36,000ft and a speed of 800km/h.

According to the drafts, the passenger version had nineteen seats in a pressurised cabin, with two pilots and a stewardess, toilet and a luggage compartment to the rear.

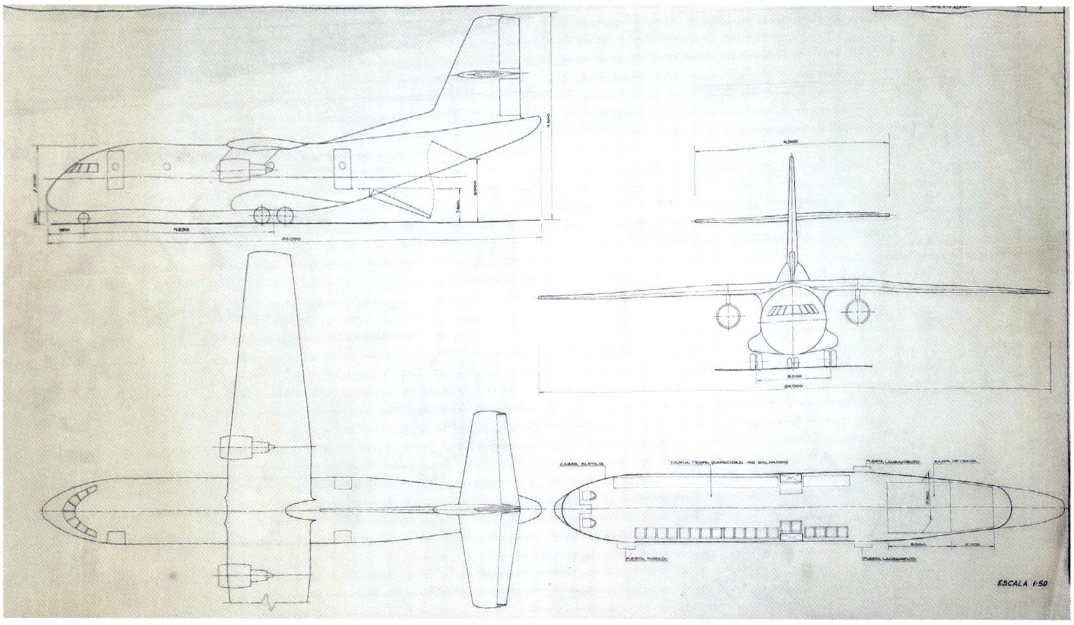

One of the high-wing studies for the IA-59 project, with the wheels retracting into the fuselage and seats for forty soldiers.

The bomber and reconnaissance variant had a pressurised front cabin for the pilots, radio operator and rest of the crew and a vertical camera, and two bomb bays, one with two rows for up to four 500kg bombs each ahead of the wing, and a smaller one for up to two 500kg bombs behind. Over the wing was a fuel tank with 4,500kg capacity.

Based on this idea, in June 1972, the Argentine Air Force issued the Operational Request OIDFA 34 for a 'transport and assault aircraft'. The requirement was for an aircraft that would meet the tactical needs of the Air Force while maintaining characteristics that would make it suitable for commercial air transport. It was due to enter service between 1976 and 1980 and versions for SAR and aerial photography were envisaged. It had to operate on short and unprepared runways, and have a loading ramp for air dropping. The passenger capacity was to be between twenty-four to thirty-six in low and high density, with toilet, or fifteen to eighteen stretchers with three or four doctors. In troop transport configuration it was to carry at least thirty-four equipped soldiers and the crew would be two pilots, a mechanic and cargomaster. The engines had to be turbofans, protected from the ingestion of FOD and the design had to contemplate the use of extra fuel tanks. The OIDFA 34 proposed that it be high wing and twin engine and the plan was to order between twenty to twenty-five aircraft.

A plan for a wind tunnel model dated 10 May 1972 indicates that the studies had already began before the request was issued and the proposal received the designation IA-59. In November 1972 the preliminary project was delivered by the IIAE,

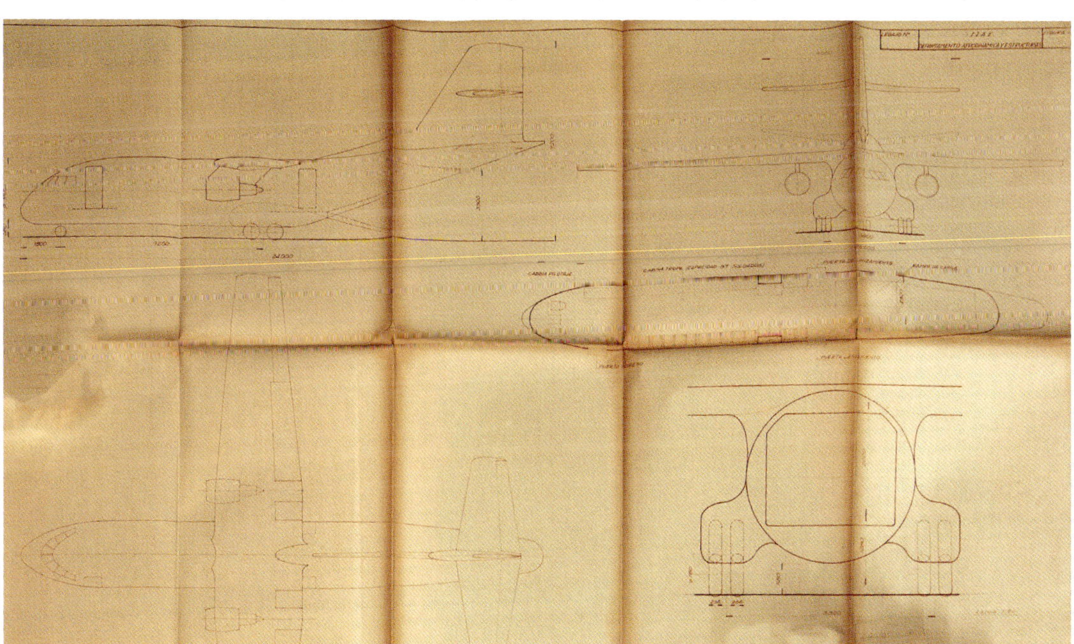

Another high-wing study for the IA-59, with the wheels retracting into fairings on the sides of the fuselage.

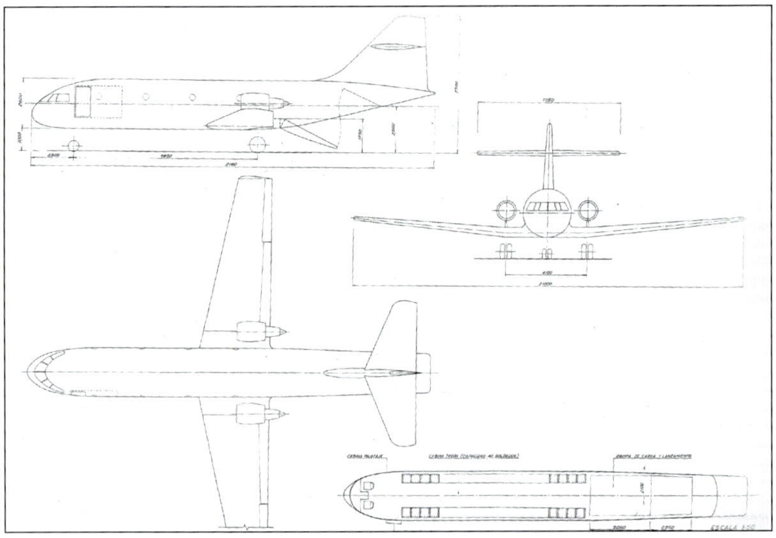

Three views of the unpressurised assault version of the IA-59, with a bigger rear ramp.

signed by Major Levi Jorge Casalotti and the technical direction was in the charge of Reimar Horten and José Tamagno. Although the request was for a high wing, the team preferred to work on a low-wing aircraft and Horten proposed, to reduce the risk of FOD while operating on unprepared runways, to use the solution used on the VFW-614, which was currently on the final stages of development, having flown for the first time in 1971.

The German aeroplane was born within the Entwicklungsring Nord (ERNO) group, comprising Focke-Wulf, Hamburger Flugzeugbau (HFB) and Weser as the E.614 and later known as WFG-614, before changing its name to VFW-614 and, although the first design had the engines on the sides of the fuselage, in 1963 a redesign included the non-conventional solution of placing the engines above the wings and to the back, to protect them from FOD ingestion. Also, Horten proposed to use the same engines, the Rolls-Royce/SNECMA M45H, which were especially designed for the VFW-614, of 3,500kg of thrust each, since the IA-59 was similar in size and weight (the VFW-614 had a maximum take-off weight of almost 20 tons and the IA-59 would be 17 tons. The fuel capacity proposed was for 2,200-litre fuel tanks in each half-wing.

The passenger version carried two pilots and a folding seat for a third crew member and passenger passenger seats, stewardess seat, bathroom, buffet and cloakroom, with a rear hold of 14m3 for luggage. The possibility of a 2.5m × 1.8m side cargo door was envisaged.

The plane would be 21m long, 6.8m high and with a wingspan of 21m, with a wing area of 61.1m2. The cabin would be 10.5m long, 2.4m wide and 1.9m high, with a volume of 40m3. The empty weight would be 9,450kg when configured for passengers and 8,700kg for cargo, with empty operational weight of 12,750kg and 12,000kg respectively and a payload of 3,250kg and 4,000kg respectively, with a maximum take-off weight of 17,000kg and 16,000kg for landing.

The military transport version had a loading ramp of 2.1m × 3.25m in the rear part, with another door of 2.1m × 2.25m at the front. The cargo cabin would be 50m3, 11m long and the adoption of aerodynamic brakes on the wing or tail would be considered. Capacity for forty troop seats or twenty stretchers; or two Jeep, Rastrojero or Unimog-type vehicles; or two A-4 Skyhawk engines was considered. Loads of 1,000kg at a time could be dropped from the ramp. The length

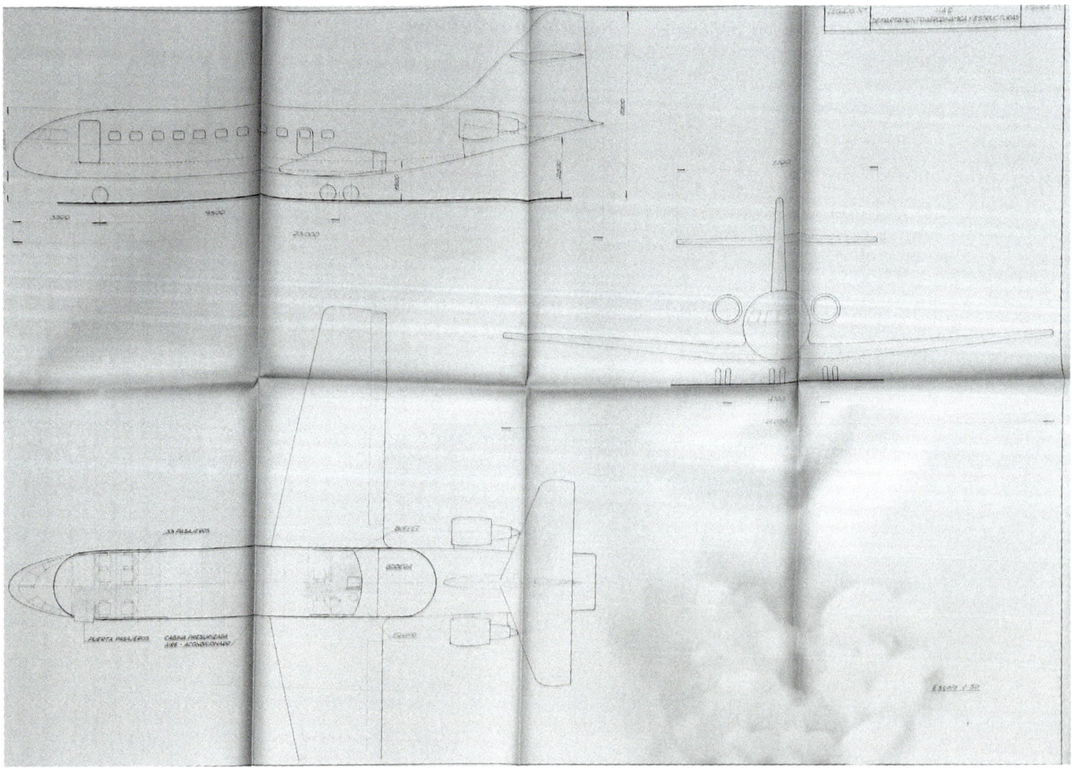

The design of the assault version of the IA-59 in its final configuration, with the engines on the sides of the fuselage, and with an internal layout for thirty-three passengers.

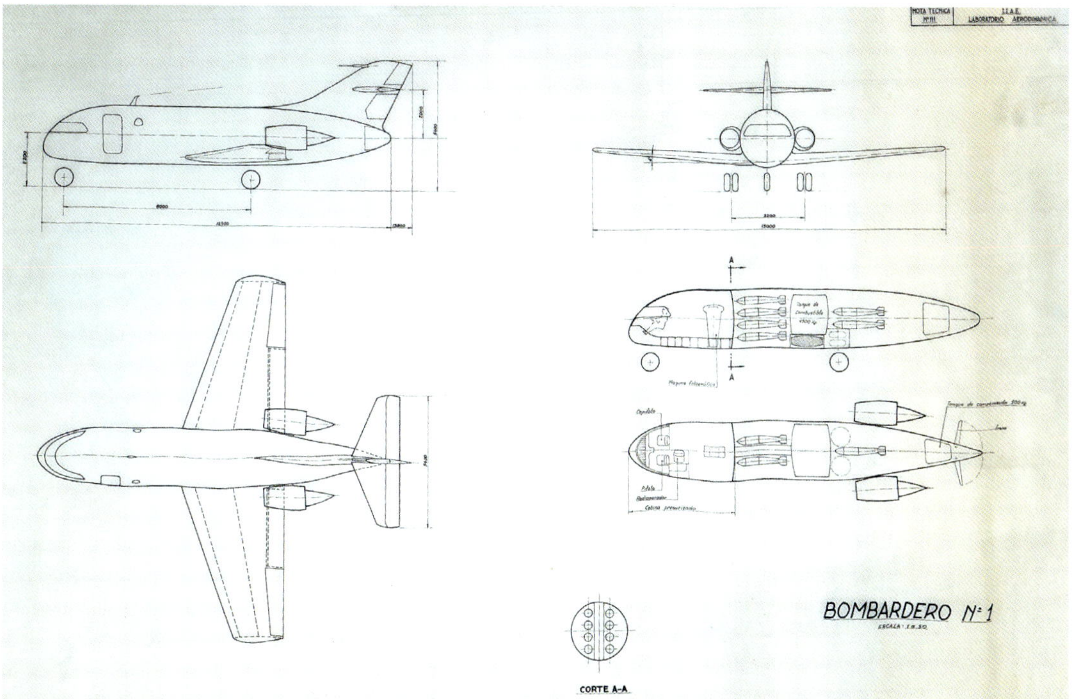

A bomber version of the initial proposal for a multi-purpose aircraft that led to the IA-59 project.

would be 21.8m and the height would be 7.3m, with the wingspan the same. The empty weight would be 8,700kg and the other weights were the same.

It was suggested that the military variant was developed first, which was not pressurised and was simpler. It was considered that the most complex thing to design would be double-groove flaps, because the factory had never built any before.

The team considered that a low wing had better flying characteristics and they did not see any advantage in a high wing. It was considered that the high wing required special structures under the wing so that the stresses caused by the weight of the wing, engines and fuel were transmitted to the landing gear. A vertical load-bearing frame was required to ensure rigidity. The diameter of the fuselage was larger, 3.1m, but this frame reduced the space of the cargo hold in that area, leaving 2.5 to 2.6m of usable width. The larger diameter made it necessary to lengthen the fuselage since aircraft flying at more than 500km/h must have a ratio between length and diameter of the fuselage greater than 7. The total weight was going to be 20 tons and the aircraft would require servo commands. The high-wing proposal was intended for up to thirty seven or forty soldiers, depending on the version, and included a passenger version with forty-one seats.

The designers also included an analysis of a high-wing proposal, but set this aside in favour of the low-wing version. The high-wing design had both alternatives of stabilisers on low, mid and upper positions and the main landing gear with four wheels in tandem or two side by side, with the first being on fairings to the sides of the cabin and those side-by-side retracting inside the fuselage, reducing the space below the cargo hold as the floor had to be raised. The high-wing proposal was 24m long and had 26m of wingspan, with a height of 9.2m.

On 7 February 1973, the FAA's Material Commander, Brigadier Horacio Guerra, stated that the preliminary project submitted by the IIAE was based on a different criterion from the operational requirement, since the requirement was for a light military assault transport but a fast troop and cargo transport was proposed and a domestic airliner.

The requirement was for it to be high wing and with a span from empennage to the ground of 3.3m, but the preliminary project raised the advantages of a low wing.

The preliminary design did not have a pressurised cabin for the assault version, the payload was increased by 2,000kg (the request was for 2,000kg and the cargo and assault version was 4,000kg, while the passenger one was 3,250kg) and the empty

An internal layout of the passenger version of the multi-purpose aircraft proposed in 1971.

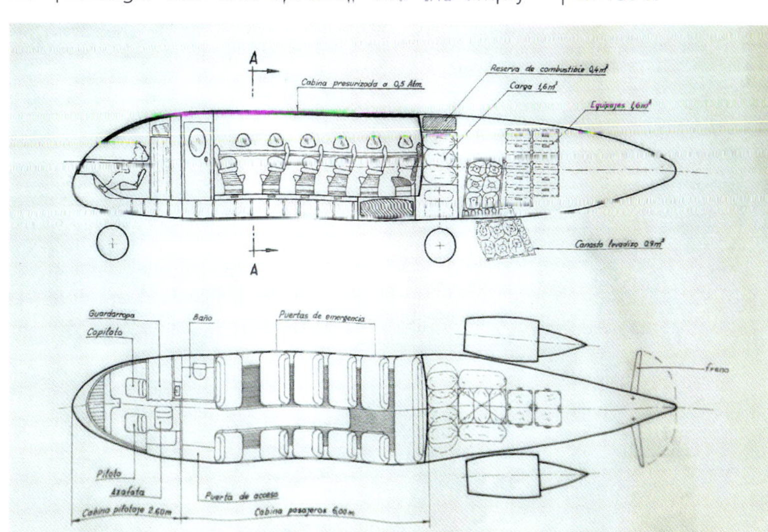

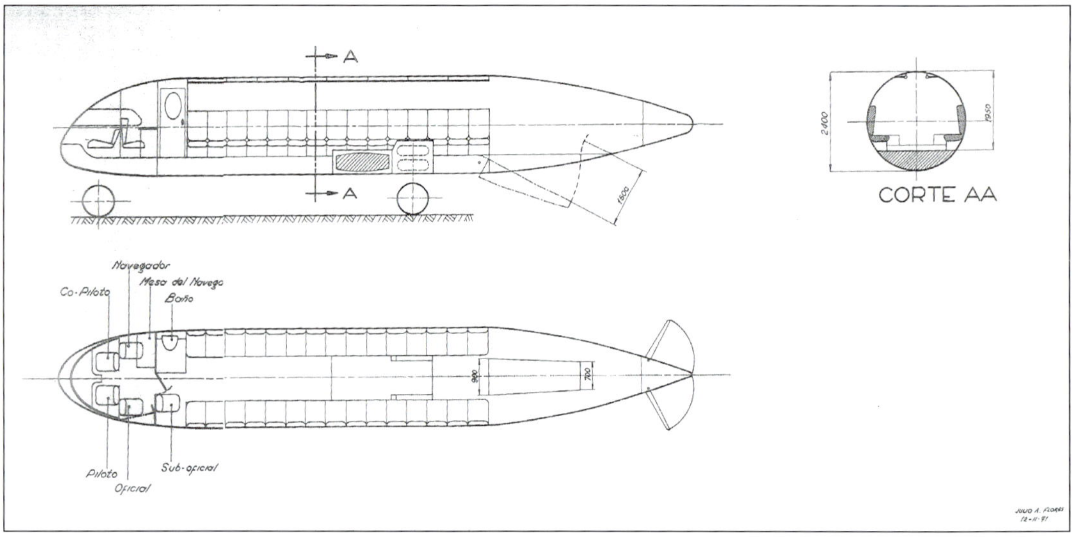

Internal layout of the troop transport version of the multi-purpose aircraft, with a rear door to drop paratroopers. *Archive Gonzalo Rengel*

weight by 700kg in the military version and 1,450kg in the civilian version. The take-off and landing runs were superior at 100 and 300m respectively, and the range in the military version was 200km less than required. He also stated that the wing located so far back was not convincing due to the variations that could occur in the centre of gravity when launching a payload. The IIAE proposed giving twelve months to finish the tunnel models, moving surface models, cabin mock-up and preparation of assembly plans, which was considered impossible to meet. Guerra requested that the preliminary draft be revised to bring it into line with the request.

The IIAE replied that the civilian version did not have a ramp to facilitate pressurisation and because the ramp reduced the space in the hold. They considered that pressurisation was feasible on the version with rear ramp, but that it would greatly increase the weight and technological difficulties. The performance data would depend on the engine to be used and the flaps, and that the data presented on the preliminary project was just to be used as a basis.

The top speed would be 720km/h and the passenger transport version would have a pressurised cabin and 12,000m of service ceiling. The transport version would have a take-off run of 800m with maximum weight and a landing distance of 1,000m, while the assault one would be 800m in both cases. The range with forty-five minutes of reserve would be 2,300km with 1,600kg of cargo at 9,000m altitude in the transport variant and 1,300km at 3,000m in the assault one.

To fulfil the request that the rear part would be high enough for a truck to approach the rear ramp for loading, the team worked on a modification of the main landing gear, so it could rotate longitudinally until only one of the wheels was in contact with the ground, extending the longitude of the whole landing gear and raising the tail until the upper part of the cargo door was 3.3m from the ground. In this late version, the engines were placed on the sides of the fuselage instead of over the wings, in a more conventional layout.

Besides the transport, a plan showing the IA-59 with two missiles inside the fuselage suggests that thought was given to a bomber version.

Despite of this change, the project was abandoned shortly after and in the end the Argentine Air Force

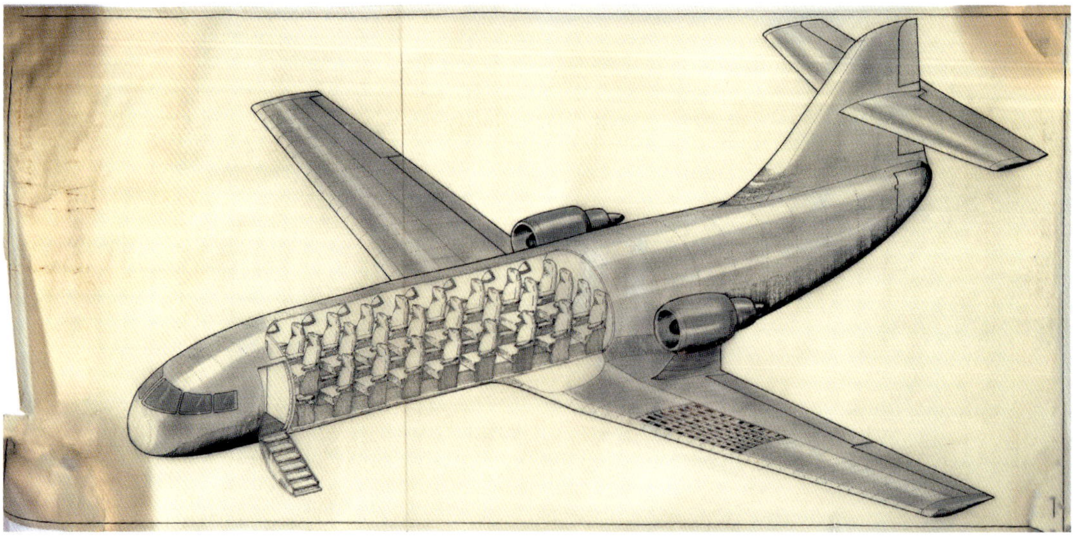

Illustration showing the internal cabin of the IA-59 for twenty-eight passengers. The windows were triangular, similar to those on the Sud-Est Caravelle.

Wind tunnel model of the IA-59 project, preserved at the Centro de Investigación Aplicada of the Argentine Air Force. The position of the engines was copied from the VFW-614. *Santiago Rivas*

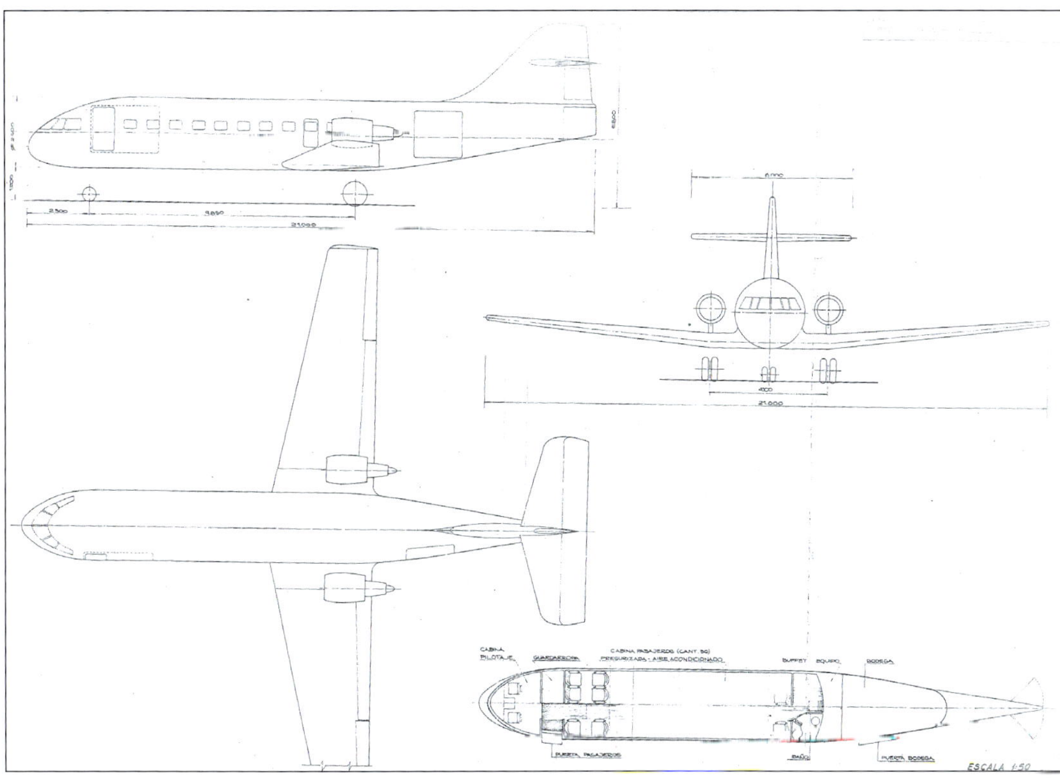

Three views of the proposed configuration of the IA-59.

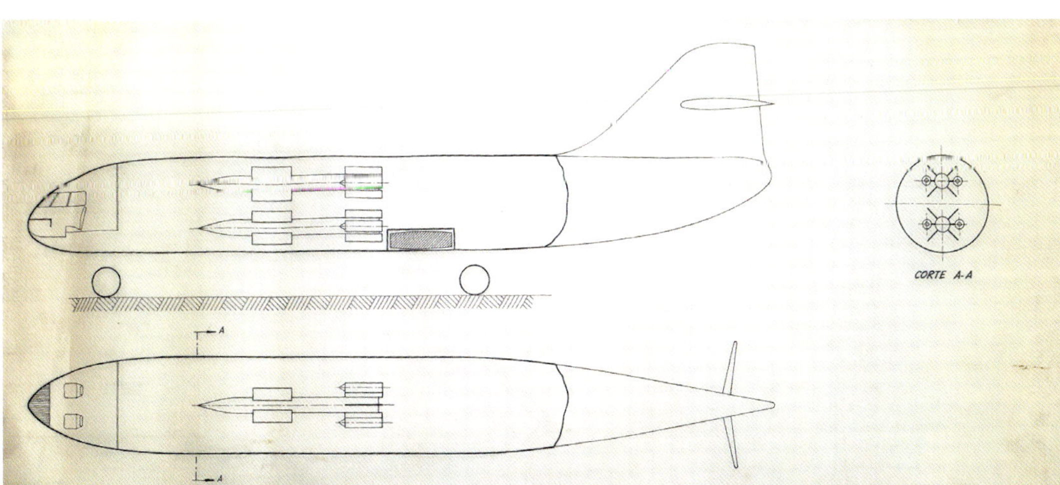

A layout of the IA-59 with two missiles in the cargo hold, which has no cargo floor and the weapons occupy the entire height of the fuselage, suggesting a bomber version was considered.

The first prototype of the IA-X-59 target, with a single vertical fin and without the piston engine. It was tested until destruction to check the flight performance. After the booster rockets accelerated the drone it glided until landing.

decided to buy the Fokker F28 in 1975. Currently, two wind tunnel models survive, as well as some plans and documents.

IA-X-59 drone

The IIAE had started to work on the research of radio guidance and control systems in the 1960s and in September 1970 Reimar Horten proposed the development of a supersonic target. While it was planned to be destroyed, it could be also landed at slow speed (200km/h) if needed, with no parachute for recovery, and was to be capable of reaching 1,800km/h (Mach 1.5) at 15,000ft, with thirty minutes of endurance. The engine was to be a statoreactor using butane and was expected to be launched by a plane such as the Pucará from a height of 21,000ft or with a rocket like the Orión II, developed by the IIAE, attached to the back of the target. The plane was planned to fly in a circle of 300km diameter at Mach 1.5 and of 2km at landing speed.

The target was to be built in Duralumin, with a delta wing and fuel tanks on the wingtips with 40kg capacity. The wingspan would be 1.7m, with a length of 1.6m and a diameter of 40cm, with a wing area of 1.5m2. The empty weight was 110kg and the take-off weight was 150kg. In the case a launch by an Orión II rocket, the rocket and its fuel had an extra weight of 116kg. This idea, which was very advanced, was not approved as it was beyond the needs of the Argentine Air Force, which did not have anti-aircraft systems against supersonic threats by 1970 (by then, only Peru in Latin America was operating supersonic fighters, with their Mirage Vs).

Around 1974 the development of a radio-controlled flying target for anti-aircraft artillery practice began. The work was in the charge of Justo Demetrio Díaz and Ricardo Olmedo of the Grupo de Fabricaciones and the type received the designation IA-X-59. In 1975 construction of a first prototype began, being a cantilever high-wing monoplane, with torpedo-shaped fuselage and a tail with one fin and stabiliser. It had single-spar Duralumin wings of constant section and cord, fitted with ailerons. The fuselage was of circular cross-section, with four main

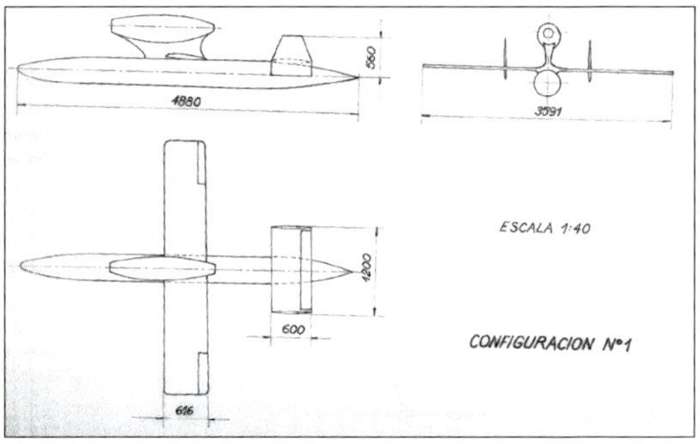

One of the IA-X-59 proposals with a jet engaine positioned above the fuselage. *Archive Gonzalo Rengel*

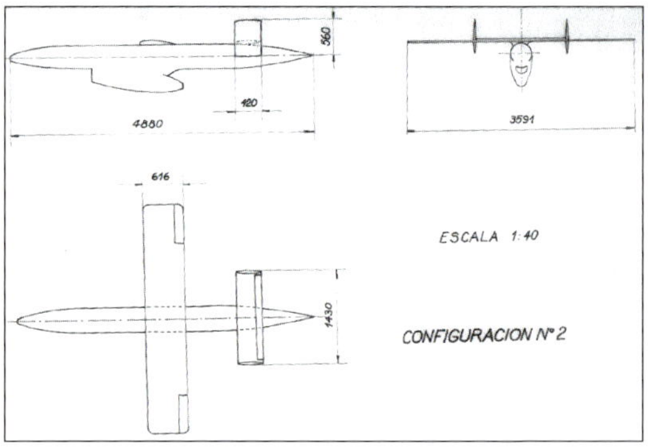

A proposal for the IA-X-59 with a turbojet under the fuselage. *Archive Gonzalo Rengel*

longerons. A steel central section formed the 40-litre fuel tank, tapered forward and the rear sections were of Duralumin. An all-Dural tail unit comprised the tailplane, with an electrically actuated elevator mounted on top of the rear fuselage, and a rectangular fin. It was designed to float, to permit its recovery from water. The wingspan was 3.6m, length 4.06m, wing area 2.25m2, maximum launching weight 170kg and landing weight 150kg. The maximum level speed was 320km/h and the stall speed was 120km/h, with a maximum rate of climb of 1,200 m/min. The service ceiling was 7,000m and the range was 320km, with an endurance of one hour.

The first flights, which were made on 9 December 1976, were made without an engine and only a jettisonable booster rocket system for launch. In 1977 a second prototype was finished with dual vertical fins and received a 72hp four cylinder two-stroke McCulloch O-100-2 piston engine, which drove a two-blade, fixed-pitch wooden propeller. Recovery was by means of a parachute deployed from the rear part of the fuselage.

The radio command guidance system used a 30W FM/FM ground transmitter operating in 138-167 MHz bandwidth. The received/decodifier separated command signals into two control channels, plus another that stopped the engine and deployed the recovery parachute. A back-up system to initiate the recovery sequence automatically if radio control was broken was included. An on-board autopilot acted under command from ground radio controller to govern pitch and roll, while vertical gyro provided attitude signals that, when amplified, governed the electrical actuators.

A third prototype, similar to the second, was built and tested, and, although the tests were successful, the project was cancelled in the 1980s due to lack of budget. Currently, the third prototype is preserved at the museum of the Centro de Investigación Aplicada of the Argentine Air Force next to FAdeA.

Meanwhile, two turbojet variants were studied in 1979 by engineer 1st Lt Miguel Serra and engineer Rubén Carrasco, with an engine of 156kg of thrust, a maximum ceiling of 6,000m and a MTOW of 252.6kg, to reach a speed of 800km/h or Mach 0.7 at high altitude. As the engine could not be installed inside the fuselage due to its size and the idea was to minimise the redesign of the drone, they decided to install the engine outside the fuselage. One option was with the engine above the fuselage, and one with a turbojet under the belly. The recovery parachute was to be installed in the tail, with the fuel tank in the middle of the fuselage and the control systems in the nose. The wingspan was to be 3.59m, length 4.88m and the height was 1m for the version with the engine above and 82cm for the one with the engine below. Empty weight was calculated as 111.6kg and the maximum 252.6kg. The type was to be used both for anti-aircraft artillery and air-to-air training, but the possibility was also considered of adding underwing pylons to carry different payloads, for use in reconnaissance and attack duties.

The third prototype of the IA-X-59 being taken to a field for tests above an early Rastrojero pick-up truck, built at the factory.

The second IA-X-59 at the museum of the Centro de Investigación Aplicada of the Argentine Air Force. *Santiago Rivas*

Supersonic flying target proposed by Reimar Horten in 1970. *Archive Gonzalo Rengel*

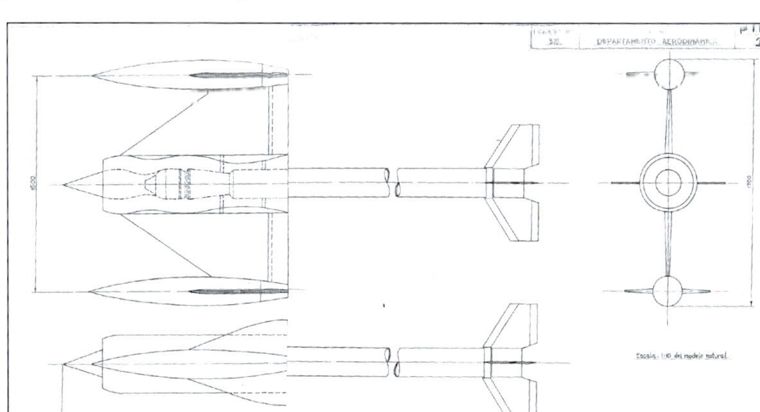

35 IA-60

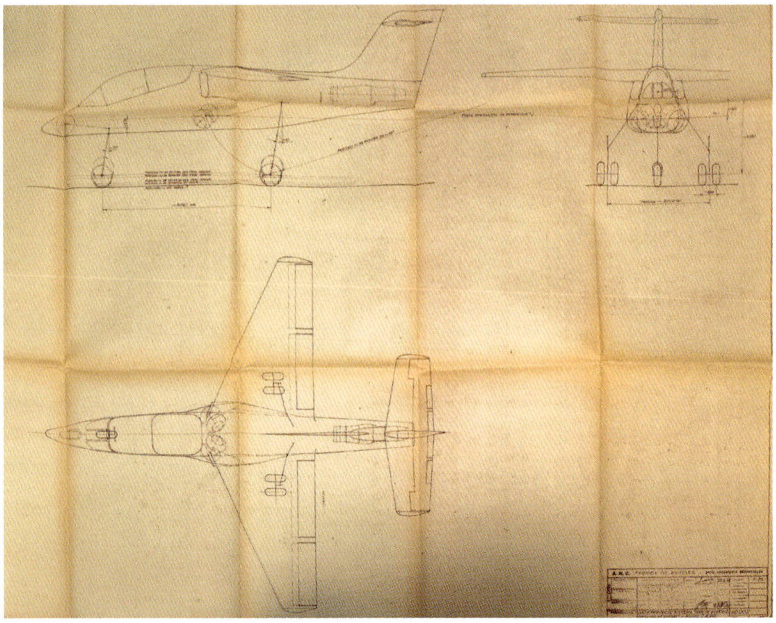

On this plan of April 1975 the IA-60 design received new air intakes and the landing gear was redesigned with two wheels on the main legs for operations on unprepared runways. The engine exhaust was also modified. *Archive Eduardo Ruiz*

Convinced that the Pucará's wing created limitations to the performance of a larger jet, Ruiz began work on a new idea with more radical changes. As he explained in a memorandum dated November 1973, the idea was to make it a subsonic bomber, with a view to later supersonic development, the definitive design of which he hoped to start in 1978 and begin serial production in 1983. Then he planned to develop a supersonic version between 1984 and 1988. In a 1974 paper Ruiz changed the dates, expecting to start work in 1976 and have the aircraft ready in 1981. There he stated that the supersonic aircraft was expected to reach Mach 1.2 or about 1,400km/h, with a weapons capacity of 3,000kg, by changing the planform and profile.

Keeping the fuselage and tail of the Pucará, Ruiz proposed the installation of a single Rolls-Royce/Turbomeca Adour Mk.102 turbofan with 7,305lb of take-off thrust, with afterburner, and 3,810lb of maximum continuous power. The engine at the time was used by the SEPECAT Jaguar and the Mitsubishi T-2, while the Adour Mk 151 version without afterburner was used by the Hawker Siddeley Hawk, which at the time was just starting its test programme. The engine exhaust would be at the rear of the fuselage, which was cut down from the original Pucará.

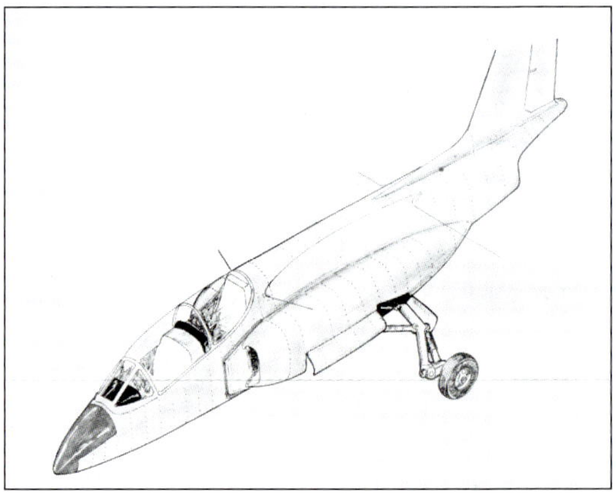

A drawing made by Héctor Ruiz of the first idea for the IA-60. The plane retains the basic Pucará fuselage and tail, with air intakes on the sides of the fuselage, new landing gear and a new wing. The exhaust is under the tail. *Archive Eduardo Ruiz*

In this regard, Ruiz took into account the Hawk's cockpit design to compare it with the Pucará's in terms of visibility, finding that the Pucará had better downward vision in the forward position and sideways vision in both positions.

Ruiz decided to go for a completely new arrow wing. It also added a fairing on each side of the fuselage, with the engine air intakes at the front and the space for the main landing gear further back, in a configuration similar to that of the IA-63 Pampa.

The planned aircraft, which received the designation IA-60, was intended not only to replace the A-4B and C Skyhawk in the Argentine Air Force, but also to serve as an advanced trainer, replacing the Morane-Saulnier Paris.

Among the specifications detailed by Ruiz, the aircraft had to be able to operate from unpaved runways, with a maximum speed of no less than 525 knots, approach speed of 110 to 120 knots, maximum dive speed of 540 knots, maximum real speed at 10,000ft of 475 knots, climb time to 10,000m of less than six minutes and stall speed at 10,000ft of 95 knots. The range in clean configuration and with internal fuel had to be greater than one hour forty minutes, the take-off distance at sea level, over a 15m obstacle, on a grass runway, had to be equal to or less than 1,000m and of 1,500m at 5,400ft of altitude. The service ceiling had to be greater than 12,000m and, at maximum load, greater than 9,000m. The radius of action on Hi-Lo-Hi missions, with maximum load, was to be greater than 600 nautical miles (1,112km), while the range in ferry flight was to be at least 1,600 nautical miles (2,965km). The launchable payload was to be about 2,000kg and it was expected to reach up to 6Gs in manoeuvres, with the possibility of carrying a nose camera in a reconnaissance version and up to five extra tanks between four underwing and one ventral pylons.

An empty weight with the crew of 3,850kg or less, a maximum take-off weight of 8,350kg and a maximum landing weight of 5,550kg was envisaged. The operating temperature limits would be -20°C on the ground and -55°C in flight and up to 50°C.

The estimated service life was 4,000 hours and 5,500 take-offs/landings, with a usage of 200 hours per year, with a basic inspection every 100 hours, a structural inspection every two years and a major inspection every six years.

The plan was to start engineering work in May 1975, have a mock-up ready in August of that year, a glider in February 1976, commissioning of the prototype in December of that year and first flight in February 1977.

By April 1975 Ruiz had substantially modified the original idea, with a shorter engine exhaust, air intakes directly below the wing and fuselage junction, a redesign of the rear fuselage, some modifications to the forward fuselage design, and a main landing gear with two wheels on each.

He also changed the wing design, working from the A-4 Skyhawk wing, as can be seen from the final design and sketches of the A-4 wing in his files together with the IA-60 documentation. However, the wing finally designed had less chord than that of the A-4, although it retained the initial concept. The installation was on top of the fuselage.

It also modified the design of the horizontal stabiliser, incorporating a 33° arrow, and by June 1975 the entire engine exhaust and the front of the fuselage were again modified, with a larger lower part, as it had been decided to equip it with two DEFA 552 30mm cannon. This part was slightly modified again in October of that year. Also, during that year, it was decided to change the engine version to the Adour RT.172-26 or Mk 804, with 8,040lb of maximum thrust with afterburner or 5,320lb without afterburner.

Meanwhile, in August 1975 the Air Force General Staff sent some opinions about the project, including several doubts about the design, such as the fact that, given the size of the aircraft, it was estimated that the actual weight could be higher than planned. The Staff also enquired about the possibility of incorporating two extra Sidewinder-type missile pylons and whether the belly mount could carry 2,000 or 4,000lb bombs. The possibility of carrying a ventral photo pod or on the right inner mount and machine gun pods in the centre pylon or under the wings was also considered. There was consultation on the possibility of considering a carrier-borne version, with no afterburner and single-seat versions, the possibility of towing targets and the possibility of fitting an in-flight refuelling probe.

The next change, in November, was to the air intake, which was moved forward and lower, to the side of the co-pilot's seat, while retaining its rectangular shape. Two wind tunnel models were produced with this configuration, a 1:10 scale model for the subsonic tunnel and a smaller one, with metal wings and stabiliser, for the supersonic tunnel.

During the tests with the larger model, Ing. Carlos Paoletti and Dr José P. Tamagno found that there was a loss of lift in the wingtip area, near the ailerons, for angles of attack between 13° and 20° and an appreciable instability at 28°, attributable to the loss of effectiveness of the horizontal empennage. This led to the evaluation of different wing configurations. Finally, the problem was solved with a wing combining aerofoils and leading-edge extensions.[6]

[6] The FMA IA-60, by Gonzalo Sebastián Rengel at www.zona-militar.com/2015/08/11/fma-ia-60

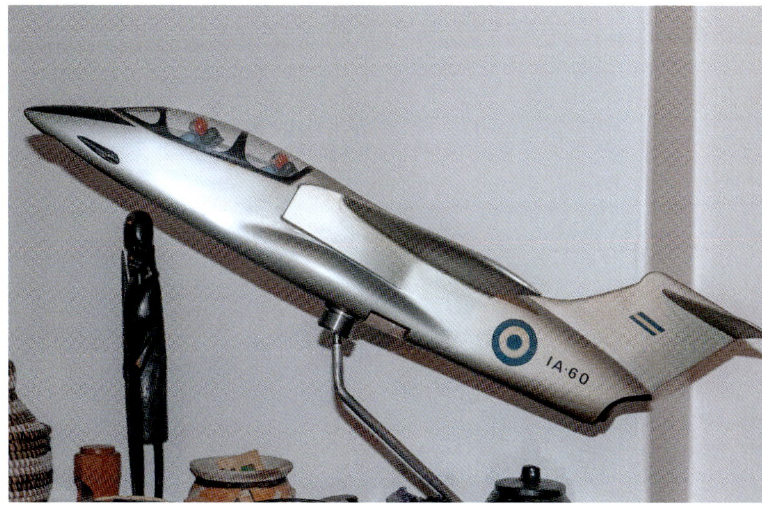

A model of the IA-60 preserved by the family of Héctor Ruiz. *Santiago Rivas*

During 1976 the programme progressed very slowly and in September a report by IIAE advisor Rodolfo Freyer made several criticisms of the project, pointing out that since the I.Ae.33 Pulqui II no work had been done on an aircraft with speeds and characteristics like those expected in the IA-60, and much of the necessary knowledge had been lost. It also indicated the lack of experience in designing a structure such as the one proposed, with openings in the underside for the landing gear and engine installation. The report showed the lack of personnel to carry out the design development of the structure, for which there were only eight engineers and ten design technicians.

The reality what became evident was that the factory did not have the capacity to develop a jet of these characteristics, as, since the end of the Pulqui II project at the end of the 1950s, it had only worked on low-performance designs, which required less precision in manufacture and had less structural stress. This situation, plus the departure of engineer Ruiz from the factory when he was assigned to the IV Air Brigade, led to the programme being halted at the end of 1976. It was finally abandoned in 1979 when it was decided to work with Dornier on the development of the IA-63 Pampa, since the German company could contribute the knowledge that did not exist at the FMA.

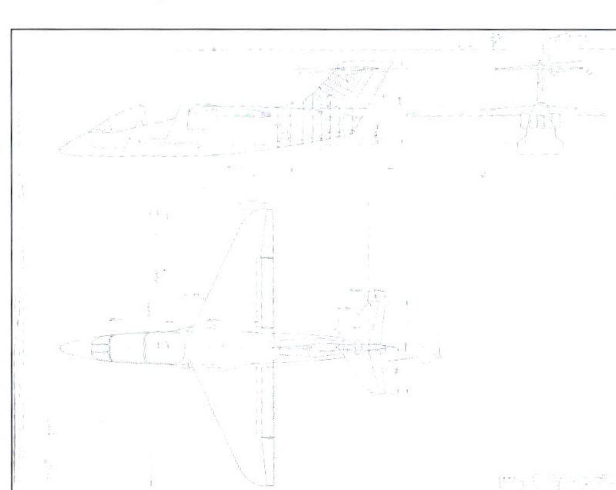

This scheme of the IA-60 from May 1975 shows many other changes, with a new wing, based on that of the A-4 Skyhawk, a new tailplane, new fairings for the main landing gear and different engine exhaust. *Archive Eduardo Ruiz*

6 Trying to keep on track

36 **IA-61 basic trainer and IA-62 advanced trainer**

The 1980s were times in which the factory developed several projects, but unfortunately, despite this being one of the most recent periods, it is also one in which less information was kept. Some proposals never went beyond the drawing board, but no trace of them survive. When the FMA was privatised in 1995, many archives were destroyed and a lot of history was lost forever, and, as all projects were cancelled, it is very probable that all the documentation related to them was also lost. This means that there is no information available on projects such as the IA-64, IA-65, IA-69, IA-71 and IA-72, although they should have existed as designations were correlative. At the same time, the project ATL (Avión de Transporte Ligero, Light Transport Aircraft) evolved beyond just and idea and models of it were even shown in fairs, but no documentation found about it include an IA- designation.

Meanwhile, by mid-1970s, the designation IA-61 was allocated to an idea for a basic trainer, to replace the Beechcraft B45 Mentor in service with the Argentine Air Force, but nothing more could be found.

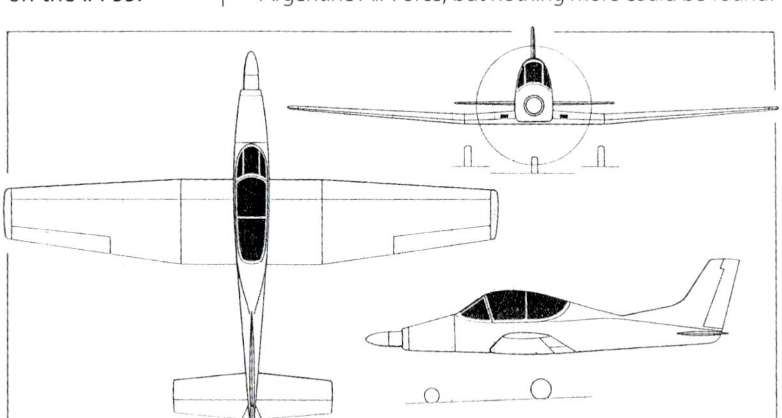

Three views of the initial IA-62 proposal, based on the IA-55.

IA-62 trainer

By late 1976, the Argentine Air Force issued an operational request for a basic trainer with about 150 knots of cruise speed and more than 200 knots at maximum speed, to be able to be used for air-to-air and air-to-ground shooting instruction and be able to operate from all types of runways. It would carry two 7.62mm machine guns, the landing gear would be a retractable tricycle, the wing was cantilever and it was an all-metal aircraft. It would be intended for +6 and -3G without external loads and +4 and -2 with charges.

A service ceiling between 6,000 and 8,000m was requested and it was desirable that it be pressurised, so it was considered that it should be a turboprop, although a 260hp Avco Lycoming AE IO-540D4B5 piston engine with Hartzell propeller was also considered. With a turboprop it was also thought that the design would be in a class of trainers with 250 knots of maximum speed.

On 1 February 1977, J. Castan and E. Guillard from France presented the analysis between the Pratt & Whitney PT6-A25 and the Turbomeca Astazou XIVR. The first had a mechanical power limit of 550shp and a thermal of 787shp and the second had a maximum continuous thermal power of 708shp or 787shp of maximum take-off power, with a mechanical power limit of 1,000shp as it was in the XVI G of the Pucará. With a power of 550shp, the PT6 consumed 286 gallons of fuel per hour and the Astazou 266. At take-off, the free-turbine PT6 had more traction due to a higher rotational speed. The direct turbine engine, as was the Astazou, had greater efficiency in reverse pitch during landing. In flight, the behaviour was similar. For dives the direct turbine was considered better, because it was more stable, it could dive without excessively increasing the speed, and the plane could fire its guns without being affected by the behaviour of the engine.

This, together with the advantages of the Astazou being used by the Pucará, led to the decision to use this engine for the project.

By early 1977 the preliminary design was presented, being a plane with a fuselage based on the one of the I.A.55 designed by engineer Olmedo, but with a canopy with a slightly different shape, tricycle landing gear and a new wing. It was expected to have the general plans finished by 1 April 1977, to allow the start of work on detailed plans. A model of the plane was showed at Le Bourget salon in June 1977.

At the preliminary design stage, the team aimed for an empty weight of 1,300kg, a maximum of 1,950kg in clean configuration and 2,600kg with external loads. The type would have a cruise speed of 300km/h and a maximum speed of 360km/h, a diving one of 600km/h and a minimum of 110km/h. The take-off distance with a 15m-high obstacle was estimated at 550m and the landing distance 500m, while the range would be 1,200km and the endurance five hours, with a service ceiling of 8,000m.

The Astazou XIVR engine with a 2.44m diameter Ratier Forest 23LF propeller would be used. It would have two machine guns on the 7.62mm wings and two underwing pylons for rockets and bombs, with a weapons capacity of 550kg.

A mock-up was expected to be built in 1977 and the prototype ready in 1979, followed by a second prototype and a ground test cell that same year.

Because the position of the engine meant that a longer nosewheel had to be installed to increase the clearance between the propeller and the ground, the basic design was modified with the engine on top of a higher cowling, also with a modified cockpit and canopy, while the wing had external sections with positive dihedral.

The project started to suffer delays and by the end of the decade there was almost no progress, while at an unknown date, closer to 1980, the project received a complete reformulation and a redesign with a new canopy and a completely new tail. While some models and plans were made, the project was cancelled in the early 1980s, when the decision was taken to cancel the IA-62 and to modernise the B45 Mentors with a turboprop engine (described in Chapter 45), but later that was also left behind and the decision was taken to buy the Embraer EMB 312 after an agreement was reached with the Brazilian government in which they were going to buy the Pampa in exchange, something that, in the end, never took place.

A model of the IA-62 preserved at the Centro de Investigación Aplicada of the Argentine Air Force. *Santiago Rivas*

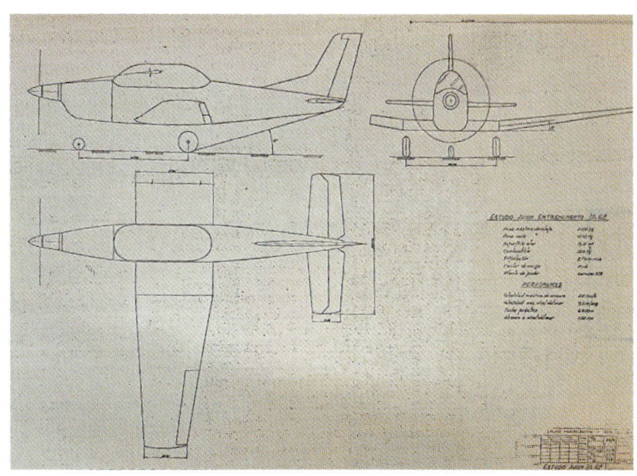

An improved design of the IA-62, with the engine higher to increase the clearance to the ground of the propeller. The wing was also modified, as well as the canopy.

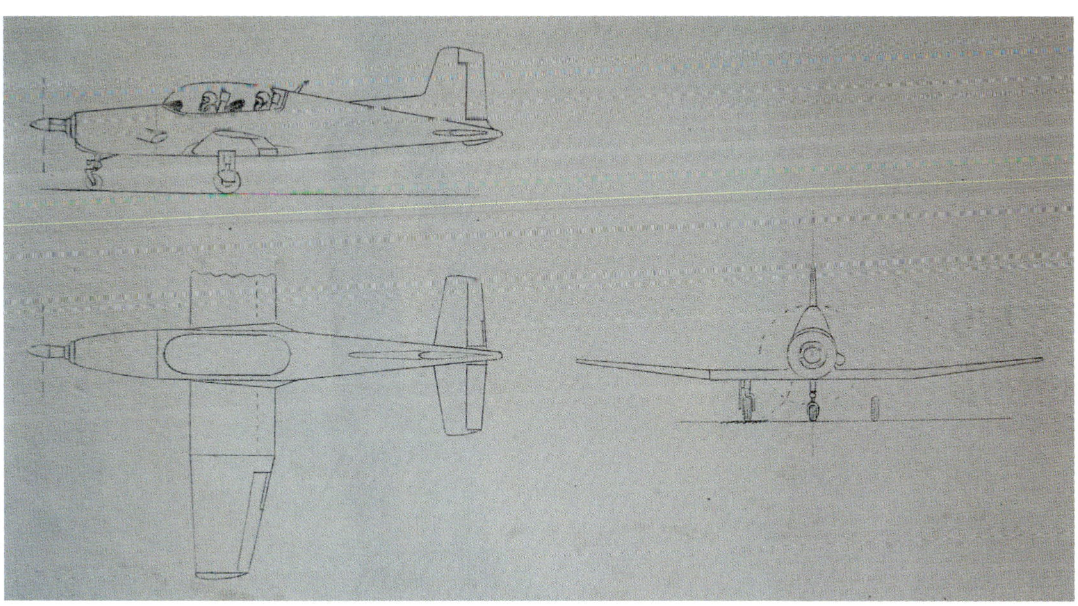

The definitive version of the IA-62, with a redesigned fuselage and tail and a modified wing.

37 IA-63 Pampa

A replacement for the Morane-Saulnier Paris

From the early 1970s, the Argentine Air Force started to analyse the replacement of the Morane-Saulnier MS.760 Paris as its advanced trainer. As has been described, first a jet version of the Pucará was considered, but this evolved into the more capable IA-60. However, the factory considered that the plane was too advanced for them to develop it alone. In 1979 the force released an operational request asking the FMA to develop and build an advanced trainer with some attack capacity, to enter service in 1984 and with the last deliveries in 1986. The request stated that 'for the basic and advanced stages of instruction, the training jet may have modest performance (MS.760 or Fouga Magister type, etc). The aircraft must be suitable for aerobatics, formation, instrument, night and navigation training, as well as for training in tactical procedures, shooting and bombing, with the ability to train in air-to-air procedures being desirable. It was important that the plane must be cheap, around $1 million each, as that way it would be possible to use more jet hours in basic and advanced training and thus increase the number of aircraft. The tactical capacity and in particular the load-bearing should not penalise the project, although they would be desirable.'

The request also stated that the air force preferred a twin-engined type, air intakes as high as possible for operation on unprepared runways, two seats in tandem, zero-zero ejection seats, night flight capability, an oxygen system for one pilot at maximum endurance, anti-G system, capacity to use extra fuel tanks under the wing, a pressurised cockpit and good visibility for both pilots. The performance included a cruise speed of over 300 knots and maximum above Mach 0.8, stall speed in landing configuration of between 85 and 95 knots, take-off and landing distance with a 15m obstacle of less than 1,300m, service ceiling of around 10,000m, range at 4,000m of 800 nautical miles, with G limits of +7 and -3 with no loads and of +4.5 and -2 at full load, wind limit of 30 knots for take-off and landing, temperature limits of -50°C and +50°C flying and -20°C and +50°C on the ground and capacity for inverted flight for at least twenty seconds.

As for the weapons capacity, it was stated that the plane had to be equipped with two 7.62mm internal machine guns, a sight for air-to-air and air-to-ground capacity, weapons pylons and the capacity to tow a target.

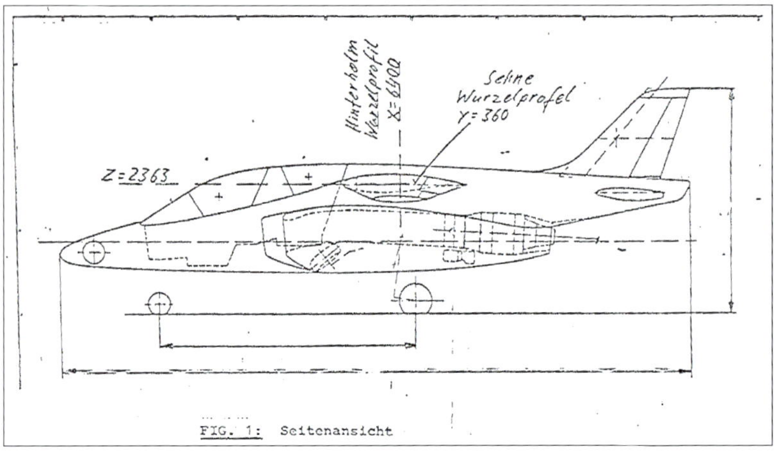

Initial layout of the IA-63 made by Dornier in 1980, with the canopy and air intakes similar to the Alpha Jet and a smaller vertical fin.

Dornier support

As the analysis of the IA-60 project stated that the factory could not develop such a plane in the requested time-frame, they started to look for external support with the design and development of the plane, which received the designation IA-63, and Vicecomodoro Ricardo Valenzuela was appointed as head of the project. After contacting different aircraft industries, on 30 March 1979 the presidential decree 746/79 designated Major Orlando Ovidi to travel to Friedrichshafen, Germany, to set up training courses at Dornier for the programming and preliminary design of the IA-63.

In June 1979 Dornier, which was finishing the production of the Alpha Jet together with Dassault, delivered a proposal during the Paris Salon at Le Bourget, which was analysed, and was followed with the configuration proposals in October of that year. The company proposed seven possible configurations, which included four with a single engine, two of them with high wing and three with two engines, one of them with high wing. Although the selected version had some resemblance with the Alpha Jet, all the proposals had a straight wing.

To power the IA-63, two engines were considered for the single-engine versions: the Garrett

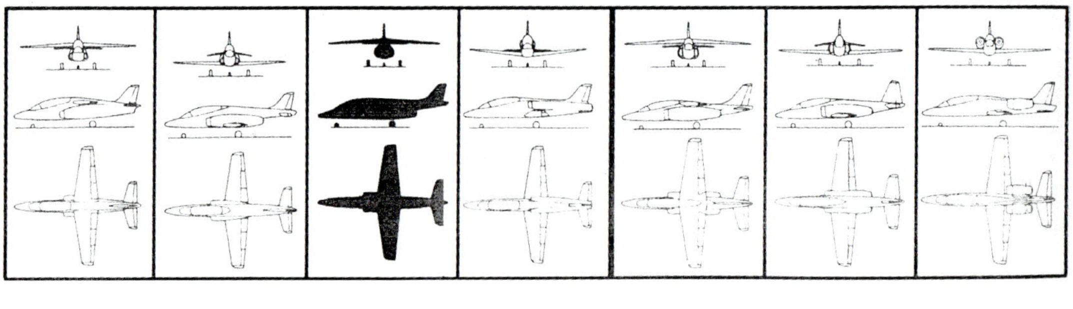

Different configurations analysed for the IA-63 project, with four with a single engine and three with two engines.

TFE-731-2-2N of 3,500lb of thrust that was used on the Learjet 35 or the Pratt & Whitney Canada JT-15D-5 of 2,900lb that was under development. The FMA preferred the last model, because it was more modern, but the constructor could not accomplish the delivery dates that the development of the IA-63 requested, so it was left in favour of the Garrett. For the twin-engined versions, the JT-15D-1 of 2,200lb was considered.

In a note sent to Dornier on 21 August 1979 by Brigadier Major Antonio Burgos, Materiel Commander of the Argentine Air Force, he suggested the use of the JT-15D because its versions were similar in size, with different power, and could be used to develop a family of aircraft based on the IA-63.

By then, it was planned to make the first flight in 1982, the series production in 1984 and fly the first series production plane in 1985.

After the proposals were evaluated, one was selected with a high wing and a single engine, because there were some proven jet power plants that gave the necessary power, and in March 1980 the preliminary design was finished. At this stage, the idea of internal weapons was abandoned.

This collaboration was augmented after the signing of an agreement on 5 May 1980 and both companies began to collaborate on development of the type. The IA-63 programme meant also the actualisation of the infrastructure of the FMA on the design and construction procedures. Big numeric milling machines were bought, a computer centre was organised, and the bigger wind tunnel was modernised.

Six wind tunnel models were built to evaluate the different aerodynamic configurations and one of them was sent to Modane, France, in September 1980, to test the performance in a corkscrew, while the engineers and technicians of FMA worked together with those of Dornier at Córdoba and at Friedrichshafen, in Germany. In the European city the Argentine personnel perfected the details of the project thanks to the German experience on the Alpha

The first mock-up of the IA-63 cabin, built in Germany, with a canopy like the Alpha Jet.

Ejection seat tests of the IA-63, to check that the seat and pilot could eject safely from the cabin.

One of the mock-ups of the Pampa that was exhibited at Le Bourget in 1981.

The instrument panel of one of the Pampa prototypes with the first sight installed on the type. Note that the weapons panel, which was below the sight, is not installed.

Jet, which had the same configuration in some respects. Meanwhile, in September and October 1980 the first wind tunnel tests were made in Córdoba.

Dornier also made a mock-up of the cabin in early 1981, which had the canopy divided like the Alpha Jet, but this idea was rejected shortly after. Together with the wind tunnel models, five 1:1 scale mock-ups were built at Córdoba to facilitate the development of flight controls and hydraulics, electricity, avionics, fuel and air conditioning, while a mock-up was presented at the Paris Air Show at Le Bourget in 1981 painted in light blue and white, on the first public presentation of the IA-63. There it caught the attention of the specialised press, which called it the 'mini Alpha Jet', although it already had the new canopy made in one piece.

That year the Área de Material Córdoba projected the construction of four prototypes and two fuselages for ground tests. In June the first budget for the programme was approved, which was of 131.756.973.000 pesos, allowing the start of big-scale development with the wind tunnel models. The use of the CAD-CATIA system for computer design led to some changes to the tail, the air intakes, an augment of the incidence angle and changes to the nose and wing.

A revision of the operational request by 1980 specified that the design must consider the possibility of adding radar and a refuelling probe to future versions.

By then, a first flight was expected for 1983, but due to budget cuts the finalisation of the first prototype was delayed, while the fourth, which was expected to be equipped with the Pratt & Whitney JT15D-5, was cancelled. In this year the CEV received new technology and its people were trained in France on it, to improve considerably on the way they tested the aircraft after the Pucará flight test programme.

While the plane was originally designed to use the Martin-Baker MkAr 8LM ejection seat, the war with the United Kingdom in 1982 led to the decision to change this, so, while the first two prototypes flew with the Martin-Baker seats, from the third prototype they used the Stencel SIIIS-31A63.

The first prototype was started in Germany, to be assembled at Córdoba. The same was to be done with the other two and with two airframes that would be used for ground training, one for the installation of the electronic equipment and the other to train the people at the FMA on the structure assembly. A forward fuselage was also built for tests, including the testing of the windscreen against impacts.

Meanwhile, the Argentine Air Force announced that it would need sixty-four aircraft to replace the Paris and possibly thirty-six more to complement the A-4B/C Skyhawk on attack and air defence missions.

Initially the plan was to incorporate the first twelve planes at the Escuela de Aviación Militar

An IA-63 airframe used to train the personnel at Córdoba, which was built by Dornier in Germany. *Santiago Rivas*

Roll out of the Pampa on 14 August 1984.

(EAM, Military Aviation School) and replace the Paris of that institution, following with the replacement of the planes of the Escuela de Caza (Fighter School) at the IV Brigada Aérea at Mendoza.

On 30 May 1984, the first prototype, serialled EX-01 (constructor number 2001) was rolled out, and was taken to the Departamento Ensayo de Estructuras (Structure Tests Departament) to carry out the vibration tests. Meanwhile, the Equipo de Ensayos en Vuelo (Flight Tests Team), which would be the responsible for testing the IA-63, worked together with the designers to understand how they had to fly the plane, and thanks to the results of ground testing areas of concern in the flight controls were known, so they planned to investigate them on the first test flights. In July, the preliminary flight manual for the first flight was finished, including a big part of the engine performance, because the test pilots carried out some tests in Learjets to find out more about the power plant.

The IA-63 Pampa

The Pampa is a single-engine, straight-wing, tandem two-seater, equipped with hydraulic systems for all the control surfaces, including the Fowler-type flaps, spoilers and landing gear. It also has a turbine to ensure hydraulic pressure and emergency power in case of engine failure in flight. The wing has a Dornier DoA-7/8 transonic profile. The structure is completely of metal, semi-monocoque, with a twin-spar wing with two of the three fuel tanks for 225 litres each (the third, flexible and of 418 litres, is in the fuselage beside the cockpit), and two extra tanks of 207.5 litres each can be installed inside the structure to bring a total internal capacity of 1,383 litres, which can be loaded in no more than three minutes through a single intake by gravity. Also, the aircraft can fly inverted for ten seconds with maximum power.

The landing gear is for unprepared runways and ground steering is made by differential braking, although a commanded nosewheel was tested but not adopted. In case of emergency it can be lowered by gravity.

It was designed under the safe life concept with a coefficient of 5 (the fatigue tests were made until the airframe reached five times the original safe life), making possible a total of 8,000 flying hours or 11,000 landings. Static tests determined a maximum load factor of 6G, although a test programme can extend the service life to 14,000 hours, with a load factor of 6.5G for combat missions.

Take-off speed is 204km/h, climb rate 1,500m/min at 6,000ft and 1,000m/min at 15,000ft. At 30,000ft the load factor is 3G. Although the maximum is 5G, test pilots reached 6G at 647km/h. Close to the limit, at 4.8G the control column becomes heavier to make it difficult for the pilot to exceed the maximum.

The engine weighs 328kg and provides 1,590kg thrust at take-off, and 340kg at 36,000ft at 0.8 Mach. It can operate between -20°C and 50°C at sea level and between; 50°C and 10°C at 45,000ft. It can be started directly using the 11.5Kw battery.

The crew has a Garrett air conditioning system, fed by the engine, which also sends oxygen to the

Head-up display installed in 1994 on the Pampa as part of the SINT programme.

First flight of Pampa EX-02 on 7 August 1985.

anti-G equipment and to seal the cabin. Avionics were mainly Collins.

The plane has four underwing pylons and one ventral, with the external wing ones for 250kg and the internal ones for 400kg. The ventral pylon can carry 400kg and can carry the 30mm DEFA 553 cannon with 145 rounds.

The Pampa flies

On 14 August 1984 the official presentation of the IA-63 took place, and the plane was rolled out from Hangar 90 at the factory. While it was originally considered to name it Coraje, for the courage shown by the Argentine Air Force in the Malvinas/Falklands War, in the end it was decided to name it Pampa. The same month, engine tests were carried out and by the end of September ground tests began. The tests pilots, Vicecomodoro Genaro M. Sciolla and major Horacio Oréfice, started with engine tests and slow taxiing to test the brakes and controls. On-board equipment and the power requested to control the plane on the ground were controlled. After that, high-speed tests were made, evaluating the aerodynamic control surfaces, finishing with a take-off run with enough fuel to fly if they had to take off. Because the runway was not long, it was planned to make a small jump, but in the end, tests were made to the rotation speed, where the nose was raised and the elevators were tested, leaving everything ready for the first flight. On early September, both pilots had travelled to Germany to fly the Alpha Jet, to familiarise themselves with an aircraft with similar characteristics.

Finally, on 6 October everything was ready. A Morane-Saulnier Paris was to escort the Pampa throughout the flight, while a Bell 212 helicopter would be ready for search and rescue in case of an accident.

Vicecomodoro Sciolla took the plane to the head of the runway with 80 per cent of power and the pilots of both aircraft kept maximum power on for two minutes to check there were no problems. When the chase plane was ready to follow the Pampa, the pilot released the brakes. They climbed to 9,000ft and then started at this altitude with some smooth turns, raising the landing gear and flaps to leave the plane in a clean configuration. There they made some tight turns at higher speed and verified the hydraulic system. Then they climbed to 13,700ft and went from 0.5 Mach to 0.6, testing the stability and control, and later the spoilers, the response to configuration changes, and lowering the gear and flaps approaching stall. After fifty minutes of flight they landed successfully.

On 10 October at 1200 hours, the Pampa made the first official flight for the Air Force authorities and the Córdoba province governor, with similar

The three Pampa prototypes flying together close to the FMA.

characteristics of the other but reaching Mach 0.63 on a low flypast, escorted always by the Paris and showing great manoeuvrability, surpassing the limits established for this first phase of tests.

Later, the CEV started the test flights that would include performance tests, 'flutter' behaviour, engine vibrations and system settings, while the Structural Tests Airframe was finished and began tests by the beginning of 1985.

In May 1985, after only fifty flight hours, EX-01 was sent on a C-130 to Oberpfaffenhofen, Germany, to undergo some tests at the Dornier factory and paint it with the company paint scheme of white, red and blue, to be shown in flight during the XXXVI Salon of Le Bourget.

Shortly after the return of EX-01, on 7 August at 1650 EX-02 (c/n 2002) flew for the first time from the runway of the Military Aviation School, for one hour, piloted by captain Julio C. Lombardi and 1st Lt Omar Gelardi. It took off with a weight of 3,966kg and flew at 296km/h at 9,000ft. Then they reached Mach 0.6 (690km/h) and tested the spoilers, flaps and landing gear. EX-02 was used for performance tests and to draw up the flight manual.

Because of budget cuts and because the Paris of the EAM were to be replaced by thirty Embraer EMB-312 Tucanos, by then it was decided that the Pampas would go directly to the IV Brigada Aérea, while the first series would be of only eighteen planes, followed by another eighteen if the budget made it possible. The cost of the programme was $190 million and the cost per plane was about $3.5 million. Both prototypes were assigned in 1986 to the IV Brigada Aérea on commission at the Centro de Ensayos en Vuelo with 200 assigned flying hours.

Between 17 and 21 March EX-02 visited FIDA 86 exhibition at Santiago de Chile, while on the 25th of this month EX-03 (c/n 2003) flew with 1st Lt Luis M Cismondi and Lt Rubén Lianza at the controls. On one of these flights, they climbed to 9,000ft and then, at 400km/h reached 15,000ft and a speed of 690km/h. It was equipped with UPC (Stencel) SIIIS-31A63 zero-zero ejecting seats in place of the Martin-Baker MkAR 8LM and eight cameras on the fuselage and wings. This prototype was used for armament and avionics tests. Meanwhile, the construction of the Dynamic Tests Airframe (Célula de Ensayos Dinámicos, CED) was very slow because the lack of parts.

In April 1986 negotiations began with the Comando de Material of the FAA to sell the licence to build the plane in Brazil, the United States and Iran. In the first case , this would be in exchange with the Tucanos, to replace the Embraer EMB-326 Xavante and, in the second, to replace the Cessna T-37 Tweet.

During September, studies were made to evaluate the operation of the Pampa at the IV Brigada Aérea and to prepare the unit for the arrival of series

Pampa EX-02 at the FIDA 86 exhibition in Chile in March 1986. *Alberto Martín*

A model of the Pampa with radar.

When the Pampas were sent to Le Bourget '89, they also travelled to Tel Nof air base in Israel, where this picture was taken over Jerusalem from a Fouga Magister of the Israel Defense Force/Air Force. The Israelis asked the Argentines to leave one of the Pampas for an extensive evaluation to replace the Magisters, but the authorities did not authorise it. The plane was being flown by Major Rogelio Marzialetti, carrying an Israeli pilot in the back seat. *Via Luis Cismondi*

A unique picture of the third Pampa prototype flying together with an Alpha Jet near Friedrichshafen. The Pampa has pilot Luis Cismondi in the front seat and Dornier test pilot head Wolf Havenstein in the back seat but flying the plane. The picture was taken from another Alpha Jet of the Luftwaffe. *Via Luis Cismondi*

production planes, while FMA began the construction of components for the first six examples. Meanwhile, performance differences with the Garrett TFE 731-5 engine of 4,304lb of thrust were studied, with the help of Dornier, changing the engine to this one for series production was considered but later ruled out.

Into service

The first series production plane (c/n 2006, the serials 2004 and 2005 were used on the test airframes), serialled E-801, was finished during 1987 and made its first flight at the CEV on 24 December, while tests on the Dynamic Tests Airframe, delivered in August, began.

Also, in June EX-01 was again sent to Le Bourget for its second participation at the European exhibition. By the end of this year E-802 was 80 per cent finished, E-803 70 per cent, 804 at 18 per cent, 805 at 11 per cent and 806 at 4 per cent, while parts of the aircraft up to E-812 were in production.

The tests on the three prototypes continued, flying 200 hours and, of those, the most important were the evaluation of the DEFA 553 30mm cannon in a ventral pod on EX-03. Also, in November the Argentine president, Dr Raúl Alfonsín, flew in EX-01, the first civilian to fly in the Pampa. This flight was followed in 1988 by the visit of Brigadier General Daniel J. Sherlock, commander of the 832nd Air Division of the USAF, and Captains Lynn Anne Merten and Patrick K. Doty; Merten being the first woman to fly the trainer.

During the first months of 1988 E-802 and 803 were finished and started testing prior to their

Pampa cutaway.

delivery to Escuadrón II of Grupo 4 de Caza of the IV Brigada Aérea, created in June. Delivery took place in July at the FMA together with E-801, with the aircraft entering service immediately to train the instructors and begin the preparation to use the Pampa for the Curso de Estandarización de Procedimientos para Aviadores de Combate (Combat Aviators Procedures Standardisation Course, CEPAC) in place of the Paris.

American tour

To demonstrate the Pampa and look for possible customers, the Fábrica Militar de Aviones planned in 1988 a tour of two of the prototypes through America, which also responded to an invitation by the United States to show the plane there. Directiva 440 of the Air Force ordered the use of EX-02 named Mancha and EX-03 Gato, commemorating the two Argentine horses that crossed America from Buenos Aires to New York in 1925. They departed from Córdoba to Jujuy together in a C-130 Hercules on 20 September 1988, then they were flown to La Joya Air Base and then to Lima, both in Perú. Then they flew to Guayaquil, Ecuador, and to Howard AFB in Panamá, San José de Costa Rica and then Tampico, Mexico. From there they flew to Kelly AFB in Texas and on to Memphis, finally arriving at Andrews AFB in Washington DC, where demonstrations began. From there they went to Randolph AFB and to Corpus Christi NAS, and in total eighty-two USAF and US Navy pilots, three from Canada, one from New Zealand, one from Northrop and three journalists flew it. Major General Hall, test pilot of the USAF, said of the Pampa that 'controls are simple, the instrument location very adequate for a training plane. Easy to taxi, the visibility is excellent on the ground and in the air. Very good power and speed, it's docile to manoeuvre, to enter corkscrews and easily exit. The touch and go is very good.'

The tour continued home via Guayaquil, with stops at Tampico, Guatemala and Howard AFB on the ferry flight, and six pilots of the Ecuadorian Air Force tested the Pampa, which was a possible replacement for their old Lockheed T-33s. Then they went to Colombia, where six pilots flew it from Apiay Air Base, where the force operated the T-33, followed by Caracas, Venezuela, where ten officers of the FAV tested it, as the air force was interested in the type to replace the Jet Provost. On 17 October it was presented at Base Aérea Las Palmas of Lima, Perú, a country that was analysing the prospect of incorporating it into Grupo No. 51 of its Air Force to replace the Aermacchi MB-339, which was very expensive to operate. In Peru another six pilots flew it and, after that, both Pampas returned to Córdoba, arriving on 29 October, after 28,850km, flying 196 hours fifteen minutes carrying 118 guests on 145 flights with 319 landings. There were only five minor recorded failures on EX-03 and four on EX-02.

One of the first series production Pampas armed with two rocket launchers and the ventral gun pod. This pod was used only for tests and more than thirty years would pass until it was finally adopted operationally. Also, the rocket launchers were used only briefly at the beginning of the operational career of the Pampa.

Deliveries

After that trip and the promotional campaign of the FMA through its subsidiary Tecnología Aeroespacial S.A. (TEA), the United States, Australia, New Zealand, Israel, Colombia and Venezuela requested information about the plane for possible purchases.

By the end of that year E-804 and E-805 (c/n 2009 and 2010) were finished, while E-806 was 85 per cent complete. They conformed to Block 4, which differed in having tails built in Argentina, while the previous aircraft had Dornier-made ones. The landing gear was built by SHL of Israel, which produced fourteen units for the prototypes and production examples until E-811, with the idea of building them locally from E-812, expected from December 1989.

In February 1989 E-804 and 805 were delivered, while E-806 to 812 (Block 5) were finished during the year. Parts for E-813 to 818 (Block 6) were at 71 per cent. The plan was to deliver E-818 in 1990 and finish this series.

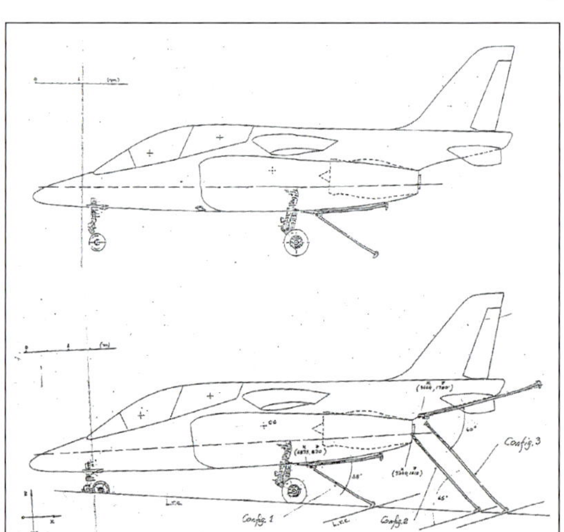

Diagrams of the proposed naval version of the Pampa.

Naval Pampa

The development of the IA-63 by the Fuerza Aérea Argentina attracted the attention of the Comando de Aviación Naval Argentina (COAN), which needed a replacement for the Embraer EMB-326 Xavante, which could not operate on aircraft carriers. Between 1989 and 1990 the COAN, together with of the Pampa for use on the ARA *25 de Mayo* carrier.

First the desirable minimal operational performances and characteristics of the model were determined. Then the location of the arrestor hook, with a correspondent study on approach conditions and the procedures during deck landings. Also, the catapult bridle hook location was studied with the launch conditions.

The requested performances were for two options, one for basic training, with pilot, pupil, and complete fuel (750kg), reaching a maximum weight of 3,800kg on launch and landing. The other was for weapons training and light attack, with pilot, gun with ammunition and two pylons with one 250kg bomb each and complete fuel, reaching 4,950kg on take-off and from 3,800kg to 4,400kg on landing.

Preliminary studies of the structural modifications showed that the landing gear location was the correct in relation with the centre of gravity. The arresting hook had to be attached to the 6875 station on the main landing gear frame, ahead of the engine cowling. Although this location meant that the nosewheel had to suffer a big force during landing, there were no other resistant parts backwards. Another place, under the engine, was rejected because it would produce a lot of pitching. The ideal place where the braking force line passed through the gravity centre was in the middle of the engine exhaust, so any solution was not the best. This was because the Pampa was not developed as a naval plane from a beginning. The hook would be 1.73m long and have a maximum inclination of 38°.

The approach speed was 99 knots, 1.15 times the stall speed, with 40° of flap and an inclination angle of 4.8°, at 80 per cent of power with 700kg of thrust. The maximum admissible load for the main landing gear would increase by 15 per cent, while the nose wheel would have 100 per cent more, because of the hook location, and both the front and main landing gear must be modified. Because the maximum compression of the nose wheel leg would be out of the cable zone, even if the hook caught the first of them, there was no problem of running over the cables during braking.

Catapult conditions were also evaluated in all the different situations to locate the bridle hooks.

The conclusions that the team reached was that the plane was very adequate for carrier use and that the basic design would allow the structural modifications for the new stresses to which it would be submitted.

Only the experimental verification of the obtained data would be needed, detailing the necessary modifications to the structure and other parts of the plane, including avionics, anti-corrosive protection, pitch indicator, verification of performance (after the construction of a prototype), detailed design and cost evaluation. The plan was to build twelve aircraft.

Despite the satisfactory results of the study, a reduction in the defence budget made development impossible, although the Navy maintained its interest in the idea. In 2000 the force showed again interest on the Pampa, but now without embarked capacity, but with another engine, avionics and reinforced landing gear to carry out carrier landing practice on land, because the ARA *25 de Mayo* had been decommissioned and sold for scrap in 1999.

Exhibitions and J-PATS

In June 1989 EX-02 and 03 were again taken to the Salon at Le Bourget and after that, due to the interest of the Israeli Air Force, they travelled to Tel Nof Air Base, near Tel Aviv, with stops in Naples and Athens. The Pampas were tested extensively and the Israelis asked for one of the prototypes to be left with them so they could continue to evaluate it, but the FMA authorities did not accept the request as they needed it to finish flight testing.

Meanwhile, the USAF launched the PATS (Primary Aircraft Training System) programme to replace the old Cessna T-37 and, with this in mind, the FMA made plans to augment the production to nine planes per month and build the 538 requested initially by the United States from the winner of the competition. Because it was necessary to work with a local company, negotiations were held with LTV and McDonnell Douglas. FMA signed an agreement with the first manufacturer on 30 April 1990, under which the American company would build under licence most of the 800 planes that were now requested in the competition, at a cost of about $7 billion, because the US Navy joined the programme to replace its T-34C Turbo Mentors, too. Because of this the programme became the J-PATS, with the J of Joint.

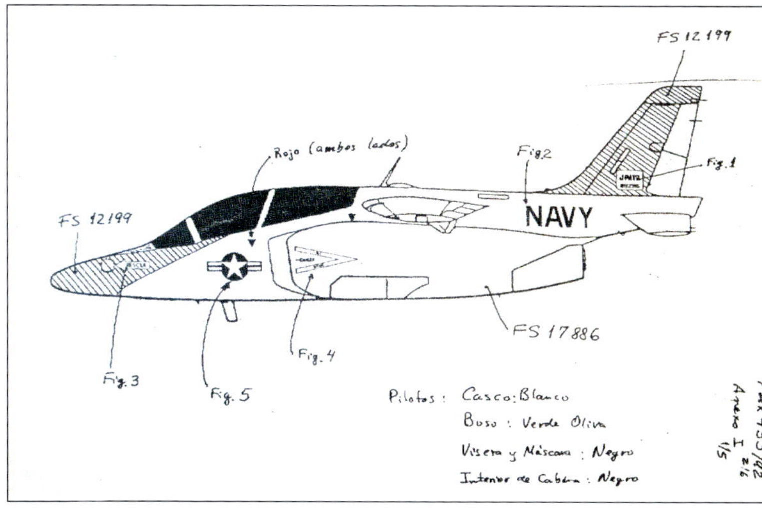

Paint scheme proposed for the Pampas for the US Navy.

To again show the plane in the United States, between 19 and 22 July 1990 EX-01 participated on the Dayton Air Show, while on 22 August a C-130H Hercules took it to Le Bourget and on the 29th it flew to Farnborough to participate in the British air show. In Paris the Pampa made some test flights commanded by Comodoro Juan C. Sapolski.

During that year, as was repeated in almost all the following shows until 2022, the IA-63 Pampa took part in the FIDAE exhibition in Chile, with either prototypes or series production aircraft.

While the Pampa caught the attention on the rest of the world, constant budget cuts at home led to a need to pause production after the delivery of E-814, with E-815 and E-816 still on the production line and the production of parts for all the series

Pampa E-812 in flight over the USA during tests for the J-PATS programme. *LIV*

A Pampa landing on Route 40, which is north of the runway of the IV Brigada Aérea and linked to the airport by a taxiway.

finished. By these times, the new government of president Carlos Menem, who flew in an IA-63 in August 1989, decided to privatise the FMA and pause the construction of forty-six planes until the plant was sold.

Meanwhile, on 31 August 1992, during rehearsal flights prior to the Farnborough exhibition, E-813 crashed at the British airport of Bournemouth, killing the pilots, Comodoro Sapolski and Omar Gelardi.

The Pampa 2000

To participate in the J-PATS, the FMA and LTV developed the Pampa 2000, a more advanced version that was adjusted to North American requests, equipped with Martin-Baker MKUS 16LC ejection seats, which were lighter, more comfortable, had a quick-release button and were easier to use; Garrett TFE731-2-2B engines with 400lb of extra power; an on-board oxygen generating system (OBOGS); digital Bendix/King avionics with a flight management system that included an air data computer; a flight director computer; GPS; an attitude heading reference system (AHRS); a multipurpose control and display unit; a com/nav integrator, digital EADI and EHSI displays; and a new polarised canopy. The price of this version was about $3 million.

EX-02 was sent together with E-812 and 814 to be evaluated in the United States. The first only received some equipment changes, while the others were completely modified into Pampa 2000s.

On 25 May 1993 E-812 made the first flight of a Pampa 2000 commanded by LTV test pilot John Hoffman and on 30 July it was officially presented to the Argentine and US authorities. During that year almost 400 US pilots evaluated the Pampa 2000 and some other countries, like México, Taiwan, Canada and Israel, demonstrated their interest in the plane if it won the competition. Venezuela, Bolivia, Paraguay, Brazil and South Africa also showed interest, the first to replace their T-2 Buckeye, Bolivia to do the same with their T-33, while Brazil and Paraguay wanted to replace their Xavantes. South Africa also needed it to replace the Atlas Impala.

On September 1993 the Pampa 2000 started a tour through some USAF and US Navy bases, beginning with Andrews AFB.

In 1994 the winner was set to be announced but some budget cuts in the United States delayed the decision until 1995. The competitors were the Grumman/Agusta S-211, which, together with the Pampa was considered as leading the competition, Rockwell/ DASA with the Fanranger, Northrop/ Embraer with the Super Tucano, Lockheed/Aermacchi with the T-Bird II based on the MB-339, Beech/Pilatus with the PC-9 Mk.2 and Cessna with the Model 526 Citationjet, the only twin-engined proposal. Although most in the United States preferred a jet, finally the government opted for the Pilatus model, called T-6 Texan II, because of its lower costs. By this reason the Pampa lost much of the possible customers, which amounted to the potential of selling more than 200 planes, besides the 800 for the United States.

The three planes returned to Argentina and received their standard equipment, but the EX-02 remained out of service. The other two kept the gold-tinted canopies that made them different from the rest, but this was later adopted by the rest of the fleet.

Budget problems

In 1994 a Head-Up Display (HUD) from Elbit Systems was evaluated in E-805 as the first stage of the SINT programme (Sistema Integrado de Navegación y Tiro, Shooting and Navigation Integrated Programme). This was continued with the installation in EX-03 of the whole system, with a HUD that comprised the PDU (Pilot Display Unit) and the FCP (Front Control Panel), a CMC (Central Mission Computer) and a PSVS (Power Source Video Signal). This example also received a Canadian Marconi CMA-734, a Lear Siegler 6000T1 gyroscope, a B&D 2800 air data computer, a TRT AHV6-611 radio altimeter, a VD 341226 angle of attack (AOA) indicator, a Collins VOR/ILS and an Eldec ID9-127-27 fuel flux indicator. On the sides of the nose, the plane received the AOA sensor, a pitot tube, static takes and a temperature probe

In July 1995 the FMA was adjudicated to Lockheed Aircraft, which created Lockheed Aircraft Argentina S.A. (LAASA), later Lockheed Martin Aircraft Argentina S.A. (LMAASA), but the production line was still halted and later it was disassembled, with the parts of E-817 (c/n 2022) and 818 (c/n 2023) used as spares for operational examples. E-815 (c/n 2020) was almost finished, but some parts were also used for spares and E-816 (c/n 2021), whose final assembly had hardly started, was also cannibalised.

By 1997 the IV Brigada began activities with only one plane in service, reaching five during the year and receiving EX-02 from the CEV for operational use, but this example was still out of service. It was painted in operational colours, but the differences with the series planes and the fear that the plane had been submitted to stresses beyond its limits carried its rejection by the brigade.

To solve a problem with the ejection seat cartridges, the possibility of interchanging the Stencel seats with the Martin-Baker Mk-BR8LCs of the Embraer Tucanos was investigated because of a delay in the delivery of seats sent to the US company for overhaul, but it was determined that it was not possible.

By that time, the lack of spares led the Argentine Air Force authorities to think of a replacement for the Pampa and the United States offered a batch of twenty-three Douglas TA-4J Skyhawks in 1998, but the offer was rejected because they were in very poor condition.

The impossibility of finding a replacement and the necessity to finally replace the Paris led to negotiations with LMAASA for the restart of the Pampa programme, starting with the delivery of E-815, which was finished using some parts of EX-02 that was still grounded. The other two prototypes were still used by the CEV for tests.

After negotiations, an agreement was reached to put into service the twelve planes of the Escuadrón II, reaching by July 1999 a total of ten for the parade over Buenos Aires on 10 August 1999, for the Air Force Day. They were joined by E-815, delivered in a ceremony on 30 September 1999, but it only served as a replacement for E-808, which was lost in an accident on the 17th of that month at Capilla del Rosario, Mendoza. The accident was caused by an engine stop because of a defective part in the turbine. The aircraft was flown by USAF Major James Hetherington, who was on commission at the IV Brigada Aérea, and Alférez Sergio Florentino of the FAA, who both ejected safely.

New Pampas, Pampa NG and AT-63

In 1995 Captain Rubén Lianza proposed an update to the Pampa because the stopping of the production line with so few deliveries was complicating maintenance, as some providers of spares were charging very high prices and with long times to deliver the parts. This was the case

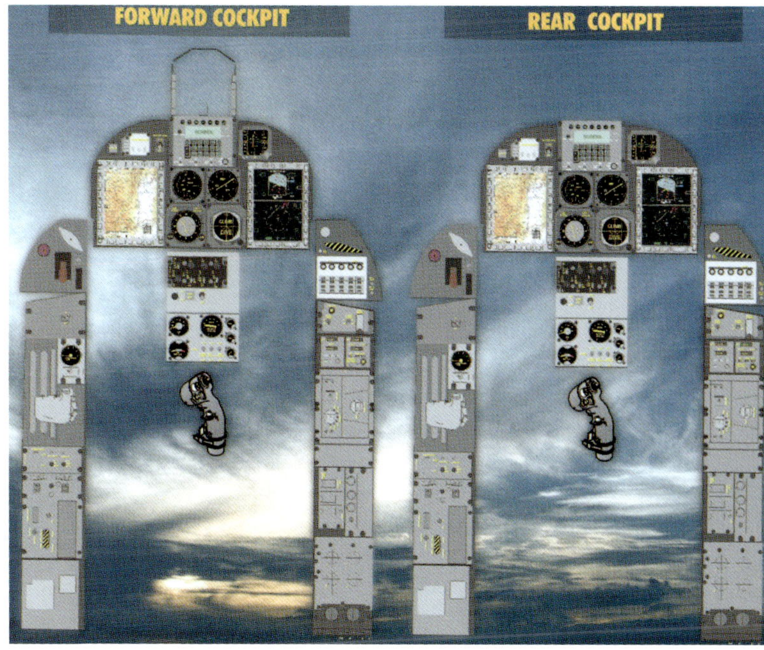

Cockpit layout of the AT-63.

Layout of the upgraded missionised version proposed by Captain Lianza in 1995, which was the basis of the Pampa NG.

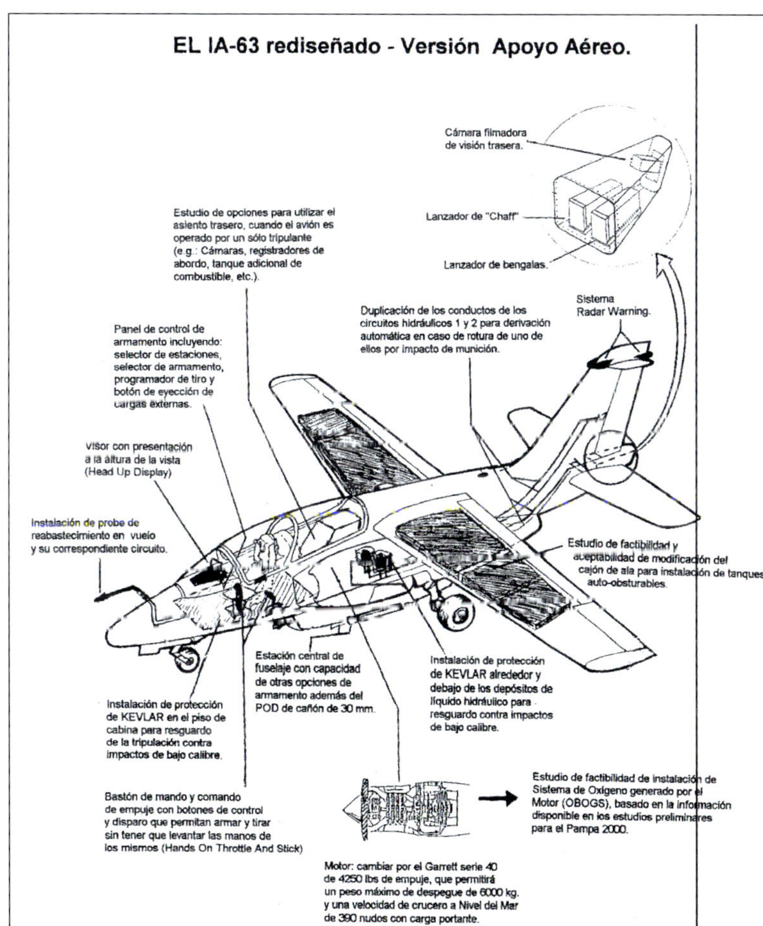

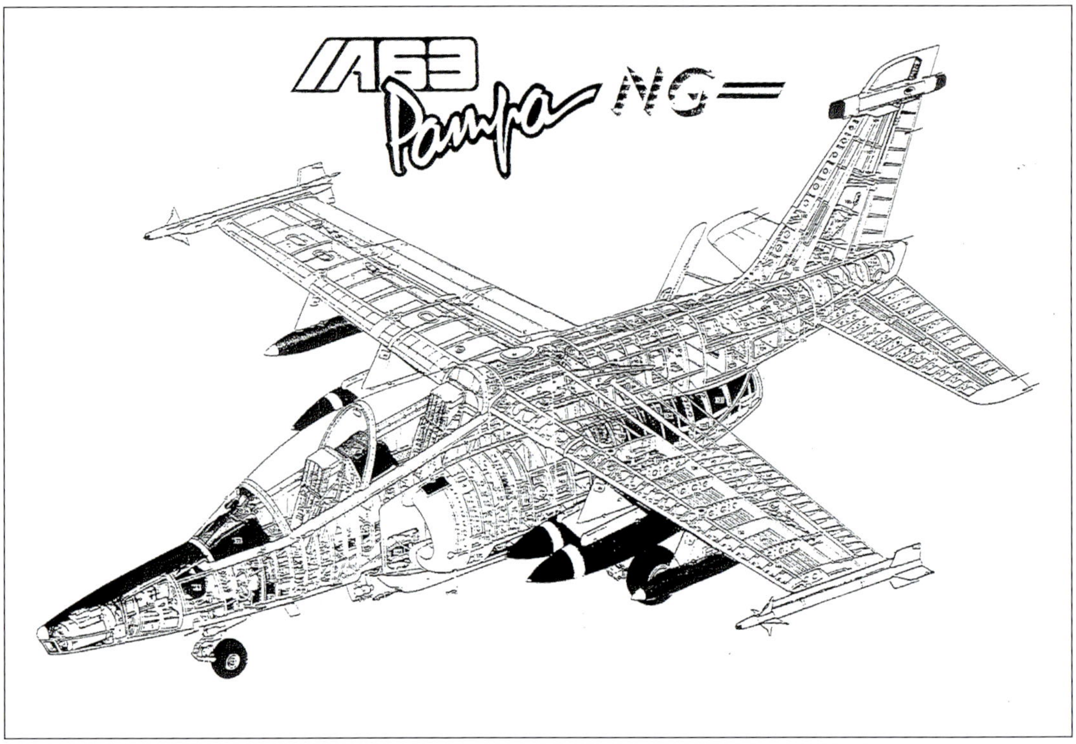

First layout of the Pampa NG, with wingtip missile pylons.

with the Messier Hispano Bugatti brake blocks, of which each cost 68,000 USD and the delivery time was two years. Some companies were even refusing to build them as the production numbers were so low, as was the case with the actuator of the cabin canopy from Aviac. Lianza also stated that the aircraft had some minor problems that had not been resolved regarding longitudinal control and during rolls, and said some technical manuals were never delivered by the factory. Lianza proposed to use some systems of the Pampa 2000, with the horizontal stabiliser inclined 20°, with the trailing edge upwards, a polarised canopy to reduce the solar radiation inside the cabin, a new windscreen prepared for impacts at up to 400 knots and without the heating system that affected the forward vision. He also proposed changing the engine for a Garrett TFE 731-40-2N of 4,300lb thrust and the ejection seats for the Martin-Baker MkUS 16LC.

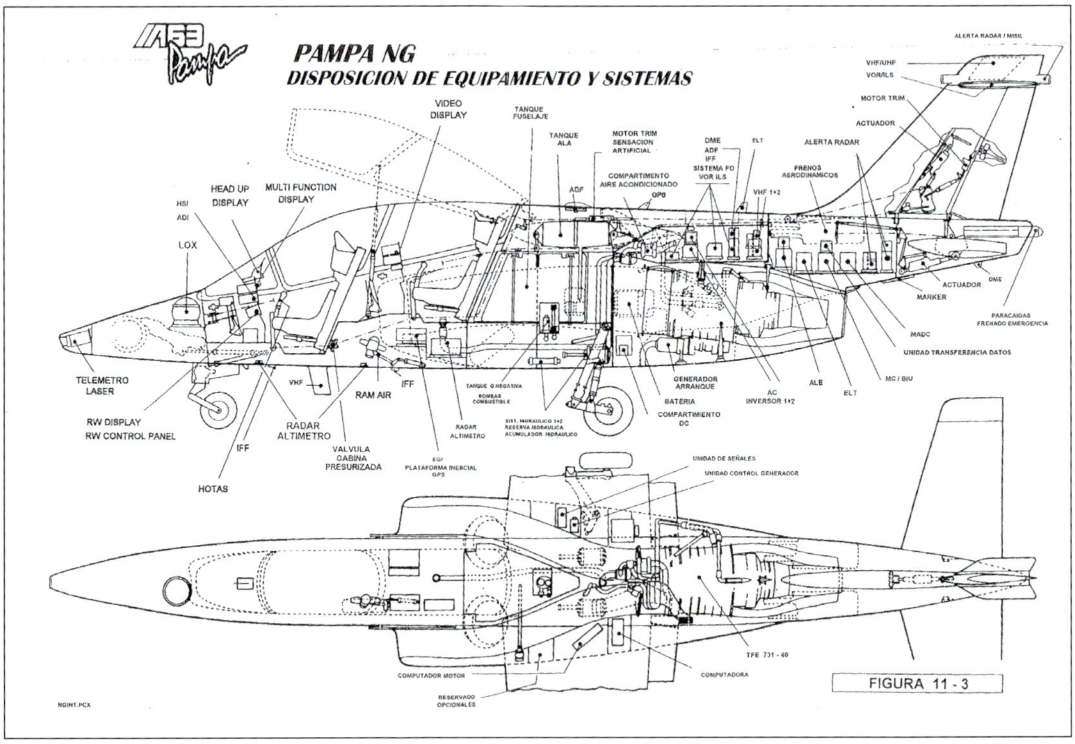

Pampa NG equipment layout.

He also planned a light attack version, which he called 'missionised', with a HUD, HOTAS commands with the weapons controls on the stick and throttle lever, Kevlar armour for the cabin floor and hydraulic system tanks and a duplicated hydraulic system. He also proposed to make studies for self-sealing tanks, an on-board oxygen generating system, the possibility of using the rear seat position for extra tanks or other systems when used with a single pilot, a rear-view camera, refuelling probe, radar warning receiver (RWR) and chaff and flare dispensers.

After Lianza's proposal, in 1996 LMAASA started to work on how to install these changes, for both the training version and the missionised one for close air support, with a limited air-to-air capability. In 1998 this idea was presented as Pampa NG (New Generation) and had two variants: NG A for training, like the current type, but with some modifications to avionics and the engine, and the NG B with more attack capacity and more power.

Engineer Nicolás Topa, who had already worked on the original Pampa project, was put in charge of the new programme and prepared the Informe Técnico I.T. FA-56/96 together with a team of twenty-one engineers and nine technicians.

They designed a new wing profile with a different leading edge with a nose drop, to increase lift and improve the loading at low speed, while it was also modified to reach up to 7Gs. Also, to add air-to-air capability, the addition wingtip pylons was studied, but this was later rejected in favour of adding a third underwing pylon, closer to the wingtip, for the missiles. It was also planned that pylons 2 and 6 would be modified to carry missiles too as well as external fuel tanks of 300 litres. As the plane was to be heavier, the main landing gear was modified with reinforcements and changing the engine for the Honeywell TFE 731-40 (later called TFE 731-40-2N) of 4,300lb thrust was also considered. Also, the team studied the possibility of adopting the Honeywell F124-GA-100 of 5,500lb thrust, but this meant a big modification to the plane. It was also planned to install a braking parachute to improve operations on short runways.

The mission equipment and avionics were to be upgraded, with a laser rangefinder in the nose, RWR in the tail, Tracor AN/ALE-40 (N) chaff and flares dispensers, and the cabin was to receive Elbit Systems avionics with one multifunction display, a new HUD, GPS and the mission computer installed on the A-4AR Fightinghawks of the Argentine Air Force. Later, the cabin was modified with a second display. Also, the weapons systems were to be improved to use guided weapons and it was expected the aircraft would be able to carry up to 2,000kg of weapons.

Alférez Fabián Pocatino, Mariano Mobilia and Diego Campasso were commissioned to develop the extra fuel tanks and system and they developed ones with 300kg of fuel capacity (around 365 litres) performing successful wind tunnel tests, but this idea was not adopted.

From 2000 the Pampas returned to life thanks to the support of LMAASA, which restarted the production of spares, mainly after a contract was signed on 15 July 2000 worth $250 million that lasted until July 2005 and included 3,407,000 work hours (including work on maintenance of the Hercules fleet of the Argentine Air Force and the IA-58D Pucará modernisation programme), which included the construction of a new series of twelve modernised planes and the modernisation of the twelve in service, plus EX-02, to the Pampa NG A level, while the contract also stated that the company had to work on selling the plane abroad, too.

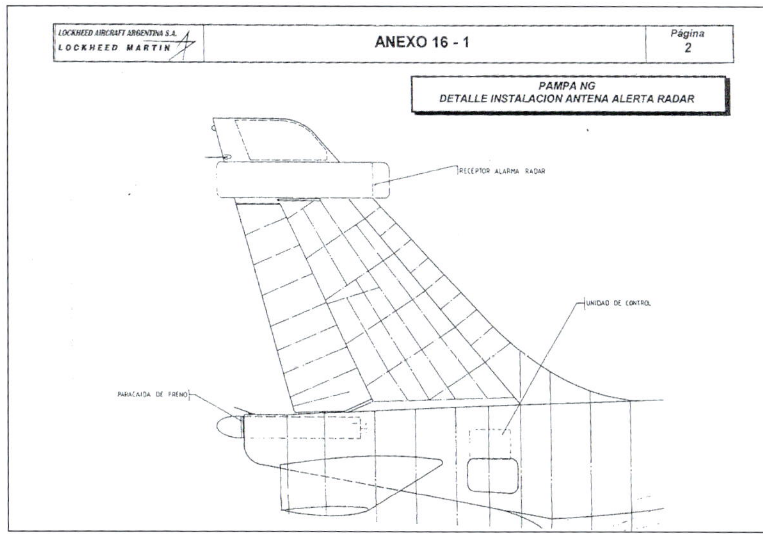

RWR antenna and parachute installation on the Pampa NG.

The plan was to finish E-816 (c/n 2021) and use it as a prototype for the new series with delivery to the CEV in 2001, while production should continue at a rate of two per month, starting with E-817 and 818.

At Farnborough 2000, James Taylor, by then president of LMAASA, and Argentine defence minister, Ricardo López Murphy, announced the signing of the contract and the development of the new version, also announcing that the Comando de Aviación Naval Argentina was again interested on the plane.

To exhibit the plane with the aim of selling it, on September 2000 E-815 was taken to South Africa in L-100-30 Hercules TC-100 of the FAA. The intention was to offer it to African air forces that could not buy more advanced planes.

By the end of 2000 the programme was renamed Pampa 2000, like the J-PATS one, and it was

Locally built FAS 250 bomb with parachute, being tested on the Pampa.

The third prototype of the Pampa seen during tests in 2010 at the Military Aviation School. *Santiago Rivas*

announced that the delivery of the first prototype, EX-03, would take place on 22 November 2001 after performing tests at the CEV between 30 July and that date. EX-02 would follow but first would be converted to the series standard after an overhaul. The original plan was to deliver EX-02 on 2 April 2002 and then continue with the modernisation with the series planes while the production line was organised again. The aim was to finish E-816 on 28 March 2003 after the delivery of the first six modernised Pampas. The plan stated that the last had to be E-827, on 18 April 2005.

Later, the programme was renamed again, now as AT-63, to be offered as an economic trainer and close support aircraft to complement the T-50 in development by Lockheed Martin. The idea was that the plane could cover the training necessities of F-16 operators, using some similar equipment. It could also serve as an attack plane for small air forces that did not have the capacity to operate more sophisticated types.

One variant, based on the NG A, was offered to some Latin American and African countries for about $3 million each. It was to have missionised avionics, improved attack capabilities, a digital 1553B Mil Bus computer, a HOTAS system, a modern instrument panel with two LCDs on each position, a new 5in multimode HUD and a TFE731-2C engine of 3,500lb of thrust, although the version for the Argentine Air Force was going to keep the original engine.

Wind tunnel tests of the extra fuel tanks.

The attack AT-63 had all what was included in the NG B plus ECM, improved combat damage resistance, a weapons capacity of 1,900kg, HOTAS and the possibility to install an inflight refuelling probe. The price was going to be $7 million.

Meanwhile, LMAASA started to offer the plane to another countries, beginning with the Fuerza Aérea Colombiana, with an offer for thirty AT-63 Pampas in 2001, followed on 19 October with the flight of KC-130 Hercules serial TC-70 to Colombia, carrying E-807. The team was commanded by Vicecomodoro Posa and demonstrations were made by Major Lianza and Captain Sanchez.

Also, an offer was made to República Dominicana for eight planes to replace its Cessna A-37Bs. Also, on 21 May 2002 the E-806 was sent to El Trompillo Air Base in Santa Cruz de la Sierra, in Bolivia, to be evaluated as a replacement for its Lockheed T-33s. However, the US weapons embargo on Bolivia impeded the export, as the Pampa had many US-built components, and instead they bought the Hongdu K-8 from China.

Pampa II

The Argentine crisis of 2001 and 2002 led to a suspension of the work and LMAASA started to renegotiate the contract. In 2003 a new modernisation programme was developed, but keeping the designation AT-63.

This new version included a INAS (Integrated Navigation and Attack System), which includes a HUD, GPS, Honeywell HG-764 EGIR radio altimeter, integrated weapon management system, a Mil Std 1553B data bus, mission computer, a 5in × 7in MFD with mission planning software, HOTAS controls and other improvements.

Also, as some potential customers requested the possibility of installing a radar, in 2001 LMAASA developed a modification of the nose to fit an AN/APG-67(V)4 multimode radar and a mock-up of the new bigger nose was shown at FIDAE 2004 besides EX-01. However, it was never tested, although this modification was offered over the years until 2009 and a model of the Pampa with the radar was shown at different exhibitions.

Meanwhile, on 10 December 2004 EX-01 was lost when it crashed at Base Aeronaval Punta Indio while it was being shown to the Chinese military and the pilot, 1st Lt Juan Pablo Martínez, lost consciousness while performing aerobatics. Five days later, EX-03 was rolled out at the factory as the prototype of the AT-63 modernisation and it made its first flight on 23 June 2005.

The second plane to be modernised was EX-02, which was also converted into the series standard and received the serial E-816, flying again on 13

One of the first Pampa Serie II on its presentation at Buenos Aires on28 April 2007. *Santiago Rivas*

February 2006 wearing a new camouflage in two tones of grey, which was adopted by the aircraft to be modernised. The plan was to deliver one or two modernised planes per month and finish the work on twelve planes by the beginning of 2007.

Also, the restart of the production line was announced, first with the completion of the four planes that were not finished yet (c/n 2021 to 2024, whose constructor numbers were changed to 1021 and 1024) and following with another six of new construction (c/n 1025 to 1030) that LMAASA said it would try to sell abroad.

Shortly after, on 28 April 2007, the first three modernised planes were delivered to the Argentine Air Force, now designated IA-63 Pampa Serie II, later known as IA-63 Pampa II, in a ceremony in which the last Morane-Saulnier MS.760 Paris were retired. The planes were E-812, E-815 and E-816, which were followed during the year by E-803, 805, 806 and 814.

The delivery of the first aeroplane built as a Pampa II took place on 16 November 2007, with E-817 (former E-816, c/n 1021) and, as no sales abroad were made, all, up until E-822 (c/n 1026), went to the Argentine Air Force, with sales finishing in 2009.

As the weight of the plane was increased, work began in late 2009 to replace the engine with the Honeywell TFE 731-40-2N, with FADEC, with no temperature or throttle movement limitations, which was limited to 3,950lb of thrust. The plan is to make it able to deliver the full 4,300lb in the future, but that means making a modification to the air intakes to avoid a stall of the compressor. The planes already upgraded to Pampa IIs were progressively modified with this engine.

The production contract was expanded to another ten airframes (c/n 1027 to 1036) with the intention of offering them for export again but they were not completed by the time the company was handed back to the Argentine state on 15 December 2009, being renamed Fábrica Argentina de Aviones Brigadier San Martín (FAdeA). In 2012 the production of a batch of another forty planes was announced, and a contract was signed in 2012. However, this was later cancelled and in 2014 a contract for only eight airframes was signed. Together with the ten contracted in 2009, the contract only covered the production of the airframes, but none of the associated systems. Also, another contract signed shortly later added another six. Currently, sixteen have been completed (c/n 1027 to 1042), with main components built of c/n 1043 and 1044 and some parts made for 1045 and 1050.

Cabin of the Pampa II. *Santiago Rivas*

The Pampa II serialled E-820 was delivered painted with the colours of the Cruz del Sur aerobatic team, as it was expected to re-equip the escadrille, which operated F-86F Sabres and Sukhoi Su-29ARs in the past, with Pampas, but this was cancelled shortly after. *Santiago Rivas*

When the Argentine government changed in December 2015, the direction of the factory was also altered and it focused on delivering planes instead of building airframes only for them to be stored.

By 2010, the idea of the close support version of the AT-63 was revived in what was now called the Pampa GT (Generación Táctica) but a lack of budget meant this did not progress.

Enter the Pampa III

On 10 October 2013 the aircraft c/n 1027 (which was assigned the serial E-823) was rolled out as a demonstrator of the Pampa III version, which had a full glass cockpit from Elbit, while it was shown with an Elbit Targo helmet with HMD. Also, Zvezda K-36LT ejection seats were installed, but they were only mock-ups and were discarded, and Martin-Baker AR-10ML (version of the Mk-10 for the Pampa) seats were installed instead, built under licence in Italy by Sicamb S.p.A., replacing the Stencel ones.

The main changes from the Pampa II were to the avionics and cockpit, with three multifunction displays instead of one, plus the HUD and Upfront Control Panel, a Data Acquisition Unit that gathers all the information, an Air Data, Attitude and Heading Reference Systems (ADAHRS) and a magnetometer on the wingtip, with all the information duplicated, a new

Pampa II serialled E-811 at FAdeA, with the FN Herstal D-HMP-250 pods and seven-tube 70mm rocket launchers. *Santiago Rivas*

Presentation of the Pampa III demonstrator (plane c/n 1027) on 10 October 2013. *Lisandro Amorelli.*

mission computer from Elbit with improved software, two Rockwell Collins VHF-4000 and one ADF-4000, new brakes for the wheels, a new canopy lock system to make the plane capable of flying at up to 42,000ft, a new alarm and failures indication panel and an ejection seat sequencer. The instruments were also prepared for operation with night vision goggles.

For air interdiction, the software of the mission computer permits the planning of very precise bombing missions in an air superiority environment, with up to 10m of precision for dropping dumb bombs.

The programme progressed slowly, with the third prototype of the Pampa being modified to a Pampa III and flying for the first time on 18 August 2015. The new government decided to go ahead with the project and on 31 March 2016 the demonstrator, now with serial EX-04, performed the first flight, being the first series production Pampa III. By 2018 the model was finally certified.

In 2019 and 2020, Fadea, the Argentine Air Force and the local company FixView worked on providing the plane with reconnaissance and targeting capacity through a pod to be installed under the belly.

At the same time, production was restarted and on 5 December 2018 the first three Pampa IIIs were handed over to the Argentine Air Force, starting with tests by the Centro de Ensayos en Vuelo. Finally, on 15 February 2019 the model entered service at the Escuadrón I of the Grupo 6 de Caza of the VI Brigada Aérea at Tandil, Buenos Aires.

The unit had been using Pampa IIs as interim planes since the Mirage family of fighters was retired by the end of 2015 and, while they were waiting for the selection of an air superiority fighter, the force decided to equip them with the improved Pampa III to increase their capacity. The Pampa III is also serving as a stopgap until a new fighter is ordered.

As the planes are now more focused on attack and air patrol missions, the serials of the Pampa IIIs were changed. While the Pampa IIs are serialled from E-801 to 822, with the E meaning Entrenamiento (Training), the new ones were initially A-700 onwards, with the A meaning Ataque, but A-700 was later re-serialled A-706.

Deliveries continued during 2019 and by early 2021 they reached the sixth Pampa III, upon which the VI Brigada Aérea sent the three Pampa IIs they had back to the IV Brigada Aérea.

From the c/n 1030 onwards (A-701), the Pampas started to use a canopy built in Argentina (previously it was imported) and landing gears made by IAI Landing Gear Systems from Israel.

By 2019 a plan was again developed to modify the underwing pylons 2 and 4 to make them able to carry extra fuel tanks, but again this was not adopted.

Pampa III Block 2

In 2019, work began on the development of what was called the Pampa III Block 2, which has increased capabilities based on an Elbit Live Virtual Constructive (LVC) training solution. This is via Embedded Virtual Avionics (EVA), which is a computer installed in the back of the plane, that includes a virtual radar based on the APG-68(V)5, virtual RWR and a datalink with about 50 miles of range to connect all the planes flying on a mission with the base and also to the simulators, so the pilots training on them can operate together with aircraft in the air. The virtual radar and RWR could be displayed on the Tactical Situation Display, which currently works with the aircraft transponders to simulate a radar screen.

It also has virtual air-to-ground modes (a ground moving-target indicator and for maritime targets),

The third prototype of the Pampa, now as a Pampa III Block 2, with the ventral gun and two Colibrí 7.62mm machine gun pods.

collision avoidance, virtual ground threats and a flight status monitor for the ground station.

To test the datalink, as the CEV only had EX-03, another plane was needed, so the plane with c/n 1027, which was stored at FAdeA, was returned to service in February 2021 and serialled EX-04. On 25 June it was officially delivered to the CEV as the second Block 2. Both EX-03 and EX-04 received a new paint scheme in March 2021, based on the scheme that the prototypes wore originally.

In 2022 EX-03 was also used to test the ventral pod for the DEFA 553 30mm cannon. Originally, four pods were made in the 1980s in Israel, but, as the company that made them did not build them anymore, FAdeA studied the design and is now producing a new version of it, with some improvements.

Also, they started to test the Tordo pod for a 7.62 MAG machine gun and work was still under way at the end of 2023. After this pod, work will continue on the Alacrán, to fit a 12.7 Browning M2 machine gun, which is under development. The CEV is also testing the FN Herstal D-HMP-250 pods on EX-03, to increase the range of weapons available with the plane. In the future, chaff and flare dispensers, will be added and these are under development, while there are also plans to integrate guided weapons and the capacity to launch AIM-9M Sidewinder missiles.

Last deliveries

In 2020, a contract was signed for the completion of c/n 1027 and from c/n 1034 to 1038, together with the modernisation of three older examples to Pampa III Block 2 standard, which were E-809, 811 and 812. Of them, by the end of 2023 c/n 1034 and 1035 had been delivered, with the other three in final assembly and, of the modernised ones, E-809 was delivered and E-811 was making the test flights before delivery.

In 2022, the Argentine Air Force decided to reopen the X Air Brigade at the Río Gallegos Military Air Base, in the southern end of Patagonia, which saw the arrival of the first three FAdeA IA-63 Pampa IIIs on 7 February 2023. These planes were all delivered equipped with 30mm gun pods in the belly.

The factory is still working on the development of a simulator for the plane, with two already ordered by the Argentine Air Force.

Export market

Between 2015 and 2019, an effort was made to export the Pampa and in July 2019 the first export contract was signed with the government of Guatemala for two planes, but with the aim of reaching a total of eight. Unfortunately, internal political problems in Guatemala ended with the cancelation of the order, but the Guatemalan Air Force expects to restart the process in the future. The government has an urgent need for planes to control its airspace, with more than forty illegal aircraft being detected operating in the country in 2019, some of them fast types such as Super King Airs and executive jets.

Also, in 2019 Bolivia was offered one plane as a payment for extra gas supplied to Argentina in that year, but Israel vetoed the operation due to the close relationship of former Bolivian president Evo Morales with the Venezuelan and Iranian governments.

Eight Pampa IIIs were also offered to Paraguay in 2019, with the option of being paid in electricity produced at the Yaciretá dam, which belongs to both countries. The Paraguayan Air Force needs an urgent replacement for their retired Xavantes and AT-33s to control their air space. Another country that has interest is Uruguay, which needs to replace their A-37B Dragonflies and is aiming to buy six, but no progress has been made since negotiations started in 2016.

With a long history of interest in the model, the Peruvian Air Force requested in 2019 a quotation for eighteen planes to replace their Aermacchi MB-339s and A-37B Dragonflies, while there was also interest from the Ecuadorian Air Force to replace their retired BAC Strikemasters with a jet trainer. Mexico is another Latin American country with a long-time interest in the Pampa and d between 2019 and 2021 negotiated the possibility of the planes being assembled there. In Central America, El Salvador and Honduras have also looked at the plane with interest.

Outside the region, Paramount Group of South Africa signed an agreement with Fadea to promote the Pampa in Africa and it offered the plane to the South African Air Force, but it was not successful on gaining a customer. In November 2019 officers of the United Arab Emirates Air Force visited FAdeA to request information and quotations for the Pampa and also asked about the possibility of the Pucará being built again.

Now, FAdeA aims to get a contract to modernise the remaining Pampa IIs to the Pampa III Block 2 standard, to take the first Pampa IIIs to that standard too and finish the remaining airframes whose completion was not contracted yet. After that, the future of Pampa production is uncertain.

The Pampa III Block 2 serialled A-708, the former EX-04, flying over the glaciers of the southern Andes in July 2023. The plane is now part of the Grupo 10 de Caza of the X Brigada Aérea. *Santiago Rivas*

Two Pampa IIIs of the VI Brigada Aérea flying over the South Atlantic in 2019. *Santiago Rivas*

38 IA-67 Córdoba and ATL

While the FMA was working with Aero Falcon and Volpar Inc. on the development of the IA-66 Pucará, the two partner companies designed a multi-role transport aircraft using as many common parts as possible with the IA-66, in order to use the tools and tooling from the Pucará production line, with the same Garrett engines as this version and thus reduce costs on a 36 per cent, while shortening the design time for the new model. The preliminary study presented in September 1980 by Volpar was called IA-67 Córdoba and envisaged the construction of three prototypes in just over a year at a cost of only $12 million, with the cost of assembly 36 per cent lower than for a new model (costing $36 million against 50). It would replace the IA-50 G-II and DC-3/C-47 in the Argentine Air Force, as well as being offered on the civilian market and abroad. Also, they studied the possibility of using the plane for firefighting and made a comparison with the Canadair CL-215.

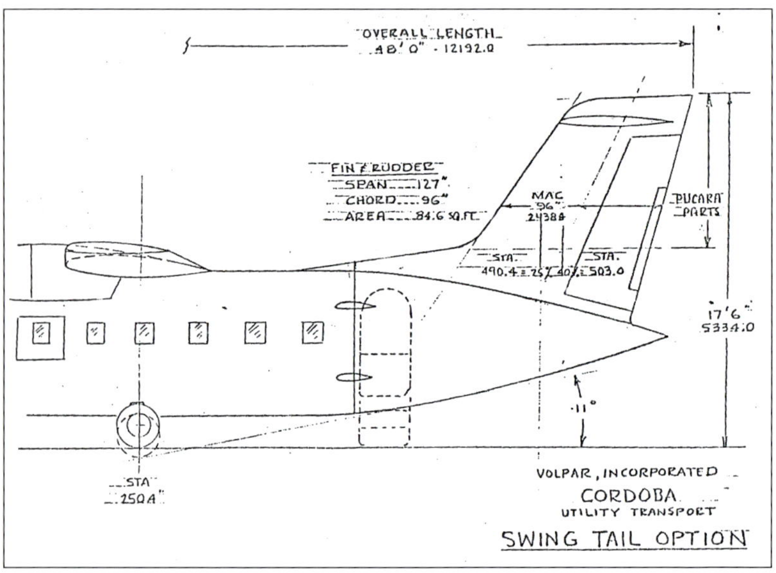

ABOVE Proposal of the IA-67 with one swing tail in place of the two booms with two tails. *Archive Santiago Rivas*

The design specified an aircraft with a configuration similar to that adopted by the Israeli IAI Arava, with two tails, using the vertical stabiliser of the Pucará. It also incorporated the wing and engine nacelles of the IA-66. The work presented by Volpar specified a five-stage plan for development, the first of which was a pre-prototype study, a prototype construction programme, a production programme, a certification programme and a final marketing stage. They expected to fly a prototype in 1981 and start series production in 1982.

The plane was to be powered by two Garrett TFE-331s of 1,045 shp each, with a maximum cruise speed of 390km/h (217 knots), a range with maximum payload of 1,400km, a take-off run with 15m obstacle of 900m, a service ceiling of 7,500m and a climb rate of 10m/s at sea level. The internal cabin was to have a section of 2.28m × 2.28m, with 2,000kg of maximum payload and capacity for twenty-three seats, for a MTOW of 8,172kg.

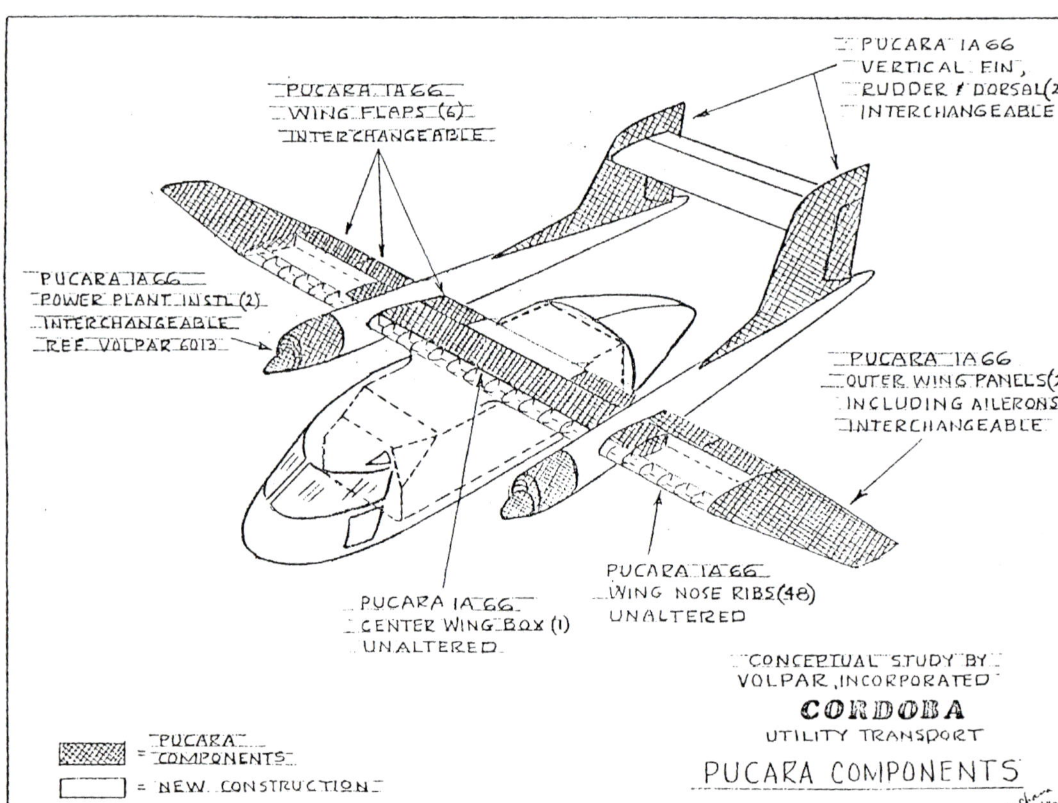

RIGHT A description of the IA-66 Pucará components expected to be used in the IA-67 Córdoba. *Archive Santiago Rivas*

For firefighting, the plane was expected to carry up to 2,750 litres of retardant, half the capacity of the CL-215, but also was half the MTOW and its cruise speed was 100km/h faster.

In response to the proposal, the FMA conducted an analysis and compared the model with the Arava, the CASA C-212, the Embraer Brasilia and the Shorts Skyvan, concluding that their performance was superior and costs were much lower. Volpar subsequently built models for wind tunnel testing and a single-tail version, using a Pucará vertical fin and stabiliser, was considered, with a swing rear fuselage for accessing the cargo hold with large loads.

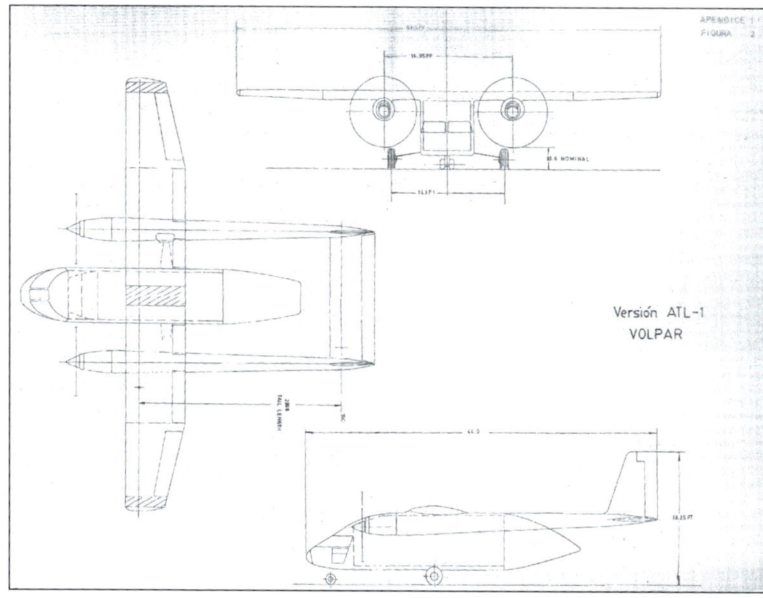

The ATL-1 proposal by Volpar, evolved from the IA-67 Córdoba.

The ATL

The proposal by Volpar attracted the interest of the FMA, which created the programme ATL (Avión de Transporte Liviano, Light Transport Aircraft), although they never used the designation IA-67 again in the documentation of the programme. The project by Volpar evolved slightly with changes to the tail, with a new vertical surface not inherited from the Pucará and some other changes to the fuselage, maintaining the configuration with two tails. This proposal was 13.41m long, had a wingspan of 16.3m and a height of 4.95m. The MTOW was 8,000kg.

By 1982, the IIAE started to work on another proposal, which initially resembled the IA-52 but with a longer fuselage, and slightly different tail. Also, thanks to the support of Dornier, with whom they were working on the IA-63 Pampa project, this proposal had a wing with a Do-A5 supercritical profile design, which was developed as TNT (Tragflügel Neuer Technologie) wing design in the 1970s and tested on a Dornier 28 before being installed on the Dornier 228, whose first prototype flew for the first time on 28 March 1981. This wing had the advantage of reducing the drag by up to 30 per cent (depending on the angle of attack), allowing a 50 per cent increase in laminar flow.

This proposal had a length of 14.25m, with a wingspan of 19.5m, a wing area of 42m2 and a height of 5.45m. Like the Volpar project, this was also proposed with two different Garrett engines, the TPE331/11 of 1,050shp and the TPE331/14 of 1,250shp. With the first engine the plane reached a MTOW of 8,700kg, which was 9,100kg with the second. The payload was 2,000kg and 2,200kg respectively.

After the second proposal was presented on December 1982, the proposal by Volpar was designated ATL-1 and the one of the IIAE was called ATL-2. Depending on the engine, each proposal was subdivided into ATL-1 or ATL-2/11 and ATL-1 or ATL-2/14.

The ATL-2 proposal made by the IIAE. Note the TNT wing designed by Dornier.

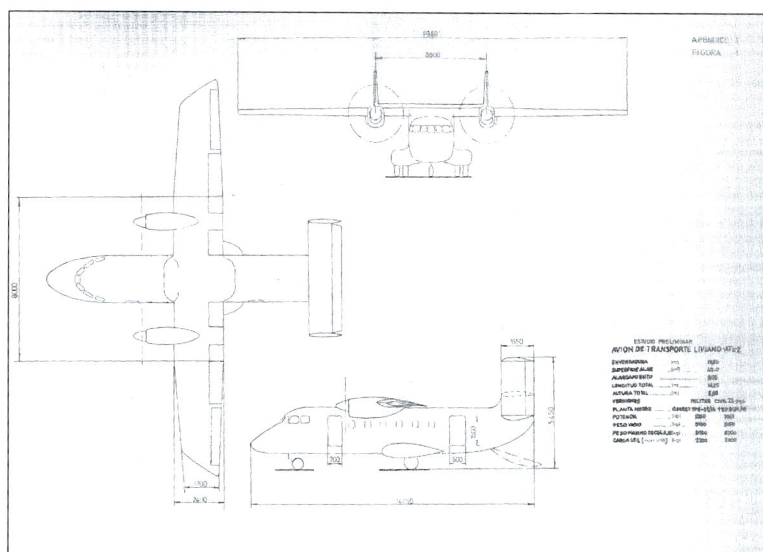

A model of the ATL preserved at the museum of the Centro de Investigación Aplicada. It has the horizontal stabilisers at about a quarter of the height of the vertical one instead of on the sides of the rear fuselage. This model was shown at Farnborough in 1984 and other exhibitions. *Santiago Rivas*

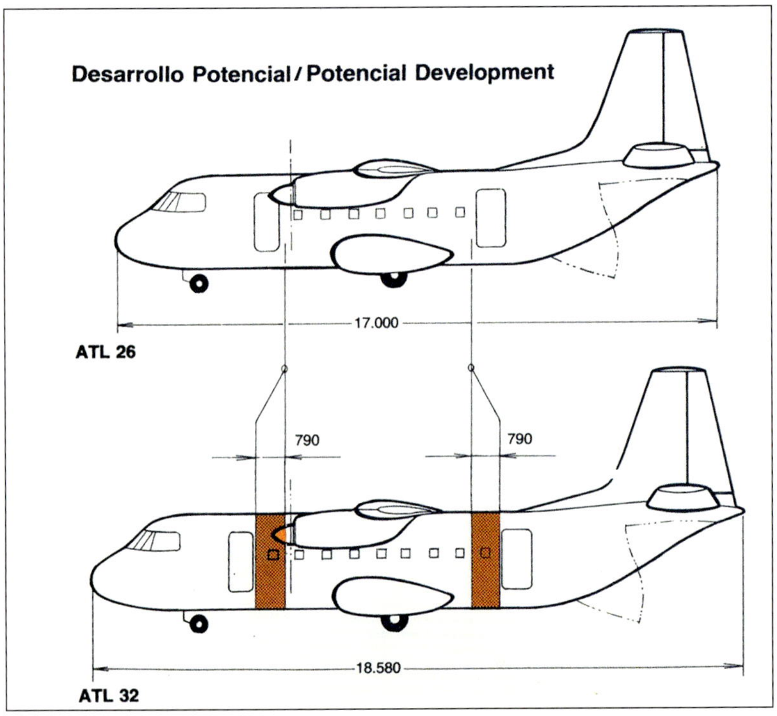

Side view of the ATL including the enlarged proposal, for thirty-two passengers.

An analysis between the ATL-2/11 and 14 made in a file numbered 398 in December 1982, determined that, while the less powerful ATL-2/11 version did not attain some of the requested performances, it could be developed as a more modest cargo plane with capacity for up to twenty-three seats and a MTOW of 8,300kg.

Another file, numbered 399, compared the two proposals of the ATL and considered that the ATL-2 was able to reach the target of being able to operate from unprepared runways of 900m thanks to the design of its wing, while it was not possible with the conventional NACA profile wing of the ATL-1. While the ATL-1/14 had a climb rate of 12.2m/s against 11.5 of the ATL-2/14 and a slightly higher service ceiling (11,500 and 11,300m respectively) due to its reduced weight, the ATL-2/14 performed far better at high speed and was 14 knots faster, with 275 knots against 261 of the ATL-1/14. The ATL-1/11 could not reach the requested speed of 220 knots, with 214 knots.

After this analysis, the proposal by Volpar was discarded and in early 1983 a longer version of the ATL-2, for twenty-nine seats, with a fuselage of 16.54m length, was proposed.

At the same time, a new proposal was made, which was a high-wing aircraft with a single tail and cargo ramp in the rear fuselage, similar in some respects to the CASA CN-235 but smaller and with a pressurised cabin. The fuselage was 16.75m long in the first layouts, later extended to 17m, with a wingspan of 19.65m, a wingspan of 42m2 and a height of 7.1m. The engines were also the TPE331/14, the empty weight was 5,800kg and the MTOW was 10,000kg, with a maximum payload of 3,000kg plus a maximum fuel load of 1,400kg. The maximum cruise speed was estimated on 255 knots with a climb rate of 10m/s, a service ceiling of 10,000m, a take-off run of 900m and a landing one of 830m. Maximum range was 1,400km and maximum endurance was four hours.

The internal cabin had a length of 7.95m with 1.11 extra metres of the rear ramp or baggage hold, totalling 9.06m.

In the civil transport version, the cabin was designed to carry up to twenty-six passengers with up to four crew members and had a toilet, with a luggage compartment in place of the rear ramp, which was removed. For cargo, it had a rear ramp and space for up to three LD1 containers, while for medical evacuation it would have capacity for fifteen stretchers and five attendants.

The military version would have room for twenty-six paratroopers.

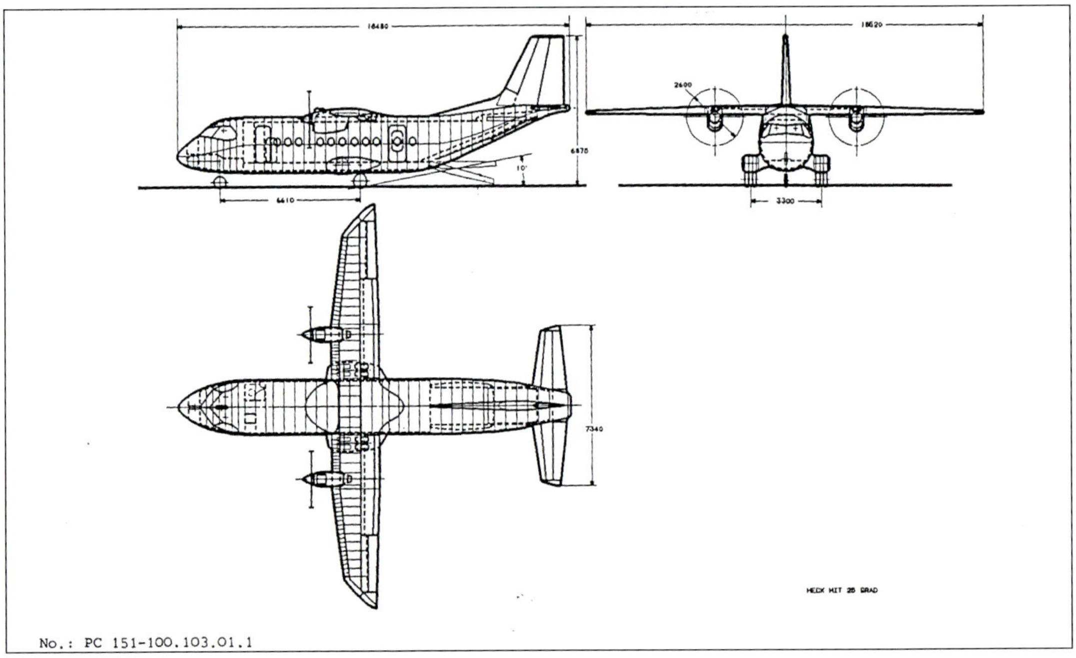

Three views of the Dornier proposal for the ATL, with the TNT wing, new tail design and slightly different nose.

A longer fuselage version was also planned, for up to thirty-two passengers, with a fuselage 18.58m long.

A model was shown at Le Bourget during June 1983, when it was announced that the FMA was in talks with Peru and Venezuela for possible joint ventures, while the company estimated a market of at least 100 aircraft, including the Argentine Air Force to replace the Douglas DC-3.

During that year and in 1984, wind tunnel tests were made, including models with the horizontal stabiliser installed on the sides of the fuselage and others with them a quarter the way up the vertical fin.

On 4 September 1984 Garrett made a proposal for the installation of the more powerful TPE331-15AW engine which was under development and delivered up to 1,400shp at 5,000ft (1,712shp at sea level), having the same power section but increased capacity gearing and water/methanol augmentation, while they announced they were working with manufacturers to develop more efficient propellers.

The company expected to compete with models like the Embraer EMB-120 Brasilia, Casa C-212, Saab SF-340, DHC-6 Twin Otter and Antonov An-28 both in the civil and military markets, with a small plane that could be easily configured for passengers and cargo.

In September 1983, Dornier delivered an analysis of their TNT wing modified for the ATL, with a centre section extended by 1.55m from that of the Dornier 228, with the engine gondolas moved outwards accordingly and 10 per cent heavier.

The involvement of Dornier grew considerably and in 1984 they worked together with the FMA on a redesign of the plane, with the TNT wing, a new nose and a new swept tail. The new design was 18.48m long, with a wingspan of 18.52m and a height of 6.87m.

Although there were negotiations to reach an agreement with Dornier for a joint venture, or to contract the German company only to support with the design, the programme slowed down in 1984 and only some wind tunnel tests were made until 1986, when the factory decided to cancel the ATL in favour of the IA-70/CBA-123.

A model of the ATL-2 proposal.

The IA-67 ATLR proposal

In December 2009, after the factory returned to the Argentine state, the company showed the draft of a new project called IA-67 ATLR (Avión de Transporte Liviano Regional), which took its basis from the ATL project and developed with different changes that made it like a smaller version of the ATR 42 aircraft. The project proposed four versions: the ATLR-L for twenty-six passengers, the ATLR-LE for thirty-two passengers, both without rear ramp, the ATLR-C for twenty-six passengers of 3,500kg of cargo and the ATLR-CE for thirty-two passengers or 4,000 of cargo, both with rear ramp. The design did not use the TNT wing but a conventional one and had a T tail.

FAdeA also planned the possibility of developing versions for maritime surveillance, anti-submarine warfare, COMINT and ELINT.

Due to the lack of funding, this proposal never went beyond the drawing board and was abandoned shortly after.

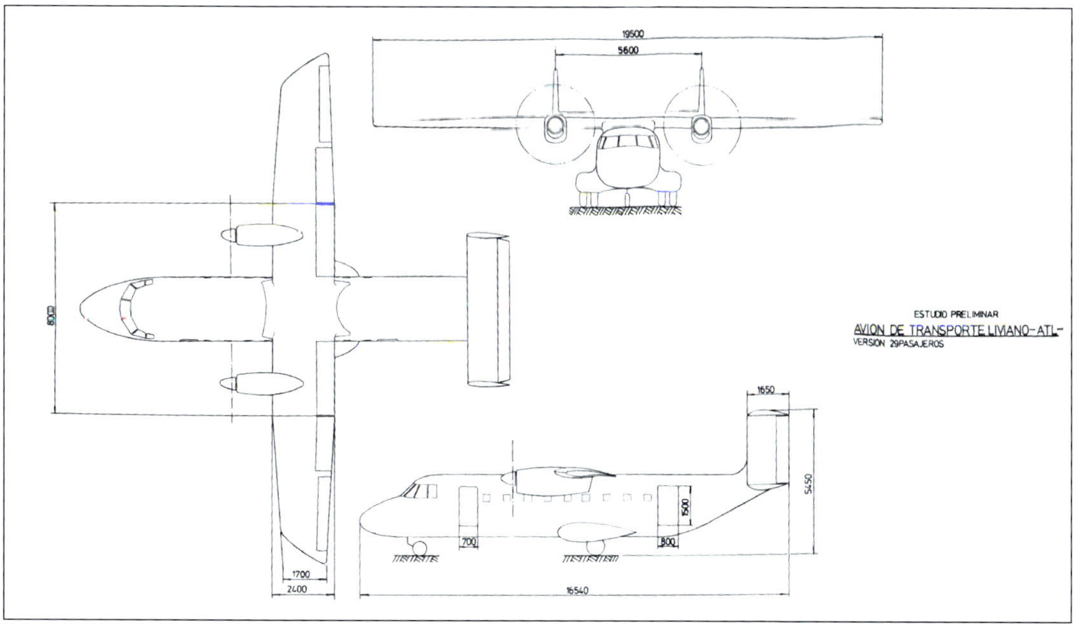

A longer version of the ATL-2 proposal for twenty-nine passengers.

39 **IA-68**

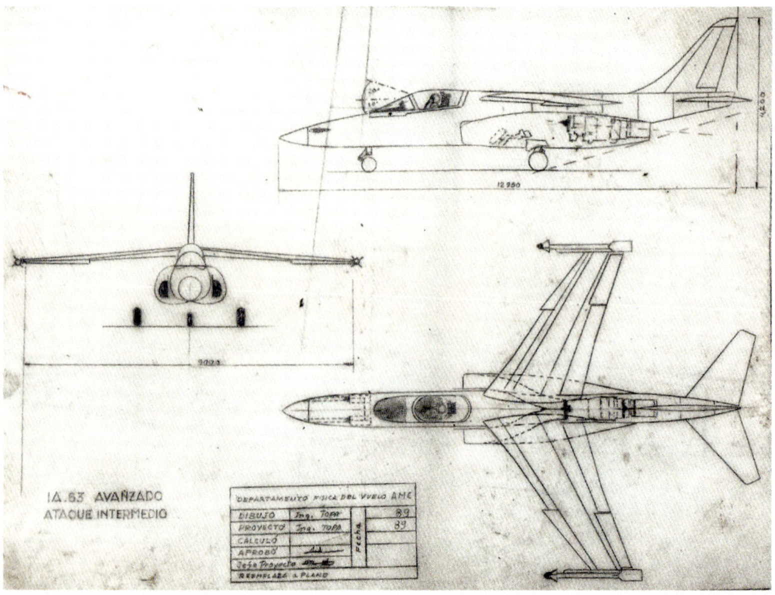

Layout of the Pampa Avanzado of 1989, keeping the wings and stabilisers of the original layout but with a new front fuselage and the vertical fin of the Pampa.

After the decision to cancel the IA-60, the Argentine Air Force was still looking for a replacement for the Douglas A-4B and A-4C Skyhawk fleet and the intention was to do it with a locally built plane. In September 1984 engineer Nicolás Topa, who had taken part in IA-63 Pampa development, worked on a draft of what he called the IA-63 Avanzado, aiming for a light attack aeroplane using the IA-63 Pampa as a basis but extensively modified, producing as a result a totally different aircraft.

This project was also called Avión de Ataque y Apoyo Táctico by the Argentine Air Force but in later documents appears as the IA-68. The initial configuration was of a plane similar to the Aeritalia – Aermacchi – Embraer AMX: single seat, with a radar in the nose, a length of 12.92m, wingspan of 9m, height of 4.7m, a swept wing with an angle of 36.3° on the leading edge and 19° on the trailing edge and a dihedral of -4°. The empty weight was 4,500kg, the normal take-off weight 5,340kg, the MTOW was 9,650kg, the maximum wing loading was 460kg/m2, the internal fuel was 2,150kg and it was expected to carry up to 750kg of fuel in external tanks.

The planned performance included a maximum speed of 1,093km/h, a penetration speed of 926km/h at low level, a maximum Mach of 0.95 at 9,144m or Mach 1.2 in a dive, with a cruise Mach of 0.82. The climb rate was 80m/sec, the service ceiling was 15,000m, the take-off distance was 915m and for landing it was 1,100m. The maximum ferry range with external fuel was 2,778km and the radius of action was 1,020km.

The design was expected to carry up to 4,000kg of weapons on four underwing pylons, plus two on the wingtips for missiles and one under the fuselage, while it would have two 30mm internal guns with up to 200 projectiles each.

The planned engines were a Turbo Union RB.199 turbofan of 4,300kg of thrust or a General Electric GE 404-100 of 4,814kg.

By March 1986 a preliminary design was readied, while, at the same time, the Argentine Air Force

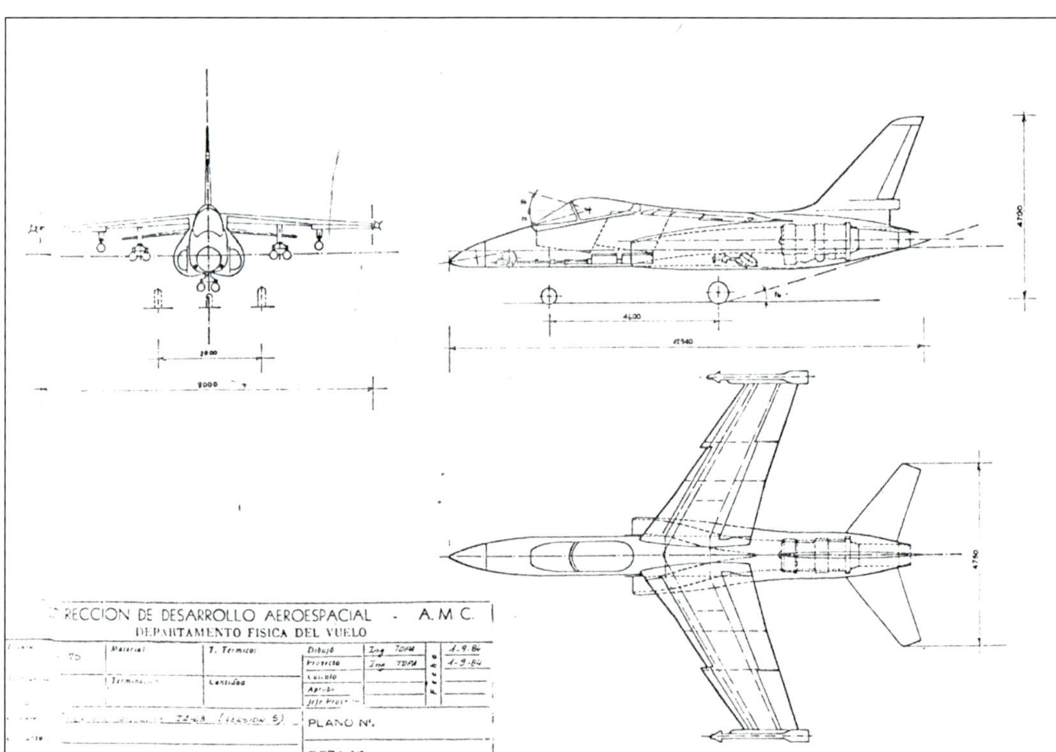

First layout of an advanced Pampa, dated 1 September 1984, described in some documents as IA-68. The configuration was similar to that of the AMX.

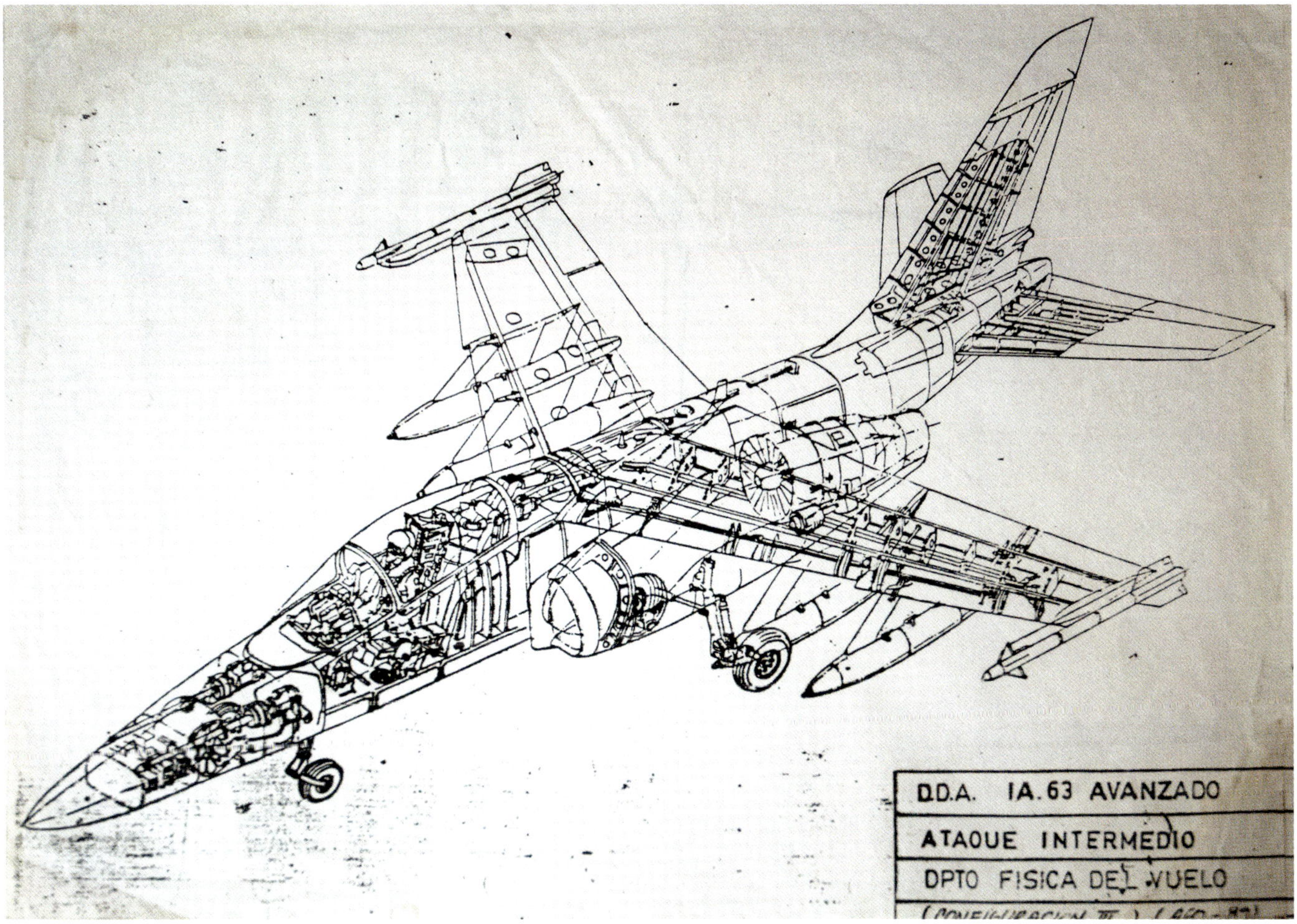

Cutaway of the Pampa Avanzado of 1989.

studied possible participation in the AMX programme, through the Área de Material Córdoba. This was ruled out by 1987 and Topa continued working on his proposal. By 1989 he presented another design, described as the IA-63 Avanzado, which had a modified fuselage, with a different nose with two 12.7mm machine guns in place of the front seat of the Pampa, in the upper part of the nose, a different cabin than the previous design and a Pratt & Whitney B-100-PR engine with the aim of reaching a maximum speed of 1,600km/h. The wing, stabilisers and vertical fin and air intakes were the same as in the IA-68.

Another proposed configuration kept the tail and wing of this proposal and the landing gear of the Pampa, but with a frontal area similar to that of an F-16 Fighting Falcon, with the air intake under the cabin.

These plans never went beyond this preliminary stage due to the budget cuts that the factory suffered because of the economic crisis in Argentina in 1989, which was followed by the cancellation of almost all projects and privatisation. Nevertheless, this idea stayed in the mind of Topa, and returned with less ambition in the form of the Pampa NG in 1996.

Another draft of the Pampa Avanzado, with the nose similar to that of the F-16. *Archive César Arreguez*

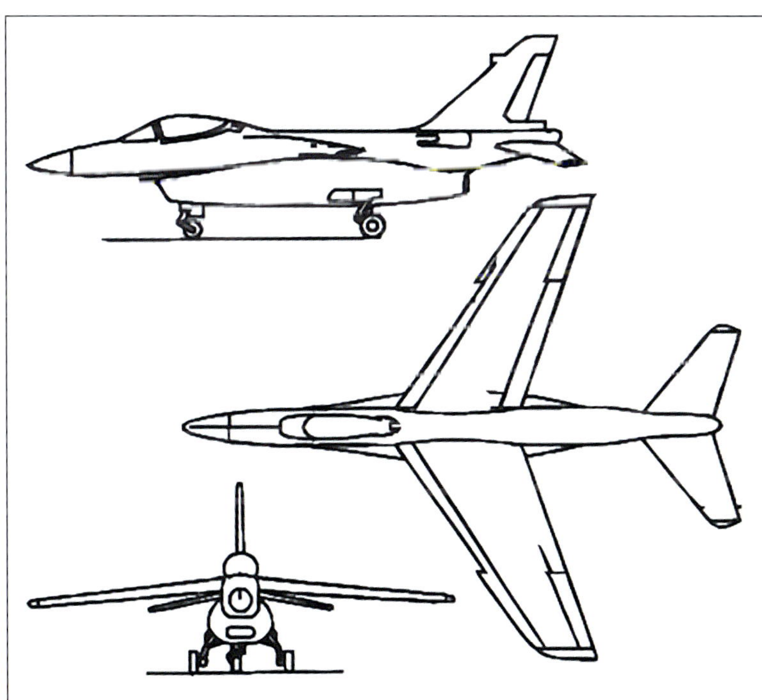

40 **IA-70/CBA-123 and CBA-130**

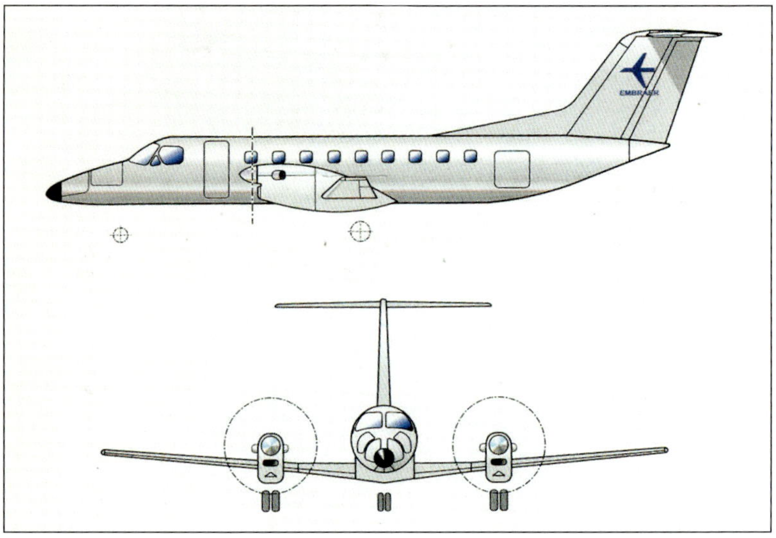

ABOVE The first configuration proposed for the EMB-123, with two engines on the wings. *Illustration Lauro Ney Batista*

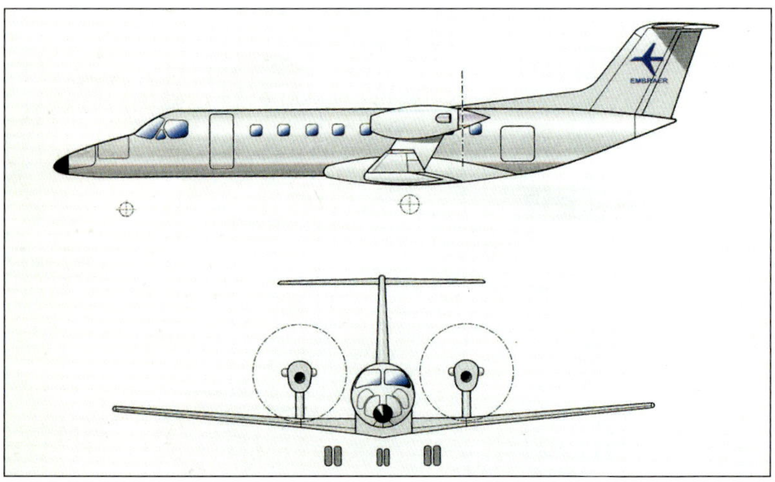

ABOVE The second proposed configuration for the EMB-123 with the engines on configuration over the wings. *Illustration Lauro Ney Batista*

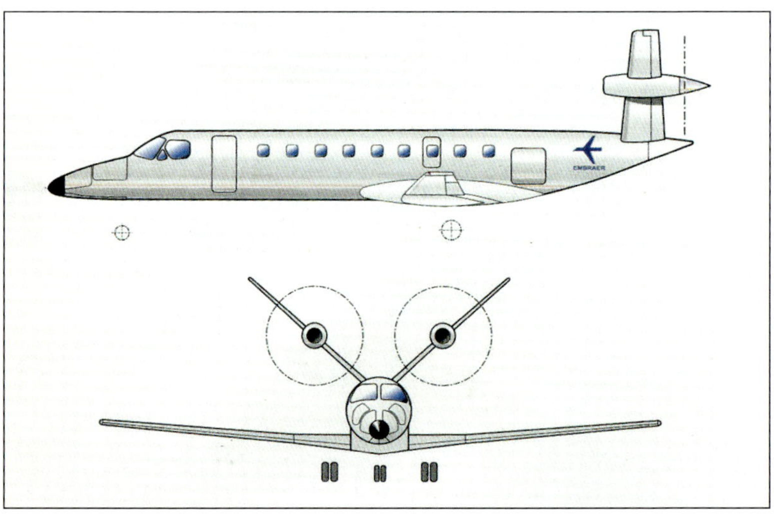

LEFT The third proposed configuration for the EMB-123 with V tail and the engines on the tail. *Illustration Lauro Ney Batista*

An Embraer project

When the Brazilian company Embraer was formed in 1969, its first project was the EMB-110 Bandeirante, a light turboprop that, in some ways, was born to compete with the IA-50 Guaraní II as the initial design and three prototypes, designated EMB-100, had almost the same cargo capacity (nine seats and a toilet in the passenger cabin. The EMB-110, meanwhile, was bigger and had capacity to carry up to twelve passengers (sixteen in the EMB-110C and nineteen in the EMB-110P1 version), thanks to its wider fuselage, with rows of three seats instead of only one on each side of the aisle. This, and a much better marketing and sales campaign, made it far more successful, with almost 500 examples built in all its versions. However, Embraer understood that there was a need for a plane with a pressurised cabin and in 1975 proposed the EMB-120 Araguaia with twenty-one seats, which shared the fuselage, wings and tail with the EMB-121 Xingu; the EMB-123 Tapajós, the latter with up to eighteen seats in a high-density configuration or ten in a more comfortable one; and the EMB-125 with twenty-six seats. Due to budget constraints, only the EMB-121 was built, being the first pressurised design of Embraer. The other two were cancelled, with the designation EMB-120 being used for the larger thirty-seat Brasilia.

By 1978, Embraer presented a pressurised proposal of the Bandeirante, called the EMB-110P3, but the shape of the fuselage had limitations to be pressurised and could only fly at up to 16,000ft with a pressure equal to that of 8,000ft, although the service ceiling was 22,600ft. This evolved into an improved version proposed in 1980, with a new T tail, like the Xingu and Brasilia, but it was cancelled shortly after because the company was focused on the production of the two other pressurised models.

By 1985, after the development of the Brasilia and Xingu was finished and resources were available to continue with new projects, the company returned to the idea of a nineteen-seat pressurised turboprop and went back to what had been studied in the design of the Araguaia and Tapajós, using the same metal semi-monocoque fuselage but with new wings and equipped with Pratt & Whitney Canada PT6A-67 engines of 1,200shp with four-bladed propellers of 2.7m of diameter. Composite materials were used in some parts that were not subjected to stress and was to be equipped with an APU to operate from airfields with no ground support. The passenger cabin was 9.12m long, with a 1.72m diameter and a maximum height of 1.65m, with nine seats on the left side and ten on the right,

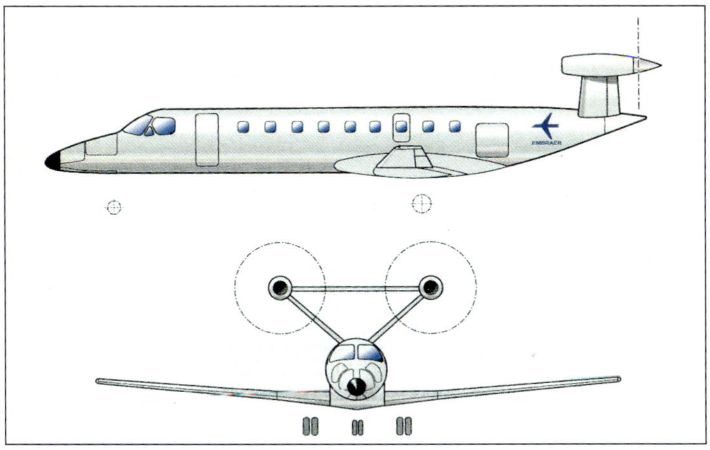

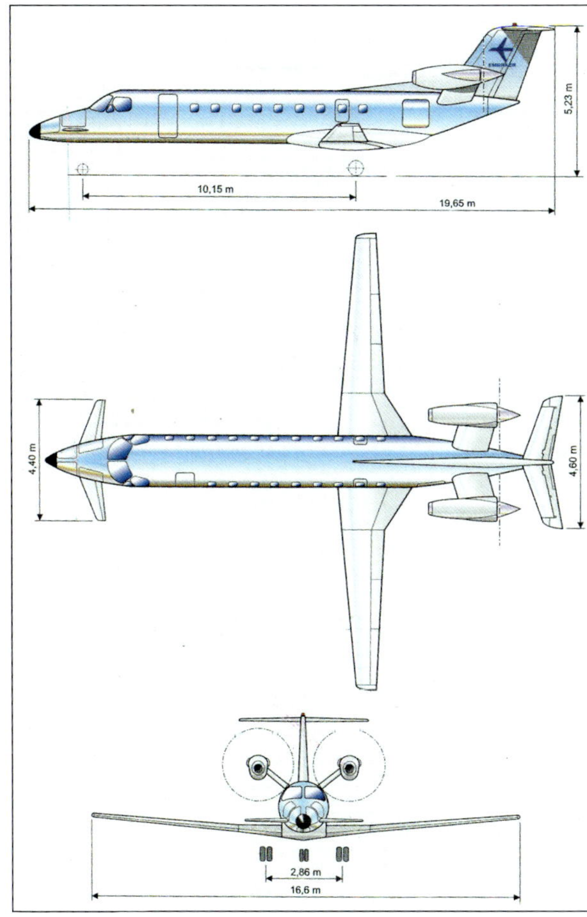

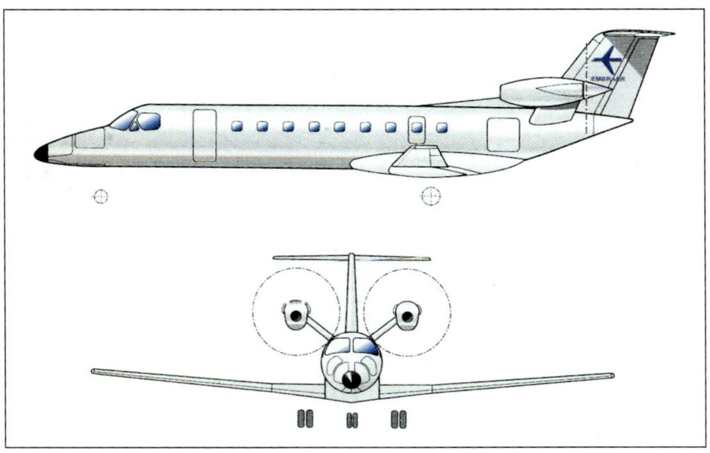

TOP LEFT A very unorthodox configuration proposed for the EMB-123 with a triangular tail. *Illustration Lauro Ney Batista*

TOP RIGHT An EMB-123 configuration with canards, to improve the performance. *Illustration Lauro Ney Batista*

ABOVE The first EMB-123 proposal with the engines on the sides of the rear fuselage, in pusher layout. *Illustration Lauro Ney Batista*

RIGHT The concept demonstrator of the EMB-123 with EMB-121 Xingu wings. *Illustration Lauro Ney Batista*

BELOW Wind tunnel model of the EMB-123 with canards, preserved at the Centro de Investigación Aplicada of the Argentine Air Force. It was tested there to analyse this proposal before it was decided to adopt the EMB-120 fuselage with a shorter cabin. *Santiago Rivas*

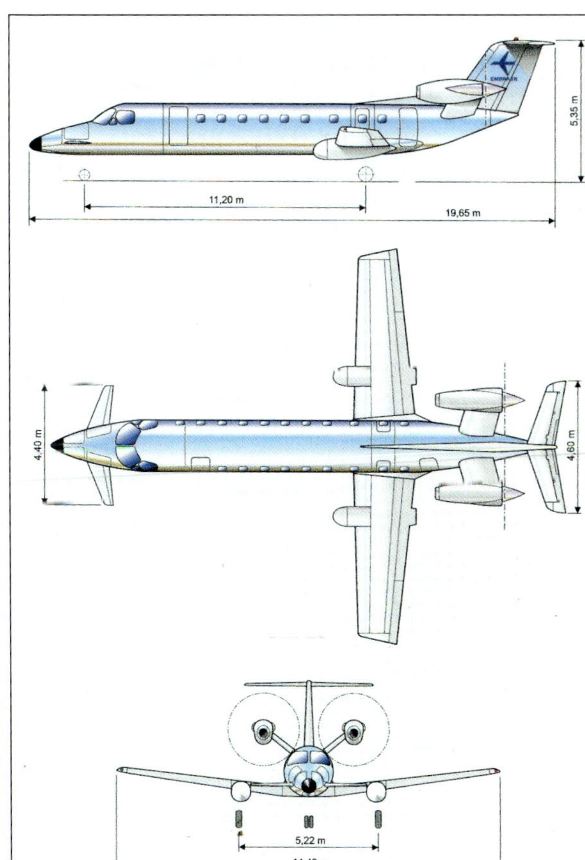

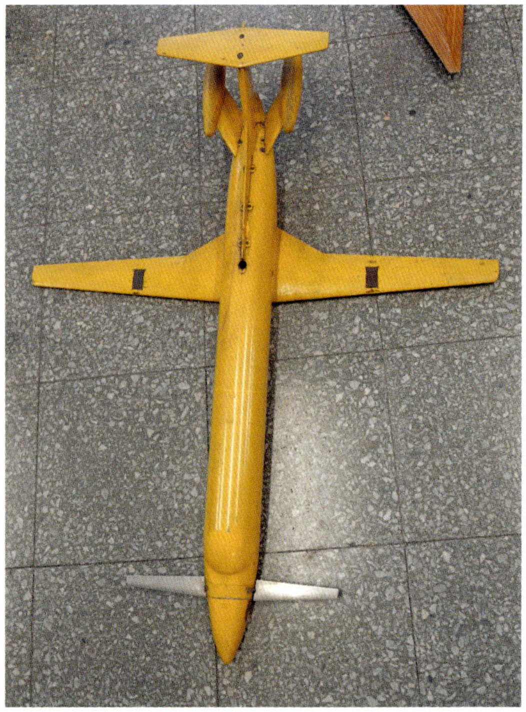

Wind tunnel model of the EMB-123 with canards, preserved at the Centro de Investigación Aplicada of the Argentine Air Force. It was tested there to analyse this proposal before it was decided to adopt the EMB-120 fuselage with a shorter cabin. *Santiago Rivas*

plus a steward seat and an electronics rack to the front, behind the pilots.

The pressurisation enabled the cabin to have sea-level pressure up to a height of 21,000ft or one equivalent of 8,000ft when flying at up to 40,000ft. Six configurations were initially studied.

The first version was the most conservative, with the two engines on the wings, but separated from the fuselage to reduce the noise inside the cabin, but this generated a problem in controlling the aircraft in asymmetric flight, increasing the minimum control speed, while the space for flaps was limited, increasing the stall, take-off and landing speeds. The second proposal had the engines in a pusher configuration and installed above the wings, reducing the size of the wing, but the pylons added too much weight and drag, as they had to be high, so the propellers were out of the turbulence generated by the wing.

Two other configurations were very unconventional, the first having a V tail with the engines installed in the middle of each tail in a pusher position. However, this meant the tail was not very efficient, with a tendency to roll, especially during single-engine operation. Also, it could have vibration problems, could not use a de-icing system on the tail and the tail needed to have a very strong structure, meaning it would be heavy. The fourth configuration was a variation of the former, with a horizontal stabiliser linking the two engine nacelles, meaning that the tail was a triangle. This made for a more robust tail structure, and more efficient tail and simpler control systems, but the rolling problem continued as did the heavy tail.

The fifth configuration had the engines installed on the sides of the rear fuselage, in a pusher configuration, but this, as the wing was also located at the rear, created too much weight at the back of the plane and moved the gravity centre backward. However, it allowed for bigger flaps to reduce the stall speed. An advantage was the reduction of the noise in the cabin, thanks to the position of the engines. The sixth and last configuration was similar but added canards on the nose to improve the performance with the centre of gravity so much to the rear. The wingspan was 16.6m, with a wing area of 22m^2, with fowler flaps and a 1,300 litres fuel tank in the centre part of the wing, divided into two compartments. The canards had a span of 4.4m with 19° of sweep and a surface area of 2.9m2. The empty weight was to be 4,300kg, with an operational empty weight of 4,560kg, a MTOW of 7,000kg and a landing weight of 6,800kg. The maximum cruise speed was 611km/h, with a range of 555km with maximum cargo, and a cruise altitude of 35,000ft, taking off and landing, at sea level, on a 1,200m runway at maximum weight.

The controls were mechanical, but the flaps were controlled by fly-by-wire. The avionics were to be digital from Collins, including EFIS (Electronic Flight Instrumentation System) and EICAS (Engine Indication and Crew Alerting System) with six multifunction displays and a HUD for the pilot. The plane was the first in its category to be designed to be certified with FAR Part 25 rules, which were used by the big passenger jets.

Embraer planned to first build a concept demonstrator, which was to use EMB-121 Xingu wings with fairings for the wheels, to reduce the construction costs and timing and to prove the concept of the position of the engines and the canards. This would be followed by two prototypes, two static and fatigue tests airframes, an iron bird and an electrical rig for system tests, an engineer mock-up to test the installation of the equipment and wind tunnel models.

The EMB-120-3 test aeroplane (PT-ZBA c/n 120001), used to test the installation of the Garrett TPF351-20 in the rear fuselage position. *Embraer*

A joint programme

By late 1985, the Brazilian government saw that Embraer could not undertake any new developments, as it was also focused on the AMX project with Aermacchi and Aeritalia and the economic situation of the country and also of state-owned Embraer was not the best. On 17 January 1986 the president of Embraer, Ozires Silva, signed an agreement with the Argentine defence minister, Roque Carranza, for co-operation between the Brazilian company and the Argentine companies Chincul (which, as well as Embraer, was producing Piper types under licence) and the Área de Material Córdoba (AMC).

In February 1986, a meeting was held in São Paulo between the teams of both companies, followed by another at Córdoba in late March, and by the end of April Embraer presented the EMB-123 project to the Brazilian Air Force, revealing that the type was to be the first to be developed together with Argentina. Also considered was the possibility of adding the AMC to the AMX programme and the production of parts for the EMB-120 Brasilia, for which just the passenger seats were built in the end. It was agreed that Argentina would take charge of 33 per cent of the EMB-123 project and production and Brazil the remaining 67 per cent. The plan was that Argentina would produce the wings and tail surfaces, with Brazil in charge of the fuselage.

The Brazilian government approved the plan to co-produce the EMB-123 and the idea was also approved by the FMA and the Argentine government. On 1 October 1986 the presidents of Argentina, Raúl Alfonsín, and of Brazil, José Sarney, signed an agreement between both countries and officially launched the project, which received the designation IA-70 at the AMC.

During the first half of 1986 wind tunnel tests were carried out with a model at Córdoba, which is still preserved. With the Brasilia now in production and proving successful, by mid-1986 it was decided to redesign the project, using the nose, tail and fuselage of the Brasilia, which had the same diameter as the Xingu but with a different structure, with the original wing planned for the EMB-123.

The basic layout was exhibited at Farnborough Air Show between 31 August and 7 September 1986, showing a shorter Brasilia, with a new wing with supercritical profile and the engines on the sides of the rear fuselage. Also, it was decided to use the same passenger seats of the Brasilia, which were narrower than those originally planned, meaning it was possible to have a shorter fuselage as the nineteen passengers were now accommodated in six rows of three seats each, with four seats at the rear end of the cabin, making it possible to eliminate the canards.

It was also planned to develop an executive transport version, with different cabin configurations, for six or eight passengers and a stewardess.

The initial market studies considered a need for ninety aeroplanes in Argentina (the Argentine Air Force planned to buy twenty to augment and replace the IA-50 G-II), 120 in Brazil and at least another 200 in the rest of the world to replace or complement the Bandeirante. It would have a basic price of \$3.3 million, while the intention was to have the first series production aeroplane ready by 1990.

The new design was to have a cargo capacity of 2,000kg, with a passenger cabin 1.73m wide and 6.74m long, 2.38m shorter. A folding seat for a stewardess was to be installed close to the access door, while the cabin would have a toilet and galley.

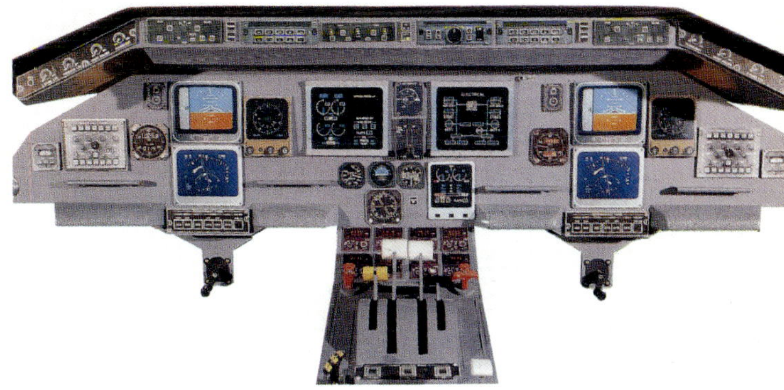

ABOVE The final instrument panel of the CBA-123.

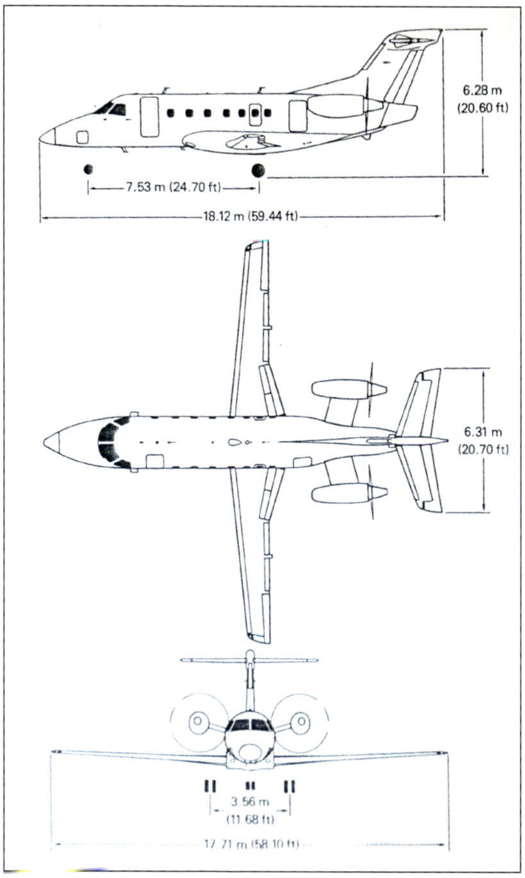

LEFT Three views of the CBA-123.

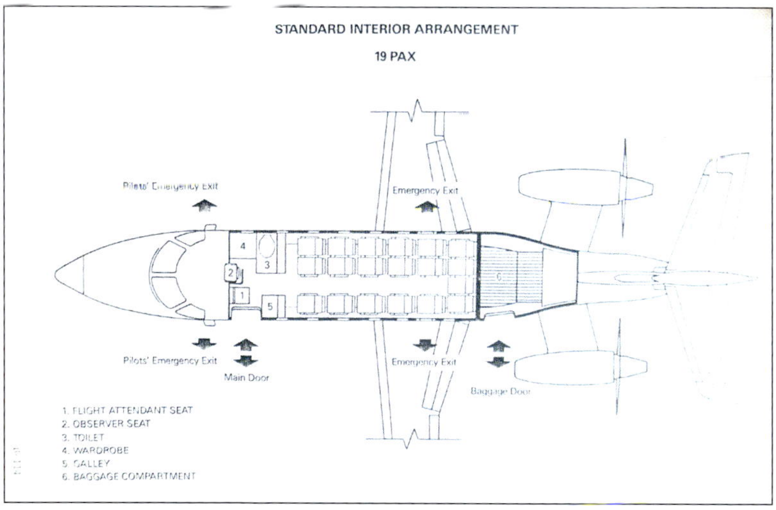

BELOW Internal layout of the CBA-123 in nineteen-seat configuration.

Construction of the first two prototypes at São José dos Campos in Brazil. *Archive Mario Vinagre*

Pressurisation was planned to have the pressure of 7,200ft while flying at 36,000ft. A cargo hold of 6.3m3 and 450kg capacity was planned for the rear fuselage.

The new design was expected to reach a cruise speed of 630km/h and a maximum one of 750km/h, with a range with maximum cargo and at cruise speed of 830km.

On 21 May 1987 the final agreement was signed to start the project, in which it was decided that, while the construction percentages would be the same, FMA would produce section I of the central fuselage and sections I and II of the rear fuselage and the tail, with Embraer building the nose, section II of the central fuselage, and the wings, engine nacelles and rudder. The project was now renamed CBA-123, with CBA meaning Cooperación Brazil Argentina, leaving behind the designations EMB-123 and IA-70. The name Paraná was suggested as a name, as this was a region shared by both countries, but this was never adopted.

In September of that year the final selection of the engines was made, the Garrett TPF351-20 of 1,300shp each, which were specifically developed for the type, with pusher six-blade Hartzell HC-E6A-5 propellers, with FADEC (Full Authority Digital Engine Control) making it possible to reach a cruise speed of 647km/h at 27,000ft. This made the type more efficient than any of its competitors and it almost reached the performance of a light jet.

By early 1988 the design of the rear fuselage had been modified with a ventral fin, but this was changed by the middle of that year to a new design that was different from that of the EMB-120 and without a ventral fin, which was the final configuration.

The final design had a wingspan of 17.72m, a wing area of 27.2m2, a length of 18.09m and a height of 5.97m. The empty weight was 6,230kg and the MTOW was 9,000kg.

To test the installation of the engines, an EMB-120 Brasilia, designated EMB-120-3, was modified with the addition of an extra engine on the left side of the rear part of the fuselage, but in a tractor configuration, flying for the first time on 4 January 1989 under the command of Embraer's test pilot Gilberto Pedrosa Schittini.

Three prototypes were to be built, two of them (constructor numbers 801 and 802) at Embraer in São José dos Campos, and one (c/n 803) at the FMA, while two static and fatigue airframes (c/n 804 and 805) were to be built.

Running the engines of the first prototype of the CBA-123 prior to the first flight on 18 July 1990.

The CBA-123 flies

Construction of the first prototype began in March 1989, with the first subjoints started in July, while in February 1990 the FMA delivered the components it had built. The economic crisis that both countries were facing by then, with Argentina suffering hyperinflation in 1989, slowed the project, but on 21 June 1989 the FMA received a loan from local banks to finance their part of the project, and on 22 June 1990 the first prototype of the CBA-123 was rolled out, serialled PT-ZVE.

On 18 July 1990 the type made its first flight from São José dos Campos piloted by Embraer chief test pilot Gilberto Pedrosa Schittini with co-pilot Luiz Alberto

Madureira and engineer Luiz Fernando Tedeschi. On the 30th it was officially presented and named Vector, in the presence of the Argentine and Brazilian presidents, Carlos Menem and Fernando Collor de Mello. On 10 August the plane flew non-stop the 2,100km to the facilities of the FMA in Córdoba in slightly more than four hours, at an average speed of 578km/h (with 28km/h of headwind) and at 9,145m of altitude, to be presented at the Argentine Air Force Day. The plane took off with a weight of 9,600kg, 600kg over the MTOW, but carrying 1,100kg of test equipment.

This flight was used to test the aeroplane on long flights as it was planned to send it for exhibition at Farnborough in September 1990, where the CBA-123 was introduced to the world after flying from Brazil to the United Kingdom with six stops and with five crew members. By then, the prototype had already flown fifty hours. The presentation, for which the plane received a paint scheme of white, red and blue (the first flights were without paint), was a great success and caught the attention of the international press.

The second prototype, serialled PT-ZVB, flew for the first time at São José dos Campos on 15 March 1991 and received a different paint scheme, of white, yellow and orange. This plane, unlike the first, was equipped with the APU at the rear end of the fuselage, which the first prototype received later. Shortly after, between 15 and 22 June of that year, it was presented at the Paris Air Show.

By that time, the plane had obtained letters of intent for 154 units, while the companies considered there was a potential to sell about 400. However, the financial situation of Embraer and the FMA was very complicated, and both countries had decided to privatise them. Also, the CBA-123 was a very advanced aircraft and, while that made it more efficient and safer than any of its competitors, it also made it too expensive, making it impossible to secure contracts.

By 1991 progress had started to slow, but in May 1993 studies were made for a larger version, called CBA-130, for thirty seats, with General Electric CT7-9 engines in the same location as in the CBA-123 but in a front-drive propeller position.

The first flight of the first CBA-123 prototype on 18 July 1990. The plane was not yet painted.

The first flight of the second prototype of the CBA-123, without paint. *Archive Mario Vinagre*

The crisis of both companies not only slowed down the programme, but also affected potential sales, as airlines started to lose interest in the CBA-123 and no contracts were signed. Also, budget cuts to the Argentine and Brazilian Air Forces meant they did not place orders either, leading to the cancellation of the programme by the end of 1993.

Currently, the first prototype is preserved at the Memorial Aeroespacial Brazileiro museum next to

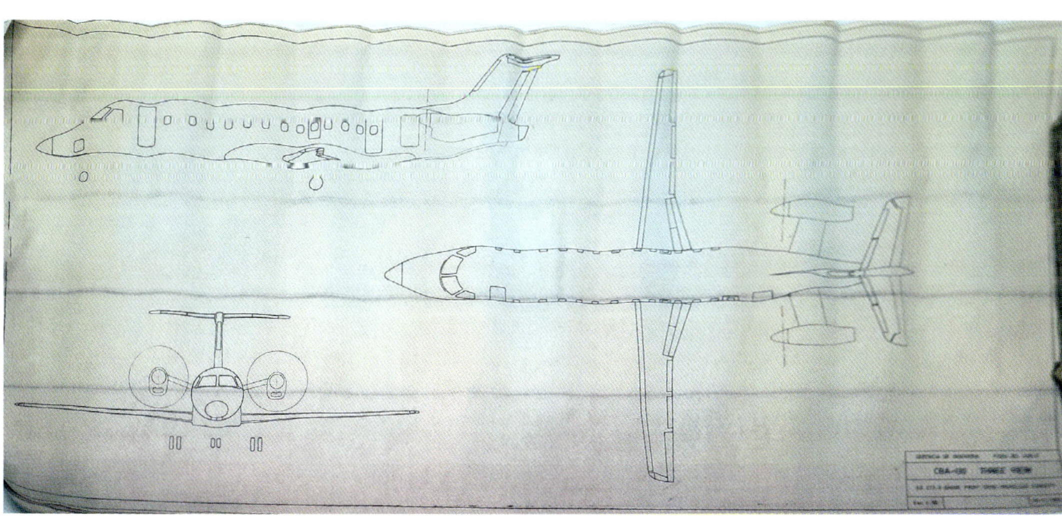

Three views of the proposed CBA-130 of 1993. This idea led to the development of the EMB-145 family.

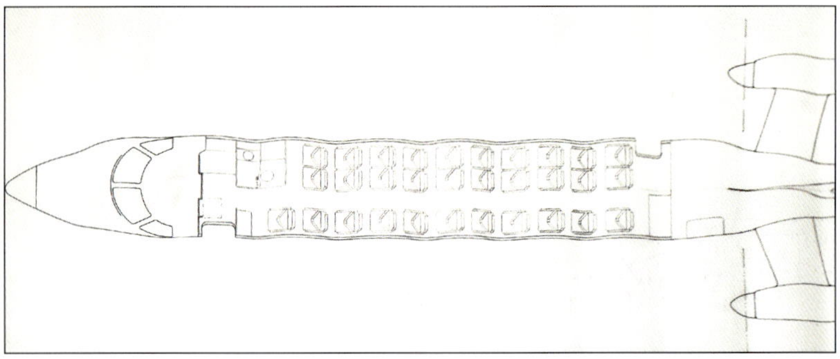

Internal layout of the CBA-130, with 31 thirty-one seats and a toilet.

Embraer facilities in São José dos Campos, while the second was restored and preserved at the Museu Aeroespacial at Campo dos Afonsos in Rio de Janeiro. The third unfinished prototype lay abandoned at the factory in Córdoba for many years until in 2013 it was completed externally and placed as a monument in front of the engineering faculty at Córdoba University.

The CBA-123, while it was a commercial failure, was a technical success, being a very advanced aircraft that pioneered many technologies for aircraft of that size. The experience gained was later exploited by Embraer to develop the EMB-145 family a few years later.

The first prototype of the CBA-123 in flight. *Embraer*

The first prototype of the CBA-123 during its visit to Córdoba on 10 August 1990.

The second prototype of the CBA-123 at Le Bourget 91. *Danny Grew*

ABOVE The first CBA-123 in flight over São Paulo. *Embraer*

LEFT The second prototype of the CBA-123 preserved at the Museu Aeroespacial in Rio de Janeiro. *Santiago Rivas*

7 New millennium, modest ideas

41 **IA-73 Unasur 1**

By the early 1990s, as the fleet of the Beechcraft B45 Mentors of the Argentine Air Force were showing their age after more than thirty years of service, the FMA again started to think about a replacement, after the plan for the IA-61 was not approved. By the first half of 1993, the FMA had produced the layout of a basic trainer with a piston engine and two seats in tandem, which received the designation IA-73, however the decision to privatise the company stopped all work and the project was shelved.

In December 2009, when the company returned to the Argentine state as FAdeA, the Mentors were still in service and in need of urgent replacement. Company engineers Ricardo Bonaiutti and Nicolás Topa proposed restarting the IA-73 project, with an estimated development cost of between $10 million and $12 million. The idea was given the go-ahead by the new direction of the factory and work was restarted. Shortly after they proposed redesigning the plane and adding a turboprop version for basic training, besides the original one for primary training, to replace the Embraer EMB-312 Tucano.

A proposal for the IA-73 from 1993. By then the factory had entered the privatisation process and the project was cancelled. *Archive José Martínez*

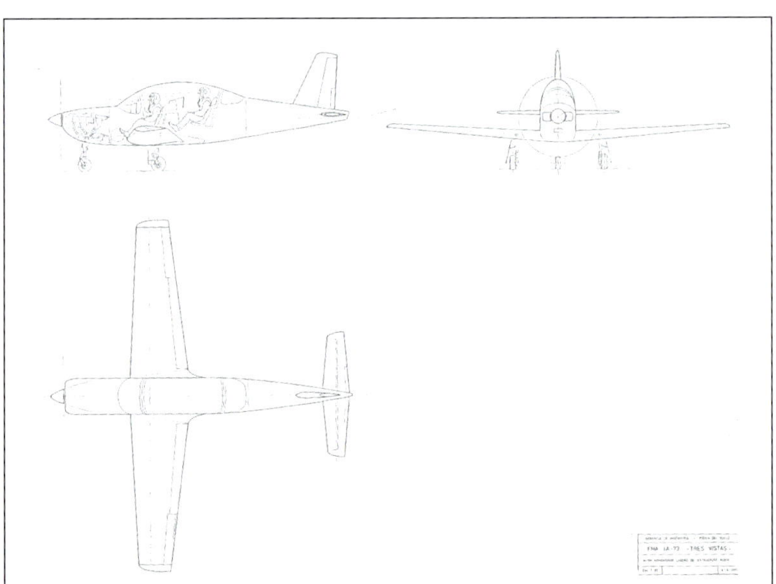

The redesign included a new nose, modified wings, a cabin with the rear seat much higher than the front one and a T tail. Also, the engineers proposed developing two light transport versions, called Avión Liviano Multipropósito or ALM (Multipurpose Light Plane), keeping the nose, tail and wing, with a new fuselage. One version had two pilots side-by-side and five seats in a rear cabin and a door to the left of the fuselage, and the other had up to ten seats, with two doors to the left.

By mid-2011, a new redesign was made, returning to a tail with the stabiliser in a lower position and a wing like the original project. Also, the two transport variant proposals were abandoned.

Meanwhile, in November 2011, the Ministers of Defence of the South American Defence Council (Consejo de Defensa Sudamericano, CDS) of the Unasur organisation, of which most Latin American countries were part, agreed to work together to strengthen the defence industrial sector to generate areas of strategic partnership and promote complementary work. This was reflected in the 2012 Action Plan, in which a Regional Working Group was created to prepare a feasibility report for the design, development and production of a primary-basic training aircraft. Initially, the team was made up of engineers and military aviators specialised in training from Argentina, Brazil, Chile, Colombia, Ecuador, Paraguay, Peru, Uruguay and Venezuela.

FAdeA proposed to use the IA-73 project as a basis, which was accepted, and the plane then received the designation IA-73 Unasur I, with work being started on the definition of the project. The countries who were interested in the programme were reduced to Argentina, Brazil, Ecuador and Venezuela, but Brazil stated it only had interest in the development but not on buying it, as it pretended to buy an indigenous design. The Brazilians announced they could invest $38 million,

Argentina $16 million and Ecuador and Venezuela $3 million each, amounts that are surprising as originally it was calculated the total development cost would be up to $12 million. Also, Argentina revealed that the Argentine Air Force was planning to order fifty aeroplanes plus two prototypes, for a total of around $115 million, with an estimated unit cost of $1.8 million. Venezuela stated they wanted twenty-four and Ecuador eighteen. Besides FAdeA, the companies Redimec of Argentina, CAVIM from Venezuela, DIAF from Ecuador and the Brazilians Akaer, Avionics and Novaer were to take part.

On 30 October 2012, on the eighty-fifth anniversary of the factory, a full-size mock-up of the turboprop version was presented.

Versions and characteristics

By then it had also been announced that three versions were planned, one with a 300hp piston engine with a three-blade propeller, with a maximum speed of about 180 knots and an operational ceiling of 20,000ft. Another was with a turboprop engine of 450shp with a five-blade propeller, with an option for one of 320shp, with a maximum speed of 240 knots, an operational ceiling of 27,000ft and a maximum of 31,000ft. Both had the option of installing ejection seats. The third was a civil four-seat aircraft, with two pilots side-by-side and two passengers behind, with the same piston engine as the first version. This version could also be used for training if the operator preferred a side-by-side solution instead of a tandem one.

Both training versions had a wingspan of 9.3m with a wing area of 12.8m and a height of 3.4m, while the piston one was 8.7m long and the turboprop was 9.15m. The internal fuel was 360 litres and the turboprop version could carry up to

TOP The first redesign of the IA-73 made in 2010 with a T tail.

ABOVE Light transport proposal using the IA-73 nose, tail and wings, with capacity for two pilots and five passengers.

LEFT A bigger transport proposal based on the IA-73 of 2010, for up to ten seats.

Proposal from 2011 for the IA-73, which was adopted by the Unasur consortium and named Unasur 1. They include a four-seat light transport, a turboprop basic trainer and a piston-engined primary trainer.

160 litres in external tanks. The empty weight was 870kg for the piston version and 840kg for the turboprop, with both having the same operational weight for training missions. The stall speed without flaps was of 62 knots and 54 knots with flaps on both versions, while the take-off distance for the piston engine version was 430m and for the turboprop was 340m. The range with internal fuel and thirty minutes of reserve was 1,100km for the piston version and 790km for the turboprop, with endurance of nine and five hours respectively.

All were to be equipped with a glass cockpit and would be equipped with four underwing pylons to drop weapons or to carry extra fuel tanks, with the piston version capable of carrying 300kg and the turboprop 400kg. They would be fully aerobatic and have a Kinematics Command System adaptable by means of external adjustments and an adjustable wing load via an interchangeable wingtip kit.

The requirement of the Argentine Air Force also stated that the IA-73 must have the capability of operating with a single-pilot in the front seat, in all possible configurations and missions, and the capability to operate on paved and unpaved runways, with an extension of 800m for take-offs and landings in MTOW and ISA +25 conditions. It must be able to perform at least two sorties of one hour in clean configuration or two of forty minutes in armament configuration within a local flying area, and in compliance with flight instruction (two crew members) with forty-five minimum fuel reserve minutes. It also stated that it must allow inverted flight for at least ten seconds and that the aircraft must be capable of withstanding at least +6 and -3G in configuration without loads and +4.5G and 2G in MTOW. It must have the capability to store flight data (in a standard removable memory unit) for later use and the turboprop-powered version had FADEC, with the engine being capable of granting a rate of climb not less than 1,600ft per minute at MTOW, ISA+15 to 15,000ft of altitude. Endurance was expected to be at least three hours with a range with no extra tanks of 450km with forty-five minutes of reserve or 990km with extra tanks and fifteen minutes of reserve. The Expected Operational Life Time Cycle of the plane was 18,000 flight hours, with a total number of flights of at least 42,000 and 53,000 landings, with a service life of at least twenty years.

The IA-73 was thought of as an Integrated Training System (ITS) composed of a multirole aeroplane for primary-basic pilot training (from elementary skills to navigation system operation, and basic aiming and shooting) and a platform for flight simulation: simulation training that facilitates primary basic pilot skills at the Academy, enabling training in a digital environment.

Full-size mock-up of the IA-73 Unasur 1 shown at the eighty-fifth anniversary of the factory on October 2012. *Lisandro Amorelli*

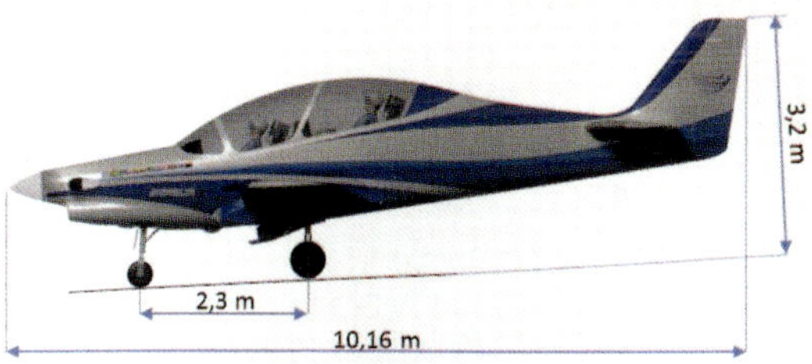

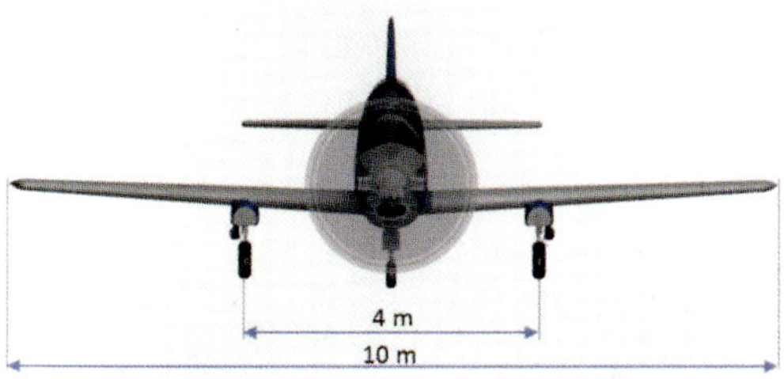

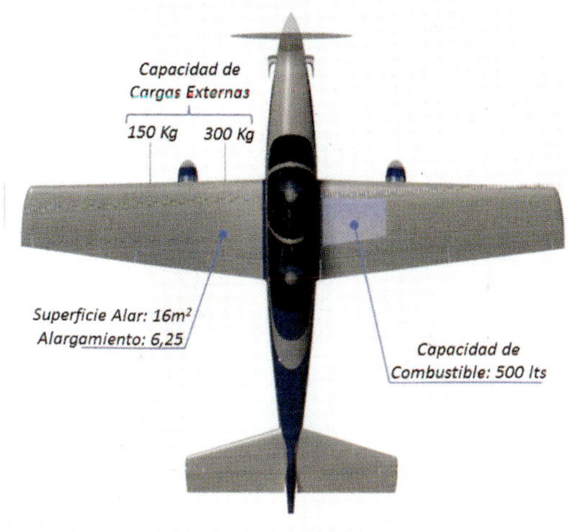

ABOVE An illustration of the two versions of the IA-73 Unasur 1 trainer.

LEFT Redesigned version of the IA-73 of 2014 after the other potential operators presented their requests. The project was cancelled by the end of 2015.

In 2014 FAdeA showed a redesign of the plane, based on the requirements of the other countries participating in the project. The new design had only a turboprop version, with a 550hp engine, equipped with ejection seats, with a rear seat more elevated, and a new design of the entire tail and of the nose. Also, the main wheels retracted forward into fairings under the wings that stood out from the wing leading edge.

It was 10.16m long, had a wingspan of 10m, a height of 3.2m and a wing area of 16m2. It would have four underwing pylons, two for up to 300kg of load and two for up to 150kg, while the fuel capacity was 500 litres. The maximum cruise speed was 235 knots, with a climb rate of 2,500ft/min, a stall speed without flaps of 64 knots and with flaps of 55 knots. The take-off run at sea level, ISA conditions and with a 15m obstacle was 360m and, for landing in the same conditions, 480m. The range was 1,480km, the endurance was four hours, the service ceiling was 27,000ft and the operational limit was 25,00ft. The load factor was +7 and -3.5G for aerobatics and +4.4 and -1.8G with full load. The maximum sustained G was 3. The empty weight was 1,100kg and the MTOW was 1,700kg for aerobatics and 2,600kg with full load.

The end

While it was planned that the prototype would be ready by July 2013, with deliveries by 2015, the programme started to suffer delays, while in the second half of 2014 the company Unasur Aero S.A was created to manage the project, although the designs were still being made by FAdeA.

By 2015, the final design was not ready but a prototype was expected by 2016, to be certified by the end of that year. However, the project was progressing too slowly and the change of government in Argentina in December 2015 meant the country left the Unasur organisation and the project was cancelled at the same time..

Side view of the ten-seat transport aircraft developed from the basis of the IA-73.

42 **IA-74, IA-100 and IA-100B Malvina**

In 2013, FAdeA signed an agreement with Embraer for the production of the rear ramp, avionics racks, nose landing gear doors, tail end cover, spoilers and flap fairings for the KC-390. This meant the company had to modernise its infrastructure, including clean rooms, operate CATIA programmes and Ansys Fluent CFD analysis and simulation, and a state-of-the-art autoclave was added. Also, new engineers were contracted, and technical personnel were trained in the new technologies.

With this, the company recovered the capacity to work on pre-impregnated composite materials, which was developed in the 1980s but then lost in the following decade.

With the IA-73 growing into a turboprop for basic training, a group of engineers of FAdeA suggested developing a different aircraft for elementary training, with all the airframe made of composite materials, for which it was planned to initially develop a concept demonstrator.

On 10 December 2014 the programme was officially launched, and the technology demonstrator was designated IA-100, for the first time not following the sequence of designations that had been in use since the 1940s, but it was planned that the series production version would be designated IA-74. A team of about thirty people including engineers and technicians worked on the design, which took 35,000 work hours and a budget of $2.1 million.

The technology demonstrator of the IA-100 was the first plane designed and built by the factory for more than thirty years. While it had many design and construction problems, it was a first step to develop the IA-100B. *Santiago Rivas*

The programme was divided into four stages, the first of them being the development and construction of the technology demonstrator, with side-by-side seats, a 180hp Lycoming AEIO-360 B1F engine with a Hartzell Trail Blazer two-blade propeller with full glass cockpit and IFR capacity. The second stage aimed for a plane for the civil market, with simplified avionics, while the third stage was the military elementary trainer, with full glass cockpit and IFR capacity. The fourth and last stage was the development of a four-seat liaison aircraft with a more powerful engine, with options such as retractable or fixed landing gear and simplified avionics or full glass cockpit.

The IA-74 was to be identical to the IA-100, but to reduce the price was to have a more basic navigation system and although in the military version it was to keep the 180hp engine, in the civilian version a 125hp version was planned. Also, the IA-74 was not be built with the lamination technique of the IA-100 but the material was to be injected to achieve uniformity of thickness and obtain about a 30 per cent reduction in the weight of the fuselage.

On September 2015 the technology demonstrator was shown for the first time in Buenos Aires at the Defensa de la Industria fair and it received the civil experimental serial LV-X596. After that, the plane was taken back to the factory to start structural tests, but they showed some construction problems and many parts had to be rebuilt, so the planned date

The first flight of the IA-100, on 8 August 2016. The plane only flew five times, showing some handling problems and lack of front view. *FAdeA*

for the first flight in December 2015 was delayed. In June 2016 the plane started ground tests, which ended on 1 August and at 10.30 a.m. on the 8th of that month civil pilot Pablo Reynoso made the first flight, which lasted fifty-eight minutes and reached 5,000ft. This was the first occasion in which an aeroplane from the factory was flown for the first time by a civil pilot who did not belong to the company.

The plane made five test flights until February 2017 and proved hard to control, while the forward visibility was extremely poor. A test campaign of forty flight hours was planned with the integration of the three-axis autopilot system, the internal and external lighting system, the ELT and Storm Scope system and a night vision camera, with the aim of reaching FAR 21 certification as an experimental aircraft. However, the factory decided to stop funding the programme and the plane never flew again.

The IA-100 demonstrator was built with a fuselage made in two longitudinal parts, joined by different structural frames, together with a glue section. It had a low cantilever wing with laminar profile, and electrically operated slotted flaps and winglets. The wing had three spars; a main carbon fibre one, with IPN (or double T) structural profile, which fitted inside the fuselage and overlapped with the main spar of the other wing assembly, to then be joined together through two structural bolts. A posterior spar in omega profile, which ran the total length of the wing, and a shorter anterior spar in C profile, in both cases tacked to the root of the fuselage, were integrated by five main wing ribs plus five secondary wing ribs.

The type had a two-seater side-by-side configuration for better communication between student and instructor, with a one-piece windscreen, and a canopy made of a single piece of plexiglass with an opening handle on its upper front part, sliding backwards. The avionics were a Garmin G3X composed of three multifunction displays of 10.6in (26.9cm), with a synthetic vision system (SVX). Below the central display were a Garmin GTN-750 and a GTN 650 for GPS/NAV/COMM information. It also had a Bendix King Master Display from DME (Distance Measuring Equipment). The integration of this avionics package was carried out by the local company Redlmec.

IA-100B Malvina

In 2020 the development of a new version of the IA-100 was launched, headed by engineer Juan Vidal, which was called IA-100B, although the specifications were what was originally intended with the IA-74 version. In 2022 it was renamed IA-100 Malvina. The plane took some conceptual ideas from the initial demonstrator but is an entirely new aircraft. It was born from a requirement of the Argentine Air Force, which aims to have a single primary trainer to replace the Tecnam P-2002 Sierra and the Grob G-120TP in the Joint Basic Course of Military Aviator (CBCAM). The force aims to incorporate twenty-five aircraft and FAdeA hopes to also sell the aircraft on the civilian market and be able to export it.

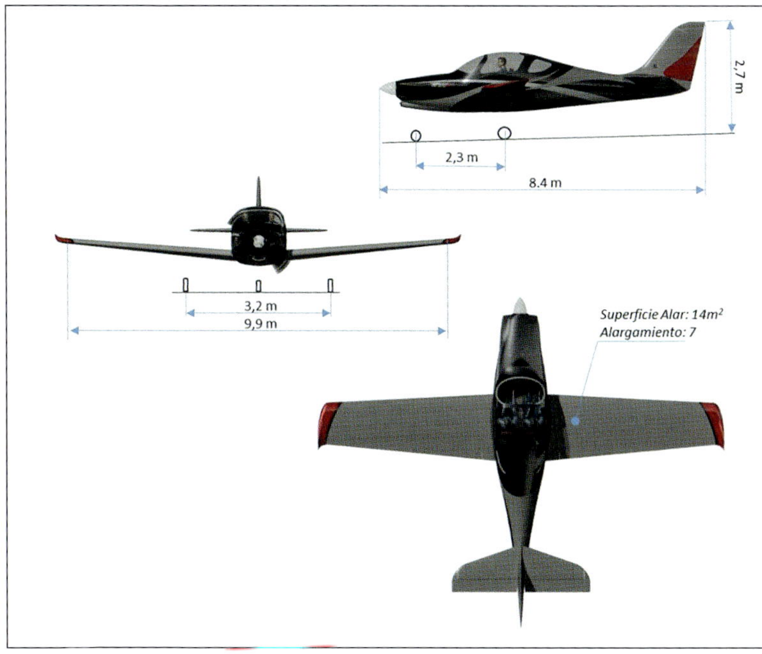

Three views of the first layout of the IA-100B Malvina, as proposed in 2020.

The plane will be made of about 85 per cent composite materials, using the much more advanced prepreg process to build the parts, which provides much better quality than wet laminate.

The new plane has a cabin with improved visibility, with a higher canopy, with customised VFR/IFR digital avionics in a cabin also designed by Redimec, which is simpler than the one in the technology demonstrator, with side-by-side seats plus a third seat in the rear for liaison. The engine is a Lycoming AEIO-540-D4A5 of 260hp with a Hartzell propeller, prepared for inverted flight for aerobatics.

The plane is expected to reach a speed of 155 knots, with a stall speed of 57 knots, with a range of 1,060km, an endurance of four and a half hours, a service ceiling of 18,000ft and a load factor of +6G and -3G.

In 2020 it was planned to have the prototype ready by 2021 and start deliveries in 2022, but this proved too optimistic and construction of the prototype began by mid-2023, with a roll-out planned for mid-2024.

Render of the IA-100B Malvinas as presented at FIDAE 2022 in Chile.

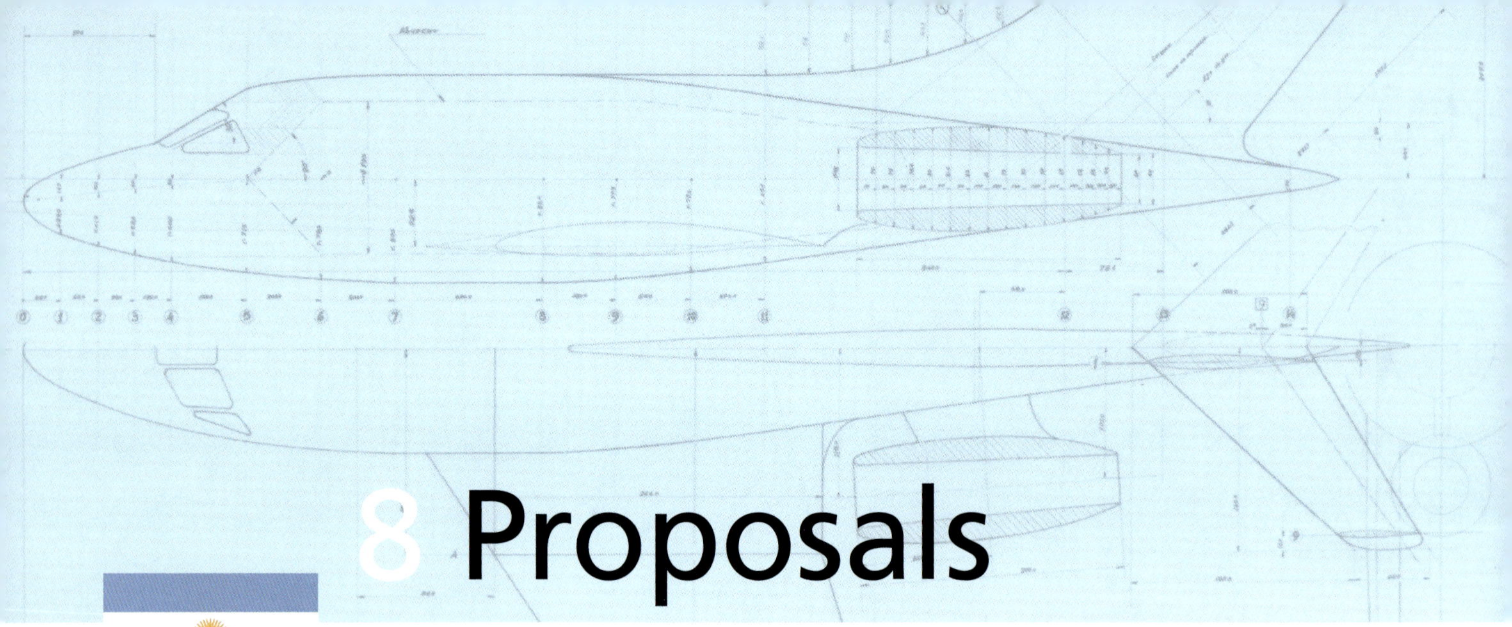

8 Proposals

43 **Proposals by Reimar Horten and others**

Over the years, there were several studies of aircraft that never went beyond a simple study, a proposal or a draft. Many have already been covered in other chapters, and many were lost as most of the archives of the factory were thrown away or stolen. In many cases, only some plans were preserved and in others there is a simple mention of them in the official documents of the factory.

Among those not included in other chapters, in 1946 studies were made by the Gabinete de Estudios e Investigaciones Aerodinámicas (GEIA, Aerodynamic Research and Studies Cabinet) of the FMA for a twin-engined light transport, which did not receive a designation but was described as the Anteproyecto Avión GEIA II. The plans of this design are all dated as August and September 1946 and describe an all-metal, low-wing monoplane powered by two Armstrong Siddeley Cheetah XXV engines of 400hp, with a wingspan of 16.59m, a length of 12.8m and a wing area of 38.79m2. The wing and stabiliser design was like that of the I.Ae.24 Calquin but the vertical fin was totally different, as well as the fuselage. The cockpit had two pilots side by side and the rear cabin was 5.8m long and 1.52m wide with space for six seats and a toilet. The access was by a door on the left side at the back of the cabin and there was a cargo compartment in the nose. This idea never went beyond a proposal, although at least four plans are preserved in the FAdeA archives.

Later, in 1948, different studies were made, detailed in the memoirs of the Instituto Aerotécnico for that year. They reveal that the transport aircraft was cancelled, that a project for a single-engine observation aircraft was considered but no progress was made and that a dive bomber was planned to be developed in 1949, but no further mention of them was made in other documents.

Among the plans of Cesare Pallaviccino for the jet version of the Ñancú, a plan was found of a side view of a bomber, of which no more details were found.

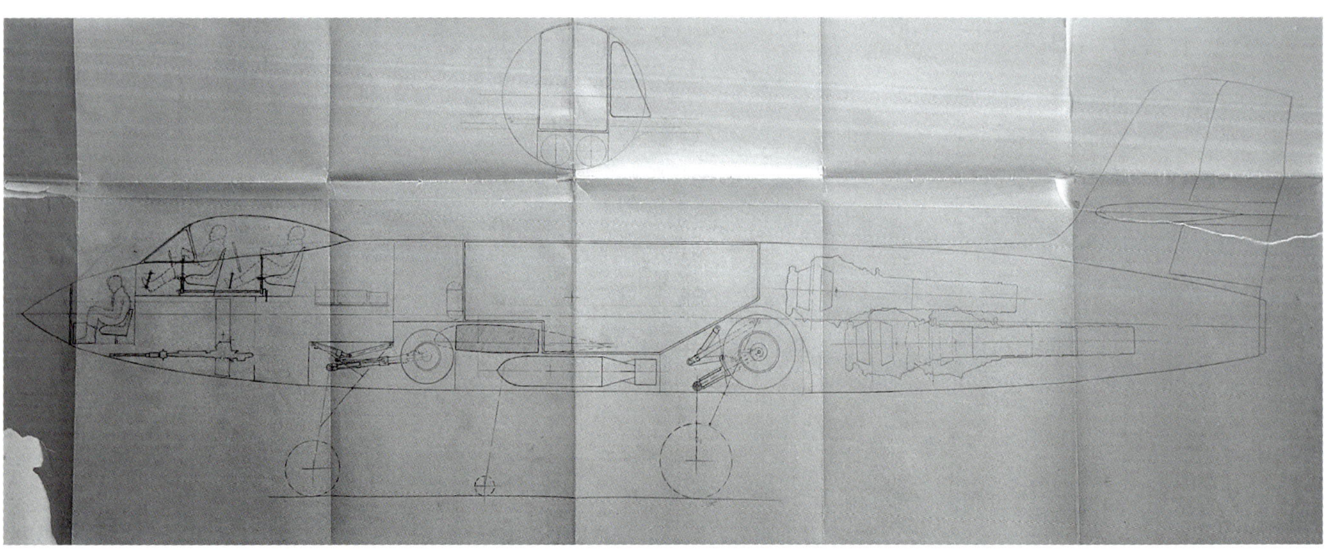

A plan for a bomber aircraft found among Cesare Pallaviccino plans.

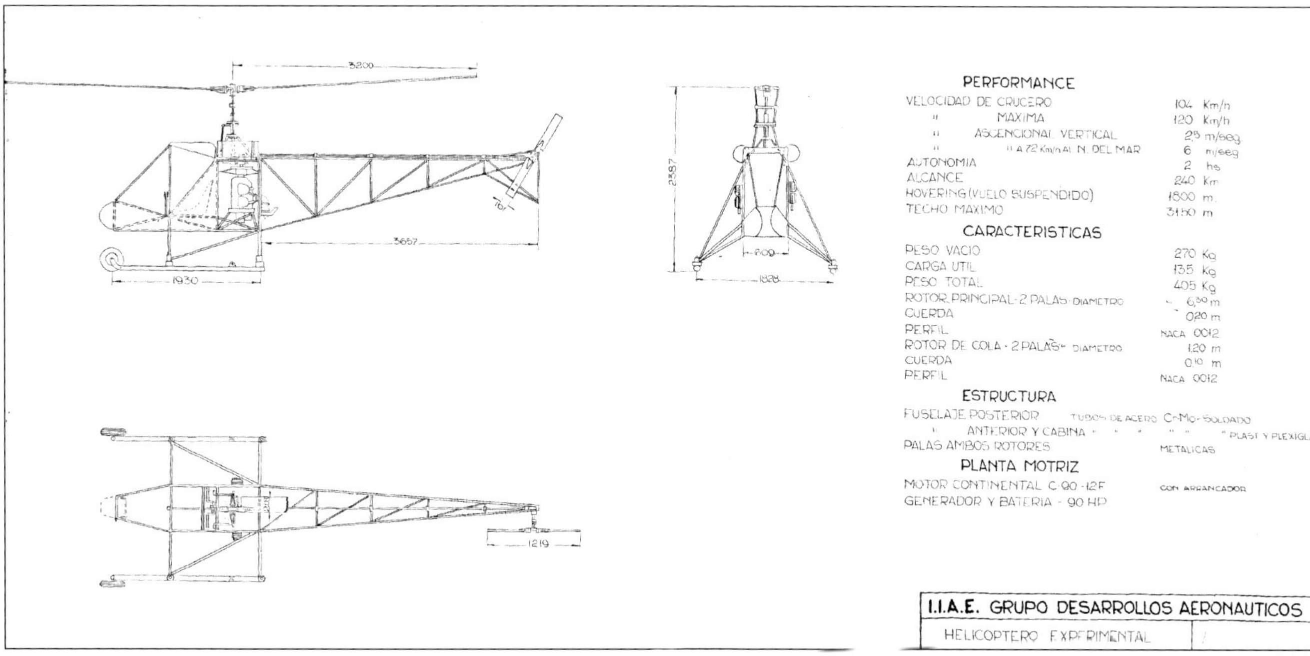

Three views plan of the single-seat helicopter proposal of 1963. *Archive José Martínez*

The plane had three Derwent V or Nene II engines, a bomb bay in the lower part of the fuselage, a wing placed in almost the middle of the fuselage, at least two 20mm guns and three crew members, with one in the nose and two in a tandem cabin. The landing gear was bicycle with small retractable wheels on the wingtips, like the Lockheed U-2. The wing was straight, and the air intakes were on the sides of the upper part of the fuselage.

Between 1961 and 1963 the factory studied the possible development of VTOL aircraft, helicopters, and hovercraft, with proposals for a single-seat and two-seat helicopters.

The single-seat helicopter was planned for experimental use, while the second was to be for agricultural purposes, with the engines, transmission and rotor blades purchased abroad.

Of the single-seat helicopter, a three-view plan was preserved, showing a basic design with a structure made of steel tubes, with a cabin partially covered with plastic and Plexiglas, and a Continental C90-12F engine of 90hp moving a two-blade main rotor. The empty weight was 270kg, with a payload of 135kg for a maximum weight of 405kg. The fuselage was 5.58m long, 0.6m wide with the base of the skids being 1.82m. The height was 2.38m, and the main rotor diameter was 6.3m.

It was expected to achieve a cruise speed of 104km/h and a maximum of 120km/h, with an endurance of two hours, a range of 240km, a maximum ceiling of 3,150m and a maximum hovering height of 1,800m.

Horten's proposals

Reimar Horten, whose relationship with the FMA lasted from his arrival to Argentina until the early 1980s, made several proposals, besides those already described in other chapters.

Plan with three views of the Anteproyecto Avión GEIA II proposal of 1946, which never went beyond the draft.

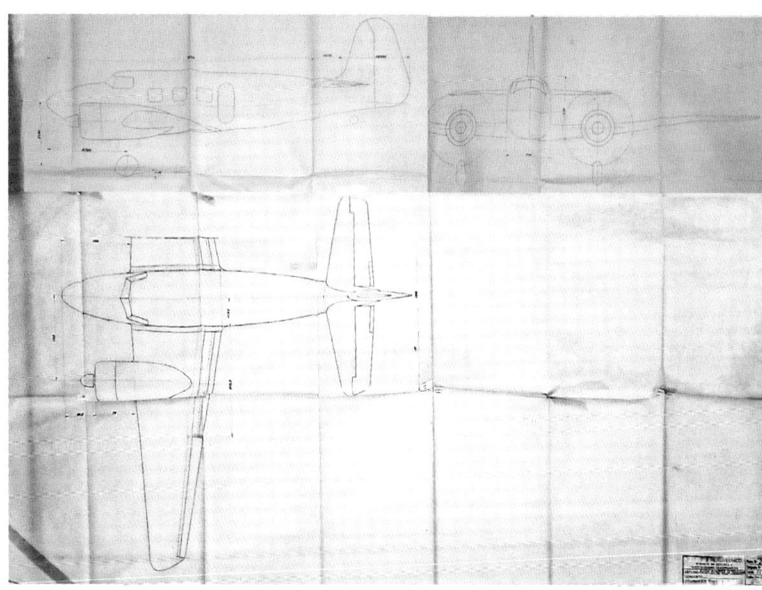

Among them, one was a twin-engined flying wing for advanced training and reconnaissance, presented in 1949. The plane had two El Gaucho engines inside the wings, with an air intake below the wings for cooling the engines and propellers in a pusher position. It also had wheels from the I.Ae. DL22 aircraft and it was planned to install two 12.7mm machine guns inside the wings, while the tail cone of the fuselage was made of Plexiglas for observation and the observer could lie down to fire two 12.7mm machine guns for the defence of the aircraft against fighters.

Internally it could carry four occupants, two of them facing forward and two facing backwards,

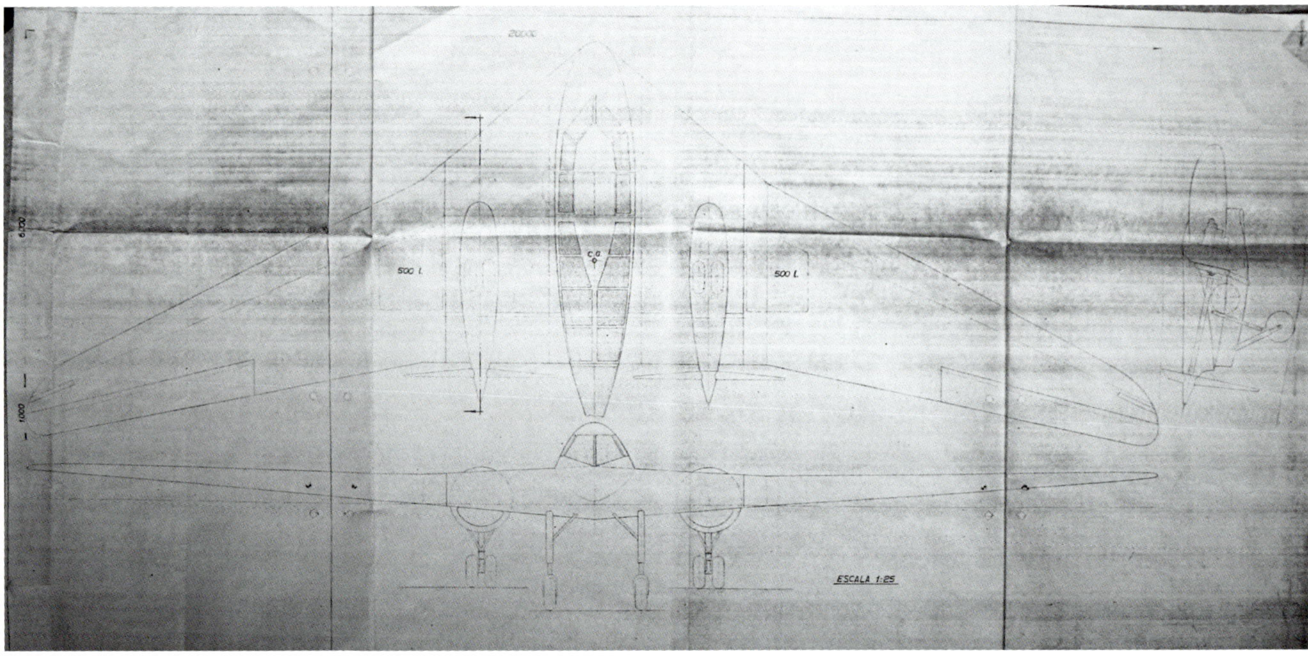

Horten XII four-seat flying wing proposal of Reimar Horten of December 1949. *Archive Diego Horten*

A plan of Horten's training and reconnaissance flying wing proposal of 1949. *Archive Ricardo Burzaco*

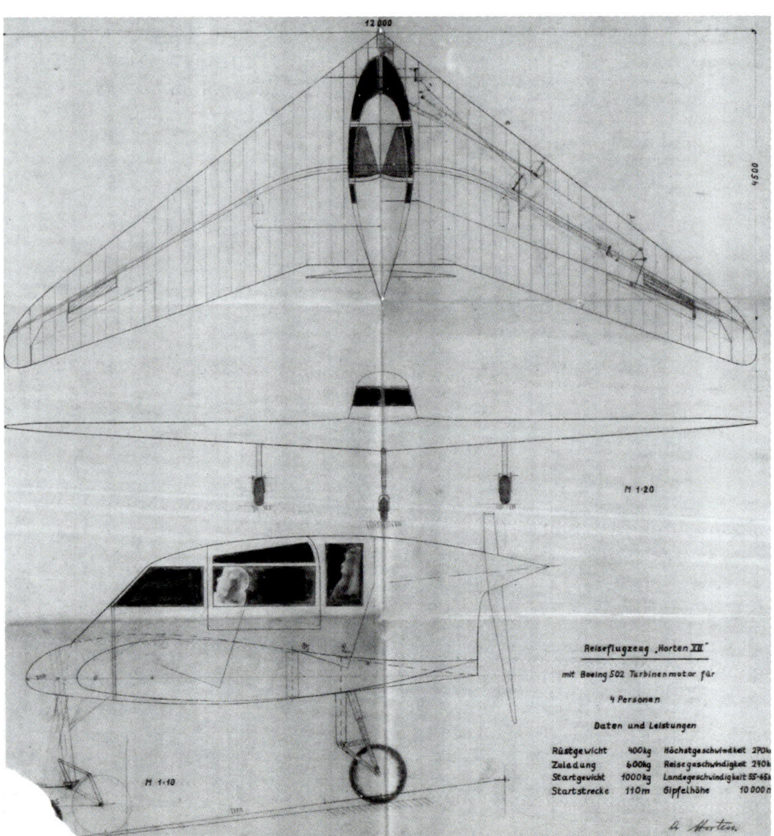

one behind the other. The construction could be of wood or metal.

The wingspan was 20m, with a wing area of 54.5m2, a length of 6m, an empty weight of 2,800kg, with a fuel capacity of 730kg plus 800kg of armament. The maximum speed was expected to be 365km/h, with a cruise speed of 330km/h and a landing speed of 100km/h. With 4,200kg of weight the maximum ceiling was calculated on 8,300m and the operational one was of 7,600m, while with 4,600kg they were 8,000kg and 7,400kg respectively.

In December 1949 Horten also drew a design for a four-seat flying wing he called Horten XII, which would have been powered by a Boeing 502 turboshaft engine of 175shp with a propeller in a pusher position at the rear end of the fuselage. The plane was designed to have a 12m wingspan and a length of 4.5m, an empty weight of 400kg and a payload of 600kg, for a MTOW of 1,000kg. Maximum speed was 270km/h and the highest cruising speed was 240km/h, with a stall speed between 55 and 65km/h. The service ceiling was 10,000m.

In 1950 Horten also proposed an assault glider, also a flying wing, with a 24m wingspan and a cabin of 15 cubic metres capable of carrying 3,000kg of cargo, for a MTOW of 5,200kg. The maximum speed was 300km/h and the landing speed was 100km/h. The fuselage had a cargo hold capable of carrying a small vehicle and had a cockpit for two pilots. As the idea of the assault gliders was being left behind after the end of the Second World War, the FMA did not accept his proposal.

Another assault glider was proposed by Horten in 1959, this time to carry only infantry, with a maximum capacity of eight people. It was expected to be 12m long and 2.4m high, with a wingspan of 20m, wing area of 28.48m2, an empty weight of 650kg and a maximum of 1,400kg. The maximum

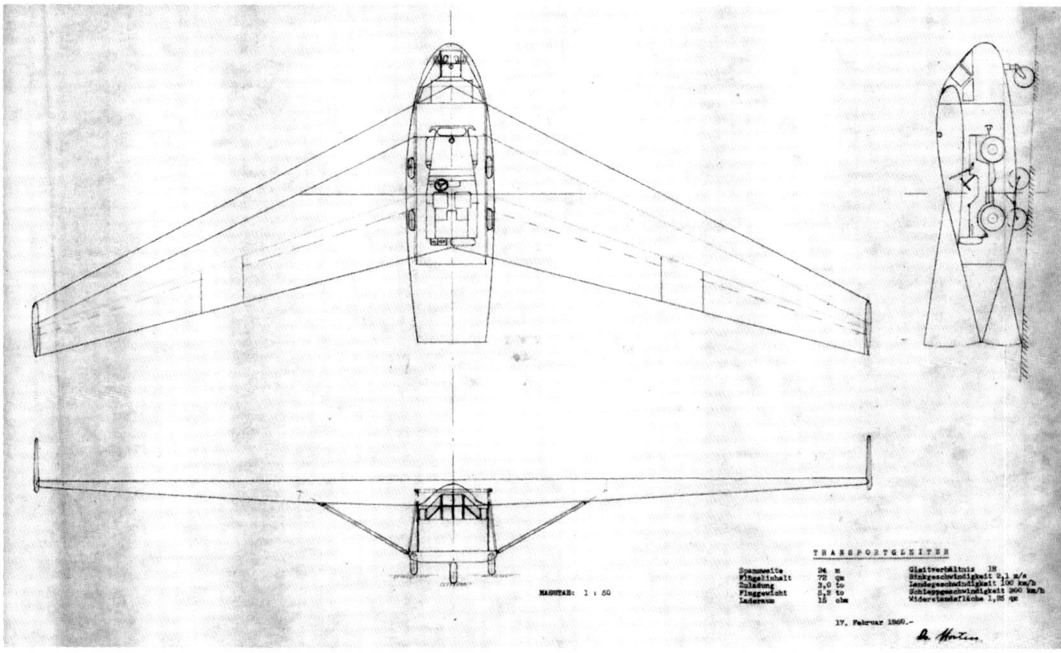

Assault glider proposal of Reimar Horten of 1950. *Archive Diego Horten*

speed was of 307km/h, the towed speed was 206km/h and the cruise speed was 185km/h, with a landing speed of 88km/h and a minimum speed of 82km/h. This project was never considered as the idea was obsolete when Horten proposed it.

In 1958 he also proposed a crop duster of very unconventional design, with a Lycoming O-435 engine, with an empty weight of 800kg, a payload of 650kg and a MTOW of 1,600kg, with a cabin for two crew members.

In 1959 Horten also proposed an innovative design, which received the designation I.A.50, which was later used on the Guaraní II. It was a twin-engine executive jet with six seats, using the vertical fin and stabiliser of the Pulqui II and a swept wing. It was projected to be powered by two Pratt & Whitney J-60 engines of 1,827kg thrust or General Electric J-85 of 1,135kg of thrust without afterburner or 1,748kg with it.

While this idea was discarded, in 1963 Horten proposed a more conventional light jet transport for two pilots and nine passengers in a pressurised cabin, in a particular configuration, as three seats were in the back of the cabin and three on each side. The middle of the fuselage was occupied by a fuel tank

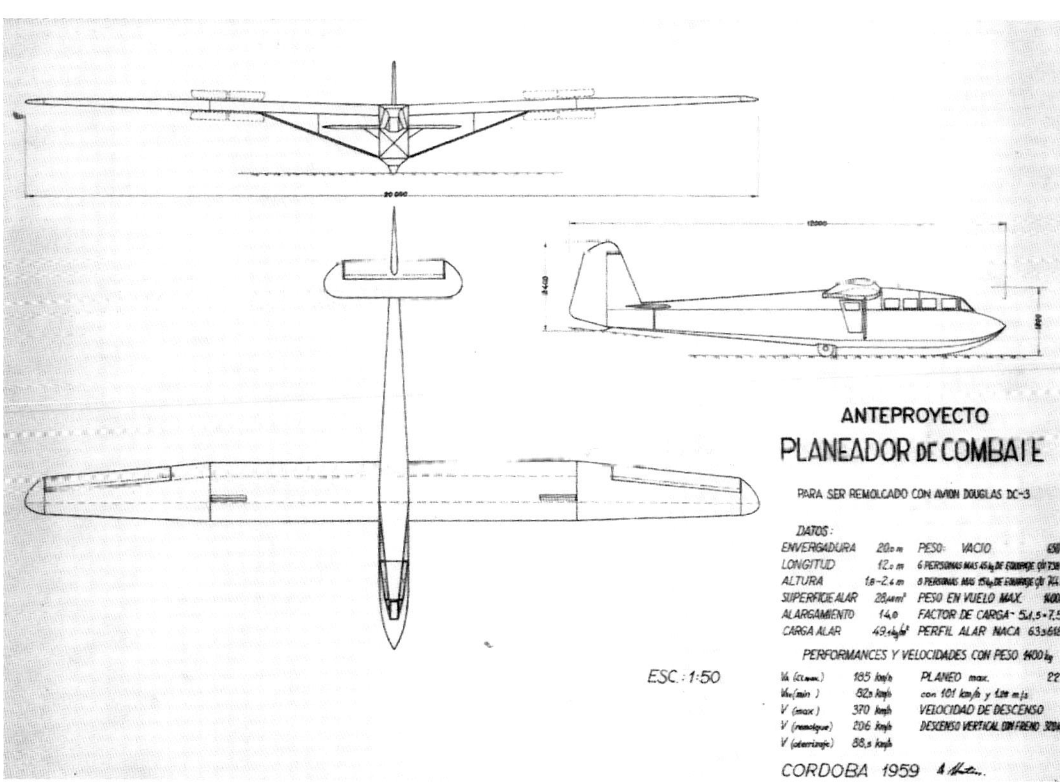

Combat glider proposal of Horten from 1959. *Archive Diego Horten*

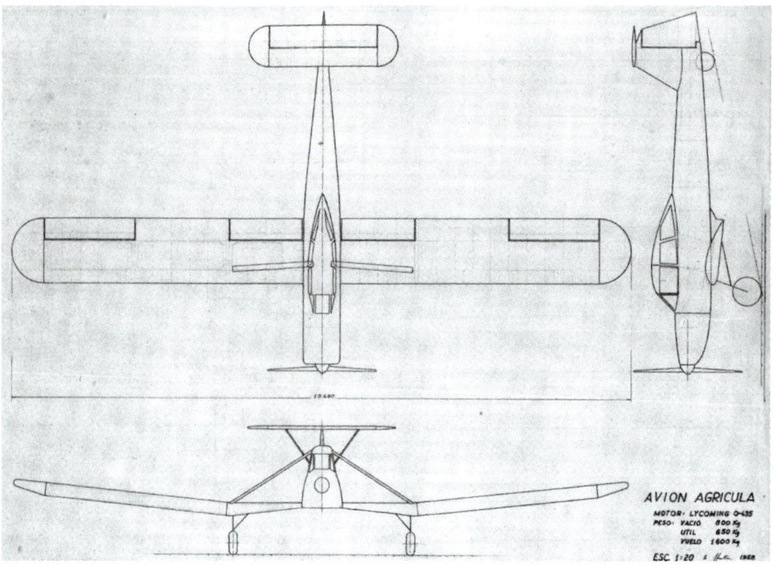

Crop duster proposal by Reimar Horten from 1958. *Archive Diego Horten*

and there was a cargo hold in the back. The plane had a straight wing like the one used by the I.Ae.35 and two Turbomeca Aubisque engines of 1,635lb of thrust. It had a wingspan of 18m with a wing area of 33.3m2 and a length of 14.4m. The empty weight was of 3,500kg and the MTOW 6,800kg. The maximum speed was 833km/h and the maximum cruise was 821km/h, with 2,382km range.

In 1965 Horten presented another proposal, also for an executive jet, with a different wing and fuselage, with two triangular windows on each side, a new tail and different landing gear. The engines were the same, but he expected to reach a maximum speed of 660km/h and a cruise speed of 550km/h, with a maximum range of 2,931km. The wingspan was 17.5m, the length 17.2m, the height was 4.8m and the wing area was 40.8m2. The empty weight was 3,847kg and the MTOW was 7,000kg. The cabin was for two pilots plus nine passengers in normal configuration, or fifteen in a high-density layout.

With the aim of providing the Argentine Naval Aviation with a jet trainer that could operate on the ARA *25 de Mayo* aircraft carrier (the force had the Aermacchi MB-326 that could only operate on land), in September 1974 Horten envisaged a trainer project equipped with a Turbomeca Astafan jet engine, with a cabin using the windscreen and part of the canopy of the Beechcraft Mentor, with folding wings with extra fuel tanks on the wingtips. The wingspan was 11m, length 8.8m, height 3.5m and wing area 19m2. The empty weight was 1,700kg and the MTOW 2,500kg. It would be capable of taking off in 600m with a 15m obstacle, had a maximum speed of 640km/h and a cruise of 560km/h, a service ceiling of 14,000m, a range of 1,500km and an endurance of three hours.

Horten's four-engine transport

Leaving behind his ideas for flying wings, on 12 December 1956 Horten presented a proposal for a medium transport aircraft for thirty-four passengers to operate both on domestic routes and to other countries. The idea was to have an aircraft capable of operating from unprepared runways and, while he stated the plane must be comfortable for the passengers, it must not be luxurious to reduce the operational costs. He said that he expected a range

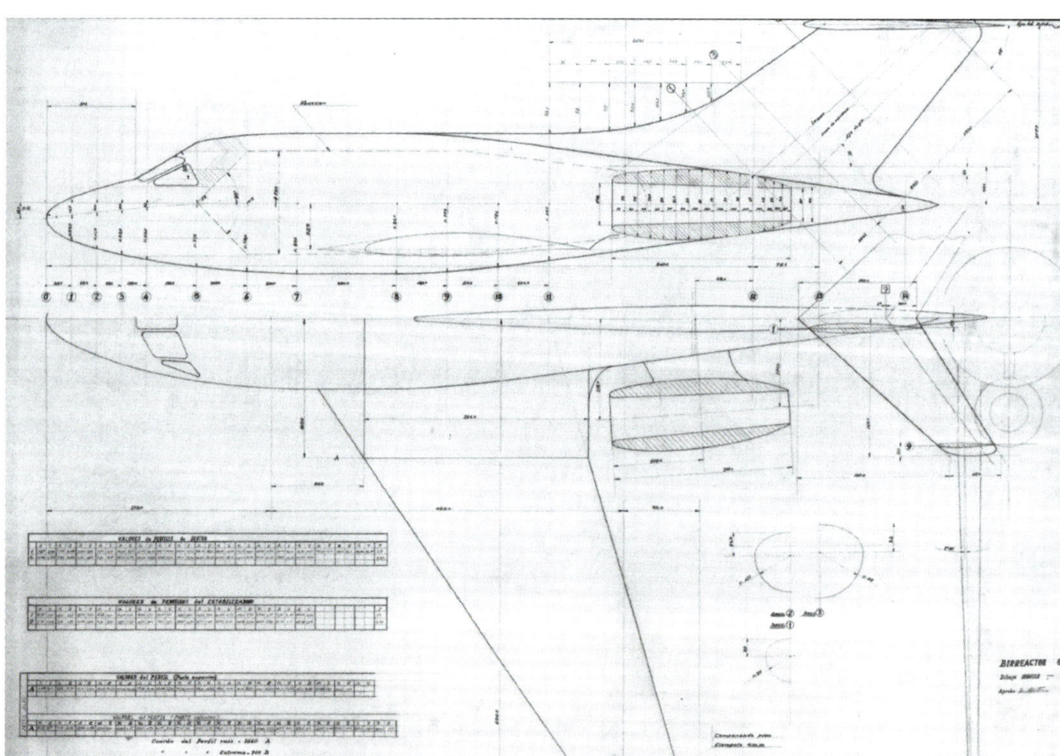

Executive jet proposal of Horten from 1959 using the tail of the Pulqui II, which received the designation I.A.50, later used on the Guaraní II. *Archive Diego Horten*

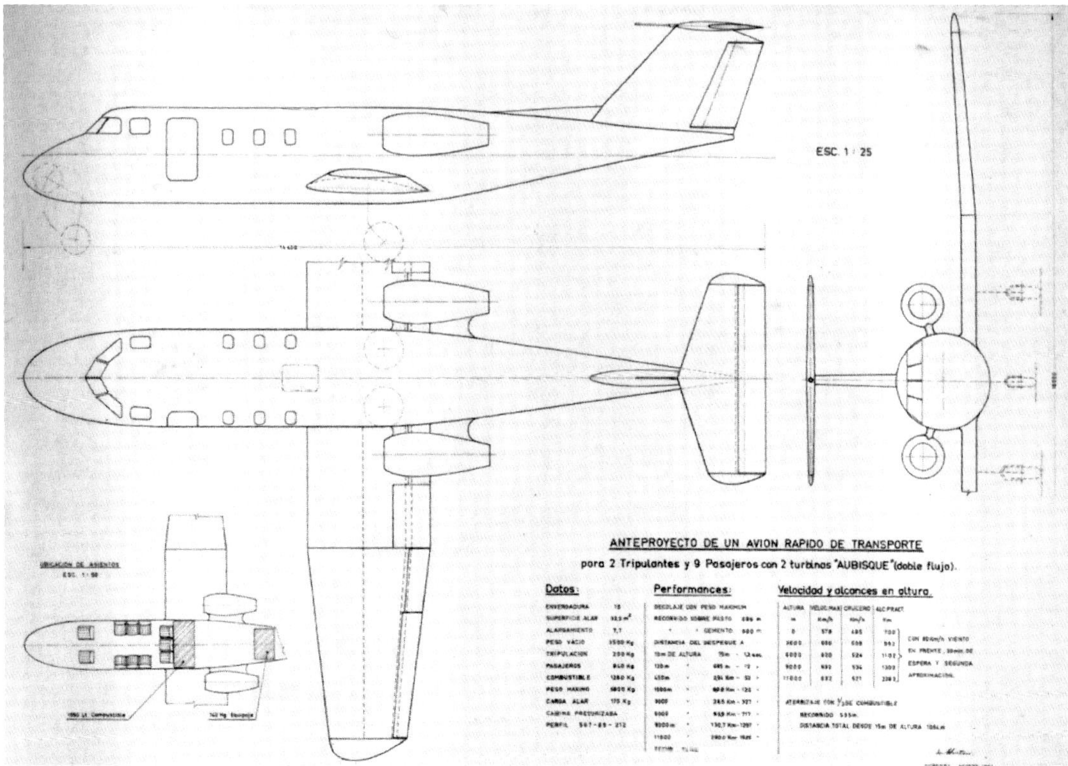

Executive jet proposal by Reimar Horten from 1963. *Archive Diego Horten*

of 1,350km with full load, to be extended to 1,600km with extra tanks of 1,100 litres on the wingtips and the operational altitude was expected to be between 9,000 to 10,500ft. With fewer passengers, the range could be 2,385km. For a ferry flight, it was 3,350km.

The plane was to be equipped with four I.Ae.R-19 El Indio engines with three-blade propellers of 3m of diameter, but he also considered the use of other engines, like the Armstrong Siddeley Panther and Pratt & Whitney Twin Wasp, with 3.5m diameter propellers.

It was to be of all-metal construction, with a wingspan of 30m and a surface of 97.2m2, divided into three sections, with the mid one having a span of 14m, with two spars. Behind the inner engines was the space to retract the main landing gear (which used the same wheels as the Gloster Meteor)

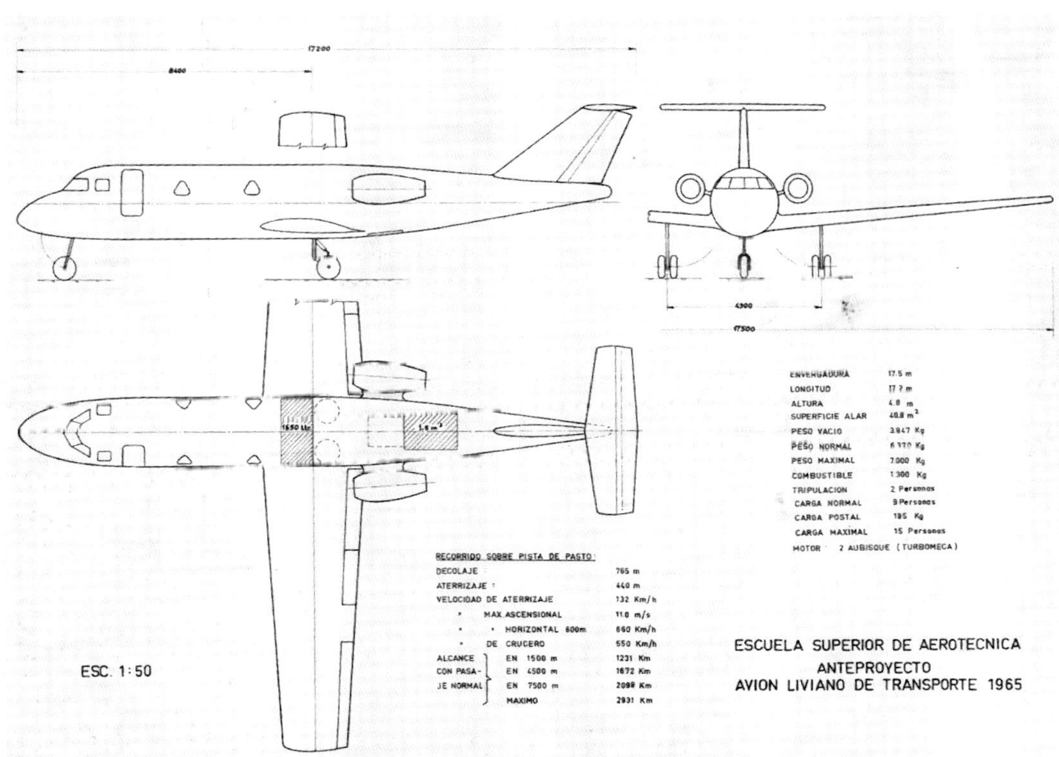

Horten's executive jet proposal of 1965. *Archive Diego Horten*

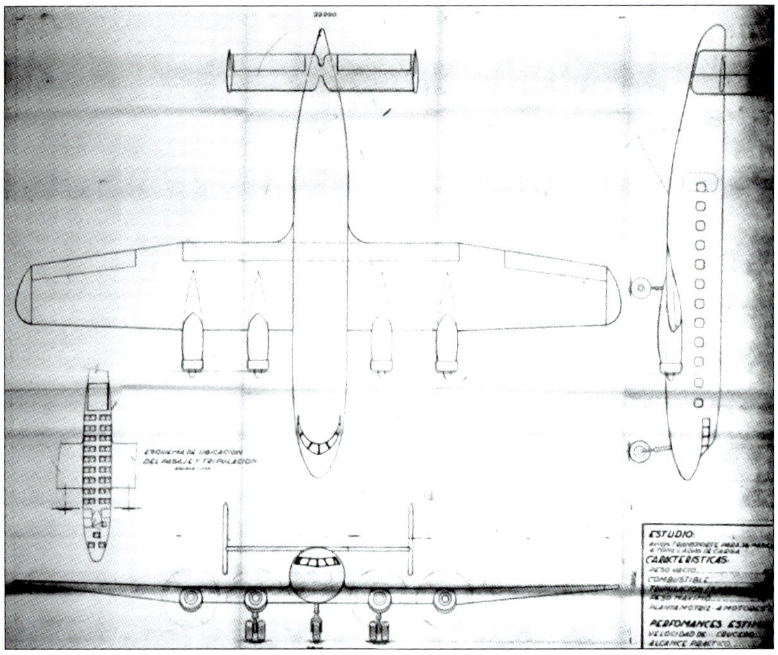

Four-engine transport plane proposed by Horten in December 1956. This was the version for thirty-four passengers, with the possibility of adding extra fuel tanks on the wingtips.

and on the outer ones were fuel tanks with 800-litre capacity. Another tank of 500 litres was installed in each semi-wing. The outer wings would be 7.8m long and a single spar and would have a 350 litres fuel tank in each.

The fuselage was 22m long, with a cockpit for a pilot, co-pilot, navigator and mechanic/radio operator, followed by a small cargo hold of 3.5m3 for 300kg of mail plus a kitchen and a seat for the stewardess.

The passenger cabin was 9.4m long with eight rows of four seats plus one of two seats to the right at the back, with the door to the left. Originally, Horten considered installing seventeen windows of 30cm × 40cm, nine on the right side and eight on the left, one for each row of seats, but on the plans the plane also has a window at the rear of the fuselage, where the toilet was located on the right side (a wardrobe was also placed in the back), and one where the kitchen was located.

The empty weight was estimated at 9,590kg, plus 300kg for the crew, 3,060kg for the passengers, 300kg for mail, 50kg for water and food and 2,300kg for fuel, for a maximum weight of 15,600kg. The take-off run with a 15m obstacle and MTOW was estimated at 685m on a grass runway and around 630m on a paved one.

The economic cruise speed with 14,450kg was 325km/h at 2,400m and the maximum was 355km/h at 1,900m. The landing speed was 140km/h.

Horten proposed to work in the first year on the aerodynamic studies and detailed design, to build a prototype in the second year of the project. After flight tests, ground tests were to be made to define

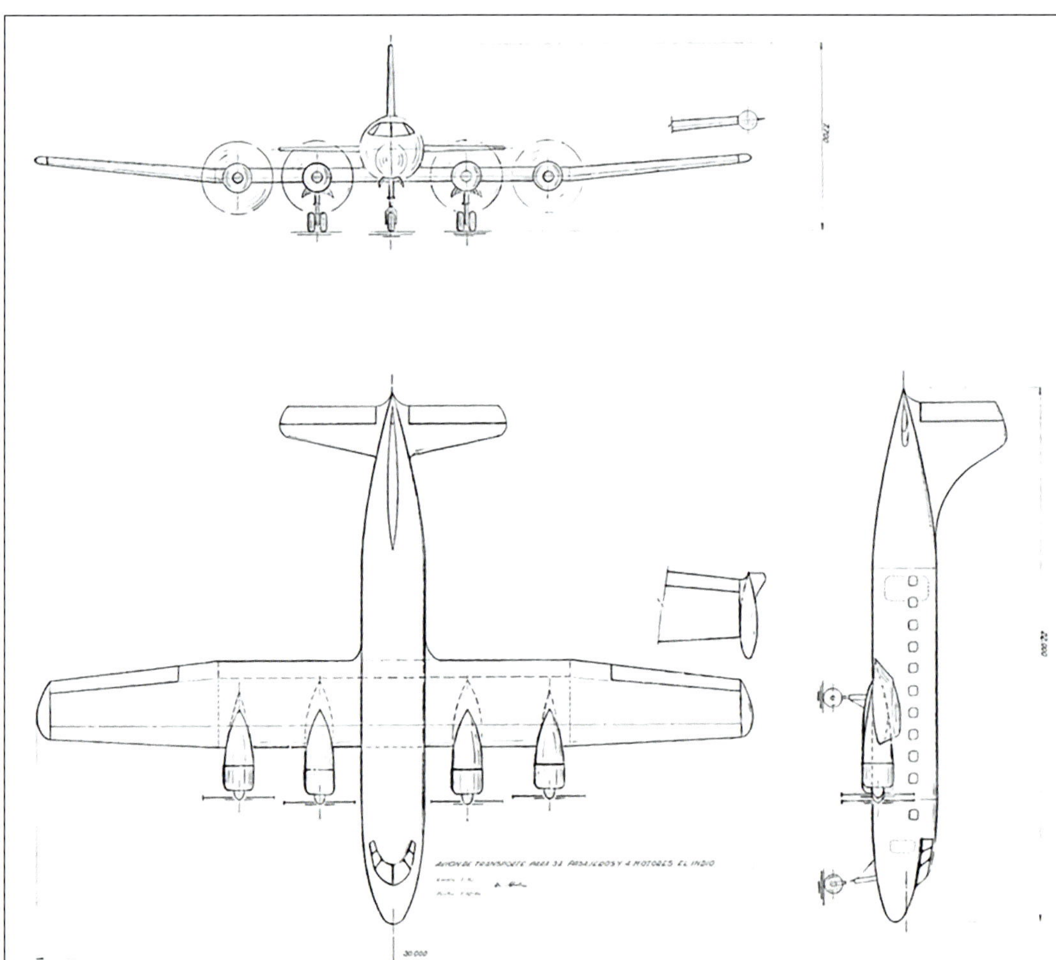

Four-engine transport proposal by Horten with two vertical fins and rear ramp, for up to thirty-eight passengers. *Archive Ricardo Burzaco*

the final modifications to be made and then he would build three pre-series aircraft in the third year, of which one should be flying by the end of that year and the other two in the fourth year, when series production could begin.

The plans show a conventional design like a Douglas DC-4, while there is another plan, dated October 1956, showing a slightly longer aircraft, for thirty-eight passengers, with an extra row of seats in a fuselage of 23.6m long and with a bigger wing, with a 33m wingspan. The internal layout showed a modification to the location of the toilet, which was now in the front part of the fuselage. For this version there is also another drawing with a different tail, dated 20 October 1956, with two vertical fins and a larger rear fuselage with a rear ramp, so the plane could be used for both cargo and passengers. The length was 24.65m. The internal layout, the front part of the fuselage and the wing were the same.

A strange fighter

Between 1971 and 1972 Reimar Horten worked on a strange design, of which a few plans remain but no written information was found. Four different configurations were found, all with a delta wing with canards and two vertical fins. The main landing gear retracted inside the fins, like in the Caza sin cola (see Chapter 17), while the shape of the trailing edge of the wing resembled that of the I.Ae.37.

The most interesting thing is that the plans indicate a swing wing, which could change the angle of attack considerably, including the central part of the rear fuselage, with the engines. Also, the canards could change the angle of attack.

One of the drawings, dated 1971, shows a single-seat plane, of which a plan shows a gun installation, with two turbofans over the rear fuselage. Another plan of the same version shows bigger engines and a different shape of the fairing behind the cockpit. This plane was 8.5m long and had a wingspan of 7m.

A tandem two-seat version was also considered, for which exist plans with two and one engines, with four guns in the nose, and a plan of 1972 shows a version with two seats side by-side and a different rear fuselage.

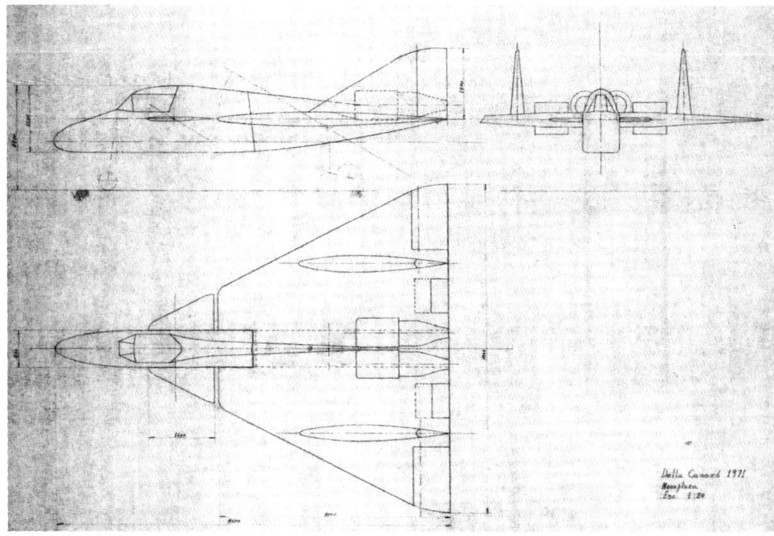

Jet fighter design made by Horten in 1971, with a swing wing and engines above the rear fuselage.

A side-by-side two-seater variant proposed in 1972 of the swing-wing aircraft by Reimar Horten.

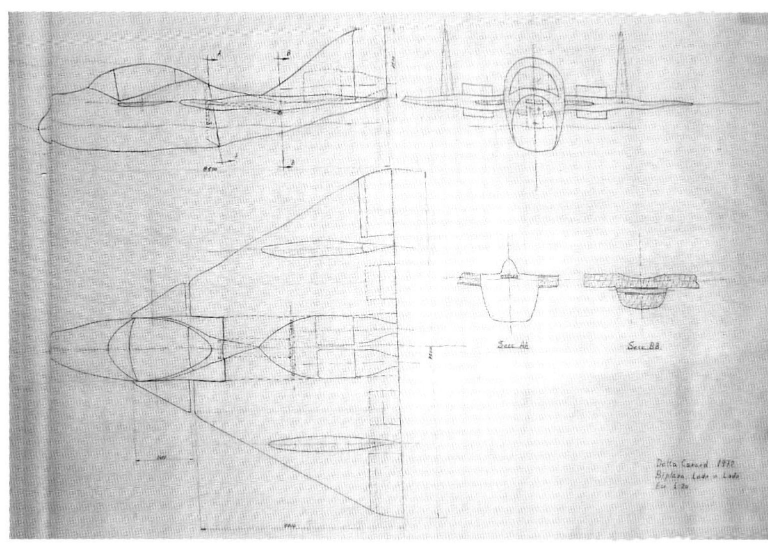

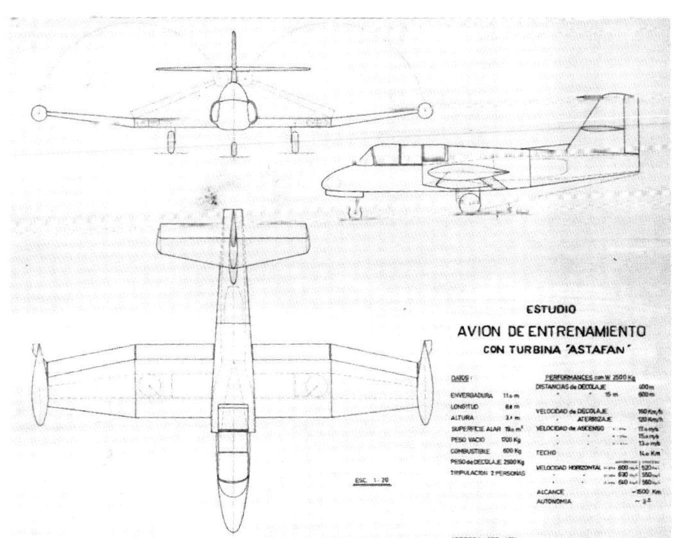

Advanced trainer proposal made by Reimar Horten in 1974 for operations on aircraft carriers. *Archive Diego Horten*

9 From abroad

44 Under licence

Among the aircraft built by the FMA and later FAdeA, there were several built under licence and some others only assembled or just modified or modernised. At the beginning, when the factory was organised, the directors were aware that they could not start with their own designs, as they still did not have the capacity to do so, so they decided to first acquire licences to produce planes from other manufacturers to gain experience.

Thus, in 1927, before the factory was inaugurated, an Army Acquisition Commission went to Europe and acquired a series of licences to produce the Avro 504R, the Breguet XIX, the Dewoitine D.21C-1 and the D.27, while locally there were talks with Virgilio Mira, who was building his own design called Golondrina, to produce it at the FMA, but no agreement was reached.

The FMA Avro 504R serialled 30 of the Argentine Escuela de Aviación Militar after receiving the Armstrong Siddeley Genet Major in 1935.

Avro 504

In the case of the Avro 504, the intention was to produce 100 504R Gosport aircraft and in 1927 the factory began the production of a series of seventeen and another of fifteen planes, with the first, serialled 11, making its first flight on 20 August 1928 piloted by Sergeant Segundo Yubel. The first series was delivered to the Escuela de Aviación Militar (EAM) during the year, replacing the older Avro 504Ks but only three of the second series were delivered in 1929, due to a lack of personnel at the factory, with seven finished in 1930, three delivered in 1931 and two in 1932. This completed the production of the type, as the Army had bought the Avro 626 Trainer and was also thinking of producing its own trainers with the Ae.M.E.1.

The poor performance of the Ae.M.E.1 led to the decision to improve the capabilities of the Avro 504R and re-equip it with a new engine. Tests were made with a 140hp Armstrong Siddeley Genet Major, which was installed in most of the planes in service, while the last built were delivered with this engine.

Later, using parts remaining from the construction of the planes and, most probably, from retired airframes, in 1937 two extra Avro 504Rs were built and delivered, but, with the arrival of the Focke-Wulf Fw 44J from that year, in 1938 the Gosports were stored and the last were scrapped by 1944.

Bristol F.2B Fighter

In 1920 the Argentine Army had received a single Bristol F.2B Mk III Fighter, followed between 1921 and 1924 by another twenty-eight, which by 1929 were in a very poor condition. In 1930 the factory started to rebuild four planes from the remains of wrecked ones, which were followed by another six in 1931, with all receiving new serials, from 29 to 38, and considered as new aircraft. The first of them flew for the first time on 13 December 1930. It is not clear the reason why the FMA decided to rebuild such old models by that time and some researchers have suggested that the Paraguayan government was interested in buying planes from the FMA to re-equip their air arm. A delay in delivering them the Dewoitine D.21s they were interested in led to the option to sell them rebuilt F.2Bs, but in the end negotiations were not successful and the planes were delivered to the Argentine Army.

Dewoitine D.21C-1

In 1926, Argentina purchased seven Dewoitine D.21C-1s plus four D.25s and the licence to produce both the D.21 and the D.27. The D.27 was an even more advanced fighter, equipped with a 500hp, twelve-cylinder V-shaped Hispano Suiza HS 57 engine, the prototype of which only flew for the first time in Switzerland in 1928. In the end, the D.27 series would not be manufactured. Along with the licence for the aircraft, one was obtained for the production of the Lorraine-Dietrich 12Ed engines of 450hp that would equip them, making them the first series-produced aircraft engines in South America.

Although the licence to produce the D.21 in the country had been active since 1927, economic problems slowed down the start of work until 1929, when the fine-tuning of its construction began and work began to produce the engine, to the point that on 28 December that year the first Lorraine-Dietrich manufactured in Argentina was finished. Tests began shortly thereafter and the engine was approved on 15 February 1930.

The Dewoitine D.21s were the first all-metal aircraft produced in Latin America and gave the FMA considerable experience, which would serve as the basis for the construction that followed years later, such as for the Curtiss Hawk 75-O. Initially there were many problems in starting production, due to the fact that the drawings that Dewoitine had delivered were insufficient and defective. Many parts were purchased directly from the manufacturer, which delayed production by four months. In addition, due to failures in the aircraft in service, locally designed copper radiators had to be built to replace the original ones, in the same way that many local modifications had to be applied.

The first of the four Bristol F.2Bs rebuilt by the FMA in 1930, before it was delivered with the serial 29.

Throughout 1930 FMA personnel worked hard to finish the series of thirty-two aircraft and forty-two engines, with construction of the first completed on 2 October. On the 15th, the aircraft made its first flight, piloted by Sergeant José Honorio Rodríguez. After a few more test flights, on 20 October it was officially presented to the national and army authorities, as well as to the press. However, it was not handed over to the army until 28 December. Shortly before, on 15 November, the prototype was presented at the Aviation Exhibition at the Chrysler building in Buenos Aires, along with a Lorraine-Dietrich engine among other things. In addition, on 23 December, the second aircraft rolled off the assembly line, which carried out a formation flight with the first example during the

A formation of FMA-built Dewoitine D.21s over Paraná Air Base.

The plane c/n 52 was finished with an Argus As 8B inline engine instead of the Siemens Halske Sh-14a one. It was called Focke-Wulf con motor lineal. *Fábrica Militar de Aviones*

delivery of the latter, while at the end of the year there were another thirty fuselages and eleven wings finished, five of them ready to be assembled and many other components.

Besides the production for the Argentine Army, in 1929 Paraguay negotiated the purchase of five D.21s, although no agreement was reached since the Argentine government prioritised the delivery of aircraft to the Argentine Army. Sometime later, in 1934, when Paraguay was in the middle of a war with Bolivia, they tried again to buy a batch of fifteen aircraft, although, given that Argentina was not only neutral, but one of the countries that was mediating for the signing of a peace agreement between the two nations, the request was not granted.

On 11 May 1931 the first eight aeroplanes had been delivered by the FMA to the Argentine Army, reaching fifteen examples on 29 October and finishing the delivery of thirty-two aircraft in 1932. Thanks to the large number of parts in stock and using materials from decommissioned aircraft, in 1937 the FMA built six additional D-21s, which were delivered at the beginning of the year and serialled from 33 to 38. The D.21s continued to operate sporadically until the late 1940s and in 1941 they were sent to the Army Mechanics School, where they remained until at least 1943 for ground instruction of the new aviation mechanics.

Focke-Wulf Fw 44J Stieglitz

Because of the need to replace the old Avro Gosport basic trainers, among other models, on 7 April 1936 an international tender was opened for the purchase of twenty basic trainers, the competition including the Bücker Bü-131 Jungmann and the Focke-Wulf Fw 44J Stieglitz, which were tested at the Escuela de Aviación Militar at El Palomar, near Buenos Aires, and the FMA. The Stieglitz was considered the winner and an order for twenty planes was made by mid-1937, including the demonstrator.

After the negotiations ended, it was agreed that the first planes would be completely built in Germany, while the second batch of ten would be assembled at the FMA using parts provided by Focke-Wulf and some built locally. Also, the licence to produce the model was acquired, not only to equip military aviation, but also for civil operators. An order was made for ninety Siemens Halske Sh-14a engines of 150hp, instruments, wooden parts for the wings and the steel tubes for the fuselage to assemble a first batch of seventy extra aeroplanes, totalling ninety, but the plan was to reach a total of 500 examples, something that became impossible later due to the restrictions in getting some parts because of the war in Europe.

On 5 October 1937 the steamer *Westerwald* arrived in Buenos Aires harbour with the wooden parts to start the assembly of the first local series, arriving at the FMA two weeks later, while on 11 October the steamer *Cap Norte* arrived with the remaining parts. Work to assemble the first plane started on 5 October, once the materials were approved by the FMA laboratories, and the plane was ready after thirty-four days, including the first metal propeller built in Latin America. An initial batch of ten metal and fifty wooden propellers was built.

Finally, on 16 December the first plane claimed as built by the FMA (in fact most of the plane was built in Germany, with locally built parts and assembled locally) made the first flight, piloted by Sergeant Santiago Germanó. This plane received the serial 21 and construction number 11.

Deliveries continued through 1938, with increasing locally built parts, with ten delivered to the Escuela de Aviación Militar, finally replacing the Avro Gosports. The first plane was used at the FMA for tests and twenty planes were delivered to the aero clubs of the Dirección General de Aeronáutica Civil, an organisation controlled by the Army Aviation but dedicated to promote civil aviation.

In 1939 deliveries continued until all the series of ninety planes were delivered (twenty built in Germany and seventy with parts made in Argentina).

The plane with construction number 52 (with serial 62 allocated, but never used) was finished with an Argus As 8B engine of four inverted cylinders and 140hp, because, due to the war in Europe, Siemens said they could not deliver more engines. Later, this aircraft was also tested with a de Havilland Gipsy Major II and exhibited with it from 19 October to 11 November 1940 at a fair in Buenos Aires. It was retired in early 1943.

Another modified plane was that serialled 51 (c/n 41) which, by order 3989/38, became a single-seater for use by the famous local female pilot Carola Lorenzini for a flight to link the fourteen Argentine provinces (by then the country only had fourteen provinces and nine National Territories, later converted into provinces), with the front seat replaced by an extra fuel tank.

In 1940, the problem to get more engines became evident, but the licence to produce the Sh14 was obtained and steel parts for a new series of one hundred planes were received, while they started to be produced locally. Meanwhile, five engines were obtained from Germany and, using locally built parts and some that could be obtained from Germany, it was possible to deliver five more planes during the year, all to the Dirección General de Aeronáutica Civil (DGAC).

The first locally built Siemens engine, called I Ae Sh14, was tested for the first time on 2 October 1940 with success, leading to a series of fifty built locally. Also, fifty Warner Super Scarabs of 145hp were purchased in the United States, but further attempts to buy more of them were vetoed by the US government, which was not happy with Argentina's neutrality in the war.

The problems with obtaining parts stopped production, but it was resumed in 1942, when on 22 September the planes 96 and 97 were delivered to the Escuela de Aviación Militar, followed by other sixty-two all to the Army Aviation. However, as there was no need to operate all of them, most were put into storage. The remaining forty-six Fw 44Js were almost ready at the factory, but problems with getting some parts and the fact that they were not needed mean they were not completed.

The factory activities were reduced again in 1943, as they were now in full development of the I.Ae. DL-22, and the examples 155 to 168 were delivered during the year. Finally, deliveries of 169 to 190 took place during 1944.

Before 1945, the planes Ee-30, Ee-48, LV-TDC, LV-IEC and LV-WDC, which had suffered accidents, were completely rebuilt. With this experience and with the intention of using extra airframes that were delivered from Germany before the war but were not finished, it was decided to complete them with wooden wings imported from Lithuania, as the original ones delivered with those airframes were in bad condition. The planes Ee-29, Ee-39, Ee-63, Ee-148, Ee-178, LV-TCC, LV-FDC, LV-XCP and Ee-182, were rebuilt using the constructor number of the former plane but now assigned to what were almost completely new aircraft. Also, a small series of twelve new planes was built, serialled Ee-67, 68 and from Ee-191 to 198.

The type served with the Argentine Air Force until 1961 and some still fly with civil owners.

The Focke-Wulf con motor lineal was later tested with a Gipsy Major II engine, as seen in the picture. It was retired in 1943. *Archive Fernando Benedetto*

Ee.104 after 1945. The plane was stored for some years before being pressed into service and saw only three years of service *Archive Santiago Rivas*

Formation of nine Curtiss Hawk 75-Os, in which those with serials from 631 to 650 were built by the FMA.

Avro Cierva C.30A

In 1936, the Argentine Juan Regés Aymá, who had met Juan de la Cierva in the United Kingdom and, convinced of the use of the autogiro, bought a C.30A, suggested engineer Bartolomé de la Colina, head of the FMA, buy a licence to build the type in Argentina. Regés Aymá demonstrated his autogiro to the Argentine Army, which ordered two, and de la Colina started to discuss with him a possible contract with de la Cierva, followed by his successor, Major Alfredo Paladino.

Regés Aymá met de la Cierva on December to discuss the creation of a joint society to sell the autogiros built in Argentina and on 8 December 1936 they reached an agreement, after which de la Cierva invited Regés Aymá to travel to the Netherlands on the following day, where he had to sign an agreement for the licence production of the autogiro in that country. The Argentine could not travel, as he had to depart for Paris, and de la Cierva was killed when the KLM aeroplane carrying him to Amsterdam crashed, ending the aspirations for the licence production of the Avro Cierva C.30A in Argentina.

Curtiss Hawk 75

In 1933, when Curtiss was selling its fighter biplanes in the region in countries like Chile, Bolivia and Colombia, contract number 463 was signed between the Dirección General de Material Aeronáutico of the Argentine Army and Curtiss Wright Export Corps, in which the latter donated the licence for the local production of the Hawk II and the Hawk Trainer, but production never started.

By the mid-1930s, the fleet of the Argentine Army Aviation was becoming obsolete, leading to a debate inside the government leaded by Agustín P. Justo about the necessity to buy new planes for the Army and the Air Force. According to the official registries of the Army Aviation, by 1935 the force was equipped with the FMA Ae.M.Oe.1 for observation and Ae.M.E.1 for training, with Dewoitine D-21 and D-25 fighters, while the Breguet XIX was being replaced by fifteen FMA Ae.M.B.1 Bombi bombers and the Junkers W34. Two Junkers F13 with three FMA Ae.T.1 and a single Ae.M.S.1 for medical evacuation comprised the transport force. As trainers, the fleet comprised the remaining Avro Gosport (some built locally under licence) and the Avro Trainers, used by the Escuadrilla de Aplicación and the Escuadrilla de Pilotaje of the Escuela de Aviación Militar respectively. The school was based at Base Aérea Militar (BAM) El Palomar, on the outskirts of Buenos Aires.

The discussion led to the sanction on August 1935 of law 12,254 for the purchase of planes and weapons for the Army and law 12,255 for the Navy, on what should be a joint purchase, using a budget determined by law 11,266. As a stopgap measure an urgent purchase of fighters was ordered and the Curtiss Model 68A Hawk III was offered together with the Fiat CR-30, the Dewoitine D-371 and D-500, which resulted in an order for ten Hawks.

On 7 April 1936 an international tender was opened for the purchase of twenty-two bombers, thirty fighters, thirty attack planes, three navigation and bombing trainers, twenty basic trainers, thirty advanced trainers, two autogiros, five transports and three planes for light transport and liaison. Meanwhile, the Dirección de Material Aeronáutico, on 17 November, purchased in Denmark Madsen 11.35mm and 7.65mm machine guns, to be used first in the Ae.M.O.1 and Ae.M.B.1 Bombis and later in other planes.

The offers arrived from most factories and this included:

Single-engine bomber: Northrop Gamma, Vultee YA-19, Breda Ba-65, Bellanca 28-70, Curtiss Model 60, and unknown models from Breguet, Koolhoven (most probably the FK-52) and an offer from a company described as Tri American Aviation Inc.

Twin-engined bomber: Bellanca 77-140, Savoia-Marchetti SM-81 with Isotta Fraschini, Fiat or Gnome engines, S.79B with the same options of engines, Fiat Br.20, CRDA Cant Z.1011, Caproni Ca.135, Junkers Ju86K, Glenn Martin 139W, Fokker TV, Koolhoven FK.50B and Breguet 460.

Fighter: Seversky SEV-X-BT, PZL P-24 with Gnome engine, Fiat CR-32, Curtiss Hawk IV, Vought V-143, Fokker D-21, Blériot Spad 510, Koolhoven F.K.58 and an offer from Tri American Aviation Inc for a plane with a Pratt & Whitney engine.

Light attack and advanced trainers: Curtiss CW-19R, Northrop Gamma, Seversky BT-8, IMAM Ro.37 with Piaggio engine, Henschel Hs 122, an unknown model of Fokker, and a model described as a Tri American Aviation Inc for a plane with Wright engine.

A commission was organised under the command of Colonel Víctor Majó, to check the proposals and then test the planes taken to the country. They later included the purchase of basic and advanced trainers, transport planes and bombing trainers.

The main factories of the world showed their models at BAM El Palomar, which included the Seversky SEV-X-BT two-seat fighter (serial NR189M, predecessor of the P-35), the Curtiss Model 79

Hawk IV (serial NR188M), the Fiat CR-32 (testing the plane MM2973 of the Pattuglie Acrobatiche), the Vought V-143 fighter (serial NR56V), an unidentified Swedish Air Arm Junkers Ju86B-3 bomber, the Savoia-Marchetti S.79B twin-engined bomber (serialled I-AYRE), the Breguet 462 (F-AKIB), the Martin 139W bomber demonstrator (serial NR15553), one IMAM Ro.37 (serial I-APLA with a radial engine Piaggio P.XR of 700hp and nine cylinders), a Curtiss CW-19R (serial NR11781), a North American NA-18, a Northrop Gamma 5B (serial NR14998), the Vultee YA-19 (serial NR14980), a Bücker Bü-131A Jungmann and a Focke-Wulf Fw 44J Stieglitz (serial D-ENOY).

Tests began on Monday, 7 September 1936 at Base Aérea Militar El Palomar, near Buenos Aires, starting on that day with the Vought V-143, the Curtiss Hawk IV, the Seversky SEV-X-BT and the North American N.A.18. After these tests, during one week, from 14 September were tested the Northrop Gamma, the Vultee YA-19 and the Martin 139W, while from 21 September the Ju 86, Breguet 462 and Curtiss CW-19R were flown.

The tests lasted until the end of the year, with those selected the Curtiss Hawk IV (but only the demonstrator was purchased), the Martin 139W (whose demonstrator was also bought by the Navy), the Northrop 8A derived from the Gamma, the NA-18 (the demonstrator NC2080 was purchased followed by an order for thirty improved NA-16Ps) and the Fw 44J (the demonstrator, serialled D-ENOY, was purchased). For the navigation and bombing trainers, the Fw-58 Weihe was ordered, although no planes were exhibited in Argentina, and for transport, the Ju 52/3m.

In the case of the fighter, the Hawk IV did not impress and in 1937 Curtiss sent the demonstrator, serialled NR1277, of the much better Hawk 75-H. The results of the evaluation were good and the Argentine Army decided to sign contract 699 to buy the demonstrator, plus twenty-nine extra examples designated Hawk 75-O. Also, by contract 670 the licence was obtained to produce the model locally, of which the plan was to build 200. To make this possible, Decree 951 of 25 June 1938 authorised an investment of 500,000 Argentine pesos to buy the tools and machinery to build the aeroplanes at the FMA, including a new press with 600 tons of pressure, a profiler with 150 tons of pressure and electric wielding equipment. Of the 25,000 parts that made the Curtiss Hawk, 10,000 were built at the FMA and the rest were bought from suppliers. The Wright Cyclone GR-1820G-5 engine of 875hp was also built under licence.

Because the plane was much modern than those built before, personnel from the FMA was sent to the Curtiss factory to be trained. A first series of twenty planes was started in early 1940, which were to be armed with two Madsen 11.35mm machine guns in the cowling and two of 7.65mm on the wings, but the later were changed to two 12.7mm Colts because they were more reliable.

On 10 August 1940 the first locally built Curtiss Hawk 75-O was finished and flew for the first time six days later piloted by 1st Lt Eduardo Correa. During the following tests, Lt Col Raúl Solá made a dive reaching 670km/h without problems. Shortly after, on 19 September, the plane was presented at El Palomar Air Base and by the beginning of 1941 they started to be delivered to the Argentine Army. By the end of the year, nineteen of the twenty were finished.

In 1942 the production ended with the last of the twenty but further production was ruled out as the progress of the Second World War showed that the Hawk 75-O was becoming obsolete. Also, the war limited the availability of materials to continue production, especially metals with which to build parts.

In 1947 the Argentine Air Force started to receive the new Gloster Meteor, a huge step forward from the Hawk, but the latter continued serving as trainers and the last were only retired in 1954.

Junkers Ju 52/3m

Due to the need to increase the transport capacity of the Argentine Army Aviation, on 19 September 1938 decree 12601 was issued authorising the purchase of five Junkers Ju 52/3ms, to be assembled at the Fábrica Militar de Aviones with Wright Cyclone GR-1820G-3 engines of 857hp each, built under licence. The Argentine Ju 52s were the first with a big-diameter nose, because of the engine, the only others being the Spanish examples, equipped with Elizalde engines. They also had Junkers three-blade engines and the plane serialled 165 had a bigger cowling on the central engine.

The airframes arrived in Buenos Aires in May 1939 and after being assembled they were assigned to the Agrupación Instrucción of the Escuela de Aplicación, at BAM El Palomar. The planes received serials from 164 to 168. In 1950 T-164, 166 and 168 were transferred to the Agriculture Ministry for crop-dusting duties against locusts, followed in 1952 by T-167, and they were retired in January 1956.

Four of the five Junkers Ju52/3ms assembled by the FMA.

Schleicher Rhönbussard, Schneider SG-38 Schulgleiter, Planeador Experimental and DFS-30 Kranich II

After a German mission visited Argentina in 1934 to develop soaring in the country, this started to grow fast and the demand for gliders grew accordingly. Gliders were imported, mainly from Germany, while there were some local projects, too. In 1938 the Sección de Vuelo sin Motor (Engineless Flight Section) of the Dirección General de Aeronáutica Civil requested from the FMA the construction of a series of Schleicher Rhönbussard gliders using plans that the Club Argentino de Planeadores Albatros (the main soaring institution of Argentina by then) had purchased in Germany. The proposal was accepted by Colonel Antonio Parodi, commander of Army Aviation, and Lt Col Alfredo Paladino, Director of Army Aeronautical Material, and in 1939 the construction of three gliders began at a very low pace, because the factory was focused on the production of the Fw 44J and preparing the series of Hawk 75-Os.

On 28 September 1940 the first example flew for the first time and was delivered shortly after to the Sección de Vuelo sin Motor, who sent it to the Albatros club. The other two were finished in late 1941 and delivered in 1942, one to Albatros and the other to the Club de Planeadores Córdoba. One of them still survives, flying in the United States with the serial N6257T, after wearing the Argentine serials LV-OAJ and LV-DAJ.

Later, in 1945, the Secretaría de Aeronáutica contracted with different local factories for the production of a series of Schneider SG-38 Schulgleiter gliders. They included the factories of Sfreddo y Paolini, Aero Talleres Argentinos, IMPA and the Fábrica Militar de Aviones. The later built ten examples, which received constructor numbers 01 to 10 and civil serials 0301 to 0310, and they were delivered to different clubs. In 1961 the first five of them were donated to the Club de Planeadores Paysandú of Uruguay, but they were never delivered as their condition was poor by then.

While production of the SG-38 was being prepared, in 1945 the Instituto Aerotécnico studied to make some structural improvements to the type and built a prototype, which was called PE or Planeador Experimental (Experimental Glider), receiving serial number 00. After tests, this glider received the civil serial 0311 but its fate is unknown.

When in March 1951 the first Argentine Congress of Engineless Flight took place at Villa Rumipal in Córdoba, the Dirección Nacional de Aviación Civil decided to buy ten DFS-30 Kranich II gliders from the Spanish company AISA. The wooden gliders, serialled 1 to 10, arrived in Argentina in very poor condition as during their transport by ship they were damaged extensively by water. Reimar Horten inspected them and suggested that IAME could rebuild five of them. Work progressed slowly and they were delivered by 1955, but three of them had to be retired shortly after due to structural problems.

The first Schleicher Rhönbussard built by the FMA in 1940, delivered to the Club Argentino de Planeadores Albatros.

Licensed ideas after the Second World War

At the end of the Second World War, Argentina was creditor of the United Kingdom, for the goods that the country sold to them during the war. Argentine neutrality was supported by the British, as Argentinian ships carrying goods to the UK were not attacked by German submarines. To pay the debt, the UK offered to pay with manufactured products, because it did not have currency at that time, but talks were also held over licence production of different British types.

In 1946, the British received a request by the Argentine government for different types of aircraft, including 150 reconditioned Miles Magisters plus 150 new, a quantity later increased to 500 and to be built under license in Argentina at the FMA. However, it was later decided that they would be constructed at a factory to be built by the company Messars, Hannequin and Co. In the end, only the first 150 reconditioned aircraft were bought.

After that, a document from 10 January 1947 and repeated in a memorandum of 22 February indicated that the country was interested in, among other types, 380 single-seat Gloster Meteors and twenty-two seaters. At a meeting by the directives of Evans, Thornton & Cía. (representatives of some of the British companies in Buenos Aires) with Brigadier Bartolomé de la Colina (Argentine Secretary of Aeronautics), Juan Ignacio San Martín (head of the FMA) and their teams, de la Colina said they were also interested in the Avro Type 700 project, which was a proposed replacement of the Anson with two 475hp Cheetah 26 engines and

Percival P.40 Prentice T.Mk.1s, assembled at IAME, while in service at the Military Aviation School. Behind there are some I. Ae. DL-22s.

seats for twelve passengers. As he was told the model was not expected to be put into production, he replied that it could be built in Argentina at the FMA. By that time, a plan was being developed to build a factory by the Hawker Siddeley Group and the Argentine government as a mixed company and the plan was to start building twenty-five Avro Ansons and then 300 Meteor Mk.IVs (with another eighty and the two-seaters to be built in the UK), so the loss of interest in the Anson was the first change to those plans. Also, the Argentinians said that any signature of a contract for the factory and the purchase of the light transport aircraft would depend on British authorisation of the sale of the Meteors and Avro Lincoln bombers.

A reply from Avro to the report of that meeting stated they did not have any improved version of the Anson (as the Type 700 never went beyond a proposal) and that the two-seat Meteor development was in its early stages and deliveries could not be made before mid-1948. The two-seat Meteor was, according to a memorandum of Hawker Siddeley, to be probably name Mk.5 (in the end was the T. Mk.7 and flew on 19 March 1948) and that the RAF was gaining interest in it (in the end, Argentine did not buy the two-seater and the RAF was the first operator).

In the end, the project to build a factory in Argentina was rejected and no further orders for the Meteor were made, including the idea to buy the two-seater. The licence to build their Derwent V engine was obtained, but only parts were made for use as spares. The FMA also made a plan to convert one of the planes into a two-seater to be used in observation missions, but this was cancelled.

Meanwhile, in 1947 negotiations took place with Filippo Zappata to obtain the licence for the production of the Breda-Zappata BZ.308 four-engined transport aircraft, which was a project by then. They continued in 1948 and even some plans were delivered to the FMA, but the negotiations were terminated during that year. In 1950 an order of planes for the newly created Aerolíneas Argentinas was negotiated, but this did not progress neither.

Percival Prentice

With the intention of replacing the Focke-Wulf Fw 44J Stieglitz as its basic trainer, in 1948 a contract was signed by the Argentine Air Force for one hundred Percival P.40 Prentice T.Mk.1 basic trainers, making it the largest foreign operator of the type. The first two planes were tested in the UK before delivery, with British class-B serials G-23-1 and G-23-4, and all were delivered disassembled before the end of 1948. They were taken to IAME, where they were assembled and delivered to the Escuela de Aviación Militar.

The first, with serial E.e-301 was delivered by the end of 1948 and between 28 March and 31 December 1949 another eighty-two were delivered, with the last seventeen shipped in 1950. The serials were shortly after changed to E-301 to 400.

The planes proved extremely reliable and there were very few major accidents, despite them being used by cadets on their first flights.

In 1955 five were transferred to the Ministerio de Aeronáutica for civil use, with civil serials, followed by three more in 1956. By that time, the problem in getting spares increased and the Air Force decided to buy ninety Beech B45 Mentors to replace them.

In 1961 the twenty-five Prentices that were in better condition were put for sale but there were no buyers, so almost all of them were scrapped.

T-33 and Morane-Saulnier MS.760 Paris

In the early 1950s, the operation of the Gloster Meteor, of which the Argentine Air Force had no two-seater, showed the need for a jet advanced trainer. On 29 January 1954 the US Air Force visited Argentina with the Alas para América (Wings for America) flight of Lockheed T-33A Silver Stars and the type was tested by some Meteor pilots. Shortly after, in April of that year, Cyril Chapellet, vice president of Lockheed Aircraft Corporation, visited IAME and talked with its directors about the possibility of producing the T-33A in Argentina.

In August 1954, a report was delivered by Lockheed estimating the production costs for a series of 100 aircraft in five years, delivering two per month and with the first deliveries after two years of signing the contract. Interestingly, the report highlighted that the aircraft production of IAME by that time was limited to the I.Ae.33 Pulqui II and I.Ae.35 prototypes, with the last all-metal aircraft produced in series being the Curtiss Hawk 75-O more than ten years ago. While they considered the engineers, chiefs of the workshops and mechanics were very good, they found that the factory had too few workers and component assemblers. They also found that, while the factory had enough space to produce the I.Ae.35 and the T-33 at the same time, there could be problems when they also considered the production of cars and other products and aircraft maintenance, which they proposed should be moved to another location within the factory.

The last of the thirty-six Morane-Saulnier MS-760 Paris to be built by DINFIA seen at Hangar 90 of the factory. They were mostly assembled with parts provided by Morane-Saulnier, with only some components built locally.

Lockheed estimated an investment of $19.8 million for the production of the 100 aircraft, but by 1954 there was no budget to move ahead. In 1956, the new head of the Argentine Air Force decided to restart the project, but also to look for other options.

In September 1957, Morane-Saulnier presented at the Aeroparque Jorge Newbery of Buenos Aires the prototype of the new MS.760 Paris, serialled F-BGVO, which was being toured across Latin America. The aeroplane showed not only its capacity as a trainer, but also the Argentine Air Force liked its capacity to carry up to four people for liaison.

An agreement was reached for the purchase of twelve examples built in France and to be assembled at the FMA, and the licence to produce another thirty-six at DINFIA, the first with French components but increasing the local production of parts. Deliveries of the French-built examples took place between 1958 and 1960, while the local production was being prepared, these being the first jet aircraft to be built in series in Latin America.

In November 1960 the local construction of the Paris began, with the first example of this series (serialled E-213) being delivered in March 1961, finishing production in mid-1963 with the delivery of E-248. However, some of them would not fly until 1967 due to a lack of engines and in the meantime they remained stored at DINFIA.

The type served for training at the Escuela de Aviación Militar and the IV Brigada Aérea, with the last serving with the latter unit until being retired in 2007 when the first IA-63 Pampa IIs were delivered. Some of them were modified at the FMA for target towing, with a 15m × 2m sleeve for air-to-air shooting practice. The FMA designed and installed an external bracket placed at the right rear of the fuselage, with the tow-cable reel located inside. The system was operated by a crew member by means of a reel, an auger and a pedal – which acted as a speed regulator for the deployment of the sleeve. The proximity between the folded sleeve and the exhaust nozzle of the right engine led to the installation of a deflector to divert hot gases away from the sleeve. In addition, a system that injected diesel into the exhaust nozzle generated smoke so that the aircraft carrying out target practice could more easily find the tug over the sea.

Beechcraft B45 Mentor

Due to the need to replace the I.Ae. DL-22 and the Percival Prentice at the Military Aviation School of the Argentine Air Force, and the cancellation of the I.Ae.44 in 1955 when Kurt Tank left Argentina, the force started to look for options, seeing that it was faster and easier to get the licence of a design that was already developed than to start again with a new project. After analysing the market, the force saw the Beechcraft B45 Mentor as the most interesting type and in 1956 they made contact with Beechcraft Aircraft Corporation through its representative in Argentina, Will L. Smith Sociedad

One of the Mentors built in Argentina seen in 2010. *Santiago Rivas*

Anónima. A contract was signed in early 1957 for a total of ninety aeroplanes, of which twenty-five were to be built in the United States and the other sixty-five in Argentina, with increasing participation of the factory in producing the components.

In 1957 the planes built in the United States started to arrive, totalling nineteen by the end of the year. During 1958 Argentine production was prepared, with the first locally built Mentor being flown for the first time on 31 October 1959, piloted Commander Raúl Enrique Borsani.

The aircraft received construction numbers from Beechcraft, with the twenty-five aeroplanes built in the USA receiving the numbers CG-165 to 189, being serialled E-001 to 025 at the Argentine Air Force. Those built in Argentina were from CG-190 to 199 and CG-224 to 278. The planes built in Argentina also received constructor numbers from DINFIA, from AG-1 to 65, with CG-190 having the constructor number AG-1. Their serials were from E-026 to 090.

Deliveries began in 1960, with a total of twenty-eight, with thirty-two more in 1961, three in 1962 and the last two in 1963. They were initially sent to the Escuela de Aviación Militar but some were also sent to the 1° Grupo de Ataque of the VII Brigada Aérea. In 1962 eight planes were assigned to the Curso de Aspirante a Oficial de Reserva (CAOR, Reserve Officer Aspirant Course) to train civil pilots as reserve officers of the Air Force, which was undertaken at the Base Oficial de Aviación Civil (BOAC, Civil Aviation Official Base) at Moreno, Buenos Aires. Those planes received civil serials of the kind used by state-owned aircraft, starting with LQ-.

In 1996, due to the age of the planes, which were reaching thirty years of service, a Service Life Extension Programme was contracted with LAASA to modernise thirty of the surviving aircraft, including a complete overhaul of the airframe and installing new or overhauled engines. Works began in 1997, with E-060 being the first delivered, and ended by 2004.

In 2008 a structural inspection was ordered and cracks were found, so the US company Blackwell was contracted to provide a reinforcement kit to extend the life of thirty planes (including a T-34A received from Uruguay and used by the CEV) for an extra 3,000 hours. The Mentors received new main wing spars and reinforcements of different parts. Sixteen were delivered in 2009 and another eight were delivered in 2010, but as they had become heavier, they could not perform aerobatics with an instructor and a cadet and were limited to operations such as shooting practice, so they could not be used properly for basic training as was their mission. Also, an accident led to the decision in 2011 to stop work on the modification of the remaining planes and retire them.

Despite this, by 2012 E-086 had been returned to service with experimental serial EX-086, followed in 2014 by EX-034 and in 2020 by EX-044, for use by the CEV and, with them, in 2020 the decision was taken to create an historical squadron. They were presented on 13 August during the parade for the Air Force Day and on 29 August 2023 they were transferred to the BAM Morón. Although the intention was to restore a total of eight Mentors, this did not happen. In December 2023 the planes E 030 and 045 were put up for sale.

Stroukoff YC-134

By the beginning of 1958, due to the need to improve the transport capacity of the Argentine Air Force, they started to analyse different types that could be built under licence and officials from the US company Stroukoff Aircraft Corporation visited DINFIA and offered their new project YC-134, which was an improvement of the C-123 Provider that they had designed for Fairchild. Although negotiations took place during 1958 and some announcements were even made that a contract was set to be signed, this did not take place.

The Farman replica built in 1962 flying at DINFIA. Currently it is preserved at the National Aeronautics Museum.

Farman replica

In 1960, together with the creation of the National Aeronautics Museum, Vicecomodoro Alberto González Albarracín proposed that DINFIA build a Farman Model 1912 for the fiftieth anniversary of the creation of the Military Aviation School, that would take place in 1962. Engineer Ambrosio Taravella, who had experience with the production of Farmans at the School workshops in the 1910s, guided the work and the Museo de Armas de la Nación (Nation's Arms Museum) donated two Gnome 50hp rotative engines and one of them was returned to service using some parts of the other. On 10 August 1962 the plane was exhibited during the celebrations for the Air Force day and on 8 September it was flown by test pilot Major Rogelio Balado. After a few flights, the plane was stored at the Military Aviation School until in 2003 it was finally taken to the National Aeronautics Museum in Morón, Buenos Aires, where it is preserved.

The Morane-Saulnier MS-885 Super Rallye assembled at DINFIA, seen shortly after being finished in 1962.

Morane-Saulnier MS-885 Super Rallye

After the good experience with Morane-Saulnier and the production of the MS.760 Paris, DINFIA received a proposal from the French company for the production under licence of the new MS-885 Super Rallye, which could be offered on the civil market in Argentina. In early 1962 the sixth pre-series production aircraft was sent to DINFIA and assembled there, being serialled LQ-HJH on 13 March 1962. The plane was to serve as the basis for the series production, but this never took place in the end and the company decided to move ahead with licence production with Cessna. The Super Rallye was flown by DINFIA with personnel from the CEV until 1964 and from then until 1966 was out of service, being sold on 15 December 1967 to José Girardotto as LV-HJH. The plane still exists and operates from General Rodríguez airfield in Buenos Aires.

Cessna production

On 24 January 1961, Cessna Aircraft Company decided to create the company Cessna Argentina S.A.I.C. and build an aircraft factory in Mendoza, Argentina, to produce the model 172. It also requested the support of the Argentine State to finance development of the facilities. They also stated that they would contract DINFIA and other local industries for the construction of different parts and said that other models could be produced in the future.

The plan they presented to the Argentine government was to start production in 1962 and they planned to build 837 aircraft until 1966, while their market study described that between 1957 and 1960 Argentina, Brazil, Chile, Paraguay and Uruguay imported 925 light aircraft, of which 680

Cessna 182 production at Hangar 90 of DINFIA. A total of 148 were assembled with some locally built parts. Many are still flying.

were Cessnas and 400 of them went to Argentina, so they considered a market of 168 aircraft per year only in Argentina.

This proposal did not get the support from the Argentine government that Cessna expected, but negotiations continued and in 1965 an agreement was reached for the production under licence at DINFIA of the model 182. They were to be named IA-53, but this was cancelled and they were instead called A182.

A first stage planned the assembly of eighty aircraft with airframes sent from the United States, with a second stage of 100 from assemblies built by Cessna, and a third stage of 320 aircraft, for which most components would be built in Argentina. The contract stated that DINFIA could request of Cessna the purchase of its production to be sold in the Latin American market, while DINFIA would sell the aircraft in Argentina.

After the first components arrived from the United States on 13 June 1966, a first series of twelve aircraft was started to be assembled. In August 1966 the first aircraft, an A182J, was finished and delivered on 2 September with constructor number A182-0001, being serialled as LQ-IPJ on the 13th of that month by the Secretaría

One of the Cessna A182Ns assembled at DINFIA, with serial LV-JED and c/n A182-0136 in front of one of the hangars of the CEV. This aircraft still exists and had a minor accident in Morteros, Córdoba, in 2022.

de Aeronáutica for use at the Base Oficial de Aviación Civil (BOAC). In 1970 the plane went to the Argentine Air Force as PG-341. Until 1968 DINFIA assembled a total of 116 aircraft, all from structures provided by Cessna, with fifty-six being A182Js, forty A182Ks and twenty A182Ls.

In February 1972 a new agreement was signed with Cessna, approved by the government with decree 1,152 of 2 March, and it also included the production of the 150 and 188 models, while it was expected to reach 500 A182s. In 1972 twenty A182Ns were delivered, but the economic and political crisis of the country stopped the production and it was only restarted in 1974 with ten A182Ns. Finally, in 1976 another two A182s were finished, but the last (c/n A182-0148) was only delivered to the Argentine Air Force in 1979. In total 148 Cessna A182 were assembled, all with Continental O-470-R engines of 230hp. Three unfinished airframes remained at the FMA and were later scrapped.

The plan expected the production of 320 Cessna 150Ls and A150L Aerobats and seventy Cessna 188B AGtrucks, and in January 1973 the first Cessna A-150L was delivered to the Aero Club Apóstoles with serial LV-LAV. In February it was the first A-A150L Aerobat, with serial LV-LAU.

In 1972, eighteen A-150Ls (c/n A-1501001 to A-1501018) and six A-A150Ls (c/n A-A1500001 to A-A1500006) were delivered, followed by twenty-one and three respectively built in 1973 (c/n A1501019 to A-1501039 and A-A1500007 to A-A1500009 respectively) but the last A-150 was delivered in June 1977 and the last A-A150 Aerobat in December 1974. All were equipped with a Continental O-200-A engine of 100hp.

In the case of the A188, the plan was to start replacing the old crop dusters that were modifications from aeroplanes not originally designed for that mission. The locally assembled planes were designated A-A188B AGtruck and equipped with a Continental IO-520-D of 300hp. In December 1972 the first aircraft was delivered to Gibiqui Aérea SRL as LV-LBD and the last went in July 1978 to Fumigaciones Rosquin SRL as LV-LYV. This was a total of thirty-four aeroplanes, of which eight were finished in 1972, ten in 1973, six in 1974 and ten in 1976. Their constructor numbers were A-A1880001 to A-A1880034.

Cessna 150s after being finished at DINFIA and ready to delivery.

As with the Cessna 182s, the economic crisis of the country made the sale of the planes very difficult and the assembly lines were closed by the end of the 1970s without reaching the quantities expected.

Many of the Cessna 182s went to the Argentine Air Force, who used thirty-nine of them over the years and some are still in service. Since 2018 the remaining fleet of eighteen has been modernised by the force with the support of the local company Redimec with new avionics from Garmin, with most of them already returned to service. Also, some of those of the three models that went to the civil market are still being flown.

Fighter and trainer proposals

Since the 1960s, there were many proposals to build fighters and trainers but none of them became a reality due to the lack of budget in almost all cases. The first proposals came in the mid-1960s, when the Argentine Air Force was looking for a replacement for the ageing Gloster Meteor and analysed the North American F-100 Super Sabre (rejected on account of its relative age), the McDonnell Douglas F-4 Phantom II (whose sale was refused by the USA), the English Electric Lightning, the Mirage III, the Saab 35 Draken and the Lockheed F-104 Starfighter. The Northrop F-5 was initially included among the options, but, despite its cheaper price tag, it was soon turned down as a result of the clear superiority of the competing designs.

By 1968, Peru was receiving its first batch of Mirages, while Brazil, Venezuela and Colombia were all examining purchases of the fighter. These factors, together with the decisive participation of the Israeli Mirage III during the Six-Day War and a powerful campaign of lobbying by Avions Marcel Dassault, led to the FAA's decision to purchase the aircraft.

The original plan called for around 100 Mirage IIIEs and Ds to be built locally at the FMA. The quantity was later reduced to fifty, but with limited available budgets, the FAA abandoned the licence-production proposal in 1967 and instead signed a pre-contract for a batch of Mirage IIIE and Mirage IIID aircraft.

Shortly after, in 15 October 1969 the Argentine Air Force issued a request for an offer to North American Rockwell Corps for the purchase of fifty T-2C Buckeye trainers to add the Morane-Saulnier Paris on the CEPAC (Curso de Estandarización de Procedimientos para Aviadores de Combate, Combat Aviators Procedure Standardisation Course, which was the fighter pilots course), to have an aircraft with better characteristics to prepare new fighter pilots, and also at the V Brigada Aérea to

improve the training to the pilots that were to fly the Douglas A-4B Skyhawk. The possibility of licence production was stipulated.

In May 1970 Rockwell delivered its proposal, in which twenty were to be delivered flying for a total cost of $10,860,000, and the other thirty would be assembled at the FMA. These would be sent in two batches of kits from Rockwell factory in Columbus, the first at a total cost of $8,130,000 and the second batch at $8,250,000. Plus, a badge of spares for $6,770,000 and tools for $1,665,000 was offered, for the maintenance of the planes for two years with an average of 400 hours per plane. Plus, some equipment had to be bought from the US government for a total of $8,364,000. Also, training for technicians was included and the FMA had to send five technicians to Rockwell to be trained on the assembly of the planes, while the company was to send three technicians to Argentina for one year to provide assistance on the introduction to service of the planes and five technicians for six months to the FMA to assist with the assembly. The training of the pilots was to be made by the US Navy under an agreement with the US government.

Deliveries of the planes completed in the USA were planned to start in August 1971, finishing in January 1972, while in February of that year the kits of the planes to be assembled in Argentina started to be delivered. The last kit of the first batch was to be delivered in September, together with the first of the second batch, finishing the deliveries in August 1973. The delivery of those planes by the FMA would have to be determined later.

Each kit was to consist of the following sets: the front and middle part of the fuselage, the rear of the fuselage, horizontal stabiliser, elevator, vertical stabiliser, rudder, ejection seats, compressor section door, combustion chamber section door, exhaust nozzle door, cabin canopy, ailerons, flaps, main landing gear with wheels and doors, exhaust nozzles, instrument panel, turbine quick change kit, primary structural components and lower fuselage.

Despite the interest, the offer was not accepted and the FMA kept looking for a solution based on the IA-58 Pucará.

After the cancellation of the IA-60, in the early 1980s, the FMA started studying an indigenous replacement for the Mirage fleet, under the designation SAIA 90 (Sistema de Armas Integrado Argentino, Argentine Integrated Weapons System), but the lack of capacity to develop a supersonic fighter led to talks with Dornier when both companies were working on the IA-63 Pampa. The Germans offered the local production of their proposal for the TFK-90 (Taktisches Kampfflugzeug 90) programme of 1979 for the Luftwaffe. The plane was developed with assistance from Northrop, initially with a single tail and vectored thrust engine nozzles and later modified with two tails and ordinary nozzles, with a shape similar in some ways to the Northrop YF-17 Cobra, although the expected performance was different.

With the Germans entering the European Fighter Aircraft (EFA) programme, this aircraft was proposed to it, but rejected and Dornier started to look for a customer for the project and discussed its sale with the Argentine Air Force.

The Air Force was interested and asked for an aircraft with a sustained turn speed of Mach 0.9 at 18,000ft; high acceleration rate between Mach 0.9

One of the Cessna A188s assembled at DINFIA seen in 2018. *Santiago Rivas*

A cover of the proposal made in 1964 by Sud Aviation for the production of the Alouette II in Argentina.

to 1.5 at 27,000ft: high deceleration, independent of relative speed; reasonable combat autonomy with internal fuel tanks; and minimal radar and IR section. The armament planned was a 27mm Mauser cannon with 150 rounds, two short-range IR missiles, four-medium range, radar-guided missiles and up to 5,000kg of air-to-ground weapons. The aeroplane must have a radar with air-to-air mode capable of detecting 5m2 targets at a distance of 90km without being detected by enemy ECM, and it also had to have the ability to track six targets that could be identified with an associated IFF. For the air-to-ground role, a radar capable of capturing the ground profile was desirable.

The engines were to be two turbofans of 5,600kg of thrust (possibly General Electric F-404), to reach a maximum speed of Mach 2. The empty weight was calculated in 7,800kg thanks to the use of composite materials. In the proposal for this aircraft Dornier suggested the use of 65 per cent carbon fibre-reinforced plastics (CFRP), 20 per cent aluminium and the rest in various materials such as titanium. The front fuselage would have 60 per cent CFRP, the centre 18 per cent and the rear 10 per cent, completed with other materials used in the wing, while the horizontal empennage would have 55 per cent CFRP and the vertical fin would have 70 per cent. The same materials would be used for the air intakes and the landing gear.

The FMA estimated that the project was to take about twelve to fifteen years to be finished from the moment the specifications were approved, which by 1987 had been delivered by Dornier, until the last production aircraft was delivered. Although the total quantity was not disclosed, as it was planned to replace the entire Mirage fleet (Mirage IIIB/C/D/E and IAI Dagger/Finger) and the Skyhawks, which should have been at least 100 aircraft. It was expected that a prototype could be flown by 1989 and deliveries could start by 1991.

While negotiations with Dornier were under way by the mid-1980s, the FMA also started talks with McDonnell Douglas for the possible licence production of the A-4M Skyhawk and with the AMX consortium to produce the AMX, with the aim of replacing the A-4B and C in service with the Argentine Air Force, but the budget reductions of the Argentine Armed Forces and the economic crisis in the country prevented the signing of a contract with any of them.

Many years later, in 2008, as the Argentine Air Force still needed to replace its Mirage fleet, Israel Aerospace Industry (IAI) proposed the production of IAI Kfir fighter aircraft using airframes from existing Kfirs or Mirages (the latter using those in service with the Argentine Air Force). A meeting between representatives of the company and the Argentine Defence Ministry took place on 11 December of that year and they proposed to develop a new and improved version, with new avionics, HMDS (Helmet-Mounted Display System), HOTAS commands, MFCDs (Multi-Function Colour Displays), UFCP (Up Front Control Panel), mission computer with integrated navigation, communications and shooting system, fly-by-wire controls, refuelling probe, ECM and self-protection systems, a new tail to carry a General Electric F414 engine, new air intakes, and some structural changes to extend the life of the original airframes for 8,000 extra hours, with an operational cost of $4,100 per hour. The investment to be made in each aircraft was around $22.8 million. IAI also suggested that this solution could be offered to other customers and stated they were building two prototypes that were to fly in 2010.

The Argentine Air Force found this project expensive for aircraft that were of an old design and thought the potential export market was too small, so the proposal was not accepted.

In 2011, during the eighty-fourth anniversary of FAdeA, the president of the company, Raúl Argañaraz, announced that they were in talks with the Chinese company Chengdu Aircraft Corporation for the licence production of the FC-1/JF-17 fighter aircraft, which he called Pulqui III, and at least forty were to be produced. Although the company kept talking about this intention until 2013, no progress was made and the idea was ditched.

French proposals

As the factory was exploring the possibility of building helicopters in the early 1960s, in 1964 the French company Sud Aviation made a proposal to DINFIA to build the SA.3180 Alouette Astazou, with a plan in three stages for a total of sixty helicopters in four years. The first stage was only the assembly of twenty aircraft from kits provided by Sud Aviation, while in the second, DINFIA was to produce most of the structure. The third stage comprised the production of all the helicopter by DINFIA except the main transmission, main rotor blades and engine. The proposal was finally not accepted for unknown reasons.

Another French proposal was made in May 1980 for the licence production of the project Aerospatiale AS35, which the French company had been developing since 1979 and which in 1981 was merged with the Aeritalia AIT230 to become the ATR 42. Aerospatiale offered two options, one being only the assembly of the aircraft and the other with the production of some components, like the wing leading edges, flaps and ailerons. They considered there must be a minimum of forty planes ordered within Argentina to consider the viability of the proposal, which would be distributed in three stages. The first stage was of three planes, which were to be assembled and painted. The second, of nine planes, included the production of the interiors, assembly of the aircraft and equipment and painting. The last stage, of twenty-eight planes, consisted of production of the moving parts of the wings and the interior, assembly and painting.

Aerospatiale also considered the possibility of ordering the production of the components built in Argentina to equip aeroplanes produced by them in other parts of the world.

The start of production was proposed by 1983, with the first kit to be assembled by the FMA to arrive in April 1985 and the last of the first stage in November of that year. The second stage was to start in October 1985 and end in December 1986, with the third stage starting in January 1987.

The first three planes were to be sold at a price of 22.6 million Francs each and the technology transfer was to be paid by the FMA at a cost of 16 million Francs. The rest of the kits, tools, spares and equipment had to be paid at a price of 65 million Francs.

Aerospatiale also proposed an association with the FMA for the sale of the AS35 in South America and for after-sales support.

While the forty planned planes were to be of the passenger version, Aerospatiale also showed a design of the cargo transport version with a rear ramp, which could have been of interest to the Argentine Air Force. This proposal was not accepted in the end and the factory moved on to work on the IA-67 programme, which was also cancelled.

In 1984 Aerospatiale made another proposal, this time for the production of the Epsilon basic trainer to replace the B45 Mentor. The plan had four stages, with the first twenty planes including parts built in France, with the first five with only minor parts built by the FMA and the assembly of the planes. The second comprised eight planes with the entire fuselage and other parts built in Argentina, while the third, of seven planes, would also include the wing and tail made in Argentina, with only some parts provided by the French company. The fourth stage, from the twenty-first plane onwards, added the final production of the wing middle part.

Helicopter projects

On 22 April 1988, decree No. 492/8, created the company FAMA SA to develop projects that were to be built by the FMA and that FAMA would later sell, with 44 per cent of the shares in the hands of Aeritalia/Agusta. The Italians proposed the local production of parts of the ATR 42 transport plane and also the production of the A129 LBH (Light

CZ-11 Pampero, the local designation given to the CATIC Z-11 assembled in 2012. The helicopter is currently stored at the factory. *Lisandro Amorelli*

The first Puelche assembled by FAdeA seen in August 2012 during an exhibition. *Santiago Rivas*

Battlefield Helicopter) Utility, a transport version of the A129 Mangusta attack helicopter, sharing the same engines, transmission, rotors and landing gear. It had slightly larger dimensions and greater capability than the A109, which was already in use by the Argentine Army. The plan was to develop the LBH version for the Argentine Army, capable of carrying, besides troops, a chin turret for a machine gun plus pylons on the sides of the fuselage to carry rockets, missiles or machine guns for light attack and anti-tank duties. For the Argentine Navy, a naval version was planned with a radar in the nose, an ESM system by Eletronicca Spa., capacity to carry anti-ship missiles, rockets and torpedoes. And, finally, for the Argentine Air Force, a utility version for transport and C-SAR operations.

The new helicopter would have capacity to carry between twelve and fourteen soldiers or 2,300kg of cargo or 2,000kg of external cargo, having an empty weight of 2,550kg and a MTOW of 4,850kg. It was to be equipped with two LHTEC CT800 turboshafts to reach a speed of 154 knots and a maximum range of 1,250km.

In July 1988 the CEO of Gruppo Agusta SpA, Raffaello Teti, delivered the production proposal for the helicopter to the Argentine Defence Ministry, with the aim of equipping the three Argentine Armed Forces with it. The proposal comprised a production of 200 helicopters for Argentine users and 400 extra airframes to be sent to Italy to be finished with the installation of the tail and main rotor. The price of each of them would be between $4.5 and 5 million.

Although there was a lot of interest from Argentina in the proposal, the problems faced by the country and the FMA by 1989 impeded the signing of a contract.

Together with the approach to China made by the management of FAdeA in 2011, the company also negotiated the assembly of the CATIC Z-11 helicopter, an unlicensed Chinese copy of the Airbus H125 Ecureuil. An example was sent disassembled to Argentina and assembled by FAdeA in two months, presenting it on 12 October 2012, where it was given the name CZ-11 Pampero. The helicopter received the experimental serial LV-X497 and FAdeA stated the type was to be sold to the Argentine Armed and Security Forces, as well as to civil operators. However, that that led to complaints by Airbus, which considered it unfair competition to offer a type that was a copy of their product.

However, FAdeA announced that they planned to start series production in 2013, adding locally built components.

On 10 May 2013 the type was exhibited to the Argentine Air Force at the VII Air Brigade in Moreno, Buenos Aires, on 17 April it was shown to the press and on 16 August it was exhibited at Morón during the Argentine Air Force celebrations. However, tests of the helicopter that showed poor performance, the lack of certification, together with the problems with Airbus and accusations of corruption that were aimed at FAdeA's president, Raúl Argañaraz, brought an end to the project and on 25 March 2014 the serial was cancelled. Since then, the helicopter has remained stored at FAdeA.

On the same day of the presentation of the Z-11, 12 October 2012, it was announced that an agreement had been reached between FAdeA and Cicaré S.A., a local light helicopter factory, for the series production of the Cicaré CH-12 two-seat helicopter, but, as with other projects announced during that time, this did not move forward.

Puelche

When FAdeA was created in December 2009, the Argentine agriculture sector was growing considerably and crop spraying activity was also experiencing an expansion. However, there was a need to replace many older types, especially those modified from aircraft not built for air spraying, as were many Piper PA-11s and 12s, Cessna 182s and other types. By then, the Argentine company Laviasa, from Mendoza, had purchased from Piper the type certificate of the PA-25 Pawnee, which they had started to build as the Laviasa PA-25-235 or -260 Puelche, according to the power of the engine.

As Laviasa did not have the capacity to produce the plane in large quantities, an agreement was signed in 2012 in which the company would deliver twelve airframes to FAdeA, where final assembly would take place. Also, FAdeA would find financing for the planes, arrange the production certification and find customers.

After those twelve examples, FAdeA would continue with the complete construction of the type at their facilities.

The first plane, a PA-25-260, was finished in 2012 and used as demonstrator, with serial LV-CZB and c/n 260-12030, while the second, initially

One of the Grob G-120TPs assembled by FAdeA, seen in 2021 flying alongside a T-6C Texan II, both being operated by the Military Aviation School of the Argentine Air Force. *Santiago Rivas*

serialled LV-CZC and with c/n 260-12031, was modified for glider towing and delivered to the Argentine Air Force with serial PG-461, being also a PA-25-260.

On 8 April 2013 the first example purchased by a civil operator was delivered, with serial LV-FMQ, and the Argentine Air Force received another in 2015, serialled PG-462 (c/n 260-12036) and another in 2018, serialled PG-463.

Interestingly, two were sold to a Colombian owner in August 2017 (one of them was tested with the Argentine serial LV-HFW), being the first exported aircraft by the factory since the Pucarás sold to Sri Lanka, and one was exported to the Rempel company of Paraguay in 2018, serialled ZP-BOV. In 2017 another was delivered to a private owner with serial LV-GAK.

The first PA-25-235 delivered was serialled LV-FQL and was followed by another two, one of them being serialled LV-FZQ.

As FAdeA could not get financing, except for the plane sold to Paraguay and two sold to private owners, only twelve were delivered (nine PA-25-260s and three PA-25-235s, half with fixed-pitch propellers and half with variable pitch), with the last in 2023. Another five unfinished structures remain at FAdeA.

Grob G-120TP

After the retirement of the Mentors in 2011, the Argentine Air Force started to look for an urgent solution and an offer was received for ten Grob G-120TP-As, but the force did not accept it. The planes were then sold to FAdeA, which was contracted by the force on a pay-per-hour basis and they were assembled at the factory from kits provided by Grob. On July 2013 the company started to assemble the first four, which received the serials E-501 to 504, and they were delivered to the Air Force on 16 August. On 19 December 2014 the other six, serialled E-505 to 510, were delivered but E-509 was lost in an accident on 19 October 2017. The others are still being used by the Military Aviation School, with all the maintenance performed by FAdeA.

45 **Modifications and modernisations**

Over the years, the factory developed several modernisation and modification programmes, some of them already described in other chapters when the types affected were those built by them. In some cases, some were only proposals and were not accepted.

Among them, one of the types more often considered for modifications and modernisation was the Beechcraft Mentor, of which the modernisation of the planes of the Argentine Air Force was discussed in the previous chapter.

Besides them, in 1961 Reimar Horten proposed to develop a jet trainer with a single Turbomeca Marboré engine, using the wings, tail and cabin of the Mentor with a new fuselage. The projected plane had a length of 9.05m, a wingspan of 9.1m and a height of 3m, with a wing area of 15.6m2. The empty weight was 620kg and the MTOW was 1,500kg. The maximum speed was 410km/h and the cruise one was 334km/h, with 1,000km of range and three hours of endurance, with a service ceiling of 30,000ft.

In 1962 DINFIA studied the possibility of modifying the design to produce a four-seat version, which was basically a return to the Bonanza. Unfortunately, no plans for this proposal were found, but the memoirs of the factory for that year include the project as one that was under study.

Shortly after, in June 1963, another study was made to install a Turbomeca Astazou in the Mentor to improve its performance, with the plane reaching a length of 8.77m. The idea of installing a turboprop engine in the Mentors serving with the Argentine Air Force was again considered in the late 1970s but, again, was discarded.

Meanwhile, with the Argentine Navy considering modernising its fleet of Beechcraft T-34C-1 Turbo Mentors received in 1978, in 2020 the force and FAdeA developed a modernisation programme for these planes. This will include a new VHF1 and 2, UHF, intercom, new instruments, the installation of a GNSS (Global Navigation Satellite System), new navigation systems and engine indicators. An Aspen Avionics EFD 1000 (PFD) system will be installed, with an RC Allen RCA 2610 Backup Attitude Indicator, a United Instruments 9552 Turn and Tilt Indicator, a Mid Continent C2400 Magnetic Compass, a Thommen 5C16 Airspeed Indicator, a United Instruments 5934 Altimeter, a UMA Instruments T08-210-60W Vertical Speed Indicator, a Thommen B15 stopwatch, a Rockwell Collins VHF4000E VHF radio, a Bendix King KTR-909 UHF radio, a Northern Airborne Technology ACP53 intercom and audio system, an Electronic International MVP50 colour engine information display unit, a Rockwell Collins NAV4500 and DME 4000 navigation system, Bendix King KDF806 ADF, Avidyne IFD410 GPS, ADS-B Out Avidyne AXP322 and ELT system.

A retired Turbo Mentor was sent to FAdeA to be used to test the equipment and works were expected to start in 2022, but they were delayed to 2024. An aircraft is to serve as a prototype and another three will be modified.

In 1961 the Argentine Air Force received a batch of fifty-two North American T-28A Trojans, but their engines were in poor condition and the airframes were showing their age, so engineer Héctor Ruiz proposed modernising them with Turbomeca Bastan turboprops. Unfortunately, no information was preserved, except

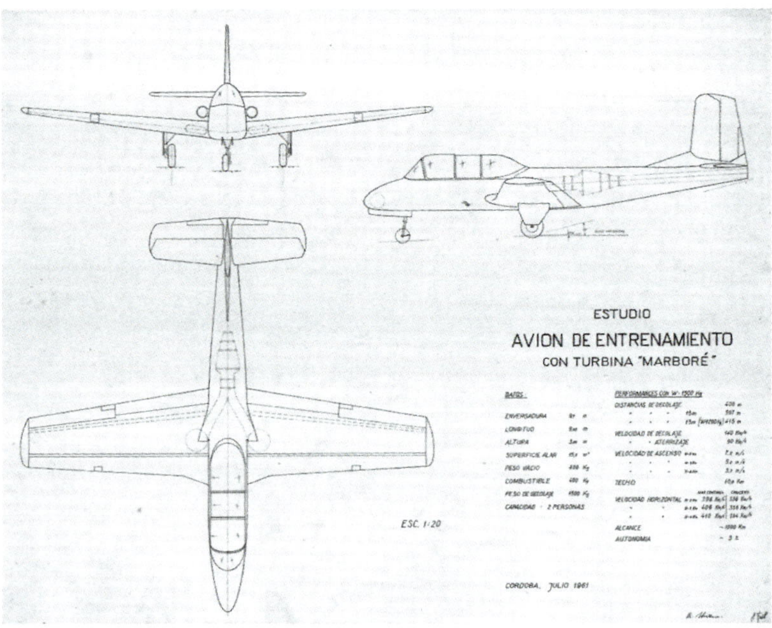

A jet aircraft based on the Beechcraft Mentor proposed by Reimar Horten in July 1961, using the cabin, wings and tail of the basic trainer but with a new fuselage. *Archive Diego Horten*

Turboprop version of the Beechcraft B45 Mentor proposed by DINFIA in 1963, with an Astazou engine. *Archive José Martínez*

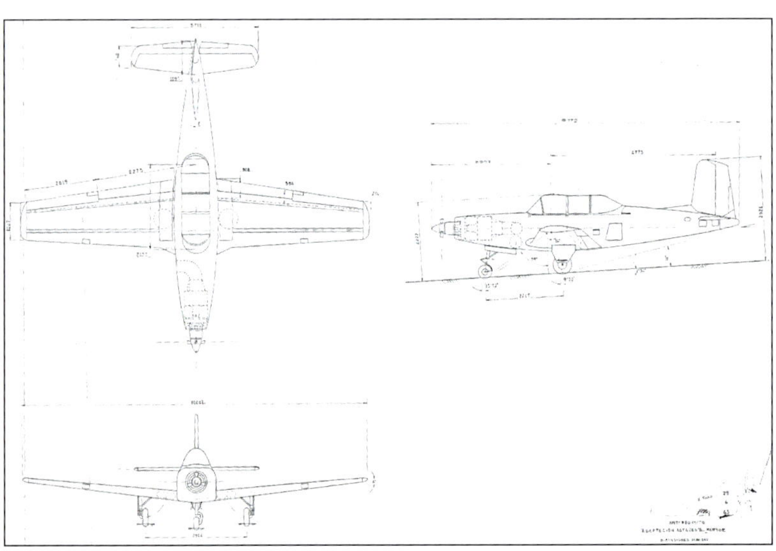

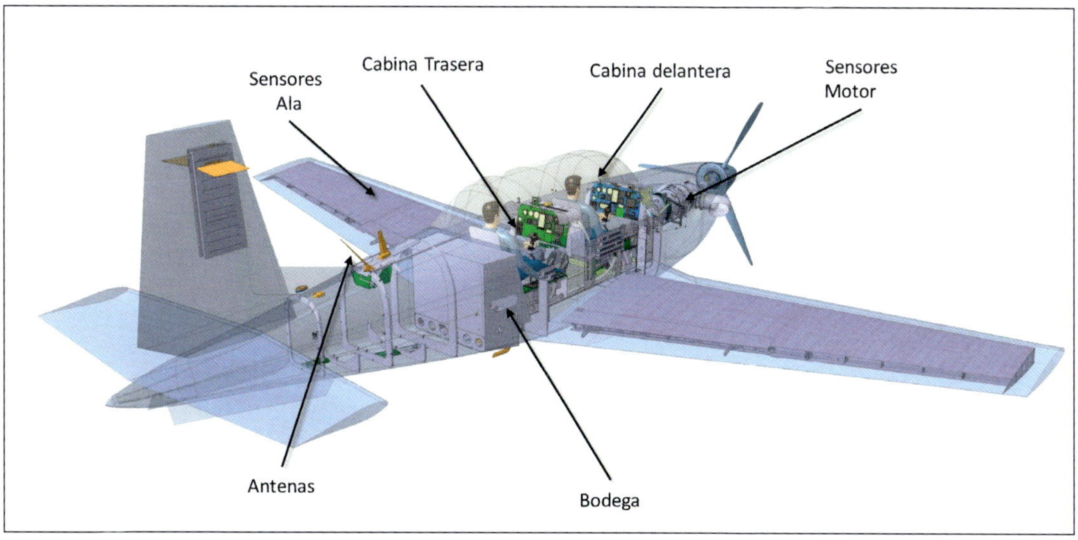

LEFT A render of the Turbo Mentor modernisation project.

BELOW A model of the T-28A modified with a Turbomeca Bastan turboprop proposed by engineer Héctor Eduardo Ruiz.

pictures of a model with one configuration and another model with a different configuration that is in the hands of Ruiz's son, Eduardo Ruiz.

A plan dated 17 April 1969 shows a proposal for a modification of the Douglas DC-4 with two Rolls-Royce Dart 12 engines of 3,200shp, instead of four Pratt & Whitney Twin Wasps, giving an extra 15km/h of cruise speed. The type was being retired by the Argentine Air Force and the proposal was to give them an extra life, but it was discarded as the force had received the first Fokker F27 and Lockheed C-130E Hercules in 1968.

A-4AR Fightinghawk

In the early 1990s, the Argentine Air Force began thinking about replacing the Douglas A-4Bs and Cs and had the F/A-18 Hornet and F-16 Fighting Falcon in mind, but the US government denied the sale of these aircraft and instead offered fifty-four A-4Ms (forty-eight A-4Ms and six OA-4Ms) instead. The Air Force, not happy with the equipment in the type, requested its modernisation and immediately the Ministry of Defence began to seek bids from different companies for a contract. Initially, the offer from Smith Industries and the US Navy was the most interesting and, in October 1992, McDonnell Douglas and CASA of Spain made an offer to improve the A-4 in Spain, also including the modernisation of the Mirage III of the VI Air Brigade. In 1994, McDonnell Douglas made another bid, this time for twenty-three modernised Kuwaiti A-4KUs, but it was rejected due to the condition of the aircraft, which were finally acquired by the Brazilian Navy in 1998.

After a long negotiation, the Argentine Air Force signed a contract with Smith Industries and purchased thirty-six A-4Ms and four OA-4Ms from the US Navy for $70 million. At the same time, the Minister of Defence accepted Lockheed Aircraft's proposal to take control of the Fábrica Militar de Aviones (FMA, Military Aircraft Factory) and modernise the A-4s in the United States and Argentina. Lockheed Aircraft Argentina (LAASA, later Lockheed Martin, LMAASA) was created and signed a contract for $214 million for the modernisation of the aircraft, part in Córdoba and the others in Ontario, California.

On 2 August 1995, the first A-4M, serialled C-905 and named 'Gaucho 02', flew to Ontario from Davis Monthan and on 6 September 1995, C-906, named 'Gaucho 01', did the same (however, the main wing spar had serious structural problems and the aircraft was replaced by another that

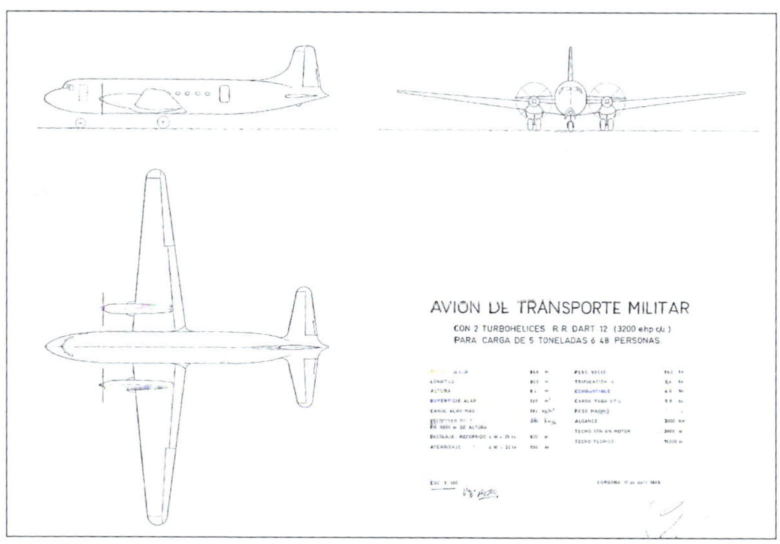

A proposal to equip the Douglas DC-4 with Rolls-Royce Dart turboprops in 1969. *Archive José Martínez*

Another variant of the T-28A modification with a turboprop, which is kept by Ruiz's son. *Santiago Rivas*

received that serial). On 30 September, the first four aircraft arrived at LAASA for modernisation.

The modernisation of the type, now named Fightinghawk, included a total overhaul of the fuselage and the addition of new avionics, which included the ARG-1 radar, a limited version (by British pressure) of the APG-66, but which was later improved in Argentina. The instrument panel received two LCD Head0-Down Displays (HDD), an Up Front Control Panel (UFCP) and a Head-Up Display (HUD). In addition, the Fightinghawk has HOTAS (Hands on Throttle and Stick) commands, AN/ARL-93(V-1) radar warning receiver (RWR), two EGI-2 laser inertial platforms with GPS, IFF and the provision of chaff and flares dispensers, although they were never used in the country. The aircraft also has a digital mission computer, with a ground mission mapping system, where the pilot enters mission information and then transfers it to the aircraft using a data transfer module (DTM). Above the engine compartment, the Fightinghawk has an integrated ECM system and a radar jamming system. All avionics are connected by a fibre optic network and use a 1553 data bus.

The first four A-4ARs (C-906, 908, 917 and 918) and one OA-4AR (C-903) were delivered on 12 December 1997 at the Lockheed Martin Skunk Works facility in Palmdale, California, and then flown to Argentina. Subsequently, on 3 August 1998, the first A-4AR was delivered by LMAASA in Córdoba (C-922) and the last was delivered on 7 January 2000 (C-905 and 916). Once the entire fleet was in service, the Air Force decided to keep eighteen in storage and eighteen in service due to a lack of budget and pilots. The type is still in service.

Fokker 50 SIGINT for Peru

In early 2020 FAdeA was contracted by the Israeli company IAI Elta to modify a Fokker 50 of the Peruvian Navy into a SIGINT (Signal Intelligence) platform. The Israelis made the design of the modification and provided the equipment to FAdeA, which built all the parts to carry the antennas and all the structural modifications, installed the equipment and carried out the flight tests.

The plane, serialled AE-567 (c/n 20253) of the 11th Naval Air Exploration Squadron, of the 1st Naval Air Group of the Peruvian Navy, based at the Jorge Chávez Airport in Lima, arrived in September 2020 and, although it was planned to finish the work in April 2021, the COVID-19 pandemic delayed it.

The aircraft received a SATCOM antenna on top, ELINT Elbit Systems Emerald AES-212 antennas on the sides, ESM and RWR antennas at the front and tail and an optical sensor turret at the front.

On top it received a Satint antenna, a GPS antenna, a LOS, UHF, IFF1 antenna and a new anti-collision light, while underneath were installed COMINT VU DF (direction finding) and P-Band, an HF antenna, six Laser Warning Systems (LWS, two in the front, two in the middle and two in the rear),

Modernisation of the McDonnell Douglas A-4M Skyhawks into A-4AR Fightinghawks at Hangar 90 of LMAASA by 1997.

Delivery of the fifth C-130H Hercules modernised, the fourth by FAdeA as the first was upgraded in Canada. Another is expected to be modernised between 2024 and 2025. *Santiago Rivas*

two Elbit PAWS IR missile warning systems (MWS), chaff and flare dispensers, DME 1 & 2 and ADF.

In the cabin it carries six system operators, with their respective racks and screens, while in the cockpit it carries the controls to launch chaff and flares.

On 17 March 2022 the plane made its first flight after the modifications and it was delivered on 19 April.

AB-206

Faced with the retirement of the Agusta A109As, which stopped flying in the first decade of the twenty-first century, the Argentine Army began in 2009 to negotiate the purchase of twenty second-hand Agusta Bell AB-206B-1s from the Italian Carabinieri, although the process was significantly delayed and only in 2017 were they acquired for a total of 2.6 million Euros, including spare parts and training.

As part of an agreement for the transfer of two Bell Huey 2 helicopters from the National Gendarmerie to the Army, five of the AB-206Bs were transferred to the Ministry of Security, although the machines are not being used. The other fifteen were left in the hands of the Army, which also decided to modernise them with Garmin 500 avionics, new communications equipment and a complete overhaul, including the change of the interior and the overhaul of the engine and transmission. The modernisation work was contracted to FAdeA and the cabin modernisation was developed by Redimec, except for one example that was modernised in Italy before delivery and used there for training.

At the beginning of 2020, the first modernised and locally overhauled example was delivered, along with the modernised one in Italy, followed by two more in April of that year. In July 2020, the modernisation of another four was contracted, in addition to the recovery of the fifth copy of the Ministry of Security, for a total of $1.5 million, which were completed in May 2023. Work is currently under way on an additional example and the contract for the remaining five is expected.

All aircraft were delivered to the Escuadrón de Aviación de Exploración y Ataque 602 (602nd Scout and Attack Aviation Squadron), although some are loaned to the Army Aviation School for training alongside the five Bell 206B-3s of that unit. While it was planned to deliver some units to the Army Aviation Sections in the interior, this has not happened.

C-130 Hercules

In 2014 the Argentine Air Force decided to modernise five of its remaining Lockheed Hercules and the company L3Harris was contracted to provide the modernisation kits. The first aircraft (KC-130H serial TC-70) was modernised in Canada and delivered in 2016 and, after that, the work on the remaining aircraft was carried out at FAdeA. The first plane was another KC-130H (serial TC-69), followed by the C-130Hs TC-61 and 66, with the last, C-130H TC-64, delivered on 23 December 2022. A sixth kit was purchased in that year and initially it was planned to install it in the force's single L-100-30, but as another C-130H was leased from the US government in 2023 and in May 2024 it was expected to execute the purchase option, the plan is to install the kit in that plane.

The modernisation includes a new cabin with six multifunction displays, new navigation and communications equipment, a Honeywell APU with a GCU (Generator Control Unit), and a Northrop Grumman APN-241 multimode radar. The KC-130Hs received a FLIR Star Safire III sensor turret too, for SAR duties.

One of the Agusta Bell AB-206s modernised at FAdeA with support from Redimec. *Santiago Rivas*

10 Beyond aircraft

46 A wide range of production

Besides aircraft, FAdeA built many other products over the years, from weapons and aircraft engines to very different products, like cars, motorbikes, tractors and boats.

Aircraft engines

The first production besides aircraft was closely related to them and was the Lorraine-Dietrich 12Ed engine of 450hp, whose licence was obtained with the licence of the Dewoitine D.21C-1, but the engines were also used on other aircraft with the idea to standardise the types of engines. The first was the FMA Ae.T.1, followed by three types of the Argentine Navy: the D.21C-1 (although they were not built in Argentina), the Supermarine Southampton Mk.III and the Fairey IIIF. However, in the latter the engine did not have enough power and they were later changed for the Armstrong Siddeley Panther IV.

The first Lorraine-Dietrich 12Ed engine built at the FMA.

Curiously, the engine was also used in the DL.43 Nahuel tank, which was entirely developed by the Argentine Army, which saw the need to have tanks in the middle of the Second World War but it was impossible to buy them abroad.

The next engine built under licence was the Wright Cyclone SGR-1820F3 of 715hp in 1939, which was used by the first five Junkers Ju 52/3ms and later installed in the Junkers K43 and the FMA Ae.M.B. Bombi when they needed an engine change.

A licence to build the more powerful Wright Cyclone GR-1820G-5 of 875hp, for use in the Curtiss Hawk 75-O, was also acquired.

The first locally developed engine was the I.Ae.R-16 El Gaucho, which was in fact a locally built Wright Whirlwind R-975-E3, of which Argentina got the licence in 1938 but their production was delayed. When the Second World War began it was not possible to secure the tools and training to build them, so, using the engines in service with the North America NA.16-1P of the Army and plans that were received, a local engine of 400hp was built. The first El Gaucho engine was started for the first time on 27 June 1944.

In 1940 licence production of the Siemens Sh 14 Bramo engine, called I Ae Sh14, also began for use in the locally built Focke-Wulf Fw 44J. A total of fifty were built by the FMA.

The Cyclone SGR-1820F3 served as the basis for the I.Ae.R-19 El Indio engine, which was basically a copy of the Cyclone with some minor improvements. After a prototype was built with 510hp, called I.Ae.R-19 SD/1 and started for the first time on 11 June 1947, followed by another with 680hp and called SR/1A, the first production version of the El Indio

The engine production line at the FMA in the 1940s.

engine was the CR/1C of 750hp with a reductor and the engine was used in the I.Ae.35 aircraft, although some other projects were expected to use it, too. A final version was tested, called CR/2, which reached 840hp and was planned to be used in the I.Ae.39 and I.Ae.42, which were never built, while in factory documents a version called X-08 is named as being developed in 1961 but it was never built

Prototype engines were made of the I.AE. 0-1600 R X-1 in December 1957, for 65 to 75hp and four cylinders opposed, and the I.AE. 0-4000-R of 160hp, which was planned for the I.A.45 Querandí and I.A.46 Ranquel and was a copy of the Lycoming O-320. A more powerful engine, called IA 0-6000DX/1, was tested on 19 September 1959, with three prototypes also being tested in 1961, but no more details are known, although possibly it was a local version of the Lycoming O-360 used in the I.A.45 X-II or the Continental O-470 of the B45 Mentor.

Although the licence to build the Rolls-Royce Derwent V and Nene II was acquired and some tooling was built in 1950 to build the engines, while a jet engine factory was organised, none was built and the factory only assembled some in 1955 and performed overhauls to the engines used by the Meteors and the Pulqui prototypes. In December 1952, work began on jet engines, with the study of the IA T-2 started, but these works were transferred to the Dirección General de Fabricaciones Militares belonging to the Army by 1955 and were cancelled sometime later.

Cars

On 30 November 1951 the Fábrica de Motores y Automotores, later called Fábrica de Automóviles, was created to build engines and cars, and construction of the facilities began on 2 December. Design of the first cars progressed very quickly and on 1 February 1952 the construction of the first prototypes began. The tests of the first car engine, called M-700, were started on 23 February, this being a two-cylinder of 24hp of 700cm3 for use in the first car to be designed.

Initially the company developed a series of vehicles called Institec, which used the mechanics based on models from DKW but externally it was based on the Chevrolet of 1951, and comprised the Sedan Institec, the Chatita Institec (a pick-up truck) and the Rural Institec (a version of the Chatita with a closed back). On 10 March 1952 they started the

The prototype of the Rural Gauchita, presented in 1952 but never built in series.

The unveiling of the Chatita Institec in 1952 at IAME.

production of the Rastrojero Willys (a pick-up designed to use the Willys 65hp from 2,500 Empire tractors imported from the USA that were not being used) and the Rural Gauchita, which was a closed version of the Rastrojero, of which only a prototype was built with Borgward D4M18 engine.

On 9 April the Sedan Institec was tested for the first time and was named Justicialista (the name of the political party of President Juan Peron), using a brand logo that was the same as the political party. Shortly after, on 12 April, the first Rural Institec was tested, followed on 19 April by the Chatita Institec. They were considered ready on 26 April and presented to President Peron on 30 April, while on 2 May IAME organised the first car exposition of Argentina in Buenos Aires to show the cars produced. This was followed on 23 August by another exhibition in which they showed the first

ABOVE Two Sedán Institecs in Buenos Aires, of two different series, with the engine hood different as well as the front part. Curiously, the cars were delivered with the badge of the Justicialista political party of Perón as the car's brand.

RIGHT A Justicialista Gran Sport coupe.

A convertible version of the Justicialista Gran Sport coupe with V8 engine. *Santiago Rivas*

cars made with plastic bodywork. This work led to the development of the Justicialista Gran Sport coupe, presented on 3 April 1953, based on a DKW design and with a Porsche engine. A convertible version was also developed with a detachable hardtop and this was built in small quantities.

As the engines of the Institec cars had little power, a more powerful one with four cylinders in V, called M-800, was developed and tested from 3 January 1953. On 26 April the first Chatita Furgón was unveiled, being similar to the Chatita but with a closed box at the rear.

From the basis of the Justicialista Grand Sport, in 1954 they built the Gran Turismo, which was awarded the first prize for elegance in the World Car Exhibition at the Waldorf Astoria in New York in February 1954.

On 14 April of that year the company presented a locally designed V8 engine of 100hp and 3,000cm3, which was installed in the two prototypes of the Grand Sport GT, a new and innovative coupe, which proved too expensive for the country at that time and never went beyond the prototype.

Later, on 18 July 1953, the first Rastrojero with diesel engines was launched, of which the first twenty-three were delivered on 31 October 1954.

During 1953, engineers Eugenio Grosovich and Gianfranco Bricci developed the Aerocar, which had a propeller at the rear for propulsion and a 65hp Continental engine to move it. The car was presented in 1954 but, despite being innovative, it was considered dangerous and impractical for use on the streets.

In 1955, after the revolution of September, the Sedan Justicialista was renamed Graciela and, by then 154 had been built with M-700 engine and twenty-five with the M-800. The Graciela also received some restyling, especially to the front. Of the Chatita Pick-up, 2,660 were built, while 726 were built of the Chatita Furgón. In addition, 152 Rurals were built with a M-700 engine and twenty-five with the M-800. Of the Justicialista Grand Sport and Convertible, a total of only 167 were built.

The Rastrojero was the most successful, with 2,365 examples with a Willys engine built between 1952 and 1954, 26,067 of the NP 62 version with Borgward D4M 1.8 diesel engine built between 1954 and 28 November 1967, 3,430 Diesel NP 66s with Borgward D301 E1 diesel engine built between 1965 and 1969, and 704 NP 66 diesels with double cabin between 1965 and 1969. In 1963, the first export of Rastrojeros took place, with a batch sent

One of the two prototypes of the Grand Sport GT with the V8 engine.

The Aerocar seen on the apron of the factory. The car was considered too dangerous for use in the city, due to its propeller.

to Peru on 30 September together with Puma motorbikes. Over the years, others were exported to Cuba, Chile, Uruguay and Bolivia.

The Graciela continued under production until 1961, when the factory delivered the last of 2,280, which kept the original design but had a Wartburg 3 engine, produced in East Germany. Then, the licence to produce the Wartburg 311 car was obtained and called Graciela Wartburg or GW, but the new design was a commercial failure and only 646 were delivered between 1962 and 1964.

In 1967 the Rastrojero was completely redesigned and produced in single cabin, double cabin, with a closed back for cargo and an ambulance version, powered by a Borgward D4M engine. The first example, called P63, was shown on 13 November of that year. When DINFIA was divided into the FMA and IME on 31 December 1967 production of cars remained under IME and was not related to the Fábrica Militar de Aviones. By then, 12,848 Rastrojeros of the new versions had been built.

Production of the Rastrojero continued until 1979, with a military version proposed in 1978 (a prototype was built, with four-wheel drive and other improvements) and the prototype of an updated version was proposed in 1980, but production was

One of the Rastrojero Diesels of the first series, built in 1963 before the model had a restyling in 1964, and behind a Rastrojero of 1978, built by IME, after car production was separated from the aircraft factory in 1967. *Santiago Rivas*

cancelled. Also, other vehicles were added, with the Ratrojero Frontalito series of light trucks and buses, but not related to the FMA. In 1982, after two years without production, IME was finally closed.

Tractors and trailers

In early 1952 IAME made a survey through a group of experts that travelled National Route 9 from Buenos Aires to Córdoba, entering each rural establishment to ask which was the tractor that worked best and was easiest to copy. The most voted for was the Lanz Bulldog D9506, of German origin, so it was decided to import two Lanz tractors from Uruguay and one of them was completely disassembled and its parts scattered on the floor of an unoccupied shed at IAME's facilities. All the industrialists with the possibility of manufacturing some parts were summoned and many of them were provided with machines, materials and tools. On 19 June 1952 work began to 'build' the first tractor, which was called Pampa, and on 11 August 1952, the Tractor Factory was created.

The front part of the second Lanz, the only place where the German brand appeared, was replaced by a locally machined one, which read 'Pampa – IAME – Industria Argentina', framed by an insignia containing a gear crossed by two wings. On 7 October 1952, the work was finished (replacing the blue colour with a striking orange) and the first Pampa tractor was put into operation in the city of Buenos Aires, keeping it running for several days at the foot of the Obelisk, with an Argentine flag next to it. Two days later, a contract was signed with Fiat in which the Italian company would help in the development of the tractor production line.

An IAME Pampa tractor preserved at the National Aeronautics Museum. *Santiago Rivas*

On 31 December of the same year, the first fifteen units manufactured locally were completed, which went out to the country on an experimental basis.

Subsequently, the factory moved its infrastructure to Estación Ferreyra, to the east of the city of Cordoba. Its foundation stone was blessed on 21 January 1953 in the presence of the Minister of Aeronautics, Brigadier Juan Ignacio San Martín, and the President of Fiat, Professor Vittorio Valleta. The plant had been purchased, turnkey, from Fiat, including all the machinery to produce the tractors.

A pre-series production Puma motorbike, followed behind by examples of the first, second, fourth, and fifth series. *Santiago Rivas*

Puma motorbikes being finished at the factory.

A year later the Fiat company signed a contract with IAME, acquiring the site in Cordoba to build the large Fiat Concord Someca Tractor Factory, which exists to this day.

Meanwhile, on 28 July 1953 they unveiled the first trailer, which was produced for Argentine farmers.

In October 1959, DINFIA handed over the facilities to Fiat and moved to a new factory that would be sold again in 1961 to Perkins, at which time the manufacture of tractors ended. The number of Pampa tractors manufactured from 1952 to 1963 was 3,760 units. A few survive today in museums and on some farms.

Motorbikes

Together with the cars and tractors, it was decided also to build motorbikes and on 15 June 1952 the production of the Puma motorbike was started. It was based on a Guericke with Sachs engine and a licence for the later was obtained by the companies Televel and Sequenza, with the local version called Puma. On 1 October the first was tested and the first pre-series of twenty was finished on 5 October, being delivered to employees of IAME for testing. After the type was improved on 27 May 1953 the creation of the Fábrica de Motocicletas was authorised and construction of a first series was started. This series was finished on 27 March 1955 after 10,036 had been delivered, including some Puma tricycles to carry small cargoes on the front. On 1 August the second series was started with some modifications and a third series was planned with some other improvements, but it was cancelled after some prototypes were made. On 1 August 1959 the fourth series was started, with more restyling, more powerful engines of 98cm3 or 128cm3, new seats and fuel tank, while the production of the second series continued until 1963, totalling 56,928 bikes.

In the meantime, on 9 March 1962, the fifth series of the Puma was started, being the most powerful, with a 200cm3 engine, while in 1963 the last of the 11,332 bikes of the series 4 with 98cm3 was delivered. The production of the series 4 with 128 cm3 continued until 1966, with 25,423 units. On 22 May 1965 the Puma number 100,000 left the production line, being one of the series 5. However, in that same year, series 5 production was finished, with 1,936 units delivered, and this ended motorbike production at DINFIA.

A Puma of the fourth series with one of the fifth series behind. *Santiago Rivas*

Prototype of the VES-X1 being rolled out in the mid-1970s.

Hovercraft and boats

On 5 December 1952 an outboard engine for boats, called Surubí, of 35hp, was built, but its series production was abandoned.

In 1953, the Taller de Motonáutica (motorboating workshops) was created, overseen by the car production management. On 22 November of that year, they presented a racing speedboat made of plastic fibre and developed another types of boats, of which thirty motorboats of two seats and seventeen small sailing vessels called Tero, all with plastic fibre, were delivered in 1954. Also, some other small boats for fishing, rowing boats and canoes were built, but in 1955 it was decided to close the workshops.

In 1962 studies of hovercraft were started, with some models tested in the wind tunnel. Later, in the mid-1970s, the Argentine Navy started to explore the use of hovercraft and requested from FMA the possibility of developing a series of vehicles for use in river operations as well as for landings. The factory started to work on the ideas and decided to make a technology demonstrator, which they called VES-X1 (Vehículo de Efecto Suelo) ,which was built of plywood, fibreglass and metal. The VES-X1 had two engines, one being a Continental O-470-13 of 225hp of the type used in the Beechcraft B45 Mentor to power the propeller that created the air cushion, the other being a 4-cylinder engine from a Volkswagen Combi to move it.

This vehicle was tested and the lessons learned were used in an improved version of the same, of which some wind tunnel models were made. This had a closed cabin with three seats, one for the pilot in the middle and one on each side. This version was to be equipped with a Tornado Interceptor SOHC 230 engine, which was bought to be installed but was never used. The VES-X1 was stored for many years under the main wind tunnel of the factory, but it was taken outside around 2015 and left in the open, being destroyed by the weather. By 2022 an attempt was made to restore it, but it was in such

A model of the VES X-2 at the Centro de Investigación Aplicada.

A racing speedboat prototype presented in 1953 and preserved until today.

poor condition that it was impossible and only a few parts were saved.

From this, the VES-X2 was projected by 1977, with two engines with a transmission that moved both the propulsion propeller and the one for the air cushion, plus a larger cabin for five occupants. Plans of it are also dated in 1979.

A wind tunnel model of an assault hovercraft for landing, with two vertical engines for the air cushion, was also built and its remains are stored at the Centro de Investigación Aplicada of the Argentine Air Force, together with a wind tunnel model with four vertical engines.

Missiles

In the years of expansion after the Second World War, the FMA started to develop different weapons, some in collaboration with the Army controlled Fabricaciones Militares. Among them, on 12 August 1947 the División Proyectos Especiales No. III was created to develop rockets and the first work was a liquid fuel rocket engine of 335kg of thrust, called AN-1, designed under the lead of the Polish engineers Ricardo Dyrgalla (who had studied the captured German rockets while serving in the Royal Air Force before being contracted by Argentina in 1946) and Estanislao Kulcycki, for the Tábano air-to-air guided missile project. Development took place and on 20 October 1949 tests were made on the ground, while a launch was made on 18 March 1950 of a glider prototype of the Tábano, without the engine, from an I.Ae.24 Calquin (see Chapter 11), followed shortly after by the Tábano with the rocket installed. Dyrgalla also built a test rocket called AN-3 with only 40kg of thrust and a bigger one, called OM-1, of 500kg thrust.

In 1950 another rocket engine was made for the PT-1 (Proyectil Teledirigido 1, later PAT-1) gliding bomb built also by Fabricaciones Militares, which was based on the Henschel Hs 293-A and was developed by a team commanded by Werner von Baumbach and the Henrici brothers, engineers of Henschel. German engineer Günther Dietrich worked on the engine at the División Proyectos Especiales No. III, developing different types of propellants, such as hydrogen peroxide, oxygen methanol, and hydrazine.

The PAT-1 lost about 90m in height before the rocket engine developed its maximum power. Once the propellant was exhausted, the fuel tank on the belly was detached and the bomb glided towards the target at a speed of 850 to 900km/h. Engine ignition lasted twelve seconds.

The first launch of a PAT-1 was made by the end of 1954 on the General Soler range; it was supervised by the German Mendel brothers, in charge of the project after von Baumbach's death in an accident on 20 October 1953 during testing of the bomb. The bomb did not have a warhead and, in its place had 200kg (440lb) of concrete to simulate the weight. It also did not carry fuel. Flying over the range at 15,000ft, the Lancaster launch aircraft started a dive and the first Latin American air-to-surface missile separated from the pylon. Guided by the pilot, it flew its first metres, but the launch was not a success because the bomb lost control and it flew over the nearby town of La Cautiva, passing at very low altitude, frightening the habitants and finally destroying a railway. Tests were resumed in 1956 with three launches but the project was cancelled shortly after.

Meanwhile, German engineer Günther Dietrich proposed building a local version of the V-1 flying bomb, which was to be powered by a pulsejet engine and was called PAT-2. The División Proyectos Especiales No. III worked on a mixture of ammonium nitrate, calcium nitrate and dinitrobenzene for the explosive, with an electrical impact fuze, an omnidirectional mechanical impact fuze, and a delay fuze driven by a clockwork mechanism. The system was interconnected, so that one of the three fuzes always detonated. The engine developed 500kg of thrust for forty-five seconds. For the tests, Dietrich and designer Guido Galán developed an 80kg thrust pulsejet that was installed on an Institec car chassis for the ground tests, but the idea was abandoned by 1955. Also, pulsejets of 14kg of thrust (valve operation) and 16kg (gunshot type) of thrust were built and tested, the first to drive helicopter rotors, and the latter to be used in the self-propulsion of gliders.

During 1953 and 1954, the División Proyectos Especiales No. III and Fabricaciones Militares developed a wire-guided missile called PA-X4 (Proyectil Argentino X4) with 5km range, commanded by the pilot of the aircraft using a joystick. The rocket had a warhead of 25kg and a proximity fuze, but the project was abandoned before a prototype was built.

On 30 May 1960, Reimar Horten proposed a supersonic missile with a delta wing and powered by a Rolls-Royce Soar R.Sr.2 jet engine of 820kg of thrust, which was to be guided in its first stage by radio and gyroscopes, while in the cruise stage it was to be guided by gyroscopes, aneroid capsules and chronometers, and in the final stage it was to be guided by an on-board radar. The launch was planned to be from a platform on the ground with 40m-long rails and it was to be boosted by two solid fuel rockets of 2,300kg of thrust each for 1.6 seconds. The airframe was to be built of metal and plastic and capable of reaching Mach 2.5, with the fuel in the wing, the radar and navigation systems in the nose and a 500-kilo warhead in the middle, with the jet engine in the back. The length was 4.8m, wingspan 2.8m and height 2m (including the booster rockets). The front fuselage had a diameter of 0.45m and the rear part 0.65m. The empty weight was 1,000kg plus 200kg of fuel and 400kg for the launch ramp and the boosters. The launch speed was to be 200km/h, with a cruise of 1,600 km/h and a dive speed of 2,000 km/h on the approach to the target. The ceiling was 15,000m.

The missile was to be launched from a ramp of 20° and after being accelerated by the rockets would be flying with its own jet engine at 200km/h, climbing at 55m/seg, and after four minutes it would reach an altitude of 33,000ft and a speed of 1,000km/h, accelerating then to 1,400km/h after flying for 170km. Then the missile was due to fly for eleven minutes for another 250km and then start the dive towards the target, reaching a speed of 2,000km/h, flying for another 20km. It was deigned to fly a total of 450km but with a maximum range of 500km, but that could be extended to 1,000km by reducing the warhead to 300kg. Horten also specified that an air-launched version could be developed, too. This idea was not approved and no further development took place.

Guns

By the mid-1940s production of guns also began in the factory at the Fábrica de Máquinas y Herramientas of the Instituto Aerotécnico, the first being a series of Colt 7.65 × 54mm machine guns for use in the I.Ae. DL-22, which were locally called Colt DL 7.65. Also, an unlicensed series of Colt Browning AN-M2 12.70 × 99mm machine guns was built for use in anti-aircraft systems and in the I.Ae.24 Calquin around 1944 and 1946.

They were followed in 1950 by a prototype of a submachine gun of 9mm, which was not produced in series, and in that same year by three Mauser MG-151/20 guns of 20mm, locally called I.Ae. Mk.151, of which two were to equip the Pulqui II and the other was for ground tests. Work was headed by Hans Göttschalk and engineer Rudolf Voigstberger, the first having worked at Focke-Wulf with Kurt Tank. Tests were made on the ground during the year and the other two were installed in the first prototype of the Pulqui II but never used. In the end, this project was abandoned as the country did not produce the 20 × 82mm ammunition needed, and the aircraft used Hispano Suiza guns instead.

Also, in 1955 the factory developed the VF-1 Justicialista rifle, which was a modification of the

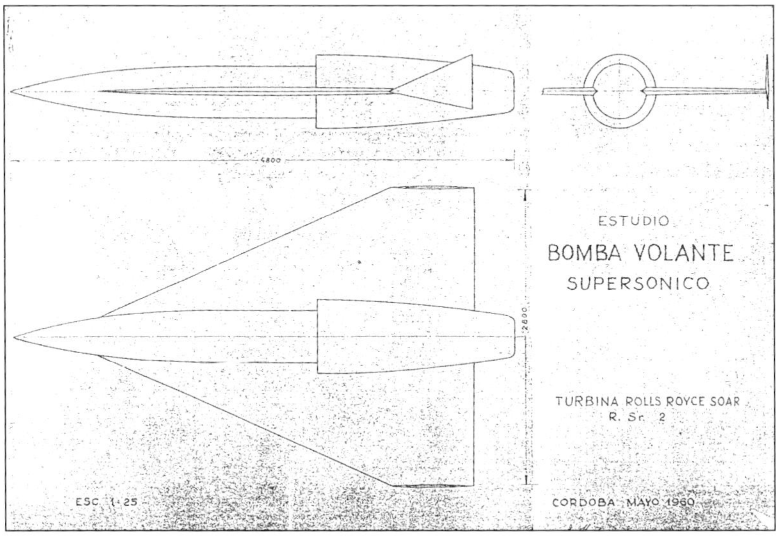

Three views of Horten's supersonic flying bomb proposal.

The VF-1 Justicialista rifle prototype, made copying the M1941 Johnson rifle but with a barrel for 7.65 × 53mm ammunition.

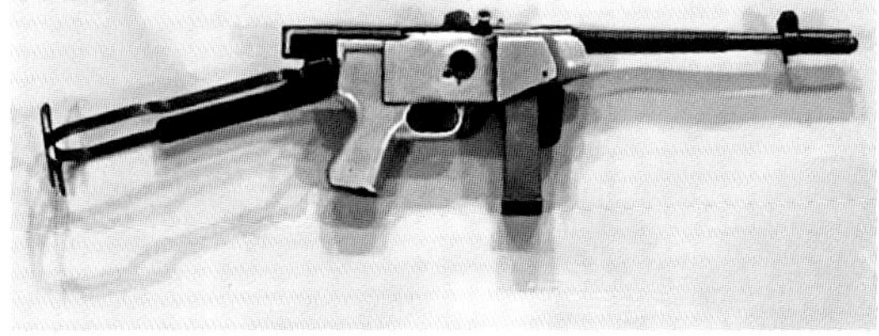

A prototype of a submachine gun made in 1950.

The AM-1 Tábano air-to-air missile, with a rocket engine developed at IAME with Ricardo Dyrgalla on its side.

A car made at IAME using the chassis of a Sedan Institec to test a pulsejet engine.

Different types of bombs designed and built at the Planta de Producción de Armamentos. From the front to the back, they are the FAS-250, FAS 800A, FAS 850 Dardos I, FAS-300 and FAS 260

M1941 Johnson but with a barrel for 7.65 × 53mm ammunition. However, the results were poor and the development was cancelled.

Bombs and rockets for aircraft

In 1953 IAME also started to build bombs, with the first napalm canisters being tested on 2 September 1953 on I.Ae.23 Calquins, followed in 1956 by others for the Gloster Meteor, but they were abandoned in 1957 as they were not considered safe for use.

No further weapons were developed until the late 1960s, when the IA-C-1057 Aspid 57mm rocket was developed, based on the British SCAR. The first launch was made on 23 March 1970 at the Pampa de Achala range in Córdoba, and the ARM-657 Mamboretá launcher was developed for it. It was widely used on Beech Mentors, Hughes 500s and other aircraft.

Meanwhile, the idea to produce napalm bombs was considered again and on 28 June 1970 six prototypes of the new ARM INC 220kg canister were tested from a Douglas A-4B Skyhawk at the V Brigada Aérea. They were later followed by the ARM INC 100kg and ARM INC 50kg canisters.

Development continued with the ARM-7105 Yaguareté rocket launcher for Pampero rockets of 105mm built by CITEFA (the research and development centre of the Argentine Armed Forces) and on 27 October 1975 locally made fuzes were tested with different bombs.

On 8 March 1976 the Planta de Producción de Armamentos was created as part of the Fábrica de Armamentos y Equipos at new facilities located 3km to the west of the FMA.

Comodoro Aldo Zeoli with an Alfa Centauro rocket in 1961.

There they started to build the rockets and napalm bombs plus the PG 250 BK-BR, PG 125 BK-BR and PG 50 BK-BR general-purpose bombs of 250kg, 125kg and 50kg respectively, plus the penetration ARM-BJ-125 of 125kg.

During the 1980s they built the FAS 300 cluster bombs of 250kg, the FAS 500 cluster of 500kg, the FAS 250 retarded by parachute (based on the Explosivos Alaveses 250kg bomb), the FAS 850 Dardos I of 227kg stand-off bomb propelled by a rocket and with a range of 15km, and the FAS 260 bomb of 37kg, retarded by parachute and then boosted by a rocket for impact at about 260m, based on the French Brant BAP-100. Also, the FAS 280, based on the former but to be used against armoured targets, and the FAS 800A of 250kg and B of 125kg general-purpose bombs with optional parachute-retarded tail.

Bomb production had stopped by 1994, when the Fábrica de Armamentos was sold to the company CITEA.

Rockets

In 1959 the Instituto Aerotécnico started to work on the idea of developing rockets for meteorological research and engineer Comodoro Aldo Zeoli headed the research, developing a first rocket that was named Alfa Centauro APEX-A1-02 and was 1.7m long. It was launched on 2 February 1961 at Base Santo Tomé on a private farm at Pampa de Achala, Córdoba, and was the first launch of a space rocket in Latin America, and 20km in altitude. Shortly after, on 13 October a first two-stage rocket was launched, also built at DINFIA, the Beta Centauro APEX A1-S2-015 of 3.81m, which reached 25km. This development led to the change of name of the Instituto Aerotécnico into the Instituto de Investigación Aeronáutica y Espacial (IIAE, Space and Aeronautic Research Institute) on 3 November, by decree 1329.

As Pampa de Achala was not far from populated areas, to launch rockets with more range a more suitable place was needed, and on 27 July 1961 the Centro Experimental de Lanzamiento de Proyectiles Autopropulsados (CELPA) was created at the Destacamento Aeronáutico Militar (DAM) Chamical in La Rioja province.

The experience gained from the Alfa and Beta Centauro led to the development of the two-stage Gamma Centauro, which was the first operational rocket. Two were launched from Chamical on 15 November 1961 and reached an altitude of 30km.

In September 1963 four more Gamma Centauros were launched, followed by another three on June 1964, while between 6 and 8 February 1965 three Gamma Centauros were launched from Matienzo base in the Antarctica and others were launched from Chamical. Also, during 1964 the DIM (Dardo de Investigación Meteorológica) rocket was developed for meteorological research.

A new rocket, called Orion I, was launched for the first time on 20 October 1965, reaching an altitude of 80km, and it was followed on 19 May 1966 by the much-improved Orión II, which reached 100km. Another Orion I was launched on 7 June and on 12 October an Orion reached 112km with a payload of 16kg. To evaluate the performances of the Orión II, three were launched at NASA's Wallops Island field in Virginia, while another three were launched on 10 October from Tartagal, Salta province.

The experiences with the Orións led to the Bio-Ciencia project to send animals to space, with the aim of putting a man into space in the future. On 22 March 1967 the first tests were made to check the functioning of the payload, a small capsule for a mouse. On 11 April a first test, called Bío I, was carried out using a

ABOVE The Cóndor II prototype, which was never tested in the end and was delivered to the United States in 1990.

Yarará rocket developed for the Argentine Army, to test the capsule carrying a mouse, and it reached 2,300m of height and an acceleration of 20Gs. The mouse was recovered safely, and the experience was repeated with another mouse on 19 May using an Orión II rocket, but the separation of the capsule for recovery failed and the mouse was killed.

While another Orión rocket, with a 22kg payload, reached an altitude of 55km on 14 December, two days later a new rocket developed by the IIAE, called Rigel, was tested, reaching 295km with a payload of 30kg. The Rigel was a rocket with two stages, the first being a Canopus one, which was an enlarged Orión II. The Canopus could be used as a rocket, was capable of carrying a 50-kilo payload and was expected to reach an altitude of 110km, or it could be used as a booster for the Rigel. After some tests on the ground with the Canopus, it was decided to work on an improved version, called Canopus II.

Another CELPA launch site was created at Mar Chiquita, near the city of Mar del Plata, on the Atlantic coast, and on 23 January 1968 the first launch of an Orión II was made from there, followed on 21 April 1969 by the first Canopus II, which had a length of 4.72m, from the same site.

Following the experiments to put animals into space, on 21 May the Experiencia Orión II- Bio II was made with another rat, followed by another on 25 August, while on 21 October the Operación 5/69 Canopus Bio was made to test the systems for the Bio II project, again using a mouse. Finally, on 23 December, the Bio II project launched a monkey to an altitude of 60km in a flight that lasted thirty minutes.

From the basis of the Rigel, the Castor rocket was developed, which was intended to put a payload of between 50 to 75kg to a height of 500km. The first stage had four Canopus II engines, with a second

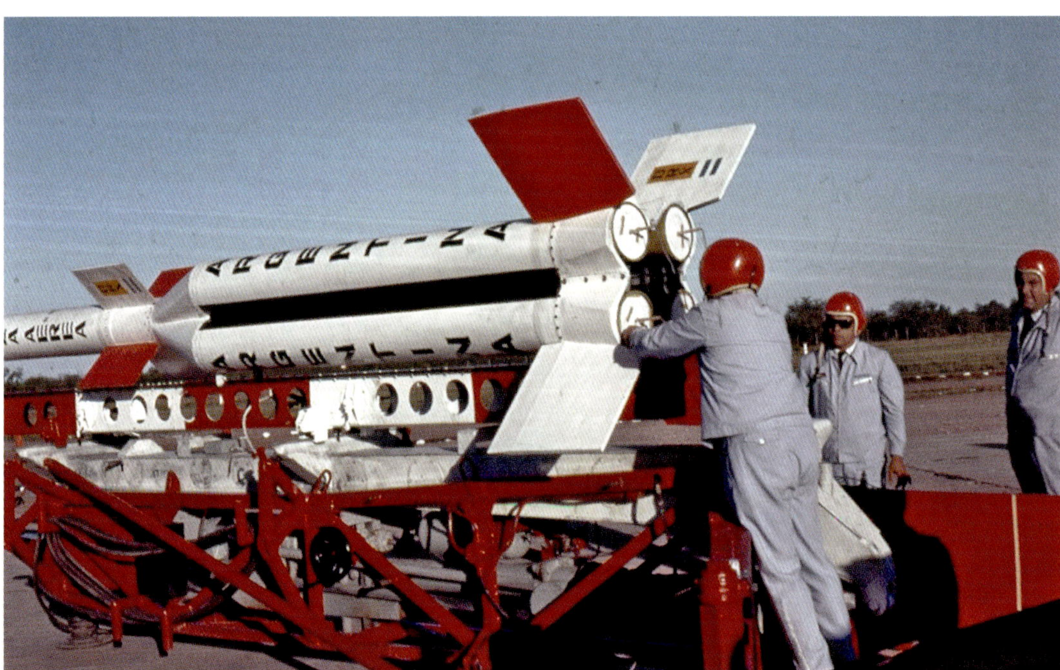

Technicians preparing a Castor rocket.

stage with a single engine of the same type. A first launch of a Castor, designated X-1, was made on 22 December 1969 to test the first stage, with the second without the engine, reaching 50km in height. This was followed by another, Castor X-2, on 16 December 1970 during the Operativo Ñahui at Chamical, in which a Canopus rocket was launched with a photo camera to take pictures from high altitude. Three days later another Castor was launched, reaching 40km, and on 22 November 1973 the first operational Castor, with the two stages, reached 480km in height with a payload of 68kg on the Operativo EGANI, a joint mission between the IIAE, the Comisión Nacional de Actividades Espaciales (which operated the payload) and the Max Planck Institut from Germany.

In the meantime, during 1971 and 1972 more Canopus II and Rigel rockets were launched, followed by others in 1974 and a launch of the Castor 02 on 30 September 1975 as part of the Operativo EGANI 3/75, reaching 470km in altitude and a payload of 56kg. The Castor 03 was launched on 3 October from Marambio Base in the Antarctica.

Two Castor rockets were launched in Peru on 21 and 22 March 1979 at Punta Lobos, reaching a height of 290km.

During 1974, the CLAG (Cohete de Lucha Anti Granizo, Anti Hail Fight Rocket) I and II were developed and many were launched from 30 April 1976.

Meanwhile, thanks to the experience gained with these rockets, the first development of a ballistic surface-to-surface rocket was achieved by the IIAE, with the SS-40 rocket, of which on 19 June 1974 two were launched, reaching distances of 48km and 57km . More tests continued, with an improved SS-50 tested on 24 March 1975. They used an Antares engine, developed from the Canopus engine but to use locally produced propellant instead of imported.

From the basis of these rockets, the Tauro was developed, to carry a 120kg to 150kg payload to an altitude of 100km. The rocket had a total weight of 1,200kg and a length of 7.66m. A stabilisation and recovery system was installed with German support. The Tauro rockets were tested until the programme was cancelled in 1981.

All these experiences were used in the Cóndor programme, which has two objectives, one being to have a vector to put satellites of up to 200kg into an orbit between 300km and 1,000km of height, and the other to have a mid-range ballistic missile to reach targets up to 1,000km distance. In 1980 the development of a first rocket, called Cóndor I, was started to test the stabilisation and guidance systems as well as the bigger rocket, and evolved into the Alacrán or Cóndor I-AIII, which was an improved

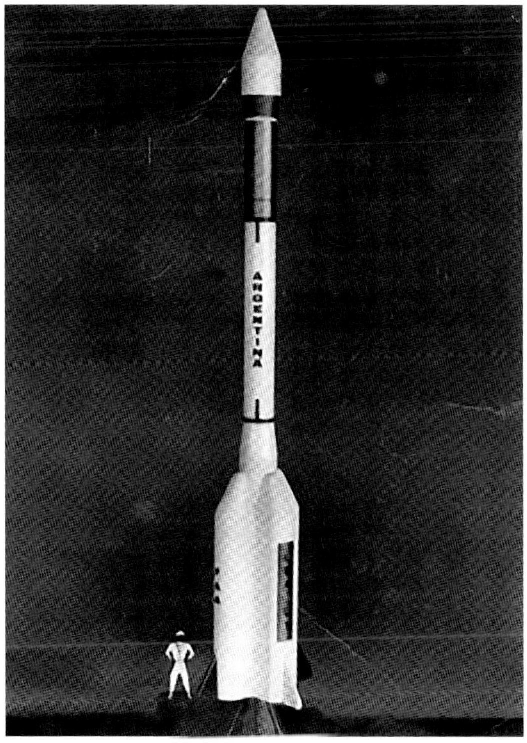

Model of the Lanzador Satelital Argentino (LSA-01), with two booster engines using those of the Cóndor II, then a second stage with a Cóndor II engine and a third with the engine of the Alacrán. It was expected to be able to put a payload of 200 kilos at between 300 and 1,000km of height.

rocket and capable of carrying a 250-kilo warhead to a distance of 100km. It was also aimed at testing the use of composite materials in its construction, something that the FMA was learning to use thanks to the IA-63 Pampa project, the use of inertial navigation systems, servo-actuator-operated control surfaces and the casting of the compound propellant in the engine tube. The rocket to put payloads into space was called Lanzador Satelital Argentino (LSA-01), and had two booster engines using those of the Cóndor II, then a second stage with a Cóndor II engine and a third with the engine of the Alacrán.

Facilities to launch the Cóndor I and the Alacrán were built on the coast of Patagonia at Cabo Raso, but the creation of the Missile Technology Control Regime in 1987 meant that the United States and the United Kingdom started to pressure Argentina against the project, as the former considered that the Cóndor II was a copy of the Pershing II missile, since Argentina had the support of MBB in its design, which also took part in the US-built missile programme.

A plan to launch the Cóndor I and Alacrán in 1988 was finally cancelled by the Argentine government and pressure to cancel the Cóndor II grew as it was revealed that Egypt and Iraq were supporting the development of the missile through German companies that were providing support. Finally, in 1990, due to pressure from the United States, the project was cancelled, ending all rocket development by the IIAE.

Appendix 1
Individual histories

Ae.C.1, Ae.M.E.1, Ae.C.2. Ae.C.3, Ae.C.3G and Ae.C.4

Serial	Received	Retired	Notes
	28-10-31	1934	Ae.C.1. Used by the FMA.
	1932	1934	Ae.C.1 Prototipo. Took part in the Escuadrilla Sol de Mayo.
R226	12-32	18-12-46	Ae.C.2. Sold to the government of San Juan province. Had an accident on 28-3-34 at La Paz, Mendoza, pilot Renato Balleri unharmed. Plane stored at the FMA until retired in 1946.
	4-32	1945	Ae.C.2 Tenga Confianza. Made the tour of the fourteen provinces. Stopped flying in 1935. Officially retired in 1945.
1	9-10-32	1945	Ae.C.2, Ae.M.E.1. Took part in the Escuadrilla Sol de Mayo. In 1934 to the Grupo 1 de Observación y Bombardeo at BAM General Urquiza. Stopped flying in 1935. Officially retired in 1945.
2	1933	1933	Ae.C.2, Ae.M.E.1. Took part in the Escuadrilla Sol de Mayo. Written off in 1933.
3	1933	1945	Ae.C.2, Ae.M.E.1. Took part in the Escuadrilla Sol de Mayo. In 1934 to the Grupo 1 de Observación y Bombardeo at BAM General Urquiza. Stopped flying in 1935. Officially retired in 1945.
4	1933	1945	Ae.C.2, Ae.M.E.1. Took part in the Escuadrilla Sol de Mayo. In 1934 to the Grupo 1 de Observación y Bombardeo at BAM General Urquiza. Stopped flying in 1935. Officially retired in 1945.
5	1933	1934	Ae.C.2, Ae.M.E.1. Took part in the Escuadrilla Sol de Mayo. In 1934 to the Grupo 1 de Observación y Bombardeo at BAM General Urquiza. Crashed on 6-6-34 and written off.
6	1933	1945	Ae.C.2, Ae.M.E.1. Took part in the Escuadrilla Sol de Mayo. In 1934 to the Grupo 1 de Observación y Bombardeo at BAM General Urquiza. Stopped flying in 1935. Officially retired in 1945.
7	1934	1945	Ae.M.E.1. In 1934 to the Grupo 1 de Observación y Bombardeo at BAM General Urquiza. Stopped flying in 1935. Officially retired in 1945.
8	1934	1945	Ae.M.E.1. In 1934 to the Grupo 1 de Observación y Bombardeo at BAM General Urquiza. Stopped flying in 1935. Officially retired in 1945.
--	27-3-34		Ae.C.3. Operated by the FMA. With Armstrong Siddeley Genet Major engine.
--	12-8-34	15-3-37	Ae.C.3. Delivered to Aero Club Posadas. With Armstrong Siddeley Genet Major engine.
R275	22-4-35	2-38	Ae.C.3. Delivered to the Centro Universitario de Aviación. With Armstrong Siddeley Genet Major engine.
R284	28-8-35	13-7-37	Ae.C.3. Delivered to the Aero Club Argentino. With Armstrong Siddeley Genet Major engine. Destroyed in an accident on 13-7-37
R270	9-12-34	2-38	Ae.C.3. Delivered to the Aero Club Pigüé. With Armstrong Siddeley Genet Major engine.
R300	1935	15-3-37	Ae.C.3. Delivered to the FMA and later to the Aero Club Coronel Suárez. With Armstrong Siddeley Genet Major engine. Equipped with a canopy to close the cabin.
--	1935		Ae.C.3. Delivered to the FMA. With Armstrong Siddeley Genet Major engine.
R312	10-7-36	15-3-37	Ae.C.3. Delivered to the Centro Universitario de Aviación. With Warner Super Scarab engine.
R310	30-6-36	15-3-37	Ae.C.3. Delivered to the Aero Club La Plata. With Warner Super Scarab engine.
R309	19-6-36	15-3-37	Ae.C.3. Delivered to the Aero Club Mendoza. With Warner Super Scarab engine.
R320	24-8-36	15-3-37	Ae.C.3. Delivered to the Aero Club San Francisco. With Warner Super Scarab engine.

Serial	Received	Retired	Notes
R316	21-7-36	15-3-37	Ae.C.3. Delivered to the Aero Club Argentino. With Warner Super Scarab engine.
R70	6-11-36	1938	Ae.C.3. Delivered to the Dirección General de Aeronáutica Civil. With Warner Super Scarab engine.
R342	10-9-37	1938	Ae.C.3. Delivered to the Aero Club Pergamino. With Warner Super Scarab engine.
R328	29-9-36	29-9-36	Ae.C.3. Delivered to the Aero Club Comodoro Rivadavia. With Warner Super Scarab engine.
--	--	--	Ae.C.3. Never finished.
	21-1-36	1942	Ae.C.3G. Used by the FMA.
	1936	1942	Ae.C.3G. Used by the FMA.
	1937	1942	Ae.C.3G. Used by the FMA.
	17-10-36		Ae.C.4. Used by the FMA.

Ae.M.O.1, Ae.M.Oe.1, Ae.M.Oe.2 and Ae.M.S.1

Serial	Received	Retired	Notes
1	7-7-34	1937	Ae.M.O.1, first series. First prototype. First flight on 24-1-34. Delivered to the Grupo 1 de Observación at Paraná, received on 18-7-34 and transferred to the BAM Los Tamarindos until retirement.
2	7-7-34	1937	Ae.M.O.1, first series. Delivered to the Grupo 1 de Observación at Paraná, received on 18-7-34 until discharged.
3	7-7-34	1937	Ae.M.O.1, first series. Delivered to the Grupo 1 de Observación at Paraná, received on 18-7-34 until discharged.
4	7-7-34	1938	Ae.M.O.1, first series. Delivered to the Grupo 1 de Observación at Paraná, received on 16-7-34 in the Training Section. Between 22-9-34 to 30-9-34 on commission to Las Lomitas Aerodrome in Formosa. To the Grupo 3 de Observación of the BAM Urquiza on 3-6-35 until retirement.
5	7-7-34	27-9-34	Ae.M.O.1, first series. Received on 19-8-34 at Los Tamarindos. Crashed with total destruction.
6	7-7-34	1937	Ae.M.O.1, first series. Received on 19-8-34 at Los Tamarindos. Crashed on 28-8-34 when it collided with a hangar and was repaired.
7	7-7-34	1937	Ae.M.O.1, first series. Received on 19-8-34 at Los Tamarindos.
8	7-7-34	1937	Ae.M.O.1, first series. Equipped with machine gun mount in the observer's station. Delivered on 19-8-34 at Los Tamarindos.
9	7-7-34	21-6-36	Ae.M.O.1, first series. Delivered to the Military Aviation School. Equipped with machine gun mount in the observer's station. Crashed at the FMA, mechanic Sergeant Luis Ortúzar killed and pilot Sergeant Ricardo Baldán injured.
10	7-7-34	1937	Ae.M.O.1, first series. Delivered to the Military Aviation School, sent to the Grupo 4 de Observación on 15-4-35.
11	7-7-34	14-1-37	Ae.M.O.1, first series. Delivered to the Military Aviation School, sent to the Grupo 3 de Observación at BAM Urquiza on 3-6-35. Crashed at Cordoba, pilot 1st Lieutenant Alberto Grande and observer Sergeant Pablo Bolo killed.
12	7-7-34	1934	Ae.M.O.1, first series. Delivered to the Military Aviation School. Accident on unknown date.
13	1935	9-4-46	Prototype of the Ae.M.Oe1. At the Military Aviation School in 1939, sent to the Regimiento Aéreo 1 on 20-3-41, to the Grupo 1 de Observación in 1942 and to the Escuela de Pilotos Militares in 1943, then returned to previous assignment until retirement.
14	1935	9-4-46	Ae.M.O.1. At the Military Aviation School in 1939, sent to the Regimiento Aéreo 1 on 20-3-41 and to the Escuela de Pilotos Militares of the BAM Colonel Pringles until retirement.
15	12-6-35	14-3-47	Ae.M.O.1. Registered in the Grupo 4 de Observación on 12-6-35 from the FMA, in the Military Aviation School in 1939 damaged after an accident, sent to the Regimiento Aéreo 1 on 20-3-41, sent to the Escuela de Pilotos Militares of the BAM Colonel Pringles in 1943 and on assignment to the Military Aviation College on 2-10-43. Overturned at Fort Tiburcio during a forced landing on 14-7-44, repaired and sent in 7-45 to the Grupo 1 de Observación. Assigned to the Regimiento 3 de Ataque on 16-2-46 and crashed on 12-9-46 in Costa Araujo, Mendoza. Sent to BAM Urquiza on 17-6-47 for recovery after the retirement. Retired with 1,377 flight hours.
16	12-6-35	9-7-37	Ae.M.O.1. Equipped with machine gun mount at the observer's station. Registered in Los Tamarindos, sent to the Military Aviation School on 20-8-35 and on 5-11-35 to BAM Urquiza. Crashed during the 9 July parade, pilot Sergeant 1st Francisco Vallejos killed.
17	12-6-35	10-12-47	Ae.M.O.1. Equipped with machine gun mount at the observer's station. On 12-7-35 sent to the Military Aviation School. In the Regimiento 2 of BAM Urquiza in 1939, sent to the Regimiento Aéreo 1 on 20-3-41 until 1943 when was transferred to the Escuela de Pilotos Militares of the BAM Colonel Pringles. On 16-2-46 to the Regimiento 3 de Ataque and on 28-6-46 transferred to the Grupo 1 de Observación. Crashed. Retired with 1,457 flight hours.

Ae.M.O.1, Ae.M.Oe.1, Ae.M.Oe.2 and Ae.M.S.1

Serial	Received	Retired	Notes
18	1935	15-10-45	Ae.M.O.1. Equipped with machine gun mount at the observer's station. At the Military Aviation School in 1939, sent to the 1st Air Regiment on 20-3-41 until 1943 when he went to the Escuela de Pilotos Militares. Accident at Villa Reynolds. Pilot Ensign Jose Mendiondo dead, down 9-4-46.
19	1935	9-4-46	Ae.M.O.1. Received on 3-6-35 in the Grupo 1 de Observación of Paraná, at the Military Aviation School in 1939, sent to the Regimiento Aéreo 1 on 20-3-41, transferred to the Escuela de Pilotos Militares of the BAM Colonel Pringles in 1943 until his discharge.
20	3-6-35	14-3-47	Ae.M.O.1. Received by the Grupo 3 de Observación in Urquiza. At the Military Aviation School in 1939, sent to the Regimiento Aéreo 1 on 20-3-41 and to the Escuela de Pilotos Militares of the BAM Colonel Pringles in 1943. On 2-10-43 on assignment to the Military Aviation College until the end of 1944. On 7-12-46 to the Regimiento 3 de Ataque. Retired with 1,649 flight hours.
21	15-4-35	29-8-47	Ae.M.O.1. Delivered at El Palomar, on 4-6-35 to Grupo 4 de Observación. At the Military Aviation School in 1940, sent to BAM Pringles on 20-3-41. On 2-10-43 in commission to the Military Aviation College until the end of 1944, in 4-45 to the Grupo 1 de Observación and on 7-12-46 to the BAM Reconquista. On 9-30-47 to BAM Urquiza for recovery after its retirement. Retired with 918 flight hours.
22	1935	22-8-36	Ae.M.O.1. Delivered at El Palomar, on 4-6-35 sent to Grupo 4 de Observación. Accident in Paraná, Entre Ríos. Pilot Lieutenant Jose Montiel killed.
23	1935	9-4-46	Ae.M.O.1. At the Military Aviation School in 1939, suffered a minor accident on 9-11-40. Sent to the Regimiento Aéreo 2 on 20-3-41. In 1942 transferred to Grupo 1 de Observación. Sent to the Escuela de Pilotos Militares on 12-4-43, arrived on 18-6-43. Accident on 23-10-43 in Villa Mercedes. Pilot Cabo Domingo Festín dead.
24	3-7-35	14-3-47	Ae.M.O.1. Delivered to the BAM Urquiza, on 2-6-35 to the Military Aviation School. Went to BAM Los Tamarindos on 20-8-35 and to the Military Aviation School in 1939. Sent to the Regimiento Aéreo 2 on 20-3-41 and then to BAM Los Tamarindos and on 31-3-42 to the Grupo 1 de Observación. Crashed on 8-10-42, repaired and sent to BAM Pringles on 18-6-43. In 2-45 to the Grupo 1 de Observación and on 16-2-46 to the Regimiento 3 de Ataque. Retired with 1,262 flight hours, sent to Paraná on 2-9-47 for recovery.
25	1935	18-10-35	Ae.M.O.1. Registered at BAM Urquiza, sent to the Military Aviation School on 2-6-35 and to BAM Los Tamarindos on 12-7-35. Accident in Villavicencio, Mendoza. Pilot Assistant Sergeant Antonio Irigoyen and Observer Sergeant Rogelio Iramain killed.
26	1935	9-4-46	Ae.M.O.1. Registered at BAM Urquiza, on 2-6-35 to the Military Aviation School, on 5-11-35 sent to the Grupo 3 de Observación at BAM Urquiza. At the Military Aviation School in 1939. Sent to the Regimiento Aéreo 2 on 20-3-41. On 31-1-42 to the Grupo 1 de Observación and on 12-4-43 to the Escuela de Pilotos Militares at BAM Pringles, where it arrived on 18-6-43. To the Military Aviation College on commission from 2-10-43 to the end of 1944, in 2-45 to the Grupo 1 de Observación. Accident on 6-7-45 20km south-east of BAM General Urquiza. Pilot Major Armando Pitamella and Sergeant Francisco Stazzone killed.
27	1935	9-4-46	Ae.M.O.1. Registered at BAM Urquiza, on 2-6-35 to the Military Aviation School, on 5-11-35 sent to Grupo 4 de Observación in BAM Urquiza. In 1940 sent to the Military Aviation School and to the Regimiento 3 de Ataque in storage. Sent to the Regimiento Aéreo 2 on 20-3-41. On 31-1-42 to the Grupo 1 de Observación and on 12-4-43 to the Escuela de Pilotos Militares at Pringles, where it arrived on 18-6-43. In 4-45 to Grupo 1 de Observación.
28	1935	1946	Ae.M.O.1. Equipped with machine gun mount in the observer's station. Commissioned into the Grupo 1 de Observación, sent to the Military Aviation School on 8-11-35. At BAM Urquiza in 1946.
29	20-4-35	7-8-47	Ae.M.O.1. Joined the Grupo 1 de Observación, sent to the Military Aviation School on 13-11-35. Sent to the Regimiento Aéreo 2 on 20-3-41, then to El Palomar and the Grupo 1 de Observación in 1942. On 12-4-43 to Pringles, where it arrived on 18-6-43. In 1945 to the Grupo 1 de Observación, to the Regimiento 3 de Ataque on 16-2-46 until 28-4, when it went to the Grupo 2 de Observación until 28-2-47. Retired on 7-8-47 with 1,342 flight hours.
30	1935	27-10-36	Ae.M.O.1. Joined the Grupo 1 de Observación, sent on 13-11-35 to the Military Aviation School. Accident in Achiras, Cordoba. Second Lieutenants Alejandro Fernández and Norberto Núñez killed.
31	3-11-35	27-1-48	Ae.M.O.1, modified with Ae.M.Oe.2 tail. Received at BAM Urquiza and sent to the Military Aviation School on 7-11-35. Sent to the Regimiento Aéreo 2 on 20-3-41, then to El Palomar and in 1942 to the Grupo 1 de Observación. On 12-4-43 to BAM Pringles and then on commission to the Military Aviation College until 1944. Sent to the Rio IV Regional Workshop until 11-14-46 when returned to Pringles. Transferred on 7-3-47 to BAM Urquiza. Decommissioned, it was without an engine, with 1,131 flight hours.
32	3-11-35	19-12-47	Ae.M.O.1. Registered at BAM Urquiza and sent to the Military Aviation School on 7-11-35. Sent to the Regimiento Aéreo 2 on 20-3-41, then to El Palomar and in 1942 to the Grupo 1 de Observación. On 12-4-43 to BAM Pringles and then to Grupo 1 de Observación again. To the Regimiento 3 de Ataque on 16-2-46. Minor accident on 2-8-46 in Lavalle, Mendoza. Damaged on 6-3-47 when collided with trees near BAM Los Tamarindos and fell into a ditch. Pilot Ensign Waldino Núñez and observer Major Corporal Guervara unharmed. Sent to BAM Urquiza on 9-30-47. Retired with 1,183 flight hours.

Serial	Received	Retired	Notes
33	1935	9-4-46	Ae.M.O.1. Admitted at BAM Urquiza, on 7-11-35 to the Military Aviation School and to El Palomar in 1941. Sent to Grupo 1 de Observación on 3-20-41 and on 4-12-43 to BAM Pringles. Sent on commission to the Military Aviation College on 2-10-43 until the end of 1944. Crashed in Villa Mercedes, San Luis, on 10-3-45. Pilot Major Corporal Dante Carnevali killed.
34	1935	17-6-36	Ae.M.O.1. Crashed in Santa Rosa, Mendoza. Pilot Lieutenant Ivar L. Alvarez killed.
35	1935	9-4-46	Ae.M.O.1. Received at BAM Los Tamarindos, sent to the Military Aviation School on 4-11-35. Sent to Grupo 1 de Observación on 20-3-41 and then to El Palomar. On 19-2-42 was transferred to Grupo 1 de Observación until discharged on 9-4-46.
36	15-4-35	28-2-48	Ae.M.O.1, modified with Ae.M.Oe.2 tail. Received at BAM Los Tamarindos, on 4-11-35 at the Military Aviation School. Sent to Grupo 1 de Observación on 20-3-41 and then to El Palomar. On 19-2-42 to the Grupo 1 de Observación and on 3-46 to the BAM Pringles, Damaged on 5-8 46, repaired, transferred on 7-3-47 to the BAM Urquiza. Decommissioned, it was without an engine, with 1,780 hours of flight time. It was the aircraft that flew the most hours.
37	15-4-35	?	Ae.M.O.1. Received on 2-11-35 at the Military Aviation School. In 1941 was sent to El Palomar and on 19-2-42 to the Grupo 1 de Observación. Accident in 1943.
38	15-4-35	11-3-48	Ae.M.O.1. Received on 2-11-35 at the Military Aviation School. Sent to Grupo 1 de Observación on 20-3-41 and then to El Palomar. On 7-12-46 sent to BAM Pringles. Decommissioned, it was without an engine, with 1,573 flight hours.
39	15-4-35	25-1-47	Ae.M.O.1. Received on 2-11-35 at the Military Aviation School, in 1941 at El Palomar until 19-2-42, when it went to the Grupo 1 de Observación. Between 31-12-46 and 24-1-47 in Grupo 2 de Observación. Retired on 28-3-48, it was without an engine, with 1,217 hours of flight time.
40	6-11-35	3-11-39	Ae.M.O.1. Received at the Military Aviation School on 6-11-35. Accident in Río Segundo, Córdoba. Pilot Corporal Carlos Salas killed.
41	1937	19-9-46	Ae.M.O.1, wore NACA ring. Accident on 14-6-38 on Timbó Colorado Island, in the Paraná Delta. Pilot 1st Sergeant Miguel Mantulak killed and observer Sergeant Argentino Ramírez unharmed. Repaired. At the Military Aviation School in 1939. Sent to Grupo 1 de Observación on 20-3-41 and then to El Palomar. On 1-4-42 to Grupo 1 de Observación until discharged on 19-9-46.
42	15-4-35	4-47	Ae.M.O.1. First flight on 5-7-34. In 1939 at the Military Aviation School. Sent to Grupo 1 de Observación on 20-3-41 and then to El Palomar and on 19-2-42 to Grupo 1 de Observación. On 12-4-43 to the Military Aviation College and in 1944 to the BAM Pringles for the Escuela de Pilotos Militares, remained at Pringles until its retirement. Retired with 1,600 flight hours.
43	10-3-37	3-5-47	Ae.M.Oe.1. Sent to the Regimiento Aéreo 3 on 20-3-41. In 1942 was assigned to the Agrupación Entrenamiento, not delivered by the FMA. In 1944 at the Pringles Escuela de Pilotos Militares. Accident on 28-6-44 at the Escuela de Pilotos Militares, Villa Mercedes. Pilot Sergeant Anuar Chaer killed. Sent to BAM Gral Urquiza. Retired with 865 flight hours.
44	----	5-12-36	Ae.M.Oe.1. Damaged at the FMA before delivery, pilot Lieutenant Eneo Hernández Barbieri killed.
45	10-3-37	19-9-46	Ae.M.Oe.1. In 1939 at BAM Urquiza, on 20-3-41 at BAM Pringles and in 1944 at the Pringles Escuela de Pilotos Militares until February 1945, when moved to Grupo 1 de Observación. Was decommissioned by Resolution 1691/46 on 19-9-46 but in December of that year it was listed at the BAM Pringles, where it went on 7-12-46. It does not appear in 1947.
46	10-3-37	26-2-47	Ae.M.Oe.1. In 1939 in the BAM Urquiza, the following year assigned to the Regimiento 3 in depot. On 3-20-41 at BAM Pringles. In 1944 at the Escuela de Pilotos Militares of the BAM Col. Pringles until March 1945 when assigned to the Grupo 1 de Observación and from there to the BAM Reconquista. Accident on 11-9-46 in La Potasa, General Obligado department, Santa Fe. Pilot Sergeant Angel Leguizamón and Corporal Luis Villa killed. The wreckage of the plane remained at the BAM Reconquista.
47	15-4-35	13-10-48	Ae.M.Oe.1. In 1940 in the Regimiento 3 (BAM El Plumerillo) in depot. Sent to Regimiento Aéreo 3 on 20-3-41. In 1942 assigned to the Agrupación Entrenamiento of the BAM El Palomar, on 10-6-43 from the Escuela de Pilotos Militares to the Military Aviation College until 1944 when returned to that school. On 26-2-45 to the Grupo 1 de Observación. Retired with 595 flight hours. Crashed on 21-3-45 in Paraná. Pilot Ensign Angel Varisco and Assistant Petty Officer Observer Enrique Purdie killed.
48	1936	18-11-37	Ae.M.Oe.2. First flight in 1935. Crashed in Campo de Mayo, Buenos Aires, 1st assistant mechanic César Ferrari killed and pilot Sergeant Juan Gonzalez jumped via parachute.
49	1937	1946	Ae.M.Oe.2. Until 1941 at the Military Aviation School. Sent to Regimiento Aéreo 3 on 20-3-41. In 1942 at the Agrupación Entrenamiento, in 1944 at the BAM Pringles with the Escuela de Pilotos Militares. From 1945 to 1946 at BAM Pringles.
50	15-6-37	3-5-47	Ae.M.Oe.2. In 1940 in the Grupo 1 de Observación at BAM El Palomar. On 20-3-41 to BAM Pringles in storage and in 1943 to the FMA. In 1944 at the Escuela de Pilotos Militares of the BAM Pringles and on 26-2-45 to the Grupo 1 de Observación at the BAM Urquiza. At the end of 1945 was sent to the BAM Reconquista. Retired with 855 flight hours.

Ae.M.O.1, Ae.M.Oe.1, Ae.M.Oe.2 and Ae.M.S.1

Serial	Received	Retired	Notes
51	20-6-37	26-5-48	Ae.M.Oe.2. Until 1941 at the Military Aviation School. Sent to Regimiento Aéreo 3 on 20-3-41. In 1942 was assigned to the Agrupación Entrenamiento, which did not receive it from the FMA. In 1944 at the BAM Col. Pringles at the Escuela de Pilotos Militares and in March 1945 was assigned to the Grupo 1 de Observación. Discharged on 26-3-46 by the unit. Decommissioned, it was without an engine. Ended with 959 flight hours, it was one of the last three to fly.
52	1937	1946	Ae.M.Oe.2. At BAM Urquiza until 3-20-41, when moved to BAM Col. Pringles for storage. In 1944 was assigned to the Escuela de Pilotos Militares of that base and on 26-2-45 to the Grupo 1 de Observación at BAM Urquiza.
53	1937	15-10-43	Ae.M.Oe.2. At BAM Urquiza until 3-20-41, when moved to BAM Col. Pringles to storage. Destroyed in an accident at the EAM, pilot Second Lieutenant Raul Newton Sola killed.
54	15-4-37	26-5-48	Ae.M.Oe.2. At BAM Urquiza until 3-20-41, when sent to Pringles for storage. In 1944 joined the Escuela de Pilotos Militares in that unit and on 26-2-45 was sent to the Grupo 1 de Observación. It was sent for a time to BAM Reconquista until 1947. Decommissioned, it was without an engine. Retired with 1,136 flight hours, it was one of the last three to fly.
55	8-3-37	26-5-48	Ae.M.Oe.2. Until 1941 at the Military Aviation School. Sent to Regimiento Aéreo 3 on 20-3-41. In 1942 was assigned to the Agrupación Entrenamiento, which did not receive it from the FMA. On 6-4-43 assigned to the Escuela de Pilotos Militares of the BAM Col. Pringles and on 10-4-43 to the Military Aviation College out of service. In March 1946 was transferred from the Directorate of Military Aeronautical Institutes to the BAM Urquiza, which repaired it and sent it to the Grupo 1 de Observación, which discharged it on 10-11-47. Decommissioned, it was without an engine. Retired with 575 hours of flight time, it was one of the last three to fly.
56	1937	?	Ae.M.Oe.2. At BAM Urquiza in 1939.
57	1937	1946	Ae.M.Oe.2. At the BAM Urquiza until 3-20-41 when it went to the BAM Col. Pringles for storage. In 1942 was assigned to the Agrupación Entrenamiento at El Palomar but was not sent by the FMA, where it was. In 1944 at BAM Pringles, damaged after an accident, until 1946.
58	15-6-37	9-4-47	Ae.M.Oe.2. At the Military Aviation School until 1941. Sent to Regimiento Aéreo 3 on 20-3-41. In 1942 was assigned to the Agrupación Entrenamiento at El Palomar, which did not receive it from the FMA, where it was. At the Escuela de Pilotos Militares of the BAM Col. Pringles in 1944, at BAM Col. Pringles until February 1945 when it went to Grupo 1 de Observación. In 1946 was assigned to the BAM Reconquista. Retired with 1,253 flight hours.
59	1937	10-7-46	Ae.M.Oe.2. At the Military Aviation School until 1941. On 17-5-40 suffered an accident and was repaired at the FMA. Sent to Regimiento Aéreo 3 on 20-3-41. Joined the Agrupación Entrenamiento in 1942 and the Escuela de Pilotos Militares at BAM Pringles in 1944.
60	15-6-37	9-3-47	Ae.M.Oe.2. At the Military Aviation School until 1941. Suffered a minor accident on 28-10-40. Sent to storage at BAM Cnel. Pringles on 20-3-41 and in 1942 assigned to the Agrupación Entrenamiento (El Palomar) although it did not receive it. In 1944 was again at Pringles at the Escuela de Pilotos Militares and in March 1945 went to Grupo 1 de Observación. Retired with 850 hours of flight time.
61	1937	1947	Ae.M.Oe.2. At the Military Aviation School until 1941. In storage at the BAM Cnel. Pringles on 20-3-41 until 1945 when it was in the charge of the Directorate of Military Aeronautical Institutes, out of service. In March 1946 by OR269 was sent to Grupo 1 de Observación. Retired in 1947.
1	26-11-35	8-8-47	Ae.M.S.1. Delivered to the Military Aviation School. In 1939 at the Grupo 1 de Observación. In 1944 to the Escuela de Tropas Aerotransportadas, renamed Escuela de Paracaidistas in 1945. In 1946 to the Agrupación Entrenamiento, stopped flying in that year and retired in 1947.

Ae.T.1

Serial	Commissioned	Retired	Notes
	18-5-33	25-7-36	Named General San Martín. Took part in the Escuadrilla Sol de Mayo. To the Grupo 1 de Observación in 9-35. Retired.
	1934	25-7-36	Named Deán Funes. To the Grupo 1 de Observación in 9-35. Retired. Used for ground training until 1945.
	1934	25-7-36	Named Jorge Newbery. To the Grupo 1 de Observación in 9-35. Retired.

Ae.M.B.1/ Ae.M.B.2 Bombi

Serial	Commissioned	Retired	Notes
201	1935	1937	First prototype, first flight on 9-6-35. Received a lot of modifications until reaching the definitive configuration. Written off in an accident in Paraná on 5-6-37. Crew wounded.
202	6-3-36	1947	Modified to Ae.M.B.2. Minor accident on 24-8-37, repaired. Was O-202.
203	6-3-36	1948	Modified to Ae.M.B.2. On 20-5-36 had a minor accident at FMA, repaired. On 26-9-36 lost a wheel while landing, repaired. On 16-2-39 broke landing gear during trials after modification, repaired. Was O-203.
204	6-3-36	1941	Modified to Ae.M.B.2. Crashed on unknown date.
205	6-3-36	1947	Modified to Ae.M.B.2. Used for paratrooper launch. Two emergency landings on 15-6-44 at Paraná. Damaged while landing on 20-7-44, repaired. Was O-205.
206	6-3-36	19-9-46	Modified to Ae.M.B.2. Landing gear broken on 12-1-37, repaired. Minor accident on 21-4-39. Grounded from 1939 to 1942 at Mendoza, minor accident in 17-4-42, repaired, sent to FMA on 11-9-43, never flew again and retired. Was O-206.
207	6-3-36	1937	On 2-5-36 broke the landing gear at Mendoza, repaired. On 21-9-36 lost a wheel while landing, repaired. On 21-12-36 crashed at Despeñaderos, Córdoba. Mechanic killed, the other four crew members jumped using parachutes.
208	6-3-36	1946	Modified to Ae.M.B.2. Used for paratrooper dropping. Emergency landing on 20-4-39 close to San Luis, repaired. Minor accident on 20-6-39, repaired. Was O-208.
209	6-3-36	1947	Modified to Ae.M.B.2. On 26-9-36 damaged while landing, repaired. Lost a wheel while landing on 24-1-40, repaired. Was O-209.
210	10-4-36	29-4-37	Crashed on 9-7-36 at El Palomar during take-off, written off.
211	10-4-36	8-8-47	Modified to Ae.M.B.2. Used for paratroopers dropping. On 9-9-40 had a minor accident, repaired. Damaged while landing on 5-9-44, repaired. Was O-211.
212	20-5-36	1948	Modified to Ae.M.B.2. Used for paratrooper dropping. Damaged while landing on 19-10-36, repaired. Was O-212.
213	20-5-36	1943	Modified to Ae.M.B.2. Minor accident while landing on 25-8-39, repaired.
214	20-5-36	1947	Modified to Ae.M.B.2. Minor accident on 17-6-36 at Mendoza, repaired. Lost a wheel while landing on 28-9-36, repaired. Was O-214.
215	20-5-36	16-9-39	Modified to Ae.M.B.2. Crashed during an emergency landing on 7-9-39, hitting a windmill close to Soler, Córdoba, crew injured.

Front view of a Bombi.

FMA 20 El Boyero

Serial	C/No.	Enlisted	Retired	Notes
T-01, t-01, LV-ZLF	1	2-11-40		First prototype. Built at the FMA. Belonged to the FMA without serial, delivered to the Argentine Air Force as T-01 and in 1945 as t-01, to the Aeronautics Ministry on 8-3-56 and later sold to a private owner. Still in service.
LV-YGA	2	1941	1996	Second prototype. Built at the FMA. Delivered to Sfreddo y Paolini S.A. on 22-4-42 for use as the basis for their own production. Later sold to different owners.
LV-NZP	003	14-10-47		First aircraft built by Petrolini Hnos. Sold to a private user. Retired in the early 1960s.
LV-RJP	004	24-12-47		Used by Petrolini Hnos. Later sold to Aero Club Goya.
t-18, ME-2 Ob, AE-2 Ob, GN-1P	005	1-4-49	1965	Delivered to the Argentine Air Force. On 19-1-56 to the Argentine Army as ME-2 Ob and later as AE-2 Ob. On 17-9-59 to the Gendarmería Nacional as GN-1P.
t-19, LV-ZMT	006	1-4-49	22-10-62	Delivered to the Argentine Air Force. Sold to Aero Club Islas de Ibicuy as LV-ZMT on 31-10-58. Destroyed in an accident at Tigre, Buenos Aires, on 22-10-62. Two killed.
t-24, LV-ZMW	007	1-4-49		Delivered to the Argentine Air Force. Delivered to Secretaría de Aeronáutica as LV-ZMW on 31-10-58.
t-20, LV-ZLI	008	1-4-49		Delivered to the Argentine Air Force. Sold to Aero Club Curuzú Cuatiá as LV-ZLI on 9-4-56.
t-25	009	1-4-49		Delivered to the Argentine Air Force.
t-21, ME-3 Ob, AE-3 Ob, GN-2P	010	1-4-49	1965	Delivered to the Argentine Air Force. On 19-1-56 to the Argentine Army as ME-3 Ob and later as AE-3 Ob. On 17-9-59 to the Gendarmería Nacional as GN-2P.
t-22, LV-ZMU	011	1-4-49		Delivered to the Argentine Air Force. Sold to Aero Club La Carlota as LV-ZMU.
t-23, LV-ZMV	012	1-4-49		Delivered to the Argentine Air Force. Sold to Aero Club as LV-ZMV.
LV-YSO	013	26-7-51		Delivered to Aero Club Junín. In service at Aero Club Concepción.
LV-YSP	014	29-11-51		Delivered to Aero Club Bahía Blanca. Still in service at Aero Club Río de la Plata.
LV-YSR	015	16-7-51		Delivered to Aero Club Tucumán.
LV-YSS	016	26-7-51		Delivered to Aero Club Tandil.
LV-YST	017	29-11-51		Delivered to Aero Club Sáenz Peña.
LV-YSU	018	29-11-51		Delivered to Aero Club Argentino.
LV-YSV	019	29-11-51		Delivered to Aero Club 9 de Julio.
LV-YSW	020	29-11-51		Delivered to Aero Club Tres Arroyos.
LV-YSX	021	29-11-51		Delivered to Aero Club Bolívar.
LV-YSY	022	29-11-51		Delivered to Dirección General de Aeronáutica Civil.
LV-YSZ	023	29-11-51		Delivered to Aero Club Patagones.
LV-YTD	024	16-7-53		Delivered to Aero Club Corrientes.
LV-YTE	025	29-11-51		Delivered to Aero Club Goya.
LV-YTF	026	29-11-51		Delivered to Aero Club General Alvear.
LV-YTG	027	29-11-51		Delivered to Dirección General de Aeronáutica Civil.
LV-YXI	028	11-10-50		Delivered to Aero Club Villa María.
LV-YTJ	029	24-10-50		Delivered to Aero Club 9 de Julio.
LV-YTZ	030	11-10-50		Delivered to Aero Club Concepción del Uruguay.
LV-YTS	031	24-10-50		Delivered to Aero Club Nogoyá.
LV-YTN	032	11-10-50		Delivered to Aero Club Salliquelló.
LV-YTY	033	11-10-50		Delivered to Aero Club Río Tercero.
LV-YTM	034	24-10-50		Delivered to Aero Club Pigüé.
LV-YTH	035	11-10-50		Delivered to Aero Club Coronel Suárez.
LV-YTV	036	11-10-50		Delivered to Aero Club 9 de Julio.
LV-YTI	037	24-10-50		Delivered to Aero Club San Nicolás.
LV-YTT	038	24-10-50		Delivered to Aero Club Dolores.
LV-YTR	039	11-10-50		Delivered to Aero Club Gualeguay.
LV-YTO	040	11-10-50		Delivered to Dirección General de Aeronáutica Civil.

Serial	C/No.	Enlisted	Retired	Notes
LV-YXG	041	11-10-50		Delivered to Aero Club Coronel Pringles.
LV-YTW	042	11-10-50		Delivered to Aero Club Victoria.
LV-YTP	043	29-11-51		Delivered to Aero Club Argentino.
LV-YXF	044	13-3-51		Delivered to Dirección General de Aeronáutica Civil.
LV-YTL	045	24-10-50		Delivered to Aero Club Santiago del Estero.
LV-YTX	046	24-8-51		Delivered to Aero Club Mendoza.
LV-YXE	047	11-10-50		Delivered to Aero Club Rafaela.
LV-YTU	048	24-10-50		Delivered to Aero Club González Chávez.
LV-YXH	049	11-10-50		Delivered to Aero Club Olavarría.
LV-YXJ	050	28-11-50		Delivered to Aero Club La Plata.
LV-YXL	051	28-11-50		Delivered to Aero Club González Chávez.
LV-YXD	052	28-11-50		Delivered to Aero Club Monte Caseros.
LV-YXM	053	28-11-50		Delivered to Aero Club Santo Tomé.
LV-YXN	054	28-11-50		Delivered to Aero Club Posadas.
LV-ZEP	055	28-11-50		Delivered to Aero Club Rufino.
LV-ZER	056	28-11-50		Delivered to Aero Club Salta.
LV-ZES	057	28-11-50		Delivered to Aero Club Santa Fe.
LV-ZET	058	29-11-50		Delivered to Aero Club Córdoba.
LV-ZEU	059	28 11 50		Delivered to Aero Club Orán.
LV-ZEV	060	28-11-50		Delivered to Aero Club Chaco.
LV-ZEW	061	28-11-50		Delivered to Aero Club Esquina.
LV-ZEX	062	28-11-50		Delivered to Aero Club Villa Mercedes.
LV-ZEY	063	13-3-51		Delivered to Aero Club Río Colorado.
LV-ZEZ	064	13-3-51		Delivered to Aero Club Las Flores.
LV-ZFD	065	13-3-51		Delivered to Aero Club Cañada de Gómez.
t-26, ME-4 Ob, AE-4 Ob, LV-IOC	066	1949		Delivered to the Argentine Air Force. On 19-1-56 to the Argentine Army as ME-4 Ob and later as AE-4 Ob. In 1965 sold to a private owner.
t-27, LV-ZLJ	067	5-5-51		Received military serial but not used by the Argentine Air Force. Delivered to Aero Club Oberá on 9-4-56.
t-28, LV-ZLL	068	5-5-51		Received military serial but not used by the Argentine Air Force. Delivered to Aero Club Rufino on 9-4-56.
t-29, LV-ZLM	069	5-5-51		Received military serial but not used by the Argentine Air Force. Delivered to Centro de Aviación Civil Mercedes on 9-4-56.
t 30, LV ZMX	070	5-5-51		Received military serial but not used by the Argentine Air Force. Delivered to Centro de Aviación Civil San Juan on 31-10-58.
t-31, LV-ZLN	071	5-5-51		Received military serial but not used by the Argentine Air Force. Delivered to Aero Club Bolívar on 9-4-56.
t-32, LV-ZLO	072	5 5-51		Received military serial but not used by the Argentine Air Force. Delivered to Aero Club Puán on 9-4-56.
t-33, LV-ZLP	073	5-5-51		Received military serial but not used by the Argentine Air Force. Delivered to Aero Club Sol de Junio on 9-4-56.
t-34, LV-ZMY	074	5-5-51		Received military serial but not used by the Argentine Air Force. Delivered to Aero Club Ceres on 31-10-58.
t-35, LV-ZMZ	075	6-5-51		Received military serial but not used by the Argentine Air Force. Delivered to Aero Club General Villegas on 31-10-58.
t-36, LV-ZLR	076	6-5-51		Received military serial but not used by the Argentine Air Force. Delivered to Aero Club San Nicolás on 9-4-56.
t-37, LV-ZLS	077	6-5-51		Received military serial but not used by the Argentine Air Force. Delivered to Aero Club Plaza Huincul on 9-4-56.

FMA 20 El Boyero

Serial	C/No.	Enlisted	Retired	Notes
t-38, LV-ZNA	078	6-5-51		Received military serial but not used by the Argentine Air Force. Delivered to Aero Club Balcarce on 31-10-58.
t-39, ME-5 Ob, AE-5 Ob, LV-IOB	079	6-5-51		Delivered to the Argentine Air Force. On 19-1-56 to the Argentine Army as ME-5 Ob and later as AE-5 Ob. In 1965 sold to Aero Club Bragado and later to Aero Club Carlos Tejedor.
t-40, ME-6 Ob, AE-6 Ob, GN-3P	080	6-5-51		Delivered to the Argentine Air Force. On 19-1-56 to the Argentine Army as ME-6 Ob and later as AE-6 Ob. On 17-9-59 to the Gendarmería Nacional as GN-3P.
LV-ZFE	081	13-3-51		Delivered to Aero Club Necochea. Later to Aero Club Río Colorado.
LV-ZFF	082	13-3-51		Delivered to Centro Universitario de Aviación.
LV-ZFG	083	13-3-51		Delivered to Aero Club San Rafael.
LV-ZFH	084	13-3-51		Delivered to Dirección General de Aeronáutica Civil.
LV-ZFI	085	13-3-51		Delivered to Dirección General de Aeronáutica Civil.
LV-ZFJ	086	29-11-51		Delivered to Aero Club Villa Mercedes. Later to Aero Club Necochea.
LV-ZFL	087	16-7-53		Delivered to Aero Club Puerto Madryn.
LV-ZFM	088	29-11-51		Delivered to Aero Club Trenque Lauquen.
LV-ZFN	089	29-11-51		Delivered to Aero Club Jujuy.
LV-ZFO	090	29-11-51		Delivered to Aero Club La Cumbre.
LV-ZFP	091	29-11-51		Delivered to Aero Club Carhué.
LV-ZFR	092	29-11-51		Delivered to Círculo de Aviación Rosario. Later to Aero Club Coronel Dorrego.
LV-ZFS	093	29-11-51		Delivered to Aero Club Rosario.
LV-ZFT	094	29-11-51		Delivered to Aero Club San Rafael. Later to Aero Club Carlos Casares.
LV-ZFU	095	29-11-51		Delivered to Aero Club Coronel Dorrego.
LV-ZFV	096	29-11-51		Delivered to Aero Club Carhué.
LV-ZFW	097	29-11-51		Delivered to Aero Club Huinca Renancó. Still operational.
LV-ZFX	098	29-11-51		Delivered to Aero Club Plaza Huincul.
LV-ZFY	099	29-11-51		Delivered to Aero Club General Villegas.
LV-ZFZ	100	29-11-51		Delivered to Aero Club Cruz Alta.
LV-ZGD	101	29-11-51		Delivered to Aero Club Paraná.
LV-ZGE	102	29-11-51		Delivered to Aero Club Mendoza.
LV-ZGF	103	29-11-51		Delivered to Dirección General de Aeronáutica Civil.
LV-ZGG	104	29-9-52		Delivered to Aero Club Reconquista.
LV-ZGH	105	29-9-52		Delivered to Aero Club La Consulta.
LV-ZGI	106	29-9-52		Delivered to Aero Club Mercedes.
LV-ZGJ	107	29-9-52		Delivered to Aero Club San Martín.
LV-ZGL	108	29-9-52		Delivered to Dirección General de Aeronáutica Civil.
LV-ZGM	109	29-9-52		Delivered to Aero Club Bahía Blanca.
LV-ZGN	110	29-9-52		Delivered to Aero Club Corral de Bustos.
LV-ZGO	111	29-9-52		Delivered to Aero Club Bragado.
LV-ZGP	112	29-9-52		Delivered to Aero Club Olavarría.
LV-ZGR	113	29-9-52		Delivered to Aero Club Azul.
LV-ZGS	114	29-9-52		Delivered to Aero Club La Rioja.
LV-ZGT	115	29-9-52		Delivered to Aero Club Bella Vista. Later to Aero Club Malabrigo.
LV-ZGU	116	29-9-52		Delivered to Aero Club General Roca. Later to Aero Club Sunchales.
LV-ZGV	117	29-9-52		Delivered to Aero Club Pampeano.
LV-ZGW	118	29-9-52		Delivered to Aero Club Santa Fe.
LV-ZGX	119	29-9-52		Delivered to Aero Club Orán.
LV-ZGY	120	29-9-52		Delivered to Aero Club Goya.

Serial	C/No.	Enlisted	Retired	Notes
LV-ZGZ	121	29-9-52		Delivered to Aero Club Pehuajó.
LV-ZHD	122	29-9-52		Delivered to Aero Club La Plata.
LV-ZHE	123	29-9-52		Delivered to Aero Club San Francisco.
LV-ZHF	124	29-9-52		Delivered to Aero Club La Plata.
LV-ZHG	125	29-9-52		Delivered to Aero Club Marcos Juárez.
LV-ZHH	126	29-9-52		Delivered to Aero Club Formosa.
LV-ZHI	127	29-9-52		Delivered to Aero Club Cañada de Gómez.
LV-ZHJ	128	29-9-52		Delivered to Aero Club General Pico.
LV-ZHL	129	29-9-52		Delivered to Aero Club Paso de los Libres.

FMA 21

Serial	C/No.	Enlisted	Retired	Notes
323	34-410	3-3-38		Built as North American NA-16-4P. Crashed on 3-11-45 killing pupil Cabo Nicolás Nuzzolese. The instructor was unhurt. Sent for repairs and modified as FMA 21 with new wing and retractable landing gear. Received on 10-1-45. Crashed in 1947, repaired.

I.Ae. DL-22

Serial	C/No.	Enlisted	Retired	Notes
Ea-700	000	3-8-44	02-02-57	Only prototype. Used for tests at the Instituto Aerotécnico. Crashed at Río de la Plata, in front of domestic airport when the engine stopped. Test pilot Hans Scheidhauer and mechanic Alberto Fiocchi, both civil, injured.
Ea-701	001	3-8-44	1958	Crashed on 2-1-50. Preserved at the Museo Nacional de Aeronáutica in Buenos Aires.
Ea-702	002	3-8-44	1946	Donated to the Fuerza Aérea de Chile el 20-8-45. Used briefly and retired.
Ea-703	003	3-8-44	16-7-48	Equipped with Cheetah engine in 1945 and Whirlwind in 1946. Crashed on 6-5-46 at Villa Luzuriaga, Buenos Aires, killing Alferez Alberto Iglesias and René Riva, written off on 16-7-48.
Ea-704, LQ-XZA	004	3-8-44	23-4-55	Equipped with Whirlwind engine in 1947. In 1955 delivered to Dirección de Aeronáutica Civil as LQ-ZXA. Crashed at Bower, Córdoba, killing Suboficial Principal Alberto Della Valle and civilian Juan Vazquez Gutenberg.
Ea-705	005	3-5-45	1957	First plane with Cheetah. Retired in 1957.
Ea-706	006	3-5-45	1958	Retired in 1958.
Ea-707	007	3-5-45	1957	Sent to storage at the II Brigada Aérea in 1956.
Ea-708	008	3-5-45	30-1-46	Crashed at Bajo Hondo, San Juan, killing Teniente Sergio Gutierrez and Capitán Osvaldo Guerisoli. Retired on 2-10-47.
Ea-709	009	3-5-45	1957	Equipped with engine Whirlwind en 1947. Crashed on 11-9-54 with 26 per cent damage. Repaired and retired in 1957.
Ea-710	010	3-5-45	1952	Donated to the Fuerza Aérea del Perú in 1945. Retired by the end of 1952, abandoned and destroyed years later.
Ea-711, FAB 1436	011	3-5-45	7-7-47	Donated to the Força Aérea Brasileira in 1945. Used until 1947.
Ea-712	012	5-6-45	05-06-58	Crashed at Lavalle, Mendoza, when the oil system broke. Eighty per cent destroyed, not repaired. Pilot unhurt.
Ea-713	013	6-6-45	1957	Flew until 1955 and stored.
Ea-714	014	6-6-45	1957	Flew until 1956 and stored.
Ea-715	015	8-6-45	1957	Flew until 1955 and stored.
Ea-716	016	8-6-45	1950	Equipped with Whirlwind engine in 1947.
Ea-717	017	8-6-45	1957	
Ea-718	018	8-6-45	1957	
Ea-719	019	8-6-45	1950	Crashed at 1946, repaired. Crashed on 14-9-49 at Escuela de Aviación Militar. Not repaired.
Ea-720	020	2-7-45	1957	Equipped with Whirlwind engine in 1948.

FMA I.Ae. DL-22

Serial	C/No.	Enlisted	Retired	Notes
Ea-721	021	2-7-45	1958	
Ea-722	022	2-7-45	1957	
Ea-723	023	2-7-45	1956	Equipped with Whirlwind engine in 1947.
Ea-724	024	4-7-45	23-12-48	Equipped with Whirlwind engine in 1947. Crashed at BAM Reconquista, pilot unhurt.
Ea-725	025	6-7-45	29-1-48	Equipped with Whirlwind engine in 1947. Destroyed at San Miguel del Monte, Buenos Aires, on 27-10-47, killing Alférez Rodolfo Agnese.
Ea-726	026	6-7-45	26-7-47	Crashed on 21-6-46 at Merlo, killing Suboficial Ayudante Mario Báez and Teniente Oscar Ruiz. Retired in 1947.
Ea-727	027	6-7-45	20-08-57	Crashed on 9-4-50, repaired. Crashed at Aeroparque Jorge Newbery in Buenos Aires when going off the runway because of crosswinds. Fifty per cent damage, not repaired.
Ea-728	028	8-7-45	01-04-57	Crashed at Guadalupe, Córdoba, because of poor maintenance. Pilot Alférez Abelardo Maliandi and Cabo Principal Eduardo Frick unhurt. Fifteen per cent damage, not repaired.
Ea-729	029	8-7-45	1955	Crashed on 24-9-54, not repaired.
Ea-730	030	8-7-45	1957	Crashed on 29-8-47, retired on 16-7-48. Recovered in 1949 and returned to service. Retired in 1957.
Ea-731	031	8-7-45	1947	Crashed on 17-10-46 at San Vicente, Córdoba, killing Alférez Alfredo Rodríguez and Soldier Miguel Marcigliano. Retired in 1947.
Ea-732	032	3-11-45	6-11-48	Crashed on 25-10-46 to the north of Córdoba, killing Cadet Julio Rusconi and injuring the instructor. Retired in 1948.
Ea-733	033	3-11-45	1957	Flew until 1955 and stored.
Ea-734	034	3-11-45	1948	Retired in 1948 at the Escuela de Aviation Militar.
Ea-735	035	3-11-45	15-9-47	Crashed on 11-10-46 at Camino Los Molinos, Córdoba, killing Cadet Rubén Paterlini. Retired in 1947.
Ea-736	036	3-11-45	14-10-47	Crashed on 29-8-47 at Reconquista, killing Alférez Harry Ávila and soldier Luis Monicaust, written off.
Ea-737	037	3-12-45	1957	Sent to storage in 1955 until 1957, flew during that year until it was retired.
Ea-738	038	3-12-45	1957	Equipped with Whirlwind engine in 1947. Crashed at El Palomar on 20-9-56 with 15 per cent damage, not repaired.
Ea-739	039	3-12-45	1951	Crashed on 20-9-51.
Ea-740	040	3-12-45	1957	Flew until 1955 and stored.
Ea-741	041	3-12-45	27-05-58	Crashed at IV Brigada Aérea while landing, 20 per cent damage, not repaired.
Ea-742	042	3-12-45	11-06-58	Emergency landing at the IV Brigada Aérea when the engine stopped in flight, 35 per cent damage, not repaired.
Ea-743	043	3-12-45	1957	Flew until 1955 and stored.
Ea-744	044	3-12-45	29-8-54	Destroyed at San Jaime field aerodrome when the pilot was dazzled by the reflectors of the anti-aircraft artillery. Pilot Alférez Hector B. Muruo and Alférez Federico G. Roa killed.
Ea-745	045	3-12-45	1957	Crashed on 18-8-54 at Campana, Buenos Aires, 25 per cent damage, not repaired, retired in 1957.
Ea-746	046	3-12-45	1957	Flew until 1955 and stored.
Ea-747	047	3-12-45	1958	Equipped with Whirlwind engine and fixed landing gear in 1948, later received retractable landing gear again. Flew until 1955 and stored, recovered in 1958, flew until it was retired in that year.
Ea-748	048	3-12-45	1957	Flew until 1955 and stored.
Ea-749	049	3-12-45	1956	Flew until 1955 and stored.
Ea-750	050	3-12-45	11-10-57	Crashed at II Brigada Aérea after malfunction of the landing gear. Twenty-six per cent damage, not repaired.
Ea-751	051	2-3-46	1957	Crashed at BAM General Urquiza on 31-5-47. Flew until 1955 and stored.
Ea-752	052	5-4-46	1958	Equipped with Whirlwind engine in 1947. Flew until 1955 and stored.
Ea-753	053	5-4-46	22-09-58	Equipped with Whirlwind engine in 1948. Crashed at Paraná due to engine failure, with 25 per cent damage, not repaired.
Ea-754	054	5-4-46	1957	Equipped with Whirlwind engine in 1948. Flew until 1955 and stored.
Ea-755	055	5-4-46	1950	

Serial	C/No.	Enlisted	Retired	Notes
Ea-756	056	5-4-46	22-07-58	Crashed at Laguna Setúbal, Santa Fe, due to indiscipline in flight. Pilot Alférez Oscar Álvarez and civil Carlos Reynoso killed.
Ea-757	057	5-4-46	1947	
Ea-758	058	5-4-46	1956	Flew until 1955 and stored.
Ea-759	059	5-4-46	1957	Mid-air collision with FMA 20 El Boyero serialled t-31 on 26-6-51. Repaired. Flew until 1955 and stored.
Ea-760	060	5-4-46	1957	Flew until 1955 and stored.
Ea-761	061	5-4-46	25-1-50	Crashed at Mendoza and written off.
Ea-762	062	12-6-46	1957	Flew until 1955 and stored.
Ea-763	063	8-4-46	19-10-51	Crashed at Paraná, Entre Ríos, killing Alférez Hugo Cacciamani and Cabo Principal Alberto Anca.
Ea-764	064	8-4-46	1-10-48	Crashed at Reconquista on 21-6-47. Repaired and crashed on 1-10-48 at Gobernador Gordillo, La Rioja, killing 1° Teniente Mario Romanella and Alférez Miguel Tebar.
Ea-765	065	8-4-46	1958	Crashed at Helvecia, Santa Fe, on 3-9-54, repaired. In storage during 1956, returned to service in 1957.
Ea-766, LQ-XZB	066	8-4-46	1955	Transferred to Ministerio de Aeronáutica as LQ-XZB on 7-2-55.
Ea-767	067	5-5-46	1958	Flew until 1955 and stored.
Ea-768	068	5-5-46	1957	Flew until 1955 and stored.
Ea-769	069	5-5-46	1957	Flew until 1955 and stored.
Ea-770	070	8-5-46		Retired between 1952 and 1953.
Ea-771	071	8-5-46	16-7-48	Destroyed in an accident in 25-3-47.
Ea-772	072	8-5-46		Retired between 1952 and 1953.
Ea-773	073	2-6-46	2-3-52	Crashed at Reconquista, killing Alférez Osvaldo Razzella and Cabo Principal Enrique Ramírez.
Ea-774	074	2-6-46	2-6-47	Destroyed in an accident on 21-2-47 at BAM Gral. Urquiza, Alférez Jorge Segat y Ragomir Hure unhurt.
Ea-775	075	2-6-46	1957	Flew until 1955 and stored.
Ea-776	076	2-6-46	1957	Flew until 1955 and stored.
Ea-777	077	2-6-46	1957	Flew until 1955 and stored.
Ea-778	078	2-6-46	2-6-47	Destroyed in an accident.
Ea-779	079	2-6-46	1957	
Ea-780, LV-XZL	080	10-5-46	1948	Delivered to DGAC on 2-9-47. Destroyed by a storm at Morón on 19-3-48.
Ea-781, LV-XZI	081	10-5-46	1948	Delivered to DGAC on 2-9-47. Crashed at San Fernando on 7-6-48, not repaired
Ea-782	082	10-5-46	1950	
Ea-783	083	10-5-46	1949	Crashed at BAM El Palomar on 22-11-47 with minor damage, not repaired.
Ea-784	084	10-5-46	1949	
Ea-785	085	17-5-46	05 09 55	Crashed at Paraná when the engine stopped, causing 60 per cent damage. Pilot Alférez Basilio H. Fernández unhurt.
Ea-786	086	17-5-46	1957	Flew until 1955 and stored.
Ea-787	087	17-5-46	3-10-48	Equipped with Whirlwind engine in 1947. Destroyed in an accident when fell into a house on 20-5-48 at Moreno, killing Alférez Cristóbal Martín, Reserve Alférez de Hugo Marcolina and two occupants of the house.
Ea-788	088	17-5-46	1957	Flew until 1955 and stored.
Ea-789	089	17-5-46	1957	Flew until 1955 and stored.
Ea-790	090	2-6-46	29-8-51	Crashed killing Alférez José Luis Deporel and Alférez Ricardo Hudson.
Ea-791	091	20-5-46		Retired between 1952 and 1953.
Ea-792	092	20-5-46	1950	Equipped with Whirlwind engine in 1948.
Ea-793	093	20-5-46	1957	Equipped with Whirlwind engine in 1948. Flew until 1955 and stored.

I.Ae. DL-22

Serial	C/No.	Enlisted	Retired	Notes
Ea-794	094	20-5-46	18-3-48	Destroyed in an accident.
Ea-795	095	20-5-46	1957	Crashed at II Brigada Aérea on 8-7-56 with 30 per cent damage, not repaired.
Ea-796	096	20-5-46	1956	Equipped with Whirlwind engine in 1947.
Ea-797	097	23-5-46	1950	Crashed at Escuela de Aviation Militar on 8-9-48, stored at Grupo 1 de Observación and later retired.
Ea-798	098	23-5-46	1957	Flew until 1955 and stored.
Ea-799	099	23-5-46	07-07-57	Crashed at II Brigada Aérea when it went off the runway on 7-7-57. Fifteen per cent damage, not repaired.
Ea-800	100	23-5-46	03-09-58	Crashed at II Brigada Aérea when the left leg of the landing gear broke. Fifty per cent damage, not repaired.
Ea-801	101	3-1-47	1958	
Ea-802	102	8-2-47	1957	Crashed at Escuela de Aviación Militar on 10-5-55 with fifteen per cent damage, repaired.
Ea-803	103	8-2-47	1958	
Ea-804	104	8-2-47	29-06-55	Crashed at Rafael García, Córdoba, when part of the covering of the right wing was lost. Pilot 3rd Year Cadet Eduardo J. Vera and Observer 3rd Year Cadet Edilberto R. Vottero killed.
Ea-805	105	8-2-47	1957	
Ea-806	106	12-2-47	1949	Crashed on 16-9-49 at Escuela de Aviation Militar.
Ea-807	107	12-2-47	8-5-48	Destroyed in an accident on the runway of the Escuela de Aviación on 30-3-48, killing 1° Teniente José Aparicio.
Ea-808	108	12-2-47	1952	Destroyed, killing the two cadets that were flying the plane.
Ea-809	109	12-2-47	1958	
Ea-810	110	12-2-47	1957	
Ea-811	111	12-2-47	4-8-52	Crashed at Mendoza and written off.
Ea-812	112	9-3-47	1958	
Ea-813	113	9-3-47	1958	
Ea-814	114	9-3-47	22-9-48	Crashed at Escuela de Aviación, killing Comandantes Carlos Ramacciotti and Raúl Ríos.
Ea-815	115	9-3-47	1956	
Ea-816	116	14-3-47		Retired between 1952 and 1953.
Ea-817	117	14-3-47	1958	
Ea-818	118	14-3-47	1958	
Ea-819	119	14-3-47		Retired between 1952 and 1953.
Ea-820	120	14-3-47	3-9-47	Destroyed in an accident at Instituto Aerotécnico on 30-4-47. Crew unhurt.
Ea-821	121	6-1-48	2-8-51	Delivered to the Escuela de Aviación only in 18-9-50. Crashed at Santa Mónica, Córdoba, killing Cadet Gustavo de la Peña and another cadet.
Ea-822	122	6-1-48	4-5-55	Crashed at DAM Tandil due to loss of power caused by low fuel pressure. Ninety per cent destruction. Crew unhurt.
Ea-823	123	6-1-48	1957	
Ea-824	124	6-1-48	1949	
Ea-825	125	6-1-48		Retired between 1952 and 1953.
Ea-826	126	6-1-48	1956	
Ea-827	127	6-1-48	31-07-57	Crashed at América, Córdoba, when the engine stopped in flight. Pilot Captain Mario G. Álvarez and mechanic Cabo 1° Norberto Cataldo killed.
Ea-828	128	6-1-48	11-10-51	Crashed at Córdoba, killing Teniente Manuel Alfonsín and Cadet Emilio Negri.
Ea-829	129	6-1-48	1956	
Ea-830	130	6-1-48		Retired between 1952 and 1953.
Ea-831	131	6-1-48	1957	
Ea-832	132	6-1-48	1955	Crashed on 21-8-54.

Serial	C/No.	Enlisted	Retired	Notes
Ea-833	133	6-1-48	1957	
Ea-834	134	6-1-48	1957	
Ea-835	135	6-1-48	15-7-48	Destroyed in an accident on 5-6-48. Pilot unhurt.
Ea-836	136	6-1-48	20-3-52	Crashed at Escuela de Aviación, killing Cadet Néstor Hernández.
Ea-837	137	6-1-48	6-9-48	Destroyed in an accident.
Ea-838	138	6-1-48	1957	
Ea-839	139	6-1-48	1957	
Ea-840	140	6-1-48	1950	
Ea-841	141	1950	1957	
Ea-842	142	2-8-49	1957	
Ea-843	143	2-8-49	1957	
Ea-844	144	2-8-49	1957	
Ea-845	145	2-8-49	14-11-56	Crashed at IV Brigada Aérea when the engine failed on take-off. Pilot Major Francisco García killed and Suboficial Principal Oscar Gallucci wounded.
Ea-846	146	2-8-49	1957	
Ea-847	147	2-8-49	1957	
Ea-848	148	2-8-49	1957	Flew until 1955 and stored.
Ea-849	149	2-8-49	1957	
Ea-850	150	2-8-49	1957	
Ea-851	151	2-8-49	1957	Flew until 1955 and stored.
Ea-852	152	2-8-49	1949	
Ea-853	153	2-8-49	1957	
Ea-854	154	2-8-49	1957	Flew until 1956 and stored.
Ea-855	155	2-8-49	1957	
Ea-856	156	2-8-49	1957	
Ea-857	157	2-8-49	23-8-50	Crashed at Piquillín, Córdoba, killing Teniente Ramón Díaz Vélez.
Ea-858	158	2-8-49	1957	
Ea-859	159	2-8-49	1957	
Ea-860	160	2-8-49	1958	
Ea-861	161	25-2-50	1957	
Ea-862	162	25-2-50	1957	
Ea-863	163	25-2-50	1957	
Ea-864	164	25-2-50	1957	
Ea-865	165	25-2-50	1957	
Ea-866	166	25-2-50	1957	
Ea-867	167	25-2-50	1957	
Ea-868	168	25-2-50	1957	Flew until 1956 and stored.
Ea-869	169	25-2-50	1957	Crashed on 20-1-57 at Pilar, Córdoba.
Ea-870	170	25-2-50	1957	Flew until 1956 and stored.
Ea-871	171	25-2-50	1957	
Ea-872	172	25-2-50	1957	Crashed with 40 per cent damage on 28-4-54 at El Palomar. Repaired.
Ea-873	173	18-4-50	1957	
Ea-874	174	25-2-50	1957	Flew until 1955 and stored.
Ea-875	175	25-2-50		Retired between 1952 and 1953.
Ea-876	176	18-4-50	1957	
Ea-877	177	25-2-50	1957	
Ea-878	178	25-2-50	1957	

I.Ae. DL-22

Serial	C/No.	Enlisted	Retired	Notes
Ea-879	179	25-2-50	1957	
Ea-880	180	25-2-50	1957	Flew until 1955 and stored.
Ea-881	181	1950	1957	Flew until 1955 and stored.
Ea-882	182	18-4-50		Retired between 1952 and 1953.
Ea-883	183	18-4-50	1957	
Ea-884	184	18-4-50	1957	Flew until 1955 and stored.
Ea-885	185	25-2-50		Retired between 1952 and 1953.
Ea-886	186	1950	1950	Assigned to Agrupación Entrenamiento in 1950, destroyed before delivery by the factory.
Ea-887	187	18-4-50	1957	Flew until 1955 and stored.
Ea-888	188	1950		Assigned to I Brigada Aérea only in 1951, retired shortly after.
Ea-889	189	18-4-50	1957	Flew until 1955 and stored.
Ea-890	190	18-4-50		Retired between 1952 and 1953.
Ea-891	191	18-4-50	1957	Crashed on 13-6-56 at Escuela de Aviación Militar with 20 per cent damage, not repaired.
Ea-892	192	18-4-50	1957	Flew until 1955 and stored.
Ea-893	193	18-4-50	25-06-56	Crashed at DAM Tandil when the wingtip hit the ground. Pilot Alférez Alfredo R. Pellegrino unhurt.
Ea-894	194	18-4-50	1957	
Ea-895	195	1950	1956	
Ea-896	196	1950	1958	
Ea-897	197	1950	1957	Flew until 1955 and stored.
Ea-898	198	1950	1957	
Ea-899	199	1950	4-7-48	Crashed at Mendoza and written off.
Ea-900	200	24-7-50	1957	

One of the Calquin assigned to Observation Group 2.

I.Ae.23

Serial	Enlisted	
0	1944	Delivered for tests by the Instituto Aerotécnico without serial. Delivered to the Comando de Institutos Aeronáuticos Militares on 16-4-47 for ground training. Retired on 27-1-48.

IAe-24 Calquin

Serial	Enlisted	Retirement	Remarks
–	8-7-47	8-10-47	First flight on 4-7-46. Accident in Puerto Nuevo, city of Buenos Aires.
Ex.-01 and A-01	8-9-47	1-6-55	Accident in El Plumerillo, Mendoza with 80 per cent damage. 270 hours fifty-five minutes flown.
Ex.-02 and A-02	8-9-47	1-4-54	Accident in Campo Funes, Mendoza. Pilots killed.
Ex.-03 and A-03	8-9-47	12-9-57	Accident in El Plumerillo, Mendoza, with 95 per cent damage. 824 hours 30 minutes flown.
Ex.-04 and A-04	8-9-47	4-58	
Ex.-05 and A-05	8-9-47	1953	Written off after an accident.
Ex.-06 and A-06	10-7-47	1947	Five hours ten minutes flown. Suffered a minor accident due to material deficiencies and was never repaired.
Ex.-07	8-9-47	20-4-48	Accident in El Algarrobal, Mendoza. Fell from a height of 100m after losing stability during a training flight. Crew killed. Written off on 12-11-48.
Ex.-08 and A-08	5-4-48	8-5-58	The first serial was never used. Accident in El Plumerillo, Mendoza. 387:15 hours flown. Last aircraft lost in an accident.
Ex.-09 and A-09	5-4-48	9-55	The first serial was never used. Transferred to Grupo 2 de Observación on 24-2-49. Decommissioned with 748 hours forty minutes flown.
Ex.-10 and A-10	8-9-47	25-4-49	Accident at Rodeo del Medio, Mendoza, pilots killed.
A-11	8-10-48	1957/8	
A-12	6-7-48	11-4-49	Accident in El Plumerillo, Mendoza.
A-13	6-7-48	6-7-48	Accident in El Plumerillo, Mendoza.
A-14	3-9-48	11-5-53	Transferred to Grupo 2 de Observación on 24-2-49.
A-15	6-7-48	3-10-49	Accident in El Plumerillo, Mendoza.
A-16	6-7-48	1950	Written off after an accident.
A-17	8-10-48	1957/8	Crashed on 20-11-48, repaired.
A-18	6-7-48	1957/8	
A-19	6-9-48	27-4-49	Transferred to Grupo 2 de Observación on 24-2-49. Accident on the runway of BAM Reconquista, Santa Fe. Mechanic dead, pilot unharmed.
A-20	7-8-48	1-3-58	Crashed in Capdevilla, Mendoza, with 975 hours fifty minutes flown. Pilots killed.
A-21	6-7-48	18-4-53	Crashed near El Plumerillo, Mendoza. Pilots killed.
A-22	6-7-48	1957/8	
A-23	6-7-48	21-7-48	Accident in Cruz de Piedra, Mendoza, pilots killed. Written off on 12-11-48.
A-24	23-7-48	1957/8	Transferred to Grupo 2 de Observación on 24-2-49.
A-25	23-7-48	1957/8	
A-26	6-7-48	1957/8	
A-27	6-7-48	1957/8	Transferred to Grupo 2 de Observación on 24-2-49.
A-28	7-8-48	4-58	
A-29	18-8-48	26-8-49	Accident in El Plumerillo, Mendoza.
A-30	1-12-48	14-2-52	Accident in El Algarrobal, Mendoza. Pilots killed.
A-31	25-11-48	6-9-57	Accident in Mar del Plata, Buenos Aires. 90 per cent damage.
A-32	8-9-48	28-9-48	Accident in El Plumerillo, Mendoza.
A-33	15-9-49	8-5-58	Crashed in El Plumerillo, Mendoza, with 833 hours thirty minutes flown.
A-34	22-11-48	19-1-58	Accident in Paraná, Entre Ríos, with 90 per cent damage.
A-35	18-4-49	1957/8	

IAe-24 Calquin

Serial	Enlisted	Retirement	Remarks
A-36	18-4-49	3-4-51	Accident in La Calera, Cordoba, pilots killed.
A-37	18-4-49	1957	
A-38	18-4-49	4-58	
A-39	18-4-49	29-4-49	Accident in El Plumerillo, Mendoza.
A-40	18-4-49	4-58	
A-41	18-4-49	20-11-51	Written off after an accident.
A-42	18-4-49	1957/8	
A-43	18-4-49	1951	Written off after an accident.
A-44	18-4-49	4-58	
A-45	18-4-49	20-2-54	Accident in El Plumerillo, Mendoza.
A-46	18-4-49	19-9-53	Written off after an accident.
A-47	18-4-49	4-58	
A-48	1949	17-1-50	Accident in El Plumerillo, Mendoza.
A-49	1949	17-10-55	Accident in Palmira, Mendoza, with 90 per cent damage and 746 hours thirty minutes flown.
A-50	1949	6-9-57	Accident in Mar del Plata. On board was journalist Eduardo Abella Nazar, who along with 1st Ten. Elvo Zocchi died in the accident.
A-51	1949	9-6-50	Crashed near El Plumerillo, Mendoza.
A-52	1949	16-5-50	Accident in El Borbollón, Mendoza. Pilots killed.
A-53	1949	19-6-56	Transferred to Grupo 2 de Observación on 15-9-49. Accident in General Ortega, Mendoza, pilots killed. 602 hours thirty minutes flown.
A-54	1949	26-3-51	Transferred to Grupo 2 de Observación on 15-9-49. Accident at BAM Reconquista, pilots killed.
A-55	1949	18-9-53	Accident in Trancas, San Luis.
A-56	1949	9-9-53	Written off after an accident.
A-57	1949	15-7-52	Accident in Caseros, Buenos Aires, pilots killed.
A-58	1949	4-58	
A-59	1949	23-11-51	Accident in El Plumerillo, Mendoza.
A-60	1949	1-9-49	Accident in El Plumerillo, Mendoza.
A-61	1950	14-5-58	Delivered to Grupo 2 de Observación. Accident in El Plumerillo, Mendoza. 90 per cent damage. 1,002 hours fifty minutes flown.
A-62	1950	4-4-57	Delivered to Grupo 2 de Observación. Accident in Coquimbito, Mendoza. Pilots killed. 601 hours twenty minutes flown.
A-63	18-4-60	4-58	Delivered to Grupo 2 de Observación.
A-64	1950	14-3-56	Delivered to Grupo 2 de Observación. Crashed near El Plumerillo.
A-65	18-4-60	20-7-53	Delivered to Grupo 2 de Observación.
A-66	1950	1957/8	Delivered to Grupo 2 de Observación.
A-67	1950	4-58	Delivered to Grupo 2 de Observación.
A-68	1950	5-9-57	Delivered to Grupo 2 de Observación. Accident in Desaguadero, Mendoza, with 711 hours ten minutes flown.
A-69	1950	29-9-56	Delivered to Grupo 2 de Observación. Accident in El Algarrobal, Mendoza, with 85 per cent damage and 571 hours five minutes flown.
A-70	1950	4-58	Delivered to Grupo 2 de Observación.
A-71	24-7-50	27-8-55	Delivered to Grupo 2 de Observación. Accident in San Francisco del Monte, Mendoza, with 90 per cent damage and 271 hours fifty minutes flown.
A-72	1950	4-67	Initially assigned to Grupo 2 de Observación but not delivered. It was modified for use in the AM-1 Tábano missile launches. It was then used in evaluations at the factory until it was delivered to the Non-Commissioned Officer School to be used as ground training material. Assigned to the National Museum of Aeronautics, it was destroyed during a firefighting exercise in 1967.

| Front view of Calquin A-49.

Serial	Enlisted	Retirement	Remarks
A-73	24-7-50	1957/8	Delivered to Grupo 2 de Observación.
A-74	1950	1957/8	Delivered to Grupo 2 de Observación. Accident in Pajas Blancas, Córdoba, on 10-3-52, repaired.
A-75	24-7-50	4-58	Delivered to Grupo 2 de Observación.
A-76	18-4-60	23-9-55	Delivered to Grupo 2 de Observación. Accident at the Military Aircraft Factory, Cordoba, pilots killed.
A-77	30-4-51	1-53	Delivered to Grupo 2 de Observación. Accident in Río IV, Córdoba on 28-4-52.
A-78	1950	4-58	Delivered to Grupo 2 de Observación.
A-79	1950	30-4-52	Delivered to Grupo 2 de Observación. Crashed near the town of Reconquista, Santa Fe.
A-80	1950	17-1-58	Delivered to Grupo 2 de Observación. Accident in Cruz de Piedra, Mendoza, pilots killed. 744 hours fifteen minutes flown.
A-81	1950	12-11-54	Delivered to Grupo 2 de Observación. Accident in Los Corralitos, Mendoza, with 60 per cent damage. 561 hours flown.
A-82	1950	1957	Delivered to Grupo 2 de Observación. Accident in Río IV, Córdoba, on 29-11-55 with 45 per cent damage. Repaired. 420 hours twenty-five minutes flown.
A-83	1950	25-10-57	Delivered to Grupo 2 de Observación. Accident in Río IV, Córdoba. 50 per cent damage.
A-84	1950	29-3-51	Delivered to Grupo 2 de Observación. Accident in Chaján, San Luis, pilots killed.
A-85	1950	4-58	
A-86	1950	1957/8	Damaged in El Plumerillo, Mendoza, on 15-3-51, repaired.
A-87	1950	28-9-55	Accident in Iriarte, Buenos Aires, with 80 per cent damage
A-88	30-4-51	4-58	
A-89	1950	15-4-57	Accident in El Plumerillo, Mendoza, with 60 per cent damage.
A-90	1950	4-58	
A-91	1950	1-9-57	Accident in San Agustín del Valle Fértil, San Juan, with 95 per cent damage. 654 hours thirty minutes flown.
A-92	1950	6-7-57	Accident in Haedo, Buenos Aires, pilots killed
A-93	1950	1-53	Written off after an accident.
A-94		29-3-51	Accident in Chaján, Córdoba, pilots killed.
	30-4-51	1957/8	
A-96	1950	2-10-56	Crashed near Villa Reynolds, St. Louis, pilots killed.
A-97	30-4-51	1957	
A-98	18-9-50	4-58	
A-99	30-4-51	2-5-56	Accident near El Plumerillo, Mendoza, with 8 per cent damage.
A-100	1950	1-53	Accident in Coronel Pringles, Buenos Aires on 28-6-52.

I.Ae.25 Mañque

Serial	First flight	Retirement	Remarks
–	1945	1949	In 1949 transferred to the 13th Infantry Regiment of the Argentine Army for ground tests. Scrapped shortly after.

I.Ae.27 Pulqui

Serial	First flight	Retirement	Remarks
–	9-8-47	1949	Belly landing on 15-7-55, repaired. Flew until 1960. In 1962 sent to the National Aeronautics Museum. Restored in 1996. Still in exhibition.

I.Ae.30 Ñancú

Serial	First flight	Retirement	Remarks
I-101	10-7-48	2-52	Visited Bolivia on 11-48. On 4-12-51 transferred to the Grupo 3 de Caza with serial I-101. Crashed on 2-52 at the FMA. Capitán Carlos Fermin Bergaglio unharmed.

I.Ae.31 Colibrí and Chingolo

Serial	First flight	Retirement	Remarks
–	18-9-47	1948	I.Ae.31 Colibrí. Had no serial. Used for tests and scrapped.
–	1947	1948	I.Ae.31 Colibrí. Had no serial. Used for tests and scrapped.
–	1947	1948	I.Ae.31 Colibrí. Had no serial. Used for tests and scrapped.
–	1949	1955	I.Ae.31 Chingolo. Had no serial. Used for tests and scrapped.

I.Ae.33 Pulqui II

Serial	First flight	Retirement	Remarks
–	30-10-48	1-49	First wooden glider.
–	21-1-49	1949	Second wooden glider.
–	1949	1950	Static tests airframe, destroyed in tests.
–	16-6-50	31-5-51	Prototype E-1. Crashed on 31-5-51 in Córdoba killing Captain Vedania Mannuwal, who ejected but did not separate from the seat.
–	25-9-51	9-11-56	Prototype E-2. Between 1-52 and 5-53 grounded for modifications. Between 16 and 21-9-55 took part in the revolution against president Perón. Crashed at Córdoba on landing on 9-11-56, pilot Rogelio Balado injured.
–	18-7-52	9-10-52	Prototype E-3. Crashed on 9-10-52 in Córdoba killing Otto Behrens.
–	–	–	Prototype E-4. Not finished, parts used to finish E-5.
–	18-9-59	1960	Prototype E-5. Finished using parts from E-2, E-4 and E-6 prototypes. Flew for the first time in 1960. In 1962 transferred to the National Aeronautics Museum, where now exhibited.
–	–	–	Prototype E-6. Not finished, parts used to finish E-5.

I.Ae.34 Clen Antú

Serial	c/n	First flight	Retirement	Remarks
–	1	20-6-49	1953	Built in 1-49. Modified in 1955 and designated I.A.34B.
LV-X-12	2	1949	25-11-51	Delivered to the Club Argentino de Planeadores Albatros. Had an accident on 25-11-51 at Merlo, Buenos Aires.
LV-X-13	3	1949	1953	Delivered to the Club the Planeadores Córdoba. Returned to the factory in 1953.
LV-X-14	4 and 1	19-10-51	–	I.A.34M. Sent to Spain for the World Soaring Championship in 7-52. Delivered to the Club de Planeadores Córdoba in 1953. In 2000 donated to the Museo de la Industria of Córdoba and restored to be exhibited.
LV-X-25, LV-XXB	2	9-2-52	3-7-52	I.A.34M. Sent to Spain for the World Soaring Championship in 7-52. Crashed at Cuatro Vientos on 3-7-52, pilot José Ortner unhurt.

I.Ae.35 Justicialista del Aire, Huanquero, Pandora and Constancia

Serial	Version	Enlisted	Retired	Notes
	–	–	–	Airframe used for structural testing to destruction.
1st prototype, T-550	V	1953	1968	First flight on 7-9-53, transformed with a cockpit similar to the production aircraft and rigid nose and christened Pandora. It was later transformed into the I.Ae.35-X-III Pandora version with engine nacelles raised 20cm, an extra window, another porthole-type window in the toilet and capacity for ten passengers. Then received double wheels on the nose gear. Made its first flight on 28-5-60. Delivered to the 1st Air Brigade in 1962, the 5th Air Brigade in 1963 and the 2nd Air Brigade in 1967. Minor accident at Aeroparque Jorge Newbery on 12-8-68, not repaired and decommissioned.
2nd prototype, Ea-001, E-501, F-501, F-21	I, then IV	1957	1971	Started construction in 1954 as version Ia, completed in 1956. On 23-1-59 had a minor accident in Mendoza with 9.5 per cent damage. Re-serialled E-501 that year, transformed for photo survey, then F-501 and re-serialled F-21 in 1962. After its retirement, was preserved in the Jorge Newbery Aeromodellers Club, on the outskirts of Buenos Aires. Scrapped in 1988.
Ea-002, E-502, F-502, F-22	I, then IV	1957	1971	First pre-series example. Flew for the first time on 29-3-57. Re-serialled E-502 in 1959 and F-22 in 1962.
Ea.003, Ea-043, E-503	V	1957	Between 1967 and 1970	Second pre-series example. Built in the eight-passenger V version with solid nose and dual command, re-serialled Ea-043 in 1958 and E-503 in 1959.
EA-004, E-504, F-504 and F-23	I, then IV	1957	1971	Third pre-series example. On 3-2-59 had an accident in Tucumán with 40 per cent damage. Re-serialled E-504 in 1959, then converted to photographic and re-serialled F-23.
IA-35 II, E-005, E-505 y T-551	II	1958	Between 1970 and 1972	First production example, prototype of the I.Ae.35 II, demonstrator of the attack and transport version. Enlisted on 3-24-58. Re-serialled E-505 in 1959 and T-551 in 1961.
E-006, E-506, F-506 y F-24	II, then IV	1958	1971	Re-serialled E-506 in 1959, converted to photographic and re-serialled F-24 in 1962.
E-007, E-507	II	1958	Between 1972 and 1973	Minor accident on 2-8-58. Re-serialled E-507 in 1959. It was A-3XX.
E-008, E-508	II	1958	Between 1972 and 1973	Re-serialled E-508 in 1959. It was A-3XX.
E-009, E-509, T-509	II	1958	Between 1972 and 1973	Re-serialled E-509 in 1959. On 2-6-60 had an accident in Mendoza, with 70 per cent damage. Re-serialled T-509 years later. It was A-3XX.
E-010, E-510, T-510	II	1958	Between 1972 and 1973	Re-serialled E-510 in 1959. On 23-10-59 suffered an accident in Mendoza with 20 per cent damage. Received a solid nose when was T-510. It was A-3XX.
S-11	III	1958		No data since 1959.
S-12, TS-12	III	1958	Between 1970 and 1972	
S-013, S-13 y S-513	III	1958	Between 1970 and 1972	Re-serialled S-13, became S-513 in 1963.
S-14, S-514 the TS-14	III	1958	31-12-73	Re-serialled S-514 in 1963, then received modifications to the nose and windscreen and was re-serialled TS-14.
S-15	III	1958	Between 1970 and 1972	It was A-3XX.
LQ-FMA	V	1959	21-7-63	Built with modifications to the windscreen, nose, received VIP interior and christened Constancia with the serial LQ-FMA. First flight on 10-10-59. Crashed on 21-7-63 in El Dorado, Misiones, causing the death of the pilot, Captain Juan Haiduc and all the passengers.
E-011, E-511, T-552	II	1959	Between 1972 and 1973	Re-serialled E-511 in 1959 and T-552 in 1961. It was A-3XX.
E-012, E-512	II	1959	Between 1972 and 1973	Re-serialled E-512 in 1959. It was A-3XX.
E-013, E-513, F-513, F-25	II, then IV	1959	1971	Re-serialled E-513 in 1959, converted to photo survey version and re-serialled F-25 in 1962.

The correlation of the former serials with the new A-3XX range is unknown, but at least twenty-one Huanqueros received the new serial at the end of the 1960s, including this example, A-313.

I.Ae.35 Justicialista del Aire, Huanquero, Pandora and Constancia

Serial	Version	Enlisted	Retired	Notes
E-014, E-514	II	1959	Between 1972 and 1973	Re-serialled E-514 in 1959. On 2-10-60 had an accident in Mendoza with 30 per cent damage. It was A-3XX.
E-015, E-515	II	1959	Between 1972 and 1973	Re-serialled E-515 in 1959. It was A-3XX.
E-016, E-516	II	1959	Between 1972 and 1973	Re-serialled E-516 in 1959. It was A-3XX.
E-017, E-517	II	1959	Between 1972 and 1973	Re-serialled E-517 in 1959. It was A-3XX.
E-018, E-518	II	1959	Between 1972 and 1973	Re-registered E-518 in 1959. It was A-3XX.
Ea-019, E-519	II	1959	31-5-63	Re-serialled E-519 in 1959. Accident in La Rioja on 31-5-63 with 70 per cent damage.
E-520	II	1959	Between 1972 and 1973	It was A-3XX.
B-521, F-20	II, then IV	1959	Between 1970 and 1972	Converted to photo survey version and re-serialled F-20 in 1963.
E-522	II	1959	Between 1972 and 1973	On 29-9-60 had an accident in Santa Fe with 40 per cent damage. It was A-3XX.
E-523, D-523	II	1960	Between 1972 and 1973	Re-serialled T-523 in 1963. It was A-3XX.
B-524, D-524	II	1961	Between 1972 and 1973	Re-serialled T-514 in 1964. It was A-3XX.
E-525	II	1961	Between 1972 and 1973	It was A-3XX.
E-526, F-26	IV	1961	1971	Converted to photo survey version and re-serialled F-26 in 1962.
B-527, F-27	IV	1961	1971	Converted to photo survey version and re-serialled F-27 in 1962.
B-528, F-28	IV	1961	1971	Converted to photo survey version and re-serialled F-28 in 1962.
B-529, F-29	IV	1961	1971	Converted to photo survey version and re-serialled F-29 in 1962.
E-530, LQ-GMF	II	1962	Between 1970 and 1972	Re-serialled LQ-GMF in 1962, served in the FMA, then DINFIA and had metal nose.
E-531, D-531	II	1962	Between 1972 and 1973	Re-serialled T-531 after 1964. It was A-3XX.
E-532	II	1962	Between 1972 and 1973	It was A-3XX.

Due to the lack of documentation in the Argentine Air Force archives,it was impossible to determine the corresponding A-3XX serials, although the following existed.

Serial	Notes
A-301	Retired 31-12-73.
A-302	Written off due to minor accident on 4-8-72.
A-305	Retired on 31-12-73. Preserved in the III Air Brigade in Reconquista, Santa Fe.
A-306	Written off due to minor accident suffered on 7-7-72.
A-307	Retired 31-12-73.
A-309	
A-310	Retired 31-12-73.
A-311	Retired 31-12-73.
A-312	Retired 31-12-73.
A-313	
A-315	Retired 31-12-73.
A-316	Retired on 31-12-73. Preserved in the National Museum of Aeronautics in Morón, Province of Buenos Aires.
A-317	Retired on 31-12-73. Preserved at the National University of San Juan on the Ullúm dam, province of San Juan, in very poor condition.
A-318	Retired 31-12-73.
A-319	Written off due to minor accident suffered on 18-4-72.
A-320	Retired on 31-12-73. Preserved in the II Air Brigade of Paraná, Entre Ríos.
A-321	Retired 31-12-73.
A-322	Retired on 31-12-73. Abandoned at the airport of Santiago del Estero for many years, bought by a scrap dealer in Río Cuarto, possibly scrapped.
A-323	Retired 31-12-73.
A-324	
A-326	Retired 31-12-73.

I.Ae.37

Serial	First flight	Retirement	Remarks
–	1-5-54	1959	Glider built for tests with prone pilot position. Between 7-56 and 3-57 cabin modified with pilot in seated position. Scrapped after 1962.

I.Ae.38

Serial	First flight	Retirement	Remarks
–	9-12-60	1961	Construction began in 1952, but it was finished in 1960. Project cancelled in late 1961. In 1962 it was transferred to the National Aeronautics Museum but was never sent and was scrapped sometime later.

I.Ae.41 Urubú

Serial	First flight	Retirement	Remarks
–	29-9-53		Used for tests and scrapped.
–	7-3-55		I.A.41B. Delivered to the Instituto Argentino de Vuelo a Vela. On 30-10-56 made the first crossing of the Andes by glider. In 1965 transferred to the National Aeronautics Museum but stored at Club de Planeadores Los Caranchos until being restored in 1996 for exhibition.
–	17-12-58		Tested briefly and scrapped.
–	–	–	Not finished.

I.Ae.45 Querandí

Serial	First flight	Retirement	Remarks
	23-9-57	1958	I.Ae.45, later renamed I.A.45A.
LV-X-29	15-11-60		I.A.45 X-II and later I.A.45B. Tested during 1960 and 1962 and then resumed flying in 1965. Retired shortly after.

I.Ae.46 Ranquel, Super Ranquel and I.Ae.51 Tehuelche

Serial	C/No.	Enlisted	Retired	Notes
X-I, LV-HOG	P-01	23-12-57		First flight on 23-12-57. Used by DINFIA and later delivered to Aero Club Chamical on 3-10-62. Fuselage abandoned at Aero Club Mar del Plata.
X-II, LV-ZNF, PG-421	001	31-10-59	2014	First pre-series aircraft, used by the Argentine Air Force for tests and later for glider towing. Disassembled at the Military Aviation School.
LV-ZNG	002	31-10-59		Delivered to the Secretaría de Aeronáutica. Crashed at Sampacho, Córdoba on 14-1-61, repaired.
LV-ZNB	003	31-10-59		Delivered to the Secretaría de Aeronáutica. Used for crop dusting.
LV-ZNC	004	31-10-59		Delivered to the Secretaría de Aeronáutica. Sold to a private owner.
LV-ZND	005	31-10-59	2-7-63	Delivered to the Secretaría de Aeronáutica. Transferred to the Ministerio de Obras Públicas of Córdoba province. Crashed on 2-7-63, pilot killed.
LV-ZNE	006	31-10-59		Delivered to the Secretaría de Aeronáutica. Sold to a private owner.
LV-ZNH	007	25-11-59		Delivered to the Secretaría de Aeronáutica. Sold to a private owner.
LV-ZNI	008	25-11-59		Delivered to the Secretaría de Aeronáutica. Sold to a private owner.
LV-ZNJ	009	25-11-59		Delivered to the Secretaría de Aeronáutica. Transferred to Aero Club San Nicolás.
LV-ZNL	010	25-11-59		Delivered to the Secretaría de Aeronáutica. Sold to a private owner.
LV-ZNM	011	25-11-59		Delivered to the Secretaría de Aeronáutica. Sold to a private owner.
LV-ZNN	012	25-11-59		Delivered to the Secretaría de Aeronáutica. Sold to a private owner.
LV-GZL	013	11-9-62	11-8-78	Sold to a private owner. Crashed on 31-5-74, pilot killed.
LV-GZM	014	11-9-62	12-1-68	Sold to a private owner. Crop duster. Crashed on 12-1-68, pilot injured.
LV-GZN	015	2-8-62	2-10-82	Sold to a private owner. Crashed on 2-10-82, pilot killed.
LV-GZO	016	11-1-62	5-1-07	Sold to a private owner. Crop duster. Crashed on 5-1-07 while crop dusting, pilot injured.
LV-GZP	017	11-1-62	13-1-79	Sold to a private owner. Crop duster. Crashed on 13-1-79 on Córdoba, pilot killed.
LV-GZR	018	3-9-62	10-10-04	Delivered to Club de Planeadores Mar del Plata for glider towing. Collided with an experimental aircraft serialled LV-X231 on 10-10-04 at Pergamino.
LV-GZS	019	3-9-62		Delivered to the Club de Planeadores Santa Rosa for glider towing.
LV-GZT	020	3-9-62		Delivered to the Club de Planeadores Pehuajó for glider towing.
LV-GZU, PG-424	021	3-9-62		Delivered to the Club de Planeadores Quilmes and transferred to the Argentine Air Force as PG-424. Retired before 2014.
LV-GZV	022	3-9-62	17-2-07	Delivered to the Club de Planeadores La Plata for glider towing. Had a mid-air collision with Aero Boero AB-180 LV-MFV at Trenque Lauquen while towing gliders, on 17-2-07, pilot killed.
LV-HLS	023	21-10-63	5-9-97	Delivered to the Club de Planeadores Trenque Lauquen for glider towing.
LV-HLT	024	21-10-63	16-3-01	Delivered to the Club de Planeadores La Rioja for glider towing. Modified as crop duster.
LV-HLU	025	21-10-63		Delivered to the Club de Planeadores Rafaela for glider towing.
LV-HLV	026	21-10-63	1985	Delivered to the Military Aviation School of the Argentine Air Force for glider towing, not receiving military serial. In 1980 to Aero Club Luján. Crashed in 1985 at General Deheza, Córdoba.
LV-HLW	027	21-10-63	19-1-69	Delivered to the Club de Planeadores Bolívar for glider towing. Crashed at Bolívar, pilot killed.
LV-HLX	028	21-10-63		Delivered to the Club de Planeadores Ceres for glider towing. Modified as crop duster. Serial cancelled.
LV-HLY	029	21-10-63		Delivered to the Club de Planeadores Rivadavia for glider towing.

Serial	C/No.	Enlisted	Retired	Notes
LV-HLZ, LQ-HLZ, ZP-EAJ	030	21-10-63		Delivered to the Secretaría de Aeronáutica. Re-serialled LQ-HLZ on 24-10-67. Sold to Club de Planeadores Mby Yui of Paraguay for glider towing with serial ZP-EAJ on 14-8-69.
LV-HMA	031	21-10-63		Delivered to the Club de Planeadores Zárate for glider towing.
LV-HMB	032	21-10-63		Delivered to the Club de Planeadores Junín for glider towing. To Aero Club Oliva. Crashed on 25-1-15, severely damaged.
LV-IAE	033	20-10-63	10-9-64	Used by DINFIA and on 4-5-63 German pilot Hans Scheidhauer to repeat the Raid de las 14 provincias. Crashed at El Palomar on 10-9-64.
LV-HOU	034	21-10-63		Delivered to the Club de Planeadores Cóndor for glider towing.
LV-HOV	035	21-10-63	16-4-65	Delivered to Taller Regional Quilmes of the Argentine Air Force and later to the Club de Planeadores Córdoba for glider towing. Crashed at Quilmes on 16-4-65, pilot killed.
LV-HOW	036	21-10-63		Delivered to the Club de Planeadores Córdoba for glider towing. Modified as crop duster.
LV-HOX	037	21-10-63	17-1-85	Delivered to the Club de Planeadores Paraná for glider towing. Crashed at Pirovano, Buenos Aires, on 17-1-85, pilot injured.
LV-HOY	038	21-10-63		Delivered to the Club Argentino de Planeadores Albatros for glider towing.
LV-HOZ	039	20-12-63	20-1-65	Delivered to Heinz Scheidhauer. Modified as crop duster. Crashed at Vicuña Mackenna, Córdoba. Pilot killed.
LV-HPA	040	16-9-63	5-10-63	Sold to a private owner as crop duster, crashed on 5-10-63 at Lincoln, Buenos Aires, pilot killed.
LV-HPB	041	8-8-63	12-1-66	Sold to a private owner as crop duster, crashed on 12-1-66 at Achiras, Córdoba, pilot injured.
LV-HPC	042	26-9-63	22-10-64	Sold to a private owner as crop duster, crashed on Berrutti, Buenos Aires, pilot injured.
LV-HPD	043	24-9-63	11-11-67	Sold to a private owner as crop duster, crashed on 11-11-67 at Baradero, Buenos Aires, pilot killed.
LV-HRU, LQ-HRU	044	23-7-64	9-1-68	Delivered to the Comando en Jefe of the Argentine Air Force as LV-HRU. On 7-5-65 to LQ-HRU. Crashed on 9-1-68.
LV-HRV	045	25-10-63	12-2-74	Delivered to the Club de Planeadores Rosario for glider towing. Crashed on 12-2-74 in Las Breñas, Chaco.
LV-HRW	046	25-10-63	15-7-73	Delivered to the Club de Planeadores Los Caranchos for glider towing. Crashed on 15-7-73 at Alta Gracia, Córdoba.
LV-HRX	047	25-10-63		Sold to a private owner as crop duster.
LV-HRY	048	25-10-63		Delivered to the Club de Planeadores Rosario for glider towing.
LV-HRZ	049	25-10-63		Delivered to the Club de Planeadores San Martín for glider towing.
LV-HSA	050	25-10-63		Delivered to the Club de Planeadores Otto Ballod for glider towing.
LV-HSB	051	25-10-63	3-11-68	Delivered to the Club de Planeadores Córdoba for glider towing. Crashed on 3-11-68 at Ojo de Agua, Santiago del Estero.
LV-HSC	052	29-7-65		Delivered to Aero Club Las Varillas.
LV-HSD	053	24-2-64		Sold to a private owner as crop duster. Serial cancelled in 1997.
LV-HXX	054	5-1-66		Delivered to Club de Paracaidistas Alta Gracia.
LV-HXY	055	27-9-65	10-10-74	Delivered to Aero Club Santa Cruz. Modified as crop duster. Crashed on 10-10-74 at Córdoba, pilot killed.
LV-HXZ	056	23-12-65	5-12-72	Delivered to Aero Club Ingeniero Jacobacci. Crashed on 5-12-72 near Azul, Buenos Aires.
LV-HYA	057	15-11-65	10-5-68	Sold to CATA S.A. as crop duster. Crashed on 10-5-68 at Ceres, Santa Fe.
LV-HYB	058	4-10-65		Delivered to Aero Club Marcos Juárez. Sold to a private owner as crop duster.
LV-HYC	059	15-11-64		Delivered to Aero Club Junín. Sold to a private owner as crop duster.
LV-HYD	060	22-1-65	30-10-80	Delivered to Aero Club Cosquín. Crashed at Cosquín on 30-10-80.
LV-HYE	061	17-9-65		Delivered to Aero Club Trelew. To Club de Planeadores El Aguilucho on 20-8-81.
LV-HYF	062	10-11-65	4-7-71	Delivered to Aero Club Río Gallegos. Crashed at La Esperanza, Santa Cruz, on 4-7-71, two killed.
LV-HYG	063	30-3-65		Delivered to Aero Club La Consulta. Modified as crop duster. Serial cancelled.
LV-HYH	064	9-11-65		Delivered to Aero Club Pampeano. Modified as crop duster.

I.Ae.46 Ranquel, Super Ranquel and I.Ae.51 Tehuelche

Serial	C/No.	Enlisted	Retired	Notes
LV-HYI	065	2-7-65		Delivered to Aero Club Chacabuco. Modified as crop duster. To Aero Club General Belgrano on 5-5-69, to Club de Planeadores Bolívar on 12-11-74.
LV-HYS	066	11-8-65	10-12-71	Delivered to Aero Club Bariloche. Crashed at Valle Encantado, Bariloche, on 10-12-71, three killed.
LV-HYT	067	10-6-65		Delivered to Aero Club Darregueira. To Aero Club Olavarría on 4-1-77.
LV-HYU	068	10-11-65	26-1-83	Delivered to Aero Club Choele Choel. Modified as crop duster. Crashed at Santa Eufemia, Córdoba, on 26-1-83, pilot killed.
LV-HYV	069	12-5-66		Delivered to Aero Club San Martín de los Andes. Modified as crop duster.
LV-HYW	070	6-10-65	29-2-84	Delivered to Aero Club Villa María. Modified as crop duster. Crashed on 29-2-84 at General Cabrera, Córdoba.
LV-HYX	071	9-9-65		Delivered to Aero Club Plaza Huincul. To Aero Club Pigüé on 22-11-84 and to Club de Planeadores El Aguilucho on 8-7-93.
LV-HYY	072	29-10-65		Sold to a private owner as crop duster.
LV-HYZ	073	21-7-66		Delivered to Aero Club Carmen de Patagones.
LV-HZA	074	3-2-66		Delivered to Aero Club Maquinchao.
LV-HZB	075	26-11-65		Delivered to Aero Club Concordia.
LV-HZC	076	15-12-66		Delivered to Club de Planeadores Águilas Blancas.
LV-IIM	077	23-12-65		Delivered to Aero Club Argentino. Modified as crop duster. Serial cancelled.
LV-IIN	078	13-9-66		Delivered to Club de Planeadores Trenque Lauquen. Modified as crop duster.
LV-IIO	079	21-7-66		Delivered to Aero Club Villa Regina. Modified as crop duster. Serial cancelled.
LV-IIP	080	13-9-66		Delivered to Club de Planeadores Junín.
LV-IIR	081	22-9-66		Delivered to the Centro Universitario de Aviación.
LV-IIS	082	29-9-66		Sold to a private owner as crop duster.
LV-IIT	083	14-10-66		Sold to a private owner as crop duster.
LV-IIU	084	3-11-66		Delivered to Aero Club Curuzú Cuatiá. Modified as crop duster.
LV-IIV	085	3-11-66		Delivered to Aero Club Bell Ville. Modified as crop duster.
LV-IIW	086	3-11-66		Delivered to Aero Club Dolores. Modified as crop duster. Serial cancelled.
LV-IIX	087	10-5-67	1-5-70	Delivered to the Centro Universitario de Aviación. Crashed on 1-5-70 at La Matanza, Buenos Aires, pilot killed.
LV-IIY	088	15-12-66		Delivered to Aero Club Comodoro Rivadavia. Modified as crop duster.
LV-IJE	089	7-4-67		Delivered to Aero Club Villa María.
LV-IJF	090	24-4-67		Delivered to Aero Club San Francisco.
LV-IJG	091	7-4-67		Sold to a private owner as crop duster.
LQ-IJH, LV-IJH	092	24-1-67		Delivered to Tucumán province government. Modified as crop duster. To Aero Club Chacabuco on 12-1-81.
LV-IJI	093	5-5-67		Sold to a private owner as crop duster. Serial Cancelled.
LV-IJJ	094	26-4-67		Delivered to Aero Club Reconquista. On 19-12-69 to Aero Club Rosario.
LV-IJL	095	29-5-67	12-10-67	Delivered to Aero Club Argentino. Crashed at Laferrere, Buenos Aires, on 12-10-67. One injured on the ground.
LV-IJM	096	29-5-67	9-3-74	Delivered to Aero Club La Paz. Crashed at La Paz on 9-3-74.
LV-IJN	097	22-5-67	2-12-84	Delivered to Club de Planeadores Los Tucanes. Crashed at Mancopa, Tucumán, on 2-12-84, three killed.
LV-IJO	098	29-9-67		Delivered to Aero Club 9 de Julio. Modified as crop duster. Serial cancelled, under restoration by 2014.
LV-IJP	099	26-6-67		Delivered to Aero Club Mercedes. Serial cancelled, being restored at Mercedes by 2011.
LV-IJR	100	20-7-67	5-8-72	Delivered to Aero Club Cosquín. Crashed at Villa Fontana, Córdoba, on 5-8-72, pilot and a passenger, plus a person on the ground killed, another passenger injured.
LV-IJS	101	21-7-68		Sold to a private owner as crop duster. Under restoration at Villa Mercedes in 2006.

Serial	C/No.	Enlisted	Retired	Notes
LV-JET	102	12-2-68		Delivered to Aero Club San Luis. To Aero Club Villa Mercedes. Serial cancelled.
LV-JAD	103	13-9-67	20-2-83	Delivered to Aero Club Suboficial Dalale. Modified as crop duster. Crashed at Pilar, Córdoba, on 20-2-82, pilot injured.
LV-JAG	104	15-12-67	21-1-83	Delivered to Aero Club Junín. Modified as crop duster. Crashed at Gorchs, Buenos Aires, on 21-1-83, pilot killed.
LQ-JEU, LV-JEU	105	25-1-68		Delivered to Córdoba province government. Modified as crop duster. To LV-JEU on 2-8-73.
LQ-JEV, LV-JEV	106	25-1-68	19-12-93	Delivered to Córdoba province government. Modified as crop duster. To LV-JEV on 2-8-73. Crashed at Villa del Rosario, Córdoba, on 19-12-93, pilot injured.
LV-JEW	107	5-12-67	9-1-10	Delivered to Aero Club Concepción. Had bigger rear windows and fairings on the landing gear. Modified as crop duster. Modified with Cessna 180 landing gear and Continental O-470-R engine of 230hp. Crashed at Rufino, Santa Fe, on 9-1-10. One killed on the ground.
LV-JEX	108	25-2-69	2-11-88	Delivered to Aero Club Orán. Crashed at Lincoln, Buenos Aires, on 2-11-88, pilot killed.
LV-JEY	109	18-6-69	3-3-10	Delivered to Aero Club Paraná. Modified as crop duster. Crashed at Sacanta, Córdoba, on 3-3-10 when hitting a tree while returning to land, pilot, Ricardo 'Tom' Lucero, killed. He was a retired Argentine Air Force Douglas A-4C Skyhawk pilot and fought in the Malvinas/Falklands war, being shot down and captured by British forces.
LV-JEZ	110	8-10-69	20-7-74	Delivered to Aero Club Argentino. Crashed at San Justo on 20-7-74, pilot and a passenger killed, another passenger injured.
LV-JFB	111	9-10-69		Sold to a private owner as crop duster. Serial Cancelled.
LV-JFC	112	26-1-70		Delivered to Club de Paracaidistas Catamarca. To Club de Planeadores Cóndor.
LV-JFD	113	1-10-70		Sold to a private owner as crop duster.
LV-JFE	114	24-8-72		Delivered to Club Atlético Bartolomé Mitre.
LV-JFF	115	7-8-72	2-3-74	Sold to a private owner as crop duster. Crashed at Noetinger, Córdoba, on 2-3-74.
LV-HYJ	201	15-5-65	9-2-68	I.A.46 Super Ranquel. Tested with skis for Operación Upsala in 1965 to prepare crews for Antarctic operations on Upsala Glacier, Santa Cruz. Delivered to Aero Club Comodoro Rivadavia. Serial cancelled on 9-2-68.
LV-HYL	202	15-5-65		I.A.46 Super Ranquel. Delivered to Aero Club Alto Paraná. To Club de Planeadores Cutral Có.
LV-HYM, E-301, PG-422	203	25-3-66		I.A.46 Super Ranquel. Delivered to the Secretaría de Aeronáutica and later transferred to the Argentine Air Force as E-301. In 1971 to PG-422. Crashed on 14-8-74 at Chapmaquí hill.
LV-HYN	204	2-7-66	23-12-93	I.A.46 Super Ranquel. Delivered to Aero Club San Julián. Had an accident on 24-6-79 at San Jorge, with 35 per cent damage and pilot killed. Repaired. Crashed at Colonia Celina, Buenos Aires, on 23-12-93, pilot killed.
LV-HYO	205	11-8-65		I.A.46 Super Ranquel. Delivered to Club de Planeadores Esperanza.
LV-HYP	206	26-10-65		I.A.46 Super Ranquel. Delivered to Aero Club Jujuy. Stored at Aero Club Río de la Plata in 2009.
LV-HYR	207	6-9-65		I.A.46 Super Ranquel. Delivered to Club de Planeadores Los Caranchos.
LV-IIZ	208	15-12-66		I.A.46 Super Ranquel. Delivered to Aero Club Salta.
LV-IJA	209	8-6-67	10-10-06	I.A.46 Super Ranquel. Delivered to Aero Club San Martín. Sold to a private owner and modified as crop duster. Crashed on 10-10-06 at La Angelina, San Luis, pilot injured.
LV-IJB	210	22-8-67		I.A.46 Super Ranquel. Delivered to Club de Planeadores Catamarca.
LV-IJC	211	21-12-66		I.A.46 Super Ranquel. Delivered to Aero Club Río Tercero. In 2010 being restored by the technical school of Resistencia airport, Chaco.
LV-IJD	212	21-7-67	24-1-96	I.A.46 Super Ranquel. Sold to a private owner as crop duster. Crashed at Noetinger, Córdoba, on 24-1-96, pilot killed.
LV-JAH	213	5-12-67	17-4-73	I.A.46 Super Ranquel. Delivered to Aero Club San Martín. Crashed at Rivadavia, Mendoza, on 17-4-73, passenger injured.
LV-JAI	214	5-2-68		I.A.46 Super Ranquel. Delivered to Aero Club Marcos Juárez. Serial cancelled.
LV-JAJ	215	7-2-68	3-1-92	I.A.46 Super Ranquel. Delivered to Club de Paracaidistas Alta Gracia. Modified as crop duster. Crashed at Villa Huidobro, Córdoba, pilot killed.

I.Ae.46 Ranquel, Super Ranquel and I.Ae.51 Tehuelche

Serial	C/No.	Enlisted	Retired	Notes
LV-JFG, PG-423	216	12-67	2005	Delivered to the Argentine Air Force as PG-423 for use in glider towing at the IV Brigada Aérea and later at the Military Aviation School. Retired in 2005. Preserved at the National Aeronautics Museum.
LV-X-26, LQ-IMF, PG-416, LV-IMF	001	16-2-63	20-10-88	IA-51 Tehuelche. Serialled LV-X-26 for tests. On 5-1-65 re-serialled LQ-IMF, used by the CEV. In 1970 as PG-416 and in 1981 to the Club de Planeadores Tucumán as LV-IMF. Crashed on 20-10-88 and written off.

I.A.50 Guaraní II and GII

Serial	N/S	Enlisted	Retired	Notes
LQ-HER, LV-X-23, LV-X-27, TX-110, LQ-JNG, TX-110, TX-01, T-121	00	2-62	15-10-94	Built on the basis of a Huanquero airframe and called IA-35 Guarani, made its first flight on 6-2-62. Modified to Guarani II, first flight on 23-4-63. Always served in the factory. In 1999 was placed as a monument in the town of Tancacha, Córdoba, with serial T-121.
TX-01, T-124, LQ-JLV, T-124, LQ-AMC, T-124	01	17-10-66	6-95	Built on the basis of a Huanquero airframe. First pre-series example. Finished in 3-65 and used for vibration testing as TX-01. Sent to France on 20-5-65. Delivered to the Secretaría de Aeronáutica as T-124 on 17-10-66 but officially transferred on 30-12-66, entered service with Squadron III of the I Air Brigade. Between 18-7-69 and 22-9-69 with the serial LQ-JLV. Between 6-5-70 and 7-9-71 at the FMA as LQ-AMC. Returned to the 1st Brigade as T-124 until 30-10-87 when transferred to the II Air Brigade until its discharge. It was held in storage at LMAASA until 2010, when it was sent to the EAM for ground instruction. Currently in poor condition.
LV-X-32, T-112	02	13-12-66	2-12-75	Built on the basis of a Huanquero airframe. Second pre-series example. Delivered to the I Air Brigade as T-112. Minor accident on 28-3-67. Accident on 2-12-75 in Bahía Solano, Comodoro Rivadavia, Chubut, with total loss.
T-111, LQ-JXN, T-123	03	28-6-66	15-10-94	Built on the basis of a Huanquero airframe. First serial example, registered in III Squadron of the I Air Brigade as T-111 until 31-12-70, when it was sold to the Argentine Federal Police. Commissioned on 31-8-71 in Air Squadron as LQ-JXN, until 18-6-81, when resold to the FAA as T-123. Served in the I and IV Brigades until 1988, when transferred to the II Brigade. Loaned as teaching material from the Technical Education School 3 of the II Air Brigade. It was stored in the unit until it was scrapped before 2005.
T-113, 5-T-30, T-113	04	25-10-66	11-10-74	Built on the basis of a Huanquero airframe. Delivered to II Squadron of the 1st Air Brigade. In 1971 it was loaned for evaluation to the Naval Aviation Command's Segunda Escuadrilla Aeronaval de Sostén Logístico Móvil, where it was registered 5-T-30, until 5-6-72 when it returned to the FAA as T-113. Accident in Cutral Có, Neuquén, with 70 per cent damage.
T-114, F-34	05	1-12-66	15-8-94	Enlisted in the III Squadron of the I Air Brigade. Serious accident on 5-5-71 in Las Mostazas, Buenos Aires, and sent to the FMA for recovery. Repaired and converted to photo survey version in 1972, delivered to the II Air Brigade as F-34. Retired, stored at LMAASA. Loaned to the Museum of Industry in Cordoba and rebuilt with T-121 wings in 2005.
F-31	06	22-8-67	7-1-07	First aircraft built as a photo survey version. Enlisted in the II Air Brigade. Decommissioned in 2007 and sent to the National Aeronautics Museum.
T-115	07	23-3-67	11-6-91	Delivered to the I Air Brigade, served as a transport for the commander of personnel and then the commander of air operations, based at Aeroparque, Buenos Aires. Retired, in storage at the II Air Brigade for a while and then scrapped.
T-116	08	4-10-67	15-10-94	Enlisted in the I Air Brigade, moved in 1980 to the IX Brigade in Comodoro Rivadavia and finally to the II Air Brigade until its retirement. Monument in the town of Oro Verde until it was destroyed by fire in 2009.
T-117	09	3-10-67	1998	Assigned to the III Squadron of the I Air Brigade, then to the II Brigade, to the III and again to the II until he was discharged. Monument in the town of Crespo, Entre Ríos.
T-118	10	19-12-67	1998	Enlisted in the I Air Brigade, in 1980 moved to the V Brigade and on 22-2-91 to the II Air Brigade until its retirement. Monument at the Aeroclub San Francisco, Cordoba.
T-119, LQ-JZO, LV-JZO, T-119	11	17-6-68	1-10-93	Handed over to the I Air Brigade, transferred in 1980 to the III Brigade. Accident in Crespo, Entre Ríos, with total loss, killing all twelve occupants.

Serial	N/S	Enlisted	Retired	Notes
T-120	12	6-3-68	11-6-91	Registered as a transport of the Air Operations Command, operated by the I Air Brigade. Served with the Air Defence Command. In 1986 moved to the II Air Brigade. Decommissioned and sold to Luis Murúa incomplete and disassembled, whose family keeps it in the garden of their house in Cordoba.
T-121	13	22-8-68	15-10-94	Enlisted in the I Air Brigade, in 1980 moved to the IV Brigade and on 3-1-91 to the II Brigade. Withdrawn from service and stored in the unit until it was handed over to the National Museum of Industry in Cordoba. Destroyed by fire in 2004. Wings used to rebuild F-34.
T-122	14	12-7-68	2-99	Registered as a transport of the Chief of Staff of the FAA, operated by the I Air Brigade, operating from Aeroparque, Buenos Aires. On 17-2-73 became the first domestically built aircraft to land in the Malvinas/Falklands. On 27-7-81 was operated by the II Air Brigade, maintaining its dependency, although later began to be used as a transport for the commander of air operations. Received the fuselage of T-111 because the original had corrosion. Retired and placed as a monument at the Aeroclub Argentino on the outskirts of Buenos Aires, where it is abandoned.
T-123	15	13-7-68	27-5-69	Enlisted in the I Air Brigade. Accident at the Pajas Blancas airport in Córdoba with total loss.
T-125	16	29-7-69	24-10-83	Enlisted in the I Air Brigade. It was evaluated in 1969 with skis for operation in Antarctica. Delivered in that configuration on 10-10-69. Accident at the FMA on 10-10-83, twelve deaths.
F-32	17	14-11-67	6-95	Registered in the II Air Brigade for photo survey. Decommissioned and ceded in 1998 to the IV Air Brigade for fire training until its total destruction in 2000.
–	18	–	–	Built in 1968 and used for structural testing until destruction.
F-33	19	4-7-68	In 2004	First example of the second series. Registered in the II Air Brigade for photo survey. Minor accident due to ice ingestion at the FMA on 23-7-74. Repaired in 1976, in 6-76 it suffered another minor accident. Monument in front of the I Air Brigade, with wings of T-129.
VR-15, T-110	20	8-71	4-07	Built as a radio aids verifier. Delivered to the VII Air Brigade, where later served at the National Institute of Civil Aviation, even working in Bolivia. On 18-1-90 was transferred to the II Air Brigade as a transport with serial T-110 and then on loan to the Military Aviation School, until in 2001 it returned to Paraná. Monument in the II Air Brigade.
AE-1001, LQ-JXY	21	5-11-71	1995	It was originally sold to the Argentine Army as AE-1001, but not operated. Sold to the Federal Penitentiary Service. Registered LQ-JXY on 13-1-72. Last flight on 18-6-93. At the National Aeronautics Museum.
VR-16, T-129	22	1971	2002	Commissioned in the VII Air Brigade as a radio aids verifier. In 12-90 was transferred to the II Air Brigade as a transport and re-serialled T-129. On loan in the Santa Romana private collection.
LQ-JZS, LV-JZS, T-112	23	5-6-72	15-10-94	Delivered to the Directorate of Aeronautics of the Province of Córdoba, registered LQ-JZS and named Inti Huasi on 27-6-72 and LV-JZS on 14-8-73. On 22-1-80 went to the Air Force, on 27-7-81 to the II Air Brigade as T-112, on 20-8-84 to the X Air Brigade of Río Gallegos and then to the VI Brigade, until on 26-12-89 returned to the II Brigade. Used for firefighting training in Paraná until its destruction around 2005.
LQ-MBS, LV-MBS and LQ-MBS	24	4-8-72	1995	Registered with the National Directorate of Social Emergencies of the Ministry of Social Welfare (later the Ministry of Health and Social Action) on 2-10-72. Re-serialled LV-MBS on 7-2-73 until the end of the 1980s. Minor accident in 1995 in San Fernando, Buenos Aires and discharged. As didactic material for the Air Force Non-Commissioned Officer School in Cordoba.
LQ-LAD, LV-LAD	25	6-12-72	9-83	Registered with the Provincial Directorate of Aeronautics of Salta and named Señor del Milagro (Lord of the Miracle). Discharged after an accident in 9-83. Remains turned over to the FAA for use as spares.
T-126	26	22-12-72	1998	Registered with the Argentine Air Force as the transport of the Commander-in-Chief of the FAA until 1996, when it became the transport of the commander of air operations until it was decommissioned and sent to depot to LMAASA. Monument in the town of Diamante, Entre Ríos.
LQ-LAE, LV-LAE	27	15-2-73	23-1-94	Delivered to the Provincial Aeronautics Directorate of Entre Ríos, then Líneas Aéreas Provinciales de Entre Ríos and finally Líneas Aéreas Entre Ríos. Inaugurated the Paraná airport on 12-2-73. Written off after a minor accident in 1994 when it hit a pipeline while trying to land at the airport in Santa Elena, Entre Ríos. The main gear collapsed and the plane returned to Paraná to make an emergency landing. Scrapped in 2001.

I.A.50 Guaraní II and GII

Serial	N/S	Enlisted	Retired	Notes
LQ-LAF, LV-LAF the T-114	28	23-5-73	6-95	Delivered to the Directorate of Aeronautics of the Province of Córdoba until 17-6-80, when it was transferred to the Air Force and on 25-8 to the I Air Brigade as T-114. On 30-10-88 went to the II Air Brigade and on 6-10-91 to the Military Aviation School until retired. It stands as a monument next to the Air Force Non-Commissioned Officer School.
LV-LAI	29	10-10-73	1992	Delivered to the Provincial Aeronautics Directorate of Entre Ríos, then Líneas Aéreas Provinciales de Entre Ríos and finally Líneas Aéreas Entre Ríos. Retired and made a monument at the Paraná airport. Since 2009 at the Aeroclub Paraná.
LV-LAJ, T-113	30	26-12-73	1983	Delivered to the Provincial Directorate of Aeronautics of Catamarca. On 17-6-80 passed to the I Air Brigade as T-113 and in 1982 was deployed south with a yellow band painted on the tail. Accident on 14-12-82 at the Jorge Newbery Airport in Buenos Aires. When it was transferred to the FMA to be repaired it was hit by a truck and was badly damaged, so it was decommissioned.
LV-LAL, T-127	31	5-3-74	1995	Delivered to the I Air Brigade on 2-4-74 as T-127, it was to be delivered to the Directorate of Aeronautics of the Province of Córdoba but was not delivered. In 1989 it was transferred to the II Air Brigade as a T-127 and to the service of the Air Operations Command, until its retirement in 1995. Used for fire practice at Cordoba airport. Sent in 2010 to the Aeroclub Córdoba as a monument, where it was scrapped in 2019.
LV-LAM, T-111	32	28-6-74	1990	Delivered by the factory on 21-5-74. To the Provincial Directorate of Aeronautics of Catamarca, named Santa María. On 17-6-80 was transferred to the I Air Brigade as T-111. Retired in 1990, its fuselage was changed to T-122. Using the fuselage of the latter, it was assembled and sold to G. Capello in 4-92, who used it in Santa Cruz del Lago (Córdoba) for children's games until it was scrapped in 2000.
LV-LAN, T-128	33	25-10-74	15-8-94	It was to be registered LV-LAN but was given to the I Air Brigade for use by Air Operations Command as T-128. It was then transferred to the II Brigade until its retirement on 15-8-94. In storage at LMAASA until it was transferred to the Museo Nacional de Malvinas in Oliva, Córdoba, in 2004. In 2006 it was sent to the Tiro Federal de Córdoba, in La Calera and then moved to a paintball centre between 2007 and 2018, until it was scrapped.
F-35	34	20-1-75	1999	Delivered to the II Air Brigade as a photo survey aircraft. Served until its retirement and is placed as a monument in the II Air Brigade.

T-110 in 1999 in Buenos Aires, before the stabilisers were modified, it being the last Guaraní II to receive that modification.

I.A.53 Mamboretá

Serial	N/S	First flight	Retired	Notes
	0			Airframe for structural tests built in 1965.
LV-X33, PGX-01	1	17-11-66	1976	First prototype. Modified in 1968. Delivered to the Argentine Air Force in 1970. Retired in 1976, preserved at the National Aeronautics Museum since 1980.
LV-X35, PGX-02	2	10-11-66	1976	Second prototype. Serialled LV-X35 on 20-11-67. Delivered to the Argentine Air Force in 1970. Retired in 1976 and scrapped.

IA-58 and IA-66 Pucará

Serial	c/n	Delivered FMA	Delivered CEV	Notes
A-X2	–	25-2-68	–	Wooden glider built under the direction of Reimar Horten. First it was a single-seater and then it was converted to a tandem two-seater. First flight 27-12-67. First flight in tandem configuration on 25-2-68.
A-X2, AX-01	–	19-8-69	–	First prototype, first flight on 20-8-69 with Garrett engines. Later received the Turbomeca Astazou XVI G engines on 8-2-72, re-serialled AX-01. Sent to France in 1971 for static testing. Used as a static demonstrator. Retired on 13-10-80. Exhibited at the National Aeronautics Museum since 1994.
AX-02	–	14-9-70	–	First flight on 15-9-70. Presented in March 1975 in Bolivia. Used for structural testing and destroyed. The cockpit was sent to the III Air Brigade, where it remained until at least 2010.
AX-03	–	8-12-73	–	First flight on 8-12-73. It was the first with the final configuration and internal weapons. Presented at Le Bourget '77 equipped with radar, crashed in Cordoba on 4-10-77. Pilot Captain Schmidt killed. Written off on 5-17-78.
A-501	001	12-11-74	31-7-75	First production example. First flight on 14-11-75. Presented the next day. Delivered to BAM Reconquista on 21-8-75. Participated in Operation Orion. Deployed to Santa Cruz during the 1982 war. Temporarily deprogrammed on 12-86 and definitively on 30-9-87, transferred as teaching aid to the Non-Commissioned Officers School.
A-502	002	14-7-75	6-8-75	Delivered to BAM Reconquista on 21-8-75 and assigned to the Pucará Airmobile Squadron in the CEV from 10-10-75 to 15-10. Participated in Operation Orion. Deployed to Malvinas/Falklands on 25-4-82. Damaged by the British attack of 1-5, repaired. Damaged when landing at Calderon on 9-5. Destroyed on 15-5 during the SAS attack. Written off on 9-8-82. In January 1983 the remains were blown up and buried at Pebble Island.
A-503	003	26-9-75	14-10-75	Delivered to BAM Reconquista on 15-10-75. Participated in Operation Orion. Accident in the VIII Brigada Aérea on 23-9-76. Written off on 5-4-77.
A-504	004	28-11-75	9-1-76	Crashed on 8-3-78 due to collision with A-510 doing acrobatics. Pilot ejected.
A-505	005	30-6-76	19-11-76	Delivered to BAM Reconquista on 22-11-76. Retired on 6-20-90 and used for spare parts. Parts were used to assemble a false A-514 monument in the III Brigade. Central part of the fuselage abandoned in the III Brigade, the front part used to make the Pucará simulator.
A-506	006	2-3-77	10-6-77	Delivered to BAM Reconquista on 10 6 77. Deployed to Comodoro Rivadavia on 8-4-82, on 25-4 crossed into Malvinas/Falklands. On 1-5-82 broke the nosewheel at BAM Cóndor and was used as a decoy. Named Satan Tripa. Written off on 9-8-82. Transported by a RAF Chinook to a depot in 1984, the tail broke off and fell south of the runway. Used as a target at the Rabbit Range.
A-507	007	6-4-77	13-8-77	Delivered to the BAM Reconquista in 1978. Sent to Le Bourget '77 in the C 130 TC-64. Damaged in Reconquista on 5-5-80. Scrapped.
A-508	008	24-5-77	18-6-77	Delivered on 19-6-77. Accident at Garabato Shooting Range (Santa Fe) on 7-30-80. Pilot ejected. Written off on 20-4-82.
A-509, AX-04	009	5-7-77	19-9-77	Assigned to CEV on 10-77 for weapons testing, including the torpedo in 1982. Assigned on 4-7-84 to Attack Group 3 in commission at the CEV. Deprogrammed in 1986, retired in 1992 and installed as a monument in Río Tercero as A-537.
A-509	016	7-4-78	7-8-78	Delivered on 31-12-78. Deployed to Comodoro Rivadavia on 8-4-82 and to Puerto Argentino/Stanley on 25-4-82. Damaged by a bomb on 24-5-82. Captured and cannibalised to arm A-529 as a memorial at RAF Mount Pleasant. Written off on 9-8-82.
A-510	010	24-8-77	29-10-77	Delivered on 30-11-77. Collision with A-504 on 8-3-78, repaired. Crashed in Reconquista on 10-8-90. It was retired in 1992. Front part used to assemble the false A-514 as a monument in the III Brigade.

IA-58 and IA-66 Pucará

Serial	c/n	Delivered FMA	Delivered CEV	Notes
A-511	011	3-11-77	19-1-78	Delivered on 31-1-78. Received SEMCA heating in 1982. Crossed to Puerto Argentino/ Stanley on 15-5-82. Shot down by Sea Harrier Frs.Mk.1 XZ451 on 21-5-82. Major Pilot Tomba ejected. Written off on 9-8-82.
A-512	012	28-11-77	12-1-78	Delivered on 31-2-78. Deployed to Santa Cruz during the war. Decommissioned and in 2019 handed over to the Aeroclub Cañada de Gómez as a monument.
A-513	015	20-2-78	14-4-78	Delivered 3-30-78. Sent to Comodoro Rivadavia on 8-4-82, crossed to Puerto Argentino/ Stanley on 25-4-82. Damaged on 1-5-82 and used as a decoy. Written off on 9-8-82. It was left in a warehouse on the islands, currently scrapped.
M2/5T MAB, A-514	017	18-5-78	23-6-78	Assigned to Mauritania as M2/5T-MAB. Delivered to BAM Reconquista on 31-12-78 and deployed to Puerto Argentino/Stanley on 29-5-82. Damaged on 1-6-82 due to a collision on the ground with A-532. Written off on 9-8-82. Cannibalised in the Malvinas/ Falklands after the war.
M4/5T MAB, A-515, ZD485	018	7-6-78	25-10-78	Assigned to Mauritania as M4/5T-MAB. Delivered to BAM Reconquista on 31-12-78 and deployed to Puerto Argentino/Stanley on 28-5-82. Damaged and captured. Written off on 9-8-82. Transferred by Chinook ZA707 to the Atlantic Causeway and on 12-7-82 sailed to the UK from Puerto Williams, where it arrived on 28-7. Taken overland on 1-8 to the Aircraft and Armaments Experimentation Centre at Boscombe Down and re-serialled ZD485. On 22-2-83 made taxiing tests and on 28-4 the first flight under the command of Vice Commodore Peart. It was evaluated, including on unpaved runways and in air combat, especially with Sea Harriers. Featured at the International Air Tattoo on Greenham Common on 23-7-83 and on 9-9-83 it was taken to the Cosford branch of the RAF museum.
A-516	020	8-8-78	13-9-78	Delivered on 31-12-78. Sent to the Malvinas/Falklands on 15-5-82 and damaged on 25-5-82. Used as a decoy. Written off on 9-8-82. The remains were buried in Puerto Argentino/Stanley after the war.
M3/5T MAB , A-517, G-BLRP	014	11-1-78	19-9-78	Assigned to Mauritania as M3/5T MAB. Delivered to BAM Reconquista on 31-12-78. Sent to Comodoro Rivadavia on 8-4-82, crossed into the Malvinas/Falklands on 26-4-82. Damaged at BAM Condor on 1-5-82 and again on 4-5-82. Captured. Delivered to the residents of Goose Green on 5-10-84, sold the same day to Grampian Helicopters Int., received the registration G-BLRP, though was not painted. Sent on the ship Monsumen to Puerto Argentino/Stanley on 30-1-85. Brought to England in 1987, it was taken to the Lashenden Air Warfare Museum in Headcorn, Kent. In 1989 it was bought by Rod Butterfield, who took it to the United States, where it remains in storage. Written off on 9-8-82.
M1/5T MAB, A-518	018	27-12-77	26-10-78	Assigned to Mauritania as M1/5T MAB. Delivered to BAM Reconquista in 5-79. Deployed to Santa Cruz during the war. Crashed on 23-9-87, it was planned to send it to the CEV, but this was cancelled. Repaired, flew until 14 June 1991. Sent to the FMA to be recovered to service, it was cannibalised and placed in storage. Repainted in Colombian colours in 2000, it was planned to be sent to that country for a museum but this was cancelled. Currently preserved at the University Institute of Aeronautics.
A-519, A-19	019	27-7-78	12-12-78	Re-serialled as A-19 for Farnborough 78 and equipped with radar. Crashed in Cerro Ancasti (Catamarca) on 2-6-79. Pilots Cap Digier and 1st Ten Spika killed.
A-517, A-520	021	17-10-78	19-9-78	First serial cancelled. Delivered on 31-12-78. It received Hamilton Standard heating in 1982. Sent to Comodoro Rivadavia on 8-4-82 and crossed to Malvinas/Falklands on 25-4-82. Destroyed by the SAS on 15-5-82 at the Estación Aeronaval Calderón. Written off on 9-8-82. The remains were taken to a warehouse on Isla Soledad and scrapped.
A-518, A-522	022	6-11-78	5-12-78	First serial cancelled. Delivered on 31-12-78. Sent to Malvinas/Falklands on 29-5-82. Captured and taken on 6-9-82 by Chinook ZA720 to the container ship Contender Bezant, which took it to Southampton, where it arrived on 23-9-82. It was taken to Abingdon the next day and received RAF maintenance number 8768M, taken to St Athan on 25-10-82 until it was sent to the Fleet Air Arm Museum in Yeovilton. Currently at the North East Land, Sea and Air Museums in Sunderland. Written off on 9-8-82.
A-519, A-523	023	21-11-78	12-12-78	First serial cancelled. Delivered on 31-12-78. Crossed to Malvinas/Falklands on 2-4-82 and damaged at Estación Aeronaval Calderón on 1-5-82. Damaged again during the SAS attack on 15-5-82. Written off on 9-8-82. It was taken after the war to a shed on Isla Soledad and then used as a target at a shooting range.
A-524	024	29-12-78	26-1-79	Delivered on 31-1-79. Deployed to Santa Cruz during the war. Second IA-58D Pucará Delta. Delivered on 21-10-04. Modified to IA-58E. In storage at the III Air Brigade.
A-525, AX-05	025	24-3-79	–	Modified to IA-58B in 1978, featured at Le Bourget '79. Retired on 7-11-82, its remains were scrapped in 12-96.

Serial	c/n	Delivered FMA	Delivered CEV	Notes
A-526	026	27-4-79	28-5-79	Delivered on 31-5-79. Deployed to La Plata during the Malvinas/Falklands War and crashed on 10-6-82 in Atalaya (Buenos Aires). Pilot Alf. Marchesini ejected.
A-527	027	31-5-79	13-7-79	Delivered on 31-7-79. Sent to Comodoro Rivadavia on 8-4-82, crossed to the Malvinas/ Falklands on 25-4-82. Destroyed on land by a Sea Harrier on 1-5-82. Pilot Ten. Jukic and eight non-commissioned officers killed. Written off on 9-8-82.
A-528	028	4-7-79	16-8-79	Delivered on 31-8-79. Deployed to Comodoro Rivadavia on 8-4-82 and crossed to Malvinas/Falklands on 26-4-82. Named Toto Juan. Damaged in Puerto Argentino/Stanley on 30-4-82. Captured. Taken by Chinook ZA720 to the container ship Contender Bezant, which took it to Southampton, arriving on 23-9-82. On 27-9-82 received maintenance number 8769M, then taken to the Oxford Museum on 18-10-82. Sent to the Museum of Army Flying, Middle Wallop, it is now on display at the Norfolk and Suffolk Aviation Museum in Flixton, Suffolk. Written off on 9-8-82.
A-529	029	7-8-79	24-8-79	Delivered on 31-8-79. Deployed to the Malvinas/Falklands on 2-4-82 and damaged in the SAS attack of 15-5-82 on Estación Aeronaval Calderón. Taken by a Chinook to the ship Sand Shore, which took it to Puerto Argentino/Stanley. Installed as a memorial at RAF Mount Pleasant for several years. Scrapped in the early 2000s. Written off on 9-8-82.
A-530	030	22-8-79	7-9-79	Used by the CEV for testing the Pampa telemetry system. It received Garrett heating in 1982. Delivered to the 3rd Strike Group in 1984. Damaged on 5-10-97 and decommissioned. Fuselage used at the Garabato firing range as a target without wings or tail.
A-531	031	7-9-79	17-9-79	Delivered on 30-9-79. Sent to the Malvinas/Falklands on 15-5-82 and shot down on 21-5-82 by a Stinger missile. Pilot Captain Benitez ejected. Written off on 9-8-82.
A-532	032	28-9-79	2-10-79	Delivered on 31-10-79. Sent to the Malvinas/Falklands on 27-5-82 and damaged the next day. Hit on the ground by A-514 on 1-6-82. Written off on 9-8-82. Taken to a shed on the Islands after the war, later used as a target at a shooting range.
A-533, ZD486	033	8-10-79	12-10-79	Delivered on 31-12-79. Sent to Malvinas/Falklands on 15-5-82, captured on 14-6-82. Taken by the Chinook ZA718 to the merchant ship Tor Caledonia, left Port Willliams on 20-8-82 for the UK, arriving at Felixstowe on 20-8-82. Taken to Finningley on 23-8 for exhibition and then to Abingdon. Re-registered ZD486 in anticipation of it flying, sent to Boscombe Down. Used for spare parts for ZD485. Exhibited at the Museum of Army Flying in Middle Wallop from 15-2-84, until it was scrapped in 1997. Front part in the hands of Gordon Ramsey. Written off on 9-8-82.
A-534	034	19-10-79	15-11-79	Delivered on 30-11-79. Participated in the 1980 South American tour. Deployed to La Plata during the war. Third IA-58D Pucará Delta. Deposited at the III Air Brigade.
A-535	035	31-10-79	15-11-79	Delivered on 30-11-79. Accident near San Justo (province of Santa Fe) on 7-5-80. Pilots 1st Lt Braun and Alf. Fernandez killed. Written off on 16-3-81.
A-536	036	15-11-79	19-11-79	Delivered on 30-11-79. Sent to the Malvinas/Falklands on 28-5-82 and damaged the same day. Written off on 9-8-82. Cannibalised and taken to a shed on the islands after the war, later scrapped.
A-537	037	16-12-79	28-12-79	Delivered on 31-12-79. Sent to the Malvinas/Falklands on 27-5-82 and the next day shot down Westland Scout XT629. Accident on the way back to Puerto Argentino/Stanley Pilot Ten. Gimenez killed. Written off on 9-8-82.
A-538	038	24-12-79	7-1-80	Delivered on 31-12-80. Sent to Santa Cruz during the Malvinas/Falklands War. Crashed on 29-6-88 near Reconquista.
A-539, AX-06	039	25-2-80	29-2-80	Sent to FIDA 80 and the Middle East. Converted in 1981 to IA-66 and re-serialled AX-06. Equipped with Garrett heating. Retired in 1984. Fuselage used to arm the n/s 107.
A-540	040	10-3-80	31-3-80	Delivered to the CEV on 30-4-80. Assigned to IV Attack Squadron in 12-81. Fell into the sea on 24-5-82. Pilot Alf. Valko killed
A-541	041	26-3-80	31-3-80	Participated in the 1980 South American tour. Delivered on 28-6-82. Damaged by structural failure while coming out of a shooting run at the Garabato Shooting Range on 21-9-83. Alf. Grillo killed.
AX-06	042	10-84	–	Used first as a mock-up for the IA-58C and then as a prototype. Assigned to Attack Group 3 on 4-7-84 on assignment to the CEV. First flight on 30-12-85. Retired in 1995 and cannibalised. Restored and put on display at the Technological Museum of the Río IV Material Area since August 2002.
A-542, FAU 220	043	21-4-80	16-5-80	Serial cancelled, delivered to the Uruguayan Air Force as FAU 220 on 12-5-81. Retired on 17-3-17. In deposit in Durazno.

IA-58 and IA-66 Pucará

Serial	c/n	Delivered FMA	Delivered CEV	Notes
A-543, FAU 222	044	13-5-80	29-5-80	Serial cancelled, delivered to the Uruguayan Air Force as FAU 222 on 14-7-81. Retired on 17-3-17. In deposit in Durazno.
A-544, FAU 223	045	12-6-80	8-7-80	Serial cancelled, delivered to the Uruguayan Air Force as FAU 223 on 12-8-81. Retired on 17-3-17. In deposit in Durazno.
A-545	046	30-6-80	24-10-80	Delivered on 31-10-80. Used for tests of the Martin Pescador missile and crashed on 2-7-82 in Flor de Oro (Santa Fe). Pilot Alf. Mastronardi ejected.
A-546, FAU 221	047	31-7-80	11-9-80	Serial cancelled, delivered to the Uruguayan Air Force as FAU 221 on 12-5-81. Retired. Used for fire practice. The remains are in Durazno.
A-547, FAU 224	048	30-8-80	31-10-80	Serial cancelled, delivered to the Uruguayan Air Force as FAU 224 on 23-9-81. Retired on 17-3-17. Preserved at the Aeronautical Museum of Uruguay in Carrasco.
A-548, FAU 225	049	7-10-80	11-11-80	Serial cancelled, delivered to the Uruguayan Air Force as FAU 225 on 8-10-81. Accident on 22-7-93 at the Rincón del Bonete dam, Uruguay.
A-549, ZD487	050	31-10-80	18-3-80	Delivered 4-12-81. Sent to Puerto Argentino/Stanley on 29-5-82. Captured. Taken by the Chinook ZA707 to the ship Atlantic Causeway, which transported it to the UK, arriving on 27-7-82 at Devonport. The Chinook ZA676 took it to Yeovilton and then by the Chinook ZA709 to Boscombe Down on 9-8-82. Registered ZD487, it was expected to fly, it did not do so because it suffered structural damage while being transported and was used for spare parts for the ZD485. On display at the Imperial War Museum in Duxford. Written off on 9-8-82.
A-550	051	13-12-80	18-6-80	Delivered on 11-9-81. Retired at 4-99. Assigned to the Municipality of Pilar (province of Córdoba) on 5-10-99.
A-551	052	19-2-81	1-4-81	Delivered to IV Attack Squadron in 12-81. To Attack Group 3 on 9-4-91. On deposit at FAdeA.
A-552	053	13-3-81	16-6-81	Delivered on 15-9-81. Crossed to Malvinas/Falklands on 2-4-82. Damaged by the SAS on 15-5-82 at the Calderon Naval Air Station. Written off on 9-8-82. Taken to a depot on Isla Soledad by the ship Sand Shore. Abandoned on the islands.
A-553	054	30-3-81	18-8-81	Delivered on 15-9-81. Crashed in Reconquista on 25-2-82. Alf Sabella killed and Alf Puga wounded.
A-554	055	30-4-81	25-10-81	Crashed before being delivered in Noetinger (Cordoba). Lt Fischer and Suboficial principal Orozco killed.
A-555	056	27-5-81	2-10-81	Delivered on 24-11-81. Sent to the Malvinas/Falklands on 28-5-82 and shot down that day over Goose Green. Lt Cruzado ejected. Written off on 9-8-82.
A-556	057	10-6-81	26-8-81	Delivered on 15-9-81. Crossed to Malvinas/Falklands on 2-4-82. Damaged during the SAS attack on Estación Aeronaval Calderón on 15-5-82. Written off on 9-8-82. Taken to a shed near Chartres in Gran Malvina/West Falkland.
A-557	058	30-6-81	25-9-81	Delivered to IV Attack Squadron in 12-81. Transferred to Attack Group 3 on 12-5-91. Sent to Chile in March 1998 to participate in FIDAE 98. Deposited at the III Air Brigade.
A-558	059	5-8-81	10-1-82	Delivered to IV Attack Squadron in 12-81. Transferred to Attack Group 3 on 15-2-91. Deposited at the III Air Brigade.
A-559	060	21-8-81	27-5-82	Delivered to IV Attack Squadron in 12-81. Transferred to Attack Group 3 in 1990. Retired, placed as a monument near the Military Aviation School.
A-560	061	31-8-81	12-4-82	Delivered on 12-8-82. In 1984 joined IV Attack Squadron. Accident in Comodoro Rivadavia on 4-1-90.
A-561, AX-561, OVX-501	062	24-9-81	12-4-82	Although assigned to the III Air Brigade in 1982, was only delivered by the FMA in 1986 and sent on commission to the CEV for weapons and systems testing. Assigned to the CEV in 1991, later assigned to the III Brigade on commission in the CEV. Participated in FIDAE 92 in Chile. Maintained its camouflage scheme, which it was delivered in, until 2019. Modified between 2012 and 2015 into IA-58H Pucará 2 with Pratt & Whitney engines and re-serialled AX-561. In 2019 it was renamed IA-58H Pucará Fénix, with serial OVX-501 and new camouflage in all grey.
A-562	063	30-9-81	12-4-82	Delivered on 31-12-82. Deposited at the III Air Brigade. Assigned to the Municipality of Baradero, but not delivered.
A-563	064	16-10-81	20-4-82	Delivered 6-28-82. Retired, installed in the city of Reconquista as a monument.

5T-MAB assembled, the only Pucará with Mauritanian colours. The plane was in the end delivered to the Argentine Air Force as A-518. *Jorge Figari via Carlos Ay*

Serial	c/n	Delivered FMA	Delivered CEV	Notes
A-564	065	28-10-81	20-4-82	Delivered on 15-7-82. Retired on 31-12-94. Used for static testing as part of the Pucará 2000 program. Front part used as a monument in the III Air Brigade and the rest sold as scrap metal.
A-565	066	6-11-81	30-4-82	Delivered to IV Attack Squadron in 12-82. Transferred to Attack Group 3 at 12-90. Deposited at the III Air Brigade.
A-566	067	17-11-81	7-5-82	Delivered to IV Attack Squadron in 12-82. Transferred to Attack Group 3 at 12-90. Decommissioned and placed as a monument in the town of Comodoro Rivadavia, Chubut.
A-567	068	26-11-81	29-5-82	Delivered on 15-7-82. Deposited at FAdeA.
A-568	069	4-12-81	29-5-82	Delivered on 15-7-82. Hit by a bus of line 140 in Buenos Aires on 19-8-87. Repaired and sent to IV Attack Squadron in 1988 until 15-2-91. It was a prototype of the IA-58E version. Retired from service in 2019, put back into flight on 30-6-21 to be sent to FAdeA for conversion to Pucará Fénix.
A-569	070	18-12-81	12-6-82	Delivered on 12-8-82. Transferred to IV Attack Squadron in 1984 until 15-6-91. Deposited at the III Air Brigade.
A-570	071	26-2-82	29-5-82	Delivered on 14-12-82. Accident in Laguna del Bonete on 6-1-83 (Santa Fe). Alférez Secco and Cabo Principal Muratore killed.
A-571, FAU 226	072	17-3-82	12-6-82	Delivered on 14-12-82. Loaned to the FAU as FAU 226 between 2002 and 2003. Converted to IA-58E. In the III Air Brigade, to be taken to Pucará Fénix.
A-572	073	31-3-82	12-6-82	Delivered 6-28-82. Delivered to be placed as a monument in Ciénaga del Coro, Córdoba.
A-573	074	26-4-82	17-6-82	Delivered 6-28-82. Transferred on 26-7-84 to IV Attack Squadron, where it was cannibalised. On 18-4-89 went to the FMA to be put into service, although it was decommissioned on 20-6-90. Parts were used to assemble a false A-514 for a monument at the III Brigada and the nose was employed in the EAM simulator.
A-574, FAU 226	075	14-5-82	8-7-82	Delivered on 14-12-82. Transferred in 1984 to IV Attack Squadron until 15-6-91. Loaned to Uruguay from 1998 to 2001, where it was registered FAU 226. Decommissioned and placed as a monument in the town of Ataliva Roca.
A-575	076	7-6-82	12-8-82	Delivered on 12-8-82. Deposited at the V Air Brigade. Converted to IA-58E. Its conversion to Pucará Fénix is awaited.
A-576, A-580	077	24-6-82	11-2-83	Delivered on 16-2-83. Delivered as A-576. Assigned in the papers for the Colombian Air Force, A-580 was sent in its place and the serials were exchanged. In 1990 was sent to IV Attack Squadron until 15-2-91. Fifth IA-58D Pucará Delta. Converted to IA-58E. Had a landing gear retraction incident during a start-up. On deposit at the III Air Brigade.
A-577	078	8-7-82	10-12-82	Delivered on 14-12-82. Used as a prototype of the IA-58D, presented on 12-02. First example of the IA-58D Pucará Delta version. Delivered 2-6-05. Decommissioned and placed as a monument in the town of Campana, Buenos Aires.
A-578, FAC 2202	079	30-7-82	23-12-82	Delivered on 29-12-82. Sold to the Colombian Air Force on 17-12-89 as FAC 2202. Sold to Uruguay in 2009. Deposited at the 2nd Air Brigade in Durazno. 2,311 hours flown in its career, of which 522 were after the inspection carried out for delivery to Colombia.
A-579, FAC 2203	080	24-8-82	9-2-83	Delivered on 16-2-83. Sold to the Colombian Air Force on 17-12-89 as FAC 2203. Sold to Uruguay in 2009. Deposited at the 2nd Air Brigade in Durazno. 1,921 hours flown in its career, of which 522 were after inspection for delivery to Colombia.

IA-58 and IA-66 Pucará

Serial	c/n	Delivered FMA	Delivered CEV	Notes
A-580, FAC 2201 FAU 221	081	8-11-82	8-3-83	Delivered on 16-3-83. In 1985 suffered an accident with 32 per cent damage. Sent to the FMA for repairs. Sold to the Colombian Air Force on 17-12-89 as FAC 2201, although the papers indicate that A-576 was delivered, which was re-serialled A-580. Sold to Uruguay in 2009. In 2018 painted as FAU 221 and installed as a monument in the 2nd Air Brigade. 1,034 hours flown in its career, of which 997 were after the inspection carried out for delivery to Colombia.
A-581	082	29-9-82	11-2-83	Delivered on 16-2-83. Retired on 4-99. Delivered to the Museo Nacional de Malvinas in Oliva (Córdoba) on 9-8-99. Armed with wings from AX-06 and parts from A-550.
A-582	083	11-10-82	14-3-83	Delivered on 16-3-83. Fourth IA-58D Pucará Delta. Converted to IA-58E. Retired on 12-19. Flew again on 22-3-21 and was later sent to FAdeA. Used between April and June 2021 for the evaluation of MET 1 of the INVAP ISR pod. Its conversion to Pucará Fénix is awaited.
A-583	084	29-10-82	14-4-83	Delivered on 4-20-83. Converted to IA-58E. Had an emergency in October 2018 during a firing sortie in the V Air Brigade. Made a hard landing that caused some damage to the plane, which did not fly again. Deposited at the V Air Brigade.
A-584	085	5-8-88	1988	Delivered on 19-10-92. First air-conditioned device delivered in 1995. It bears the kill mark of Scout XT629. Deposited at FAdeA.
A-585	086	1989	1989	Delivered on 12-9-91. Converted to IA-58E. Retired on 12-19. Flew again on 22-3-21 and was later sent to FAdeA for conversion to Pucará Fénix.
–	087	1982	16-9-82	Airframe used for fatigue tests until destruction.
A-588	088	1989	1990	Delivered on 15-11-91. Participated in FIDAE 88 in Chile before being handed over to the FAA. Converted to IA-58E. Deposited at the V Air Brigade. Possibly to be turned into Pucará Fénix.
A-589	089	23-5-83	13-9-83	Delivered on 3-1-92. Crashed on 16-3-06. Cabin used for firefighting training in the III Air Brigade.
A-590	090	8-6-83	24-11-83	Damaged when the nose leg retracted at the CEV. In storage at LMAASA disassembled. Loaned to the private collection of the Santa Romana ranch.
A-591	091	29-6-83	29-2-84	In March 1984 was sent to Chile to participate in FIDA 84. Delivered to the FAA on 9-9-91. It had been selected for possible sale to Iraq. Stopped flying in November 1992 with only 219 hours. Deposited at FAdeA.
A-592	092	28-7-83	29-2-84	Delivered on 14-8-91. Deposited at FAdeA.
A-593	093	18-8-83	30-4-84	Delivered on 17-12-91. Deposited at the III Air Brigade.
A-594	094	8-9-83	29-8-84	In March 1988 was sent to Chile to participate in the FIDA 88 fair. Delivered to the FAA on 4-10-91. Deposited at the III Air Brigade.
A-595	095	1986	1989	Delivered 4-4-97. Deposited at FAdeA.
A-596	096	12-12-91	1992	Delivered 6-9-91. Retired and placed as a monument in the town of Salsipuedes, Córdoba.
A-597	097	8-4-92	1992	Delivered 8-7-92. Deposited at the III Air Brigade.
A-598	098	23-10-91	1991	Delivered on 25-10-91. Accident on 8-9-10, pilot killed.
A-599	099	8-7-92	1992	Delivered 8-7-92. Deposited at the III Air Brigade.
A-600, CA-601	100	28-12-93	1993	Sold in 1992 to Sri Lanka as CA-601. Delivered in 12-92. Minor accident on 13-10-93, shot down on 14-7-95.
A-601, CA-602, CA-605	101	28-12-93	1993	Sold in 1992 to Sri Lanka as CA-602 and then CA-605. Delivered in 12-92. It was retired in 1999 and is now at the Sri Lanka Air Force Museum in Ratmalana.
A-602, CA-603	102	20-1-93	1993	Sold in 1992 to Sri Lanka as CA-603. Delivered in 3-93. It was retired in 1999 and is now at the Sri Lanka Air Force Museum in Ratmalana.
A-603, CA-604	103	20-1-93	1993	Sold in 1992 to Sri Lanka as CA-604. Delivered in 3-93. Lost in action on 15-4-97.
A-604/ A-504	104	1996	1996	Delivered on 12-12-96. Sixth Pucará Delta. On deposit at the III Air Brigade.
A-605, FAU 227	105	1998	1998	Delivered to the FAU in April 1998 re-serialled as FAU-227, using parts of FAU-221. Retired on 17-3-17. Run until 2019. Preserved in the II Air Brigade in Durazno.
A-606	106	–	–	Delivered to the FAU, used for spare parts.
A-607	107	–	–	Started in 1985 with the fuselage of n/s 039, not completed. Deposited at FAdeA.
A-608	108	–	–	Started in 1985, not completed. Deposited at FAdeA.

Presentation of the Pampa 2000 at LTV facilities in the USA. *LTV*

IA-63 Pampa

Serial	C/N	Enlisted	Notes
EX-01	2001	30-5-84	First prototype. Presented at Le Bourget '85. Used by the Centro de Ensayos en Vuelo. Crashed on 10-12-04 at Base Aeronaval Punta Indio. 1st Lt Juan Pablo Martínez killed.
EX-02, E-816	2002	8-85	Second prototype. Named Mancha on the American tour. Used on the Pampa 2000 programme. Used by Centro de Ensayos en Vuelo. Taken to AT-63 standard, later Pampa II in 2006 and delivered on 28-4-07 to the IV Brigada Aérea. In service.
EX-03	2003	3-86	Third prototype. Named Gato on the American tour. Used for weapon tests. Converted to AT-63/Pampa II prototype and presented on 15-12-04. Modified in 2015 to Pampa III, making its first flight with the new configuration on 18-9-15 with new paint scheme. Upgraded to Pampa III Block 2 and flew again on 3-21 in new colours. In service at the Centro de Ensayos en Vuelo.
—	2004	1985	Static tests airframe, used until 1989. In storage at FAdeA.
—	2005	8-87	Dynamic tests airframe, used for ground tests and as a mock-up at FAdeA.
E-801	2006	7-88	Out of service since the 1990s. Awaiting restauration and modernisation to return to service.
E-802	2007	7-88	Crashed at Mendoza on 23-11-91 while doing aerobatics, Major Héctor Hugo Luna and Lt Gustavo Javier Ottogalli killed.
E-803	2008	7-88	Had a minor accident while landing at the I Brigada Aérea on 5-6-95. Repaired. Taken to Pampa II standard. In service at the IV Brigada Aérea.
E-804	2009	2-89	Modernised to Pampa II in 2016 and delivered to the VI Brigada Aérea. In service at the IV Brigada Aérea.
E-805	2010	2-89	Modernised to Pampa II in 2007. In service at the IV Brigada Aérea.
E-806	2011	1989	Modernised to Pampa II in 2007. In service at the IV Brigada Aérea.
E-807	2012	1989	Modernised to Pampa II in 2017 and delivered to the VI Brigada Aérea. In service at the IV Brigada Aérea.
E-808	2013	1989	Crashed on 17-9-99 at Mendoza, pilots USAF Major James Hetherington and Alférez Sergio Fiorentino of the FAA ejected.
E-809, A-709	2014	1989	Grounded between 2007 and 2023, never taken to Pampa II and modernised to Pampa III Block 2, delivered on 1-2-23. In service.
E-810	2015	1989	Crashed on 14-12-94 at Mendoza due to bird ingestion. Pilot and an NCO killed.
E-811, A-711	2016	1989	Modernised to Pampa III Block 2, started flight tests in 11-23.
E-812	2017	1989	First prototype of the Pampa 2000. Taken to Pampa II and delivered on 28-4-07. Being modernised to Pampa III Block 2.
E-813	2018	1990	Crashed at Bournemouth, UK, on 31-8-92. Pilot Vicecomodoro Juan Carlos Sapolsky and Captain Darío Omar Gelardi killed.
E-814	2019	1990	Second Pampa 2000. Modernised to Pampa II. In service at the IV Brigada Aérea.
E-815	2020	30-9-99	Construction started in the 1980s. Modernised to Pampa II in 2007. In service at the IV Brigada Aérea.
E-816, E-817	2021, 1021	16-11-07	Construction started in the 1980s. Initially E-816 serial assigned, changed to E-817. Delivered as Pampa II. First flight on 18-10-07. In service at the IV Brigada Aérea.
E-817, E-818	2022, 1022	31-12-07	Construction started in the 1980s. Delivered as Pampa II. In 2011 the canopy came off and damaged the tail. Repaired. Mid-air collision with E-819 on 10-8-12 over the Military Aviation School, landed safely and repaired. In service at the IV Brigada Aérea.

FMA IA-63 Pampa

Serial	C/N	Enlisted	Notes
E-818, E-819	2023, 1023	27-6-08	Construction started in the 1980s. Delivered as Pampa II. Mid-air collision with E-818 on 10-8-12 over the Military Aviation School, landed safely and repaired. In service at the IV Brigada Aérea.
E-819, E-820	2024, 1024	20-3-08	Construction started in the 1980s. In 2012 painted with the colours of the Cruz del Sur aerobatic team as it was announced the team would be recreated with Pampas but the idea was rejected shortly after. Repainted in grey camouflage sometime later. In service at the IV Brigada Aérea.
E-821	1025	15-8-08	In service at the IV Brigada Aérea.
E-822	1026	27-10-08	In service at the IV Brigada Aérea. On 23-2-18 the canopy came off during a test flight and the engineer, who was in the rear seat, ejected. The pilot landed the plane safely and it was repaired. The mechanic landed safely.
EX-04, AR-004, EX-04, A-708	1027	25-6-21	Presented on 10-10-13 as Pampa III demonstrator but did not fly until 31-3-16. Taken to Pampa III Block 2 and used the FAdeA internal serial AR-004, presented on 25-5-21 as EX-04, handed over to the FAA on 25-6-21. Delivered to the X Brigada Aérea on 7-2-23 as A-708. In service.
E-823, EX-05, A-702	1028	12-18	Delivered as Pampa III, re-serialled EX-05 for ground tests and A-702 on delivery. Delivered to the VI Brigada Aérea. On 7-2-23 transferred to the X Brigada Aérea. In service.
E-824, A-700, A-706	1029	12-18	Delivered as Pampa III, re-serialled A-700 before delivery. On 8-22 re-serialled A-706. Delivered to the VI Brigada Aérea. In service.
E-825, A-701	1030	12-18	Delivered as Pampa III, re-serialled A-701 before delivery. Delivered to the VI Brigada Aérea. On 7-2-23 transferred to the X Brigada Aérea. In service.
E-826, AR-001, A-703	1031	9-19	Delivered as Pampa III, used the provisional serial AR-001 of FAdeA and re-serialled A-703 before delivery. Delivered to the VI Brigada Aérea. In service.
E-827, AR-002, A-704	1032	11-19	Delivered as Pampa III, used the provisional serial AR-002 of FAdeA and re-serialled A-704 before delivery. Delivered to the VI Brigada Aérea. In service.
E-828, AR-003, A-705	1033	3-20	Delivered as Pampa III, used the provisional serial AR-003 of FAdeA and re-serialled A-705 before delivery. Delivered to the VI Brigada Aérea. In service.
E-829, A-707	1034	22-4-22	First series production Pampa III Block 2, re-serialled A-707 before delivery. Delivered to the VI Brigada Aérea. In service.
E-830, A-710	1035	18-5-23	Delivered as Pampa III, re-serialled A-710 before delivery. Delivered to the VI Brigada Aérea. In service.
	1036		In final assembly
	1037		In final assembly.
	1038		In final assembly.
	1039		Airframe built, awaiting to enter final assembly.
	1040		Airframe built, awaiting to enter final assembly.
	1041		Airframe built, awaiting to enter final assembly.
	1042		Airframe built, awaiting to enter final assembly.
	1043		Only some components built.
	1044		Only some components built.

CBA-123 Vector

Serial	N/S	First flight	Retired	Notes
PT-ZVE	801	18-7-90	1993	First prototype. Assembled in Brazil. Sent to Farnborough, UK, in 9-90. Preserved at the Memorial Aeroespacial Brazileiro in São José dos Campos, Brazil.
PT-ZVB	802	15-3-91	1993	Second prototype. Assembled in Brazil. Sent to Le Bourget, France, in 6-91. Preserved at the Museu Aeroespacial in Rio de Janeiro, Brazil.
–	803	–	–	Third prototype, unfinished, to be assembled in Argentina. Restored and placed in 2013 as a monument at the Engineering faculty at Córdoba University.

IA-100

Serial	N/S	First flight	Retired	Notes
LV-X596	001	1-8-16	2-17	Technology demonstrator. Finished in 9-15. Stopped flying in 2-17. Stored at FAdeA.

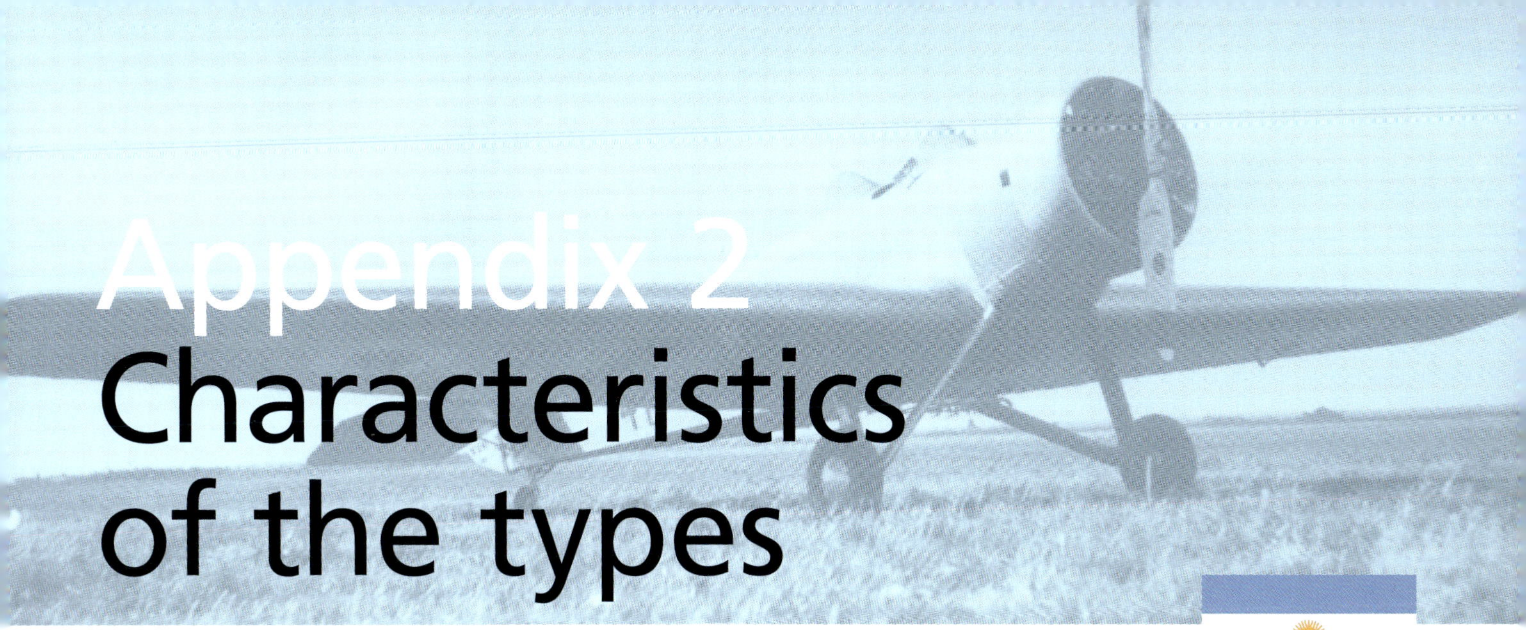

Appendix 2 Characteristics of the types

Ae.C.1

Engine	The first prototype flew with a five-cylinder Armstrong Siddeley Mongoose of 150hp with a wooden two-blade propeller and a Townend ring. Tested with a 100hp Gnome Rhône Monosoupape. The second received a 140hp Armstrong Siddeley Genet Major with a NACA cowling
Wingspan	12m
Length	7.75m
Height	3.16m
Wing area	19m2
Empty Weight	700kg
MTOW	1,120kg
Maximum speed	180km/h
Cruise Speed	171km/h
Service Ceiling	4,300m
Endurance	4 hours

Ae.C.2/Ae.M.E.1

Engine	Wright R-540E Whirlwind of 165hp and five cylinders
Wingspan	12m
Length	7.9m
Height	2.7m
Wing area	19m2
Empty Weight	650kg
MTOW	1,130kg
Maximum speed	220km/h
Cruise Speed	175km/h
Service Ceiling	5,000m
Endurance	4 hours

Ae.C.3

Engine	Armstrong Siddeley Genet Major engine of 145hp with a Townend ring
Wingspan	12.3m
Length	8.2m
Height	2.5m
Wing area	19m2
Empty Weight	670kg
MTOW	964kg
Maximum speed	170km/h
Cruise Speed	140km/h
Service Ceiling	4,500m
Endurance	5 hours

Ae.C.3G and Ae.C.4

Engine	de Havilland Gipsy Major engine of 130hp
Wingspan	12.16m
Length	7.44m
Height	2.7m
Wing area	16m2
Empty Weight	610kg
Payload	
MTOW	932kg
Maximum speed	200km/h
Cruise Speed	165km/h
Range	800km (1,000 on the Ae.C.4)

Ae.M.O.1 (2nd series)

Engine	Wright Whirlwind R-760ET seven-cylinder radial and 235hp
Wingspan	12.30m
Length	7.85m
Height	2.7m
Wing area	19m2
Empty Weight	965kg
Payload	483kg (172kg crew, 19kg oil, 47kg Madsen turret machine gun and equipment, 145kg of 202 litres of fuel)
MTOW	1,434kg
Maximum speed	209km/h at sea level, 220km/h at 2,100rpm and 500m, 200km/h at 1,000m or 2,000m, 191km/h at 3,000m, 179km/h at 3500m and 163km/h at 4,500m
Cruise Speed	179km/h at sea level and 1,800rpm, 193km/h at 1,800rpm and 1,000m
Service Ceiling	5,500m
Range	1,000km
Endurance	5.09 hours
Armament	Under-fuselage support for four bombs and a 7.65mm Madsen machine gun (Avro Trainer's 7.5mm Vickers in the early until 1936) in the observer's position and in some cases two 7.5mm Vickers twin machine guns, then 7.65mm Madsen machine guns in the hood, synchronised with the propeller

Ae.M.Oe.1

Engine	Wright Whirlwind R-760ET seven-cylinder radial and 235hp
Wingspan	11.8m
Length	7.95m
Height	3.4m
Wing area	17.52m2
Empty Weight	996kg
Payload	475kg
MTOW	1,471kg
Maximum speed	215km/h, 209km/h at sea level, 200km/h at 2,000m, 191km/h at 3,000m, 179km/h at 3,500m and 163km/h at 4,500m
Cruise Speed	190km/h
Service Ceiling	5,000m
Range	1,140km
Endurance	6 hours
Armament	Under-fuselage support for four bombs and in some cases two twin 7.5mm Vickers machine guns, then 7.65mm Madsen machine guns in the hood, synchronised with the propeller

Ae.M.Oe.2

Engine	Wright Whirlwind R-760ET seven-cylinder radial and 235hp
Wingspan	11.8m
Length	8.2m
Height	3.7m
Wing area	17.52m2
Empty Weight	1,003kg
Payload	475kg
MTOW	1,478kg
Maximum speed	220km/h
Cruise Speed	195km/h
Service Ceiling	5,000m
Range	1,121km
Endurance	5.45 hours
Armament	Under-fuselage support for four bombs and in some cases two twin 7.5mm Vickers machine guns, then 7.65mm Madsen machine guns in the hood, synchronised with the propeller

The Ae.M.O.1 serialled 41 with the NACA ring and the bomb pylon on the belly.

Ae.M.B.1 and 2 Bombi

Engine	Wright Cyclone SGR-1820F3 radial of nine cylinders and 715hp, with a three-blade Hamilton Standard propeller of regulatable pitch on land and 3.6m of diameter
Wingspan	17.20m
Length	10.90m
Height	2.80m
Wing area	35m2
Empty Weight	2,120kg
Payload	1,380kg
MTOW	3,500kg
Maximum speed	285km/h at 2,100m
Cruise Speed	240km/h at 2,100m and 1,750/1,800rpm
Service Ceiling	6,000m
Range	600km
Endurance	5 hours
Alternative loads as a bomber	Pilot, bomber/co-pilot, radio operator (total 240kg), 400kg of bombs, 30kg in ammunition and photographic material, 550 litres of fuel, full oil and 20kg of radio equipment
	Pilot, bomber/co-pilot, radio operator (total 240kg), 100kg of bombs, 30kg in ammunition and photographic material, full oil and fuel and 20kg of radio equipment
Alternative loads as a transport	Pilot, co-pilot, radio operator, one passenger, 40kg of cargo, full fuel and oil
	Pilot, co-pilot, radio operator, 3 passengers, 60kg of cargo, 700 litres of fuel, full oil
	Pilot, co-pilot, radio operator, 5 passengers, 40kg of cargo, 600 litres of fuel, full oil

Ae.M.S.1

Engine	Wright Whirlwind R-975 radial of 330hp
Wingspan	11.8m
Length	7.95m
Height	3.4m
Wing area	17.52m2
Empty Weight	1,284kg
MTOW	2,079kg
Maximum speed	200km/h
Cruise Speed	183km/h
Service Ceiling	4,700m
Range	800km

Ae.T.1

Engine	Lorraine-Dietrich 12 Eb engine of 450hp
Wingspan	17.3m
Length	9.7m
Height	4.36m
Wing area	37m2
Empty Weight	1,750kg
MTOW	2,810kg
Maximum speed	225km/h
Cruise Speed	195km/h
Service Ceiling	6,000m
Range	1,170km
Endurance	6 hours

FMA 20 El Boyero

Engine	Two prototypes with Continental A50 of 50hp and series production with A65 of 65hp
Wingspan	11.5m
Length	7.1m
Height	1.8m
Wing area	17.7m2
Empty Weight	325kg
MTOW	550kg
Maximum speed	167km/h
Cruise Speed	140km/h
Service Ceiling	4,000m
Range	650km

FMA 21

Engine	Wright Whirlwind R975E-3 engine of 456hp
Wingspan	11.8m
Length	7.95m
Height	3.4m
Wing area	17.52m2
Empty Weight	1,284kg
MTOW	2,079kg
Maximum speed	200km/h
Cruise Speed	183km/h
Service Ceiling	4,700m
Range	800km

I.Ae. DL-22

Engine	I.Ae.R.16 El Gaucho of 450hp, Wright Whirlwind R975E-3 engine of 456hp, Pratt & Whitney R-1340-41 Wasp of 550hp, Armstrong Siddeley Cheetah Mk.XXV of 475hp or Alvis Leonides 503 of 540hp
Wingspan	12.6m
Length	9.2m
Height	2.82m
Wing area	23.29m2
Empty Weight	1,520kg
MTOW	2,220kg
Maximum speed	290km/h with El Gaucho engine and 305km/h with Cheetah
Cruise Speed	260km/h with El Gaucho engine and 275km/h with Cheetah
Service Ceiling	5,200m with El Gaucho engine and 5,500m with Cheetah
Range	1,100km with El Gaucho engine and 1,168km with Cheetah
Endurance	4.15 hours
Armament	Two 7.65mm Colt DL 7.65 machine guns on the wings with 450 rounds each, one in the co-pilot position, plus underwing pylons for up to six 50kg bombs, 18 bombs of 15kg or twelve I.Ae.10 rockets

I.Ae.23

Engine	Siemens Bramo Sh-14 of 150hp with a wooden propeller of fixed pitch
Wingspan	9 m
Length	7.28m
Height	2.83m
Wing area	20m2
Empty Weight	525kg
MTOW	870kg
Maximum speed	185km/h
Cruise Speed	172km/h
Service Ceiling	3,900m
Range	675km

I.Ae.24 Calquin

Engine	Two Pratt & Whitney R-1830-65A Twin Wasp model S1C3-G radials of 1,200hp at 2,700rpm at take-off with Hamilton Standard Hydromatic 23-E-50 metallic three-bladed propellers with variable pitch and constant speed. Some carried the R-1830-43 engine
Wingspan	16.33m
Length	12m
Height	3,627m
Wing area	38.20m2
Empty Weight	5,340kg
Payload	1,860kg
MTOW	8,164kg
Maximum speed	440km/h
Cruise Speed	380km/h
Service Ceiling	10,000m
Range	1,200km
Endurance	2.15 hours
Armament	On light bomber missions it carried four locally manufactured 12.7mm Colt Browning AN-M2 12.70 x 99mm machine guns with 750 rounds each and a rate of fire between 550 and 600 rounds per minute, plus two 100 or 350kg bombs, four 50kg bombs or eighteen 13 to 15kg bombs. The maximum capacity of bombs was 740kg housed in the bomb bay. On attack missions it only carried the machine guns, but with 1,170 rounds. On assault missions it also carried machine guns with 1,170 rounds and up to ten 105mm A3F rockets or 75mm rockets under the wings. On reconnaissance missions, a camera could be installed behind the bomb bay. The installation of four 20mm Hispano 804 cannon was experimented with. The machine guns could be removed and in such cases a combination of up to ten rockets and 350kg bombs could be used

I.Ae.25 Mañque

Engine	None
Wingspan	25.50m
Length	14.70m
Height	3.84m
Wing area	79.10m2
Empty Weight	2,460kg
Payload	1,122kg
MTOW	3,582kg
Towing speed	220km/h
Minimum glide speed	61km/h

I.Ae.27 Pulqui

Engine	Rolls-Royce Derwent V of 1,587kg of thrust
Wingspan	11.25m
Length	9.69m
Height	3.39m
Wing area	19.70m2
Empty Weight	2,358kg
Payload	1,242kg
MTOW	3,600kg
Maximum speed	720km/h
Cruise Speed	600km/h
Service Ceiling	14,000m
Range	800km
Endurance	1 hour

I.Ae. 30 Ñancú

Engine	Two Rolls-Royce Merlin 130 series (134-5 port, 135-5 starboard, 12-cylinder liquid-cooled piston engines giving 2,035hp at 2,000ft each driving a four-bladed de Havilland variable-pitch propeller
Wingspan	15m
Length	11.52m
Height	5.16m
Wing area	35.32m2
Empty weight	6,208kg
MTOW	7,600kg
Maximum speed	740km/h
Cruise speed	500km/h
Service ceiling	8,000m
Range	2,700km
Endurance	5.25 hours
Armament proposed	Four 20mm Hispano Suiza HS.804 cannon with 190 rounds each. Provision for one 500lb bomb or five 83mm RP under the outer wings

I.Ae.31 Chingolo

Engine	Blackburn Cirrus Major 3 of 155hp with a metal two-blade propeller with pitch variable on the ground
Wingspan	10.7m
Length	8.12m
Height	2.18m
Wing area	16.5m2
Empty Weight	750kg
MTOW	981kg
Maximum speed	230km/h
Service Ceiling	5,180m
Endurance	1.4 hours

I.Ae.31 Colibrí

Engine	Blackburn Cirrus Major 3 of 155hp with a metal two-blade propeller with pitch variable on the ground
Wingspan	10.37m
Length	7.95m
Height	1.9m
Wing area	16m2
Empty Weight	635kg
MTOW	916kg
Maximum speed	240km/h
Cruise Speed	210km/h
Service Ceiling	6,500m
Endurance	1.5 hours

I.Ae.33 Pulqui II

Engine	1 Rolls-Royce Nene 2 of 2,315kg of thrust
Wingspan	10.6m
Length	11.68m
Height	3.50m
Wing area	25.1m2
Empty Weight	3,554kg the first prototype, 3,736kg the other three
Payload	1,950kg the first prototype, 2,675kg the other three
MTOW	5,988kg the first prototype, 6,875kg the other three
Maximum speed	1,040km/h the first prototype, 1,057 the second, and 1,080 the other two
Cruise Speed	960km/h the first prototype, 954 the other three
Service Ceiling	15,100 m the first prototype, 14,200 the second, and 15,000 the other two
Range	2,039km the first prototype, 3,090 the other three
Endurance	1.45 hours the first prototype, 2.5 the other three
Armament	4 x 20mm Hispano Suiza cannon

I.Ae.34 Clen Antú

Engine	None
Wingspan	18m
Length	4.4m
Fuselage length	3.5m
Height	1.6m
Wing area	19m2
Empty Weight	275kg, the I.Ae.34 was 220kg
MTOW	475kg
Maximum speed	200km/h
Landing Speed	60km/h

I.Ae.35 Justicialista del Aire, Huanquero, Constancia and Pandora

Engine	Initially two I.Ae. R-19 A El Indio of 650hp, the last seven carried I.Ae. R-19C of 750hp, later installed on all the others, moving a three-blade, constant-speed and variable-pitch Rotol RA 25635-1 propeller on the first and RA 25826 on the last
Wingspan	19.6m
Length	14.19m the first prototype and the Pandora and 13.98m the others
Height	4.7m
Wing area	42m2
Empty Weight	3,500kg
Payload	2,300kg
MTOW	5,800kg
Maximum speed	380km/h
Cruise Speed	320km/h with I.Ae. R-19A engine and 330km/h with I.Ae. R-19C
Service Ceiling	6,400m with I.Ae. R-19A engine and 6,500m with I.Ae. R-19C
Range	1,570km with I.Ae. R-19A engine and 1,450 with I.Ae. R-19C
Endurance	4.40 hours with internal fuel and 7:40 hours with extra tanks
Version I.a (training)	For navigation training with three crew members instructor and four pupils. Instrumental flight equipment, photographic camera and oxygen
Version I.b, later IA-35 II, attack and military transport version	For machine gun, bomb and rocket fire training. Armed with two internal Browning M3 de 12.7mm machine guns and 250 rounds reloadable in the air. One pylon per wing for one 12.7mm (5in) or four 5.6mm (2.25in) rockets on ARN-141 launchers. Four under-fuselage pylons for four 50kg pr two 100kg bombs on IA-35-35 81 launchers, including of Napalm of the same weight. Equipped with T-2A sight for bombing and a Wild sight for rocket and machine gun fire. Three crew members and up to seven passengers. Also could carry a baggage container on the pylons, never used and extra fuel tanks, used only by the first series plane, Ea-005, during tests
Version III ambulance	Three crew members, four patients and medical attendant. Also had four stretchers, a medical chest and table for doctor
Version IV photographic	Equipped with a Fairchild 225 camera for photographic surveillance. Three crew members and one camera operator
Version V for passengers (Pandora)	Three crew members and eight or ten passengers, with low-noise cabin, bar, toilet and other comfort elements

I.Ae.37

Engine	1 Rolls-Royce Derwent V of 1,632kg of thrust or two Rolls-Royce Avon of 2,950kg
Wingspan	10m
Length	Glider 10m, prototype 11.78m
Height	4.92m
Wing area	48m2
Empty Weight	3,300kg
MTOW	4,800kg
Maximum speed	800km/h with Derwent V
Service Ceiling	11,000m
Range	2,000km

I.Ae.38

Engine	Four I.Ae.R.16 El Gaucho of 450hp
Wingspan	32m
Length	13.40m
Fuselage length	11.10m
Height	3.95m
Wing area	133m²
Empty Weight	8,000kg
Payload	10,000kg
MTOW	20,000kg
Maximum speed	320km/h
Cruise Speed	265km/h
Service Ceiling	4,500m
Range	1,600km
Endurance	6.6 hours

I.Ae.41 Urubú

Engine	None
Wingspan	18m
Length	5.8m
Height	1.9m
Wing area	27m2
Empty Weight	250kg
MTOW	410kg
Maximum speed	200km/h
Landing Speed	52km/h

I.Ae.43

Engine	2 I.Ae.R.19C El Indio engines of 860hp
Wingspan	19.4m
Length	16.4m
Height	5.57m
Wing area	45m2
Empty Weight	4,005kg
Payload	1,760kg
MTOW	6,705kg
Maximum speed	323km/h at 7,000m
Cruise Speed	349km/h at 3,000m
Service Ceiling	7,500m
Range	1,150km

I.A.44

Engine	One I.A.R.19CR El Indio of 650hp or I.A.R.19C of 840hp with metal three-blade propeller
Wingspan	11.7m
Length	9.3m
Height	3.7m
Wing area	21m2
Empty Weight	1,950kg
MTOW	2,780kg
Maximum speed	440km/h
Cruise Speed	350km/h
Range	1,200km
Endurance	4 hours
Armament	Two internal machine guns in the wings and weapons pylons for twelve rockets or bombs

I.A.45 Querandí

Engine	Two Lycoming O-320 of 150hp, with Hartzell metal two-bladed propellers of variable pitch and constant speed in pusher position on the I.A.45A and two Lycoming O-360 of 180hp on the I.A.45B
Wingspan	13.54m the I.A.45A and 13.75m the I.A.45B
Length	8.84m the I.A.45A and 8.91m the I.A.45B
Height	2.80m the I.A.45A and 2.79m the I.A.45B
Wing area	19.00m2 the I.A.45A and 19.30m2 the I.A.45B
Empty Weight	1,084kg the I.A.45A and 1,170kg the I.A.45B
Payload	566kg the I.A.45A and 630kg the I.A.45B
MTOW	1,650kg the I.A.45A and 1,800kg the I.A.45B
Maximum speed	284km/h the I.A.45A and 276km/h the I.A.45B
Cruise Speed	260km/h the I.A.45A and 245km/h the I.A.45B
Service Ceiling	6,500m the I.A.45A and 7,550m the I.A.45B
Range	1,000km the I.A.45A and 1,100km the I.A.45B

I.A.46 Ranquel and I.A.51 Tehuelche

Engine	Lycoming O-320 of 150hp with a Sensenich two-blade fixed pitch metal propeller. A 180hp Lycoming O-360 on the Super Ranquel and Tehuelche
Wingspan	11.60m
Length	7.45m
Height	2.15m
Wing area	18m2
Empty Weight	560kg with seats and 600kg with crop-dusting equipment
Payload	370kg with seats and 400kg with crop-dusting equipment
MTOW	930kg with seats and 1,000kg with crop-dusting equipment
Maximum speed	195km/h
Cruise Speed	170km/h
Service Ceiling	4,000m
Range	680km
Endurance	4 hours

I.A.50 Guaraní II or G-II

Engine	Two Turbomeca Bastan VI-A of 930hp plus 75kg of extra trust with three-blade Ratier Figeac FH 86 propellers of 2.75m diameter. The first prototype flew with Bastan III, later changed to Bastan IV on this and the second prototype until the Bastan VI were installed.
Wingspan	19.59m
Length	15.49m
Height	5.76m
Wing area	42.09m2
Empty Weight	4,009kg
Payload	2,790kg
MTOW	6,700kg
Maximum speed	490km/h
Cruise Speed	475km/h
Service Ceiling	12,500m
Range	2,575km

IA-53 Mamboretá

Engine	Lycoming O-540-B2B5 of 235hp, driving a McCauley A200 FM-9047 two-blade metal propeller of fixed pitch
Wingspan	11.6m
Length	8.2m
Height	3.3m
Wing area	21.52m2
Empty Weight	844kg
MTOW	1,525kg
Maximum speed	215km/h
Cruise Speed	185km/h
Range	650km
Armament	The proposed COIN version had four 7.62mm machine guns in underwing pods and up to 208kg, consisting of T-10 rockets and 50 or 100kg bombs on four underwing pylons

IA-54 Carancho

Engine	None
Wingspan	19m
Length	8.4m
Empty Weight	300kg
MTOW	500kg

IA-55 (Ruíz proposal)

Engine	660hp Turbomeca Astazou XI engine
Wingspan	10.52m
Length	8.97m
Height	2m
Wing area	15.8m2
Empty Weight	1,000kg
MTOW	2,000kg

IA-55 (Olmedo proposal)

Engine	A 640shp Astazou X Turbomeca with a 2.5m diameter Ratier Figeac propeller
Wingspan	11.07m
Length	9.66m
Height	3.74m
Wing area	20.65m2
Empty Weight	1,235kg
MTOW	2,303kg
Maximum speed	412km/h
Cruise Speed	387km/h
Service Ceiling	6,750m
Range	1,080km
Armament	Four 7.62mm machine guns, plus a combination of two 110kg bombs, six 50kg bombs, 24 6.5kg rockets or twelve 28kg T-10s in underwing pylons. Alternatively, machine guns and a 340kg bomb under the fuselage. For training could carry the camera gun, four 50kg bombs and six T-10 rocket

IA-56

Engine	None
Wingspan	15m
Wing area	13.24m
MTOW	290 to 310kg

IA-58 Pucará

Engine	Two Turbomeca Astazou XVIG turboprops of 978hp (720Kw) each that move two Ratier Forest 23 LF-379 three-bladed propellers of 2.59m diameter and variable pitch
Wingspan	14.5m
Length	14.25m
Height	5.36m
Wing area	30.3m2
Empty Weight	4,020kg
Payload	2,780kg
MTOW	6,800kg
Maximum speed	520km/h
Cruise Speed	485km/h
Service Ceiling	8,280m
Range	3,042km
Endurance	6 hours
Armament	Two 20mm Hispano Suiza DCA-804 cannon with 270 rounds each and four Browning model machine guns of 7.62 × 51mm with 900 rounds each. Two Aero 7A-1 underwing pylons and one Aero 20A-1 ventral pylon with Alkan 105E ejectors for 500kg on the wings and one Alkan 115E for 1,000kg on the centre. A TER (Triple Ejector Rack) can be installed on the wing pylons and a MER (Multiple Ejector Rack) or TER can be installed on the central one. BK-BR bombs of 50, 125 and 250kg, general purpose bombs of 130kg, ASA FM of 225kg, AN M57 of 125kg, AN-M64 of 250kg, Mk.81 of 125kg, Mk.82 of 225kg, INC-50, INC-100 and INC-220 napalm bombs and ARM-BJ-125 fragmentation penetration of 125kg. The rocket launchers include the nineteen-tube LAU-60, 61, 66 and IIAE-238, seven-tube LAU-68 and experimental six-tube, all of 70mm. Also ARM-657 Mamboretá for IA-C-1057 Aspid 57mm rockets. The 105mm ARM-7105 Yaguareté was evaluated, and in October 1982 the possibility of operational use of the 127mm SAPBA rocket developed in the country by CITEFA was evaluated. The 2.25in SCAR and T-10 rockets were previously tested, but were not adopted for operational use. Alkan 530 grenade launchers are also used for 74mm grenades of various types

IA-63 Pampa

Engine	Initially Garrett TFE-731-2-2N of 3,500lb of thrust. Garrett TFE731-2-2B engines with 400lb of extra power on the Pampa 2000, Garrett TFE 731-40-2N of 4,300lb of thrust on the Pampa II and III
Wingspan	9.69m
Length	10.87m
Height	4.29m
Wing area	15.63m2
Empty Weight	2,921kg
Payload	1,100kg
MTOW	5,200kg
Maximum speed	815km/h
Cruise Speed	740km/h
Service Ceiling	12,900m
Range	2,112km
Endurance	4.45 hours
Armament	The plane has four underwing and one ventral pylons, with the external ones for 250kg and the internal ones for 400kg. The maximum load is 1,405kg. The ventral pylon can carry 400kg and can carry the 30mm Defa 553 cannon with 145 rounds. A TER (Triple Ejector Rack) can be installed on the inner wing pylons. Weapons include BK-BR bombs of 50, 125 and 250kg, Mk.81 of 125kg, Mk.82 of 225kg and INC-50, INC-100 and INC-220 napalm bombs. Alkan 530 grenade launcher. The rocket launchers include the nineteen-tube LAU-51/A, 60, 61 and IIAE-238, four-tube LAU-10, seven-tube LAU-32 or LAU-68 of 70mm, ARM-657 Mamboretá for IA-C-1057 Aspid 57mm rockets and 105mm ARM-7105 Yaguareté. Gun pods include Tordo and Colibrí pod for a 7.62 MAG machine gun, Alacrán pod for a 12.7 M2 Machine gun, FN Herstal D-HMP-250 pod with 12.7mm machine gun

IA-66

Engine	Two Garrett TPE-331-11-601W 1000shp and Dowty Rotol R 316 four-blade propellers
Wingspan	14.5m
Length	14.25m
Height	5.36m
Wing area	30.3m2
Empty Weight	4,020kg
Payload	2,780kg
MTOW	6,800kg
Maximum speed	550km/h
Cruise Speed	500km/h
Service Ceiling	8,28m
Range	3,042km
Armament	Same as the IA-58

IA-67

Engine	Two Garrett TPE-331-15 1045shp with Dowty Rotol four-blade propellers
Wingspan	21.34m
Length	17.5m
Height	6.5m
Wing area	41.5m2
Empty Weight	10,000kg
Payload	6,000kg
MTOW	18,000kg
Cruise Speed	390km/h
Service Ceiling	7,500m
Range	1,400km

IA-70/CBA-123 Vector

Engine	Garrett TPF351-20 of 1,300shp each, with pusher six-blade Hartzell HC-E6A-5 propellers, with FADEC
Wingspan	17.72m
Length	18.09m
Height	5.97m
Wing area	27.2m2
Empty Weight	6,230kg
Payload	2,270kg
MTOW	9,500kg
Maximum speed	647km/h
Cruise Speed	612km/h
Service Ceiling	11,125m
Range	1,852km

IA-100 demonstrator

Engine	Lycoming AEIO-360-81F of 180hp moving a two-blade propeller
Wingspan	9.4m
Length	7.8m
Height	2.4m
Wing area	12.5m2
Empty Weight	637kg
Payload	110,5kg
MTOW	950kg
Cruise Speed	250km/h
Service Ceiling	5,500m
Range	850km
Endurance	3.5 hours

IA-100B Malvina

Engine	Lycoming AEIO-540-D4A5 of 260hp moving a three-blade Hartzell propeller
Wingspan	9.9m
Length	8.4m
Height	2.6m
Wing area	14m2
Empty Weight	964kg
MTOW	1,350kg
Maximum speed	287km/h
Service Ceiling	5,500m
Range	1,090km
Endurance	4.5 hours

Bibliography

Archives and documentation
FAdeA Central Archive
Libro Histórico de la FMA 1926- 1976
Catálogo de aviones de la FMA
Libro Histórico del Comando de Material
Especificación General Avión IA-53 versión COIN, Capitán ingeniero Justo Demetrio Díaz, ingeniero aeronáutico Billy Juan Mauricio Montico, FMA, Córdoba, Diciembre de 1966.
Análisis del Proyecto IA-67 'Córdoba', Fábrica Militar de Aviones, 1981.
'A proposal to conduct a pre-prototype conceptual study for a utility transport utilizing a maximum number of Pucará IA-66 components, the Córdoba', prepared by Volpar Inc. September 1980.
Diseño mejorado de pantalla multi función para la nueva versión del sistema de navegación de la aeronave Pucará. M. D. Principi, A. C. Principi, G. M. Rodríguez, R. H. Manno and J. O. Oviedo.
All existing memories in the archives of the air units of the Argentine Air Force, the Material Areas and the Directorate of Historical Studies.
Boletines Aeronáuticos Públicos and Reservados.

Factory brochures
FMA 20 El Boyerol.
A-46 Ranquel.
IA-50 Guaraní.
IA-58 Pucará.
IA-58C Pucará Charlie.
IA-63 Pampa.
IA-66 Pucará.
IA-67 Córdoba.
ATL.
CBA-123.
Weapons of the FMA.

Articles
Ala delta de IAME, by Reimar Horten on Revista Nacional de Aeronáutica, June 1955.
Creación del Guaraní II, by Captain Héctor Eduardo Ruiz on Revista Nacional Aeronáutica y Espacial, October 1963.
Antecedentes del avión IA-50 Guaraní del Servicio Penitenciario Federal, Institution Manuscript.
Así nació la Fortaleza Volante Argentina, Carlos A. Ay, Pista 18, Nº15, Buenos Aires, summer of 1999.
Desarrollo de aviones rápidos sin cola, by Reimar Horten on Revista Nacional de Aeronáutica, September 1952.
Dos Décadas de Producción de la Fábrica Militar de Aviones, by Eduardo F Ferreti and Federico A. Giró on Revista Nacional Aeronáutica y Espacial, June and July 1962.
El Ae.C.1 y sus derivados, Oscar Luis Rodríguez, Alas magazine, issue 2, Buenos Aires, April 1994.
El Ae.C.2 Tenga Confianza, Oscar Luis Rodríguez, Alas magazine, issue 3, Buenos Aires, May 1994.
El Ae.T.1 primer trasnprote comercial de la FMA, Oscar Luis Rodrígues, Alas magazine, issue 7, September 1994.
El Boyero (FMA 20), Francisco Halbritter, Alas magazine, issue 8, Buenos Aires, October 1994.
El Guaraní, su nacimiento, su significación, by commander Rogelio M. Balado on Revista Nacional Aeronáutica y Espacial, December 1961.
El IA-63 Pampa, Armando Taurozzi, Alas special issue 1 Buenos Aires, 1994.
Flying the Pucará – The Boscome Down verdict. Ben Dunnell, The Aviation Historian No.8.
El Mosquito que quiso ser Águila, Carlos Ay, Atilio Baldini and Sergio Bontti, Pista 18, issue 6, Buenos Aires, winter 1997.
FMA, Fábrica de Maravilla Aeronáuticas, Oscar Luis Rodríguez, Alas magazine, issue 1, Buenos Aires, Marzo de 1994.
I.Ae.24 Calquin, Oscar Luis Rodríguez, Alas magazine, issue 12, Buenos Aires, March 1995.
I.Ae.24 Calquin, a la memoria de un guerrero, Fernando Benedetto, Alas magazine, issue 44, Buenos Aires, enero/febrero de 1998.
IA-46 Ranquel en Argentina, partes 1 y 2, Francisco Halbritter, Alas magazine, issues 17 and 18, Buenos Aires, August and September 1995.
Julio Argentino Noble (1895–1955) ingeniero civil, político y aeronáutico apasionado, Oscar Luis Rodríguez, Alas magazine, issue 29, Buenos Aires, September 1996.
La Gaceta Aérea, August 31, 1953 and September 23, 1953, edited by ALEA.
Los últimos Huanquero, Juan Carlos Cicalesi-Santiago Rivas, Pista 18, Nº12, Buenos Aires, January/February 1999.
Los 61 ejemplares del Ae.M.O., Oscar Luis Rodríguez, Alas magazine, issue 6, Buenos Aires, August 1994.
Os projetos da Embraer que não saíram das pranchetes, Parts 2 and 3, Mário B. de M. Vinagre, Flap magazine, issues 330 and 353, São Paulo, March 2000 and February 2002.
Revista Aeroespacio, miscellaneous numbers.

Books
AMORES, Eduardo, Fuerza Aérea Argentina, Guía de aeronaves militares, 1912–2006. Dirección de Estudios Históricos of the FAA, Buenos Aires, 2007.

AMORES, Eduardo, Fuerza Aérea Argentina, Guía de aeronaves militares, 1912–2015. Dirección de Estudios Históricos of the FAA, Buenos Aires, 2016.

ARREGUES, Ángel César, Fábrica Militar de Aviones, Crónicas y testimonios, Agencia Córdba Ciencia, Córdoba, 2007.

ARGUINDEGUY, Pablo E. contraalmirante (R.), Historia de la Aviación Naval Argentina, tomos 1 y 2, Instituto Aeronaval, Buenos Aires, 1981.

AY, Carlos, DINFIA Guaraní & IA-50 G-II, edited by Jorge Núñez Padín, Buenos Aires, 2021.

BENEDETTO, Fernando, Curtiss III, IV & H75-O Hawk, edited by Jorge Núñez Padín, Buenos Aires, 2010.

BENEDETTO, Fernando, I.Ae.27 Pulqui I & I.A.33 Pulqui II, edited by Jorge Núñez Padín, Buenos Aires, 2012.

BENTANCOR, Walter, El general de los cazas, Adolf Galland en Argentina, 1948–1955, Ediciones Argentinidad, Buenos Aires, 2013.

BENTANCOR, Walter, Suboficiales pilotos militares, 1912–1965, AMT Ediciones, Buenos Aires, 2021.

BIEDMA RECALDE, Antonio, Crónica histórica de la aeronáutica argentina; Círculo de Aeronáutica – Fuerza Aérea Argentina, Buenos Aires, 1969.

BOUND, Graham, Falkland Islanders at war, Pen and Sword Books, South Yorkshire, 2002.

BURDEN, Rodney and others, Falklands the Air War, British Aviation Research Group, London, 1986.

BURZACO, Ricardo, Las Alas de Perón, Editorial Da Vinci, Buenos Aires, 1995.

BURZACO, Ricardo, CICALESI, Juan Carlos, RIVAS, Santiago, Las Alas de Perón II, Ediciones Eugenio B, Buenos Aires, 2007.

CARBALLO, Pablo Marcos, Dios y los Halcones; Editorial Abril, Buenos Aires, 1983.

CARBALLO, Pablo Marcos, Halcones sobre Malvinas; Ediciones del Cruzamante, Buenos Aires, 1984.

DANEL, Raymond, CUNY Jean, Les avions Dewoitine, Docavia Editions Larriviere, Paris, 1982.

DE LEÓN, Pablo, Historia de la actividad espacial en la Argentina, edited by the author, Buenos Aires, 2008

FRENKEL, Leopoldo, Juan Ignacio San Martín, Buenos Aires, 1992.

HALBRITTER, Francisco, Historia de la industria aeronáutica argentina, Biblioteca Nacional de Aeronáutica, Buenos Aires, 2004.

HALBRITTER, Francisco, Los primeros 500, los aviones experimentales en la República Argentina, Ediciones Argentinidad, Buenos Aires, 2016

HORTEN, Reimar, SELINGER, Peter F., Nurflügel, edited by H. Weishaupt Verlag, Graz, 2000.

Historia de la Fuerza Aérea Argentina, tomo I, Dirección de Estudios Históricos de la FAA, Buenos Aires, 1997.

Historia de la Fuerza Aérea Argentina, tomo II, Dirección de Estudios Históricos de la FAA, Buenos Aires, 1998.

Historia de la Fuerza Aérea Argentina, tomo III, Dirección de Estudios Históricos de la FAA, Buenos Aires, 2000.

Historia de la Fuerza Aérea Argentina, Tomo VI, La Guerra de Malvinas Volume 1 and 2; Dirección de Estudios Históricos de la FAA, Buenos Aires, 2000.

Jane's All the World Aircraft, All editions from 1925 to 2010.

MARURI Juan, teniente 1° (Av) (R), Historia de la Fuerza Aérea Uruguaya, edited by the author, Montevideo, 2007.

McMANNERS, Hugh, Forgotten voices of the Falklands; Ebury Publishing, England, 2008.

MORGAN, David, Hostile Skies, The battle for the Falklands; Phoenix, 2007.

MYHRA, David, The Horten Brothers and their all-wing aircraft, Schiffer Books, Atglen, 1998

PEREIRA, Roberto, Enciclopédia de aviões Brazileiros, Editora Globo, São Paulo, 1997.

RAMSEY, Gordon, Falklands then and now, Battle of Britain International Ltd, Essex, 2009.

REIGNER, Guillermo, Reimar Horten, biografía en imágenes, edited by the author, Buenos Aires, 2023.

RIVARA, Horacio, La Luftwaffe en Argentina; Editorial Martín, Buenos Aires, 2009.

RODRÍGUEZ, Oscar Luis and MARTÍN, Eloy, Comando de Aviación de Ejército, Catálogo de Aeronaves, Buenos Aires.

VINAGRE, Mario B. de M., Guido Pessotti, mestre do design aeronáutico; Somos Editora, São Paulo, 2015.

WAGNER Wolfgang, Kurt Tank: Focke-Wulf's designer and test pilot, Schiffer Books, Atglen, 1998.

WARD, Nigel, Sea Harrier over the Falklands, A Maverick at War; London, BCA, 1992.

ZULOAGA, Ángel María, La victoria de las alas; Círculo de Aeronáutica – Fuerza Aérea Argentina, Buenos Aires, 1958.

Websites

El FMA IA-60, by Gonzalo Sebastián Rengel at www.zona-militar.com/2015/08/11/fma-ia-60

Los IA-58 Pucará a reacción, by Gonzalo Sebastián Rengel at www.zona-militar.com/2016/01/25/los-ia-58-Pucará-a-reaccion

Acknowledgements

Fabián Arregues
Francisco Halbritter
Diego Horten
Fernando Benedetto
Hernán Casciani
Daniel Gómez
Atilio Baldini
Eduardo Amores Oliver, Dirección de Estudios de la Fuerza Aérea Argentina
Ricardo Lezón
Dirección de Estudios de la Fuerza Aérea Argentina
Biblioteca Nacional de Aeronáutica
Museo del Centro de Investigación Aplicada de la Fuerza Aérea Argentina
Rolls-Royce Heritage Trust
Gregory Alegi
Dave Collins
Ricardo Burzaco
Walter Bentancor
Juan Carlos Cicalesi
Peter Kirk
José Martinez
Brigadier Horacio Oréfice (FAA)
Brigadier César Cunietti (FAA)
Brigadier Alberto Vianna (FAA)
Brigadier Guillermo Stahl (FAA)
Brigadier Miguel Cruzado (FAA)
Brigadier Alejandro Moresi (FAA)
Comodoro Miguel Navarro (FAA)
Comodoro Gabriel Pavlovcic (FAA)
Comodoro Juan Manuel Cimatti (FAA)
Comodoro Guillermo Landa (FAA)
Comodoro Carlos Tomba (FAA)
Comodoro Roberto Vila (FAA)
Comodoro Roberto Címbaro (FAA)
Comodoro Carlos Horacio Argente (FAA)
Comodoro Rubén Sassone (FAA)
Comodoro Raúl Páez (FAA)
Mayor Sebastián Ardiles (FAA)
Geselino Garbini (FAA)
Martín Liva (FAA)
Teo Maza (FAA)
Guillermo Rasia (FAA)
Suboficial Alejandro Marcori (FAA)
Suboficial Sergio Schoenfeld (FAA)
Suboficial Martín Neme (FAA)
Suboficial Matías Paczkowski (FAA)
Darío Gambini (FAA)
Coronel Hugo Parentini (FAU)
Mayor Wilfredo Guedes (FAU)
Mayor Marcelo Lorenze (FAU)
Pablo Souza (FAU)
Ricardo Moreirazerpa (FAU)
Stephanie Catherine Techera (FAU)
Roberto Moreno (FAU)
Iván Salaberry (FAU)
Pedro Cardeillac (FAU)
Germán Páez (FAC)
Germán Ribero (FAC)
Juan Carlos Ramírez (FAC)
Jaime Clavijo (FAC)
Uditha Danwaththa (Sri Lankan Air Force)
Air Chief Marshal Kolitha A. Gunatilleke (Sri Lankan Air Force)
Captain Priyantha Adikaram (Sri Lankan Air Force)
Flt. Lt David Morgan (RAF)
Buddhika Dissanayake
Lisandro Amorelli
Jona Zorzón
Gonzalo Rengel
Cees-Jan van der Ende
Sergio Bellomo
Jorge F. Núñez Padín
Sergio Baroni
Jorge Leonardi
Gabriel Lladó
Javier Franco
Gonzalo Altamirano
Sergio García Pedroche
Mauro Bia
Gervasio Dambroriarena
Marcelo Buteler (FixView)
Eduardo Ruiz (FAdeA)
Juan Remedi (FAdeA)
Federico Bima (FAdeA)
Sebastián Ugarte (FAdeA)
María José Álamo (FAdeA)
Juan Ignacio San Martín (FAdeA)
Ismael Martínez (FAdeA)
José Ignacio Bertea
Rodrigo Jiménez Sch.
Álvaro Romero
Carlos Maggi
Juan Martín Rivas
Javier Ordoñez Jimenez
Raúl Cabido, Centro de Investigación Aplicada de la FAA
Cristian Bustamante, Centro de Investigación Aplicada de la FAA

Index

British Combat Aircraft in Latin America

This book covers the story of all the British military aircraft that served in Latin America since 1940. Though the presence of British combat types is now almost gone from the skies over Latin America, its legacy will last for a long time. After World War 2, Britain was happy to sell the most modern equipment to the region giving it an advantage over the United States, hitherto the main provider of planes to Latin American air forces. This was one of the main reasons why many air forces chose to buy British combat aircraft up to the 1970s. In many countries Gloster Meteors or de Havilland Vampires were the first jet combat aircraft, while the Argentina's Avro Lancasters and Lincolns was once the most potent bomber force in Latin America. BAC Canberras had five South American operators, were the only jet bombers in use in the region and saw action several times. Combat activity by British types include Argentine planes used during the 1955 revolution and ironically Argentine Canberras in action during the Malvinas/Falklands War against British forces, Cuban Sea Furies over the Bay of Pigs, Peruvian Canberras in the conflicts with Ecuador, Chilean Hunters during the 1973 coup d'etat, Dominican Vampires, Mosquitoes and Beaufighters in internal struggles.

624 pages, hardback

ISBN: 9781902109572, £44.95/$64.95

Available at *crecy.co.uk*